Y0-CJG-213

An economic geography of Hungary

Authors of individual units:

Tivadar Bernát: II/1.2, III/2,6, IV, IV/5, VII/1,2,4
Gyula Bora: III/1,3,4,5, IV/2, VII/3,5
Lajos Kalász: I, II/1.1, II/2, IV/1,6
Zoltán Zoltán: II/3, IV/3,4

An economic geography of Hungary

Edited by
Tivadar Bernát

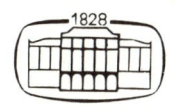

Akadémiai Kiadó, Budapest 1989

Translated by
I. Véges

Translation revised by
P. A. Compton
The Queen's University of Belfast
Northern Ireland

Second enlarged edition

HC
300.28
.M3413
1989

ISBN 963 05 4990 5

© Akadémiai Kiadó, Budapest 1985, 1989

Printed in Hungary by Akadémiai Kiadó és Nyomda Vállalat, Budapest

Contents

Preface		9
I	**The physiographic environment**	11
1	The geographical position of Hungary	11
2	Physiography and the economy	14
3	Mineral resources and their economic significance	15
3.1	Energy sources	15
3.2	Minerals	17
3.3	Non-metallic minerals	18
4	Climate and its effect on the economy	20
5	Water as an economic resource	26
6	Soils	32
7	An evaluation of the natural endowments and mineral resources of Hungary	35
	Bibliography for Chapter I	39
II	**Population and settlement**	41
1	A survey of the history and administration of Hungary	41
1.1	Historical survey	41
1.2	The system of local administration	48
2	Population	51
2.1	The natural increase of population	52
2.2	Population distribution by age and sex	55
2.3	Distribution of the population by nationality	57
2.4	Population density	58
2.5	Occupational structure	61
2.6	Internal migration	66
3	Settlement and infrastructure	69
3.1	Settlement characteristics predating the present-day structure	70
3.2	The main components of the Hungarian settlement network and their characteristic regional types	74
3.2.1	Towns	75
3.2.2	Villages	83
3.2.3	The size structure of the rural settlement network	86
3.2.4	Tanya settlements	88
3.3	Development concept of the national settlement network	91
3.4	The infrastructural provision of settlements	93
3.4.1	Service provision in towns	94
3.4.2	Service provision in villages	95
	Bibliography for Chapter II	97
III	**The spatial location of economic sectors**	100
1	Industry	100
1.1	A few basic problems	101
1.2	The dynamics of development and structural changes	103
1.3	Spatial industrial structure and the dynamics of change	108
1.4	Energy	115
1.5	Metallurgy	133

1.6	The engineering industry	143
1.7	The chemical industry	157
1.8	The building-materials and construction industries	169
1.9	Light industry	175
1.10	The industrial regions of Hungary	188
2	The food industry	192
2.1	Enterprise and ownership relationships in the food industry	194
2.2	Basic production factors of agriculture	197
2.2.1	Agricultural manpower	198
2.2.2	Land and land use	200
2.2.3	Means of production	214
2.3	Spatial location of the production sectors	218
2.4	Bread-grain production, the milling and baking industries	221
2.5	The production and processing of industrial crops	227
2.6	Viticulture and the wine industry	236
2.7	Fruit and vegetable production and the preserving industry	243
2.7.1	Fruit production	243
2.7.2	Vegetable production and the preserving industry	249
2.8	Fodder crops, and the production and processing of animal products	256
2.8.1	Fodder crops	256
2.8.2	Animal husbandry. The production and processing of animal products	266
2.9	Regions of agricultural production	282
3	Transport	288
3.1	The main characteristics of the transport network	290
3.2	The railways	292
3.3	Road transport	297
3.4	Water transport	301
3.5	Pipeline transport	304
3.6	Air transport	304
4	Tourism	305
5	International economic relations and their impact on the spatial distribution of productive forces	310
5.1	CMEA integration and its impact on the spatial distribution of productive forces	313
5.2	Economic co-operation with the developed western countries	318
5.3	Economic relations with developing countries	320
6	Trends in the spatial structure of the Hungarian economy	321
	Bibliography for Chapter III	327
IV	**Economic and planning regions – The question of regionalization**	332
1	The central economic–planning region	336
1.1	Natural endowments and resources	337
1.2	The economy	339
1.2.1	Industry	340
1.2.2	Agriculture and food processing	349
1.2.3	Transport	352
1.2.4	Tourism	354
1.3	Population	355
1.4	Settlement	357
1.5	Subregions and urban hinterlands	357
2	The Northern Hungarian economic–planning region	360
2.1	Natural endowments and resources	361
2.2	The economy	363
2.2.1	Industry	363
2.2.2	Agriculture and food processing	368
2.2.3	Transport	371
2.2.4	Tourism	371
2.3	Population	372
2.4	Settlement	373
2.5	Subregions and urban hinterlands	373
3	The economic–planning region of the **Northern Great Plain**	376

3.1	Natural endowments and resources	377
3.2	The economy	379
3.2.1	Industry	380
3.2.2	Agriculture and food processing	384
3.2.3	Transport	387
3.3	Population	388
3.4	Settlement	388
3.5	Subregions and urban hinterlands	390
4	The economic–planning region of the Southern Great Plain	393
4.1	Natural endowments and resources	394
4.2	The economy	397
4.2.1	Industry	397
4.2.2	Agriculture and the food processing	402
4.2.3	Transport	406
4.3	Population	407
4.4	Settlement	407
4.5	Subregions and urban hinterlands	409
5	The economic–planning region of Southern Transdanubia	412
5.1	Natural endowments and resources	412
5.2	The economy	414
5.2.1	Industry	414
5.2.2	Agriculture and food processing	419
5.2.3	Transport	421
5.2.4	Tourism	422
5.3	Population	423
5.4	Settlement	424
5.5	Subregions and urban hinterlands	425
6	The economic–planning region of Northern Transdanubia	430
6.1	Natural endowments and resources	430
6.2	The economy	432
6.2.1	Industry	432
6.2.2	Agriculture and food processing	439
6.2.3	Transport	442
6.2.4	Tourism	442
6.3	Population	443
6.4	Settlement	443
6.5	Subregions and urban hinterlands	444
7	Changes in the spatial structure of the Hungarian economy and society (1982—1987) (Transl. by J. Pokoly)	447
7.1	Changes in the demographic and occupational structure	448
7.2	Changes in settlement and infrastructure	450
7.3	Changes in the development and geographical location of industry	453
7.4	Regional changes in food industry	463
7.5	Changes in transport network and tourism	469
	Bibliography for Chapter IV	471

Preface

This book is designed to satisfy the increasing world-wide interest in Hungary manifesting itself during the past few years. It presents the dynamic spatial changes, accompanied by urbanization, of the transition period from a quantitative to a qualitative phase of the development of the Hungarian economy, changes in the distribution of population, in the regional structure of industry and in the locational specialization of agriculture. It reviews the most important achievements and difficulties of regional development during the past quarter of the century, the more balanced shaping of the spatial pattern, as well as the specific problems of economically disadvantaged areas.

The book has been written by scientists working in the field of research into regional planning and concerned with the solution of the related socio-economic problems for about three decades. True, the economic policy of the 1950s, ignoring objective endowments, did not require the assistance of science, yet the situation has since experienced a radical change. Scientific knowledge about the locational factors of production, the co-operation of science in taking decisions on regional development has become an urgent and indispensable social requirement. Hence, the position of geography has undergone a profound change, which finds its reflection in this book, too.

What the authors have tried to accomplish is not an „inventory-type" description, not a mere pointing out of the locations of the various production sectors. They have tried instead to place emphasis on the questions of „why" and „how" as against the traditional questions of „what" and „where", i. e. they have tried to clarify the role the individual factors play in spatial location. This approach has made it necessary for them to identify, in reviewing the geographical implication of each economic sector, the factors determining locations, on the one hand, and to delimit the spatial types, the regions of economic activities, on the other. This concept has necessarily determined the book's lay-out and its methodology, too. The elements of this concept are as follows:

— The authors have broken with the traditional method of placing emphasis on the geography of the individual sectors, of population and settlement, in which regional analysis was virtually confined to a summary of the statements made in chapters on the individual sectors.

Their book consists of two parts, mutually presupposing and complementing each other. The first, general part deals with the economic geography of the country as a whole, with its natural resources, population, settlement and the various sectors of the economy. The second, regional part discusses the relevant problems in a division of the country into regions. Spatial approach being the natural point of view of geography, it appears to be justified to register the findings of research according to regions. This requirement is fully met by this book, and in a greater detail at that than it was usually done in earlier works of a similar type.

By focusing their statements on the characteristics of the spatial structure of the Hungarian economy, the authors have avoided discussing in detail those questions which are less conducive to an understanding of regional interrelationships. Thus, less attention is paid to problems relating to economic policy, to sectoral and management economics, to the science of technology and commodities, etc., whose examination would have gone anyway beyond the space available to the authors.

As regards the method of presentation, the authors have subordinated description, the mere statement of facts, to an analysis of the spatial location of the economy in order to ensure a better understanding of geographical relationships. Compiling a book destined for foreign readers, the authors have deemed it appropriate to include in it fewer place names and statistical data than otherwise would have been warranted.

Diagrams, charts and maps relating to the selected years in the decade 1971 and 1981 help to illustrate spatial locations and orders of magnitude.

The authors are hopeful that their book with its novel approach and method of examination will do good service to the presentation of the economic geography of Hungary. It may be a useful source of information for specialists of scientific research and practice interested in Hungary, and provide at the same time a true picture of the present-day state of the country for Hungarians living abroad.

Note to the second edition

Our book, according to the preface to the first edition, was designed to satisfy a growing interest in Hungary. It served this purpose so well, that the book was sold out in less than two years. Updating the book by completely rewriting it would have caused too much delay. Yet the authors refused its unaltered publication, as the five years separating the two editions brought along new socio-economic features, institutions and tensions. In order to indicate the new tendencies, we have attached an additional chapter.

I The physiographic environment

1 The geographical position of Hungary

The Hungarian People's Republic, with an area of 93,030 square kilometres and covering one-third of the central and western low-lying parts of the Danubian or Carpathian Basin, is a typically Danubian country.

As regards its latitudinal position, the country is approximately equidistant from the equator and the North Pole. Although its territory is located within a comparatively narrow latitudinal band between 45° and 49° N, the difference between the phenological phases of individual plants is nonetheless, in general, around one to two weeks.

Since the country is elongated in an east-west direction, the effects of variations in longitude are even more marked and the sun rises 27 minutes earlier over the village of Garbolc in Szabolcs-Szatmár county in the east than over Felső-Szölnök in Vas county in the west.

Hungary is one of the land-locked countries of Europe. Nearest to it (200–250 kilometres by air) is the Adriatic branch of the Mediterranean Sea, from which it is separated by the barren Karst mountains of Yugoslavia, but although obstructing transport and partly diverting rivers from the sea, this obstacle cannot restrain Mediterranean climatic influences from reaching the country, especially in the south-western parts. Much further, at a distance of 500–800 kilometres, is the coastline of the Black Sea, easily accessible via the Danube. This sea has always held a special position in the country's river and sea transport, and does so today, with a substantial part of Hungary's mineral raw materials being transported from the Soviet Union by waterway. Of least significance economically is the Baltic Sea, at a distance of 1000–2000 kilometres. It is the Atlantic Ocean, however, at a mean distance of 1500–1700 kilometres, and especially the North Sea, which contribute most to the formation of the country's climatic character *(Fig. 1)*.

Hungary is a low-lying, predominantly flat country surrounded by higher regions, and level plains, nowhere reaching 200 metres (660 feet) above sea level, cover two-thirds of its area. Mountainous regions, mostly between 400 and 500 metres above sea-level, account for only 2000 square kilometres, and there is only one peak, the Kékes, which just exceeds 1000 metres (3280 feet) in height.

A highly important factor in the country's physiographical position is its basin-like character. This has a great and equalizing impact on climate and hydrology, and also influences water economy and flood control.

Fig. 1. The geographical location of Hungary

The country's soil map with its mosaic-like pattern shows the various and transitory character of the arable areas, while only 10 to 15 per cent of the surface has preserved its natural vegetation. All the characteristic types of the surrounding major regions can be found among its plants, but with the prevalent cultural landscape under constant extension, only very few remnants of earlier environments have been preserved.

The country is equally affected by internal and external socio-economic relationships, by the development of native productive forces and those of the surrounding countries. Looking at the nation's history as a whole, it is clear that, unlike the almost unchanged physiographic environment, Hungary's economic geography as a historical and social category has been subject to dynamic change. Her economic history and overall position have been affected by developments in internal social relations, by historical events taking place in surrounding countries and often extending over a large part of Europe, by socio-economic development and growth and, last but not least, by her geographical position also.

At the end of World War II the transformation of social relations and the rapid development of productive forces brought about major changes in the country's economic geography, as the replacement of the capitalist system by socialism and the strengthening of ties with the Soviet Union created an entirely new political and economic environment.

The location of the country has several implications for economic development. For instance, its central position in relation to the countries of eastern, western, central and southern Europe is an advantage for transit freight traffic and tourism. Closely connected with this is its central position in the transport system of the European continent and well over 20 per cent of Hungary's overall railway business is transit traffic. The country's juxtaposition between the socialist and capitalist spheres provides a favourable potential for tourism, while its common frontier with the Soviet Union, its most significant import and export partner, as well as its proximity to the other socialist countries of Europe, makes the expansion of commodity exchange and co-operation with them possible.

Hungary is one of the few European countries with no seaboard of its own, which diminishes its otherwise favourable geographical location with regard to communications. It increases handling costs and requires, in the case of less valuable raw materials, the predominant use of railway transport instead of cheaper waterway transport.

Its continental location is also disadvantageous because the country thereby lacks the resources that can be obtained from a maritime economy and the exploitation of the sea, while it is denied the possibility of extracting seabed minerals in the future, too.

Moreover, Hungary's proximity to the European Economic Community, one of the world's great economic amalgamations and market outlets, makes it possible, given the favourable communications both in terms of time and costs, for the country to maintain its traditional external economic relations and to keep to delivery commitments arising from the rapidly expanding number of co-operative production schemes. The Danube–Main–Rhine Canal, to be completed by the end of 1980s, will further improve the country's communications position not only in relation to Common Market countries, but also in relation to overseas areas, such as North, Central and South America.

The small size of the country with its relatively small population, comparatively narrow internal market and limited economic potential offer but a restricted scope for several sectors of the economy, which can only be offset by an increasing involvement in the international – primarily socialist – division of labour. But the small size of the country also contains certain potential advantages, such as the possibility for more rational organization; shorter transportation distances; easier construction and maintenance of the telecommunication network and other linear infrastructure systems; a more even distribution and density of population with a concomitant spatial balance in the size and skill level of the labour forces.

2 Physiography and the economy

Relief forms connected with the structural features and stratigraphy of the Earth's crust have an important bearing on the spatial distribution of mining, as well as being of paramount significance in influencing, and even determining, climatic conditions. Physiography also directly affects the geographical pattern of settlement and agricultural production as well as the location of the transportation system.

The effect on climate is manifest at both regional and local levels and contributes importantly to the differentiation of agricultural activity. At the macro-scale, relief has transformed Hungary into a kind of continental island climatically, surrounded by a markedly more maritime environment. Since the country occupies the middle and western part of the Carpathian Basin, at an average height of less than 200 metres above sea-level over more than half of its territory, mean temperatures are higher and precipitation lower than in the encircling mountain ranges. Because of the surrounding mountain rim, the Basin is also sheltered from the extreme effects of the wind, while the range of temperature is also greater. As for the natural vegetation, this is a wooded steppe rather than continuous forest cover, in accordance with the warmer summers and lower precipitation, although in the cooler hill country with more abundant precipitation forest does become dominant. These regularities also apply to soil distribution.

Relief characteristics have not only indirect but also direct effects on the economy, primarily in the field of transportation. Steep slopes slow down, or even halt traffic depending, of course, on the means of transport, but the relief endowment of the country is such that such obstacles are few in number, and those that do exist are usually mountains of only medium height. In such areas, however, particularly in Transdanubia, the main routes tend to follow the fault lines at the foot of mountains and hills.

The distribution of settlements throughout the country is also largely influenced, along with historical factors, by relief characteristics. In the larger part of Transdanubia, comprising Baranya, Vas, Zala and Somogy counties as well as the Bakony Highlands, small, even tiny, villages with fewer than 1000 inhabitants are characteristic, while on the Great Plain large, overgrown villages with 5000 inhabitants and more together with the surrounding population inhabiting detached farmsteads *(tanya)* are typical forms of settlement. The fact that settlement density is highly heterogeneous, ranging from 0·9 to 9·2 settlements per 100 square kilometres per district is also closely interrelated with relief characteristics. Lowest in density, but of largest settlement size, is the Great Plain away from which density increases gradually to reach a maximum in the hilly and mountainous regions, where settlement sizes happen to be smallest.

The fact that half the country's area is of quaternary formation, with older geological remnants only reaching the surface to a limited degree [30], explains why Hungary is poor in iron ore and high-quality coal deposits. Coal and mineral ores are exclusively associated with strata of secondary and tertiary age and are located in regions of such geological origin. All coal deposits, including those in the Mecsek Mountains, as well as bauxite and hydrocarbons, the only two really significant mineral resources in Central European relation besides brown coal, are located in the low mountain districts, in adjecent basins, or beneath the quaternary sediments of the Great Hungarian Plain, which are themselves insignificant from the point of view of mineral resources. This distribution of mineral resources obviously determines the location of the primary extractive sector.

3 Mineral resources and their economic significance

Although, owing to its geological structure, Hungary is not generally rich in mineral resources, does nonetheless contain valuable reserves, both in quantity and quality, of certain mineral types. The processes that took place in geological history have dictated that the topography of the country is one consisting primarily of plains and basins separated by smaller mountain ranges of limited extent. Predominant on the surface and at depths accessible for mining purposes are those strata which were formed during the more recent phases of geological history. Such volcanic activity that took place in the past did not produce major formations despite the fact that the mountains are, in part, of volcanic origin. The present area of the country was subject to periodic massive transgressions over a long period of geological time and, as a result, sedimentary rocks deposited during these phases are predominant. Also important are deposits formed by the processes of erosion, while underwater volcanic activity has left a legacy of valuable mineral resources.

3.1 Energy sources

Most of the coal-mining basins of the country are to be found in the northeast-southwest trending Hungarian Highlands and in the Mecsek Mountains. Coal reserves are estimated at about 8 to 9 billion tons, of which lignite comprises over 60 per cent, brown coal close to 25 per cent and bituminous coal only about 15 per cent. Given the current prices and those expected in the near future, about 2·5 billion tons of the total can be exploited economically. The older and better-quality deposits are to be found in Transdanubia, while younger fields of low caloric value are located in the North Hungarian Highlands.

The oldest and at the same time the only hard coal field of the Jurassic age is situated in the Mecsek Mountains. The field is highly faulted and folded and, as a result, the coal tends to be crumply and fine-grained. Three seams exist at an average depth of 600 to 800 metres, the first extending in

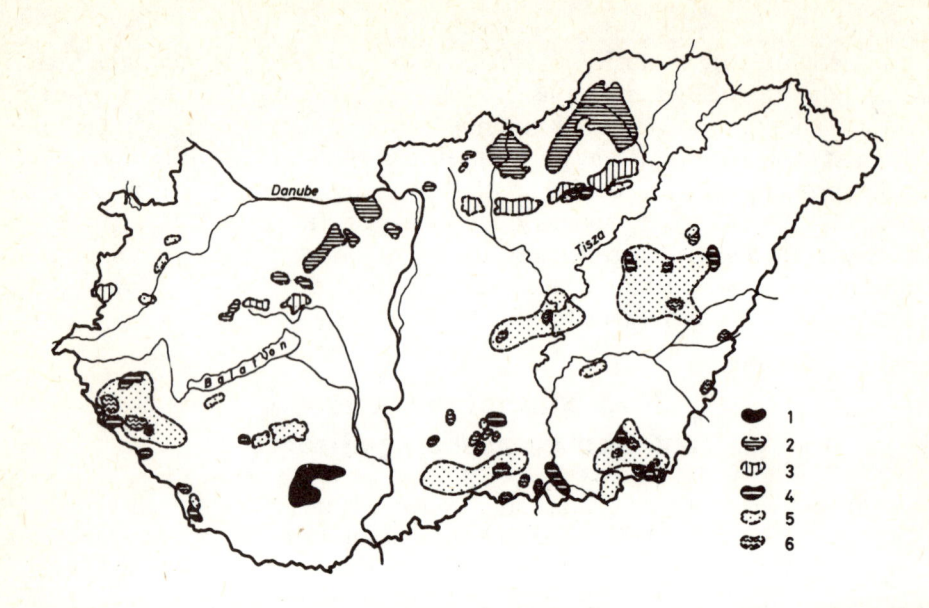

Fig. 2. Energy sources
1 — black coal; 2 — brown coal; 3 — lignite; 4 — HC field under exploitation; 5 — natural gas occurrences, 6 — petroleum occurrences

a southern direction, between Pécs and the village of Vasas, the second being found between Vasas and Komló and the third occurring along the northern edge of the range. The coal varies in quality and calorific value, the most valuable is the coking coal of the Komló Basin.

Of the other fields in Transdanubia, the reserves of the Ajka Basin, situated on the northwestern side of the Bakony Mountains, constitute a type transitional between hard and brown coal, while the country's most valuable brown-coal basins can be found at the foot of the Vértes, Gerecse and Pilis Mountains. These latter were formed during the early Tertiary period and since they tend to have a high tar content they had formerly been used primarily by the chemical industry.

During the later Tertiary, low-quality brown coal deposits of Oligocene age were formed in the Nógrád Basin, around Ózd and in the Sajó valley. Exploitable coal seams are closer to the surface than elsewhere and their inclination is slight, but the siting and the operation of modern mines is more often than not uneconomic, owing to the scattered location of the basins and the moderate thickness of the seams.

The country's lignite fields also date from the later Tertiary, and deposits with a high water content and of low calorific value can be found in the vicinity of Várpalota and Torony in Transdanubia. Extensive deposits also extend along the southern rim of the Mátra and Bükk Mountains at a depth of 30 to 80 metres *(Fig. 2).*

Peat reserves have some economic significance for the production of compost manure.

Hungary's oil and natural gas reserves were formed during the early Tertiary, and occur in various types of strata. For instance, the limited oil reserves at Bükkszék were extracted from volcanic tufa, as is the present exploitation near Eger and Bükkalja.

Extraction first began in the southern part of Zala county in Transdanubia during the second half of the 1930s, but since the mid-1960s the centre of gravity of the industry has shifted to the Great Plain, where considerable hydrocarbon resources have been proved. The most important areas of extraction are in the neighbourhood of Szeged, in the zone between the Danube and Tisza rivers, in Békés county and around Szolnok and Hajdúszoboszló.

With the application of secondary and tertiary extractive techniques, e.g. injection of CO_2 and seam-burning, the proven reserves of the early 1980s should make it possible to keep the level of oil output at about 2 million tons per annum up to the end of the century. More than three-fourths of the petroleum products exploited between 1976 and 1980 was natural gas, of which the share of inert gas has increased over recent years. The production cost of oil is, even when secondary or tertiary methods are applied, only one-fifth to one-eighth of the 1981 world-market price ($ 230). Hungary's natural carbondioxide (CO_2) occurrences belong to the richest in Europe.

Uranium is mined from rocks of late Permian age at Kővágószőlős near Pécs, where ore of sedimentary origin occurs in an enriched form in lenticular structures similar to bauxite. The deposits dip quite steeply, and mining is already approaching a depth of 1000 metres. Owing to the application of modern mining techniques, output increased threefold during the 1970s, and the present extraction rate, the potential reserves are sufficient to meet the needs of an atomic power station of about 4000 MW capacity [15]. If this rate increases, the use of the uranium deposits as a potential energy basis may be multiplied.

3.2 Minerals

Workable iron-ore deposits, interbedded with Mesozoic limestone, occur only at Rudabánya in Borsod county. The seam, extending over a distance of 4·5 kilometres, is made up of limonite, siderite and anchorite, with an average metal content of less than 30 per cent. Proven reserves are put at about 16 million tons.

Manganese rich muds and clays developed along the marshy coastal areas of the Jurassic recessed sea at Úrkút in the Bakony Mountain, but with a metal content below 25 per cent, the ore is of medium to low quality. The carbonate-rich ore is also harder to process than the oxygenous varieties.

After the Soviet Union and Romania, Hungary has the most substantial manganese reserves in Europe.

The range of mountains extending from Visegrád to the Zemplén Mountains developed during the volcanic period of the Miocene and led to the formation of limited metalliferous zones in the Börzsöny, Mátra (Gyöngyösoroszi) and the Zemplén (Telkibánya) Mountains during the late hot-springs phase of volcanism. Of the valuable minerals occurring in metallic reefs found in the above areas, lead, zinc, copper and molybdenum are the most significant. At greater depths considerable copper-ore deposits have been discovered and proved near Recsk, while the polymetallic especially the copper ores of the Mátra also contain some gold.

The tropical climate of the Cretaceous period also led to the development of rich deposits of bauxite on the then land surface, and where these have not been removed by subsequent denudation, workable quantities are to be found. But although Hungary's reserves of bauxite are substantial by European standards, they are insignificant when compared with the more well-endowed countries of the world. The bauxite occurs in the Bakony and Vértes Mountains and in the Nagyharsány area of southern Baranya county. The quality (modulus coefficient) of much of the reserves is medium to low.

3.3 Non-metallic minerals

Hungary is relatively well supplied with certain non-metallic minerals and construction materials. For instance, the reserves of bentonite, kaolin, glass sand, perlite, anhydrite and zeolite will last for several decades yet, covering the whole, or greater part of internal demand. Some, indeed, depending on price and transportation costs, can even be exported economically. The reserves of limestone, building stone, e.g. basalt and granite and andesitic and rhyolite tufas, together with sand and gravel, will ensure a stable supply of ancillary materials of the construction and metallurgical industries.

Of special significance is the frequent occurrence of bentonites developed from the underwater decay of volcanic material. This valuable industrial mineral can be found in a great many places, especially in the Zemplén Mountains (Erdőbénye and Mád), and in the northern part of the Mátra (Istenmezeje and Pétervására).

Mention should also be made of kaolin, of which sizable quantities have been discovered in the Zemplén Mountains, where they are suitable, for the most part, even for the production of fine ceramics. Kaolin is also mined in the Gerecse Mountains, where it is obtained from kaolinite quartz sandstone. Another valuable industrial raw material of volcanic origin that is commonly found is perlite, a variety of rhyolite. It is used in high-rise buildings for heat and noise insulation, as well as in agriculture for soil improvement. Extensive perlite reserves are to be found at Pálháza *(Fig. 3)*.

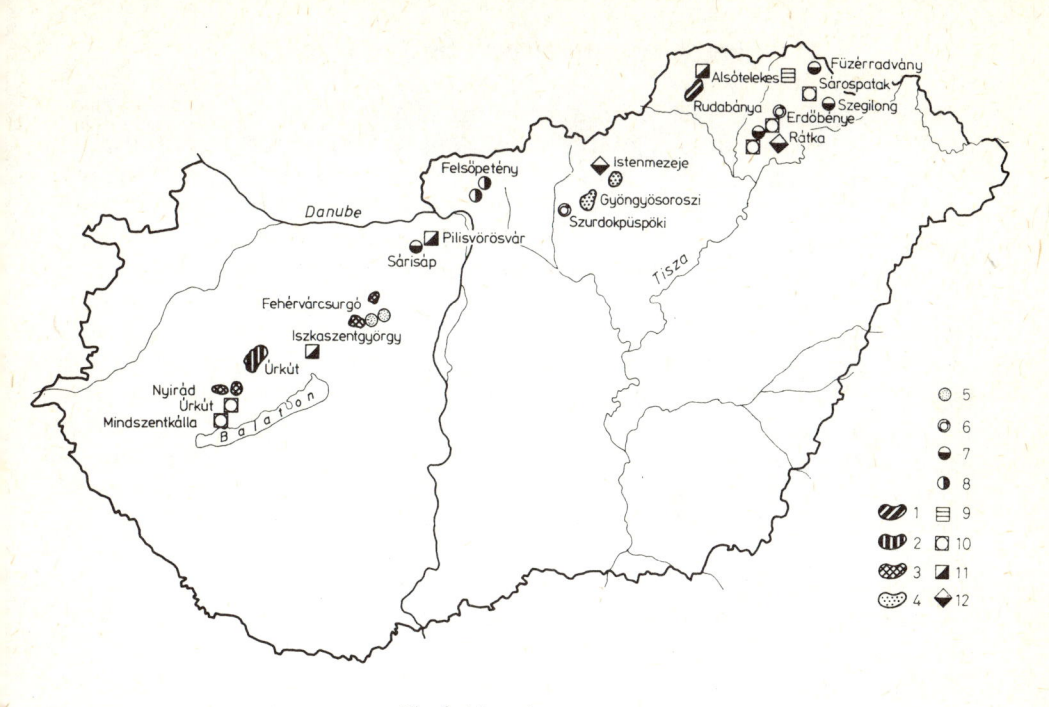

Fig. 3. Mineral resources

Minerals: 1 — iron ore; 2 — manganese; 3 — bauxite; 4 — other ores. Non-metallic minerals; 5 — quartz sand; 6 — silica; 7 — kaolin; 8 — fire-proof clay; 9 — perlite; 10 — quartzite; 11 — dolomite; 12 — bentonite

An important mineral resource of volcanic origin is silica, the largest occurrences of which are at Szurdokpüspöki in the Mátra region and at Erdőbénye and Tállya in the Zemplén Mountains. The silica or silicious sinter is mainly used as a carrier in the manufacture of herbicides and pesticides. Quartzite can be found in abundance in the Balaton Highlands, in the Velence and Mátra Mountains and near Tokaj. It is used in the form of ferrosilicon as an ancillary material in the metallurgical industry as well as in the manufacture of fireproof materials. Quartz, however, achieves its greatest value as glasssand which is quarried at Fehérvárcsurgó, while foundry sand is found primarily at Mindszentkálla in the Tapolca Basin.

Sand and gravel are abundant and easily accessible. It occurs in mountain and hill foot detrital cones, as at Pestlőrinc, Nyékládháza, in the Little Plain, and along the Rába and Dráva valleys. The gravel quarried from the bed of the Danube is essential for the building industry, especially in the northern and western parts of the country, while fine-grained river sand of detrital cone origin and from bed of the upper reaches of the Tisza as well as of the Sebes-Körös and Maros rivers is common in the eastern and southern parts of the Great Plain.

4 Climate and its effects on the economy

Several factors interact to produce Hungary's climate.

The latitudinal position of the country is the basic factor, because it is this which determines the amount of insolation and heat received, the periodicity of the four seasons as well as the relationship of the country to the global wind systems. Suffice it to say that Hungary is situated within the belt of westerly winds and cyclonic activity of the temperate zone, although the effect of the latter is limited and modified especially by the basin location of the country.

A second factor is distance from the continental interior, the Atlantic Ocean and, to a lesser extent, the Mediterranean Sea. This factor accounts for the basic continental character of Hungary's climate, for its precipitation characteristics, for the positive heat anomaly, the monsoon effects in early summer and in winter as well as for the Mediterranean effects prevailing in certain southern parts of the country.

A further significant factor is the basin location of the country, together with the low elevation above sea-level of a major part of the territory.

The passage of air masses also exerts a great impact on the climate and on day-to-day changes in the weather. A factor of constant importance throughout the year is the ,,Icelandic or North Atlantic" low-pressure area, which is the scene of the development of cyclones in the temperate zone. Equally constant throughout the year is the effect of the ,,Azores" high-pressure area, and although the impact of the Siberian high pressure system or the winter monsoon is less regular, when operating, it may cause long cold spells of particular severity. Also irregular is the effect of the so-called Iranian low pressure minimum. The characteristic features of the various air masses and resulting atmospheric conditions depend upon the nature of the source areas, and make themselves felt through fairly rapid fluctuations of temperature, the degree of cloudiness and the duration of sunshine and, last but not least, through spatial and temporal irregularities in the distribution of precipitation [2].

Atlantic or maritime influences on the climate mean that, with few exceptions, substantial amounts of precipitation fall in each month of the year. Moreover, the western winds bring warm air intensified by the Gulf Stream to a large part of Europe, which in Hungary gives rise to a positive heat anomaly of about +2 °C in annual mean temperature (9 °C to 11 °C), i.e. the difference between the mean temperature of the country and the average for latitudes 46°–48°.

Mediterranean influences result in high summer temperatures, frequent early warm autumns with much sunshine and, regularly, a secondary autumn precipitation maximum in south-west Transdanubia [2]. The Mediterranean effect loses much of its intensity towards the north-east, though there are annual periods, the so-called Mediterranean-type years, when the effect manifests itself throughout the whole area of the country.

The fact that most precipitation falls in late spring and early summer (May, June and early July), is due, primarily, to a summer monsoon effect.

Its basin position offers the country a certain degree of shelter from inclement elements. The Alps help impede the intrusion of gale force winds from the west and significantly deflect the courses of temperate depressions, thereby causing, among other things, increased uncertainty in meteorological forecasting. The Carpathians, by contrast, shut out the cold polar air masses, at least temporarily, and often deflect them towards the East.

The high mountain rim of the Carpathian Basin modifies the humidity, temperature and velocity characteristics of air masses arriving from distant areas, and moderates the various atmospheric conditions. As a result of the basin location, a rather mild föhn effect also makes itself felt which contributes to the fact that air temperatures and the inclination towards drought is higher than what it would otherwise be. The rare incidence, usually in late autumn and early winter, of temperature inversion is also closely connected with the basin location.

The relatively minor differences in relief forms, and variations in slope and exposure are of only secondary climatic consequence, and such effects are largely confined to relatively small areas.

An important characteristic of the country's geographical location is that it is situated in the zone where the Atlantic, continental and Mediterranean climates meet, and as each of these climates become alternatively predominant, so the weather can fluctuate rather unpredictably both within one single day and seasonally. Hence, a basic feature of the climate is its transitional character and consequent variability [8]. Further consequences of the country's climate are the small number of perennial plants, the variability of agricultural production and the need to heat buildings for six months of the year from the middle of October to the following April.

Of the climatic elements, atmospheric pressure has, owing to its slight range, little direct economic significance. In Transdanubia, the incidence of near-ground northwest-westerly winds is 45 to 50 per cent, while the same applies to the north-northeasterly winds in the region east of the Tisza. Owing to the channelling effect of the Dévény gate, wind velocity increases in the western part of the Little Plain, and relatively strong winds also prevail in various parts of the Transdanubia Central Highlands [2]. Especially dangerous is the north-westerly ,,Bakony wind" which blows across Lake Balaton during the summer tourist season.

Although the country's climate cannot be described as stormy, damage caused by winds is still significant. Especially harmful is the soil-destructive activity of the wind on deforested slopes, where deflation caused by the west-northwestly winds as well as erosion by sun-off, denude the soil. Very common in sandy areas is the so-called ,,sand scourge" of early spring.

Theoretically, the total possible hours of sunshine is equal to the number of the hours of day-light, i.e. 4448 hours, but as a result of the interaction of the various climatic elements the number of hours of actual sunshine is

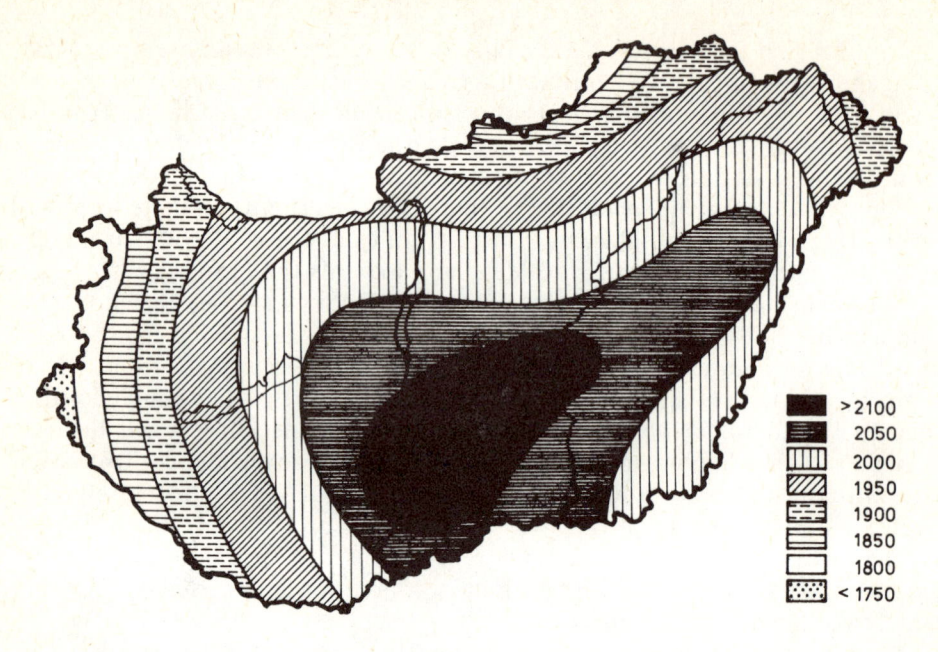

Fig. 4. Annual hours of sunshine

everywhere much less than this, and cloud cover predominates for 55 to 60 per cent of the year in most places *(Fig. 4)*. As a result, even those areas where summers are longest, i.e. the region between the Danube and the Tisza rivers as well as the southeastern lowland of the country, enjoy only 2050 to 2100 hours of sunshine a year, while the western parts of Transdanubia, in sub-alpine areas and in the north of the country, the amount may fall below 1800 hours a year. The amount of sunshine available, however, enables plants to be grown that demand much heat and light, such as grapes and other fruit, paprika (red pepper), tomatoes, maize, soya-beans, lavender, etc. The relatively favourable radiation and atmospheric conditions are also of great significance for tourism and balneology with the largest incidence of sunshine occurring in July and August, and the least during the month of December.

As regards temperature, hot summers and comparatively moderate winters are the characteristic features. The mean temperature in January which is the coldest month of the year, only falls below -4 °C in the highest mountains. Also cold, i.e. -3 °C in January and February, is the north-eastern part of the country, while January averages only -0.5 °C in the south-western frontier region. Mean temperatures during April, the most typical spring month, equal the annual mean of 11 °C in the south and 9 °C in the north of the country, and remain below 9 °C only in the higher mountainous areas. The highest temperature is to be found in the south-eastern region of the country,

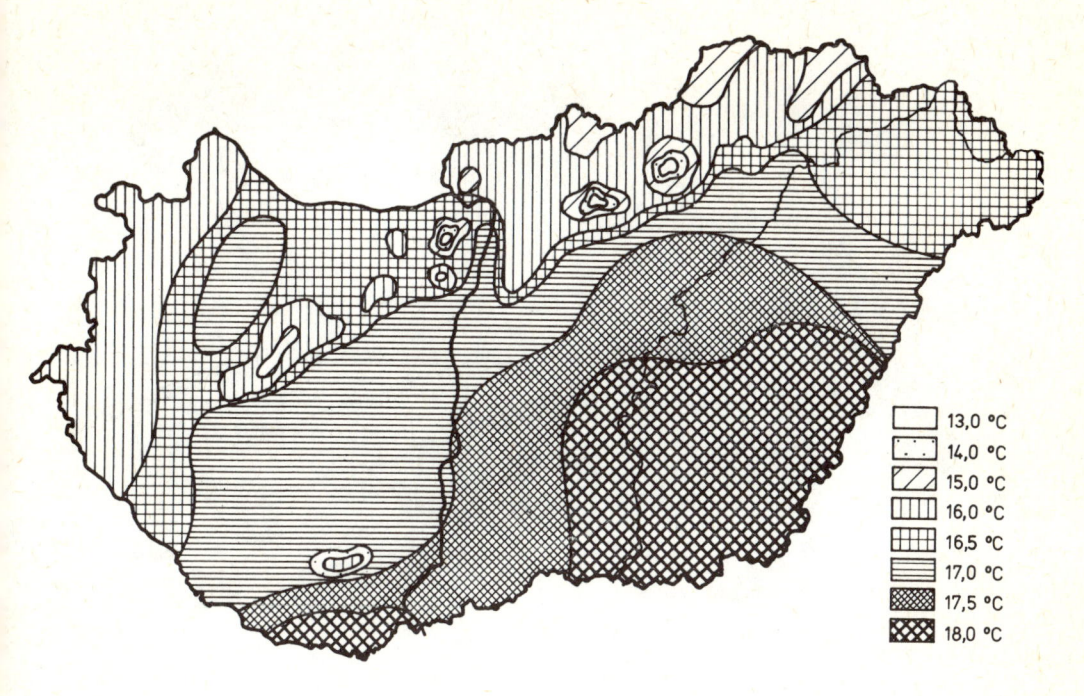

Fig. 5. Mean temperature during the growing period

where the mean July temperature rises above 22 °C in typically continental years, while the lowest, below 22 °C, occurs in the subalpine frontier regions and the North Hungarian Highlands. Typical of the autumn is the fairly persistent, cloudless and warm weather, which is very beneficial to agriculture, but less favourable autumns also happen and can cause severe losses and substantial surplus costs. Significant territorial disparities may also occur in the amounts of heat available during the vegetative period *(Fig. 5)*, being about 10 per cent more in the southeast than in the western parts of Transdanubia and the northern mountainous areas. Moreover, summer heat increases not only from north to south but also from west to east.

Of great practical significance is the timing and frequency of certain temperature thresholds. The average number of warm summer days with a daytime maximum of over 25 °C exceeds 85 in the southeast but is below 60 in the north, while the number of hot days with a daytime maximum of over 30 °C is above 30 but under 10 in the respective areas. It testifies to the severe winters of the north-eastern frontier zone as compared with the mild winters of the valleysides of the Drava and Zala rivers that the number of winter days when the temperature is less than 0 °C is 50 and 25 in the respective areas. The average frost-free period between the last spring frost and the first autumn frosts is about 40 days longer at Szeged and along the Dráva river than in the Upper-Tisza region and along the Sajó river. Of all climatic elements, the greatest territorial differences (50–100%) are in the annual

23

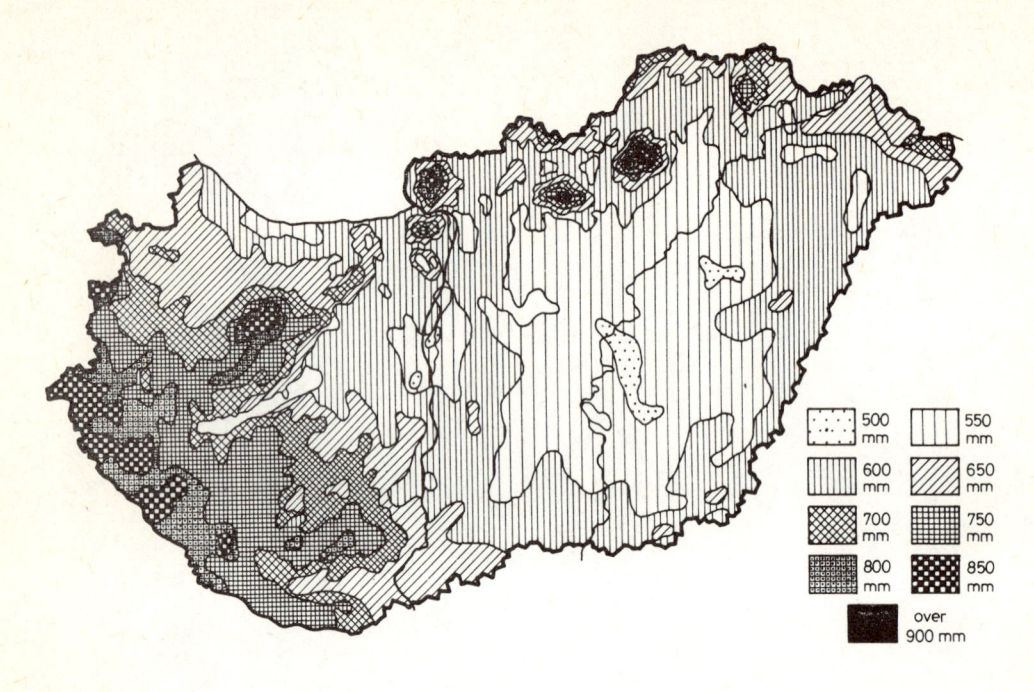

Fig. 6. Annual distribution of precipitation
(amount of precipitation in mm)

average precipitation. However, although sufficient heat and sunshine can be expected everywhere in most of the year, rainfall adequate for cultivation is much less certain during the growing period, and therefore the danger threatening agriculture is more likely to be due to insufficient precipitation than to adverse temperature conditions.

Despite the relatively small area and simple relief characteristics of the country, precipitation varies quite widely. In the driest regions of the Hortobágy and Tiszazug, the annual amount averages less than 500 millimetres but may reach as much as 900 millimetres in the eastern parts of the country (Fig. 6). Moving away from the driest Tisza-regions, precipitation increases in all directions and varies between 600 and 700 millimetres in the Szatmár–Bereg lowland, in the North Hungarian and the Transdanubia Highlands, in the gently sloping areas of Tolna and Somogy counties as well as in the greater part of the Little Plain. It is somewhat higher, i.e. 700 and 800 millimetres, in the more elevated parts of the North Hungarian Highlands, Bakony and in most of Vas, Zala and Somogy counties, and exceeds an annual average of 800 millimetres in the westernmost parts of Vas and Zala counties.

Taking the records for several years, abundant precipitation falls in each month everywhere, with a strong tendency for maximum values to be registered in late spring and early summer, and minimum values in winter. May and June are generally the wettest months, but in the westernmost parts it is July, and, due to the Mediterranean effect, October in the south-western parts of Transdanubia. Precipitation also fluctuates markedly during the growing period, ranging from 300 in the driest lowland areas to over 400–500 millimetres in the west [2, 14].

Precipitation during the winter months may fall as snow, and plays the important role of shielding autumn-sown crops from serious frost damage. The falls occur during the second half of November in the north, which is about two weeks earlier than in the south, while the last snows come around early April. The number of days with snow-cover ranges from between 15 and 30 in lowland areas to 40 to 50 in the mountains, but the snow cover may be very thin, or completely lacking, in the northeastern and south-eastern fringe of the Great Plain. An unpleasant concomitant of the winter weather in Transdanubia is the frequent snow drifts causing obstructions to traffic.

In summer, relative humidity averages less than 60 per cent in the Körös area, Hortobágy and along the middle reaches of the Tisza, and exemplifies the necessity for irrigation in these regions. During winter, on the other hand, damage is often caused to forests and overhead electric cables by hoar-frost and to communications by freezing rain.

From the point of view of agricultural production, Hungary's climate displays several favourable features. Such is the positive heat anomaly, warm continental summer and an approximately six-month-long growing period, which make it possible economically to cultivate the many temperate plants and even some sub-tropical plants too, as well as enabling autumn-sown and perennial crops to survive the winter. The large amount of heat available during the growing season and the non-coincidence of warmest and driest areas are especially favourable for plants requiring considerable precipitation during the height of summer. It is a further favourable circumstance that most precipitation falls during late spring and early summer, although there is generally sufficient precipitation throughout the growing season. The prevalence of cloudless, dry, sunny Indian summer is especially beneficial to the cultivation of vines, fruit and vegetables because their sugar, vitamin and volatile-oil content as well as flavour and external appearance are thereby enforced.

The most detrimental feature of Hungary's climate is its variable nature, especially the unpredictable distribution of precipitation. Because of continental and Mediterranean influences, the danger of drought often appears in mid-summer. A further unfavourable feature that derives from the unequal and irregular incidence of the three climatic determinants, is the extreme and unpredictable values of both temperature and precipitation. Also detrimental is the fact that the number of days of snow-covers is, in general, rather small, the cover being particularly thin in the northeastern parts of the country, from which frost damage to autumn-sown grain may ensue. Detrimental is the lateness of spring and lack of cloud cover giving rise to spring frosts; particularly great may be the damage caused when advective and radiation frosts reinforce each other. Also harmful is the relatively large number of stormy days (25 to 40) and concomitant hail. Nevertheless, the detrimental effects of the various elements of the climate are nowhere so serious as to make cultivation uneconomic [8].

Over-abundant rainfall during the summer, especially when coupled with the late occurrence of spring and the early onset of autumn, can also have unfavourable consequences. In such circumstances, the growing season is much shortened, the optimal requirements of heat- and light-demanding crops are not satisfied, fungal disease spreads more rapidly, and plant maturation may be delayed by 2 to 3 weeks, extending sometimes into late autumn. In addition, agricultural costs are increased significantly through extra sprayings, and the need to dry cereals and maize before storage.

As to a balanced appraisal of the climatic conditions for agriculture, widely different views can be encountered. Some overemphasize Hungary's geographical location and speak of the „extremely favourable" climatic conditions of agriculture. But although many crops of high quality are grown, such as tomatoes, red peppers, apples, and the various wines, the natural endowments of the country should not be overstated. Some neighbouring countries possess, with respect to certain agricultural sectors and crops, climatic and natural conditions similar to, or even better than, those of Hungary, and the country cannot boast of any exceptionally favourable endowments in general. On the other hand, it may be asserted without undue exaggeration that the natural endowments for agricultural production make it possible for Hungary to match the level of agricultural output and productivity of any country in Europe. Indeed, for certain productive branches and crops, conditions are undoubtedly outstanding.

5 Water as an economic resource

Water is a natural resource for many uses, but can no longer be regarded as a free good. Earlier, nature offered society clean water without cost and in abundance, but nowadays it requires labour and becomes increasingly expensive to store and distribute. Hungary's main water resources and also an important means of waste disposal are the major rivers that either touch its boundaries or flow through its territory, most importantly the Danube, Tisza, and Dráva rivers. The physiographic location of the country clearly limits the volume of available and potential water reserves, which therefore require conscious and planned utilization and management.

The country's natural endowments are characterized by an interesting dichotomy, for although it is rich in rivers, its water resources are rather limited. Less than 5 per cent of surface water originates within the country, which means that 95 per cent originates from without and is rather polluted. In the field of water economy, Hungary therefore has many common interests with adjacent countries and co-operation with them is deepening and becoming more effective.

Two-thirds of the country's water supply is provided by the Danube, equivalent to 18 to 20 per cent of its network's potential, while the utilization of the Tisza river and of its catchment area is almost complete, and its reserves are now exhausted. The northern parts of the country are short of water especially in summer and autumn, and a limited supply can only be secured by considerable expenditure. The demand for irrigation in areas often exposed to drought and the requirements of fish farming can usually be ensured only at the cost of the industrial and municipal consumers of the Great Plain and northern areas of the country. Owing to the basin location of the country, river discharge heavily depends on the extent of water extraction in surrounding countries, and this often exerts an unfavourable effect on the nation's water potential. Even now, and increasingly in the future, account must be taken of the factors that limit the supply of water. Demand in certain regions can only be secured by the construction of reservoirs in such valleys as the Rakaca and Lázbérc and by the extension of regional waterwork systems. At present the water supply of Pécs is transported via a 40-kilometre-long canal from the Danube and that of Debrecen via a 20-kilometre-long canal from the Eastern Main Canal. In addition, the construction of the 55-kilometre Fonyód–Kaposvár Canal to tap Lake Balaton water will be completed in 1985.

Water as an organic part of the environment is a valuable resource that must be protected by society as a whole. The population consumes approximately 6 billion m^3 of water annually, the overwhelming part of which has to be transported, unlike electricity, both to and from the consumer. Once used, it must be purified and recycled. The expenditure incurred is thus considerable and 4 per cent of the total national investment is spent on the water economy.

Hungary falls within the Danube drainage basin, which in this region is composed of the river system of the Ipoly and those of Transdanubia and the Little Plain. The major right bank tributaries of the Danube that form their own independent drainage basins are the Rába, Marcal and the Zala–Balaton–Sió and the Mura–Dráva rivers. Throughout the Hungarian section of the system terraces, both broken and unbroken, are found which are significant from the point of view of settlement, road construction, water supply, and gravel and sand extraction.

The length of the Hungarian section of the Danube is 410 kilometres. From the western border to Gönyü the main branch flows in a regulated bed, while its subsidiary – the Moson Danube – flows around Szigetköz. The gradient of this section is relatively steep, being four times greater than that between Esztergom and Budapest, and because of this together with favourable bank and bed characteristics, this section is the most suitable for the construction of a barrage and hydro-electric system in co-operation with Czechoslovakia [10]. The river is aggrading as far as Komárom, which aggravates navigation especially during the low-water periods of winter and autumn. The stretch between Vác and Budapest is inclined to develop islands and sandbanks, and no gravel is transported beyond Fajsz.

The Danube is characterised by two flood régimes. The one develops from the considered effect of the domestic rainfall maximum and the Alpine snow melt, but is of lower amplitude than the second, the spring flood, which derives from snow melt alone [2]. Under unfavourable weather conditions, a third flood period may also emerge during the winter. The maximum range so far recorded between the lowest and highest water levels was approximately 9 metres at Budapest and extremely low water levels may bring navigation to a halt, this usually occurs during the period October to December. Ice drift develops almost each year in the river, although a continuous ice cover makes navigation impossible only once in every two to three years.

For the purposes of a planned water economy, barrages are in the process of being planned or constructed, they serve the compared interests of power generation, navigation and irrigation. The joint Gabčikovo–Nagymaros hydroelectric power plant, which is being built under a Hungarian–Czechoslovak co-operation scheme, will have an energy generation capacity of about 860 MW.

Also significant is the Zala–Balaton–Sió water system. The Zala river, which rises in the westernmost part of the country, has its mouth in Keszthely Bay of Lake Balaton which is consequently undergoing siltation. The Sió, in its turn, is a regulated outflow of Lake Balaton, and a flood gate has been built where it flows into the Danube.

The Dráva, the third largest river of the country, constitutes the state boundary with Yugoslavia for much of its length. It flows in an unregulated, shoaly bed of a considerable gradient, and of its three floods the one in spring is the most violent. Without regulation it is unsuitable for navigation, but its water budget has been included in the comprehensive plans that have been drawn up for the utilization of water and the location of water-intensive industries. The regulation and economic utilization of the river is presently under way in a joint co-operation scheme with Yugoslavia.

Within the drainage basin of the Tisza only the rivers and streams of the Northern Highlands, the Bodrog, Sajó–Bódva–Hernád, Tarna and Zagyva rivers are terraced, while the other tributaries meander across wide flood plains. The water system of the Tisza, compared with that of the Danube, is rather limited, and few natural watercourses traverse the three alluvial cones of the Great Plain. The Tisza drains about half the total area of the country, but by a process of channel straightening, its course has been reduced to about two-thirds of its original length and the section within the country is now 600 kilometres long. Its long profile is only slightly graded, the fall amounting to not more than 30 metres. Indeed, south of Tokaj the gradient is as low as 2 to 3 centimetres per kilometre. Owing to the increased efficiency of inland drainage, the discharge fluctuates markedly with the range between high and low water levels at Szeged amounting to 25:1. The river also carries a great deal of suspended sediment.

Today the Tisza is regulated along the whole of its Hungarian section and is navigable as far as Záhony. Since the construction of the dam at Tiszalök in 1954 and of the barrage system at Kisköre in 1974, it has been possible to use the river for energy generation, for the extension of irrigation over large areas (the Main Canal of Jászság and Kiskunság), as well as for navigation. The Eastern Main Canal branching off at Tiszalök flows into the Berettyó river and can, in case of emergency, also supply water to the Körös. A third Tisza dam will be constructed in the Csongrád area in the late 1980s.

The first right-bank tributary of the Tisza is the Bodrog, the lower reaches of which flow within Hungary. It is a river which floods extensive areas frequently. Each component of the Sajó—Bódva—Hernád river system is steeply graded, but discharge is rather low. The Sajó and more recently the Hernád, too, are of considerable significance in the water economy of the Borsod industrial area. The Sajó is the country's most polluted river, and the problems of waste treatment are largely unsolved and require international co-operation. The Zagyva river, together with its tributaries, the Tarna, the Galga and the Tápió, also has a low discharge and displays extreme fluctuations in its régime.

The left-bank tributaries of the Tisza, the Tur and the Kraszna, are canalized along the whole of their courses and offer, in general, a meagre discharge. The Szamos, on the other hand, is a much more important tributary liable to dangerous flooding.

A particularly important tributary is the Körös drainage system. Owing to its well-constructed irrigation network, it supplies but little water to the Tisza in summer, and may indeed itself need replenishing from the latter. Its system consists of the Berettyó, and the three Körös streams, the Fast, Black and White Körös, all of which are regulated, in part canalized and protected, by embankments. The late summer flood in 1980 reached an extraordinary height and caused extensive inundation and damage. It is these rivers, together with the Eastern and Western Main Canals, the Hortobágy—Berettyó rivers and several smaller tributaries as well as the inland drainage and irrigation canals that compose the drainage system of the Körös region, the most regulated system of the country. At Békésszentandrás a barrage system with a navigable canal and several locks has been built, enabling the irrigation of large areas. The Tisza's largest tributary is the Maros, its Hungarian length is about 40 kms.

Lastly, it should be mentioned that the clearance of forests in the headwaters and upper reaches of Hungary's rivers as well as the contraction of flood plain areas has meant that floods are now more frequent than in the past.

The country's lakes originated during the early part of the Pleistocene. Their basins are shallow and hence of limited water-holding capacity as well as being exposed to aggradation. The largest of the lakes and the most significant from a scenic and economic point of view is Lake Balaton, the number-one resort and tourist region of the country. With a surface area of 600 square kilometres, it also represents a great national asset from the point of view of fishing and reed production as well. The southern line of its basin is accompanied by a 70-kilometre-long sand beach and a continuous strip of holiday resorts. Behind the sand bars, the former poorly drained inland bays are now largely converted to arable land and pasture. Much more varied are the northern and western fringes of the lake. Here the Keszthely Mountains, Tapolca Bay, the volcanic hills of Szigliget and Badacsony, the fault line of the Balaton Highlands which extends from Balatonörs to Fűzfő together with the Tihany Peninsula make the densely settled shoreline of over 100 kilometres in length an extremely varied strip of land. The average depth of the lake is only 3 metres with a maximum of 11 metres occurring in the Tihany Straight.

The main source of the lake's water is precipitation. In summer, the surface temperature can exceed 25 °C, while in winter it is covered with a rather thick sheet of ice. On the southwest side of the lake a marshy zone with only a limited area of surface water and known as Little Balaton is to be found. Thanks to its unique bird life and natural vegetation this is a protected area, but the harvesting of its reeds is of national significance.

The harmful consequences of the drainage of Little Balaton have now become evident as the drift sands and polluted water of the Zala river pour into Keszthely Bay on Lake Balaton without the benefit of eutrophication. Measures against the pollution of Lake Balaton constitute a top-priority task of environmental protection.

Lake Fertő is shallow, of indefinite outline and densely dotted with reed islands. Its total surface area is 335 square kilometres, of which only the southern quarter belongs to Hungary. Its level fluctuates as a function of weather conditions. To the southeast, the Hanság, a poorly drained, shallow and marshy area traversed by the Hanság Main Canal is attached to the lake. The greater part of the Hungarian portion of Hanság has been drained for arable and animal husbandry.

Lake Velence, with a surface area of 26 square kilometres, is situated in a depression of Pleistocene origin. The in-filling of the depression is at an advanced stage, and open water constitutes only 16 square kilometres, the rest being composed of reeds and marshy pasture. The water of the lake is derived from small temporary streams, precipitation and ground water, and two artificial reservoirs have been built to it. Its proximity to the capital makes it an important resort area, and it is also known for fishing and reed production.

Of increasing importance are the country's sub-surface waters [27]. Ground water lies between the top soil and the first impermeable layer, and can be tapped by wells. Indeed, at some places the roots of plants reach down to the groundwater level. It is used as drinking water, for irrigation and sometimes also for industrial purposes. A high ground-water level is often accompanied by the pollution of wells, as is evident from the experience of many hundreds of settlements and it is clear that the provision of piped water supplies to endangered villages is an important and urgent task.

Also of great significance is unpolluted artesian water [19]. In lowland settlements using predominantly ground or river water for drinking supply, the massive boring of artesian wells has brought about sudden development since the end of the last century. A modern drinking-water supply for the rural and urban population is provided, to a significant extent, by the country's cold artesian water resources, while the discovery and utilization of warm and hot artesian water is increasingly gaining ground for agricultural, bathing and heating purposes.

In certain low-lying regions, for instance the Körös region, Rétköz and Bodrogköz, water may cover large areas, especially during years of above-average precipitation. Such long-lasting inundation of arable land not only destroys autumn-sown cereals, but may also prevent the utilization of the land for the whole year.

Hungary is extremely rich in deep water which may be of a thermal, mineral or medicinal nature. The presence of such water is closely related to the present and past geological structure of the given area, i.e. rock structure and type, structural movements, folds and faults. Water temperature is primarily a function of depth as well as of heat-generating process taking place in the surrounding geological environment. Owing to its geological structure, Hungary is the most well-endowed European country per capita as regards thermal, mineral and medicinal waters, and springs of different qualities and varied medicinal effects can be found in practically all parts of the country.

Along the major fault line that traverses the middle of the country there are over one hundred natural or bored medicinal springs along both banks of the Danube in the Budapest agglomeration, with a combined discharge of about 70 million litres a day. The springs are supplied by the permeable rocks of the right bank of the Danube, by hot waters flowing at the deeper levels, under the Great Plain as well as from deep waters surging upwards along the fault line. Water temperature is dependent upon the proportionate mixture, varying between 14 and 76 °C, and has given rise to a whole series of lukewarm and hot-water springs which supply health resorts and open-air swimming pools, as well as being used for various drinking cures.

Near the south-western shore of Lake Balaton is situated the resort of Hévíz, with the country's most valuable calcareous and sulphurous spring water at an average temperature of 33 °C, while at Balatonfüred the carbonic acid waters derived from the after-effect of basaltic volcanism have been used for centuries [28].

During the search for oil and natural gas in the course of boring artesian wells in the deep-lying strata of the Great Plain, valuable medicinal waters and hot springs have been discovered and brought to the surface at several places. Such are the medicinal hot waters containing iodine at Hajdúszoboszló. So far more than 390 springs have been detected, and it is clear that substantial untapped potential for their further use still remains [20]. For instance, during the past few decades, several measures have been taken to utilize the geothermal energy of hot springs, and the results attained have met with international recognition. Yet these results still lag far behind the great potentialities, and the immense reserves of thermal water — about 500 billion cubic metres — could play a much greater role in satisfying the country's energy requirements.

Experience has shown that one possible way of utilizing geothermal energy is in the supply of hot water to dwellings and communal institutions and, to a lesser extent, in their heating, for instance in Budapest and Szeged. Yet the most important task remains the heating of the green houses and plastic tents used in gardening. The multiple utilization of geothermal energy produces substantial water supplies, and despite transport and investment difficulties, efforts are being made to increase its use, although it is not suitable for the production of electric energy [21].

6 Soils

Hungary is situated at the contact between the European forest and meadow soil zones, and it is these soils that cover more than 60 per cent of the country's territory [29]. Owing to the varied climate, hydrology and natural vegetation as well as the divergent and multifarious effects of the solid geology and relief characteristics, sandy, alluvial bog, marsh and alkali soils came into being, alongside the prevailing soils, producing a variety that can hardly be found in Europe as a whole [23]. Within the Great Plain even a few meters' difference in surface level can bring chernozem, meadow and alkali soils in close proximity to one another.

25 per cent of the country's area is covered by meadow chernozems. The characteristic features of this soil type, covering the region east of the Tisza, North-Bácska, Mezőföld and the Little Plain, are a favourable crumble structure, calcareous content, a humus layer to a thickness of as much as 100 to 150 centimetres and a slightly alkaline chemical reaction. Drainage is good, the soils are easy to cultivate; they are locally called „black soils", and because of their fertility they are important natural resources.

The most extensive meadow-type chernozem has developed on the loess of the Békés—Csanád region, where the thickness of this extremely fertile soil reaches as much as 150 centimetres. In the Hajdúság, the meadow chernozem has a humus layer 60 to 80 centimetres thick, but in the middle reaches of the Tisza and in the Szolnok loess area the humus layer is thinner and the crumble structure less good, while the fertile meadow chernozems of the north of Bácska may merge into alkali soils in the lowest-lying parts. From the alluvium of the Danube emerges the Baranya loess table which is also covered with a rich loess-based chernozem soil, as is the loess-covered Gerezsd, while extensive chernozems can be found in the Mezőföld [1]. The

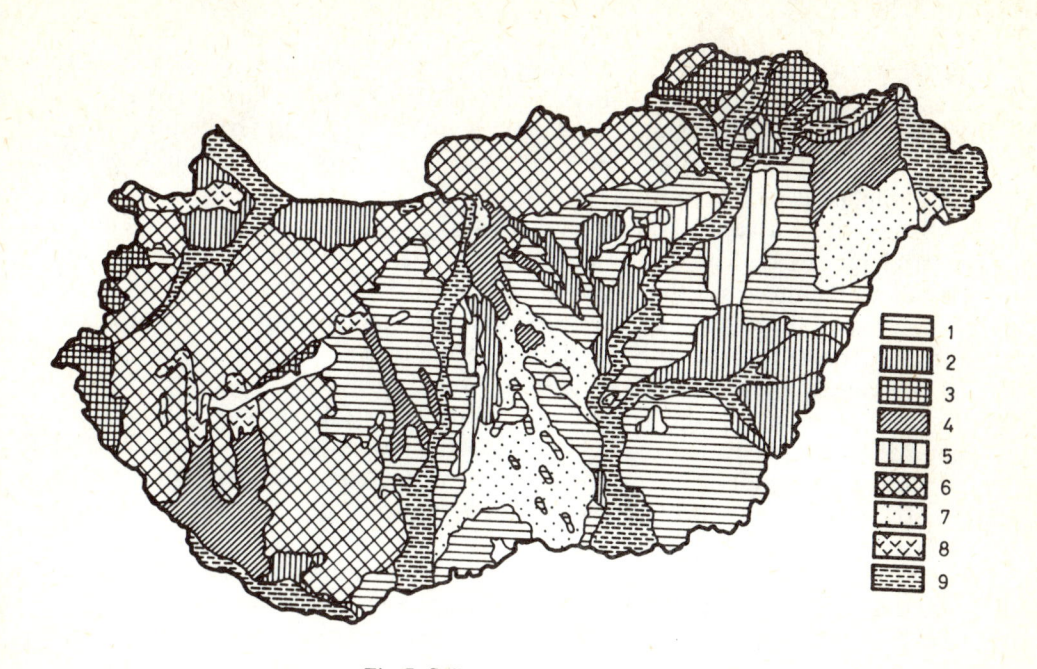

Fig. 7. Soil types of Hungary
1 — marshy soil; 2 — meadow soil; 3 — grey forest soil; 4 — rost-brown forest soil; 5 — alkaline soil; 6 — brown forest soil; 7 — sandy soil; 8 — bog soil; 9 — alluvial soil

best-quality soil type of the Little Plain is the fertile meadow chernozem of the loess terrace of the Győr–Komárom region. Also of meadow type are the alluvial soils of the Moson Plain and Szigetköz, while the former brown forest soil of Outer Somogy and Tolna counties are gradually changing into meadow soils under the impact of cultivation. Here the thickness of the humus layer can reach as much as 80 centimetres, but soil erosion is very intensive *(Fig. 7).*

41 per cent of the soils of the country are mildly acidic forest soils, although grey, strongly acid brown forest soils with a low humus content have developed in the higher and wetter regions of Transdanubia and the Northern Middle Mountains. In such cool and rainy areas as the western parts of Vas and Zala counties and at higher elevations in the Börzsöny, Mátra, Bükk and Zemplén Mountains strongly acidic rost-brown and brown forest soils have developed rather than podsols.

The dominant forest soil of the country is the slightly acid brown forest soil, which embraces not only most of the Middle Mountains and the hilly areas, but is also extensive on the fringes of the Little Plain. As a result of prolonged cultivation, they are slowly evolving into meadow soils of better structure. In addition, the proportion of brown podsolic forest soils is also increasing in Western Transdanubia and the subalpine region, where they are of high acidity, display poor drainage characteristics and low fertility and are

33

strongly eroded. The podsolic brown forest soils of Kemeneshát and of the area between Gyöngyös and Ikva belong to the poorest soils of the country. Rendzinas, soils consisting of rock debris with a very thin fertile horizon and poor drainage properties, are scattered throughout the limestone and dolomite areas of the country.

Sandy soils, a variety of skeletal soils, consist mainly of quartz grains and cover large areas. Those of the Danube–Tisza Mid-region are rich in limestone, while those of the Nyírség and inner-Somogy are acidic. As for the former sand-dune county, this has needed many centuries of strenuous effort to bring to productivity, the soil being bound together by the planting of vineyards, orchards, acacia and black-pine forest.

Large areas along the rivers are occupied by alluvial soils. They are, in general, difficult to cultivate, and can be ploughed only when adequate moisture content is present owing to a high degree of cohesion. They are mostly fertile and, owing to their low-lying location, are irrigated in a significant part.

Meadow soils have developed in damp depressions on the higher levels of the river flood plains. They are most commonly found in the Körös region, but they also cover large areas of the Little Plain and its fringes, and occur in the valleys of Transdanubia and elsewhere. Meadow soils are particularly difficult to cultivate and can be broken down by deep ploughing only under appropriate weather conditions. It is largely for this reason that such areas are generally under pasture.

Highly acidic peaty bog soils have developed on former wet areas as a result of extensive and prolonged inundation. Their organic content can reach as much as 70 per cent. Muck and peaty bog soils can be found around Lake Balaton, in the Hanság, Sárrét, Rétköz and the nature reserves of the Ecsed marshland. These types of soil have not fulfilled the hopes attached to them with respect to the growing of either sugar beet or hemp.

Alkali soils are very common in areas of continental climate and poor drainage, and are particularly associated with the Great Plain. The process of alkalization took place for the most part several thousand years ago and, to a lesser extent, as a result of the drainage works of the last century. Under present-day weather conditions, alkali soils are gradually evolving into meadow-type chernozems in arable areas and into meadow and alluvial soils in irrigated regions [23]. Of the two types of alkali soil found in Hungary, alkali (solonetz) soils of low lime content occur mostly along and east of the Tisza river, while limey-saline alkali (solonchak-solonetz) soils are mostly to be found in the Danube–Tisza Mid-region and on the high-flood plain levels of the Danube. Between these two types of limey alkali soils occupy an intermediate position. The most heavily alkaline area is the Hortobágy, where alkali soils account for more than 80 per cent of the total area. Meadow soils occur only in patches at higher levels, but even so, most of them have an alkali sub-soil.

One of the most prominent natural endowments of Hungary is the relatively large proportion of the land that can be utilized for agricultural purposes. It is very difficult to compare the quality of agricultural land between countries and even within one single country, but the sorts of criteria that must be taken account of include natural soil fertility, precipitation, the amount of heat available, duration of sunshine and relief. Also of importance are the water régime (precipitation, evaporation, and surface and ground water) and the degree of erodability and temperature. Taking cognizance of the above criteria, the agricultural land area of Hungary may be described as being somewhat better than medium quality.

7 An evaluation of the natural endowments and mineral resources of Hungary

In a synthesis and economic evaluation of the natural endowments of Hungary, the first point to be examined is the role that these factors play with respect to the growth and structure of the economy and with respect to international relations.

The recent worldwide price explosion in raw materials, and the deterioration of the terms of trade and balance-of-payments difficulties of the Hungarian national economy means that the significance of the rational management of natural resources has greatly increased. Hence, taking stock of the potentialities and limitations of the natural endowments of the country is an indispensable condition for balanced economic growth, structural transformation and the development of economic relations. The rapid and effective exploitation of favourable natural endowments and the overcoming of resource deficiencies is an important prerequisite for economic development.

Natural endowments represent for any country a stable and relatively constant factor in the drawing up of realistic long-term plans of economic growth and in ensuring an adequate and efficient adjustment to the needs of international speculation [5] Such factors significantly influence the rate and stability of growth, stability, and the possibility for eliminating disequilibria.

In this respect account must be taken of the fact that Hungary also processes imported raw materials and semi-finished products for both domestic consumption and export, and its economic development therefore depends in no small measure on the possibilities and economic efficiency of these operations. No less important is the adequate utilization of all natural resources, especially where they offer-better-than marginal additional income and comparative cost advantages.

In this scientific and technological age the elements of the natural environment that are the most significant are those which provide resources for the processes of production, yet the adequate and efficient use of all the elements and natural resources of the physical environment is indispensable for the favourable adjustment to socialist economic integration and to world economic relationships [24].

In the past few years, as a result of world economic changes, the appraisal of the economic value of raw materials — among them of mineral resources has also undergone a basic change in Hungary and, as a consequence, efforts aimed at increasing the extraction of local raw materials have been intensified [12]. How an economic policy designed to exploit and utilize the mineral resources of the country most effectively can be made to serve the solution of the basic problems of that policy has become a crucial question in economic development. In this connection it must be emphasised that during the period when the country was adjusting to the needs of international specialization, i.e. during the phase of economic intensification, raw-material exploitation shifted from one emphasising maximum physical output towards one emphasising optimal economic production. To put it differently, the exploitation of the country's natural resources, for instance the expansion of mines already operating and the opening up of new mines, is only feasible under the changed conditions if the efficiency of the national economy is thereby increased, if they can be fitted into the economic and industrial policy designed to attain these objectives.

When interpreting and assessing the natural resource potential from the point of view of economic development, account must be taken of the fact that the determination of the industrial mineral wealth of the country depends, partly, on trends in world-market prices and, partly, on domestic extraction costs which, in turn, are strongly influenced by technological progress. As a result of these two effects, the economically workable mineral reserves of Hungary are increasing, and more geological prospecting is being undertaken. The efficiency of this latter programme is exemplified by the fact that the potential value of industrial mineral wealth discovered between 1976 and 1980 is 12-times the amount expended on geological prospecting and research.

The forms of raw-material extraction geared to the selective development of the national economy can be divided into two distinct parts firstly, domestic reserves that are economically exploitable expand in quantity with rising values on the world market, while secondly, the discovery of favourable natural resources, the adoption of new techniques, scale economies, and the creation of efficient vertical integration schemes constitute the basis of the second alternative [15]. In the first case, with a cost level taken to be unchanged, the use of domestic natural resources merely replaces or diminishes the burdens brought about by changed world-market price relations, while in the second case, the utilization of the country's own reserves may mean partial or full release from the costs of purchasing them on the world market.

Whether there is any economic rationale behind the utilization of domestic reserves — i.e. the dilemma between increasing domestic production and the stepping up of imports — can only be decided after a functional appraisal of the potential. The changes that a mineral may undergo during the course of extraction — i.e. partial processing — and utilization have to be assessed as to economic efficiency by individual sectors, i.e. the economic possibility of extraction has to be deduced from the financial viability of the end product by determining the degree of efficiency during the individual stages of any process of vertical integration and by taking account of the value and profitability of the mineral raw-material base.

Related analyses reveal that where vertical integration leads to a more retired level of processing, the increase in value may be thought of as a form of mining rent. Yet, depending on world-market prices, the highest stage of processing will not always ensure the greatest profitability for all products, and in certain cases semi-finished products may have a greater income-generating capacity.

In any assessment of the mineral wealth of Hungary conflicting views can be encountered. The most common value judgement is that „Hungary is poor in mineral raw-materials", yet this should not be taken as meaning that the country suffers from a general scarcity of mineral resources. If an objective view is to be achieved, then this has to be based on comparisons, either at a national or an international level.

To what extent can domestic sources satisfy the needs? During recent years, domestic supply has met two-thirds of the demand for minerals and, within this, 50 per cent of the demand for energy-generation. Although the demand for energy satisfied from domestic sources fell from 66 per cent in 1950 to 50 per cent in 1975, this cannot account for all the economic difficulties faced by the country. Moreover, this 50 per cent ratio can be maintained, given a large-scale development up to the margin of economic efficiency and a well-thought-out structural policy, up to the end of this century [16]. The following may be considered realistic objectives, the maintenance of oil and natural gas production at the present level or even a moderate increase in the case of natural gas output; the doubling of domestic coal production; a small rise in bauxite output; the satisfaction of the demand for manganese from domestic sources and, depending of the capacity to be built, sufficient for the export of ferro-manganese; meeting the increment and later the whole of copper demand from domestic sources; an increase in the output of gallium, titanium—dioxide and vanadium largely as by-products; the raising of the production of non-ferrous minerals for both domestic consumption and export [3].

Another way of assessing the potentialities of mineral resources is to consider the extent to which their production contributes to national income. According to the Hungarian Central Statistical Office, in 1980 the value of the country's mineral wealth was 500 billion forints, or 11 per cent of the national income, and close to one third of the total value of all natural resources. Between 1970 and 1978, while national income doubled, the wealth contributed by mineral exploitation, computed at current prices, grew threefold and as a result of world-market price movements in the 1970s, the margin of economic extraction has shifted considerably.

The country's relative raw-material potential can also be assessed by examining the specific value of mineral production, either by unit area or per capita, and by comparing the values thus obtained with international data. On the basis of 1973 data, prior to the price explosion Hungary with its mineral wealth of 2891 dollars per m^2 ranked 28th among the 148 countries under survey. This was more than 2·5-times the world average of 1093 dollars per m^2. Also, with respect to the per-capita value of production, Hungary occupies an intermediate position among the world's countries [4, 5, 7].

A more realistic assessment of the country's mineral contribution to raw-material supply can be attained by computing the ratio of domestic production to net imports, i.e. by finding out the extent to which the primary sources of industrial production (ores, fuels and basic materials) are located within the national frontiers. Viewed in this way, Hungary, no doubt, has more limited mineral potential than many other countries, and will have to rely increasingly on imports in the face of further industrial development. Characterizing the country's position with regard to individual primary resources, we can state that the supply of energy sources is below the world average, although recent price changes have improved the viability of marginal reserves.

The reserves of certain metal ores, particularly bauxite, manganese, and copper, are substantial and will not be exhausted for several decades yet. On the other hand, the reserves of iron ore, polymetallic ores and several non-ferrous metal ores are either minimal, or completely lacking and are of poor quality. The position is worst with regard to the raw-materials for the chemical industry and raw sulphur, phosphates, potassium and rock salt have to be imported. By contrast, the supply of certain non-ferrous minerals like quartz sand, kaolin and bentonite as well as limestone, marl, various kinds of stone, gravel and sand for the construction industry is excellent.

Physiographical endowments must also be assessed from the point of view of domestic production, all the more so as the world terms of trade allow the rent component of minerals and several agricultural raw-materials to play a greater role. Also the utilization of favourable physical conditions may constitute the basis for a steadily growing income from tourism [17].

The income and profits from natural endowments — depending of course on adequate technical—economic utilization — have become a substantial factor in national economic achievements throughout the world. The conscious survey and utilization of nature-based productivity differences is also of vital interest to the economic development of Hungary, which makes the development of all those extractive branches necessary in which physical conditions are better than marginal when expressed in terms of prices [17, 18]. It is also necessary to specialize internationally by producing more such raw-materials and by developing those extractive activities that — by international comparison — are found under favourable natural conditions. At the same time, domestic production must replace the import of all those mineral and agricultural raw-materials that can be realized under better-than-marginal physical conditions [17], and for which the investment conditions are also more favourable, e.g. the extraction of copper ore, and the growing of soya beans and other protein fodders.

Bibliography for Chapter I

[1] Ádám, L., Marosi, S and Szilárd J. (eds) (1959): *A Mezőföld természeti földrajza* (Physiography of the Mezőföld). Akadémiai Kiadó, Budapest, 514 p.
[2] Bacsó, N. (1959): *Magyarország éghajlata* (The climate of Hungary). Akadémiai Kiadó Budapest, 302. p.
[3] Balogh, K. (1978): A földtan helyzete Magyarországon (The state of geology in Hungary). MTA X. Osztályának Közleményei, Nos 1–2, pp. 85–109.
[4] Benkő, F. (1977): Az ásványi nyersanyagokban szegény ország kérdéséhez (The issue of countries poor in mineral wealth). MTA X. Osztályának Közleményei, Nos 1–2, pp. 73–95.
[5] Bernát, T. (1980): Gazdaságunk természeti erőforrásai, térszerkezeti sajátosságai és a gazdasági egyensúly kérdése (Natural resources, spatial characteristics of the economy and the question of economic equilibrium). *Egyetemi Szemle*, I, pp. 21–30.
[6] Bernát, T (ed.) (1981): *Magyarország gazdaságföldrajza* (An economic geography of Hungary). Tankönyvkiadó, Budapest, 461 p.
[7] Borai, Á. (1977): A természeti erőforrások országos és regionális értékelése, különös tekintettel a nemzeti vagyonra (The nation-wide and regional appraisal of natural resources with special reference to national wealth). *Földrajzi Értesítő*, No. 2, pp. 161–178.
[8] Bulla, B. (1962): *Magyarország természeti földrajza* (The physiography of Hungary). Tankönyvkiadó, Budapest, 423 p.
[9] Dank, V. (1976): A hazai szénhidrogénprognózis néhány kérdése (Some questions concerning the prospects for oil and natural gas reserves). *Földtani Közlemények*, Suppl. pp. 457–463.
[10] Dávid, L. (1979): A vízgazdálkodás és az energiagazdálkodás fejlesztésének fontosabb kapcsolatai (Some important relationships in the development of the water and energy economies). *Hidrológiai Közlemények*, No. 12, pp. 543–548.
[11] Góczán, L. (1980): Mezőgazdasági területek agroökológiai kutatása, tipizálása és értékelése (Agro-ecological research, typology and evaluation of agricultural areas). *Földrajzi tanulmányok*, 18, Akadémiai Kiadó, Budapest, 150 p.
[12] Hahn, Gy. (1978): A földtani kutatás népgazdasági eredményei (The results of geological research in the interest of the national economy). *Földrajzi Közlemények*, No. 2. pp. 141–146.
[13] Jakucs, L. (1971): *A karsztok morfogenetikája. Karsztfejlődés variációi* (The morphogenetics of karst. Variants of karst-development). Akadémiai Kiadó, Budapest, 310 p.
[14] Kakas, J. (ed.) (1960): *Magyarország éghajlati atlasza* (A climatic atlas of Hungary). Akadémiai Kiadó, Budapest, 20 p., 78 maps.
[15] Kapolyi, L. (1978a): A természeti erőforrások szerepe a magyar gazdasági struktúrában (The role of natural resources in the economic structure of Hungary). *Rendszerelemzési szeminárium*, Budapest, 26 p.
[16] Kapolyi, L. (1978b): Hazai energiakincsünk szerepe energiagazdálkodásunkban (The role of domestic energy sources in our energy economy). *Energia és Atomtechnika*, No. 10, pp. 401–411.
[17] Kozma, F. (1978a): Gondolatok a természeti erőforrások hasznosításának hatékonyságáról (Some ideas about the efficient utilization of natural resources). *Közgazdasági Szemle*, No. 9, pp. 1051–1075.
[18] Kozma, F. (1978b): *Mire képes a magyar népgazdaság?* (The capabilities of the Hungarian national economy) Kossuth Kiadó, Budapest, 388 p.
[19] Láng, S. (1967): A vízkémiai változások kérdése mélyebb rétegvizeinkben (The question of hydrochemical changes in artesian water). *Hidrológiai Tájékoztató*, pp. 25–29.
[20] *Wells of Thermal Water in Hungary*. VITUKI, Budapest, 1966, 420 p.
[21] *Hydrological Atlas of Hungary*. VITUKI, Budapest, Series I–IV, 1952–1966.

[22] Marosi, S. and Szilárd, J. (1975): Balaton menti tájtípusok ökológiai jellemzése és értékelése (The ecolological characteristics and appraisal of the landscapes of Lake Balaton). *Földrajzi Értesítő*, No. 4, pp. 439–477.
[23] Pécsi, M. (1964): A magyarországi szerkezeti talajok kronológiai kérdései (Chronological questions concerning structural soils in Hungary). *Földrajzi Értesítő*, No. 2. pp. 141–156.
[24] Pécsi, M. (1974): A környezetpotenciál integrált földtudományi értékelése (An integrated geological appraisal of environmental potential). *MTA X. Osztályának Közleményei,* Nos 3–4, pp. 193–198.
[25] Pécsi, M. (1979): A földrajzi környezet új szemléletű regionális vizsgálata (A new view of the regional investigation of the geographical environment). *MTA X. Osztályának Közleményei*, Nos 1–3, pp. 163–175.
[26] Pécsi, M. (1980): A Pannónia-medence morfogenetikája (The morphogenetics of the Pannonia-basin). *Földrajzi Értesítő*, No. 1, pp. 105–126.
[27] Salamin, P. (1980): A víz szerepe a magyarországi sík-, domb- és hegyvidék felszínének alakulásában (The role of fluvial processes in the development of the plains, hills and mountains of Hungary). *Földrajzi Közlemények*, No. 4, pp. 308–330.
[28] Schulhof, O. (ed.) (1957): *Magyarország ásvány- és gyógyvizei* (The mineral and medicinal waters of Hungary). Akadémiai Kiadó, Budapest, 973 p.
[29] Stefanovits, P. (1963): *Magyarország talajai* (The soils of Hungary). Akadémiai Kiadó, Budapest, 2nd ed., 442 p.
[30] Vadász, E. (1960): *Magyarország földtana* (The geology of Hungary). Akadémiai Kiadó, Budapest, 2nd ed., 646 p.
[31] Vadász, E. (1955): Grosstektonische Grundlagen der Geologie Ungarns. *Acta Geologica*, No. 3, pp. 207–244.

II Population and settlement

1 A survey of the history and administration of Hungary

1.1 Historical survey

The first traces of man in the territory which now forms Hungary, as shown by the finds discovered at Vértesszőllős in 1962, go back in history as far as the Palaeolithic period. The Palaeolithic man already used fire and had fairly developed implements, which justifies the conclusion that he lived contemporaneously with Pithecanthropus discovered in Java, and with Sinanthropus found near Peking. In the Bükk and the Gerecse Mountains the remains of a Neanderthal-type man dating from the period 150 000 to 100 000 years B.C., and who lived in caves and made use of thermal waters have also been found. Additionally, the traces of nomadic tribes who hunted cave-bears and other big game around 100 000 B.C. have been discovered on the northern and north-western flanks of the Bükk Mountain and to the north of Lake Balaton, while the earliest primitive agricultural implements have been found in the foothills of the Mecsek Mountain and the south-western part of the Great Plain and derive from the Pre-Palaeolithic and the Palaeolithic Ages. The first signs of the domestication of animals can also be put at around that time. Various copper implements and potshreds found in excavations carried out in the Tisza region are estimated to derive from the late Neolithic and the Copper Ages (2500 to 2000 B.C.) for which there is also some evidence of hoe tillage on the loessic soils.

During the Bronze Age, 2000 to 1300 B.C., the middle Carpathian Basin, comprising Western Transdanubia (the Illyrians) and the southern Tisza region (the Thracians), was the main area of a primitive agriculture with some livestock breeding and the domestication of horses. Dwelling houses and strong points were also constructed at this time, and a fairly extensive trade was maintained with middle- and north-Germans, the routes of the amber trade passing through Sopron, Szombathely and Győr.

The last thousand years B.C. was the Iron Age, when nomadic tribes of Iranian origin, the Scythians, settled in the middle parts of the Carpathian Basin and were dominant there for three centuries. These were followed by the Celts, who came from the west and settled primarily in Transdanubia, and who used weapons and tools made of iron and were familiar with metal coinage.

The conquest of Transdanubia and its annexation to the Roman Empire under the name of Pannonia Province took place during the first century A.C. On the sites of Celtic settlements the Romans built several towns as at Savaria now Szombathely, Scarbantia now Sopron, and Arrabona now Győr. Along the Danube, frontiers were built: Ad Flexum now Magyaróvár, Brigetio now Szőny (near Komárom), Aelia Solva now Esztergom, Ulcisia Castra now Szentendre, Aquincum now Budapest, Intercisa now Dunaújváros and Alisca now Szekszárd. Also Roman foundations were Herculia Gorsium now Tác, Mogentianae now Keszthely and Combria now Veszprém.

The Romans constructed an excellent network of roads in Pannonia, which connected it with the central parts of the Empire, while veteran soldiers settled there and assimilated with the local population. Grain and vine cultivation, the latter mainly on the volcanic soils of the northern shore of Lake Balaton, were introduced in the third century. While Pannonia was under Roman rule, nomadic Bulgarian tribes settled in the south-eastern parts of the Great Plain; from 420 to 454, the greater part of the Carpathian Basin belonged to the Hunnish Empire of Attila and was subsequently occupied by various Germanic tribes — the Gepids, the Eastern Goths and Longobards.

The Avars — an eastern nomadic tribe — settled in the Carpathian Basin during the 6th century, where they became dominant between 567 and 800 A.C. At first, they practiced only stock farming, and grain was grown in Transdanubia mainly by subjected Slavs. But after the Avar domination was crushed, Transdanubia bacame first part of Charlemagne's empire, and when that in turn disintegrated and was divided, it found itself part of the Moravian—Slavic state until the Hungarians conquered the territory at the end of the 9th century, in 895—896.

The Magyars, consisting of 7 tribes and ranging from 250 000 to 300 000 in number, occupied the Carpathian Basin under the leadership of Árpád. Linguistically, these nomadic horsemen belonged to the Finno—Ugrian family of languages, and the nearest linguistic kinsmen of the modern Magyars are the Chanti and Manshi in Western Siberia, and the Finns and Estonians of Northern Europe. The original Finno—Ugrian homeland of the Hungarians is assumed to have been somewhere in Western Siberia. Subsequent migrations placed them in various regions between the Volga and the Ural, first in what is now the Autonomous Tartar Republic and Soviet Socialist Levedia, then in the area between the Black and the Azov Seas, and finally in Etelköz, the present-day Soviet Socialist Republic of Moldavia. From there, threatened by and threatening other tribes and peoples, they moved further westwards, and occupied the Carpathian Basin where they mixed with the indigenous population.

The years 907—955 are called the Age of Raids, when the Hungarian chiefs conducted campaigns for plunder, or fought as the allies or mercenaries of rival feudal principalities in Bavaria, Northern Italy, France and the Byzantine Empire during the period of feudal anarchy preceding the establishment in 962 of the Holy Roman Empire. It is the fear of the marauding Hungarians that is reflected in the litany: ,,From the arrows of the Hungarians, save us, oh Lord!". The intermingling with Slavic and western tribes brought about changes in the ethnic character of the Hungarians. The marauding raids were brought to an end by the defeat of the Hungarians at the battle of Merseburg in 933 and finally at the battle of the river Lech near Augsburg in 955.

This was followed by a new orientation begun under the rule of Prince Géza and continued by King Stephen I (1000–1038), later canonized Saint Stephen, who invited knights and missionaries into the country, and who adopted Christianity as the religion of the country. Stephen, the first king of Hungary, built castles, and bishoprics and monasteries of the Benedictine and Cistercian orders. Under his rule, a feudal economic and social order, and a feudal state were established; once Hungarian tribes at last settled permanently, they adopted agriculture along with animal husbandry, and began to play a dominant role in the region. Moreover, markets and a system of yearly or more frequently recurring fairs began to evolve around the churches and fortresses.

The feudal social and state order was reinforced during the reigns of Ladislas I (1077–1095) and Coloman Beauclerc (1095–1116), who enacted severe laws to this end, but the independence of the feudal Hungarian state had to be defended both politically and through armed struggle against the Holy Roman Empire in the middle of the 11th century, and against Byzantine attempts to impose vassalage upon it in the mid-12th century. Nomadic Cuman tribes settled in the Danube–Tisza Mid-region and in certain parts of the area east of the Tisza during the 13th century, and the strong centralized power of the crown was further weakened by feuding feudal chiefs, while the Mongol invasion of 1241–1242 destroyed a large part of the country. The work of reconstruction and the reorganization of the central power was carried out by Béla IV (1235–1270), who has therefore been termed the second founder of the country. He and his successors built castles and founded the towns of Győr and Sopron in 1272.

After the death of the last king of the Árpád dynasty in 1301, Charles Robert of Anjou occupied the throne. His consolidation of the power of the crown and reorganization of the economic foundations of the Hungarian state was made possible by the more effective collection of royal revenues and by the development of economic relationships and the emergence of the second great social division of labour. There evolved a guild industry and peasant commodity production, a money economy and the mining of precious metals gained increasing importance. Between the end of the 13th and the middle of the 14th century, Hungary progressed from a primitive to a mature and flourishing feudal state. Following the downfall of the Anjou dynasty, the crown lost much of its strength, and the struggle against the Turks began. During this period János Hunyadi — the governor of the country between 1446 and 1453 — inflicted a heavy blow upon the Turks near Belgrade in 1456, in memory of which the Pope ordered the sounding of the noonday bell. It was also between the mid-13th and the mid-15th

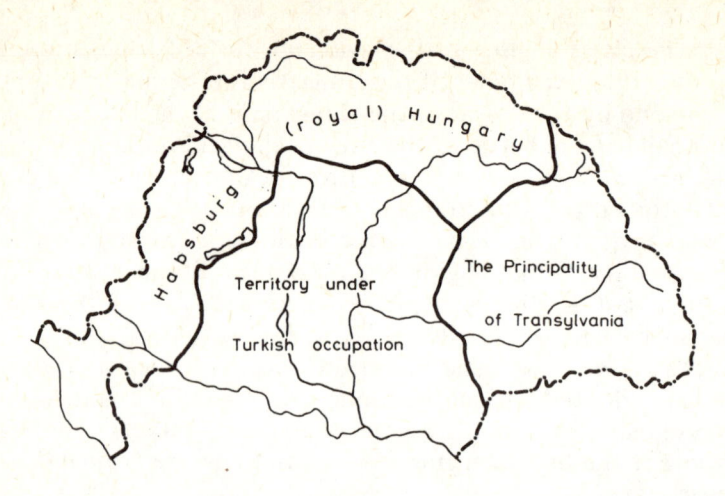

Fig. 8. The division of Hungary in the 16th and 17th centuries

centuries that the order of the nobility evolved, with the first feudal Diet being held in 1439.

During the reign of Matthias Hunyadi (Matthias Corvinus, son of János Hunyadi, 1458–1490), a centralized feudal monarchy was reestablished, when the size of the country's population and the economic power of the king were equal to those of England. Agriculture, home and foreign trade, the guild industry and renaissance culture all flourished.

After Matthias' death, the power of the crown collapsed, and feudal anarchy followed. With the rapid economic deterioration of the serfs and the limitation of their free movement, social conflicts sharpened and led to the peasant revolt of 1514 under the leadership of György Dózsa. The country, torn by social conflict, lost the decisive battle against the Turks at Mohács in 1526. With two kings elected, the country was first divided into two parts (it was at that time that the Habsburg dynasty took possession of Hungary's throne), but with the Turks occupying the castle of Buda from 1541 a threefold division was soon to become the reality. The western and northern parts of the country were attached to the Habsburg Empire under Ferdinand Habsburg (1526–1564), with Pozsony (Bratislava) as its capital, while the central areas fell under Turkish domination for 150 years. Turkish rule led to depopulation, to the massive destruction and annihilation of small villages and to the devastation of agriculture and its replacement by nomadic cattle-breeding, only the so-called market towns flourished in a relative sense. The eastern part of the country evolved into the Principality of Transylvania (1544–1692) which retained limited sovereignty and paid regular annual tribute to the Turks *(Fig. 8)*.

From the early 16th century on, the age of mature feudalism was followed by the period of late feudalism which lasted for about three centuries. This was the age of the so-called second serfdom *(Leibeigenschaft)*, which extended not only to Hungary, but to Europe east of the Elbe in general, and typically often involved a complete turning away from agrarian and social developments in Western Europe. The dependence of the serf on the landlord increased, urban development and capital formation declined, the feudal dues were extended and payments in kind to the landlord increased, trade was largely the prerogative of the landowners, profits from trade were not converted into capital, and the relative situation of the peasantry deteriorated throughout the period.

Protestantism, primarily Calvinism, led to new conflicts, and Counter-Reformation, whose main figure in Hungary was Péter Pázmány, the Archbishop of Esztergom, resulted in re-catholicization primarily in the western part of the country. During the 17th century, several wars of independence were fought against the rule of the Habsburgs. István Bocskai at the beginning of the 17th century, Gábor Bethlen, Prince of Transylvania, during the initial stages of the Thirty Years War, and Imre Thököly during the 1670s and 1680s. Miklós Zrínyi, a poet and formerly loyal aristocrat, formulated the ambitious concept of liberating the country from the Turks without the help of the Habsburgs, relying solely on own forces, and of establishing an independent Hungarian kingdom. His death in 1664 prevented him from carrying out his plan, and the absolutist rule of Emperor Lipót I followed. When liberation from Turkish occupation finally materialized between 1683 and 1686, it was with Habsburg help, and led to the acknowledgement of the hereditary right of succession of the Habsburg dynasty. Protest against absolutism created a unified social opposition and from a regional peasant uprising turned into a national war of independence between 1703 and 1711 under the leadership of Ferenc Rákóczi II, but was crushed.

The country was subsequently incorporated into the system of the Habsburg Empire under the rule of Charles III and Maria Theresa, and around the middle of the 18th century the devastated areas were repopulated by spontaneous immigration, organized internal and foreign settlement of Serbs, Croats, Romanians, Slovaks and Germans, the last being primarily Catholic „Swabians" and Bavarians. It was at that time that Hungary became a heavily multiethnic country, though it is true to say that the Hungarian group had never fully settled the Carpathian Basin. This fact was to become, with the evolution of nationalism during the age of state-building and the growth of nationalist–chauvinistic policies by the Hungarian ruling classes and of regional identity on the part of the nationalities vigorously instigated by the Habsburgs, one of the main determinants of the country's future history.

The basis of the present-day rural settlement network began to take shape during the 18th century. With more labour-intensive cultivation, first temporary shelters, and the permanently inhabited dispersed settlements, together with various types of farmsteads *(tanya)*, began to evolve in the outlying areas of the expanding market towns and villages of the Great Plain. During the boom period of the Napoleonic Wars in the 18th century, agriculture developed one-sidedly, and the emergence of a handicraft industry was prevented by the mercantilist policies of the Habsburgs, especially the dual-customs decree of 1754. Moreover, the economic policy of the enlightened absolutism of Joseph II (1780–1790), although partly beneficial, was also very harmful to the country.

After 1770 there ensued the decline and disintegration of feudalism, and from the mid-1820s onwards the so-called Reform Movement, whose intention was to change, in various measure, the economic and social conditions came to the fore. The two leading personalities of the age were the moderate reformer István Széchenyi and the more radical reformer and later revolutionary Lajos Kossuth, who wanted to achieve the full independence of Hungary from Austria. In March 1848 the bourgeois revolution broke out. the serfs were emancipated, although most of the large estates were left in the possession of the feudal landlords, the freedom of the press was achieved, and the first responsible Council of Ministers was established. Having stifled the other bourgeois revolutions, unity movements and wars of independence, the Habsburgs tried to reverse the Hungarian revolution and transformation by resorting to military force. This led to the Hungarian War of Independence which was fought between September 1848 and August 1849, and headed by Lajos Kossuth, but was crushed by the joint intervention of the Habsburgs and Tzarist Russia. After a cruel revenge, Hungary was incorporated into a unitary and centralized monarchy, but with the deterioration of the political position of Austria through the establishment of Italy in 1859–1860, and her defeat during the Prusso–Austrian war of 1866, the so-called Compromise was concluded in 1867. With this Compromise the dual Austro–Hungarian Monarchy centred in Budapest and Vienna, was established, and persisted until the end of World War I. The Austrian Emperor Francis Joseph I was crowned King of Hungary.

After the bourgeois revolution of 1849, Hungary, although fraught by feudal remnants, entered the period of capitalist development, and the abolition of the customs frontiers between Austria and Hungary in 1851 benefited the development of trade and agriculture. The 1867 Compromise, which settled constitutional relationships, promoted the influx of foreign capital and, together with internal accumulation, helped with the launching of a stronger but still dependent industrial development, in which mining, certain branches of the heavy industry and food processing were emphasized, but in which light industry was left largely underdeveloped.

After the 1867 Compromise, the territories of Croatia, Slavonia and Transylvania which had been detached earlier from the country were re-united with Hungary. In 1910, 51 per cent of the 21-million population were comprised of the national minorities, but even so the nationality question remained unresolved. With the exception of the Croats, the nationalities were given no cultural and territorial autonomy, and their situation as compared with the liberal beginnings after 1867 deteriorated further. The denial of minority rights put such centrifugal forces into motion that the historical

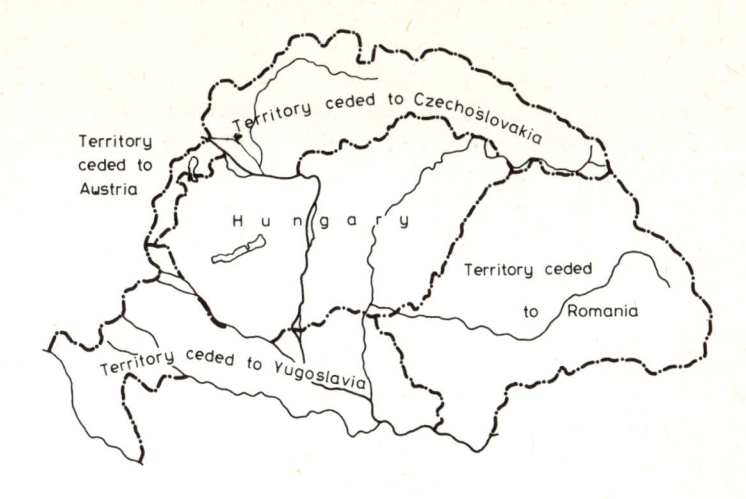

Fig. 9. The division of Hungary in 1920

state of Hungary was brought to the brink of disintegration. Indeed, this was the outcome of the peace treaties of Saint Germain and Trianon concluding World War I, for they not only liquidated the Austro–Hungarian Monarchy, but also brought about basic changes in respect of Hungary as well. Those areas of the historical state largely inhabited by the nationalities but where several million Hungarians were also living were distributed among Czechoslovakia, Romania, Yugoslavia and Austria, and Hungary's territory dwindled to less than one third of its former size i.e. to 93 030 square kilometres *(Fig. 9).*

The fall of the short-lived socialist republic of 1919 was followed by 25 years under the conservative, autocratic system of Admiral Horthy in which Fascist-like features strengthened during the 1930s and 1940s. Economic development was slow. National income increased by an average of only 1 per cent per annum during the quarter of century between 1919 and 1944, and although appreciable growth was achieved in the light industrial, electrical engineering, and chemical sectors after 1924, the agrarian crisis still persisted.

The system of large estates of feudal origin was unable to develop the productive forces of agriculture and hindered and even prevented the rise of the peasants and kept the poor peasantry and agrarian proletariat totalling about 3 million people including family members in utmost poverty and insecurity. The Horthy system chose the side of the Axis powers, and drove the country into the Second World War against the Allies in 1941. In the spring of 1944, the Germans occupied the country, and in October 1944, after Horthy had proclaimed an armistice, removed him from power and established a total fascist dictatorship.

After World War II the Hungarian People's Republic was established and, as a result of socio-economic transformation, the country embarked upon the road of socialist construction. In 1949 a new constitution was enacted and Hungary became a member of CMEA. In 1950 a land reform and monetary reform (following the world's largest inflation) were carried out, the industry and the other economic sectors were gradually nationalized and the socialist transformation of agriculture was begun.

The mistakes made during the course of socialist construction, together with foreign interference, led to the counter-revolution of 1956, but since then government policy has led to a rapid socio-economic development and has resulted in increasing social satisfaction. During the years 1958–1961 the socialist reorganization of agriculture was accomplished with a simultaneous growth in agricultural output, and by 1962 the foundations of socialism had been laid. During the 1960s, the process of re-organizing the economy with due consideration to the national-historical endowments was begun and led in 1968 to the adoption of the new system of economic management (the so-called new economic mechanism), whose essence included the harmonization of national economic planning with market relationships, greater independence and responsibility for individual enterprises, and the regulation, control and supervision of the economy by indirect methods. The period 1968–1974 was the golden age of Hungarian economic development and economic history when, as a result of rapid growth, national income increased vigorously, real wages, real income and the living standard of the various social strata rose rapidly and in a balanced manner and the socialist way of living improved.

The new world economic relations since 1973 have had an extremely unfavourable effect on the country – in all probability a more unfavourable impact than in most European countries – causing immense economic losses stemming from the deterioration of the terms of trade. While preserving and adjusting to the new relations and further developing the system of economic management, it is most important in the new situation to restore and maintain an external economic equilibrium, to preserve living standards and to construct, on the basis of an extensive updating of economic relations, a developed socialist society.

1.2 The system of local administration

Since the elimination in 1984 of districts, the Hungarian system of local administration with its traditional, centuries-old threefold division into counties, districts and towns has been simplified into a two-tier system.

Thus Hungary's local administration is composed of
– counties and county-ranked cities,
– towns, villages (including large villages, villages with independent and villages with joint councils). In addition, Budapest as the country's capital with its extensive area and 2 million inhabitants performs the same function as a county.

As January 1st, 1984, Hungary is divided into 19 counties, 5 county-ranked cities (plus the capital), 103 towns and 2957 villages (see *Table* later). Although the present-day structure of local administration shows, at the level of counties, little similarity with that which had existed a thousand years ago, it is nonetheless based on the historical divisions of royal and other feudal estates underlying the ancient county network established in the time of King Stephen I.

Although the various administrative boundaries have undergone several modifications and corrections over the centuries, yet the basic administrative units of counties and districts display but few consistent objective criteria. Before the administrative reorganization of 1950, the administrative system had been composed of 14 cities with municipal rights[*], 47 county-ranked cities, 1166 large villages and 2079 small villages, all falling within 25 counties.

At the reorganization, the number of counties was reduced to 19 because the frontier changes following the Trianon peace treaty had fragmented many counties along the frontier of the country (Abaúj, Zemplén, etc.) which were attached to the neighbouring counties. Also at the 1950 reorganization a new council structure was created, which remained in all its essential features unchanged until 1984, although some minor modifications were also made. The changes that occurred were mainly to the district network designed to supervise the administration of villages, which, with the increased independence of the villages became eventually superfluous. It is also indicative of the development of the administrative organization that at the establishment in 1950 of the council system there were councils with more or less qualified specialists in about 3000 villages, small and large alike. In 1970, their number hardly reached 2000, and in 1984 only 1379 village councils managed their own affairs and those of the neighbouring associated settlements. This decrease was also accompanied by substantive changes. As long as many, among them also small and ineffective, village councils operated, district councils were needed to coordinate and guide them. They provided assistance not only in fulfilling central duties but also in implementing the local tasks of state administration. These tasks required special knowledge which the villages of that time often did not possess. Officials specialized in administrative, building and other activities were lacking in the villages.

Since democracy was gaining ground in the state as a whole and ever greater decision power was assigned to the settlements — towns and villages —, districts as administrative units have lost their significance. This, however, does not mean that the villages were able to take over all responsibilities of the districts overnight. The administrative relation system of towns and, in a few exceptional cases, of large villages with a town rank, a system

---

[*] These cities had the same legal status and self-governing character as the counties.

that is designed to replace the districts, has to be regarded as a historically transitory process.

In the local council organization, such a district-centred network of villages and towns has been established in which the councils' management organization in the overwhelming majority of towns (105 out of the country's 109 towns) and 34 large villages in regions with few town settlements (of which 22 used to be district centres) will also perform, transitorily, the secondary administrative functions of about 10 to 15 villages (such, for example, as are related to building activities, price control, health and other social services). In this way, the territory of the country will be divided into 139 urban regions and large town-ranked villages, or to use a uniform term: urban hinterlands. Between the village councils in the urban hinterland and the council of the hinterland centre *no hierarchic but a co-ordinated relationship will develop to perform the manysided planning-developing and harmonizing activities*.

The 2957 village settlements of the country are encompassed by 1394 village councils. 681 out of them operated as independent village councils, and the authority of the 715 joint village councils extended over 2276 village settlements. Thus 1675 villages, the so-called associated villages, have no locally operating councils. It was to remedy the grievances of these associated villages that a nation-wide administrative resolution was taken in 1983 to establish an independent organ consisting of the council members of the associated villages. This authority was entrusted with the task to protect the interests of the member villages.

The reorganization of the administration system is an important means for the development of state power and for the management of the national economy. It constitutes a basic organizational framework as well as the territorial foundation of a system of management and planning. The local organs of state power are the *councils*, which are arranged in a hierarchy, but also have significant responsibilities in the fields of economic management, organization and supervision, and co-operate with the productive enterprises in the various settlements. Many of the small- and medium-sized enterprises oriented towards the satisfaction of local needs, whether they be state enterprises, co-operatives or private artisans, collectively termed council industry, operate directly under the supervision of the councils and account for about 7 per cent of the annual production value of the national industry. Councils are also responsible for the economic tasks associated with the infrastructure, such as settlement development, urban and village economy, local transport and communications as well as the satisfaction of social demands for welfare, health and culture. Since the reorganization of the system of economic management in 1968, the councils have acquired the experience needed to perform the tasks of settlement development independently.

Even this sketchy enumeration of their economic tasks should serve to demonstrate the significance that the councils of different levels have in shaping the territorial division of labour.

At present, decision-making is excessively concentrated in the hands of the county and capital councils, that is, in councils that are of territorial significance. It is indicative of the unjustifiably great economic role of the county councils that about 90 per cent of the councils' development resources are at the disposal of the council organs with allocative power. Specialists have already worked out several proposals which, though differing as to the sources, magnitude and proportions of the villages' local incomes, show an almost complete consensus with regard to the requirement of expanding the villages' authority to take independent decisions and of limiting the counties' excessive power to perform activities in concentrating, withdrawing and redistributing resources.

The number of administrative units (capital and counties)

Capital, county	Cities of county rank	Towns	Large villages with town rank	Centres of attraction and their hinterland	Villages with independent councils	Villages with joint councils	Villages total	Villages of which large villages
Budapest (capital)	1	–	–	–	–	–	–	–
Baranya	1	4	–	5	11	280	291	11
Bács-Kiskun	–	6	4	10	91	14	105	23
Békés	–	6	3	9	50	18	68	24
Borsod-Abaúj-Zemplén	1	8	1	10	62	277	339	24
Csongrád	1	4	2	7	31	23	54	9
Fejér	–	3	3	6	45	58	103	18
Győr-Sopron	1	4	–	5	35	125	160	12
Hajdú-Bihar	1	4	2	6	21	53	74	27
Heves	–	4	1	5	63	51	114	9
Komárom	–	6	1	7	30	38	68	8
Nógrád	–	3	3	6	18	99	117	6
Pest	–	8	6	13	89	82	171	53
Somogy	–	5	3	8	4	229	233	8
Szabolcs-Szatmár	–	6	1	7	48	171	219	34
Szolnok	–	8	1	8	28	39	67	21
Tolna	–	5	–	5	33	70	103	11
Vas	–	6	1	7	8	201	209	6
Veszprém	–	8	1	9	12	200	212	8
Zala	–	5	1	6	2	248	250	6
Total	6	103	34	139	681	2276	2957	318

At the census held on January 1, 1980, a population of 10 710 000 was enumerated in Hungary, a rise of 388 000 or 3·8 per cent when compared with the previous census of 1970. In terms of population numbers, Hungary ranks 13th amongst the 32 countries of Europe and of the European socialist countries only Bulgaria and Albania have smaller populations. By con-

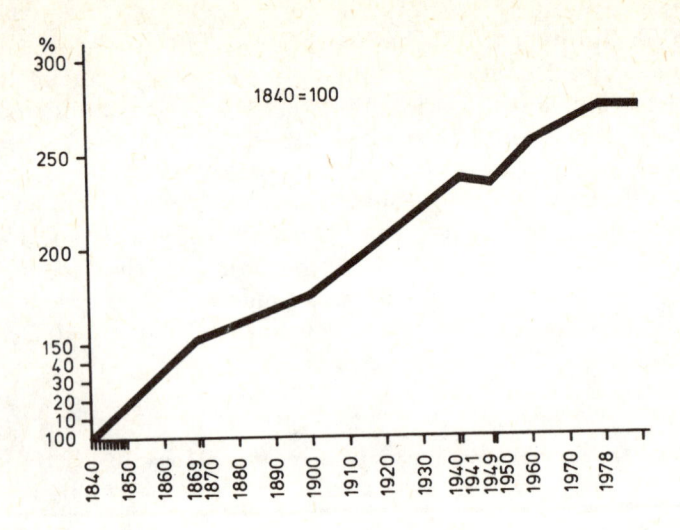

Fig. 10. Changes in the number of population (1868–1980). Data apply to the present territory of the country

trast, with a population density of 115 people per square kilometre, Hungary is one of the more significantly populated countries of Europe *(Fig. 10)*.

Population data relating to the present area of the country have been available from census sources since 1867 and as estimated data since 1840.

2.1 The natural increase of population

Rapid natural increase occurred in Hungary during the more vigorous phase of capitalist development during the last decades of the 19th and the first decades of the 20th century. Owing to improvements in public health, including effective measures against epidemics, and better living conditions resulting from industrial growth, the mortality rate strongly decreased, while a high birth rate tended to persist. As a result of these two factors, the natural population increase remained at around 11 to 12 per thousand per annum, but although this represents a high rate of growth by Hungarian standards, it was nonetheless rather low when viewed in the wide perspective of southeastern Europe.

According to tentative estimates the total Hungarian population of the world amounts to around 15 million, and of the 5 million or so Hungarians living outside the country's frontiers about 3 million constitute national minorities in the neighbouring countries of Czechoslovakia, the Soviet Union, Romania, Yugoslavia and Austria. In excess of 600 000 Hungarians live in south Slovakia, the highest densities being found near the Danube, while in the Carpathian Ukraine of the Soviet Union Hungarians number about 150 000, living mostly on the plain contiguous with Hungary and in the towns.

The largest Hungarian minority, however, of about 1 800 000 is to be found in Romania. However, they only form a cohesive group on either side of the Hargita Mountains, in the Sekler land; elsewhere Hungarian settlements are scattered throughout Transylvania, while many live in the large towns, although their share is on the decrease. According to the 1977 Romanian census, the proportion of Hungarians was 33 per cent in Kolozsvár (Cluj-Napoca), 42 per cent in Nagyvárad (Oradea), 46 per cent in Szatmár (Satu-Mare) and 54 per cent in Marosvásárhely (Tîrgu-Mureş).

Out of the 23 million inhabitants of Yugoslavia, Hungarians number between 500 and 550 thousand, most of whom live in the autonomous province of the Voivodina.

Lastly, Hungarians are to be found in the Burgenland province of Austria, although their number is less than 8000.

Between the two world wars, the birth rate declined more rapidly than the death rate, and as a result natural increase fell to an average 5 to 6 per thousand per annum. After 1945 while the mortality rate continued to fall, the birth rate rose above the level of the 1930s until 1956 and as a consequence natural increase fluctuated within the range of 7 to 10 thousand.

During the three and a half decades since 1946, movements in population numbers have been, basically, a function of the birth and mortality rates, the only exception occurring during the 1956 counter-revolution when about 190000 people left the country, of whom some 50000 have returned.

The birth rate has displayed the greatest fluctuation during the past few decades, and the following stages can be distinguished:

a) Partly as a reaction to the administrative measures of the years 1953–1956 and partly as a result of the legalization of induced abortion, the birth rate fell to a historical nadir of 12·9 per thousand in 1962, which was superseded by a stagnating rate of 13·1 per thousand level during the following three years.

b) Between 1966 and 1973, partly as a result of government measures designed to stimulate births, including child-care grants, increased family allowances, improved medical services and extended crèche facilities, and partly because of a higher proportion of women of child-bearing age, the birth rate tentatively moved upwards to 15 per thousand.

c) During the years 1974–1978 the annual number of births was up by some 20 to 40 thousand when compared with the previous years and reached a peak of 194 thousand live births, 18·4 per thousand, in 1975, but since then both the number and rate have declined. More than half the rise in the birth rate during the late 1960s and early 1970s can be attributed to the effect of population policy measures and the rest to the fact that it was at that time that the large cohorts born between 1953 and 1956 entered the child-bearing age range.

d) Between 1978 and 1980, the birth rate fell sharply to 15·7 per thousand in 1978, 15 per thousand in 1979 and 14 per thousand in 1980, and of the country has again entered a growth trough. Indeed according to the data for the first 8 months of 1980, the number of deaths actually exceeded the number of births, in 1981 it was 13·3‰.

The fluctuations in the birth rate since the early 1950s can be traced back to several factors. Fertility has been greatly influenced by the changing economic structure and concomitant social and professional restratification, commuting, massive internal migration from rural to urban areas, and by the increasing participation of women in the labour force. Thus, along with personal subjective reasons, it is clear that certain facts of a socio-economic nature, although positive and desirable in themselves, have tended to decrease the birth rate. In other words, effects, very positive in other contexts, tended to have an unfavourable influence upon population growth.

The former considerable differences between the fertility of the various social strata have diminished substantially, although average family size is still a little greater among the rural population. In one third of the families there is only one child, a fashion which is spreading, primarily in the towns and mainly among intellectuals.

The effects albeit lagged, of the variable birth rate make themselves felt in all fields of life, causing fluctuating demand for places in, for example, the maternity wards of hospitals, child institutions, and educational establishments, as well as creating wide variations in the number of school leavers taking up gainful employment.

The mortality rate has fallen by about 50 per cent since 1920, and has ranged between 10·3 and 13·5 per thousand during the past decades, i.e., somewhere close to the average level for Europe, although the ageing of the population is now making itself felt in the crude rate. (In .1981 it was 13·5‰.) Infant mortality, however, has diminished somewhat faster than general mortality, falling from 130 to 140 per 1000 live births before the Second World War to around 22—25 per thousand now. (In 1981 it was 20·8‰.) Consequently, life expectancy at birth had risen to 65—66 years for males and to around 70 for females by the end of the 1970s, i.e. to a level very little below that of most developed countries, although improvements in male longevity have virtually come to a stop over the last few years. The rise in the average age of the population, and the fall in death rates, particularly in the infant mortality rate, are clearly indicative of the economic and social changes that have materialized during the phase of socialist development.

Natural population increase has been rather uneven over the past quarter of a century. Since 1949 the population has increased by about 1·5 million, but this growth is less than it was between the two world wars. The slow rate of increase is partly due to the decline in natural increase, and partly to losses from various emigrations.

There are substantial spatial differences in the rate of natural population increase, which is generally lowest in urban settlements, although the rate in certain industrial areas may exceed that of several rural regions. Territorially, the rate has been the highest for a considerable time now in Szabolcs-Szatmár county which also displays the highest birth rate in the county. At around 8 to 10 per thousand, the rate is close to three times the national average, with Fejér, Hajdú, Borsod, Komárom and Pest counties following in that order. The new industrial towns also tend to have a rather high natural population increase. By contrast, the rate is lowest in Csongrád, Békés, Somogy and Tolna counties, while in the case of the capital the growth in population during the period 1950–1967 came exclusively from an in-migration surplus, and although the situation has improved since the late 1970s, natural decrease has again been typical.

Variations in the annual levels of natural population growth are largely a function of the large-scale fluctuations in the number of births [9]. Although the development of the birth rate can and should be assessed only in the long run, trends in the reproduction of the population have nonetheless to be taken into account. During the 1980s, the country will again experience a trough in the 20-year demographic cycle fluctuation as the girls belonging to the small cohorts born in the 1960s gradually enter the child-bearing age groups. From the early 1980s, the decrease in the population number has been continued in 1981 by about 2000 persons, 10 000 in 1982 and more than 20 000 in 1983. The further decrease should not be stopped for the beginning of 1990s; it may be diminished only in favourable case.

At present, the average number of children per family is 1·9, and the efforts and measures of population policy must therefore be concentrated on encouraging families to have three children [24, 25], this means that the model of the two- and three-child family must be substituted for the one- and two-child family type of the last decades. The government wishes to increase the number of births not so much by administrative measures but by improving living conditions, by preparing the young for family life, and by shaping the consciousness of public opinion. Assuming that the capacity of the national economy for carrying such burdens will increase in the future, the principle that the costs of the reproduction of labour should also include the costs of educating the new generation should increasingly assert itself in practice, and it is to be hoped that the factors unfavourably affecting population growth can gradually be eliminated.

2.2 Population distribution by age and sex

All the censuses so far taken in Hungary have registered an excess of females. As a result of losses during World War II, the imbalance amounted to over 8 per thousand in 1949, and although the proportions of the two sexes have since become more equivalent, the female surplus enumerated at

Distribution of population by age group (%)

Year	Under 15 years	15—39 years	40—59 years	60 years and older	15—59 years
1900	35·4	37·9	19·0	7·7	57·6
1949	24·9	38·8	24·7	11·6	63·6
1960	25·3	36·8	24·2	13·7	60·8
1970	21·1	37·0	24·8	17·1	61·8
1980	21·7	36·1	25·3	16·9	61·4

the 1970s census was still around 6 per cent. As for the future, assuming no disturbance by external factors, the relative fall in the number of females, is expected to continue, giving a sex ratio of about 1040 females to 1000 males by the end of the 1980s. It is to be noted, however, that although there is a female surplus in all counties and most towns of the country the extent of the surplus differs widely spatially and by type of settlement.

In the distribution of population, a major role is played by age composition, which influences the degree of employment, the ratio of wage-earners to dependants, and the mobilization and utilization of manpower. The age structure of the population is affected by changes in birth and death rates, by wars and by migration.

From census to census, the proportion of the elderly in the country's population has been steadily increasing. This ageing of the population can basically be traced back to two contrary processes: one is the change in mortality rates whereby the average age at death is increasing, and the other is the long-term decline in the number of births in part resulting from the fall in the proportion of younger age-groups in the total population. The economic consequence of ageing is manifest in the stagnation of the economically active population and, more directly, the increasing burden of old-age pensioners. The improvement of both family and societal living standards is also significantly influenced by the ratio of wage-earners to dependants. In 1979, for instance, almost 20 per cent of the total population were of retirement age, that is, more than 17 per cent were 60 years of age or over.

As a result of the fall in the number of births and of rising longevity, society is proceeding towards a general ageing, and it is clear that a positive phenomenon such as a longer life span can also produce a negative effect. The maintenance of an increasing proportion of elderly imposes, in the rising level of old-age pensions, a heavy burden upon an active population, which itself is either stagnating or decreasing in number, even though the national income and the fund for consumption are rising. One way of avoiding this is to ‚improve' the age distribution of the population by regulating the number of births.

At the end of the 1970s, 62 per cent of the total population consisted of males and females of economically active age. There still, however, exists a certain disequilibrium in the age distribution of the industrial and agricultural populations. The proportion of older workers is somewhat lower in industry, although it is increasing through the encouragement of retired persons to take up employment again. In agriculture, by contrast, the position is significantly worse, with the proportion of elderly workers again increasing, despite the fact that the retirement ages for agricultural wage-earners and for those working in other sectors were recently equalized. A balanced distribution of young manpower among industry, agriculture, transport and the service sector requires, over and above income relationships, effective economic and cultural policy measures.

2.3 Distribution of the population by nationality

As has already been discussed, historical Hungary was a multinational state with half its population belonging to ethnic minorities in 1910. By the period between the two world wars, however, this figure had dropped to 7 per cent of the population, and after World War II the population has been virtually homogeneous with 95–97 per cent speaking Hungarian as their mother tongue.

Of the considerable numbers of *Germans* living formerly in the country, about 170 000 who co-operated with fascism were expelled after World War II, and at the same time, under an agreement concluded with Czechoslovakia on the exchange of population, 70 000 Slovaks were repatriated.

According to the 1970 census, the size of the national minorities amounted to 56 000* and Germans still constituted the bulk of them. They live scattered in and around the capital, in the villages and towns of the Transdanubian Central Mountains, in the hilly regions of Tolna county, in the Mecsek area, in the Bácska and along the Austrian frontier.

The *Slovak* population lives in the settlements and surroundings of Békéscsaba, Tótkomlós, Szarvas and Mezőberény in the south-eastern parts of the Great Plain. They are also scattered throughout the Danube–Tisza Mid-region, and are found around the capital and in parts of the Northern Middle Mountains and in their basins lying south of them.

The *Romanian* population lives in those south-eastern parts of the Great Plain contiguous with Romania (Gyula, Elek, and Méhkerék).

The *Southern Slavs* comprising Croats, Serbs, and Slovanians live in the south-eastern part of the Danube–Tisza Mid-region, along the Drava river,

---

* It is very difficult to assess reliably the true size of the national minorities living in Hungary. In 1970 altogether 56 000 inhabitants declared themselves as non-Hungarians. At the same time, the number speaking a language other than Hungarian as their mother tongue was much higher at 156 000. According to the „liberal" estimates of nationality alliances, however, the number of Germans amounted to 220 to 230 thousands, while there were over 100 thousand Slovaks, 33 to 36 thousand Romanians and 80 to 100 thousand Southern Slavs in Hungary.

in the settlements of Vas and Zala counties bordering Yugoslavia, in a few villages near the frontier around Hegyeshalom, as well as in scattered settlements on Csepel Island and in around Szentendre.

Gypsies, numbering between 350 and 400 thousand persons, are scattered in various, mainly rural settlements of the country, although some are now urban dwellers. Substantial changes have also taken place in their occupational structure, and while segregation is decreasing, their full adjustment to society will require a longer period of time, as is also shown by the fact that many marginal elements and groups are, unfortunately, recruited from Gypsy families.

The last nationality that deserves mention is the *Greeks*, who settled in the country after the Greek civil war in 1949—1950.

The socialist state has resolved the nationality issue in the spirit of Marxist—Leninist politics, and the Constitution of the Hungarian People's Republic ensures full equality and the free exercise of their national culture for all national minorities.

2.4 Population density

As regards population density, Hungary ranks 9th among the countries of Europe, and is more heavily settled than either Czechoslovakia or Austria with their heavily broken terrain, mountainous regions and more intensively forested territories, or indeed France. Of the socialist countries of Europe, only in the GDR is population density greater at 165 persons per square kilometres *(Fig. 11)*. Although Hungary's population density is lower than that of most developed West-European countries, it is rather high, compared with the available productive forces. Thus population density constitutes no hindrance in the location of productive forces or in appropriately utilizing the natural endowments of all the regions and areas of the country.

Naturally, there are substantial regional differences in population density, reflecting variations in physiographic and socio-economic characteristics as well as varying rates of population increase, especially internal migration. The spatial distribution, moreover, reflects the territorial location of industrial productive forces, the endowments of the geographic environment and, in agricultural regions, the former distribution of latifundia as well as the intensity of production.

Population density is highest in the towns followed by the industrial areas, and rural districts with intensive cultivation. From this it may be concluded that population density is not a determinant, but primarily a function of the spatial location of productive forces, although it is also the case that a high-density area may stimulate further development of productive forces.

The areas of a high population density (140 to 240 persons per square kilometre) extend in a contiguous strip from the mining and industrial district centred on Tatabánya, Dorog and Almásfüzitő in Komárom county

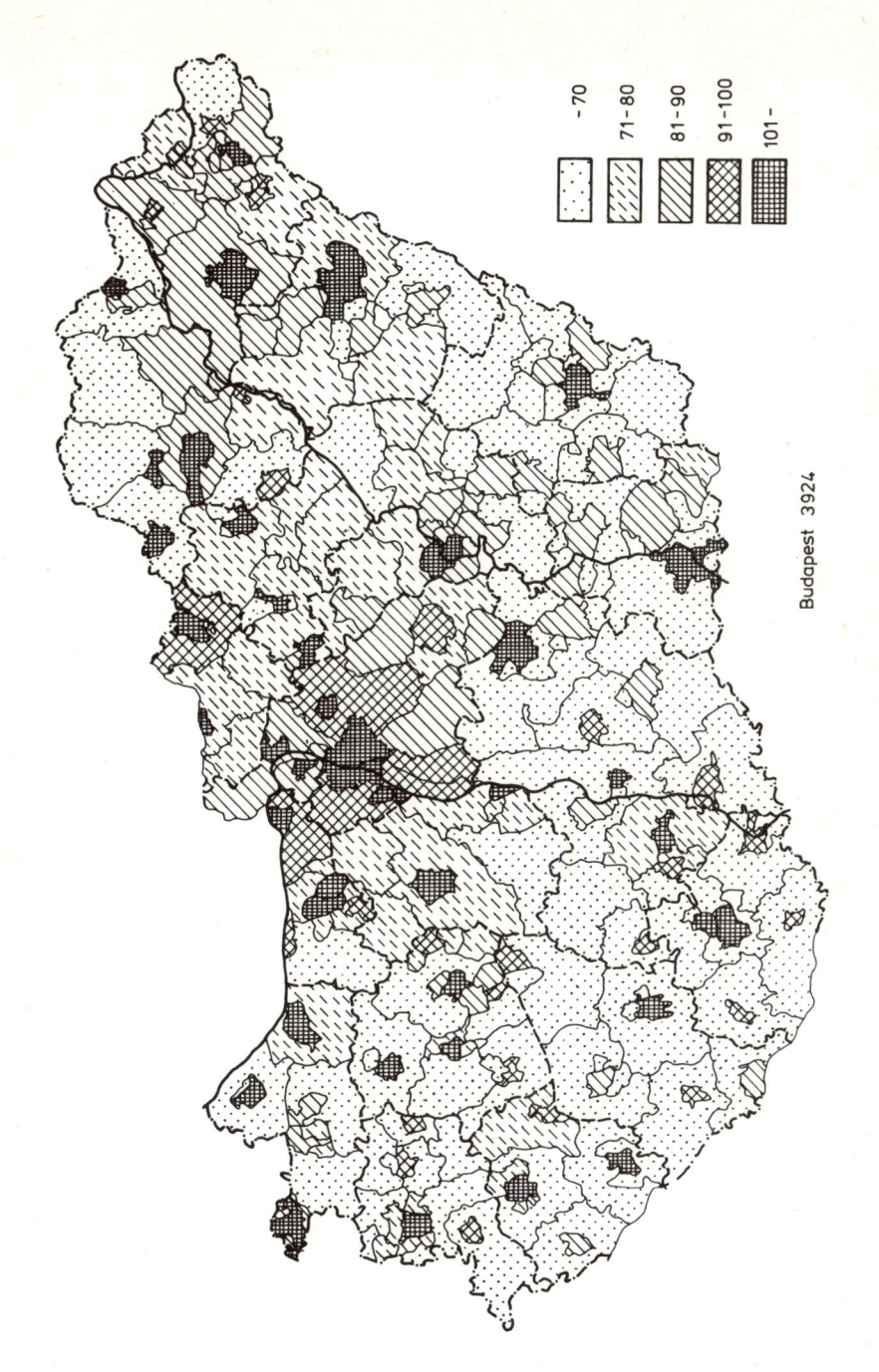

Fig. 11. Population density of districts, towns and neighbourhoods, 1981 (number of population per km²)

in the west, embraces the metropolitan area of the capital and stretches across the Gödöllő hills to the eastern part of the Danube—Tisza Mid-region. Density also remains fairly high in the Jászság, Tiszazug and the fertile regions east of the Tisza and south of the Körös rivers, as well as in the more agricultural areas of the Nyírség. Local high points can also be found in the Zagyva valley, primarily near Salgótarján and Ózd and in the valleys of the Sajó and Hernád rivers. Additionally, quite high densities are associated with the industrializing areas of the Mecsek Mountain, along the valley of the Zala river, in Győr county, along Lake Balaton and areas of local agglomeration.

By contrast, low population densities (50 to 80 persons per square kilometre) and relatively sparse habitation are to be found in the western part of Baranya county, Somogy county as a whole but especially its southern districts, the western part of the Mezőföld and, despite its significant industries, in Veszprém county also, because of the relief characteristics and considerable areas of forest. Population density is also low in the sandy and alkali regions of the Danube—Tisza Mid-region, in the partly alkalized areas lying between the Nagykunság and the Hajdúság to the east of the Tisza river as well as in the plateau and karst regions of the Northern Middle Mountains.

The most closely settled counties are Pest and Komárom, where population density exceeds 145 and 140 persons per square kilometre, respectively. Density exceeds 100 per square kilometre in Borsod, Csongrád and Győr—Sopron counties. The least densely populated county is Somogy, where population density is less than half that of Pest county.

During the course of socialist economic development substantial changes have taken place in the pattern of population density. Density has increased in Pest, Borsod, Komárom, Veszprém, Fejér and Baranya counties as a result of industrial developments and the attractive power of the capital. By contrast, internal migration produced considerable outflows of population from the more agrarian counties from the early 1960s on and, as a result, population density dropped by between 2 and 12 persons per square kilometre in Békés, Szabolcs-Szatmár, Somogy and Tolna counties.

Nevertheless, despite considerable differences in population density, it can be stated that with the exception of the Budapest agglomeration, there are neither extremely densely nor extremely sparsely inhabited areas in Hungary. The density of even the most richly settled districts, namely Buda, Vác, Monor, Gödöllő, Dorog and Hatvan, does not exceed 240 persons per square kilometre, while that of the most sparsely inhabited districts and urban areas, namely Szigetvár and Barcs, does not fall below 35 persons per square kilometre.

Although not as extreme as in many other countries, population density in Hungary thus exhibits appreciable differences. As a result of the large-scale development of the productive forces, primarily the high spatial concentration of industrialization processes which produced the simultaneous social and occupational restratification of the population largely through migration, a major differentiation has taken place in the spatial distribution of the country's population. Formerly, population density tended to rise towards the east, owing to the larger rates of population increase in the counties of the Great Plain, but during the past quarter of a century the territorial restructuring of the population has meant concentration in the so-called „industrial axis".

It is now clearly the case that densities are highest in Transdanubia north of a line from Lake Balaton to Budapest, in Pest county and in the other counties constituting the northern part of the country. The southern parts, by contrast, owing to their more agrarian character, are somewhat more sparsely inhabited, although Csongrád and Baranya counties with their significant industrial urban population are exceptions.

2.5 Occupational structure

Since the country's liberation in 1945, radical changes have taken place in the class and occupational structure of the population, as well as in the whole society owing to the socialist reorganization of production and the development of productive forces.

With laying the foundations of socialism in 1962, the class relations of society have been simplified.

During the period of socialist construction substantial social mobility was accompanied by the social-occupational restratification of the population, which has greatly increased the size of certain social strata and occupational groups, while decreasing that of others. The intensity of social mobility is reflected in the increased number and ratio of workers engaged in industry and in a corresponding decrease in the peasantry. The number of professionals and non-productive employees has also risen conspicuously, while the number of independent peasant proprietors as well as artisans and small merchants has decreased, the latter to a greater extent than was desirable during certain periods. At the end of the 1970s, wage- and salary-earners constituted 80 per cent of the active population, and close to 49 per cent of the total population. Out of every hundred active earners 57 are employed in industry, 15 are co-operative farmers, 25 professionals and employees and 3 small commodity producers.

When characterizing the present-day structure of society it is not enough merely to analyze its stratification into social classes. Within the basic class structure various socio-occupational strata have also evolved out of the position occupied in the social distribution of labour and according to the type of work undertaken, and it is therefore clear that investigations into stratification will have to pay greater regard to differences in occupational relationships and work-type in the future.

Never in the past have such rapid and radical changes in the occupational structure of the country's population taken place as in the past three decades. Of the active earning population of 5083 million in 1980 33·6 per cent were employed in industry, 8·1 in the construction industry, 19·4 per cent in agriculture, 1 per cent in forestry, 8·1 in transport and communications, 9·6 per cent in commerce, 1·5 in the water economy and 18·7 per cent in the non-productive branches such as public services.

The transformation of the occupational structure has been brought about by large-scale investment in industry and other sectors of the national economy, which has created many hundreds of thousands of new job opportunities. The increase in the number of active earners has been ensured by young people entering the labour force, by migration from rural areas and by the increasing participation of females in the workforce. As a result of the massive rise in the numbers employed, the ratio of the earning population to dependants has shifted towards the former. For instance, while in 1949 there were 134 dependants to every 100 active earners, by 1980 this ratio had dropped to 102 dependants per 100 earners. Nearly all of the economically active male population are employed, while the proportion of female earners in active population has risen from 30 per cent in 1949 to 43 per cent in 1980. As a result of educational policy, the number of pupils and students of working age has doubled and now amounts to 10 per cent of the total active population. Within the economically active population the number of agricultural manual workers has undergone the greatest change, falling by 50 per cent between 1960 and 1980, while their proportion within the active population has declined from 37 to 10 per cent over the same period, reflecting the increasing industrial character of the country's economy. However, it should not be ignored that many former agricultural earners who have moved to other economic sectors have not lost their personal contact with agriculture and constitute a specific stratum of „peasant-industrial workers".

The branch and sub-branch composition of workers engaged in industry has also changed. A marked increase can be registered in the numbers employed in telecommunications, in the fine instruments industry, the manufacture of mass metal products and in machine-building in general, as well as in the chemical and food-processing industry. By contrast, the role and weight of mining, electricity generation, metallurgy and the construction industry have declined. The proportion of active earners in industry and the construction industry is highest in Komárom and Pest counties, but is also above the national average in Nógrád, Borsod-Abaúj-Zemplén, Győr-Sopron and Veszprém counties. Agricultural workers, on the other hand, are most significant in the economy of Hajdú-Bihar county, but surpass the national average in Bács-Kiskun, Szabolcs-Szatmár, Csongrád and Tolna counties, too.

Owing to the introduction of large-scale production and the adoption of new technology, the character of agricultural work has also undergone substantial changes. Great progress has been made towards specialization, and the ratio of people employed in those non-agricultural sectors that nonetheless serve agricultural production has increased in large-scale farming units.

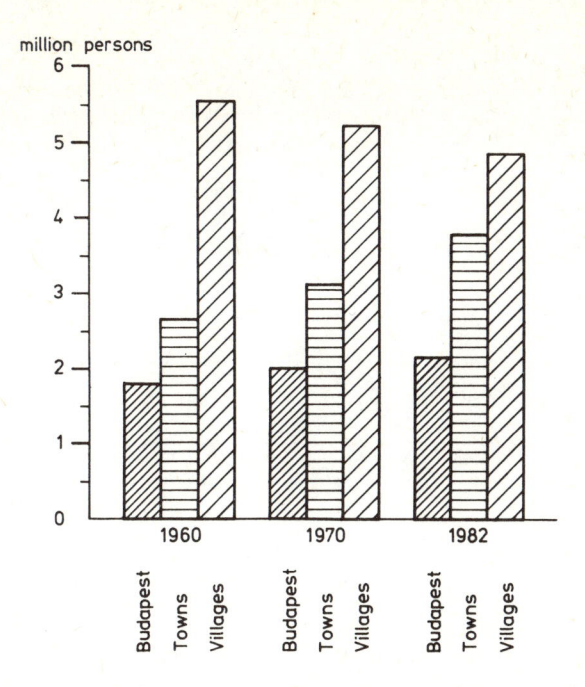

Fig. 12. The spatial distribution of population

In conjunction with these developments, the number of people with special skills has also greatly increased and is still increasing in rural areas.

It would be erroneous to identify the rural population with the peasantry, just as it would be incorrect to regard the working class or even non-agricultural manual workers as simply a predominantly urban class [1]. Thus the occupational structure of the various settlement groups cannot be differentiated by saying that non-agricultural workers live in towns and agricultural manual workers in villages, for the proportions of non-agricultural semi-skilled and unskilled workers are about the same in both towns and villages, while even the proportion of skilled workers is not that much higher in towns either. Substantial differences do exist, however, to the extent that professional and administrative-clerical workers are concentrated in towns, primarily in Budapest and in the five largest cities, while those engaged in agriculture tend to be concentrated in the villages and partly in the smaller provincial towns. Non-agricultural manual workers constitute about the same weight in both the urban and rural population; of the approximately 2·5 million non-agricultural workers 1·1 million live in the villages [1, 2] *(Fig. 12).*

As in many other countries, the employment has expanded more rapidly in the tertiary than in the productive sectors, perhaps at a faster rate than can really be justified. This faster rate of growth has mostly resulted from the rise in the numbers employed in the fields of health and education and in cultural, social and scientific institutions, and is only to a lesser extent due

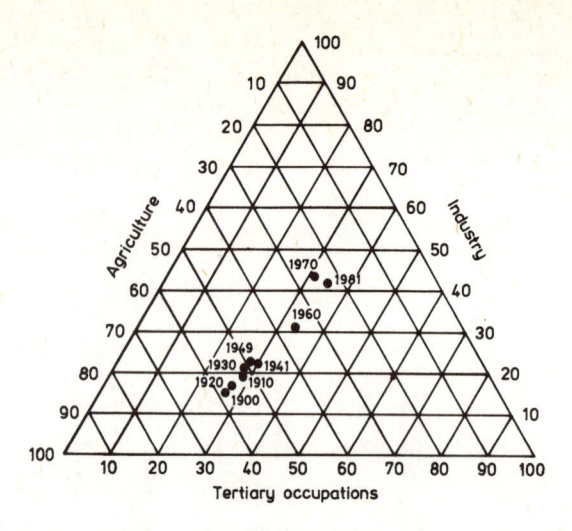

Fig. 13. Changes in the occupational structure of population (1900–1981)

to the growth of state administration. There are over 130 thousand persons engaged in education service, of which 80 thousand are teachers in primary and secondary schools, while over 100 thousand persons are engaged in the health and social services, of whom about 26 thousand are physicians *(Fig. 13)*.

The country's relatively high population density, together with the increasing skills of the workforce and its concentration in the economically more effective sectors and branches, means that the availability of labour will constitute a very important factor in further economic growth. Moreover, the structural changes consequent upon economic growth, and the world-wide spatial reorganization of productive forces and production, as well as the rapid development of science and technology, in turn necessitate a higher general level of education, a more solid basic vocational training and more convertible skills amongst the population.

In the new world economic situation, the exchange of work of different degrees of sophistication has become a crucial problem of the international division of labour. Of the factors of production, the role of the human factor, particularly the level of general education and the skills of the workforce, has become especially important everywhere and in Hungary in particular. The returns from a trained labour force appreciably exceed those otherwise achievable and as a consequence the economically more developed countries modify their production structures in favour of products requiring the research and development potential of a highly qualified labour force. But products demanding such labour can only be produced in Hungary economically if productivity is higher than the respective wage-levels. Given a substantial lag in productivity, there is little consolation in the fact that qualified labour is employed in several sectors, but at a level far behind that of the country's competitors. On the other hand, even a relative advantage in productivity cannot justify the manufacture of products where the wage-levels of competitors are so low that they offset the advantage gained from higher productivity.

In Hungary, labour is still a scarce resource although the slowdown in the rate of economic growth, along with more intensive economic development and technological renewal, have somewhat lessened the tensions in the labour market. Contrary to public opinion, especially scarce are the highly qualified, and those with a creative managerial ability, and any economic unit or country which has more of this scarce resource at its disposal enjoys a comparative advantage.

The educational and skill levels of a population can be most appropriately characterized by the highest level of education attained. In this regard, close to 80 per cent of the population of Hungary aged 15 years and over had finished at least the 8 grades of primary (general) school in 1980, while the proportion of 18-year-olds and over who had finished secondary school was around 30 per cent, and of the population aged 25 years and over 5·3 per cent had finished university or college.

In Hungary, the general level of education of the labour force barely exceeds that of semi-skilled workers, although substantial variations exist. Thus every second person engaged in industry and every third working in agriculture is skilled. Moreover, the level of qualifications may increase faster than hitherto, thanks to the sound structure of the educational system. However, a greater proportion of the economically active population would acquire a solid vocational training and raise their general level of skills were the still existing discrepancies and qualitative differences in the spatial location of the school network to be eliminated. But territorial as well as occupational mobility is of importance. Owing to the country's relatively small area, its good transportation network and the degree of industrial decentralization already attained, a change of residence entails but little inconvenience. If the spatial levelling out of living conditions continues to proceed and if housing difficulties can be overcome on a national scale, then the territorial mobility of the labour force may further strengthen.

A basic aim of labour policy has been, and still is, full employment, but the real and growing problem is the scarcity of labour, partly fictious, and partly structural and functional, caused by various factors both at a national and regional scale. Labour scarcity primarily afflicts industry, because it competes for the same types of labour as the dynamic sector of infrastructure. In addition, some co-operative industrial enterprises are not sufficiently competitive in terms of wages and incomes with many of the profitably operating large agricultural units and service activities.

Demographic processes and changes indicate that in the years to come labour will still continue to be a scarce resource. Especially during the first half of the 1980s.

2.6 Internal migration

Migrations amongst individual areas, counties, planning and economic regions and settlements are jointly referred to as internal migration. The mobility of labour is one of the most important forms of the spatial division of labour and is, consequently, a manifestation of the social division of labour.

Ever since the beginning of socialist economic development, migration has assumed unprecedented proportions and has only begun to lessen during the second half of the 1960s. The process itself has been an inevitable concomitant of Hungary's socio-economic development. Its scale, however, is connected with the character of the territorial division of labour, and with the inherited pattern of industrial location whose disparities were impossible to change over a short time span.

Industrial development, structural transformation and urbanization have been accompanied by substantial population flows throughout the world, but only produce extreme migration rates under conditions of a polarized territorial division of labour as in Hungary. During the course of economic development, the massive employment opportunities created for the comparatively unskilled during the stage of extensive economic development attracted hundreds of thousands of people to the industrial regions, urban centres and towns.

The imbalances in the territorial division of labour inherited from the past, made themselves felt for a considerable time after socialist economic development had been embarked upon, and the concentration of industrial and non-agricultural activity in general in well-defined areas led to a mass exodus from rural areas of those who could not find employment in agriculture. As those leaving agrarian occupations constituted an important source of industrial labour, migration from rural areas to the industrial centres and towns soon assumed enormous proportions.

The shift from an agricultural to an industrial or some other non-agricultural activity could for the most part take place only through some form of migration, i.e. commuting, seasonal migration or permanent resettlement [24, 45], but although internal migration over the past decades has been directed mostly towards towns and industrial areas, the numbers moving from one rural or urban community to another have also been significant as have those settling in the metropolitan areas of the cities. Indeed, a two-way flow of the skilled and mainly unskilled labour force evolved. First migration to local centres was heavier, but as their absorptive capacity was exhausted, movement to the capital and the higher-order urban centres bacame more intensive, producing what may be described as double urbanization.

The rural—urban flow resulting in permanent residence in towns has not equally affected all towns, and has been more prominent to the capital, the county-ranked towns and county seats, the new industrial towns, the centres of industrial areas and to second-order urban places. It is primarily due to migration that a marked increase has been registered in the number of the inhabitants of Budapest and of other high-order centres, and further in Dunaújváros, Komló, Kazincbarcika, Oroszlány and elsewhere. Since 1960, three-fourths of the urban population has been due to net in-migration.

Since the mid-1960s, however, migration has been directed especially towards the second-order places. To this group of towns belong such rapidly developing county seats as Szombathely, Székesfehérvár, Kaposvár, Tatabánya, Kecskemét, Nyíregyháza and Szolnok, all of which perform high-order central functions. The population increment of such places through migration has tended even to exceed that of larger centres [7]. Other medium-range centres, however, could not develop to a desirable extent. From among these the greatest rural-urban influx has been to towns in which the proportion engaged in industrial and other sectors is markedly high. To this category belong 24 towns — more than half of them county seats and towns performing transportation, recreational and tourist functions. Towns in which agrarian activity is still strong, such as Hajdúböszörmény, Kisújszállás, Mezőtúr, Szarvas, Túrkeve and Makó have generally continued to suffer depopulation and have not managed to retain their natural growth increment. Their situation has, however, improved slightly since the 1970s.

Along with the towns, the communities belonging to the metropolitan area of the capital which include Budakeszi, Pomáz, Budakalász, Göd, Gyömrő, Vecsés, Pécel and Érd as well as mining and industrial villages such as Peremarton, Lőrinci and Lábatlan, and as a result of increasing tourism, many settlements around Lake Balaton, in the Mátra Mountains and the Danube Bend, have attracted, and are still attracting, a significant number of in-migrants.

The population size of certain less developed, mainly rural, counties has hardly increased owing to large-scale out-migration. Such flows determining the rate of population growth of the counties reached the peak in the middle and second half of the 1960s, since when they have decreased in scale and intensity. The consolidation of large-scale farming, the progress made in the regional development of industry and the growth of the local centres have tended to dampen inter-county flows and thus the spatial polarization of migration. The fact that the same counties, with few exceptions, invariably register a positive migration balance shows, as in the past, that the main migration trends are persistent, and that it requires quite a long time to change fundamentally the spatial and socio-economic factors influencing migration. But the one-sided nature of migration whereby individual areas either attract or repel is diminishing, and a more balanced distribution has been achieved between population inflows and outflows. The decrease in the intensity of regional population flows has also been promoted by an increase in the ratio of intra-county migration.

The rural exodus has tended to decrease the population of villages that were already small, but it has not left unaffected the large, mammoth villages and rural market towns of Transdanubia and the Great Plain either. These features are reflected in the negative correlation that exists between the size of villages and the scale of out-migration, largely accounted for by the almost one-sided agrarian character and the poor accessibility to transportation facilities of small settlements. Massive population flows have also stimulated the pursuit of a territorial and regional policy aimed at a gradual decentralization of the economy, the attainment of which would undoubtedly be a significant achievement.

Some members of the population who have moved from rural areas to industrial districts and from urban peripheries to towns have settled permanently, but others commute between their places of residence and work, or partake of seasonal migration. The fact that the number of inter-settlement commuters has significantly increased can be attributed to a number of factors including the anarchic character of industrial location under capitalism, to deficiencies in the location of productive forces during socialist construction, to the necessity to locate industry in areas with the necessary endowments and, last but not least, to the fact that housing provision has lagged behind the demand. The size, significance and proportions of commuting are clearly borne out by the fact that in 1980 the number of daily commuters was more than one million and that, in addition, there were over 300 thousand workers commuting over longer intervals. The increase in the number of commuters was particularly high during the 1960s and the first half of the 1970s. Some change in their structure is also to be seen, for while formerly commuting was typical of unskilled rural males, the proportion of females is now increasing.

The ratio of commuters to local earners varies by region, depending on the degree of industrialization, the extent of occupational change and the location of settlements with respect to transport facilities. In Pest county, for example, over 40 per cent of the active earners are employed in places other than their places of residence, while in the more industrially developed counties of Komárom, Borsod and Fejér, 20 to 24 per cent of wage-earners are commuters.

The various commuter belts can be ranked as follows [20, 42]:

(a) residential or dormitory settlements, forming a commuter zone, can be distinguished where commuting affects 60 per cent or more of the work force;

(b) an outer dormitory belt can be defined as embracing those settlements from which 45 to 60 per cent of the gainfully employed commute to work;

(c) 20 to 45 per cent of workers especially commute to work from within the broader environment of centres of attraction, with the exception of the rural market towns of the Great Plain, in practically all the urban and industrial areas of the country;

(d) outside of (a), (b), and (c) another 5 to 10 per cent of the work-force commute to work and this embraces most of the country, with the exception of settlements that have poor communications.

The average travelling distance of commuters is 23 kilometres, but distances of 40 to 50 and even of 75 to 80 kilometres are not uncommon.

About one in eight commuters travel either weekly or bi-weekly owing to the large distance between their place of residence and place of work.

Seasonal labour has evolved in connection with the sugar, canning and confectionary industries, and with tourism. State farms and co-operatives growing vegetables, fruit and grapes on a large-scale also draw on an increasing number of seasonal commuters.

3 Settlement and infrastructure

Like the relief characteristics of the country, the macro-structure of Hungary's settlement network also falls into two regions with sharply differing characters and structure. The one is the hill area of Transdanubia and the Northern Middle Mountains, while the Great Hungarian Plain lies to the east and south of them. The characteristic differences, discernible up to now between the settlement network of these two regions, cannot be explained in terms of their natural endowments, however, but result much more from their divergent historical and economic evolution. While the western and northern parts of the country were not lastingly under Turkish occupation, their domination of the Great Plain lasted for 150 years from 1526 to 1676 and this brought about an entirely different settlement structure.

In addition, Transdanubia and the Northern Middle Mountains were typically the regions of the large estates (latifundia), while the Great Plain was mainly an area of small and medium-sized peasant holdings. Moreover, while the western and northern parts were, as a rule, loyal to the existing feudal and capitalist power systems, the Great Plain, owing to its decisively different socio-economic structure, was mostly a centre of opposition and rebellion. Differences also existed in religion with Catholicism dominant in Transdanubia and Protestantism on the Great Plain. The county towns in Transdanubia and the Northern Middle Mountains were, as a rule, episcopal seats and educational centres with rich historical endowments. By contrast, the Puritan Protestantism and poor peasantry of the Great Plain did not leave such monuments to posterity.

This dichotomy of the settlement structure has prevented up to this day the formulation of a unified character whether to analyze the settlement network. The debates and clashes within the Hungarian geographical literature of the past one hundred years have been due to the fact that specialists have always wanted to present a uniform picture based exclusively on the characteristics of either the settlement network of Transdanubia or of the Great Plain, giving rise to protests on the part of the protagonists of the other region. Thus the debate as to which settlement network was to be regarded as „most typically Hungarian" was only settled as late as 1945, when the problem was removed from the agenda. But the fact that the existence of two types of settlement has not been officially acknowledged has caused a great many problems and difficulties in the implementation of a uniform official policy of settlement development. This has proved detrimental primarily in the Great Plain, where the problems of the „tanya" system of detached farmsteads, and the possibilities that exist for modernizing the rural market towns, have not met with much understanding. This is because they require a basically different approach to the towns of Transdanubia and the Northern Middle Mountains, which, owing to their already existing industrial development and proximity to mineral deposits, have come to the forefront of socialist industrial and urban development. The different development needs of the two regions were not acknowledged officially until the beginning of the 1970s.

The most obvious way to characterize the existing differences is through a comparison of the settlement structure of the Little Plain in western Transdanubia and that of the Great Plain, since in both areas the relief forms are similar. On the Little Plain a system of large and medium-size villages predominates, while on the Great Plain large and mammoth-sized villages generally prevail. The urban network in the Little Plain can be characterized by the most developed supply figures within the country but, despite the undoubtedly large-scale development of the past decade, this cannot be said to apply to the rural market towns of the Great Plain. Moreover, while the towns of the Little Plain are rich in valuable historic monuments deriving from the former rich handicraft industry and the bourgeois strata, the rural market towns of the Great Plain, for reasons already mentioned, are poor in such features.

3.1 Settlement characteristics predating the present-day structure

The broad outlines of Hungary's settlement network first evolved between the 8th and 10th centuries when, because of the small population, a fragmented settlement network came into being, with large areas suitable for settlement left unhabited. After the establishment of the feudal state there began the formation of royal and ecclesiastical organizations. Castles and churches were built and, to ensure manpower, the feudal estates established villages. Within this fragmented settlement system there existed just a few towns which were the centres of feudal administration, and seats of the ecclesiastical authority and aristocracy.

However, the next stage of development, which was the Turkish occupation, brought about decisive changes that can still be felt today. In the 14th and 15th centuries, the development of the productive forces speeded up, towns arose around the castles, and rich mining towns were established and gained significance. However, the fragmented rural settlement network was greatly thinned by the subsequent Turkish occupation and has only survived in an original or vestigial state in those areas over which the Turks did not extend their rule, or where they stayed for just a short time as in the counties of Vas, Zala and Veszprém in western Danubia, and in the counties of Borsod-Abaúj-Zemplén and Szabolcs-Szatmár in the north-western part of the country. In the territory under Turkish occupation it was only in Baranya county that the small-village settlement pattern was revived, mainly in conformity with the ideas of new settlers of German and Southern Slav origin.

Following the Turkish occupation, the slow development of productive forces meant that the evolvement of larger urban clusters made slow headway, and at that only in the Great Plain. This was because the population of the smaller rural market towns that depended on animal-breeding multiplied as they had to absorb the inhabitants of destroyed villages, often as many 30 to 40 of them. The towns had to pay tribute to the Sultan who in return ensured their protection, and it was this that attracted the population of villages that had been destroyed. The economic basis of the rural market towns of the Great Plain was mainly agriculture, which proved very unstable as animal epidemics, natural disasters and frequent wars set back their development seriously. The most important consequence of the development of this period was the evolution of the tanya system, which will be discussed in detail later on.

In Western-Transdanubia and the Northern Highlands towns could develop in more peaceful conditions, based primarily on the guild industry and commerce, while several towns gained significance as episcopal centres during Counter-Reformation and the period of Habsburg absolutism.

The development of those centres that form the majority of the towns today showed a vigorous upswing during the 19th century phase of railway construction and during the existence of the Austro–Hungarian Monarchy (1867–1918) as a result of industrial development. During this time, Budapest became increasingly dominant within the Hungarian settlement network because, being a large city capable of developing its infrastructure, it was able to attract the benefits of industrial development. Its growth was spectacular and its population increased by over half a million within a few decades. It was the main economic centre of the Carpathian Basin where the main offices of large enterprises, banks and merchant houses were centralized. No less important was the effect derived from its function as the centre of the transportation system, and as a cultural and educational centre. Apart from Budapest, only a few towns in Transdanubia and the Northern Highlands managed to reach a significant level of industrial development. In addition, a large number of mining and industrial villages, so-called company towns with unbalanced economic structures, came to be established in the new mining districts, for instance Tatabánya and Ózd, and attained a town rank only after 1945. Others like Dorog, Nagybátony and Sajószentpéter have remained villages to the present day.

The strong effect of the expanding railway network on settlement development is apparent from the fact that several railway junctions, for example Celldömölk, Dombóvár and Hatvan, owe their fast growth and subsequent urbanization basically to the railway, while the modernization of public administration ensured the county towns a period of short-lived but effective development.

The period between the Austro—Hungarian Compromise of 1867 and the turn of the century marked one of the greatest inherent contradictions of Hungarian settlement development, in that, at a time when the industrial revolution leading to wholesale urban expansion was making rapid progress in Western Europe, in Hungary it was the market towns of the plainlands that were growing most rapidly because of the agrarian boom, including the spread of the more labour-intensive cultures like grapes, fruit and vegetables and the repeated outflow of rural population to the detached tanya farmsteads.

After the Trianon Peace Treaty of 1920 concluding World War I, the relative dominance of Budapest further increased because, formerly the leading centre of the Carpathian Basin, it now found itself the capital of a country with a much truncated area and population. Between the two world wars, Budapest was first to attract the then modern industries such as telecommunications and pharmaceuticals and the high concentration of total industrial production in its territory is indicative of the mono-centric spatial structure of the country. After the Trianon Peace Treaty, the administrative system of the country changed significantly, and the significance of the county towns of Miskolc, Pécs, Debrecen, Békéscsaba, Szeged and Győr became more pronounced as their ,,competitors", for instance Kassa, Nagyvárad, Arad and Pozsony, were annexed to neighbouring countries.

After the liberation, Hungary inherited a settlement network beset with a great many inherent contradictions. The elimination of the contradictions in the settlement system could only be carried out gradually, in several stages. The transformation and up-grading of the settlement system was also dependent on several conditions set by the level of economic development and the organization of state administration:

(a) First the ,,old grievances over public administration" had to be remedied. Some settlements which had been performing urban functions for some time were officially granted urban status, namely Hatvan, Törökszentmiklós, Orosháza, Tatabánya and Ózd. This was necessary because in Hungary the concept of a town is associated with an administrative status, from which it follows that towns receive many benefits, for example budgetary allocations.

(b) A reform of the county system also had to be carried out and this was done in 1950. Along with the fusion of several small ,,fragmented counties" which has already been mentioned, the largest county of Pest—Pilis—Solt—Kiskun was divided into Pest and Bács-Kiskun counties and, as a result, Kecskemét became a county town. The new state was distrustful of some county forms, and certain changes were thus carried out. The county town of Nógrád county was moved from Balassagyarmat to the industrial centre, Salgótarján, while the large traditional centre of Tatabánya became the county town of Komárom.

(c) It was a further problem that in several counties in the early 1950s, for instance in Fejér, Somogy, Tolna and Szabolcs-Szatmár, the county seat was the only town. Thus there were many areas deficient in urban development, which hampered the rational location of productive forces and the levelling of territorial differences in living standards. Therefore, socialist industrialization also meant the creation of several new socialist towns for example Dunaújváros, Várpalota, Komló, Kazincbarcika and Ajka, out of a number of partly industrialized and unindustrialized communities, which also helped to promote a more balanced spatial location of the urban centres [29].

(d) More and more unindustrialized historical towns had to be included in the process of industrialization so that they might further proceed towards full urban development, the rural market towns of the Great Plain such as Kiskunfélegyháza, Hódmezővásárhely and Kiskunhalas falling mainly into this category.

(e) As a result of industrialization and the planned development of the settlement network, many communities were given town status, primarily in the town-deficient areas of Szabolcs-Szatmár, Somogy and Vas counties. In total 42 settlements were granted the legal town status between 1945 and 1981.

(f) Tentative attempts were also made to transform the tanya-system to fit in with the needs of large-scale socialist production. The official view of the 1950s was that this should be achieved by eliminating the tanya settlements altogether and reorganizing them into villages, but this view had to be modified later as the tanya settlements of the Danube–Tisza Midregion in particular were more resistant to change than had been assumed. Today their long-term survival in the intensive wine- and fruitgrowing areas is taken for granted, and their electrification and connection with the road network are both under way.

(g) With the completion of the socialist reorganization of agriculture, by considerable amount of working power of agricultural requirements migrated to the industrial centres and Budapest. As a result, tendencies towards agglomeration experienced a great upswing and commuter settlements with rapidly increasing populations came into being around Budapest (for example Érd with 41, Vecsés with 21 and Gyál with 18 thousand inhabitants) and around the large provincial industrial centres.

(h) Recreational settlements have expanded enormously around Lake Balaton, along the Danube Bend and in holiday resorts with thermal baths and, although not of a town rank, most are nonetheless urban in function.

(i) The steady strengthening of integration processes is manifesting itself in the settlement network, as borne out only by the tendencies towards agglomeration but also by the merging of an increasing number of settlements, for example Tatabánya–Tata–Oroszlány and Békéscsaba–Békés–Gyula. Efforts are being made to plan their development in a purposeful and concerted way, in order to avoid superfluous rivalry.

(j) The government is striving to promote the concentration of administration in accordance with the requirements of socio-economic development by administrative—organizational measures, by establishing, for example, joint village councils, embracing up to four villages, in areas where villages are small. Moreover, urban regions are also being established in certain instances that embrace a large urban centre and its surrounding hinterland, as, for example, around the town of Pécs.

(k) To guide the long-term development of the settlement system, the Development Concept of the National Settlement Network was adopted in 1971 and will be discussed in more detail at the end of this chapter.

Through these various measures, the Hungarian settlement network can now operate as an organically integrated system not only the field of administration, but also through the hierarchical provision of, for example, educational and health services.

The functioning of the settlement network as an integrated system is further promoted by the national provision of public utilities and other services, for example the national electricity, natural gas grids, regional water supply systems and the transportation network as well as the regional organization of financial institutions, and wholesale trading.

The national settlement system is in fact composed of the individual county settlement networks. Thus there are counties, for example Győr-Sopron, where the urban network is virtually complete, and the same can generally be said of the counties of Komárom, Vas, Zala, Veszprém, Somogy and Baranya. In Tolna and Fejér, moreover, where several large villages are to be raised to town status, urban development is proceeding in a planned way but, on the Great Plain in particular (with the exception of Szabolcs-Szatmár county), and to a lesser extent in the Northern Highlands, the process of town creation is still very far from completion, although even here it is expected to be concluded by the turn of the century.

In what follows we shall discuss the main components of the Hungarian settlement network, the most frequent settlement types, noting in each case their main characteristics.

3.2 The main components of the Hungarian settlement network and their characteristic regional types

The most important components of the settlement network are the various towns of different sizes, functions and developmental levels, the villages and the dispersed or *tanya* settlements. It is their totality that constitutes the settlement network in which each settlement has its own function and place in the settlement hierarchy.

3.2.1 Towns

Although relatively few in number (there were 109 towns in 1984), with respect to their significance, central role and extensive economic and service functions, towns constitute the most important element of the Hungarian settlement network *(Fig. 14)*. According to the 1980 census, 53 per cent of Hungary's population are town-dwellers, and since their number is steadily rising, the role played by towns in the country's settlement network will further increase and assume a determining significance.

The assessment of the individual units of the Hungarian urban network has for long been a subject of considerable debate in the relevant Hungarian literature. Using the criteria of western geographers, some specialists only considered the so-called western-type town, which were in a minority, as towns in the strict sense of the term, and called into question the urban character of that uniquely East-European and Hungarian settlement form, the rural market town, identifying them in essence as mammoth villages [37].

The main spatial types of town are as follows.

(1) *Western-type towns*, which can be found chiefly in Transdanubia as well as in the Northern Highlands, are located at the focal points of the communication system. Most of them are perceived by the public as ancient settlements rich in history and of an ecclesiastical character; such are Győr, Sopron, Szombathely, Kőszeg, Veszprém, Pápa, Székesfehérvár, Esztergom and Eger. Their development speeded up significantly during the 17th and 18th centuries, hence the predominantly baroque style of their centres, which house the old ecclesiastical and public institutions, and even of many of their residential buildings. As a result of their more or less continuous historical development, these towns were able to take, from the Middle Ages on, increasing economic advantage from their location, which they made good use of during the industrial development of the 19th century. Their smooth development has for a long time been undisturbed and the capital they accumulated could thus play a positive role not only in the development of productive forces but also in the establishment of the infrastructural basis for subsequent advance. These are the towns that are functionally best supplied with piped water, drainage, roads, dwelling amenities and public institutions. The reason for this lies, primarily, in the fact that the infrastructural provision of these towns began to develop as early as the Middle Ages and could thus be adjusted to the requirements of their inhabitants and industrial production. Therefore, the great historical lags did not develop here as appeared in the Great Plain where, based on an agrarian economy, only a much poorer socio-economic structure with a much more modest demand for infrastructure could be created.

(2) *Market-type towns* are the basic settlement form of the plain, but some are still be found in Transdanubia and in the region of the Northern Middle Mountains. Thus two sub-types can be distinguished:

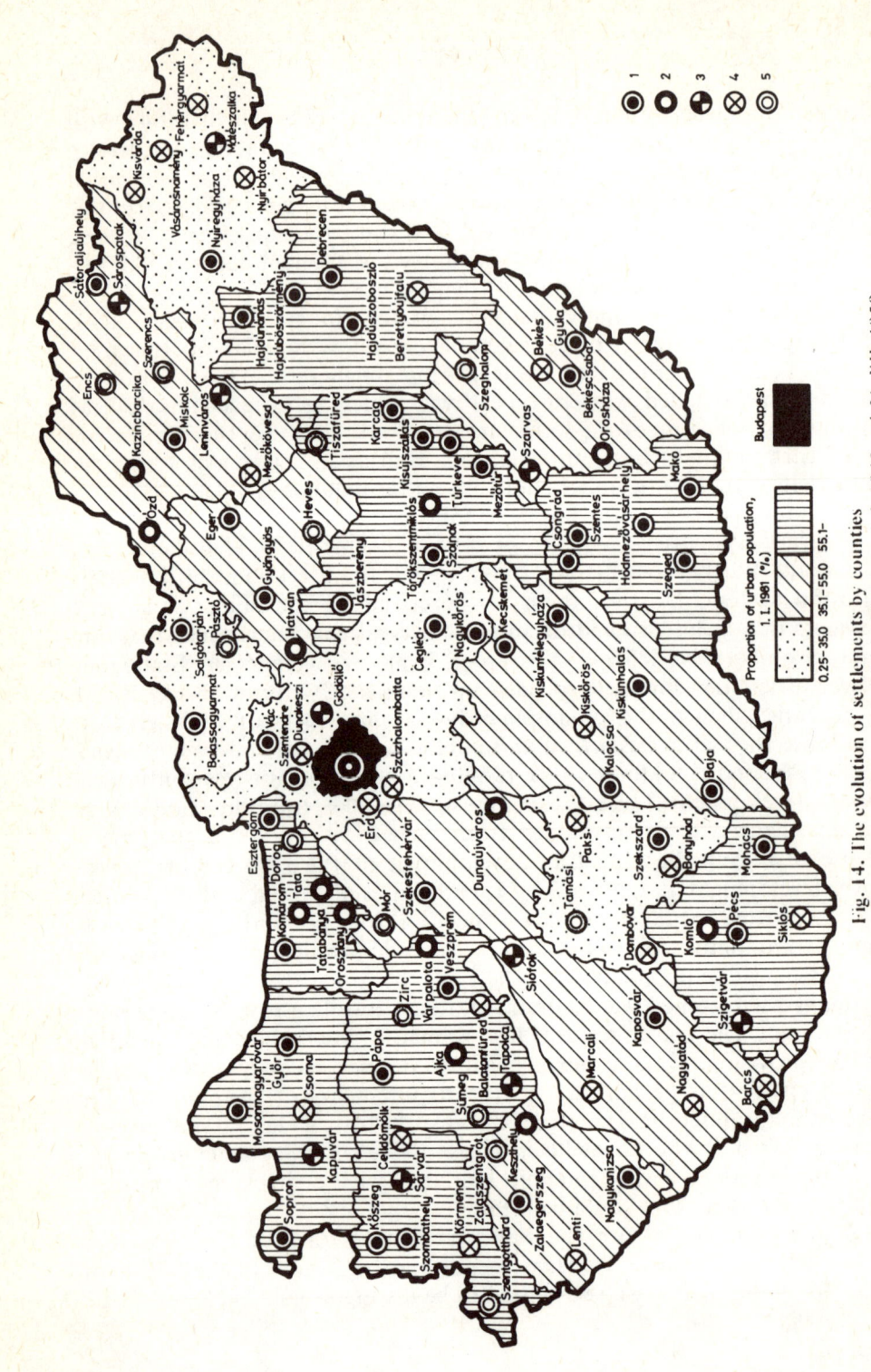

Fig. 14. The evolution of settlements by counties
1 – towns established before 1. I. 1945; 2 – towns established between 1. I. 1945 and 31. XII. 1959;
3 – towns established between 1. I. 1960 and 31. XII. 1969; 4 – towns established between 1. I. 1970 and 31. XII. 1983; 5 – towns established after 1. I. 1984

(a) *The market towns of the Great Plain* with a large surrounding area whose economic basis was ensured, up to recent times, by large-scale agricultural activity.

The history of the rural market towns dates back to the period of the Turkish occupation, and subsequent movement of the population form their protection to the tanya settlement as has already been referred to. The population that remained in the towns nonetheless retained an agrarian character and, as regards their occupational structure, they could hardly be described as urban. For instance, as late as the 1949 census, 76 per cent of their population gained a livelihood from agriculture, as did 53 per cent of them, even in 1960. The question is then what has constituted their urban character, what urban functions have they been able to perform. The answer to this question is as follows:

The market towns had large land areas surrounding them, as much as 70 thousand hectares in which lived a large tanya population. The town was the purchaser of their products, i.e. it had a market function and was the supplier of various services, consumer goods and the means of production.

They were also the centres of a small but dynamic rural handicraft industry geared to agrarian production, for example, cartwrights, blacksmiths and harness-makers, and to the demands of the local population, for instance bootmakers, tanners, joiners, furriers and tailors, while some products were even sent to other areas. Thus these towns occupied a specific place in the geographical and social division of labour.

Most market towns had secondary schools with many centuries of tradition. Since the majority of their inhabitants were Protestants, the Turks tolerated the maintenance of these schools, for example in Mezőtúr, while new schools were established as early as the first half of the 19th century. The educational function of these towns attracting pupils over considerable distances was also significant.

Being administratively independent, the market towns had an urban institutional system with a town magistrate, court of justice and police force.

The social structure of these towns had a specific character: along with a small professional and administrative–clerical stratum, a very strong rich peasant population lived in the town, but their lands were cultivated by family members or labourers living in the tanya. Social conflicts between the two strata occurred frequently. There were also large numbers of medium-sized landowners belonging to the peasant strata, who in winter lived in the town and during the agricultural season in the tanya. The proportion of artisans and small merchants was substantial and considerable social mobility occurred within the group with the above peasant strata. Upward mobility from the middle-peasant, artisan and merchant strata was, however, rather rare.

The market towns also had a characteristic morphology and structure. Their territorial extension was horizontal, with an urban nucleus in which were located the two-storied buildings that housed the public administration, schools, retail commercial services and offices of banks, and grain merchants, together with a large market square and churches. This part of the town was usually supplied with public utilities. Around this nucleus lived the administrative employees, professionals and rich peasants of the town in one-storied houses built usually on large plots with closed courtyards. Those with lower incomes lived farther from the centre, while the poor, comprising the landless peasants, day-labourers and navvies lived on the outskirts. In the wide streets leading out of the town cattle were herded to be driven out to graze on outlying common. Such towns had few paved roads. As regards drinking-water supply, artesian wells began to play an important role from the last third of the 19th century. These were visited by the population usually once a day, which provided the possibility for the establishment of interesting social habits, meetings and exchange of information.

The reason why, apart from the destruction during the Turkish occupation, the town network of the Great Plain could not evolve, lies in the fact that small-peasant agriculture was unable to accumulate sufficient capital to make this necessary and the limited demand for urban functions of a poor-peasant society could be fully met by the modest institutional services of the rural market towns. Emphasis was laid only on administrative autonomy, the market function, and educational, health and cultural provision. The agrarian production structure of the towns did not require the public provision of water supply and drainage as did the handicraft-manufacture of the guild towns, nor could the peasantry have been able to operate these services with their low incomes.

The development of the market towns was largely determined by the extent to which the extensive agriculture of the 19th century was able to evolve into more intensive cultivations. Such a changeover was promoted first of all by railway construction and by the programme for stabilizing the wind-blown sands of the Danube–Tisza Mid-region, by the switch-over to livestock stabling in the region east of the Tisza river, and by changes in the types of agrarian production. This process unfolded first of all in the Danube–Tisza Mid-region, then in Békés and Csongrád counties south of the Tisza and lastly in the Nagykunság and Hajdúság, where many structural problems had to be overcome, and in the Nyírség.

The problems of underdevelopment and infrastructural deficiencies did not become really conspicuous until after the socialist reorganization of agriculture which altered the occupational and income rationships and stimulated motorization [22]. The elimination of the infrastructural lag can only be achieved in the longer term and is aggravated by the existence of one-family dwellings with gardens, which substantially increases the costs of providing public services, although this does the benefit of making the population interested in self-financing developments.

Certain centrally located towns, for example Szeged and Debrecen, have managed to „outgrow" their market-town status, which has been helped by economic development. Of the towns of the Great Plain only Szolnok, because of its location and accessibility was never a market town. As a bridging point of the river Tisza, it became important in the transshipment of salt and timber. Moreover, agriculture could never play a significant role in its economic life owing to its small land area.

(b) *The market towns of the Transdanubian and Northern Mountains* differ from those of the Great Plain in several features, but primarily in the much smaller agricultural area contained within their boundaries, while the Turkish occupation did not promote the same concentration of productive forces. They were, in consequence of their relief characteristics, grape- and wine-producing market towns of which Tokaj-Hegyalja is the most characteristic. The phylloxera destroyed the vineyards of the historical wine-growing districts at the close of the 19th century, undermined their economic basis and, as a consequence, most reverted to village status. Others, however, such as Balatonfüred, Tapolca and Sárospatak were able, owing to other functions, to rise to urban status.

(3) *The towns associated with 19th-century industrial development*. Such towns evolved from the agglomeration and spontaneous coalescence of earlier mining or industrial villages as for instance in the cases of old Tatabánya, Salgótarján, Ózd and old Diósgyőr. Most of them were formerly typical company towns with a host of crowded houses and a very low standard of public services. Capitalist industrial development was not accompanied by a well-thought-out policy of urban development and most of these towns had to be re-developed over the past two decades.

One of their characteristics was the lack of any uniform urban structure, and it is only since the conferment of town status that such structures have been established, after many compromises and substantial cost inputs. Under this policy new town centres have been built in Tatabánya, Salgótarján, Ózd.

(4) *Planned socialist industrial towns*. The new socialist industrial towns have also been created, almost without exception, through the rapid industrialization of rural settlements, but in this case according to a definite plan and in association with large investment projects. Thus new towns such as Dunaújváros, Kazincbarcika, Komló, Százhalombatta and Leninváros are infrastructurally the best-supplied towns today [9]. It is in these towns that the highest ratios of new up-to-date flats with high service provision are to be found, although these are noneless overcrowded due to heavy in-migration and a high rate of natural increase. Institutional provision of new schools, houses of culture and health establishments is also favourable, although commercial and entertainment facilities are poorer, partly because the norms were lower when they had been built, and partly because the population had outgrown them due to its rapid increase. Nevertheless, they still belong to the category of best-supplied towns.

(5) *Budapest*, the country's capital, has to be treated separately within the urban network because of its size, national and international functions, and the problem associated with its past and future development. The Second World War inflicted heavy losses upon the capital, and although reconstruc-

tion was rapid, Budapest received relatively little attention during the 1950s because of the priority given to industrialization. Though subsequently modified, this development strategy did have the consequence that Budapest was granted a lower level of budgetary allocation for industrial investment and housing purposes than justified by the real needs [52]. Thus its industries could not develop adequately, with the consequence that their competitiveness deteriorated. Housing is still the most burning problem, and there are also serious difficulties with infrastructural supply, at least when compared with foreign cities of similar size.

Owing to the nature of its historical development, the structure of Budapest is intricate. The basic layout and residential structure of the inner districts evolved for the most part during the second half of the 19th century. The older housing stock of the peripheral districts and of the agglomeration belt, however, which were administratively attached to Budapest in 1950, is largely the product of the first half of the 20th century. Housing standards in both inner and outer districts were generally neglected before 1970 because of the great shortage of housing in the capital. Instead, from 1960 the building of new housing estates on vacant ground came to be regarded as a means of diminishing the pressure on housing. They were, therefore, often located on the periphery of the urban area and were difficult to link in with the functional circulation of the town. This difficulty was further aggravated by the fact that living-space in the new flats is rather small (between 40 and 60 square metres), and social provision level on the estates limited, with few institutions for children and underdeveloped commercial facilities.

It was at the end of the 1960s that the rebuilding and modernization on the suburbs of Óbuda, Csepel, Pesterzsébet, Kispest, Kőbánya and Újpest gained momentum.

In the early 1980s, however, we are at last witnessing the beginning of the rehabilitation of the inner districts, also, where the housing stock is over one hundred years old and is badly in need of renewal and modernization. The programme of renewal has been helped by the decrease in the volume of new investments, which has released some of the capacity of the construction industry for this task.

Nonetheless, important progress has been made especially in the building of a new underground railway system, the Metro, which has meant a qualitative leap in the standard of public transport. (In fact, the first underground railway in Budapest was opened in 1869, second only to that of London.) The new east-west line was brought into operation in 1970, while the southern section of the new north-south line was opened in 1978.

There are, however, still serious problems to solve, especially in the new housing estates, where there is still a shortage of nurseries, retail outlets, medicinal centres, telephones and cultural services. Moreover, as a result of the rapid increase in the number of passenger cars, road and bridge capacity has reached a critical level, and there is a pressing need for a motorway-ring to carry transit traffic around the capital.

*Principles of urban classification
according to function and size*

In addition to the spatial and genetic types outlined above, towns can also be classified in other ways to highlight the characteristic features that influence infrastructural requirements. The most common of these is a classification based on function and size.

In a functional classification, the production, economic, service and administrative aspects of towns have to be taken into account. Account must be taken of those functions which are most important within the context of the settlement network, i.e. the ones through which towns play a role in the settlement network as a concerted, co-ordinated system.

The functional classification of Hungarian towns is as follows:

— *Mining towns,* for example Tatabánya, Oroszlány and Komló, whose economic base is coal mining. (No other type of mining has given rise to urban development in Hungary).

— *Industrial towns,* such as Miskolc, Ózd, Dunaújváros and Győr, are usually centres of heavy industry containing the most important factories of the country.

— *Market or trading towns,* which previous historic times were the most characteristic type of urban development. They are located in linear patterns primarily at the foot of the Northern Middle Mountains, and along the fringes of the Great and the Little Plains, where the products of the highlands and plainlands were exchanged. Most of them have evolved into industrial towns since the late 19th century and include Pápa, Győr, Vác, Gyöngyös, Eger, Miskolc and Sátoraljaújhely.

— *Railway towns,* for instance, Dombóvár, Celldömölk and Hatvan, located at major railway junctions, which have taken on an increasingly industrial function owing to their favourable situation and the existence of repairshops and warehouses.

— *Bridge towns,* such as Szolnok and Komárom, which have developed into centres for the transshipment of goods, attracting thereby water- and transport-intensive industries.

— *Agrarian or semi-agrarian towns,* the present-day successors to the old plainland market towns, in which agrarian and food-processing activities constitute the primary economic basis. The number of towns of predominantly agricultural function is steadily diminishing as industry gains an increasing foothold and it is now therefore correct to classify them as semi-rural towns. Examples include Cegléd, Kiskunfélegyháza and Kiskunhalas.

— *School and university towns,* a type slowly declining, because with the large-scale expansion of secondary and higher education and its emphasis on former school towns such as Pápa, Esztergom, Kalocsa and Sárospatak, has shifted towards industry.

— *University towns* do not really exist as separate entities in Hungary as it is mainly in the larger, multi-functional towns for example Debrecen,

Szeged and Pécs, where universities can be found. The only exception is perhaps Gödöllő, with its university of agriculture.

— *Bath and tourist resorts,* including Keszthely, Siófok, Balatonfüred and Hajdúszoboszló as examples of bath and Sopron and Kőszeg as examples of tourist towns in which are preserved many features of the historical past. In the larger cities like in Budapest, Szeged and Debrecen such functions cannot be separated from the general urban environment.

We can also speak of administrative centres, for example the county and district towns. For a long time, the administrative function was the most important determinant of the Hungarian urban network, and carried greater organizational power than the economic function. It was in these administrative centres that the various financial institutions, secondary schools and hospitals were located, and it was there that most artisans lived, a class which played an important part in the provision of urban services [4].

The administrative function is now no longer decisive as it is the industrial centres that wield the strongest attraction. For example, the number of settlements performing only district-level administrative functions have been reduced considerably, because they have proved unsuitable for the provision of higher functions, and their administrative role has been taken over by nearby settlements of a more industrial character. For example, Ajka, Kazincbarcika and Komló have taken over the administrative functions of Devecser, Edelény and Sásd, respectively.

A classification of towns by size yields the following types:
— small towns with 5 to 20 thousand inhabitants;
— medium-sized towns with 20 to 100 thousand inhabitants;
— large towns or cities with 100 to 300 thousand inhabitants.

Classification by size is important because the categories have different qualitative linkages with infrastructural provision. This does not, however, apply to the basic service provision of piped-water and drainage as in all types of town efforts must be made to realize, step by step, the full supply of these services, but rather to the more selective institutional spheres of commerce, health and culture, where significant differentiation according to size is necessary.

A classification by size also exemplifies the development of the Hungarian urban network.

In the early 1950s, the five large provincial cities of Miskolc, Debrecen, Szeged, Pécs and Győr still had populations of around 100 thousand each, but by the early 1980s, Miskolc had already exceeded 200 000 and the populations of Debrecen, Szeged and Pécs were close to this figure. In addition Székesfehérvár, Nyíregyháza and Kecskemét have joined the group of cities with populations over 100 000, and Szombathely, Szolnok and Kaposvár may reach that level by the turn of the century.

The bulk of the Hungarian urban hierarchy, however, is made up of medium-sized towns with populations of between 20 and 100 000, most of which are either mining or industrial towns or semi-rural towns, or county or district seats. Basically, it is the level of their infrastructural provision which determines the developmental level of Hungarian towns in general. By contrast, there are relatively few small towns with 5 to 20 thousand inhabitants, because relatively few urbanizing centres were granted the legal status of towns before the mid-1960s, as the emphasis was being laid on the construction of the new socialist industrial towns. Thus most former small towns soon developed into medium-sized towns. Today, the majority of settlements that perform small-town functions are to be found among the large villages, numbering about 300 in all. Nevertheless, the elevating process of suitable communities to small-town status has been speeded up to late, and of the 13 settlements gaining the legal status of town on January 1, 1984 belong to the small-town category and are located in peripheral areas from which migration towards the centre is significant. The creation of such small towns should, however, play a significant role in reducing the rate of out-migration from peripheral areas.

3.2.2 Villages

During the past two decades, from 1960 to 1980, the Hungarian village network has changed drastically. Most villages are no longer inhabited by an agricultural population but predominantly by an industrial and non-agricultural population. In the past, the overwhelming bulk of the rural population, 75 per cent in 1949, was still engaged in agriculture and in the strongly polarized spatial division of labour that emerged during the belated phase of capitalist development in Eastern Europe, it was the villages that were synonymous with agriculture, foodstuffs and raw-materials, while the towns were the scene of industrial production and processing. In 1960, more than half of the rural wage-earners were still engaged in agriculture, but by 1980 this proportion had fallen to 30 per cent.

About 1500 of the country's 3100 rural settlements, i.e. close to 50 per cent, are of an agricultural character in which the majority of the population are engaged in agrarian activities. However, they are mainly composed of the small and tiny villages located in the peripheral parts of the country and barely contain 10 per cent of the total population. In the larger villages, by contrast, the greater share of workers out of agriculture dominates. Village functions have thus undergone a profound transformation, as the former one-sided activities in agriculture and forestry have given way to industrial, tertiary, transport and tourist functions, turning many rural settlements into multi-functional units [31].

Functional types of villages

– *Agrarian villages* constituted for a long time, the most typical and most common village type, on whose morphology, internal structure and provision level traditional peasant agriculture has left its mark. Its main characteristics are: traditional peasant forms of house-building and living style. In many cases the mixing of production- and residential functions in the same garden the livestock-breeding in the courtyards of homes, which greatly pollute the environment. The low requirement towards services which, on the one hand, were not required by a backward agrarian community and which, on the other hand, far exceeded the financial capability of inhabitants of settlements.

After the reorganization of agriculture in 1960–1962, significant changes in the structure of these villages began to unfold. Productive activity was increasingly removed from them and concentrated in the co-operative and state farms lying outside the village area. The dwelling stock has also undergone a process of transformation and modernization, and, with a greater provision of services, these villages were now coming to resemble the residential areas of small houses with gardens that are associated with the small towns.

The organization of agricultural work is also beginning to take on a more industrial character with the introduction of valuable modern machinery and systematic organization, while income levels are approaching and even exceeding those in industry. These processes have become one of the main driving forces behind the urbanization of agrarian villages, and large-scale farming is shaping the living conditions not only of the peasantry but also of the rural population as a whole. The rate of development is naturally influenced by the production levels of individual agrarian districts as well by village size.

Nonetheless, agrarian villages still present a rather traditional picture with their old peasant houses, wells and general stores, although agrarian-industrial centres also have modern buildings and now perform urban functions basically different from those of the old, traditional village. These new agrarian industrial settlements are centres where industrial-like production systems are applied to agriculture, of the so-called ,,systems organizers", as at Bábolna (near Komárom), Nádudvar (near Debrecen) and Bóly (near Mohács).

– *Commuter settlements.* Morphologically these are typical agrarian villages that are to be found in the hinterlands of certain large cities, for example Budapest and Miskolc, and around large industrial centres such as Dunaújváros. Here the attraction of the industrial centres had already led to a significant occupational restratification before the liberation, but particularly during the 1950s. With the organization of socialist agriculture, the rural labour force increasingly found employment in these centres, especially as industrial production was highly labour-intensive at that time, but were prevented from migrating to them because of the housing shortage. Under this process the new agglomeration belt of the capital consisting of

44 settlements experienced rapid growth, and similar agglomeration zones came into being elsewere, as in the valleys of the Sajó and Zagyva rivers, and along the upper part of the Danube between Komárom and Esztergom.

Besides proximity to the centre, the existence of cheap housing plots and favourable lines of transportation, e.g. railway stations and bus routes, also helped orientate the settlements of the agglomeration. Thus, stations have become the central areas of such settlements, that is where the shops and other service institutions are located.

On account of rapid in-migration, such commuter villages which are without any independent economic basis have been unable to provide the necessary financial resources for their own infrastructural development, and in respect of the provision of public utilities and other sevices they have incurred considerable debts.

— *Industrial villages* are relatively smaller settlements of an industrial character, containing one or more industrial plants. Although the local industry has lent an industrial character to the occupational structure of the population, this in itself has proved insufficient to transform the settlement into a central place.

There are certain industrial villages which owe their rationale to the processing of the agricultural products of the former large estates, for instance sugar refining, distilleries and starch and hemp factories. In other cases, large industrial plants, for instance, to generate electricity or manufacture cement, were set up to exploit the output of some nearby mine, but the proximity of a large town or the availability of cheap local labour also created favourable conditions for the location of engineering plants or light industry. A typical example of such an industrial village is Martfű, south of Szolnok, which was founded by the Czeh Bata Shoe Company before 1945 for the utilization of cheap local labour.

— *Mining villages* are located in districts where coal and other mines, as well as oil wells are in operation. The majority of their inhabitants usually work in mining, while their traditional rural character has been modified by the establishments and dwellings associated with the mine, and by certain public institutions of an urban character, such as technical schools, miners' houses of culture and ambulance stations. Such a settlement is Rudabánya, located north of Miskolc, where the only iron-ore mine of the country is to be found.

— *Railway villages* are performing some function associated with the railway, or are settlements located along a main railway line inhabited by railwaymen. The main organizing force of the settlement is the railway.

— *Recreational settlements*. For most of these tourism constitutes the main source of income of the inhabitants. Such settlements have usually developed only during the past few decades, in association with beaches, holiday homes and forest parks. Typical of recreational settlements are the holiday resorts located along the shores of lakes Balaton and Velence, in the

Danube Bend, at thermal spas as well as in the rugged terrain of the Northern Middle Mountains. Infrastructurally, they are some of the best-supplied villages, typical examples being Parád, Harkány and Leányfalu.

3.2.3 The size structure of the rural settlement network

Over and above their functional character, population size may also be indicative of developmental differences among rural settlements. Only large villages with several thousand inhabitants are capable of performing several different functions, while the tiny villages and scattered settlements are hardly able to provide a single function satisfactorily.

The size structure of the rural settlement network is rather diversified, as settlements with different numbers of inhabitants and population density are unevenly distributed over the country. Structurally, three rather heterogeneous types can be distinguished.

(a) Small to tiny villages are typical of those areas of Western Transdanubia and the Northern Middle Mountains where the productive endowments for agriculture are generally favourable. 72 per cent of the country's area falls into this category and one-fifth of the country's population lives in some 2300 small to tiny villages. As regards the structure and spatial location of this settlement type, it can be divided into two sub-groups.

– tiny villages and
– small villages.

In Baranya, Vas and Zala counties, where tiny villages predominate, the average population size of villages is 700 to 800 persons, and in 80 per cent of them less than 1000. The very small village areas correlate quite closely with hilly relief characteristics, but they may also occur in flat area. In such regions settlement density is twice the national density, but population density is below the national average.

Also significant is the number of dwarf villages with less than 500 inhabitants *(Fig. 15)*. In these villages it is difficult to ensure even the services meeting basic, everyday needs (see paragraph 3.4). They have no public administrative organization of their own, and two or more villages constitute a so-called joint-council community. (Nearly half the villages of Baranya county are dwarf villages, among them Gyűrűfű, the first depopulated village in Hungary.) The very small village network can no longer meet today's social requirements either in the organization of agricultural work, education and culture, or in service provision. Therefore, they may develop in the future, like the tanya in the Great Plain, into inhabited peripheral parts of independent villages.

Small villages have an average population size of over 1200, although some are considerably larger. The spatial distribution of small villages is characteristic mainly of the hilly and mountainous regions and of the small basins

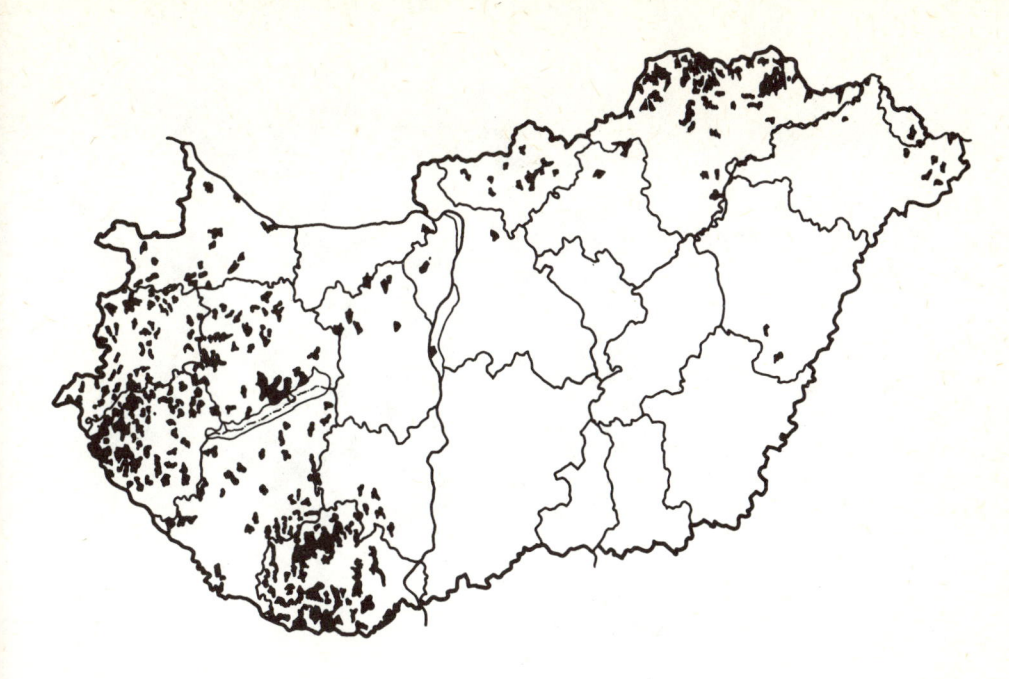

Fig. 15. The distribution of dwarf villages

surrounded by them as in Borsod-Abaúj-Zemplén, Nógrád, Veszprém, Somogy and Győr-Sopron counties, where the dense medieval settlement pattern was hardly thinned during the 150 years of Turkish occupation.

(b) With their more or less balanced geographical distribution, medium-sized villages are characteristic of Fejér, Komárom, Tolna, Heves and Szabolcs-Szatmár counties. Average population number is over 2000. The average territorial extent of tiny villages ranging from 2500 to 3000 hectares conforms with the average size of co-operative farms. Appropriate communal and public institutions can also operate within them.

(c) Large and mammoth villages are typically found in the Great Plain counties of Bács-Kiskun, Szolnok, Békés, Csongrád and Hajdú-Bihar, and partly in Pest. The large villages have average populations between 3000 and 4000 rising to over 5000 in some cases. Mammoth villages, on the other hand, have between 5000 and 10000 inhabitants, but on the Great Plain and in certain zones of agglomerations of over 10000 are to be found. The main characteristic of mammoth villages is that, despite their large size, they lack the central-place character typical of small towns with similar populations, and the view that mammoth villages and rural market towns are basically synonymous concepts is mistaken. There are fundamental differences between them, if not in outward appearance, then certainly in terms of functions.

Before the liberation, most of the best-known mammoth villages housed day-labourers who worked in agriculture in other regions of the country,

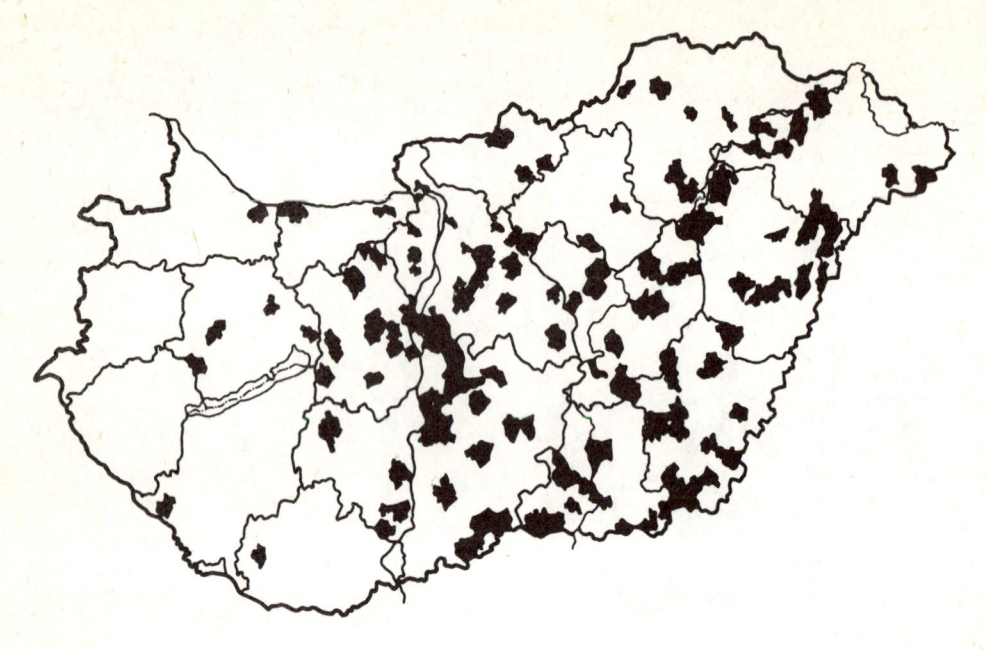

Fig. 16. The distribution of mammoth villages

and in road or railway construction, because local job opportunities were few and the amount of arable land available to them insufficient. Owing to their peculiar structure, these mammoth villages could not develop centre-place functions comparable with those of the rural market towns whose economies were based on more intensive activities.

The mammoth villages *(Fig. 16)* of today are industrial or agglomeration villages, and though their urbanization is steadily progressing, they are still without any central functions, because most of their inhabitants commute to work in other centres, as in the case of Gyál and Vecsés.

Economic growth acts on the development of settlements in a selective way. The smaller villages and tanya settlements have lost up to 30 per cent of their population through out-migration, while moderate rates of loss have been recorded by medium-sized and large villages [32]. 90 per cent of settlements with less than 1000 inhabitants, 80 per cent of villages with populations of 2000 to 5000 and 70 per cent of those with more than 5000 inhabitants have suffered substantial out-migration over the past two decades.

3.2.4 Tanya settlements

In Hungarian official statistics, tanya settlements are not regarded as independent settlement types, though many geographers hold them to be a characteristic settlement type of the plainlands. In official surveys they are classified as „outlying inhabited places". But the concept of an „outlying inhabited place" is wider than that of the tanya. In essence, all buildings used as independent dwellings and located in the outlying districts of settlements, for instance dam or railway watch houses, storage sheds, farmsteads as well as the tanya belong to this concept.

Nonetheless, the overwhelming majority of „outlying inhabited places" are tanya settlements at least in the Great Plain, where they constitute the typical settlement pattern of the outlying parts of the old rural market towns and large villages. In Transdanubia, by contrast, the smaller outlying inhabited places of the agricultural population are dwellings dispersed around the farms of the old manorial estates.

The tanya system of the Great Plain evolved over a considerable time span, as a result of Turkish domination. The areal extent of the market towns and large villages was so big that the distance between central settlement and much of agricultural land was too great for people to cover in one day, thus encouraging out-movement from the central village to town. After the Turkish wars had come to an end, the population began to swarm out to the deserted lands. First they lived only in temporary homes, but later in permanant dwellings. For a long time, they lived there only in summer, and in winter moved with their cattle to the town. Later still the old peasants settled permanently in the rural towns, while the younger generation remained on the tanya. Thus the number of people living in the tanya increased steadily, a process that was further enhanced by the fact that landless peasants working for the richer brethren continued to live on the latter's tanya. The tanya was usually built at the edge of the proprietor's land, and performed the following functions:

– it embodied, in terms of settlement geography, the territorial unity of place of work and residence;

– at the same time, it was also an agricultural unit. The owner kept his implements and animals on the tanya, while the land he cultivated lay around the tanya.

It may be questioned why the tanya has not become a modern agricultural unit during the course of subsequent development. The answer may lie in the fact that the backwardness of Hungarian agriculture was best reflected in the tanya economies. They were, in general, small farms with small pieces of land and low accumulation potentialities. With their scanty resources, the town, the county and the state could not ensure the infrastructural conditions for their development. Most of the houses in the tanya settlements were built of mud or clay and roofed with reeds or straw, and tiles only appeared as late as the turn of the 19th and 20th centuries. Drinking water was supplied from wells, and the roads were little more than tracks. The tanya inhabitants took their produce to the town market, where they also purchased their necessities, but during winter most were completely isolated from the town. In addition, primary-school education in the tanya began as late as the beginning of the 20th century. At the same time, however, life in the tanya had a peculiar quality of its own, in a close connection with nature and isolated from civilization.

After the great wave of 18th century development, the evolution of the tanya system falls into several stages. The mass diffusion of tanya settlements can be related to the land policy of the rural market towns which, from time to time during the 18th and 19th centuries, parcelled out their degraded pastures among the poor. Thus those who came into the possession of land in this way left the town and built a tanya on their small plots, and tried to cultivate the land around them as intensively as possible.

From the second half of the 19th century until quite recently, the tanya settlements played a significant role in developing labour-intensive activities, such as market-gardening, viticulture, fruit-growing and animal husbandry — and thus contributed to territorial specialization. Indeed, the last great wave of out-migration to the tanya occurred after the 1945 redistribution of land, when over 10000 new tanya came into existence.

However, during the main periods of socialist reorganization of agriculture, in 1950—1952 and 1960—1962, as well as later, the position of the tanya became critical. First the official organs felt that the tanya economy could be dispersed with after the establishment of large-scale socialist farms as these would soon be able to take over the production tasks of the tanya. They therefore envisaged the rapid liquidation of the tanya system, and the incorporation of their lands into a co-operative's system.

But these ideas proved to be rather-founded. Firstly, the large farms were unable to cultivate mechanically the old wine- and fruit-growing plots of the small peasantry, while, secondly, collective animal husbandry progressed too slowly to allow the production from the tanya economy to be dispersed with. Thus the tanya system has survived in several places and its continued existence in the form of household plots co-operating with the socialist large-scale farms is justified in those areas with intensive cultures such as the Danube—Tisza Mid-region and the Nyírség [44].

The main spatial types of tanya

— *Dispersed tanya* have evolved mainly in the hinterlands of the market-towns of Csongrád, Szolnok and Hajdú-Bihar counties. Their foundation was laid by the parcelling-out process already referred to, by which rural market towns made it possible for their poor peasantry to obtain their own land outside the town. It is characteristic of their distribution that most of them can be found on the immediate peripheries of towns and along the main roads.

The winding up of the dispersed tanya is going on most vigorously in outlying areas, where service provision, i.e. built roads, electricity supply and health services, is poorest. In the areas around the towns the tanya are better provided with electricity and transport facilities, and children can attend the local schools.

— *Linear-tanya,* which are located along built roads and agricultural tracks, form a second type. They came into being mainly on the former, large estates, where there was no comprehensive parcelling-out activity, and where agricultural labourers were allotted plots along the roads in near proximity to the towns. This is a rather common settlement form in Békés county.
— *Tanya clusters* are a settlement form occurring in the Nyírség. They also evolved on the peripheries of the former, large estates, though in a nucleated rather than linear pattern.

Obviously, the electrification and the supply with other infrastructural services of both linear and clustered tanya is relatively easier to accomplish than in the case of dispersed tanya settlement forms.

3.3 Development concept of the national settlement network

The Hungarian settlement network is thus made up of these main elements, the proportions of which vary regionally according to the level of development. However, it is felt that differences in the advancement and provision levels of settlements of the same size and function resulting from their historical development should be evened out as rapidly as possible, although it is appreciated that their complete elimination is impossible. These sets of problems have been confronted in the Development Concept of the National Settlement Network.

The Development Concept of the National Settlement Network defining the principles for long-term settlement development and adopted by the government in 1971 outlines how the process of urbanization should proceed up to the end of the century. It lays down a hierarchical system of settlements to be implemented as part of the development process and designates the high- and medium-order service centres of the country as well as specifying a system of low-order centres to serve the rural population [30].

The functions to be performed by the individual tiers of the hierarchy, as set out by the Concept, are as follows:

Budapest, as the capital of the country, naturally retains its position as the main metropolitan centre.

Below it come the five provincial cities of Miskolc, Debrecen, Szeged, Pécs and Győr which have been designated first priority high-order centres. Each has a hinterland containing some 1 to 1·5 million inhabitants and each is expected to act as a counterbalance to Budapest in a model which envisages the decentralization of regional functions. It is in these cities that the provincial headquarters of certain important institutions will be located, for instance the railways, the post office, the national banking organization, electricity and gas utilities and wholesale trading enterprises. In addition, they will become the centres offering higher education facilities, specialized health service establishments as well as being the locations of the more significant provincial theatres, museums, art galleries, libraries and radio and TV studios.

The next tier of the hierarchy is occupied by 23 second- and third-priority centres. To this category belong the county towns and other cities of equal size and rank, for instance, Dunaújváros, Sopron, Baja and Hódmezővásárhely, and their role is to offer economic, administrative and service functions at the county-scale.

Such functions are performed by the county offices of commercial enterprises, county bank directorates, county hospitals and county museums and houses of culture, and thus encompass county management activities in many specialized fields. Some settlement specialists hold the view that the number of such centres is too large relative to the small area and the population size of the country, and believe that their number should be reduced.

First and second priority medium-order centres number 64 and 39, respectively, and perform the same urban functions as the high-order centres at a spatial level intermediate between the counties and districts.

At the bottom of the hierarchy are some 144 villages, defined as special low-order centres and comparable to the concept of urbanized communities, plus 547 villages defined as low-order and 284 as partial low-order centres. Two-thirds of the villages of the country, 2060 settlements in all, are, however, envisaged to be settlements without any higher function, i.e. their functions do not extend beyond their own boundaries.

It is clear that both the number and proportion of population residing in medium- and higher-order settlements is steadily rising. Especially fast is the growth in the weight second and third priority high-order centres, which reflects the county—town-centred character of regional development policy over the past two decades.

In the distribution of settlements by number of population, settlements with 10 000 inhabitants constitute an important dividing line. Above this level, the population size of individual settlement categories has tended to increase at an accelerating rate, the only exception to this rule being Budapest with its more moderate rate of population growth. In the settlement categories with fewer than 10 000 inhabitants, settlements with populations of between 5000 and 10 000 are virtually stagnant in size, while the populations of smaller communities have declined at an increasingly faster rate.

The main deficiencies of the Development Concept of the National Settlement Network lie in the fact that it is a network rather than a settlement development concept and that it tends to apply too rigidly the principles of settlement hierarchy and Christaller's central-place theory. Today it is no longer possible to build a settlement system out of a rigid hierarchical arrangement of towns and their immediate spheres of attraction alone, for the rapid pace of socio-economic development of the past two decades has brought the processes of integration and agglomeration to the fore [38] In the various zones agglomeration, as in the valleys of the Sajó and Zagyva rivers, along the Upper—Danube, and around Lake Balaton, and also where individual urban settlements have merged together, (for example Békéscsaba—Békés—Gyula and Tatabánya—Tata—Oroszlány, the relationships among the individual settlements does not evolve according to the rigid hierarchical principles of central-place theory. Thus the Development Concept of the National Settlement Network emphasized more than was desirable the development of individual settlements and this has generated several unfavourable social and economic features, such as the proliferation of various „prestigious investments" in high-order centres designed to justify the high-order central function. A further weakness of the Concept is that it has been unable to tackle appropriately the more difficult characteristics of the settlement network of the plainlands and has tried to apply an identical normative yardstick as elsewhere to this very different settlement type. As a consequence of these deficiencies the Concept was revised and modified in 1978.

3.4 The infrastructural provision of settlements

Infrastructural provision comes in two forms: first as the provision of the so-called basic services to meet the everyday needs of the population preferably at or near to the place of residence and, second, as the provision of higher-order services that can only be made available in towns performing central functions.

Basic service provision includes the communal services of pipe-water, drainage, electricity, natural gas and district heating, together with nurseries, kindergartens, day-care centres, general schools, shops selling everyday necessities, units of the basic service industry, cinemas, houses of culture, a panel-doctor service, local transport, and the road network. But basic service provision varies greatly between towns and villages according to population size, and while the above list of services applies to the towns, the provision in smaller settlements is more modest so as to ensure the efficiency of their operation.

As for higher-order service provision, this includes shops selling clothing and industrial articles, departmental stores, motorcar service stations, vocational schools, colleges, universities, out-patient clinics, hospitals, polyclinics, theatres, concert halls, museums and hotels. It is, of course, difficult to present a comprehensive picture of the qualitative level of national and regional service provision. The establishment of higher-order services, for example, depends on a number of specific circumstances, including the production structure and the educational, health and tourist functions of any given town. A further difficulty is presented by the fact that the need for services is a dynamic phenomenon, and for this reason only a few characteristic examples of regional differences in the provision of services is given in the following.

3.4.1 Service provision in towns

Towns need a wide range of infrastructural services, the specific provision depending on their size, the sectoral structure of their economic activities, the character of their central function and the extent of their hinterland as well as on the income and demand structure of their inhabitants.

Housing forms a basic issue in this context, and for many years now the provision of flats has been most satisfactory in the county towns and not in the capital. For instance, in 1981 8.2 dwelling per 1000 persons were built in the capital, compared with 8·9 per 1000 in first priority high-order centres, 9·5 per 1000 in second and third priority first-order centres, that is the county towns, and 8—10, 1000 in first and second priority medium centres and other towns, respectively.

The proportion of flats in the towns with pipe-water supply averaged 85 per cent in 1981, but is rising to around 97 per cent in Budapest and in the new socialist towns. The corresponding proportions for other settlement types were as follows: first priority high-order centres 92 per cent, and second and third priority high-order centres 76 and 67 per cent, respectively. But within these settlement types there are considerable differences between the towns of Transdanubia, the northern areas, and the plainlands of the country. For instance, in the medium-order centres of the Great Plain counties of Szolnok and Békés, the provision of pipe-water is less than half the national average. This is because pipe-water supply is closely related to population density within individual settlements and this is low in most market towns of the Great Plain because of the predominance of single storey family houses.

The basic problem with drainage provision is that it falls behind that of pipe-water supply in most of the towns. The proportion of flats with main drainage was 66 per cent in 1981, being 93 per cent in Budapest, 72 in the first priority high-order centres, 64 and 69 in second and third priority centres, respectively, and 40 and 46 in first and second priority medium centres, also respectively.

Average annual electricity consumption in private households per head of population was 556 kWh in the towns in 1981, with consumption in Budapest much higher at 789 kWh partly due to differential tariff rates, followed by the medium-order centres, the first priority high-order and then the record priority high-order centres, the last with a consumption of 375 kWh. Thus even within the town category differences of up to 210 per cent and in certain concrete cases as much as 250 to 350 per cent exist as a result of divergent structural characteristics, such as provision of household appliances and differential use of electricity for cooking, heating and warm-water supply.

The pipe- and bottled gas consumption were 140 m^3/per capita in towns in 1981. Higher than average consumption was recorded in second and third priority high-order centres, and about average in the capital and the first priority high-order centres. It was slightly below average, however, in the medium-order centres.

The average retail-trade turnover per head of population in the towns amounted to 45800 forints in 1981. (According to the 1981 exchange rate of the National Bank of Hungary, 100 forints are equal to 2·7 US dollars.) It was 49100 forints in Budapest, 45200 forints in second priority high-order centres, 49000 forints in third priority high-order centres and only 44500 forints in the first priority high- and medium-order centres. Basically, these settlement types may be regarded as the primary commercial centres of Hungary as the corresponding figures for second priority medium-order centres and other towns are much lower.

The spatial provision of kindergarten places was rather balanced throughout the country, places per 1000 population averaging 39 in the towns in 1981, that also being the figure for Budapest.

As regards the number of hospital beds per 10000 population, the urban average was 114 in 1981, breaking down into 109 for Budapest; 122 for first and second priority high-order centres which usually have clinics also 180 for third priority high-order centres due, primarily, to the county hospitals located there; 129 for first priority medium-order centres and only 43 for second priority medium-order centres. These settlement types may be regarded as the main centres of the public health service.

All these index numbers demonstrate the outstanding role played by the county towns in the development and public supply of the countryside.

3.4.2 Service provision in villages

The ensurance of basic service provision causes the greatest problems in the areas of small villages and tanya settlements. Part of the basic service provision, for instance housing, electricity, water supply and drainage in these areas is solved individually, although some progress has already been made towards including these settlement types within the integrated service systems. The main difficulties arise over the construction and efficient operation of the basic institutional network of education, commerce and health services, and for this reason their services are increasingly concentrated in low-order village centres, where the provision of higher-level functions can be justified on populations grounds. But this solution presupposes the existence of a good road network and adequate public transport or individual car ownership so that effective links can be forged between „peripheral villages" and low-order centres, which are normally located 5 to 8 kilometres apart. This is in fact, the solution adopted by several economically developed countries with large scattered populations. As for the very villages, depopulation is not envisaged, despite the apparent uneconomic nature of service provision. Indeed, within the limits of rationality, efforts continue to be made to meet elementary infrastructural needs locally, until more adequate supply can be ensured in the central villages [16].

The rate of rural housing development had been rather low until 1960, but has since speeded up with housing stock increased by 18 per cent between 1960 and 1980. The fastest increase of 22 per cent was recorded in the large, and was slowest in the very small villages where it barely reached 4 per cent. Housing conditions were improved by the modernization of old dwellings, a process helped by out-migration of population. One-fourth of all dwellings in the villages are already equipped with bathrooms or wash-basin facilities, while two-thirds of the settlements performing low-order central functions are supplied with pipe-water, although only 25 per cent of them have mains drainage. By contrast, only one-third of the 2000 villages have access to a public water supply and only 5 per cent have a sewage system.

The composition of the housing stock is the most favourable in regions where agricultural production is high, or where the majority of rural wage-earners are employed in industry. Electricity supply, however, owing to the high ratio of dispersed settlements, is still lacking in 5 per cent of rural dwellings. In the service provision of rural dwellings bottled gas plays a prominent role, and its use for cooking and hot-water supply has resulted in a certain modernization of rural living conditions.

60 per cent of settlements nationally have their own 8-grade general (primary) school offering basic education to children in their place of residence, but a substantial number of children living in small rural settlements have to complete the upper four grades in district general schools located in the larger villages only.

A general practitioner is to be found in all low-order centres and in 90 per cent of partial low-order centres, but is available in less than one quarter of the villages. The dwarf villages are, not unexpectedly, the least well off with only 3 per cent having a district medical service.

It is characteristic of the basic service provision of rural settlements that the whole structure of the institutions providing basic services is available in the larger villages, and adequate further development is ensured, whereas in the smaller villages only the modernization of dwellings and their supply with electricity, bottled gas and drinking water can be guaranteed. Provision in the latter is thus very deficient, its supply is uneconomic, and below a certain order of magnitude even impossible. The remedy would seem to lie in the modernization of the local road network, in connecting small villages with the nearest low-order centre and in developing their transportation facilities.

Bibliography for Chapter II

[1] Andorka, R. (1974): A községi népesség társadalmi jellemzői (The social characteristics of the rural population). *Társadalmi Szemle,* Nos 8–9, pp. 69–75.
[2] Andorka, R. and Harcsa, I. (1979): A községekben zajló társadalmi változások az elmúlt másfél évtizedben (Rural social change during the last one and a half decades). *Társadalmi Szemle.* No. 5, pp. 68–78.
[3] Antal, Z. and Nagy, K. (1976): Population and demographic policy in Hungary. *Annales Univ. Sci. Budapestiensis de R. Eötvös Nom., Sect. Geogr.,* Vol. 10, pp. 110–140.
[4] Beluszky, P. (1966): Az alföldi városias jellegű települések központi szerepköre (The central role of the town-like settlements of the Great Plain). *Földrajzi Értesítő,* No. 3, pp. 329–345.
[5] Beluszky, P. (1978): Changes in urban hierarchy with specific respect to urbanizing regions in Hungary. In: Enyedi, Gy. (ed.): *Urban development in the USA and Hungary.* Akadémiai Kiadó, Budapest, pp. 45–54 (Studies in geography in Hungary 14).
[6] Beluszky, P. (1980): Néhány gondolat az Országos Településhálózatfejlesztési Koncepció felülvizsgálatakor (Some thoughts on the revision of the Development Concept of the National Settlement Network). *Területi Kutatások,* No. 3, pp. 19–38.
[7] Bernát, T. (ed.) (1981): *Magyarország gazdaságföldrajza* (An economic geography of Hungary). Tankönyvkiadó, Budapest, 461 p.
[8] Bókor, P. and Botond, Zs. (1980): Néhány – a nagyobb vidéki városok népességnövekedését befolyásoló – tényező vizsgálata (An analysis of certain factors influencing population increase in the larger provincial towns). *Területi Statisztika,* No. 3, pp. 244–253.
[9] Bora, Gy. (1976): Regional industrial structure and the development of urban systems in Hungary. *Papers of the Regional Science Association,* Vol. 36, pp. 133–145.
[10] Compton, P. A. (1976): *Some aspects of the internal migration of population in Hungary since 1957.* Statisztikai Kiadó, Budapest, 197k, 293 p.
[11] Compton, P. A. and Pécsi, M. (eds) (1976): *Regional development and planning.* British and Hungarian Case Studies. Akadémiai Kiadó, Budapest, 234 p. (Studies in Geography in Hungary, Vol. 12.)
[12] *Demográfiai évkönyv* 1978 (Demographic Yearbook 1978). Központi Statisztikai Hivatal, Budapest, 1979, 417 p.
[13] Deskins, D. R. (ed.) (1978): *Impact of urbanization and industrialization on the landscape.* Proceedings of American–Hungarian Geography Seminar, Ann Arbor, Michigan, May 8, 1978. Department of Geography, University of Michigan, Ann Arbor, 428 p. (Michigan Geographical Publication, No. 25.)
[14] Dienes, L. (1973): Urban growth and spatial planning in Hungary. *Tijdschrift voor Economische an Sociale Geografie,* No. 1, pp. 24–38.
[15] Ehrlich, E. and Szilágyi, Gy. (1980): Infrastruktúránk nemzetközi összehasonlításban, 1960–1974 (An international comparison of infrastructure, 1960–1974). *Közgazdasági Szemle,* No. 2, pp. 187–207.
[16] Enyedi, Gy. (1977): A falusi életkörülmények területi típusai Magyarországon (Territorial types of rural living conditions in Hungary). *Földrajzi Értesítő,* No. 1, pp. 67–87.
[17] Enyedi, Gy. (1980): *Falvaink sorsa* (The prospect for our villages). Magvető, Budapest, 183 p.
[18] Enyedi, Gy. (ed.) (1976): *Rural Transformation in Hungary.* Akadémiai Kiadó, Budapest (Studies in Geography in Hungary, Vol. 13.), 116 p.
[19] Enyedi, Gy. (ed.) (1978): *Urban Development in the USA and Hungary.* Akadémiai Kiadó, Budapest, 116 p. (Studies in Geography in Hungary, Vol. 14.)
[20] Enyedi, Gy. and Mészáros, J. (eds) (1980): *Development of Settlements Systems.* Akadémiai Kiadó, Budapest, 265 p. (Studies in Geography in Hungary, Vol. 15.)
[21] Enyedi, Gy., Mrs (1978): Dinamikusan fejlődő agrártérségek Magyarországon (The dynamic agrarian regions of Hungary). *Közgazdasági Szemle,* No. 4, pp. 434–450.
[22] Erdei, F. (1961): Az alföldi mezővárosok városfejlesztési problémái (The urbanization problems of the market towns of the Great Plain). *Földrajzi Közlemények,* No. 3, pp. 201–216.
[23] Erdei, F. (ed.) (1968): *Information Hungary.* Budapest–Oxford, Akadémiai Kiadó–Pergamon Press, 1144 p.
[24] *Az 1980. évi népszámlálás* (The 1980 population census). Központi Statisztikai Hivatal, Budapest, 1980–1982.
[25] Halmai–Vissi, M. (1980): A központi szerepkörű települések funkcionálása a magyar településhálózatban (The functioning of higher-order centres in the Hungarian settlement system). *Területi Statisztika,* No. 3, pp. 214–227; No. 4, pp. 324–334.

[26] Hörcher, F., Mrs (1979): A magyar városok demográfiai viszonyainak értékelése, különös tekintettel a hazai urbanizálódási folyamatra, a népesség térbeli elhelyezkedésére (An evaluation of the demographic characteristics of the towns of Hungary with special regard to urbanization and the spatial distribution of population). *Területi Statisztika,* No. 3, pp. 272–281.
[27] Klinger, A. (1977): Magyarország népesedési helyzete 1971–1975 (Hungary's demographic situation, 1971–1975). *Statisztikai Szemle,* No. 1, pp. 5–24, No. 2, pp. 117–135.
[28] Klinger, A. (1980): A népességpolitikai határozat eredményei 1973–1979 (An assessment of population policy decisions, 1973–1979). *Statisztikai Szemle,* No. 5, pp. 453–469, No. 6, 565–574.
[29] Kórodi, J. and Kőszegfalvi, Gy. (1971): *Városfejlesztés Magyarországon* (Urban development in Hungary). Kossuth Kiadó, Budapest, 136 p.
[30] Kovács, T. (1980): Magyarország településhálózata és fejlődésének főbb tendenciái (The settlement network of Hungary and its main development trends). *Statisztikai Szemle,* No. 11, pp. 1061–1080.
[31] Kőszegfalvi, Gy. (1979): A magyarországi városhálózat helyzete, fejlődésének problémái, ellentmondásai, a fejlesztés feladatai (The urban network of Hungary: developmental problems, contradictions and the tasks for the future). *Területi Statisztika,* No. 4, pp. 121–130.
[32] Lackó, L. (1975): A kedvezőtlen feltételekkel rendelkező területek fontosabb jellemző vonásai (The main characteristics of disadvantaged areas). *Területi Statisztika,* No. 4, pp. 352–362.
[33] Lettrich, E. (1969): The Hungarian tanya system: history and present-day problems. In: Sárfalvi, B. (ed.): *Research Problems in Hungarian Applied Geography,* Akadémiai Kiadó, Budapest, pp. 151–168 (Studies in Geography in Hungary, Vol. 5.)
[34] Lettrich, E. (1976): Faluhálózatunk fő vonásai (The main features of the rural network). *Földrajzi Értesítő,* Nos 3–4, pp. 313–319.
[35] Lettrich, E. (1978): Die Probleme der Verstädterung in Ungarn. *Mitteilungen der Österreichischen Geographisches Gesellschaft,* Band 120, II, pp. 281–303.
[36] Lettrich, (1979): Die wichtigsen Merkmale des Entwicklungsprozesses der Urbanisierung in Ungarn. *Geografický Časopis,* No. 1, pp. 3–12.
[37] Matheika, M. (1974): A településhálózat társadalmi–gazdasági dimenziójáról (The socio-economic dimension of the settlement network). *Területi Statisztika,* No. 3, pp. 234–244.
[38] Matheika, M. (1975): A települések közötti és településeken belüli kapcsolatok jellegéről, különböző hálózati dimenziókban (The characteristics of inter- and intra-settlement relationships in different network dimensions). *Földrajzi Értesítő,* No. 3, pp. 417–421.
[39] Matheika, M. (1979): A települések valódi területi meghatározásának módszere Pécs és Miskolc példáján. In: Pálné Kovács, I.–Rechnitzer, J. (szerk.): Az agglomeráció-kutatás módszertani kérdései (A method to determine the hinterlands of settlements using Pécs and Miskolc as an example). In: Pál–Kovács, and Rechnitzer, J. (eds.): *Methodological questions concerning research into agglomerations,* MTA Dunántúli Tudományos Intézet Értekezései, Pécs, pp. 97–103.
[40] Matheika, M. (1981): Településagglomerációk és integráns városok Magyarországon. In: Rechnitzer, J. (szerk.): Vonzáskörzetek, agglomerációk (Settlement agglomerations and integrated towns in Hungary). In: Rechnitzer, J. (ed.): *Spheres of attraction and agglomerations.* MTA Dunántúli Tudományos Intézet Értekezései, Akadémiai Kiadó, Budapest.
[41] Mendöl, T. (1963): *Általános településföldrajz* (A general settlement geography). Akadémiai Kiadó, Budapest, 567 p.
[42] Perczel, K. and Gerle, Gy. (1966): *Regionális tervezés és a magyar településhálózat* (Regional planning and the Hungarian settlement network). Akadémiai Kiadó, Budapest, 445 p.
[43] Perényi, I. (1980): Verstädterung und Städtenbau in Ungarn. *Berichte zur Raumforschung und Raumplanung,* Nos 2–3, pp. 18–22.
[44] Romány, P. (1973): *A tanyarendszer ma* (The tanya system today). Kossuth Kiadó, Budapest, 124 p.
[45] Sárfalvi, B. (1979): Die Pendelwanderung in Ungarn. *Mitteilungen der Österreichischen Geographisches Gesellschaft,* Band 121, I, pp. 94–106.
[46] Schultz, J. (1978): *Les villes de Hongrie. Le rôle des villes dans la société socialiste.* Université Paul Valéry, Montpellier, p. 140.
[47] Szabady, E. (1978): A demográfiai és gazdasági–társadalmi változások kölcsönhatása Magyarországon (The interaction of demographic and socio-economic changes in Hungary). *Statisztikai Szemle,* No. 11, pp. 1102–1112.
[48] Szabó, K. (1980): Magyarország várható népessége, 1980–2021 (Hungary's population projections, 1980–2021). *Demográfia,* No. 1, pp. 11–41.

[49] Thomas, B. E. (1964): *Römische Villen in Pannonien.* Akadémiai Kiadó, Budapest, p. 418.
[50] Zala, Gy. and Fodor, L. Mrs. (1979): Városaink fejlődésének gazdasági hatótényezői (Economic factors behind urban development). *Területi Statisztika,* No. 4, pp. 391–398.
[51] Zoltán, Z. (1972): Városaink infrastrukturális ellátottsága (Urban infrastructural provision). *Városépítés,* No. 5, pp. 26–29.
[52] Zoltán, Z. (1976): Gondolatok az infrastruktúráról (Some thoughts on infrastructure). *Budapest,* No. 12, pp. 28–29.
[53] Zoltán, Z. (1979): *Az infrastruktúra térbeli rendszerei és területi hatásmechanizmusa* (Spatial infrastructural systems and their regional mechanism). Akadémiai Kiadó, Budapest, 189 p.

III The spatial location of economic sectors

1 Industry

Industrial production and the process of industrialization unfolded very slowly and rather late in Hungary as compared with most European countries. While the industrial revolution was making rapid progress and large-scale industry had already been established in several countries of Western Europe, Hungary was just witnessing the disintegration of the guild system and the emergence of capitalist handicraft-manufacture. The suppression of the bourgeois revolution of 1848 and the loss the War of Independence further retarded the evolution of industry [12].

Appreciable industrial development only began in the 1860s and even then, contrary to the general European development trend, not with the light but with the food industry. This benefitted the proprietors of the large estates, enabling them to place their products in a semi-processed state on the market and thereby to increase their profits. But it was also favourable to Austria, Hungary's partner in the dual monarchy, as it ensured her food supply and presented Hungarian competition with the already developed industry of Austria and Bohemia, primarily the textile industry. The industrial branches first established were the flour milling industry, distilleries and sugar refining, with the canned industry and food-processing soon to follow.

Heavy industry — mainly coal-mining and the manufacture of basic materials like metallurgy and the building-materials — began to develop only in the wake of large scale railway construction during the final quarter of the last century. It was around the turn of the century that machine-building, primarily the branches requiring the most up-to-date and most developed technology of the time, e.g. the production of rolling stock, milling machinery, shipbuilding and electrical engineering, took shape. In the period immediately preceding the First World War, heavy industry further expanded and the production of military equipment became significant. Notwithstanding these developments, Hungarian industry still remained rather underdeveloped relative to that of Austria and Bohemia within the Dual Monarchy.

After the collapse of the Monarchy, the newly independent Hungarian state used high customs tariffs to protect its industry against foreign competition, and to ensure further development. But customs tariffs alone could not produce the desired results as socio-economic conditions during the inter-war period, including the survival of feudal elements within agriculture, the low purchasing power of the population, the narrow domestic market, economic agreements injurious to Hungarian interests and the increasing role of foreign capital led to unbalanced industrial development.

Between the two worlds wars, light industry and food-processing changed places within the structure of industry, induced primarily by the particularly high profits to be gained owing to low Hungarian wage rates. Industrial development in the most important branches was characterized throughout by high capital concentration, as in coal mining, bauxite and aluminium industry, the chemical industry, engineering and the defence industry, and by the influence of foreign capital, which steadily gained ground.

Along with the manufacturing industry, small-scale industry as well as handicrafts also played a prominent role. Thus in 1938, while the manufacturing industry employed 400 000 persons, the number of workers engaged in small-scale industry and handicrafts was 323 000. The handicraft industry produced partly traditional consumer goods for the peasant population, and attempted, under difficult conditions, to survive in the face of competition from the large-scale industry. In other branches, however, e. g. furniture, footwear and clothing manufacture, it achieved noteworthy results.

The Second World War inflicted heavy losses on Hungarian industry. More than one-quarter of its fixed assets and productive capacity was destroyed. Liberation was followed by a short period of reconstruction and then by the wide-spread nationalization policy of the years 1947–1950. Since then Hungarian industry has developed within the structure of a planned economy, according to the basic principles of socialist industrialization.

1.1 A few basic problems

According to Hungarian planning and statistical definitions, industry includes mining, electricity generation, the production of basic materials (i.e. most branches of metallurgy, the building-materials industry, and the chemical industry), manufacturing industry (i.e. engineering, textile and clothing industry, handicraft industry, etc.), food processing and the provision of certain utilities and services (water works, most of the repair industries, etc.).

Industry occupies a leading position within the Hungarian economy, and serves the requirements of a modern economy, and also the socio-economic construction of socialism. In 1981, industry accounted for 55·1 per cent of the gross national product, and 47 per cent of national income. It ranks first in the employment of the active working population and is especially significant in foreign trade as it is the demands of industry that determine the pattern of imports, while industrial exports provide the greater part of foreign-exchange earnings *(Fig. 17)*.

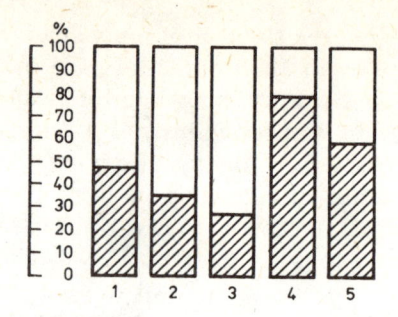

Fig. 17. The weight of industry in the national economy (1981)
1 — contribution to national income; 2 — proportion of employed population; 3 — proportion of total fixed assets; 4 — proportion of exports; 5 — proportion of total electricity consumption

In Hungary, as in the other socialist countries, industry is generally in socialist ownership, being owned either by the state or by co-operatives. Thus in 1981, for instance, 83·5 per cent of the 1 628 000 people engaged in industry were employed in state industry and 13·3 per cent in the co-operative sector. These two sectors are usually referred to as socialist industry. The remaining 3·2 per cent were employed in private small-scale industry. From the point of view of control and management, state industry is divided into two parts, the so-called *ministerial industry* (employing 93 per cent of total industrial manpower) under the supervision of various central government ministries, and *council* or *local industry* (with 7 per cent of manpower) under the direction of the county and urban councils. Part of the industrial enterprises owned by the state were formed by the nationalization or former large-scale industry, to which have been added various new enterprises established within the framework of industrial development policy. In a socialist economy, state industrial enterprises receive their capital from the state, partly in the form of investment, and partly as turnover capital. They have to give an account of their activities to the state, as their managements are appointed partly by elections and partly by state institutions.

Ministerial industry comprises, in general, large-scale industry, while council industry encompasses smaller plants together with their networks, which are designed to meet local demands and provide local services. Co-operative industry is organized into sectoral associations that perform supervisory functions. It is characteristic of the Hungarian economy that many large agricultural units, in the first place the farming co-operatives, also carry on industrial activities, for instance food-processing, the manufacture of components and industrial repair work, thereby complementing the industrial activities of the ministries and local councils. In this way, agricultural co-operatives are able not only increase their incomes but also to supplement the activity of industry proper.

The direction and control of socialist industry is implemented basically within the framework of a planned economy. The main directions of industrial development, the formulation of a long-term development strategy for the individual branches and the specification of the activities to be performed in the framework of CMEA co-operation are set out in national industrial plans. Within this basic framework of directives, individual industrial enterprises are granted a significant degree of independent decision-making. This applies to the determination of product mix, production co-operation, the use of development funds and the formulation of policies for further development and investments. Otherwise, the state performs its function of management by indirect methods using, for instance, economic regulators, incentives and preferences.

1.2 The dynamics of development and structural changes

During the three decades of socialist industrialization, Hungarian industry has undergone multifarious change and development. During the various individual periods, the crucial question has been the determination of the rate of industrial growth, and changes in its sectoral structure. Despite the results achieved, problems, errors and difficulties arose in both fields [13, 14, 15]. The period of socialist industrial development can be divided into the following main phases:

— The *first phase* was the period of dynamic development lasting from 1950 to 1960, which was characterized by a very high annual growth rate averaging 10 per cent, but surpassing 15 per cent in certain years, and by production targets of a predominantly quantitative nature. The most important source of growth was the massive absorption of new manpower, while technological development and economic efficiency were largely neglected. Industrialization was further characterized by an excessive sectoral concentration primarily on heavy industry.

— The *second phase* (1960–1968) was of a transient character. The growth rate was generally below 10 per cent, and although extensive development still continued, by the end of the period labour resources were already beginning to be depleted, the quantitative aspect of production had weakened, and the conditions and necessity for intensive development had become increasingly manifest. Within industrial policy the sectoral point of emphasis had begun to take shape; such were, for example, the so-called development programmes for diesel motors, buses and instruments *(Fig. 18)*.

— The *third phase* (1969–1973) marked the transition to intensive development. By that time labour resources had become exhausted, and as productivity and efficiency were below the international level, it was necessary to accelerate technical development, production organization and special capital inputs [91]. New industrial investment decreased, and a greater

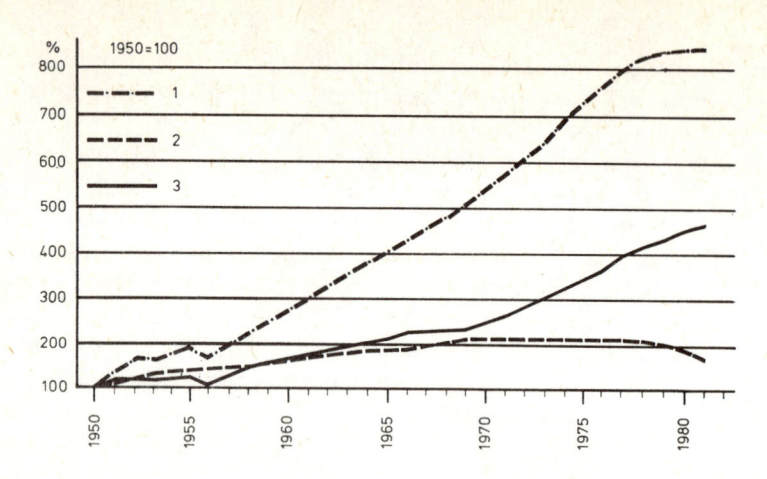

Fig. 18. Selected indicators of industrial development (1950–1980)
1 – output; 2 – number of employees; 3 – output per employee

proportion of the available funds was allocated very purposefully to the technical development of existing plants.

— During *the fourth phase* from 1974 to 1980 industrial output slowly increased at an annual rate of 4 to 5 per cent owing, among other things, to the new world economic situation. The number of persons employed in industry began to decline, primarily in Budapest, production growth came out of increased productivity, technical advance was speeded up and the objectives of production came nearer to the realistic requirements of the domestic and external markets.

The process and consequences of industrialization during the phase of extensive* development

Processes	Economic effects	Social effects	Other effects
Initially a very high, later a moderate growth rate with the absorption of new manpower. Quantitative production objectives and a mainly autarchic type of development.	Rapid change in economic structure. Forced investment policy, large number of new plants. Slowly improving productivity, inadequate economic efficiency.	Rapid changes in social and occupational structure favourable to industry.	Excessive migration from the less developed areas to the north of the country, the main scene of industrialization. Rapid urbanization in the above areas causing overcrowding in certain places, primarily in Budapest.

* The terms ‚extensive' and ‚intensive development' are used generally in socialist countries. The former means the high utilization of labour relative to capital and technology in economic growth. The latter is designed to achieve economic growth by a higher input of capital and technology relative to labour, and by a more efficient organization of production.

The process and consequences of industrialization during the transition phase from extensive to intensive production

Processes	Economic effects	Social effects	Other effects
Moderate growth rate; less new labour included in production; still surviving extensive growth in certain areas, import substitution, later to be replaced by export-oriented development.	Slow transformation of the economic structure; a decreasing number of new industrial investments; greater emphasis on the existing plants; increase in productivity although still slow, was faster than during the previous phase; improving economic efficiency.	Slowdown in social and occupational restrucuring, but still movement towards industry.	Decreasing migration; more balanced urbanization regionally, acceleration of the development of infrastructure.

The process and consequences of industrialization during the phases of intensive and selective development (fourth and fifth phases)

Processes	Economic effects	Social effects	Other effects
Low growth rate. Growth is covered by increased productivity. Fall in the number of industrial manpower. Sectoral development by selective methods, and more marked export-oriented industrial development.	New industrial investments minimized. Development is directed decisively towards changes in the product structure of existing plants. Growth in productivity is speeding up with improving efficiency.	Beginning of the transformation of the occupational structure, and consolidation of the tertiary sector.	Low migration rates; urban development separated from industrialization.

— During *the fifth phase* which the country is in at present, i. e. during the early 1980s, growth rate has dropped to 2 to 3 per cent per year and the number of persons employed in industry continues to decline not only in Budapest but also in the larger industrial centres of the countryside. Intensification has become more marked and the socio-political means have been accordingly adjusted. Development as regards sectors is now taking place in a very selective way by selective methods ensuring that manpower flows to the more efficient sectors. The basic criterion of development is economic efficiency, which has made imperative a switch-over to qualitative development and the technological changes underlying it as well as to a change in production structure [29, 50].

An important consequence of the industrialization process has been the change in the sectoral structure of the industry, mainly in favour of heavy industry. During the first stage, economic policy overestimated the role and significance of heavy industry, setting development targets at too high a level

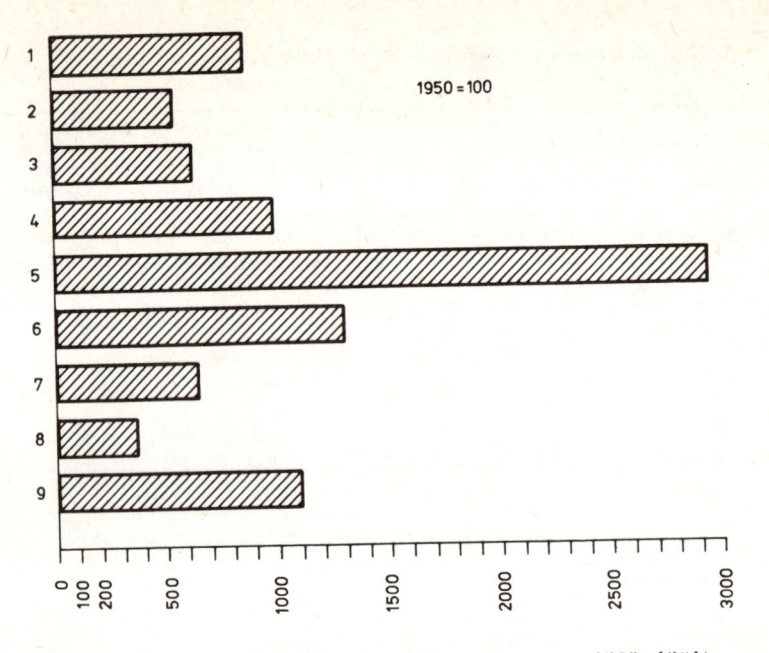

Fig. 19. The growth of output by selected industrial sectors (1950-1981)
Sector: 1 — socialist industry, total; 2 — food-processing industry; 3 — light industry; 4 — construction industry; 5 — chemical industry; 6 — engineering industry; 7 — metallurgy; 8 — mining; 9 — heavy industry

and disregarding the country's geological endowments and the capital cost of creating a heavy industrial base. As a result, disequilibria developed in the economy, and a satisfactory rise of living standards was not achieved. Since the 1960s, with the primacy of heavy industry being maintained, a more balanced structural transformation has taken place, and changes have been effected that fit in with the structural trends occurring in developed industrial countries *(Fig. 19)*.

In the present situation, structural transformation has slowed down, and the primary aim has been to bring about a structure more adjusted to real endowments and to market requirements. To attain this objective it is no longer so important further to change the so-called macro- (sectoral) structure, but rather increasingly to change the transformation of the micro- (product) structure. Instrumental in bringing this about is selective development, greater enterprise independence, giving higher play to market forces and to the ensurance of adequate economic policy measures, such as export development credits.

The relative shares of individual industrial sectors vary according to whether their importance is computed on the basis of the number of persons employed, the value of fixed assets, the performance capability of installed

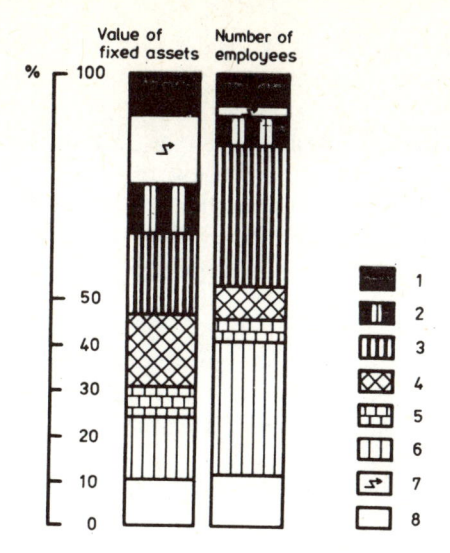

Fig. 20. The structure of socialist industry (1980)
1 — mining; 2 — metallurgy; 3 — engineering; 4 — chemicals; 5 — building-materials; 6 — light industry; 7 — electricity generation; 8 — food-processing

machinery or electrical power consumption *(Fig. 20)*. With respect to structural changes account must also be taken of the fact that there have taken place within the context of the divergent growth dynamics of the individual sectors (see *Fig. 19*).

Given these considerations, industrial development during the 1980s has to contend with the following.

— Given that the domestic energy and raw-material base can be expanded, relative to the demand, to only a limited extent, the development of industry can be realized only through an increasing volume of exports at pre-

The sectoral pattern of socialist industry, 1950–1981
(percentages of gross output)

Industries	1950	1960	1970	1981
Heavy industry	56.4	59.1	60.4	61.7
Mining	11.2	7.8	5.5	6.0
Metallurgy	13.5	13.6	10.7	9.5
Electricity generation	4.3	4.3	3.5	4.3
Machine-building industry	20.6	22.9	26.5	23.6
Chemical industry	3.5	6.8	10.9	19.1
Building-materials industry	3.3	3.7	3.3	3.2
Light industry	19.9	21.3	19.7	19.7
Food industry	23.7	19.6	19.9	18.6
Socialist industry, total	100.0	100.0	100.0	100.0

sumably high world-market prices. Thus development decisions have increasingly to take account of the special energy or import demands of sectors and their products.

— As a result of earlier demographic changes, the number of young people entering the working population will be low, while the flow of labour from agriculture to industry will not rise either. As a result, any increase in industrial output has to be achieved from a narrowing labour base and smaller industrial work force. Hence, growth can only come through increased productivity, which in turn can be ensured by improved technology and better organization of production.

— As a result of the fact set forth above, development decisions should give priority to those sectors and plants which are capable of producing products incorporating a multiple of the value of the materials used in the production process [79].

— The world market situation will give rise to new difficulties. Certain developing countries are already successfully exporting traditional products like cotton textiles, and mass electronic products, while marketing conditions in developed countries will further worsen. A requirement arising from this situation is the maintenance of the quality and technical standards of products at a constantly high level. This in turn makes it necessary to manufacture products more carefully, which is only possible if specific capital investments are increased. Since, however, resources in Hungary are limited, development must be restricted to those sectors which are able to meet in the best possible way the requirements of increasing efficiency, economical exports and modernity [26, 40].

— In taking development decisions, emphasis must be placed on the great potential that exists for further socialist economic integration. On the one hand, taking into account scale economies, the output of certain sectors and products can be increased, because of demand in socialist countries while, on the other hand, co-operation makes accessible at reasonable prices such products as have hitherto been produced at a low level of efficiency by Hungarian industry. The production of these commodities can be discontinued and imported more favourable from other socialist countries.

1.3 Spatial industrial structure and the dynamics of change

Socialist industrialization in Hungary, as in the other socialist countries, was paralleled by the transformation of the spatial structure of industry. Such a policy was necessitated by the distorted geographical division of labour in capitalist Hungary which manifested itself most conspicuously in considerable regional disparities. The reasons for this peculiar development were as follows:

— The development of both industry and of the capital, Budapest, took place at the same time historically and under identical conditions of relatively rapid expansion. Although it was an important historical achievement, the material resources of the time were insufficient to cover the substantial developments in other towns, which could have prevented the regional one-sidedness of industry. The favourable situation of Budapest was further enhanced by the excessively centralized railway network.

— Within the national boundaries of pre-First World War Hungary, industry was, on the one hand, centrally located in Budapest which grew into an oversized centre of manufacturing industry and, on the other, was of a peripheral character with the largely basic-materials industries of mining, metallurgy, and forestry located in the regions inhabited partly by the national minorities and also rich in raw materials and endowed with cheap labour. At that time the latter still partly offset the predominance of Budapest, but the intervening regions remained, in general, unindustrialized. Within the new state frontiers after the First World War, Budapest became the centre of a country with a considerably reduced area and population, in which the overcentralization of the capital therefore stood out even more strikingly. Between the two world wars, owing to the slow pace of economic growth, no equalization between regions with divergent industrial characteristics could be achieved.

— The concentration of industry in Budapest was promoted by taxation, favourable tariff rates and subsidies.

— Apart from a few branches, most industries based on Budapest developed a complex vertical structure, in which close enterprise co-operation made for more economical production.

— In the countryside, however, general underdevelopment, together with the lack of an industrial tradition, skilled manpower and innovative capability, slow capital formation, the backwardness of the settlements, and the inadequacy of urban infrastructure, were detrimental to industrialization. Although agriculture was capitalizing the low production level of the big estates and of the scattered peasant farms, the low demand of agriculture for industrial products, and thus the narrowness and slow expansion of the domestic market also hindered the industrialization of the countryside.

The geographical location of industry in the period before the Second World War can be characterized as follows: 54 per cent of the industrial labour force was employed in Budapest, while a significant belt of industrial agglomeration evolved around it. (According to the provisions of the 1949 public-administration reform, the greater part of this agglomeration was attached to Budapest.)

Apart from Budapest, appreciable industrialization only took place in areas relatively well-endowed with energy sources and mineral raw materials, for instance in Abaúj–Zemplén, Komárom, Fejér, Veszprém, Baranya, Nógrád and Borsod counties. Their industrialization was characterized by specialization and sectoral one-sidedness, because the dominance of mining and the heavy industries depressed the other branches. The only manufacturing of note outside Budapest evolved in the Little Plain.

The other regions of the country, including the Great Plain and most of Transdanubia, were industrially very backward (see *Table* on p. 114).

Since this state of affairs was in glaring contrast to the laws of socialist economy and society, the government decided that changes in the spatial structure of industry should be integrated into the activities of economic planning. This policy was based on the following fundamental principles:

— That the change in economic structure necessitated a change in spatial structure.

— In deciding the location of industry, account must be taken of geographical endowments such as natural resources, raw materials and accessibility to water.

— The formation of a rational spatial structure meant the elimination of regional disparities and a reduction in the weight of Budapest.

— In deciding the location of industry due attention had to be paid to the fact that industry is an effective and rapid means of developing economically background areas.

— Special care had to be taken to ensure that the manpower released from agriculture found employment in industry, while appropriate regional development policy measures had to be implemented to prevent the emergence of excessive migration.

— Since industrialization has a generative effect on urbanization, the urbanization of backward areas could be promoted by industrialization [32].

In transforming the spatial structure of industry, account had also to be taken of co-operation with other CMEA countries, for instance, the impact of transmission systems and specialized complexes.

The change in the spatial structure of industry by means of socialist economic planning took place according to viewpoints that complemented rather than contradicted one another and that were modified, when necessary, from time to time [8, 34].

— The change in the spatial decentralization of industry, including a decrease in the disproportionate weight of Budapest was throughout an overriding principle.

— Concentration processes were also frequent, primarily in connection with the location of large investment projects, in the framework of which large-capacity industrial complexes were established, often together with the building of new towns. These also had a significant effect on the local environments as with the mining of black-coal at Komló, the integrated iron and steel complex at Dunaújváros, the chemical complexes at Kazincbarcika and Leninváros, and the location of the aluminium industry at Ajka.

— The formation of spatial growth poles by means of industrialization first made itself felt in the 1960s, with the decision to develop the five large provincial centres of Miskolc, Debrecen, Szeged, Pécs and Győr as counterweights to Budapest. Within this concept an important role was assigned to the new plants to be located at each growth pole.

— A deconcentration process, meaning the spread of industry to underdeveloped regions and areas with surplus labour, also emerged.

— Equalizing goals to bridge, by means of industrialization, the wide income gap between individual regions, was a basic premise as well.

The process of changing the spatial structure of industry can also be divided into several phases, which only partially conform with the phases of industrialization already outlined *(Fig. 21)*.

During the first phase from 1950 to 1959, spatial transformation was also marked by extensive processes, when location decisions were exclusively taken at the highest level of economic management by the National Planning Office and the industrial ministries. The large number of new industrial plants created during this phase resulted in rapid changes in spatial structure. But, owing to the forced growth of heavy industry, the new plants were located predominantly in the already relatively developed regions with abundant energy sources and raw materials. On the other hand, the relative share of Budapest in industry fell rapidly, despite the rapid growth of industrial manpower.

The second phase lasting from 1960 to 1968 saw changes in the policy of industrial location. In 1959 the government issued a decree to industrialize former economically backward regions, notably the Great Plain, and to restrict the further expansion of industry in Budapest, and specified the smaller and technically deteriorating plants to be removed from the capital. During this period, the number of new industrial investments also began to decline, while the reconstruction of old plants was begun [60]. Moreover, owing to the restriction and also to an emerging labour shortage, enterprises sited in Budapest began to establish branchplant in the countryside. The industrialization of backward regions quickened, but since labour orientation came to the fore in decisions on industrial location, extensive development continued to prevail in the countryside. Nonetheless, regional proportions changed in favour of the Great Plain, the share of industry located in Budapest continued to decline and the decentralized character of industrial location became more pronounced [17, 63].

The third phase, from 1969 to 1975, was initiated by the change in the system of economic management which also brought about changes in investment and general decision making. The authority of the government and organs of central direction was restricted to large investments, and to those affecting the main direction of economic strategy. It was now only the locations of plants such as electric power stations, and chemical works that were determined by central decisions.

Although government subsidies, along with enterprise development funds financed some investments, there mostly comprised the reconstruction of existing plants and therefore did not involve decisions about new locations.

The greater proportion of investments was made under the authority of individual enterprises, using accumulated development funds and various bank credits. Whether an existing enterprise was to be further developed, or

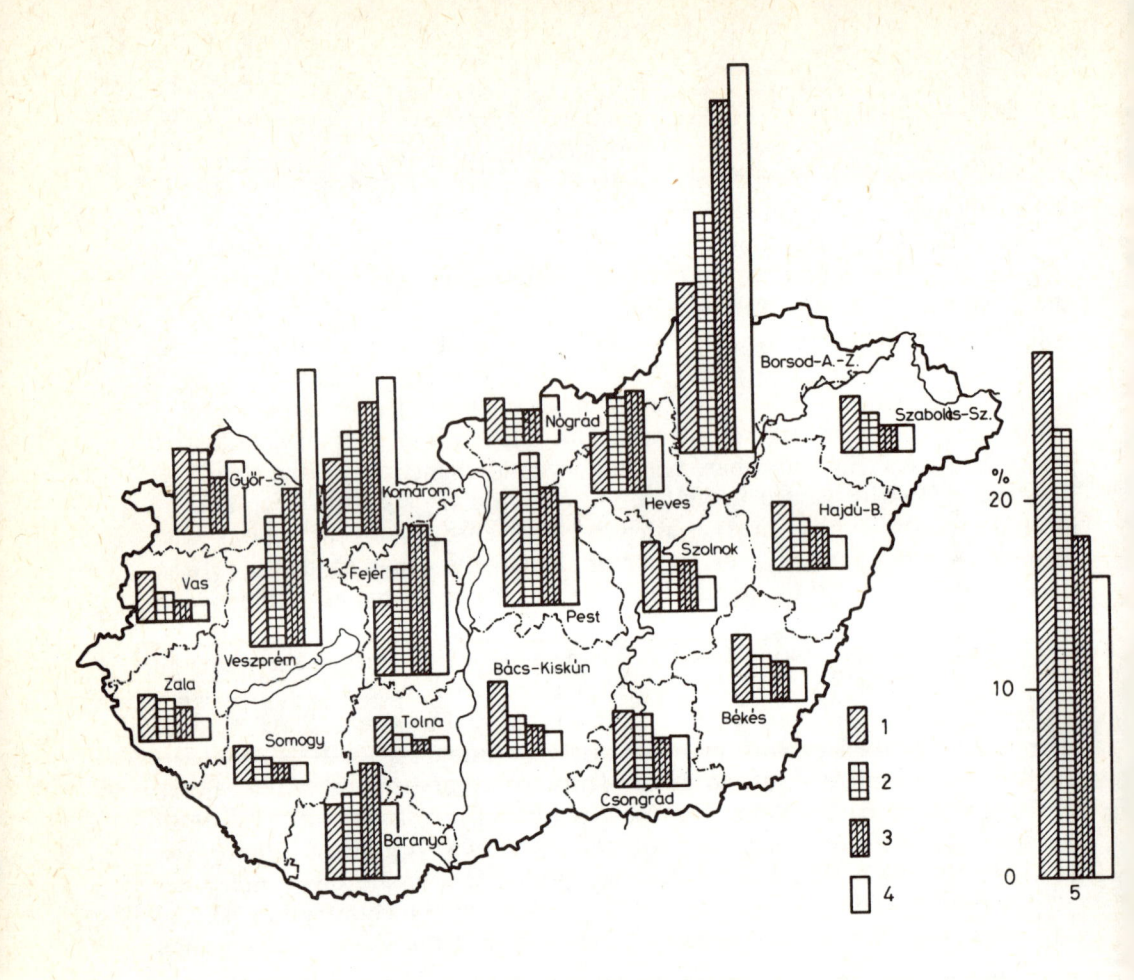

Fig. 21. The spatial distribution of industry by counties (1981)
1 — total employees; 2 — total fixed assets; 3 — driving power; 4 — electricity used by industry;
5 — value of Budapest

a new plant established, the siting decision rested with the enterprise. In order to satisfy the aims of regional policy, the government guaranteed various regional development funds and preferences [97]. But because the number of the preferential regions gradually fell to zero, the Central Office of the Regulated Market for Industrial Site Selection, operating at the individual enterprise level, was created. Its task is to gather from the various local organs the recommendations and information relating to industrial sites, collate enterprise preferences and take decisions, after due consideration, on site alternatives.

The characteristics of this stage of development were as follows.

— the number of new investments greatly increased, and development through the reconstruction of existing plants gained ground;

— the investment activity of enterprises also gathered pace.

Owing to the chronic labour shortage in the city, Budapest enterprises continued to found new plants *en masse* in the countryside where labour was still available, while even companies in the large provincial industrial centres began to set up factories in places where they hoped to acquire manpower. The enterprises made use of the various preferences, and the removal of plants from Budapest made progress. As a result of the above processes, the spatial structure of industry became more balanced, with former backward regions showing notable advances, while the share of industry in Budapest continued to decline, partly due to the labour shortage in the capital [33].

The industrialization of the countryside was also promoted by the rapid development of agriculture, as the quantity of industrial crops and animals increased in several areas, making possible the establishment of new slaughter-houses, meat-processing plants, cold-storage plants, vegetable-oil factories, complete maize-processing plants, breweries and sugar refineries.

CMEA co-operation also led to an increase in the productive capacity of several large factories. Moreover, such enterprises tended to set up within their own sphere of decision-making component-manufacturing plants, creating a new phenomenon in the industrialization of Hungary.

The establishment of provincial industrial plants by Budapest enterprises changed the direction of regional production linkages, and the earlier tight, almost closed, productive co-operation among Budapest enterprises developed horizontally to include plants in the countryside.

In 1976 the country reached its fourth stage, in which several economic problems have cropped up, bearing not only on industrial development, but also on industrial location. The changes taking place in world economy have exerted a negative effect on Hungary. Along with the deterioration of the terms of trade, other critical problems of the Hungarian industry have also emerged, namely technological underdevelopment and inadequate product quality. It has therefore become necessary, given these realities, to accelerate intensive development and to change over to the selective development policy mentioned above. A principal consequence of these policy measures is that a great proportion of future investments will, for a long time, be the reconstruction of selected sectors and plants. New investment will be reduced to a minimum [11].

The present phase can be characterized as follows:

— Changes in spatial structure are expected to be minimal, for example, the number of so-called government investments in the 6th five-year plan period from 1981 to 1985 will be confined to a few plants only. Greater efforts will be needed to improve the efficiency of industrial location, and it is this that will largely influence spatial structure [7].

— Owing to the increase in world energy prices, it will become necessary to exploit more intensively existing national resources, for instance the opening up of new brown-coal mines. This will call for extremely large investment

Changes in the spatial location of industry
(1949–1981)

Regions	The region's share			
	as percentage of population		as percentage of persons employed in industry	
	1949	1980	1949	1981
Budapest and Pest county				
Budapest	0·6	19·3	54·0	24·2
Pest county	6·9	9·2	1·7	6·0
Total:	7·5	28·5	55·7	30·2
Industrially developed counties				
Northern counties[1]	14·4	13·0	13·0	14·3
Middle Transdanubia[2]	12·7	10·6	10·2	12·4
Győr-Sopron county	4·3	4·0	5·3	4·5
Baranya county	4·8	4·0	4·3	3·9
Total:	36·2	31·6	32·8	35·1
Less developed regions				
Less developed counties in Transdanubia[3]	17·5	10·9	3·6	9·3
Great Plain counties[4]	38·8	28·4	7·9	22·6
Total:	56·3	39·9	11·5	34·7
Country's total:	100·0	100·0	100·0	100·0

[1] Borsod–Abaúj–Zemplén, Heves and Nógrád counties.
[2] Komárom, Fejér and Veszprém counties.
[3] Somogy, Tolna, Zala and Vas counties.
[4] Csongrád, Szabolcs–Szatmár, Bács–Kiskun, Békés, Hajdú–Bihar and Szolnok counties.

funds, and will, by and large, effect regions already well-endowed with energy sources and industry.

– Certain changes are likely to arise from an expected decrease in industrial manpower not only in Budapest but also in the large provincial industrial centres, which will effect regional proportion, as well.

– Those sectors producing component parts, accessories and offering certain industrial services will presumably be located in non-urban settlements with free labour resources, which will have the effect of diffusing industrial activities [6].

– The emergence and consolidation of various industrial co-operation schemes (e.g. convergent co-operation) are also likely developments.

In summary, as a result of three decades of development, not only have the most outstanding regional discrepancies of the earlier period been diminished, but a more rational spatial structure has also been established. (The changes in the spatial location of industry are presented in detail in the *Table* above.)

1.4 Energy

According to international trends, the energy consumption of a country doubles every 10 to 15 years. Despite the slowdown of Hungarian economic growth and the increase in energy demand, the long-term increase in energy consumption will be of such a scale that its ensurance will call for great economic efforts.

Energy today is one of the crucial factors in world economy. In addition, the Hungarian economy has to cope with several additional difficulties as the internal sources of energy are less unfavourable than in most CMEA countries and in several of the industrially developed countries of the West.

In Chapter 3.1 reference has already been made to the fact that most of the energy reserves in Hungary are in the form of brown coal and lignite, and only to a lesser proportion in black coal. Petroleum and natural gas reserves are not on a large enough scale to build a safe perspective upon them. Because long profiles of rivers suitable for power production are generally low and their water regimes tend to fluctuate between extreme values, their utilization for small- or medium-size power plants is possible only at the cost of very high investments.

The only available uranium deposit is not significant at the world scale, and the low level of extraction means that home processing beyond primary enrichment, i.e. removal of waste rock, is uneconomical.

The specific extraction costs of most energy sources are high by international standards, and the multiplier effects of the costs of production and transportation also raise the costs of allied products. The prices of imported energy sources are, owing to world price trends, high also, and the substitution of imports for the less economical Hungarian energy sources is, therefore, impossible. As a result, only the energy deficit can be made up from imported sources. Even so, the share of energy sources in total imports exceeds 10 per cent.

The energy sources of the country are comparatively restricted in location. The brown-coal and lignite deposits follow the range of the middle-high mountains, while black-coal and uranium ore are mined in the Mecsek Mountain. Formerly, the coal basins attracted fuel-intensive industries, and as a result the areas with power resources became the largest fuel consumers. The bulk of oil and natural gas deposits are to be found in the southern and northern parts of the Great Plain, in areas poor in other energy sources.

It was after the First World War that the various types of coal, as against other fuels like wood and agricultural waste, gained absolute predominance in the pattern of Hungarian energy consumption, with the ratio of oil and natural gas remaining low. Although the national economic plans foresaw a high growth rate in domestic power production during the 1950s, the change in energy structure was slow to take place and Hungary followed the international trend only belatedly. The cause of this was excessive reliance on do-

Proportional changes in energy sources[1]
1949 to 1981 (percentages)

Energy sources	1949	1960	1965	1970	1981
Coal in its many varieties	77·9	72·4	65·7	49·8	29·7
Petroleum and its products	8·8	18·6	22·0	29·4	35·7
Natural gas	3·8	2·6	6·3	13·6	26·2
Others[2]	9·5	6·4	6·0	7·2	8·4
Total	100·0	100·0	100·0	100·0	100·0

[1] Domestic output and imports computed in heating value.
[2] Imported electricity, timber and hydro-electric power.

mestic coal production during the 1950s and the constraints on Hungarian participation in the world economy. During the 1960s, the transformation of the power structure speeded up, a development which was promoted by the then cheap import of energy from the Soviet Union. At the same time the pattern of domestic energy sources also changed (see the table above and *Figure 22*) [73]. At present, the energy structure of the country is quite close to the world pattern. Prior to the rise in world prices, the concept whereby priority was given to imported energy sources, as against domestic production gained ground in the long-term energy plans of the country, but subsequent world market price rises have made it necessary to revise this earlier perspectives [81].

A realistic assessment of future energy trends must take the following basic factors into account.

(a) Owing to limited natural endowments, the creation of new capacity particularly in mining calls for large investment funds. Moreover, once in production, the costs of operation will also be high. Nonetheless, during the next two to three five-year plan periods, investment in power production will amount for a disproportionately high share, approximately 40 per cent, of all industrial investments.

(b) The steep rise in world energy prices made the extraction of certain domestic energy sources, primarily good-quality brown coal and lignite, favourable for open-cast mining. One may therefore expect renewed development of individual energy sources seemed earlier to be uneconomical [56].

(c) Despite the above facts, the country's energy resources will be able to satisfy only a part of future demand and the volume of imported energy is therefore expected also to rise. During the early 1980s, imported energy accounted for almost 50 per cent of consumption, and although this proportion will presumably rise, it will do so only at a slow rate. To this the following has to be added:

— Imported energy sources tend to be transported over considerable distances, from Western Siberia, the Volga—Ural region, which adds to the overall costs.

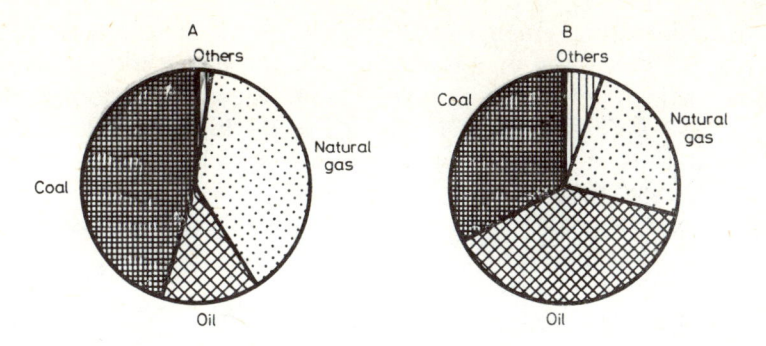

Fig. 22. The share of energy sources in the structure of energy (1981)
A — output of domestic energy sources; B — total available energy sources (ration of domestic output to imports).
Notes: „Others" in Fig. A includes timber and water. „Others" in Fig. B includes timber, water and imported electricity

— The raw-material-exporting countries of CMEA demand that their customer should also contribute to their capital investment in mining and related infrastructure and, what is more, often partly in convertible currency. Given their substitutability, a judgement has to be made as to whether the development of expensive domestic energy sources is preferable to the import of energy at high prices that bears considerable transportation costs and may also involve the investment abroad of capital assets.

— Increasing imports necessitate increasing exports of agricultural and/or industrial products. Thus, when taking energy policy decisions careful consideration must be given as to whether expensive domestic investment or imports with the above-mentioned financial implication is the more favourable alternative. Such decisions are greatly affected by trends in world prices.

(d) One factor in favour of the maintenance or even growth of imports, notwithstanding the great economic burdens involved, is the different uses of various energy sources, e.g. the greater part of oil products cannot be replaced by coal.

(e) Finally, account must also be taken of the fact that the increased exploitation of domestic energy sources may give rise to dangerous environmental side-effects, for instance, a fall in the water table in the new coal-mining areas planned for the karst mountains, and the danger of increased air pollution (e.g. acid rains) resulting from greater coal consumption.

(f) Given these problems it is not surprising that in Hungary energy consumption per head of population, which was 3,809 kg units of coal in 1981, is lower than in the other European countries belonging to CMEA and can be raised only to a limited extent.

(g) Economic growth and growth of national income may develop in the domestic and world economic interrelationship of the energy economy.

Thus a one percent increment in the national income of the country requires a 0·7 per cent increase in energy consumption, which may be regarded as a favourable ratio. Nonetheless, owing to the high proportion of imported energy, a rapid rate of economic growth could induce such rise in energy demand and thus increased energy imports as would jeopardize the equilibrium of the economy. Because of the country's comparatively unfavourable energy endowments, it is not economic to increase the share of those industrial sectors which have a high absolute or specific energy consumption within the national economy.

(h) As regards the energy balance, a relative decline in the rise of oil and natural gas is expected, owing to the enhanced use of coal. Moreover, from the early 1980s on, atomic energy will also have a role to play within the energy balance.

(i) In the interests of efficient utilization, care must be taken to ensure that individual energy sources be utilized in the best possible way, from a macro-economic point of view, e.g. it is no longer sensible to build new power plants fuelled by oil or natural-gas. The use of electric energy should be preferred to the use of oil wherever possible, e.g. railways should be electrified rather than dieselized, and trolley buses substituted for ordinary buses, because electric power can also by generated from domestic coal production.

(j) Energy conservation and rationalization policy measures should be implemented on a larger scale than before, if only because more specific energy consumption is needed for the production of one unit of national income than in the developed industrial countries.

In order to complement its scarce energy resources, Hungary is pursuing a broad policy of international co-operation with other socialist countries, the main forms of which are as follows:

— the import of energy sources within the framework of foreign-trade relations, i.e. black coal, bricketted brown coal, petroleum, oil products, and natural gas;

— participation in joint CMEA energy investment projects, e.g. the construction of the Alliance gas-pipeline from Orenburg to the western part of the Soviet Union and to several socialist countries, and the nuclear power plant at Hmelnitskiy in the Ukraine;

— bi- and multilateral CMEA co-operation in electricity generation;

— the establishment of mixed enterprises, such as **HALDEX**, a joint Hungarian—Polish project for the extraction of coal from slag-heaps in Silesia.

Although socialist co-operation is ensured by medium- and long-term agreements, it cannot meet the whole range of import demands. Thus during the second half of the 1970s oil was also imported from Arab countries, while enhanced co-operation over energy with certain western countries with Austria for instance, is also justified.

The increase in the extraction and utilization of oil and natural gas which, as we have already noted, is in part an adjustment to international trends, can be attributed to the following facts:

Firstly, the existence of economically viable domestic reserves has enabled some increase in production and consumption. Moreover, of the basic energy imports oil and natural gas can be used most economically and in the widest range and both can be transported by pipeline.

The mechanization of agriculture and rising car ownership have naturally had an impact on the consumption of oil products. Fuel oil and natural gas are also used more efficiently in several industries than either coal or coal gas. In the interests of lessening air pollution in densely populated industrial areas, in the large towns and Budapest in the first place, the spread of oil and gas heating has been promoted by government preferences. Household demand for gas has also expanded as a result of urbanization and the increased use of propane-butane gas. It may also be noted, that a modern chemical industry is a great consumer of oil and gas products and provides an important reason for raising their production and import.

Nevertheless, oil and natural gas have proved comparatively minor factors in industrial location in Hungary. This is not only because of their limited volume, but also because the domestic extraction from the Great Plan is easily piped to Budapest and the great industrial centres where it has replaced coal.

Significant and workable oil and natural gas deposits were first discovered, after long geological prospecting, in Pleistocene sediments immediately before the Second World War in the south-western part of Zala county at Lispe, Budafapuszta, Hahót, and Lovászi. In the early 1950s, further new oil fields were opened up in Zala County, near Nagylengyel, and then after the application of intensive geological and geophysical methods, additional oil and natural gas reserves were found in the Hortobágy, in the southern part of the Danube—Tisza Mid-region and in the South—Eastern Plain.

The increase in production was neither even nor free from problems. In the 1950s emphasis was placed on the extraction of the Zala oil fields, but a decrease in output with their gradual depletion was prevented by the discovery of the fields in the Great Plain. This process has also changed the geographical location of production. The oil and natural-gas reserves of the southern part of the Great Plain occupy a prominent position. A narrow strip extending in a north-south direction from Algyő to Szeged is the most productive field, accounting for 60 to 65 per cent of crude-oil output, and for 40 to 45 per cent of all natural-gas production. The oil and natural-gas fields near Üllés and Szank, accounting for one-tenth of overall natural-gas and oil production, also belong to the southern part of the Great Plain. In Békés county, in the eastern part of the Great Plain, the natural gas and oil fields of the Kardoskút — Pusztaföldvár — Orosháza area, and the natural-gas occurrences at Battonya, are significant. The fields in Békés county

Changes in petroleum and natural gas production and imports

	1938	1949	1960	1981
Petroleum production (1000 tons)	43	506	1217	2024
Natural gas production (million m^3)	8	372	342	6011
Petroleum imports (1000 tons)	174	–	1456	7754
Natural gas imports (million m^3)	–	–	200	4002

account for approximately 13 per cent of the country's natural-gas production.

The occurrences in the southern Plain are at substantial depths; for instance, in the Szeged–Algyő area gas and oil can be found in upper and lower Pannonian sandstones at a depth of 1750 to 2200 metres, and natural gas in lower Pannonian sandstones at a depth of 2350 to 2650 metres. Characteristically, the oils extracted in the southern part of the Great Plain are mostly poor in sulphur, have a paraffine base, while their output of higher fractionates, i.e. petrol, is good. Production is gradually shifting to the recently opened fields around Kiskunhalas.

The gas produced south of Debrecen at Hajdúszoboszló and Nagyhegyes in the Hortobágy accounts for one-fifth of the country's output. Its quality is good and it is suitable for both heating and the chemical industry.

In the traditional area of production in Zala county the bulk of the southern fields has been depleted owing, primarily, to ruthless exploitation during the Second World War. Only a small-scale natural-gas production of oil and natural-gas is still maintained. However, exploration is going on at depths below the ‚worked-out' fields (below 4000 metres) in the expectation of discovering additional reserves.

Of confirming significance is the highly bituminous and very viscous oil, suitable mainly for the manufacture of asphalt, of the southern Zala region near Nagylengyel and Gellénháza, which still provides about 10 per cent of the country's oil production. The oil extracted near Nagylengyel is not accompanied by natural gas.

Along with domestic output, imported crude oil and refined oil products and natural gas ensure a leading position for petroleum in the energy economy of the country. As a result of energy saving policy between 1978–82 the oil import could be reduced by 2 million tons.

The main consumers, of mazout, a residual substance of oil refinery, are the thermal power station at Százhalombatta, individual heat-intensive sector, like cement, steel, and alumina plants and the district heating plants of housing estates.

The largest consumer of natural gas is industry, particularly the steel and glass industries. Moreover, the discovery of domestic natural-gas fields has

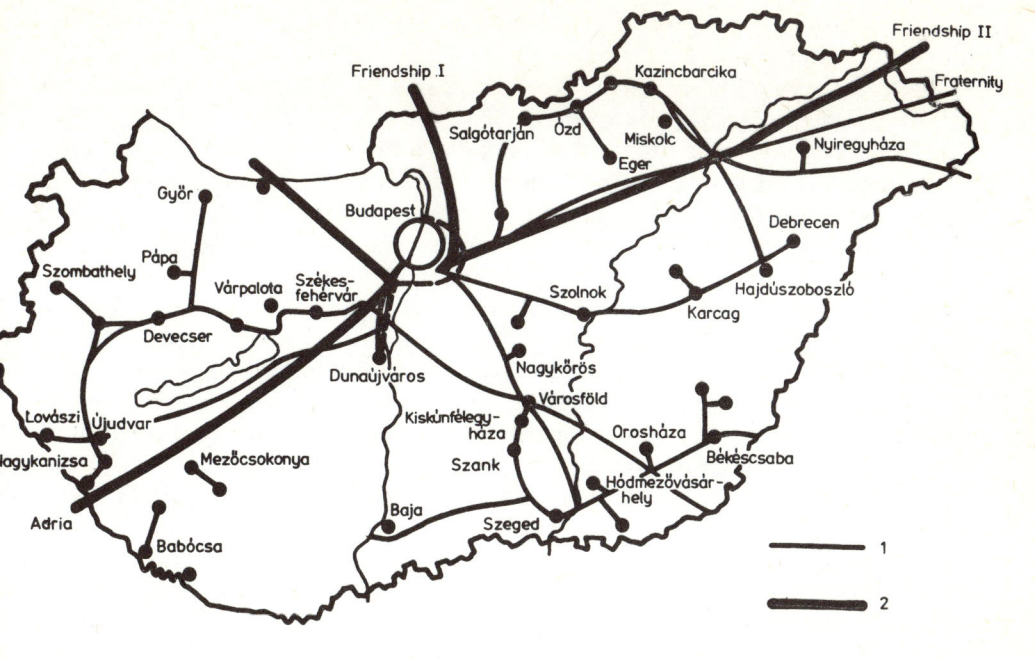

Fig. 23. Major oil and natural-gas pipelines (1980)
1 — natural-gas pipeline; 2 — oil pipeline

made it possible to switch nitrogenous fertilizer production from one based on lignite or expensive imported coke to one based on natural-gas, while air pollution in Budapest has been diminished by converting the heating systems of residential buildings in the inner districts from coal to natural gas. The expansion of the gas supply to households is in the interest of the energy economy, but in the countryside, apart from the large towns, the spread of bottled propane-butane gas consumption rather than expensive inter-urban or local piped-gas has been the favoured solution. By the early 1980s more than 60 per cent of all households had been provided with one or other type of supply.

Oil and natural-gas production and imports have made necessary the construction of a pipeline network, which is more economical than other forms of transport. By 1981 the total length of the pipeline network had reached 5629 kilometres, more than half the length of the railway system. Three types of pipeline may be distinguished according to function (see also *Fig. 23*).

a) *International oil pipelines*

The ,,Friendship" pipeline whose Hungarian section, as part of the network supplying CMEA countries, enters the country from the Carpathian Ukraine passes through Leninváros and joins the national network at Százhalombatta from which oil is transported to the refineries at Almásfüzitő.

The Orenburg pipeline supplies natural gas to the Hungarian network from the Soviet Union.

A separate pipeline from the Kissármás area of Romania supplies natural gas to Kazincbarcika via Leninváros.

The „Adria" international oil pipeline was built as a joint Yugoslav, Hungarian and Czechoslovak venture, and supplies oil to these countries from the Yugoslav seaport of Bakar. The pipeline will be significant in perspective from the point of view of Arab oil imports which it transfers directly from tankers to Hungarian refineries at a low transportation cost.

b) *The national pipeline network* connects the Transdanubian and Great Plain oil and natural-gas fields with the various refineries, and distributes the product to the capital and the other large towns and industrial centres.

c) *Local pipelines* connect a given gas field to the larger consumers in the vicinity, for instance, Hajdúszoboszló to Debrecen, and Kardoskút to Hódmezővásárhely and Orosháza.

Although not a source of energy, the occurrence of carbon dioxide gas is worth noting, since it is significant from a world economic point of view. Co_2 occurrences are rare on the Earth, and as most of them are of an insignificant volume, their industrial application is uneconomical. Based on the relatively large reserves in the Mihály—Répcelak area of the Little Plain, a processing plant has been set up at Répcelak which exports the gas in bottled or dry-ice form for cooling purposes.

Coal mining

In Hungary, coal played a dominant role for almost a century and the coal basins were for long the determining factor in the location of heavy industry and those branches with a sizeable fuel demand. The coal basins and coal varieties of the country may be characterized as follows.

a) Most coal basins are of a limited size, the number of workable seams is generally small, and average thicknesses are usually below those found in more favoured areas abroad. Reserves are also relatively insignificant. The opening up of large-capacity mines is limited, and although extraction is concentrated, operations are comparatively small, apart from open-cast lignite mining.

b) In most coal mines, seams are not only affected by faulting, but their low thickness causes difficulties in extraction. In places, the thickness of economically exploitable seams hardly reaches one metre, although at the best occurrences seams achieve thicknesses of 3 to 5 metres. The overburden usually consists of loose, sedimentary deposits, and extraction can therefore only proceed without extensive timbering. Because of such geological difficulties, the mechanization of extraction is difficult and costs are high.

Most coal basins, especially the brown-coal fields, developed in the limestone mountains of Triassic age and karst water can generally be found at the mining level. Continuous pumping is therefore necessary and very often karst water inundates the pits and paralyzes production for months.

c) The coal — so expensively extracted, owing to the above difficulties and large investments necessary — is mostly of medium quality, with a low calorific value, high ash and moisture content, and poor burning characteristics. Moreover, much of it can only be used for specific purposes. Internationally, the coal fields of Hungary rank generally rather low, and this also applies to the prime costs of production, to productivity, and to the specific cost per calorific unit of output. Decisions on the development of coal mining can only be taken selectively, treating each individual basin separately, and taking account of the demands and conditions of the given stage of economic development.

d) Certain coal varieties involve high environmental hazards. Brown coal has a high sulphur content and generates air-polluting sulphur dioxide. Other types, especially when burned in poorly operating furnaces and heating systems, spew masses of ash and soot into the air. In industrial centres and towns where coal heating is territorially concentrated, serious environmental damage is caused by the burning of poor-quality coal.

The development of Hungarian coal mining over the last three decades can be divided into three stages. During *the first stage*, from 1950 to 1965, the aim was to maximize coal output by extensive methods, mainly by employing many new miners. New pits were sunk in all fields, particularly in the Nógrád and Borsod basins, and coal mining expanded geographically. New housing estates were built around the mines and two new socialist mining towns, Komló and Oroszlány, were also founded. A negative consequence of this stage was that a non-selective development policy meant that mines which were hard to exploit and produced low-quality coal with a high production cost were also established.

The second stage lasted from about 1965 to the first energy crisis of 1973. The energy structure of the country was rapidly transformed with oil and natural gas coming to the fore. Economic policy was aimed at bringing about more economic and efficient production, a policy which seriously affected coal mining. Less, but higher-quality and cheaper coal, was needed, and this led to the rationalization of the industry, with the closure of 80 uneconomic pits producing low-grade coal, and with the concentration of investment on financially viable pits. Rationalization affected virtually all the coal basins. At the same time, the first steps were taken to exploit the large lignite reserves if Visonta suitable for open-pit mining. To avoid depression and unemployment, the government set up a development fund to encourage new industries to come to mining districts.

The third stage began around the second half of the 1970s, and coincided with the international energy crisis and unprecedented rise in world-energy prices, initiating changes in the whole world economy. Increased prices, including those for coal, created a relatively advantageous situation for a part of domestic production, and led to the development of a perspective policy for coal mining which, however, was more differentiated than before. The

Changes in the qualitative distribution of coal output
(in per cent)

Type of coal	1938	1949	1965	1981
Black coal	10·7	12·4	13·7	11·9
Brown coal	83·9	81·3	70·7	55·7
Lignite	5·4	6·3	15·6	32·4
Total	100·0	100·0	100·0	100·0
Average calorific value of extracted coal in kilojoule	17158	16523	13292	11196

main reason for mining coal is to diminish the pressure for increased energy imports on the national economy.

The prospects for black-coal mining depend on price and the prospects for coke and coking coal. In a few currently working brown-coal basins the reserves of several pits are likely soon to be depleted. New pits will therefore have to be opened, but only where large and economically workable reserves are available. It is to attain this aim that the government has launched the so-called Eocene Programme, under which the new mine at Márkushegy, south-west of Tatabánya, is already operating, while other mines will be opened in the Dorog basin, at Lencsehely as well as at the easily accessible new brown-coal sites at Nagyegyháza and Mány, south-west and east of Tatabánya, even though the coal is only of medium quality there. The last mentioned area has the additional advantage that bauxite seams occur below the coal, and the sinking of coal mines can therefore be coupled with an expansion of bauxite mining. The modern mechanized mines to be opened under the Eocene Programme will be highly productive and will presumably display favourable economic indicators.

In the structure of coal output the shares of brown and black coal are declining in the country's total production, and that of lignite is increasing, though the calorific value of the latter is low. As a consequence, the shares of the various coal types in the total calorific value of output differ from the weight ratios *(Fig. 24)*.

The rationalization and technical development of coal mining has registered several results. The concentration of production has grown, while manpower is currently 70 per cent of the 1965 maximum, although total output is a little down.

The 1960 average output of 1600 tons per underground shift had risen to 2441 tons by 1979 and 93 per cent of all underground transport is mechanized now. The ratio of open-cast coal has also grown. The most serious problem is the gradual deterioration of the average calorific value of the coal extracted, as a result of which coal mining as a whole now produces albeit temporarily, until the opening of new mines, less energy equivalent than before *(Fig. 25)*.

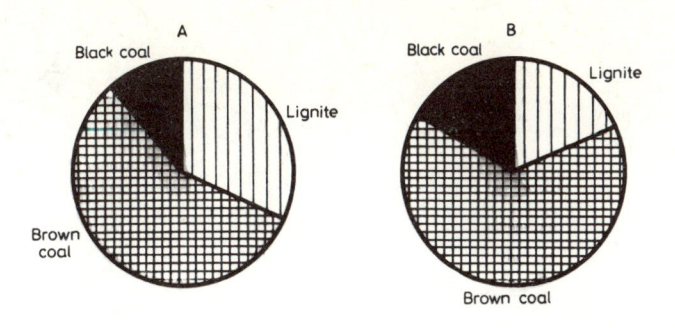

Fig. 24. The distribution of coal output by coal type, 1981
A – according to weight; B – according to calorific value

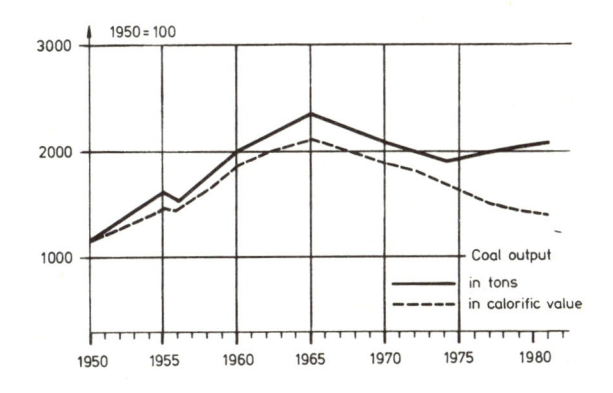

Fig. 25. Changes in coal output (1950–1981)

Coal fields that are in operation are comprised of the following (Fig. 26):

a) The Mecsek coal basin, of Jurassic age, is the country's only black-coal field, and mining is concentrated in the vicinity of Pécs and Komló. The calorific value of coal mined there is around 19000 kilojoules with the mine near Pécs producing coal of a higher calorific value, although under rather less favourable conditions. The coal has good burning properties and is used as a high-quality furnace coal. (Earlier, the basin was the main coal supplier for Danube shipping.) With its shafts of 500 to 600 metre depth, coal production near Komló represents the most concentrated mining activity in the country, the only one whose daily capacity and technical equipment reach

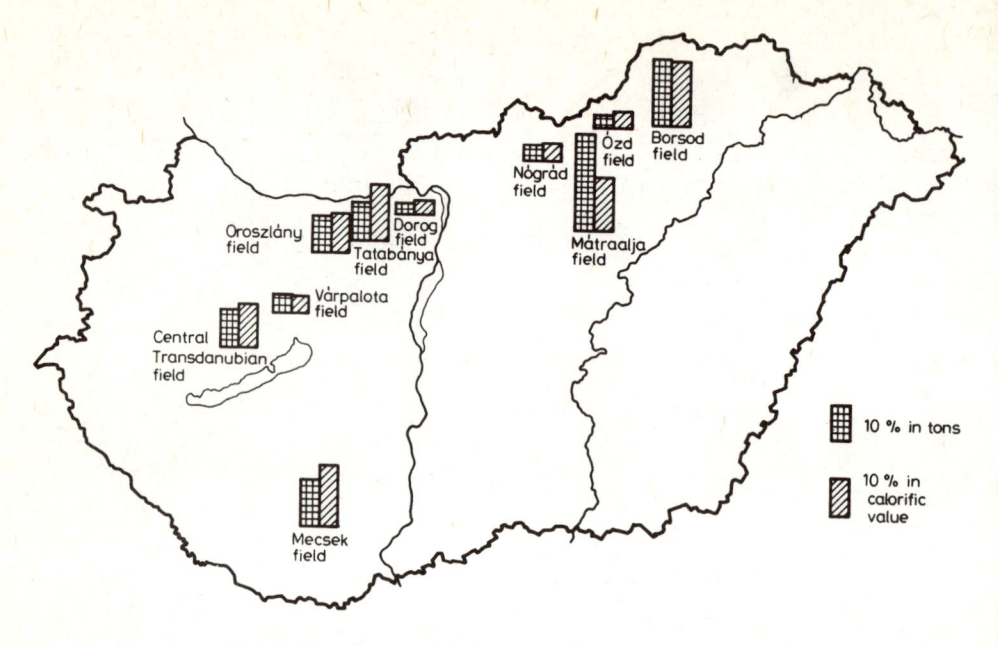

Fig. 26. The distribution of coal output by coal field (1981)

the levels of traditional coal-mining countries. The seams are thicker than elsewhere and the extraction process is better mechanized. Although of lower calorific value than Pécs coal, it is suitable for coking, and is the main supplier of the iron and steel works at Dunaújváros. New pits are to be sunk in the northern parts of the basin under the so-called Lias Programme.

b) The coal deposits of the Bakony Mountains are referred to as the Central Danubian Coal Basin. The largest is the Ajka field, which is heavily inundated with karst water. It is of Cretaceous origin, but as the conditions for coal formation were unfavourable, it only produces medium-quality brown coal.

c) The youngest of the large brown-coal basins in Transdanubia is the Oroszlány field where, in addition to the pits opened in the 1950s, the modern mine at Márkushegy is now operating. The calorific value of its coal exceeds 13 000 kilojoule, but the coal itself is shaly and is used in powdered form primarily as a fuel for thermal power plants.

d) Brown-coal mines with long historical antecedents can be found in the Tatabánya basin, which played a very important role in the industrialization of that area and in the supply of Budapest. The calorific value of the coal mined there averages around 17 000 kilojoules, burns well, and was an important supplier of the railway network. Currently, its coal is mainly used locally in plants depending on considerable heat such as cement works and thermal power stations.

The distribution of productive coal fields
(million tons)

Fields	1938 Output	%	1949 Output	%	1960 Output	%	1981 Output	%
Mecsek	1·0	11·1	1·5	12·5	2·8	10·1	3·1	12·0
Dorog	1·7	17·8	1·7	14·1	2·0	7·7	0·6	2·3
Tatabánya	1·9	21·2	2·7	22·9	3·0	10·3	2·4	9·2
Oroszlány	–	–	–	–	3·9	10·2	2·8	10·8
Middle Transdanubia	0·7	8·4	0·8	7·3	2·7	10·1	2·4	9·3
Nógrád	1·4	14·7	1·7	14·0	3·4	14·7	0·9	3·5
Borsod	1·3	13·5	1·9	16·5	4·3	16·9	4·6	17·8
Ózd	0·6	7·1	0·8	6·5	1·1	4·2	0·7	2·7
Mátra region*	0·2	4·3	0·1	5·0	2·0	7·8	7·1	27·5
Várpalota	0·4	1·9	0·6	1·2	2·3	8·0	1·3	4·9
Total	9·3	100·0	11·8	100·0	26·5	100·0	25·9	100·0

* In 1981 only Visonta.

e) The coals of the Nógrád field in the Northern Middle Mountains generally have a high ash content and are of poor burning quality, with a calorific value below 13 000 kilojoule. The field is of a limited extent, it is difficult to sink productive mines; production costs are very high and the policy of closing marginal mines affected this field most of all. The mines still working are located in the Kisterenye, Mátranovák and Nagybátony areas. The basin mainly supplies the local industries of the Zagyva valley.

f) The Ózd field produces relatively good-quality brown coal with an average calorific value of 14 000 kilojoules. The coal mined near Egercsehi and Ózd is of higher quality than in the rest of the basin.

g) The Borsod field is located in the middle of the Sajó valley, mainly to the east of Kazincbarcika. Reserves are of different quality and are rather scattered in location. Some coals are of a medium calorific value and good burning characteristics, but most are low-quality brown coals with a calorific value of around 12 000 kilojoules. The main consumers are the heavy industry of Borsod county and local households.

h) Lignite deposits which are currently worked are concentrated in two basins. At Várpalota, where both underground and open-cast mining is performed, the lignite is of high water content, of about 8000 kilojoules calorific value, and is used to fuel local thermal power stations.

The county's largest lignite mine is at Visonta, in Mátraalja. Although this lignite is of low calorific value, about 7500 kilojoules, it can be used economically in the local thermal power stations. Indeed, since mining is by the strip mining method, production costs relative to calorific value are the lowest in the country.

There are two other extensive lignite fields in the country — estimated at several thousand million tons each — located in the vicinity of Bükkbárány, at the south-eastern foot of the Bükk Mountain, and at Torony in Vas county, respectively. Mining may soon begin in co-operation with Austria, although this will depend on future world energy prices [86].

Besides domestic production, imported coal is also an important source of supply. Black coal is imported from the Soviet Union, Czechoslovakia and Poland, while bricketed brown coal is supplied by the GDR.

About 80 per cent of the coal is used by industry, the largest proportion of which is used to fuel thermal power stations. Private consumption, about 12 per cent of the total, ranks second. From the 1950s on, private consumption has increased rapidly for a time, but as fuel oil gained ground in household consumption, the use of coal declined. Coal consumption by the railways has also fallen, owing to the change-over from steam to electric and diesel-electric traction.

Electricity generation

Electricity generation as a secondary energy source is equally important for developing the various sectors of the economy and for improving the living conditions of the population. The main problems surrounding its domestic development arise from the following factors.

a) The needs of the economy and society require that sufficient electrical energy should be available to meet the demands in all parts of the country at all times of the year. To fulfil this requirement, the country should be supplied from an electricity grid, and capacity should be planned in such a way that peak-period consumption might be met and, further, that the system should have adequate reserves to lessen the hazards of breakdowns. The generating system in Hungary can meet these requirements only in cooperation with other socialist countries.

b) In planning electricity generation, account must be taken of the expected growth of both production and private consumption. The increase in demand for electricity is closely connected with the general growth rate of the economy and with that of industry in particular. It follows from the country's general energy position that the growth of industrial output should be accompanied by a relatively moderate increase in electricity generation, the fulfilment of which calls for the modernization of consumption system and for a careful selection of sectors to be developed, priority being given to those with low specific electricity demands. By the close of the 1970s considerable progress had been made and a one per cent increment in industrial output could be accomplished with a 0·6 to 0·7 per cent increase in electricity consumption.

c) International experience shows that technical development and more efficient energy consumption require the conversion of an increasing proportion of basic energy sources into electricity. In the late 1970s, approximately one-third of the overall energy consumed was in the form of electricity.

There remains the crucial question, however, as to which fuels should be used in thermal power stations. Clearly, any decision must be closely related to the country's energy endowments, to the possibilities of international co-operation, costs of basic energy sources as well as to changes in world prices. Owing to the variability of the above factors, Hungarian energy policy has changed several times since planned economy was introduced [91].

In accordance with the country's fuel situation and with its coal reserves, thermal power stations use poor-quality brown coal mined at Oroszlány, Ajka and Borsod, so-called „small coals" unsuitable for other industrial uses, and lignite of low calorific value which is uneconomic to transport over long distances and which is mined at Várpalota and in the Mátra. Electricity generation is the country's largest coal-consuming sector.

Natural gas and fuel oil also have an important role to play. The economic efficiency of gas and oil, as compared with coal, manifests itself in a higher calorific value, simpler and cheaper transportation, less air pollution and simpler generating equipment. There is, for example, no need for mills to pulverize coal, which in turn requires the consumption or energy. (The generating station at Tiszapalkonya is fuelled by coal and natural gas, the one at Százhalombatta by mazout and natural gas, that at Leninváros by mazout.) Owing to the high price of imported petroleum, however, no further oil-fuelled stations will be built in the future, despite their above advantages. At the same time, since coal output, too has its limits, the use of nuclear energy is an increasingly likely development.

d) During the past few decades, technical advance in thermal power-plant equipment has made rapid progress throughout the world. Following this international trend, Hungary has also improved its generating equipment made possible by this domestic manufacture of turbines and generators. Further increase in the size of installations is, however, unlikely. Although turbines of 1000 MW capacity are in use in many developed countries, such turbines are at present unsuitable for Hungary, given the limited scale of its electricity network, and their use is a matter for the longterm future.

The primary consideration in the siting of power stations is that of fuels, and half the country's capacity is located in coal minery areas at the fort of the middle mountains and in the Mecsek district. Most generating stations, owing to their large demand of fuel consumption, are based not on individual pits, but rather on coal fields, where coal classification facilities, as at Ajka, Oroszlány, Tatabánya, Kazincbarcika and Pécs, ensure uniform quality. Mazout-fuelled power plants are more appropriately located in the vicinity of oil refineries.

Thermal power stations require enormous quantities of water for the production of steam and for the cooling plants condenser system — and water is therefore an important locational factor comparable to fuel supply. If the demand for water is to be met entirely from a natural water source,

Changes in generating capacity and electricity output

	1938	1949	1960	1981
Installed capacity in MW	493	559	1479	5344
Output in billion kWh	1·3	2·4	7·6	24·3
Import needs in kWh	–	–	0·5	7·9
Specific coal consumption in joule	–	21075	17196	11553
Electricity consumption per head of population, in kWh	150	271	760	2556

for instance a river, then the daily requirement may be of the order of several hundred thousand or even a million cubic metres. When there was no possibility of obtaining water at or near the coal field, the earlier practice was to site the station at the nearest river with a large enough water budget as for example in the case of Tiszapalkonya. The more expensive solution of transporting water from a distance was only resorted to when there were also other large water consumeres within the vicinity, as was the case with the water-main built between Mohács and Pécs, supplying Danube water not only to the thermal power station near Pécs, but also the town itself. More recently, however, the installation of the water-efficient Heller–Forgó air-condenser has made the location of power stations possible in water-deficient areas as, for example, near Visonta.

The increasing size of power plants together with their equipment enhances siting difficulties. In the case of coal fuelling, the volume of coal to be transported amounts to many millions of tons, but oil fuelling also requires the transportation of several hundred-thousand tons of oil, while adequate water supply also encounters steadily increasing difficulties. In the future, only large-capacity power stations are likely to be constructed and, except for the new nuclear power plants to be built, will be located on the brown coal and lignite fields.

The large generating stations of the country have been integrated into a uniform grid system of 110 kW and 220 kW capacity, which confers several advantages: the generation and consumption of electricity is co-ordinated and the so-called load-distribution centre which monitors and manages the supply is located in Budapest; in the case of breakdowns, current can be channelled to the effected areas, while the system is linked in with the international network.

Given the country's energy problems, imported electricity plays an important role in meeting electricity demand, along with increased domestic production. Co-operation with the socialist countries takes on various forms. The Hungarian grid system is part of the United Energy System (CDU) established within CMEA, with its management centre in Prague. Within this framework, Hungary receives electricity according to demand, and although a net recipient, also supplies it when necessary. Participation in the energy system ensures the electricity needed at peak times and also provides assurance against breakdowns.

Of greater significance, however, is the volume of electricity continuously imported from the Soviet Union. The Hungarian and Soviet grids are interconnected at several points, the largest of which is the 750 kW AC grid between Vinyitsa in the Ukraine and Albertirsa in Hungary. This line is significant not only from a technical viewpoint, it is one of the highest-voltage transmission lines of Europe, but it also ensures the growing demand for electricity within the country.

A smaller-scale co-operation has been established with Yugoslavia, while, taking advantage of the possibilities offered by the divergent energy bases, international co-operation with Austria has been expanded. In summer when Austrian hydro-electric power plants are over-producing, surplus energy is supplied to Hungary. When these plants discontinue power generation, they can be overhauled to ensure safe operation. In winter, when water is scarce in Austria rivers, it is the Hungarian network which supplies energy to Austria from Saturday noon to Sunday midnight each week, which is used to refill the storage reservoirs of peak-capacity power stations.

One of the most important projects for future electricity supply is the Paks nuclear power station with a planned first-stage capacity of 860 MW. The first block with capacity of 430 MW was completed in 1983. The crucial consideration when siting the plant was the Danube, which alone can ensure the vast amount of water demanded by the station.

99 per cent of the country's electricity output stems from thermal power stations. Hydro-electric plants are of the a small capacity and usually meet local demand only. As river regimes within the country fluctuate between wide margins, storage barrages and dams to prevent floods have to be erected, which raises the construction costs of hydro-electric power plants to such an extent that it is only ecenomic to build them in conjunction with other engineering establishments: for instance, if the plant also serves the purposes of irrigation and the expansion of shipping, thus spreading construction costs. It was within this broader framework that the Tiszalök, connected with the Eastern Main Canal, and the Kisköre power stations on the river were constructed on the river Tisza.

The best hydro-potentialities are to be found in Transdanubia. In co-operation with the Czechoslovak energy industry two hydro-electric power plants with a combined capacity of about 900 MW are under construction along the common Hungarian–Slovak section of the Danube between Gabčíkovo and Visegrád–Nagymaros. Unfortunately there are great likelihood, that serious environment risk will be involved by the dams and power stations. A peak-capacity power station with a storage reservoir in the Visegrád area will become part of this scheme later [82].

Electricity generation can be broken down into the following regions (*Fig. 27*).

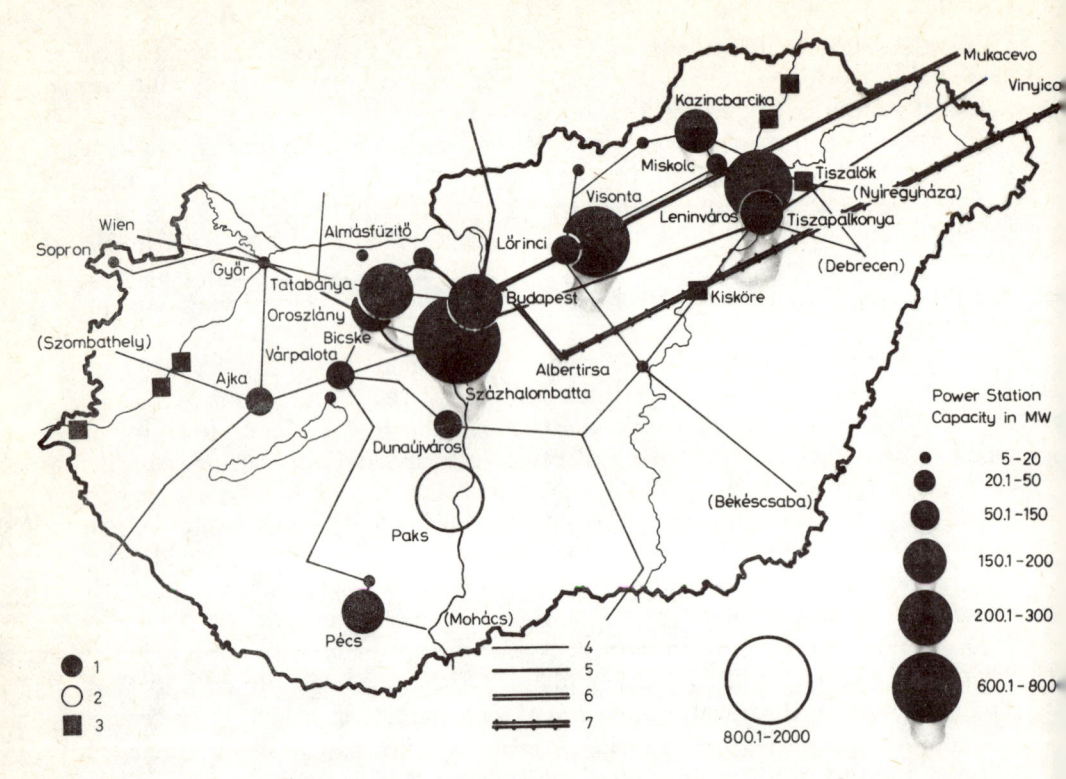

Fig. 27. The spatial distribution of electricity generation capacity (1981)
1 — power station in operation; 2 — power station under construction; 3 — hydro-electric power station; 4 — 120 kV voltage; 5 — 220 kV voltage; 6 — 400 kV voltage; 7 — 750 kV voltage

(a) *The northern electricity-generating district.* The power stations of this region are fuelled by lignite from Mátraalja, poor-quality brown coal from the Ózd and Sajóvölgy area, i.e. the local coal fields, and natural gas and mazout. The largest stations are the Gagarin Power Plant in Visonta, of 800 MW capacity based on Mátraalja lignite, and the oil- and so-called high nitrogen content inert natural gas fuelled Tisza Power Plant of 860 MW capacity. There are also operating in the district several medium-capacity thermal stations, for instance the Mátravidék Power station at Lőrinci. The main consumers are the chemical, iron and steel, mining and building-materials industries.

(b) *The central electricity-generating district.* Typical of this district is that its power stations are supplied with coal from almost all parts of the country. The largest, of 1900 MW capacity, is the Duna Power Station at Százhalombatta. Along with the utility and industrial power plants there are also heating power plants. Despite a substantial generating capacity, the greater part of the electricity demand of the district, due to the large consumption of the industries, transport and population of Budapest, is met by the national grid system.

(c) *The Northern Transdanubian electricity-generating district.* Power stations are sited on the Tatabánya, Oroszlány, Dorog and Central-Transdanubian coal fields, and capacity will be further enhanced when the 1500 MW power station to be erected at Bicske is commissioned in the late 1980s. The electricity consumption of the district is very high, because it is here that the energy-intensive aluminium industry is located, together with plants of the mining and building-materials industries.

(d) *The South-Transdanubian electricity generating district.* Here power stations are fuelled by the shaly coal gained as a by-product during the mining of black-coal. The importance of this area will undoubtedly be enhanced by the commissioning of the Paks nuclear power station.

1.5 Metallurgy

Indicative of the significance of Hungarian metallurgy is that this branch engages close to 100 000 persons. It is also the most energy-intensive sector and is deeply involved with wide-scale domestic and international co-operation.

The leading branch of metallurgy is the iron and steel industry, the development and regional problems of which are summed up in the following sections.

a) Metallurgy is an extraordinarily raw material-intensive branch needing millions of tons of iron ore, foundry coke, iron scrap, limestone, and alloy materials, totalling about 13 million tons per annum, only part of which can be met from domestic sources.

The only iron-ore mine in Hungary is located at Rudabánya and turns out mainly limonite and siderite. Most types of ore mined there cannot be smelted in their crude form, and have to be dressed by various techniques. A 40 to 45 per cent ore concentrate is produced at Rudabánya, while limonite, together with imported ores, is processed by a central ore-dressing plant near Miskolc. Domestic production meets less than 10 per cent computed in metal content, of the country's needs. Further expansion is prevented by limited reserves but even where this is possible, it would be uneconomical, because the ore deposits must be mined underground.

The main source of imported ore is the Krivoy Rog area of the Soviet Union. To ensure the long-term supply of ore, Hungary has provided credit for the expansion of Soviet iron-ore mining.

One third of metallurgic-coke demand is met by the Danube Iron Works and the expansion of the coking plant is under way. The greater proportion of coking coal is therefore again imported from the Soviet Union, Poland, Czechoslovakia and the Federal German Republic.

One of the most important metals needed for steelmaking is manganese. Manganese ore is mined near Úrkút in the Bakony Mountain, but a larger part of the higher-quality, oxidized receives has already been depleted, and only lower-quality, carbonate ores are produced. As facilities for the smelting of manganese ore, do not exist in the country, part of the ore mined is exported. At the same time, ferro-manganese is imported, as are the other raw materials for the production of steel-alloys.

Most of the iron scrap needed for steel production comes from domestic sources in the form of waste iron supplied by metallurgy, various manufacturing plants and other branches of the economy.

Metallurgy also needs large amounts of fuel. Steel works and rolling mills use mazout and natural gas, while the latter has also been introduced to iron blast furnaces, because the demand for coke has diminished, and the reduction process is speeded up. The demand for limestone can be fully met from domestic supplies.

b) The development of metallurgy was for a long time a much debated issue of Hungarian industrialization policy. Disparities in capacity between the engineering industry as the main metal consumer and metallurgy as its supplier arose as early as the Second World War, and the need further to develop steelmaking was already realized at that time. The economic policy of the 1950s overestimated the significance of iron metallurgy, however, and expansion went far beyond the endowments and the economic capacity of the country. Since then, development has been more realistic, taking account of domestic demand and the possibilities of the co-operation with other CMEA countries. Investment has been carried out in several stages. During the 1950s, emphasis was placed on the production of pig iron and steel-making and during the 1960s on sheet products, which were required by modern engineering branches as well as for export. More recently, reinforcing round-iron production and high-quality steel-making have come to the fore, while the demand for section-steels, for instance, rails, is again increasing. With the expansion of the various natural-gas pipelines and infrastructural networks (water, gas, etc.) and the spread of central heating and piped-water supply, the demand for pipes of different diametres is constantly rising.

In recent years there has been a stable demand for steel products on the world market, and taking advantage of this Hungary has exported a substantial quantity of rolled steel products to capitalist countries. In certain cases this trade was only marginally economic, but the earnings thereby obtained contributed to improving the trade balance of the country. The post-boom situation has provided evidence that in the future only high-quality and alloyed steel products will be successful in export markets, and in consequence of this the sixth five-year plan has stressed the importance of a faster rate of development of high-quality steels.

c) Despite the results so far attained and the technological advances, Hungarian metallurgy has been unable to match the quality and specification of the world's leading steel-makers. Hungarian plants are still of small to medium capacity, technological development has been relatively slow and continuous casting has been adopted belatedly. Moreover, while the most up-to-date steel-making technology, the so-called LD converter has been adopted in more than half the world's steel-producing capacity, it was only introduced in Hungary in 1981.

Economical production is also limited by factors stemming from the country's internal economic structure and raw-material endowments. In modern Soviet and Japanese plants large blast furnaces equalling the capacity of all domestic blast furnaces combined are in operation. The technical and economic parameters of these gigantic blast furnaces are incomparably better, but Hungary cannot adopt them, owing to insufficient domestic demand for steel and the limited availability of raw materials. Yet it is still possible to ensure more economical production partly by means of technical development and partly by shaping a modern product range, including in particular special alloy steels [54].

The future development of iron and steel making is connected with the facts outlined above. An increase in the production of pig iron is, owing to raw material shortage, not justified, although steel-making may expand at a moderate rate.

Hungarian metallurgy co-operates closely with other CMEA countries, and special mention should be made of the Intermetall organization. It is this organization which co-ordinates the production and exchange of rolled goods among participating countries, and has been responsible for a considerable increase in trade in steel among socialist member countries.

Since 1981 steel-making has undergone substantial technical changes with the introduction of LD converter technology to the steel plants at Diósgyőr and Dunaújváros, and the closure of some units bare on the Siemens process. But steel-making using the coverter technique needs larger quantities of pig-iron and whereas the old Siemens technology used pig-iron and scrap in a ratio of about 6 to 4, the adoption of LD technology has meant in further shift towards pig-iron. The increased demand for pig iron can be met temporarily from domestic production, but as steel making rises, it will become necessary to import pig iron or enriched pellet ores. A significant growth is expected in the making of electric steel.

The geographical distribution of the Hungarian iron and steel industry was first oriented towards raw-material sources. This was characteristic of the Borsod plants and, before the First World War, also of those at Gömör (now in Czechoslovakia), Vajdahunyad and Resica (now in Romania). At the turn of the century, steel-making without pig-iron production was developed at Csepel, where its rationale was the engineering industry of Budapest. During the first five-year plan there began the construction of the Danube Iron Works at Dunaújváros, whose location is, primarily, transport-oriented. The main locational factor was the fact that ore could be transported directly from the Soviet Union via the Danube, while the precise location of the plant was a site mide-way between the source of coking-coal in the Mecsek and the main consumer market, Budapest. The iron works were also

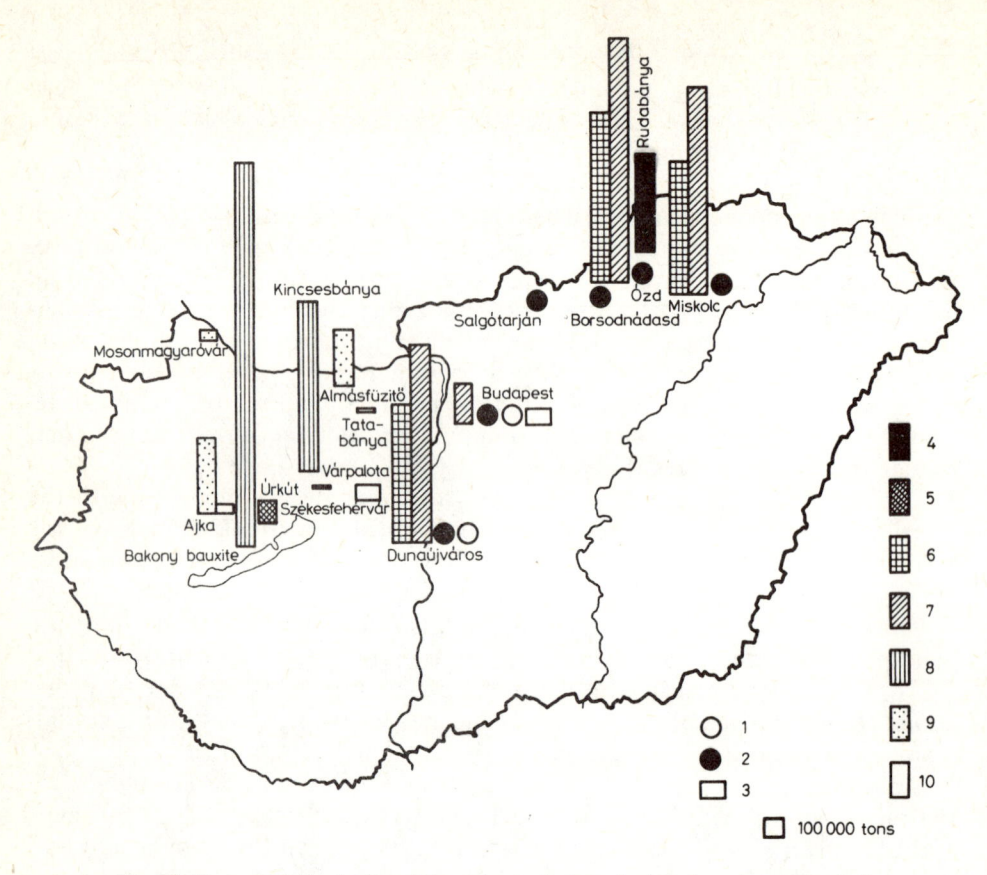

Fig. 28. The spatial discription of the output of selected minerals and metallurgical products (1981)
1 – tubes; 2 – rolled products; 3 – aluminium rolling mill; 4 – iron ore; 5 – manganese; 6 – crude iron; 7 – steel; 8 – bauxite; 9 – alumina; 10 – aluminium

instrumental in helping the development of an economically underdeveloped and previously completely unindustrialized region of the country. *(Fig. 28)*

An international trend in the development of iron and steel manufacture is the establishment of a vertical structure, in which all technological phases are integrated. The Danube Iron Works is the only such integrated plant in Hungary where coke, pig-iron and steel production, hot and cold rolling mills and tube and pipe manufacture can all be found combined on the one sites. The integrated works is complemented by an ore-dressing plant, a factory producing fire-resistant materials, a power plant supplying steam and electricity to the surrounding town and plants, and a chemical works processing the by-products of the coking process.

Because of a lack of coking coal, only a partial vertical integration could be accomplished in the iron and steel works in Borsod.

Changes in the domestic output and import of the most important raw materials and products
(in thousand tons)

	1938	1949	1960	1981
Iron-ore: domestic output	297	339	516	422
Iron-ore imports	40	600	1900	3765
Manganese: domestic output	15	71	123	71
Coking-coal: domestic output	–	–	500	645
Coking-coal imports	...	700	1000	1056
Pig-iron: domestic output	500	400	1300	2193
Steel: domestic output	600	900	1900	3643
Rolled-products: domestic output	300	500	1200	2816

Nonetheless, the Borsod industry as a whole constitutes a regional vertical integration, in which apart from coke production, iron-ore mining, and the manufacture of pig iron, steel, rolled products, wires, iron- and steel-castings, pressed- and wrought-iron, and various steel products are all carried on in close co-operation with each other. The production profile of the Lenin Metallurgical Works at Diósgyőr is pig iron, steel, alloy steel and rolled products. The country's largest electric furnace is to be found in the works and supplies the largest alloy-steel rolling mill. The new integrated steel works, with its oxygen-converter and electric plants, is capable of producing steels of the highest quality.

The Ózd Works produces pig iron, steel, rolled products, plates, rods for reinforced concrete and wire. Emphasis is placed primarily on the production of the last two items. The small-capacity Borsodnánás Plate Plant co-operates closely with the Ózd Works and producing various plate types in special sizes. The Salgótarján Works, which was originally located on local coal reserves, carries out, along with a small-capacity steel-making the processing of steel products supplied from Ózd, and produces primarily cold-rolled steel strips, drawn and galvanized steels and various finished steel products.

The Csepel Works in Budapest, the country's largest engineering factory operates its open-hearth steel mill, a rolling mill and a tube factory. The steel mill processes mainly scrap as well as pig iron supplied by other plants. Steel-making in Budapest has, presumably, no long term future, although the development of further tube manufacture seems to be justified.

An indispensable material for steel-making is ferro-alloy, which is manufactured only in Salgótarján where ferro-silicon is mainly produced.

The foundry industry, comprising iron, steel and other metal foundries, occupies a border position between the iron and steel and engineering industries. In technology, it is closer to iron and steel manufacture but its products have more direct applicability in the engineering industry. Whereas, rolling mills turn out standardized steel products, which undergo further processing in engineering factories, the foundries, by contrast, manufacture products according to the form, size and quality, specification – demanded by engineering concerns, which are them incorporated, without further processing, in engineering products. It is there relationships that determine the geographical location of foundries which can be classified as follows.

a) One group of foundries is closely integrated with the technological cycle of three iron and steel plants namely, the Lenin Works, the Danube Iron Works, and the Salgótarján Works. Castings are usually produced from electric steel, which increases quality and reliability.

b) Another group of foundries is integrated into the technological cycles of various large engineering works, for instance, the large-capacity steel foundries of the Hungarian Railway Carriage and Machine Works (RÁBA) in Győr, and the electric founderies of the Ganz-Mávag and Csepel Works.

c) The third group is comprised of independent foundries working mainly in iron and other metals. Although they are scattered all over the country, there is a significant concentration in Budapest amounting for about half their total output, for instance, the plants of the Foundry Enterprise, the Steel Foundry and Tube Factory and the Engine-casting Factory. The most significant foundries outside Budapest are those in Miskolc, Győr, Salgótarján, Kecskemét (the latter supplies iron castings for bath tubs), Pápa and Kisvárda.

Non-ferrous metallurgy

Non-ferrous metallurgy in Hungary is concentrated one-sidedly around aluminium manufacture, mainly bacause of the availability of abundant bauxite. — With the exception of newly discovered copper ore the country is poor in other non-ferrous metals, those that are found being of too low quality for economic exploitation. The development of additional branches of non-ferrous metallurgy would therefore necessitate considerable ore imports and it has been found more expedient to rely on their non-ferrous metallurgy industries of other socialist countries, mainly the Soviet Union, Poland and Bulgaria, which are better endowed with raw materials. The non-ferrous resources and dressing plants of western countries are mainly in the hands of large multinational corporations, which seldom sell crude or dressed ore to outsiders. Moreover, most branches of non-ferrous metallurgy are energy-intensive, which, owing to the scarce energy resources of the country is a further reason which makes their development unjustified.

Domestic bauxite ores are of sedimentary origin, are yellow-reddish in colour, are of varied composition, and developed during the Cretaceous Period. Their main constituents are: aluminium hydroxide, iron oxide, silicon oxide and the oxides of other metals like vanadium, titanium and gallium. The main bauxite deposits are in the limestone and dolomite mountains of the Bakony, Vértes, Gerecse and Villány. They belong to the group of so-called karst bauxites, and can be found in numerous but small-volume deposits. They are usually only a few square kilometres in extent, and many of a lenticular shape and small diameter are relatively deep below the surface.

Bauxite cannot be smelted directly: the first stage in the process is the removal of aluminium oxide from the ore using caustic soda (NaOH) as a catalyst, the so-called Bayer process. The efficiency of the process depends on the silicon dioxide (SiO_2) content of the ore, which absorbs part of the caustic soda used, and is lost in the course of processing. A high silicon oxide content therefore reduces the efficiency of alumina production. Bauxite quality is determined by the ratio of aluminium oxide to silicon oxide, the so-called „modulus", in which a modulus exceeding 10 denotes a high quality ore. The average modulus of bauxite now mined in Hungary is 7.4, which, by international standards, is rather low, reserves of the better-quality bauxites previously mined, now being exhausted. In the early 1950s, two tons of bauxite were sufficient to yield one ton of alumina, but this has now risen to three tons. Another problem is that most mines are worked underground, rather than being opencast.

Bauxite mining began in Hungary in the mid-1920s for the most part utilizing German and Swiss capital. Most of the output was exported, and domestic consumption was low throughout the capitalist period. The post-war planned economy, however, foresaw the growth of domestic bauxite mining in conjunction with the need for the development of a domestic aluminium industry and with the international requirements of the economy. The significance of bauxite exports has, thus diminished and the countries of destination are now Czechoslovakia, the GDR and Poland.

Bauxite mining is concentrated in two large areas. One extends north of Székesfehérvár, where the Mór trench and the Bakony Mountains meet, and where production is from deep mines worked near Iszkaszenthegy and Kincsesbánya. The other area is in the southern part of the Bakony Mountains in the Halimba–Nyirád–Szőc district, where both underground and open-cast mines are operating.

More recently new reserves have been discovered in the northern Bakony Mountains in the vicinity of Bakonyoszlop and Fenyőfő and south-east of Tatabánya in the Gerecse Mountains at Nagyegyháza. At the latter place the bauxite occurs below a brown-coal deposit. With the opening up of both areas in the second half of the 1980s, the geographical distribution of mining will undergo a fundamental change.

A multi-phase vertical integration process is now used in the transformation of bauxite to aluminium, each phase being carried out in a different geographical, technical and economic context. The first phase involves an production of alumina and requires considerable water, steam, and caustic soda. Of the above demands, water, in particular, is a locational determinant, while the demand steam requires the proximity of fuel sources or a power station supplying steam. Caustic soda, on the other hand, has a double economic significance in that rock salt has to be imported as does the electricity needed for the electrolysis of the salt either indirectly as fuel generating electricity or directly as electric current.

The second phase is smelting, which converts alumina into aluminium. Its primary characteristic from both a locational and economic point of view, is its high consumption of electrical energy, as the process takes place by means of electrolysis. Thus any increase in aluminium production has immediate consequences for the Hungarian energy industry which is already faced with serious difficulties in many fields, and presupposes a growth in output of domestic coal production, or the import of electric current. Furthermore, necessary auxiliary substances like anodic substance, cathode coal, cryolite, etc. are also mainly imported.

The third phase is the manufacture of so-called semi-finished products (plates, bars, tubes, wires, and castings) requiring expensive machinery and skilled labour, as well as other metals for the production of various alloys of magnesium, manganese, and copper, which constitute a further import demand.

The fourth phase, the manufacture of aluminium products, belongs only partly to the aluminium industry as it is a raw material in many manufacturing processes, being used by the cable, vehicle, and electronics industries.

The most critical phase from the point of view of development is the conversion of alumina into aluminium, where the economics are marginal because the large amount of electricity used in the process must be produced from coal or imported fuels. To develop aluminium production to an extent commensurate with the extensive bauxite reserves would therefore be uneconomical on account of its energy-intensity nature and high production costs. Furthermore, despite a price rise, aluminium is still the cheapest non-ferrous metal, whose world price is determined by countries that are much better endowed than Hungary [55].

Nonetheless, the development of the aluminium industry is justified by the availability of bauxite, the only significant raw material possessed by Hungary, as well as by increasing domestic and CMEA demands. It also follows from the specifes of the individual phases of integrated production that while the manufacture of alumina and of semi-finished and finished aluminium products can be undertaken economically, the smelting of aluminium is less justified on economic grounds. The solution to this has been sought within the framework of international co-operation whereby Hungarian alumina is smelted in foreign countries, but the aluminium produced is made available to the Hungarian economy.

The first co-operative agreements were concluded with Czechoslovakia (bauxite exports to the alumina plant in Ziar nad Hronom), with the GDR (bauxite exports to the alumina plant in Lauta) and with Poland. The latter was in force from 1960 to 1980, under which Hungary supplied alumina to Poland and received in exchange block aluminium. But most important for the development of the Hungarian aluminium industry has been the co-operation with the Soviet Union, under which Hungary exports 330 000 tons of alumina for smelting in the Soviet Union, mainly to Volgograd. All the aluminium thus refined is re-exported to Hungary. The basis for accounting

Changes in the balance sheet of the aluminium industry
(1000 tons)

	1938	1949	1960	1981
Bauxite output	304	561	1190	2914
exports	362	326	500	498
Alumina output	7	31	218	792
exports	3	2	120	626
Crude (block) aluminium				
output	1	14	50	74
imports	0	0	1	154
exports	0	3	10	86
Semi-finished products output	0	9	33	139
exports	0	0	4	33

the transaction is the world price of alumina and block aluminium respectively.

This agreement effectively solved the dilemma concerning the development of the second phase of the vertical integration process: the construction of the necessary power-generating capacities and of a new aluminium furnace were affected outside the boundaries of Hungary. Despite substantial transportation costs, the aluminium smelted in the Soviet Union using the electricity generated from its hydro-electric power plants and transported back to Hungary is cheaper than producing it in Hungary with electricity generated from domestic or imported energy sources. In fact the aluminium smelting of Hungarian alumina in the Soviet Union is tantamount to the export of electricity to Hungary. The agreement has made it necessary to step up alumina production and to expand existing rolling-mill capacities. As a result of such co-operation, aluminium output not only satisfies domestic consumption, but is also increasing exported to socialist countries and to the west.

In order to meet the growing demand for aluminium both at home and abroad, a new foundry with a capacity of about 100 000 tons, will be necessary in the years of late 1980s.

It is most favourable for the Hungarian economy if aluminium is exported in the form of semi-finished or finished products. Given the world-market prices of the late 1970s in U.S. dollar term and assuming the cost of bauxite to be 100 yields the following prices: alumina 600 to 650, foundry aluminium 3200, semi-finished products 4200 and finished products 5000 to 6000. When aluminium is exported in a highly finished form, mining rent can already be realized. But in a realistic assessment of Hungarian endowments it is also necessary to realize that the export efficiency of highly finished products is constantly deteriorating, as their production involves a substantial import content of electricity, alloying materials, and the depreciation of expensive imported machinery and equipment.

Most plants were established during the capitalist period, and are sited in accordance with the locational factors relating to the individual phases of the production process. Alumina production is carried out in three plants. The largest capacity is concentrated at Ajka, where two factories are operating. The siting rationale is the nearby mining of bauxite in the southern part of the Bakony Mountains and the Ajka coal field. It is the steam produced as a by-product from the generating station based upon Ajka coal field that supplies the heat energy for the alumina plant, while the water needed for the process is pumped up from the bauxite mines. The construction of a second plant was made necessary by the Hungarian—Soviet aluminium agreement, which called for the growth of domestic alumina production. This factory also produces high-value gallium as a by-product. The alumina factory at Almásfüzitő uses the Danube as its source of water, while bauxite is supplied for the most part from Fejér county. The smallest alumina plant is located at Mosonmagyaróvár, and was the first to be installed as early as the 1930s in an abandoned factory building. Water demand is also ensured by the Danube, while the plant also produces vanadium oxide (V_2O_5) and corundum as by-products.

Aluminium smelting is carried out in three plants, each based on an electricity generating station fuelled by locally produced brown coal. The foundries are also connected to the national grid to ensure continuity of production. In order to render aluminium metallurgy economical, the furnaces have undergone large-scale technical development, as a result of which the specific use of electric current per ton of aluminium produced has fallen from 22 000 kWh/ton in the 1950s to 15 500 kWh/ton at present.

The largest foundry is operating at Várpalota and is linked with the Inota generating station which used local lignite resources, while that at Tatabánya is based on energy generated on the Tatabánya coal field.

The foundry at Ajka is attached to the old alumina factory and uses energy supplied by the Ajka power station. Geographically, the site at Ajka is an optimum location because the proximity of local coal, bauxite, alumina and industrial water minimizes transport costs. The complex is also connected with a large-capacity aluminium foundry.

The manufacture of semi-finished products is concentrated at the Light-Metal Works at Székesfehérvár, the geographical centre of the vertical integration of aluminium production, where a large-capacity rolling, pressing and drawing plant is also operating. With its products, the rolling mill at Székesfehérvár constitutes a plant of considerable weight within the aluminium industry of Europe. There are two aluminium rolling plants in Budapest, the one at the Csepel Works, the other at Kőbánya where aluminium foil for the food-packaging industry is its main product.

Richest in workable non-ferrous metal ores is the Mátra Mountain, where small quantities of lead and zinc ores are mined and then dressed at Gyöngyösoroszi. The mining of copper ore with a small gold content has a long tradition at Recsk and recently an extensive though workable deposit of low-grade copper ore has been discovered there. These reserves will make

Hungary self-sufficient in copper in the foreseeable future and even a net exporter of small quantities. After the process of exploring and mine-construction, copper-ore mining itself is expected to begin in early 1990s.

1.6 The engineering industry

In Hungarian planning and statistical practice, the comprehensive term *engineering industry* stands primarily for industries manufacturing metal into finished products, and thus includes the industries producing machinery and equipment, railway, road and other vehicles, electrical machines and appliances, electro-engineering, telecommunications, vacuum- and precision-engineering and miscellaneous metal products. The branches of the engineering industry produce the bulk of the means of production and therefore promote the modernization and growth of the technical basis for the development of productive forces and the economy as a whole. The engineering industry, by producing telecommunication and household appliances as well as the other technical means of everyday life, promotes the rise of living standards.

In the history of Hungarian industrialization, the engineering industry made its appearance during the last third of the 19th century. Paralleling with the development of a large-scale flour-milling industry, there began the production of the milling machinery, especially the manufacture of cast-steel grinding rollers, an innovation of world-wide significance, while the expansion of the transportation network, primarily the construction of railways, led to the production of various types of conveyance. By the turn of the century, the first steps had been taken in the production of electric machinery, incandescent lamps, electric railway locomotives (the electrification of the world's first major railway line, the North-Italian Valtellina Railway was undertaken by the Ganz Factory in 1902) and electric tramcars. Although the Hungarian agriculture of the time was largely unmechanized, the manufacture of ploughs, threshing machines and steam-powered traction engines was nonetheless soon begun. Moreover, due to the world political situation and the endeavours of the Monarchy, an appreciable armaments industry was also founded, tied closely to the engineering industry. Between the two world wars, the engineering industry regressed, and only reached the production level of 1913 as late as 1938. Its product range, however, was widened by such branches as the manufacture of radio sets, cables, telecommunication appliances and telephone exchanges, diesel locomotives, and multiple units and aircraft. Throughout the period of capitalist development, the industry was characterized by two important factors: the high participation of foreign capital, largely German, British, Dutch and Swiss, and low productivity. Its competitiveness on the international market could be only ensured by the fitful appearance of novel products and a wage level far below the European average.

The significance of the engineering industry for the national economy is summed up in the following paragraphs:

In 1981, it employed as many as 505 000 persons, or 32 per cent of the labour force of socialist industry, and accounted for 27·7 per cent of the production value of the socialist sector. The engineering industry also plays a decisive role in the country's foreign-trade turnover, with 33 per cent of its output exported. The increasing participation of the machine-building industry in Hungarian exports is an important economic phenomenon, because this branch is capable of producing finished products whose value is several times that of the raw materials used. In an economy like that of Hungary, whose growth can only be ensured by high-cost energy and raw-material imports, the development of branches producing high-value commodities is indispensable. It is the task of economic policy to ensure that this happens within the limits of reality, and to take account of the fact that the engineering industry can do this more efficiently than many other industrial branches. One of the realities is that the engineering industry makes further import demands over and above the imported materials incorporated in domestically manufactured products and components by buying from abroad various steels, non-ferrous metals, synthetic materials, components, capital equipment and licences. Thus in assessing the external economic significance of the engineering industry, the import content of individual products should also be considered. The economic efficiency of exports requires that the quality and modernity of products marketed abroad should be such as to guarantee that the prices obtained not only serve the interests of the individual but the national economy as a whole, too. A crucial problem of the late 1970s was that serveral of its less up-to-date products, and products manufactured at a high prime cost, did not satisfy the above requirements. As regards the reasons for this, reference has to be made first of all to the fact that it is most difficult to raise the quality of products to the latest technical and market requirements and maintain them at that standard. In view of the rapid development of technology, the performance of this task encounters several economic and technical constraints. The up-grading of products to an international level calls for enormous investment, continuous product development and scientific research, as well as management which take into account the demands of the market. Therefore, only those branches should be developed, that are able to meet domestic production realities and world-market requirements alike. The small dimensions of the country and its economy make the manufacture of high-value products representative of the most advanced level of science and technology impossible, and this applies to products such as aeroplanes, rockets and certain electronic equipment, as well as the adoption of the latest technologies in the chemical industry, because they require particularly large capital investments and a scientific research background. Instead, the development of those branches is needed which correspond to the limited potentialities, and whose quality can be maintained at an international level.

In order to overcome these difficulties it is imperative to assert consistently, by way of a long-term programme, the basic principles of an intensive and selective development policy, which means in practice that emphasis will have to be placed, first and foremost, on shaping the right product (micro-) structure. Owing to the limited availability of resources, it will only be possible to realize the product structure of selected engineering factories by, among others, moving labour from the less to the more efficient plants. It is expected that the manufacture of many uneconomical products will be discontinued, in addition to the manufacture of those products that have already ceased within the context of CMEA specialization, or as a recognition of their uneconomic nature. These include combine harvesters, motorcycles, railway passenger carriages, tramcars and certain small household appliances and mass products. Although problems resulting from a policy of selective development are spread nationwide, they affect the engineering industry of the Budapest agglomeration most decisively.

Through their extensive linkages, the development of certain branches of the engineering industry are also capable of boosting other branches, i.e. they exert a multiplier and accelerator effect. These branches have a dynamic effect on the other branches with which they are in production co-operation. As a result of economic but mainly technical progress, the composition of these dynamic branches changes from time to time, and whereas formerly it was the road vehicle industry, today it is the electronic industry that performs this role.

As the main consumer of their products, the engineering industry is closely tied to the metallurgy and foundry industries, and also co-operates with other industrial branches, such as chemicals, synthetic materials, and rubber manufacture. But more intensive than its co-operation with other industrial branches is the co-operation that takes place within the engineering industry itself. The international development of the engineering industry in modern times is characterized by a definite separation of the manufacture of components and accessories from their assembly into finished products, a separation which is steadily assuming increasing international proportions. Although with a time lag, the development and structural transformation of the Hungarian engineering industry is also following the international trend. Co-operation within the engineering industry is closely linked with the increasing of specialization of individual plants, a process which moreover also has regional implications, especially in relation to main and branch plant activity.

In the case of many products we are witnessing the manifestation of a tendency of worldwide significance for the development of the engineering industry, i.e. the expansion of large-batch or mass production. The increased efficiency of the Hungarian engineering industry also requires that the greater part of its production change over to ever larger batch sizes, but in the case of many products, this comes up against the serious difficulty of the limited absorptive capacity of the relatively small domestic market.

Changes in the manufacture of some important engineering products

Product	Unit	1949	1960	1970	1981
Lathes	number	764	2724	3210	1912
Milling machines	number	374	1177	985	272
Boring machines	number	983	3054	3644	3389
Ball bearings	in millions	8	15	16	27
Motor-car diesel engines	in thousands	–	11	17	26
Lorries	number	996	2923	3815	2401
Buses	in thousands	0.2	2	6	11
Radio receivers	in thousands	67	212	206	180
Television sets	in millions	–	139	364	421
Incandescent lamps	in millions	22	64	148	415
Semi-conductors	in millions	–	2	26	114
Washing machines	in thousands	–	144	164	256
Electric refrigerators	in thousands	–	9	241	504
Bicycles	in thousands	137	254	275	286
Cables	in thousand tons	...	25	66	96
Electric supply meters	in thousands	270	460	347	629
Tape recorder	in thousands	–	–	60	555

Although the production runs of a few products have been raised to a satisfactory level in recent decades, for instance buses, vacuum engineering products, television sets, rural types of electric machinery and instruments, large-batch mass production has not yet become general practice. This statement, of course, does not preclude the possibility of individual or small-batch manufacture of certain products, provided it is justified by efficiency criteria.

Specialization within the CMEA has expanded the dimensions and marketing potentialities of several products of the Hungarian engineering industry, because it is in the interests of socialist countries that engineering products are manufactured in larger batch sizes, with greater productivity and lower production costs. Within the programme of long-term targets, the CMEA also organizes co-operation among member countries in the field of engineering. The utilization of this possibility to transform the product structure of the Hungarian engineering industry should be readily grasped, because the demand within socialist countries ensures a safe market for products manufactured in large batch sizes.

The Hungarian engineering industry, over and above product specialization, effectively co-operates with CMEA countries in the joint production of components and the manufacture of certain products; buses, components for passenger motor cars, rear axles and electronic computers are produced in this way. Agencies furthering co-operation within the field of engineering include *Intranszmas* for materials handling equipment, *Agromas* for certain agricultural machinery, *Intertextilmas* for textile machinery, and *Interatomenergia* for installations related to atomic plants and atomic-energy research.

Besides production co-operation with socialist countries, the Hungarian engineering industry also seeks opportunities to establish production contacts with the engineering industries of Western countries on the basis of mutual advantage. Such links have been established with the Volkswagen, Volvo, the Fiat, the Siemens companies, while high-precision machine tools are produced co-operatively by Krupp and the Csepel Works.

Besides the purchase of foreign licences Hungary has also managed to sell licences to firms in the West. Several large plants in Hungary are carrying out assembly work for West German and Swiss machine companies, and the creation of joint Hungarian and Western enterprises, mainly with Austrian, Italian and West German firms is becoming more common in the field of investment projects, like factory installations and the construction of electricity generating plant. But the greatest drawback of co-operative agreements with the Western countries is that they are usually at best medium-term, whereas longer-term arrangements would be more beneficial to Hungarian industry.

For a long time it was the engineering industry that boasted the fastest rate of industrial growth, and it is only recently that it has been overtaken by the chemical industry. After the reorganization following nationalization, new sectors, such as bus and roll-bearing manufacture, and the machine-tool industry sprang up. During the 1950s, engineering like other industrial branches was characterized by quantitative growth and the development of wide range of products, none of which was given priority. As a result, development was slow and product quality poor. Moreover, branches whose products had been of rather high quality fell victim to the quantitative approach and could not maintain their former standards. By the early 1960s, however, product differentiation was already emerging within the CMEA, although the selection of branches to be developed was not always successful, and the technological problem of technical lag continued to accumulate. But since then, due mainly to the modernization of economic management, several branches of engineering have undergone a fast technical, quantitative and qualitative development, for instance by purchasing from abroad the right to manufacture a number of high-quality products and by accelerating domestic product development. The results of this process have manifested themselves in the improvement of the economy, in both exports as well as public supply. Within engineering, production co-operation has expanded, and council- and co-operative-owned industries have also joined successfully in several machine-building programmes either as suppliers of components or as end-product producers. At the same time, a number of the less adaptive firms with obsolete product structures have ceased manufacture. The qualitative problems of the engineering industry stood out most conspicuously after the 1973 energy crisis and subsequent pricing problems and deterioration of marketing conditions. Another deficiency was that decisions were end-product-oriented, with enterprises striving to turn out primarily end-products, which had the consequence that ancillary industries manufacturing components, or undertaking repair and maintenance work developed insufficient capacity. A further retarding factor was the clumsy management of oversized enterprises which adjusted less successfully to the changing conditions. During the 6th five-year plan (1981—1985), economic policy will concentrate on the creation of these ancillary industries.

A task of similar importance has been the rationalization of the spatial structure of the engineering industry. During the capitalist period, the engineering industry was characterized by its excessive concentration in Budapest, primarily because of the advantages that this offered. Thus the complex development in the capital made it easier for individual plants to develop production linkages, thus ensuring more economical and cheaper production. Also the necessary ancillary industry, often in the form of small family undertakings, was available.

With the establishment of new factories, for instance the ball-bearing plant in Debrecen, a change in the geographical location of the engineering industry began as early as the first five-year plan and had become noticeable by the mid-1960s. Owing to an increasing labour shortage, engineering firms in Budapest found that the best policy was to site new plants away from the capital, thereby making use at the same time of the preferences associated with regional industrial development policy. The new plants located in the provinces, while partly producing components or acting as partners of the parent companies in Budapest, mostly manufactured end-products.

The geographical location of the engineering industry in Hungary is only partly determined by those factors which are generally accepted as locational determinants. This can be partly explained by history, partly by the small size of the country and its economy, and partly by its specific continental location. The specific factors acting upon the spatial location of the Hungarian engineering industry are summarized in the following paragraphs.

Manpower has remained the principle factor since the first stage of engineering development up to the present. At the close of the last century, it was the surplus manpower in Budapest, stemming for the most part from migration, that exerted a strong pull on the engineering industry. Later on, in the 1930s as well as after the Second World War, the existence of skilled manpower in the capital continued to attract engineering firms. Since the mid-1960s, however, the labour shortage in the capital has induced enterprises to look more towards the regions, especially the less industrialized areas of the Great Plain and Transdanubia.

Opportunities for integration and co-operation were for long only considered as factors of location in relation to the Budapest agglomeration. This was particularly manifest in the 1950s, when the engineering industry in Budapest underwent a quantitative development, and linkages among individual branches created a regionally closed circle of co-operation. Linkages with other industrial branches in the same region were effective locational factors only in a few fields, for instance, the linkage between the heavy machine industry and iron and steel in the Miskolc–Diósgyőr area involving the processing of wrought- or pressed-steel products and steel castings.

A new phenomenon, however, is the so-called convergent integration which appears to be promoting spatial linkages among the large plants assembling and manufacturing components. Several large engineering enterprises, usually participating in CMEA co-operation projects, have created a system of branch plants that are located quite close to the parent firm, which helps promote the industrialization of the countryside and also provides employment to the local labour force. The plants of the Győr-based Hungarian Railway Carriage and Machine Works (RÁBA), which are located in the Little Plain, those of the Videoton Radio and Television Factory in Székesfehérvár and the Bakony Works for Metal and Electrical Appliances in Veszprém located in Central Transdanubia and the plants in the Jászság of the Jászberény Works for Refrigerating Machinery provide good examples of this trend.

Close spatial linkage with the consumer market is a common locational factor internationally and was of importance in accounting for the development of the Hungarian engineering industry in the Budapest agglomeration. At the close of the 19th century, Budapest was the centre of the Danube shipping trade, which attracted shipbuilding, while the construction of the railway network with Budapest at its centre drew to it the manufacture of locomotives and rolling stock. Similarly, since the 1960s, large-scale housing construction in Budapest has attracted industries manufacturing installations for water supply and central heating.

Otherwise, this sort of linkage can only be witnessed in the agricultural machine manufacturing industry of the Little Plain, where the early intensive development of agriculture created a demand for machinery, which in turn stimulated agricultural machine production. This process is still occurring in the region where, as a result of the broiler- and corn-production system used by the Bábolna State Farm, the development of agricultural machinery production has again picked up.

Market factors also manifest themselves in the fact that the railway vehicle repair-service industry has been sited at the larger railway junctions. Although the centre of this sector is Budapest, the repair-service industry is located throughout the provinces. Currently a similar phenomenon can be observed in the geographical location of the road-vehicle service industry, which has developed as a complex network serving the capital, the county and larger towns, and the centres of foreign tourism.

Important locational factors for advanced engineering firms are the scientific background and innovational bases. Formerly, owing to the regional concentration of scientific and innovative capabilities in Budapest, these factors worked exclusively to enhance the engineering industry of the capital. For instance, innovations helped transform the Ganz concern from a small enterprise producing flour mills into one manufacturing electrical machinery and railcars. At present it is the Hungarian Railway Carriage and Machine Works (RÁBA) in Győr that exhibits a similarly impressive development based on innovations.

Since the Hungarian engineering industry has a relatively short history, production and technical traditions as developed in certain European countries, for example the countries-old watch-making industry of Switzerland, or toy manufacture in Saxony and Thuringia, have exerted a relatively small effect on the location of engineering in the country. In the current development period, however, one can start to speak of the locational effect of industrial traditions. The Videoton Radio and Television Factory in Székesfehérvár has become the centre of the computer industry, because as a plant formerly manufacturing electronic appliances it already had a production experience and a tradition. The raising of the production structure of several provincial engineering plants to a higher technical level has also been promoted by the industrial experience gained in the past.

Apart from general infrastructure, such as the water supply, drainage, electricity supply and a road networks, the engineering industry does not have any special requirements as for example large quantities of water. The transportation factor has also been of minor significance in the siting of most branches of engineering. Even the material-intensive plants, or the plants assembling masses of components can achieve a decrease in their transportation costs if their sites are appropriately chosen in the future, too. The most modern branches of electronics and instrument manufacture, with their light-weight components and finished products are not transport-intensive, and can make use of the existing road network. There is no need for the construction of expensive factory sidings, or locations close to railway lines. this fact has been duly considered when dispersing engineering plants to the provinces.

The geographical location of the engineering industry at the opening of the 1980s can be summarized as follows *(Fig. 29)*.

(a) The engineering industry continues to be highly concentrated in Budapest and its aggglomeration belt where almost all engineering branches are represented. Production linkages within that area are invariably strong, but linkages with newly-founded provincial plants, primarily factories producing components, have become more open territorially, and widespread co-operation is developing between Budapest and the countryside.

(b) The second most important engineering area is the Little Plain with motor-vehicle production as its dominant branch. Around this branch are grouped the majority of plants such as the Hungarian Railway Carriage and Machine works (RÁBA) in Győr with its convergent integration. Also significant are the manufacture of agricultural machinery at Mosonmagyaróvár and Szombathely, miscellaneous hard metal wares production at Mosonmagyaróvár and the manufacture of electrical appliances and components at Pápa and Szombathely.

(c) Although co-operation is less typical, the northern industrial area with its production potential and multifarious structure is beginning increasingly to satisfy the engineering demands of the district. Plants in Miskolc, Eger, Gyöngyös and more recently Salgótarján, and in several of the more minor

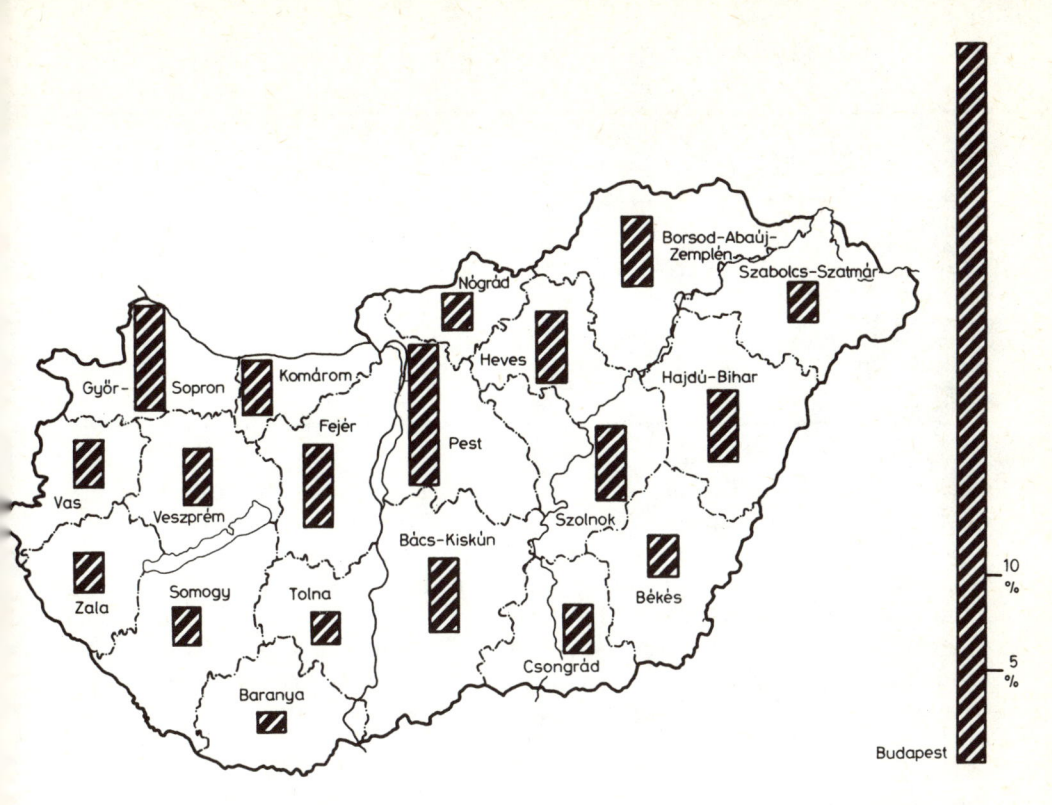

Fig. 29. The spatial distribution of the engineering industry by number of employees, in per cent (1981)

towns produce heating installations, electric engineering components, automatic systems, pneumatic elements, medical instruments and electronic products.

(d) In addition to the three industrial areas, other major provincial centres of the engineering industry are Székesfehérvár producing electronics, buses and machine-tools; Veszprém involved with passenger motorcar components; Pécs concerned with electronics, vacuum engineering, anf food-processing machinery, Kecskemét producing telecommunication equipment, miscellaneous products and machine-tools; Debrecen and environs where ball bearings, washing machines, medical instruments are manufactured, and Szeged producing cables and miscellaneous metal products. Other centres of some significance are Jászberény manufacturing electric refrigerators, Nagykanizsa which produces incandescent lamps and oil-mining equipment, and Vác with electronics and containers.

(e) Locational factors specific to the Hungarian engineering industry can also be distinguished. Reference has already been made to the importance of manpower, but another factor is the fact that compared with other

151

Distribution of the engineering industry in Hungary by main branches
(1981)

Branches	Percentage of gross production value	Percentage of manpower employed	Percentage of gross value of fixed assets
Machinery and equipment	22·4	25·4	24·4
Transport equipment	27·6	20·0	29·7
Electric machinery and equipment	14·5	12·2	12·9
Telecommunications and vacuum engineering	14·6	19·6	15·7
Instruments industry	8·8	11·6	8·1
Miscellaneous metal products	12·1	11·2	9·2
Engineering industry, total	100·0	100·0	100·0

socialist countries, Hungary has emphasized less the concentration of production, and has instead created large enterprises comprising individual product-groups and often whole industrial sub-branches as, for instance, the Hungarian Machine Tool Company and the Electrical Equipment and Machinery Company. Along with the development of their central plants, such enterprises have also established several new, usually medium-scale, productive units. Since large enterprises initiating convergent integration have also established ancillary plants, it follows that engineering production in Hungary is comparatively decentralized.

Engineering enterprises can be further characterized by the structure of their plants as follows:

— enterprises consisting of one plant;

— enterprises based on an internal division of labour in which plants may specialize in the production of end-products or components. For example, the United Incandescent Lamp and Electrical Company carries out product development and the manufacture of the most sophisticated products in Budapest, but also has plants in Gyöngyös producing semiconductors, in Nagykanizsa plants manufacturing incandescent lamps, and in Kaposvár producing electronic valves as well as plants manufacturing components in Kisvárda and Vác;

— enterprises whose plants are linked by convergent integration (see the above-mentioned examples);

— enterprises where the manufacture of the latest products is carried out in Budapest or at the headquarter plant of the enterprise, while less exacting products are manufactured elsewhere, for example the branch plants of the Hungarian Optical Works located at Dunaújváros and Mátészalka;

— enterprises whose product development and planning is done in Budapest, while production itself is carried on elsewhere, for instance the Institute for Electric Automation has product development plants in Budapest and a manufacturing in Eger;

— enterprises where the manufacture of the end-product is carried out in Budapest and that of components elsewhere.

As indicated by the table, the manufacture of transport equipment, a traditional branch, occupies a leading position in the output of the engineering industry, while the share of such modern branches as electrical machinery, telecommunications and vacuum engineering, and the instruments industry is still relatively low.

The territorial location of the engineering industry may be presented by the distribution of its major branches:

(a) The production of machinery and equipment is very extensive as it embraces the manufacture of calorific machines (apart from locomotives and motorcar engines), power generating and metallurgical equipment, machine tools, equipment for the chemical, food-processing and building industries, lifting equipment, steel structures and ball bearings. These branches are highly significant as they are the main producers of power and work machines, and are mainly located in Budapest. In taking decisions about further development, selectivity has to be the primary consideration.

Steam turbines up to 210 MW capacity for electricity generating stations and canning factory installations are produced in Budapest by the Láng Machine Enterprise. Several plants of this branch of engineering, located both in Budapest and elsewhere, are also involved in the production of nuclear power-plant equipment, predominantly of traditional energetic appliances and instruments as well as automatic equipment serving the reactor. Boilers for turbines of 210 MW capacity are produced by the Budapest plant of the Hungarian Shipyard and Crane Factory.

Machine-tool production is gradually shifting emphasis from the manufacture universal types (lathes, milling, boring and grinding machines) to the production of more modern, high-value, high-precision and partly automated types (the so-called numerically controlled (NC) lathes, single-purpose and aggregate machines), although some setbacks have been experienced. The factories of the Machine-Tool Manufacturing Works integrating most plants of this industry are located in Budapest, the largest user of machine-tools. Also in Budapest is located the Machine-Tool Factory of the Csepel Works. Significant plants are also located in Esztergom, Székesfehérvár and Győr. The major plants of tools making are operating in Budapest, Békéscsaba and Kecskemét.

The Diósgyőr Machine Works (DIMÁVAG) of Miskolc produces rolling-plant equipment, drawing-machine lines, equipment of the cable industry, axles and wheels for railway rollingstock and pumps.

Bearing production is growing rapidly and ball bearings are made in Debrecen and roller bearings in Diósd. The Hungarian ball-bearing industry participates in the CMEA Alliance of Bearing Industries, which co-ordinates the production and standardization of bearings in socialist countries.

Several products of the iron- and metal-structure industry, for example bridges, have gained an international reputation, while the branch also produces factory and more recently light-structure buildings. The largest plants are operating with the ambit of the Ganz-Mávag Locomotive and Machine

Factory in Budapest and the Hungarian Railway Carriage and Machine Works in Győr (RÁBA). The high-quality output of the branch is evidenced by the Erzsébet Bridge in Budapest, by radio and television transmitting towers and many new factory buildings. In the interests of the production of light-structure buildings, new plants have been established in Dunaújváros, Kecskemét and Székesfehérvár.

The modernization of agriculture makes it necessary to raise steadily the level and volume of agricultural equipment manufactured domestically. The introduction of large-scale agriculture has increased the need for higher-capacity tractors, ploughs, disk cultivators, sowing machines, fertilizer- and manure-spreaders and sprinkling equipment for irrigation, the manufacture of the last developing especially fast during the 1960s. Considering the benefits to be derived from a division of labour among the socialist countries, much agricultural equipment is bought abroad, for example combine harvesters from the Soviet Union and potato and sugar-beet harvesters from the GDR and Czechoslovakia. Nonetheless, domestic manufacture has not been able to keep up the rapid development of agriculture, and for all its noteworthy achievements is far from satisfactory. The growth of agriculture in Hungary, which has been outstanding even by international standards, requires the production of advanced equipment, but because of domestic failures much of the equipment needed for the various industry-like production system has had to be imported from the western countries, and several manufacturing licences e.g. for the production of the American heavy-duty Steiger tractor were purchased. Plants manufacturing agricultural equipment are located in Törökszentmiklós, Debrecen, Makó, Hódmezővásárhely, Szolnok, Mosonmagyaróvár, Szombathely, Veszprém and Kaposvár, while tractors are manufactured by the Hungarian Railway Carriage and Machine Works (RÁBA) in Győr.

(b) Manufacture of equipment for the transport industry is a rather extensive branch of engineering, whose significance is enhanced by its export-orientation. In view of international trends and the potentialities offered by the domestic market, a selective change within its product structure began with vehicle manufacture. Along with significant technical advances at home, an important role has been assigned to the development of CMEA agreements and foreign licencing arrangements, and by means of the latter, the lead time needed for certain modern products has been substantially curtailed. For example, the manufacture of the MAN diesel engine under licence has solved the engine problems of the Hungarian commercial vehicle industry.

The geographical location of the vehicle industry is also characterized by a considerable concentration in Budapest, although the construction of modern factories in other parts of the country is rapidly increasing. In Budapest, the Ganz-Mávag Locomotive and Railway Carriage and Machine Factory manufactures 6000 kW capacity electric and 2000 kW capacity diesel-electric locomotives and multiple railcars. During its history, this factory has delivered steam locomotives and later diesel railcars to all continents with the exception North America. Other manufactures include water turbines, compressors and more recently lifts. The centre of commercial vehicle production is the time-honoured Hungarian Railway Carriage and Machine Works (RÁBA) in Győr. Transformed from its earlier profile of rolling-stock production, its main products are now diesel engines, and transmission gears rear axles, substantial quantities being exported to the USA, the Soviet Union and other socialist countries. The factory also produces heavy-duty tractors and commercial vehicles. The plants producing buses, heavy trucks and tractors can install the engines and sub-assemblies, produced by RÁBA Engineering into their own products.

The second great enterprise of the road-vehicle industry is the IKARUS Car Body and Vehicle Company, transformed from a small Second-World-War aeroplane factory in 1945. It produces buses for urban and long-distance transport as well as trolley-buses, and exports three-quarters of its production, mostly to the Soviet Union and the GDR. IKARUS buses are running in Europe, Africa and Asia and even in the USA, while assembly plants are operated, in co-operation with Cuban and Iraqi enterprises, in Havana and Bagdad. The factory's main plants are in Budapest and Székesfehérvár. IKARUS maintains wide co-operative relations with the other plants of the commercial vehicle industry, RÁBA in Győr, for example, supplies the diesel engines, and with other engineering branches.

The Csepel Motor Works, located at Szigethalom, produces vehicle chassis (for IKARUS), gearboxes, other components and also assembles them.

The Hungarian motorcar industry does not produce passenger cars, because domestic demand (at around 100 000 new cars annually), is not large enough to justify production in the numbers typical of the motorcar industry today. Domestic demand is therefore met by the motorcar industries of the other socialist countries. At the same time, the increased volume of imports has led Hungary to develop co-operative arrangements with several socialist countries in the large-scale manufacture of certain components, the export of which is set against the import of passenger cars. The Hungarian industry has especially close links in the production of components with Soviet and Polish producers manufacturing car under Italian licence. The most important Hungarian component manufacturer is the Bakony Metal and Electric Works in Veszprém, and its instruments plant in Budapest.

Shipbuilding is also a branch of transport engineering, and is carried out by the Hungarian Shipyard and Crane Company with yards in Budapest, Tiszafüred and Balatonfüred. The enterprise produces primarily cranes, containers and boilers and to a lesser extent river tugboats, and barges. Bicycles are manufactured in the Csepel Work.

(c) The production of electrical machinery and equipment, investment goods and household appliances alike, is a traditional and today extensive branch of the Hungarian engineering industry. About half the output is concentrated in Budapest, where the Ganz Electrical Works produces heavy-duty engines, equipment for electric and diesel-electric locomotives, generators and transformers of up to the 400 kW size. Subsidiary plants have also been established in Kaposvár, Szolnok, Cegléd and Kunszentmiklós, which are gradually counterbalancing the heavy concentration in Budapest. Cables are manufactured in Budapest, Szeged, Balassagyarmat and Miskolc, and other electric equipment in Budapest, Szentes and Szombathely.

The production of modern household appliances – washing machines, refrigerators and water heaters – has a short history, dating back to the late 1950s, when it began to enter the product structure of several plants, but most of these products are produced today in large lot sizes. An important characteristic of this branch is that most of its associated plants and enterprises are located outside Budapest. Washing machines are produced at Téglás (near Debrecen), refrigerators in Jászberény, electric heaters in Pápa, cooling compressors in Eger, and the electric motors for households appliance in Iklád.

(d) Electronic engineering, based primarily on the application of semiconductors, is the most dynamic subsector of the engineering industry throughout the world. Its products can be found, not only in telecommunication equipment, but in practically all fields of modern industry in the automation and monitoring processes of production. This branch is also the producer of electronic computers.

As elsewhere, electronic products occupy an increasingly prominent place in the Hungarian engineering industry. They are not material-intensive, and because of the highly skilled-labour and scientific requirements, a great part of their production is concentrated in Budapest. The concentration in Budapest is also justified by the close linkages this branch has with precision engineering, the instruments industry and component-manufacturing enterprises which are also based in the capital. Nonetheless, to create a more locational structure, plants and component-manufacturing factories using local manpower have been built in the provinces.

Television receivers (including colour sets), micro- and short-wave telecommunication equipment and computer peripherals are produced in Budapest by the ORION Radio and Electrical Company. Radio sets, television receivers and electronic computers are manufactured in Székesfehérvár by the VIDEOTON Radio and Television Company, and tape recorders and other products by the Budapest Radio Engineering Company. Other electronic engineering factories are operated as ancillary plants by the above enterprises in Szombathely, Vác, Salgótarján, Kecskemét and Pécs.

Telephone exchanges are produced in Budapest, and other telephone equipment and railway-safety devices are manufactured in the Budapest and provincial plants of the Telephone Company.

The most important enterprise producing vacuum engineering products is the United Incandescent Lamp and Electrical Company (Tungsram), which, with its incandescent lamps, radio valves, transmitter tubes, semi-conductors, chips and vacuum-engineering machinery has gained a reputation not only in

Europe but throughout the world. Along with its factories in Budapest it has also established several plants elsewhere in the country. The enterprise exports many of its products to all parts of the world, and collaborates with joint ventures companies in Austria, Ireland, the USA and Pakistan. In addition, it has installed several incandescent lamp factories in the Soviet Union, India and Africa.

(e) The most important products of the instruments industry are instruments regulating and controlling oil and natural-gas pipelines, instruments serving nuclear and space research, scientific research and geophysical prospecting, devices for educational purposes, cash registers and, in co-operation with western companies, typewriters.

Owing partly to traditions and partly to the demand for skilled labour and a scientific base, the largest enterprises are located in Budapest, i.e. the Gamma Works, Mechanical Measuring Instruments Company, Electronic Measuring Instruments Company, and the Ganz Measuring Instruments Works in Hódmezővásárhely, a weighing-machine factory, and in Gödöllő a factory manufacturing electricity supply meters.

Among precision-engineering and optical products mention must be made first of all of the various lenses, geophysical and geodesic instruments and spectacle frames produced primarily by the Budapest plants of the Hungarian Optical Company. The production of medical instruments in Budapest, Debrecen and Miskolc also has a special place in the instruments industry and comprises valuable export items. An important role is also played by the instrument-making artisans' co-operatives.

(f) A widely ramifying activity is performed by the industry producing miscellaneous metal manufactures. Its plants are dispersed throughout the country in Budapest, Szécsény, Salgótarján, Sátoraljaújhely, Berettyóújfalu, Kecskemét, Bonyhád and Mosonmagyaróvár. An active part is played in the production of mass metal manufactures by council and co-operative industry and also by the ancillary plants of the large state farms and agricultural co-operatives.

1.7 The chemical industry

The most dynamic sector of Hungarian industry, one closely connected with all aspects of the economy, is the chemical industry, whose output has increased 29-fold since 1950. Its advance is made all the more dramatic by the fact that, compared with the chemical industries of the more advanced countries of Europe, it was comparatively undeveloped until recent times, and was only able to meet the country's demand for a few basic chemicals like sulphuric and hydrochloric acid. A significant step in the development of the industry was the creation of the manufacture of synthetic ammonium and nitrogenous fertilizers between the two world wars, when smaller coal-processing plants, attached to gas factories, were established. Yet oil-refinery capacity was inadequate, an organic chemical industry was lacking, very few of the synthetic materials of the time were produced, and chemical imports were very substantial. The only branch of note was the pharmaceutical industry whose products were placed on the international market as early as the inter-war period. The significance of the development of the chemical industry for the national economy of the country is discussed in the following paragraphs.

a) The chemical industry in a modern economy, and thus in the Hungarian economy, too, performs a „multiplier" function, and the spin-off from growing investments and output exerts an effect far beyond the industry itself, touching all other sectors of the economy and even the non-economic fields. Hence

— it raises the general standard of industry by its exacting requirements in terms of technical and quality levels and skilled labour;

— it stimulates the output and technical level of allied sectors. For example, the equipment demanded by the chemical industry has boosted the development of certain metallurgical processes, such as alloyed steel, and certain engineering branches (though not the production of machinery for the chemical industry and of fittings and instruments);

— because of its high productivity, it is capable of raising the productivity of industry as a whole;

— the transport of certain chemical products, e.g. ethylene is, for safety reasons, possible only in special high-pressure refrigerated cars, and their use raises the technical standards of the transport industry, moreover; the chemical industry has also stimulated the development of the pipeline network;

— the chemical industry also favourably affects the efficiency of several other fields;

— the research demand of the industry gives an impetus to the advancement of higher education, the training of skilled manpower and to scientific discovery.

b) The development of the chemical industry is justified despite unfavourable domestic raw-material endowments and a high import propensity, because of its capability of producing artificial substances, which can effect an improvement of raw-material supply of the country. For example, the paper industry with its heavy reliance on the world market has been helped by the development of synthetic packaging materials. The import of natural fibres is diminished by the manufacture of man-made fibres, while plastics can be used as substitutes for some non-ferrous metals.

c) It is a characteristic feature of several branches of the chemical industry that efficient production presupposes large production capacities. This is partly due to factors of a technical nature, but the practice in countries with a developed chemical industry and world prices also make it necessary. In Hungary, however, owing to the limited domestic market, there is, apart from a few branches typically carrying on small-capacity production, little need or possibility to construct plants of such large optimum size. These limitations can be overcome within the context of the socialist international division of labour — by product specialization, by joint ventures and inter-plant co-operation. Co-operation can ensure that plants of optimum capacity are built in the participating countries, with surplus output being disposed of in the framework of planned commodity exchange.

A further difficulty arises from the fact that the number of the various chemical products runs into several thousands, and although the main sources of material supply are other CMEA countries, expensive chemicals, mostly in comparatively smaller quantities, have to be imported from Western countries. For the pharmaceutical industry, for instance, CMEA co-operation has brought significant progress primarily in large-scale production, but the manufacture of many products has not yet begun, or is on a small scale, and the possibilities remain of developing further co-operation over a wide range of products [2].

Along with the above arguments for and the possibilities of development the problems and constraints on development should also be pointed out. One of the main characteristics of the chemical industry is its capital intensive nature and need for large investments for development. Future development is obviously limited by the ability of national economy to bear such financial strains. A further limiting factor is the rise in the price of the most important raw materials, particularly oil products, while a danger also exists of saturating of the market with certain, mainly petrochemical products, to the detriment of their price structure.

d) Mention has also been made of the environmental hazards of the chemical industry. Many of the chemicals produced are dangerous to man and life in general, and the industry is itself a major environmental pollutant. In the location and operation of chemical plants, environmental considerations must therefore be given a high priority.

e) In 1981 the chemical industry accounted for 19·1 per cent of the gross production value of Hungarian industry, while its share in the energy consumption of industry was 23 per cent. By contrast, it employed only 6·9 per cent of total industrial manpower.

Compared with other branches (cf. the graph in Chapter 1.1), the chemical industry is very capital-intensive, and requires a high level of technical equipment. From an economic point of view it is significant that the primary and finished products, except for oil and natural gas used as raw materials, account for more than 15 per cent of Hungarian imports and almost 10 per cent of exports.

The locational factors of the chemical industry. The chemical industry in general and in Hungary also is located in concentrations rather than in a dispersed form, because of the specific locational requirements of the industry. Formerly, it was located almost exclusively in Budapest and Transdanubia, and except for a few urban gas works, small oil refineries and pharmaceutical plants, the chemical industry had no plants east of the Danube. Currently, however, it is to be found not only in the above centres, but in the Great

Changes in the output of the main products of the chemical industry
(1949 1981)

Product	Unit	1949	1960	1970	1981
Sulphuric acid (100 %)	1000 tons	49·0	164·3	454·4	572·7
Caustic potash	1000 tons	8·1	19·8	67·8	180·0
Nitrogenous fertilizers (in terms of agent)	1000 tons	26·0	57·0	350·0	588·7
Phosphorous fertilizers (in terms of agent)	1000 tons	15·0	45·0	167·0	157·5
Polyvinyl-chloride (P.V.C.)	1000 tons	–	2·0	14·0	157·8
Ethylene	1000 tons	–	–	3·0	262·0
Polyethylene	1000 tons	–	–	5·7	52·9
Chemical (synthetic) fibres	1000 tons	–	0·4	5·6	28·8
Polypropilene	1000 tons	–	–	–	47·5
Benzol	1000 tons	2·0	4·4	14·8	87·5
Tyres	1000 pieces	4·0	250·0	450·0	467·0
Antibiotics	1000 kg	–	216·0	532·0	468·0
B_{12} vitamin (crystallized)	1 kg	–	9·0	508·0	486·0
Synthetic detergents	1000 tons	2·3	8·1	36·3	93·8
Paints	1000 tons	3·6	10·8	56·2	130·6

Plain and the northern regions alike. The reasons for and factors behind the geographical location of the chemical industry are discussed in the following sections.

Raw-materials, almost exclusive coal, were an important locational factor during the earlier phases of the development of the industry. Thus the two nitrogen plants at Pét and Kazincbarcika were based on coal. The former, located on the lignite fiels at Várpalota, represented a significant technological advance in the 1930s, as it was the first synthetic ammonium plant to be based on poor-quality lignite. At the same time some of the smaller coal-based plants were either closed, or their production profiles changed, as was the case with the plant at Dorog, while the oil refinery at Zalaegerszeg was based on the highly-viscous, difficult-to-transport petroleum at Nagylengyel.

— The most decisive locational factor in the chemical industry is *water* The specific comsumption of water is so high that, given the domestic hydrographical endowments, large-capacity chemical plants can only be built in limited numbers. Owing to the present location of the chemical and other water-intensive industries, conditions suitable for the future establishment of large-scale chemical plants are only to be found along the southern sections of the Danube and the Tisza, and in the Dráva region. Plants typically sited close to water are the synthetic fibre factory at Nyergesújfalu on the Danube and the integrated chemical works at Balatonfűzfő beside Lake Balaton.

— The significance of *manpower* as a locational factor varies from branch to branch, and those plants manufacturing basic materials because of their capital intensiveness have little demand for labour. The bulk of their processes are automated and labour is needed only for control and maintenance. If there is a problem it is the need for qualified labour, which is mostly secured by resettlement.

By contrast, plants producing finished products generally employ an appreciable amount of manpower that is easily trained and in the industrialization of the countryside several plants of this type processing synthetic materials and manufacturing household chemicals and cosmetics were located there.

— *Transport* also played a role in the location of the industry in earlier periods. The oil refineries on the Danube at Szőny, Almásfüzitő and the ones located in Budapest which were destroyed during the war or dismantled afterwards were based on oil carried in barges on the Danube.

— Technologically, production in most branches of the chemical industry can be made more efficient if interrelated processes are combined in one complex. In this way equipment is better utilized, the consumption of heat and electricity diminished and transportation costs minimized. Moreover, the by-products from certain processes are used as raw materials for others and wastage is thereby reduced. Some chemical plants are vertically-integrated from the raw material stage to the finished products, while others are built in the form of combination linkages whereby the processes of several products or product groups are joined together. The third form comes into being when complexes, often consisting of a number of plants, are located on one source from which a product suitable for the production of various basic materials can be turned out either in a vertical or combinatory way. The forms discussed above are at the same time locational factors in as much as one technological process exerts an attractive effect on the others.

Production linkages have also played a significant role in the location of all aspects of the chemical industry in Hungary, for instance, the Szolnok chemical trust is based on the vertical integration of sulphuric acid and superphosphate production, attached to which are synthetic cryolite, powder-paint and detergent manufacturing plants. The Olefin plant in Leninváros is sited next to the oil refinery, which provides raw materials for further manufacturing processes.

That the consumer market has had a locational effect can also be demonstrated directly or indirectly, as in the location of gas works, the paint and cosmetics industries of Budapest, and the chemical fertilizer factories in Transdanube, built to serve the more developed agriculture of the Little Plain.

Infrastructure influences the location only of smaller plants, or those that are tied to the public-service network of a settlement. In general, chemical complexes, owing to their large size, have build their own utilities (water, gas, steem and electric current) to meet large-volume consumption and also for operational safety. Other branches of infrastructure are usually built as subsidiary investments. For instance, the development of the chemical industry induces the building of the two new towns of Kazincbarcika and Leninváros, and elsewhere has led to the construction of new housing estates.

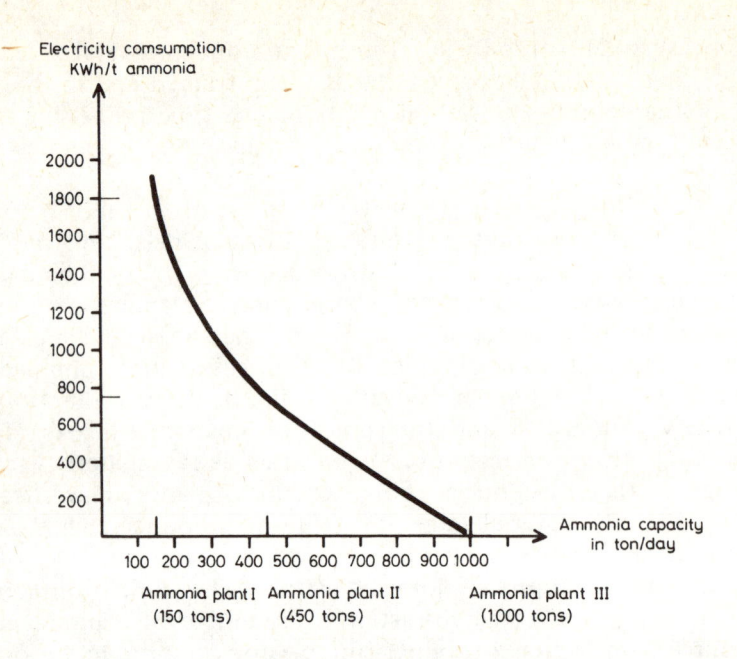

Fig. 30. Correlation between capacity and electricity consumption in the production of ammonia at the Pét Nitrogen Works

The significance of *innovations* as a locational factor is hard to demonstrate, but it certainly had, and still has, a role in the expansion of the pharmaceutical industry in Budapest, and also accounts for the location of the pharmaceutical plant at Tiszavasvár.

Let us now turn to a discussion of the main branches of the chemical industry in Hungary. The inorganic chemical industry has only achieved large volume production in the case of chemical fertilizers, primarily due to the deficiency of raw-materials, although sulphuric acid is produced in large quantities mainly for the manufacture of superphosphates and industrial explosives. Polish and Soviet sulphur and Soviet pyrite are the basic raw-materials used (the plants are in Szolnok, Budapest and Peremarton).

The modernization of agriculture demanded a rapid expansion of the nitrogen industry, based on the production of ammonia (NH_3) and already the whole of the nitrogen industry is based on natural gas. It is a characteristic of this branch that, apart from its basic materials, its economic efficiency is a function of plant size, on which the consumption of electrical energy, one of the most important factors, depends (see *Fig. 30*). In the next decade it is unlikely that any new plants will be built, or existing ones expanded, because it has been agreed that the Soviet Union will supply sufficient nitrogenous fertilizers to meet any increase in Hungarian demand. In return the domestic chemical industry will deliver more specialized products to Soviet agriculture. This solution is favourable to Hungary, because the production of ammonia is more energy-intensive than that of insecticides, for example.

One of the nitrogenous fertilizer plants operating in Transdanubia is the Pét Nitrogen Factory at Várpalota, whose capacity has been built up in several stages. It now produces over one million tons of chemical fertilizers a year measured in natural units. It is supplied with natural gas by pipeline from the field near Kardoskút.

Integrated into the Borsod Chemical Works in Kazincbarcika and the Tisza Chemical Trust in Leninváros, additional nitrogen factories have been built close together in Borsod. The smallest, integrated into the first complex, utilizes natural gas from Hortobágy, while the other, integrated into the second complex, processes natural gas imported from Kissármás in Romania. The first is located on the Sajó river, the second is on the Tisza river and use the electricity of the Tiszapalkonya thermal power station.

The nitrogen industry has radically changed in structure over time. Firstly, it produced only one synthetic fertilizer, i.e. Pét salt or calcareous ammonitrate needing much powdered lime. Although its production is still continuing, currently fertilizers with a higher nitrogen content are more important, for instance, carbonide, which is also used as fodder in small quantities in animal husbandry, or as special, easily soluble fertilizers (for top dressing). Recognizing the requirements of moderne agriculture, a complex (N–P–K) fertilizer is also manufactured. The potassium needed for fertilizer production is processed from potash imported from the GDR and the Soviet Union.

Earlier, the chlorine-alkali industry was rather underdeveloped because of the lack of domestic rock salt and the large amounts of electric power needed for electrolysis. A chlorine-alkali plant is operating in the Budapest Chemical Works, in which chlorine (hydrochloric acid) and caustic soda (NaOH) are produced by the electrolysis of salt. Similar products are manufactured by a plant at Balatonfűzfő, which, besides using them for its own purposes, also supplies other factories.

Caustic soda is needed in large quantities for alumina production, a demand that used to be met by imports. However, a large-capacity plant has been built in Kazincbarcika within the framework of the Borsod Chemical Works, where the manufacture of P.V.C. from chlorine and imported salt, yields caustic soda as a by-product. This production process, although consuming considerable electricity, is indispensable because chlorine imports are difficult to materialize, while the output of the three plants fully covers the caustic soda needs of the aluminium industry, even leaving some for export.

Sodium carbonate (Na_2CO_3) is not manufactured in the country, because the domestic demand is fully met by the large-capacity sodium carbonate factory at Devnya in Bulgaria, in which Hungary made a considerable financial investment.

Mention must be made here of the production of chemicals for agriculture purposes. Since the range of products rapidly changes, progress is usually ensured by the purchasing of manufacturing rights from the large international companies. Agricultural chemicals are manufactured either within the framework of an integrated chemical complex or as part of the pharmaceutical industry. Examples include the Balatonfűzfő works producing herbicides and the Budapest Chemical Works manufacturing selective maize herbicides, while the North-Hungarian Chemical Works, Chinoin, at Dorog and the Alkaloid Pharmaceutical Factory at Tiszavasvár produce various other useful chemicals. Of the other branches of the inorganic chemical industry mention must be made of the Forte Photographic Film and Paper Factory at Vác.

The organic chemical industry is concerned with carbon compounds and their industrial use, as well as with the syntheses of organic compounds.

The processing of chemical from coal, which was once the most important branch throughout the world, has developed only moderately in Hungary. The reason lies in the fact that it was mainly brown coals that were available, which are less suitable than black coal for the production of chemicals. The largest coal-processing plant is operating in Dunaújváros, which produces various basic substances for further processing from the tar gained during the manufacture of coke, and with the construction of a new coking plant, is undergoing further development. With the cessation of the manufacture of coal gas and the closure of the brown-coal distilleries, this branch of the chemical industry is now concentrated overwhelmingly in Dunaújváros.

Oil refining. In addition to the traditional products of petrol, diesel oil, household fuel oil and mazout, the oil refining industry produces petrochemicals, either for further processing or as finished products. Domestic refining capacity approached 12 million tons per annum at the end of the 1970s.

The Danube has already been shown to be an important locational factor in siting oil refineries together with raw-materials. In the case of the Danube Oil Refinery at Százhalombatta, however, which receives crude oil through the Friendship Pipeline, the prime locational factor is nearness to the capital, i.e. it is market oriented. In addition, it ensures the mazout supply of the large thermal power station operating at the same site. It also produces higher octane petrol and, along with the usual cracking products, lubricating oils, orthoxylol and various aromatic compounds within the framework of its petrochemical programme.

The Komárom Petroleum Refining Company operating on the Danube at Almásfüzitő, produces motorcar engine oils along with petrol.

The most recent plant to be built is the Tisza Petroleum Refinery in Leninváros, which supplies low octane petrol mainly for the Olefin plant of the Tisza Chemical Trust.

A smaller and older oil refinery at Várpalota (Pét) is asssociated with a high-pressure chemical plant producing fatty alcohol for synthetic detergent production. The bituminous and high-viscous oil from Nagylengyel is refined at Zalaegerszeg, producing among other things asphalt used as a road-paving material.

The further development of oil-refining capacity depends upon the transforming of the energy structure of the country, although further investment is unlikely in the near future as a pipeline carrying refined products from the Soviet Union has recently been completed. It is, however, possible that new petrochemical products will be integrated into the technological system of certain oil refineries. As part of the recent development programme, the idea of constructing a high-pressure (cracking) refinery has also been raised in Százhalombatta, for although a very expensive investment, it would ensure the more economical production of refined products. A small volume of the products of the petroleum refining industry (e.g. aromatic compounds) is exported to European capitalist countries.

The synthetic materials industry is especially important in Hungary, owing to the scarcity of natural primary materials. Despite this, domestic consumption of synthetic materials developed slowly belatedly as it is an industry which is very capital- and raw-material-intensive. Formerly, the now almost classical synthetics of bakelite, plexiglass and resins were produced mainly in plants located in Budapest, supplemented by the initially small-capacity plant of the Hungarian Viscosa Company at Nyergesújfalu.

The more recent development of this branch, in line with international development trends, has been made possible by the creation of a petrochemical base, which has become known as the so-called Olefin programme [28]. As part of this programme several plants were established between 1970 and 1980, primarily within the framework of the Tisza Chemical Trust and the Borsod Chemical Works. The olefin chemical industry is structured in three stages:

— the first stage is based on the low octane petrol produced by the Tisza Petroleum Refinery from which are derived the basic substances of the olefin process — the so-called double-bond, open-chain — in the form of enthylene, propylene, and C_4 fraction butylene-butadiene;

— during the second stage the above substances are synthesized into polyethylene, polypropylene and P.V.C. by the process of polymerization;

— the third stage produces the finished products, such as foil, pipes, sacks, floor covering, synthetic yarns, carpets, textiles and packaging materials.

During the phase of expansion, the synthetic materials industry was faced with two key problems, namely raw materials and plant size, both of which were overcome under an agreement concluded with the Soviet Union. Given the international technical standards of the time, it should be noted that this was the only way of constructing a large-capacity plant of economic size. An annual production capacity of 250 000 tons of ethylene, 125 000 tons of propylene and 80000 tons of C_4 fraction derived from about one million tons of low octane petrol had to be built. Basic materials in such large volume will only be needed by the Hungarian economy in the distant future.

According to the agreement, the surplus output will be bought by the Soviet Union, who in return will supply various basic petrochemicals, finished products and synthetics. A smaller agreement has also been concluded with Poland. Besides ensuring economical plant size, the olefine co-operation scheme has made it unnecessary to construct plants for the manufacture of products supplied by the partner states and has freed the Hungarian economy from the necessity of making large investments. A further benefit from co-operation, over and above the possibility of satisfying the domestic demand for most synthetic materials, is that the country is freed from several hundred million dollars' worth of western imports can, in addition, also effect exports to western countries.

The basic plants of the olefin process were built as part of the Tisza Chemical Trust in Leninváros. The basic factors in its location there were firstly, the proximity of a thermal power station, providing the basis for a chemical industry, secondly, a new town that was under construction, which ensured the necessary technical and infrastructural background, thirdly, the convergence of the Fraternity gas pipeline and the Friendship II. oil pipeline at Leninváros, fourthly, the existence of a long-distance electricity transmission line from the Soviet Union. The source of industrial water is the Tisza river, although this does constitute a considerable environmental hazard in that the olefine plant is located above the Tisza II reservoir of the Kisköre dam system. The Tisza Chemical Combine produces the ethylene, propylene and C_4 fraction basic to the olefine process as well as polyethylene and polypropylene. It also houses the country's largest capacity for the manufacture of synthetic finished products.

Developed in three stages, the Borsod Chemical Works is the centre of P.V.C. production, each stage representing a step in the technological development of P.V.C. manufacturing. The basic substance of the first stage is acetylene, which is produced by the smallest plant from a calcium carbide, an uneconomical process because of the heavy consumption of electricity; the second, in which the finished product is produced by the partial oxidization of natural gas; the third and the largest stage is that in which P.V.C. is manufactured from ethylene supplied through a pipeline by the Borsod Chemical Combine. Part of the P.V.C. output is used in the production of finished goods, mainly pipes. It is worth noting that capro-lactame, the basic substance of nylon-type synthetic fibres, is produced in the nitrogen plant of the Borsod Chemical Combine.

In the North-Hungarian Chemical Works at Sajóbábony synthetic substances, primarily foam rubber, are produced from imported polyurethane.

Within the framework of olefine agreement, the Tisza Chemical Combine supplies ethylene to a chemical trust at Kalus in the Ukraine by pipeline and propylene and C_4 fraction by rail. In return, the Soviet Union supplies polyethylene, polystyrol, acryl nitrile, ethylene glycol and synthetic rubber. Although the basic raw materials would be available, the creation of a synthetic rubber industry is not envisaged for the time being, partly because domestic demand does not justify the construction of a plant of economical size, and partly because synthetic rubber of different quality would be needed. The establishment of Hungarian synthetic rubber production will only be feasible in the framework of product specialization.

The basis of the Hungarian synthetic fibres industry is the Hungarian Viscosa Factory at Nyergesújfalu. Although the manufacture of viscosa rayon has been discontinued as uneconomical, viscose-based cotton and wool-type cut fibres are still produced. In addition, rayon-type nylon fibres are made from domestic caprolactame and a wool-type polyacryl nitrile fibre, produced from Soviet raw materials. Part of these PAN fibres are supplied to Poland, which in return delivers polyester terylene fibres. Since the domestic manufacture of synthetic fibres does not satisfy internal demand, further development of the plant is justified.

The processing of synthetic materials is carried on in medium- and small-sized plants in various places throughout the country. The largest enterprise is the Hungarian Synthetic Materials Manufactures with plants in Budapest, Debrecen, Szombathely and Kecskemét. In addition, co-operative and private small-scale industries also process synthetic fibres materials, mainly plastic.

The rubber industry is based almost exclusively on imported raw materials. Crude rubber is bought either from Malaysia or through the rubber exchanges, while synthetic rubber is supplied by the Soviet Union, the GDR and the FRG, and blacking by the Soviet Union. The largest plants of the Taurus Rubber Manufacturing Enterprise, the country's only rubber manufactures are in Budapest, where lorry tyres are produced, Szeged is noted for its technical rubber products and Nyíregyháza produces motor-car tyre tubes, tyres for agricultural machinery, and camping articles. The latter two plants were so sited as to tap local manpower. In order to ensure large-scale production, the Hungarian rubber industry does not manufacture tyres for passenger cars, which are bought instead from the countries exporting cars to Hungary, but concentrates on tyres for lorries, buses and agricultural machinery. The Hungarian industry is one the largest suppliers of camping articles to the world market.

A most significant branch of the economy recognized as of world standard also is the pharmaceutical industry with its long-standing tradition. Indeed, Hungary ranks in 11th to 12th place in terms of world output and 6th in terms of exports of pharmaceutical products. Moreover, in terms of per capita value of pharmaceutical exports, Hungary is preceded only by Switzerland. The industry exports two-thirds of its output, comprising 4 per cent of the overall exports of the country. Its products are of high-value as well as being competitive and it constitutes the country's most economical export sector. The Hungarian medical, pharmaceutical and biological sciences provide the research background to this successful branch of the chemical industry.

The raw-material supply is ensured by various enterprises and economic sectors. For instance, Nitrokémia and the North-Hungarian Chemical Works provide important basic substances, as does agriculture with medicinal plants, and the food industry, with products derived primarily from the slaughter industry. Besides domestic sources some basic and semi-finished products are imported mainly from western countries. In order to expand the domestic material base, the pharmaceutical industry has also taken over several smaller chemical plants in Budapest and elsewhere, e.g. the coal distillery at Dorog.

Pharmaceutical production is largely concentrated in plants in Budapest, the most important of which are the Chinoin Pharmaceutical Works, Kőbánya, Pharmaceutical Work (Richter), the United Works of Pharmaceutical Chemistry, also with a plant manufacturing dietic products at Körmend, Phylaxia Vaccine Manufacturers and Human Vaccine Manufacturers.

Of the provincial pharmaceutical factories mention must be made, first of all, of the Alkaloid Pharmaceutical Works at Tiszavasvár, built, as a result of a local enterprise, in the 1930s. Its main product was morphium extracted from the seed capsule of the poppy, with which it dominated world morphium production for a long time. Today morphium production is less important owing, among other things, to the decrease in labour-intensive poppy cultivation. Other products manufactured by the plant are basic substances extracted from medicinal herbs plants and drugs, as well as herbicides and insecticides. In the production of agricultural chemicals, the factory is in a close co-operation with the large British concern, Imperial Chemical Industries, Ltd. The Biogal Pharmaceutical Works, the only producer of antibiotics in the country, was established in Debrecen in the 1950s.

The Hungarian pharmaceutical industry has export connections with practically all countries of the world, developed and developing alike. To preserve existing and to acquire new markets, the industry has, together with the Medimpex Foreign Trade Company, also built up joint interests in the form of pharmaceutical factories and trading companies in the Western countries. Apart from drugs, the sale of licences and patents also yields substantial earnings. To retain its international reputation, the industry maintains a constant programme of research and development so as to be in a position to place new and more efficient products on the market. In the country's economic development programmes, however, the branch has not yet been accorded the priority it deserves.

1.8 The building-materials and construction industries

The building-materials industry is the only branch for basic materials, because the demands of other branches are rapidly growing, e.g. steel structures, concrete bars, pipes and fittings, synthetic materials, and aluminium and sanitary installations. In terms of value, the share of the traditional building-materials industry in the supply of the construction industry has fallen below one-third [4].

Although the building-materials industry can be divided into several sub-branches, there are nonetheless several common factors affecting the development and geographical location of the industry as a whole.

For instance, the building-materials industry uses, in general, large quantities of raw-materials, which during the production process suffer an insignificant loss of weight, apart from the energy sources used. The industry is therefore raw-material-oriented.

Again most of the necessary raw materials occur in large quantities, are easy to extract, and are, compared with the raw materials of other branches, cheap to produce; for instance, clay and sand are the world's cheapest materials. Therefore, their transportation over long distances is too costly and processing is most economically performed on the spot, of the basic-materials industry of the country whose raw materials are, in the vast majority ensured domestically. Relatively few materials, like asbestos and magnesite are not locally available and have to be imported, as do others for which there are strict quality specifications as in the case of iron-oxide-free white glass-sand and fine-grained kaolin. Otherwise the natural endowments of the country ensure a fairly even distribution of the necessary building materials.

The principal task of the building-materials industry is to supply the construction industry. In contrast to other industrial branches this leaves little room for participation in the international division of labour either with regard to the import of raw materials or the export of finished products, the most important of the latter being glass-ware, artistic and sanitary porcelain, and more recently concrete structural elements. As a result of a constantly expanding capacity, the building-materials industry can meet the greater part of domestic demand.

The national economic significance of the sector is not diminished by the fact that the modernization of the construction industry has diminished its demand which also underscores the raw-material-orientation of the industry.

In addition, within the building-materials industry a distinction must be made between the extraction of raw materials, done almost exclusively by open-cast techniques and the building-materials industry proper, which processes them. The two branches are seldom separated geographically in the interest of cutting transportation costs, and most plants of the building-materials industry are on the site of raw material extraction. Extraction without any processing plant is only in use in quarrying and when the raw materials have several different uses, for example gravel, glass sand, foundry sand and mineral aggregates.

The branches of the building-materials industry usually transform silicic and calcium compounds, or rocks containing them, into building-materials, a process needing substantial heat. Most processes are therefore very fuel-intensive, for example, the manufacture of cement, glass, brick, and ceramics. Moreover, some owing to their high heat consumption, are located most economically in the vicinity of fuel sources, for instance, the glass industry. Therefore it was where marl, clay, limestone and coal occurred jointly that the building-materials industry developed, as along the Danube between Dorog and Lábatlan, and around Tatabánya and Miskolc. Formerly, domestic coal was used exclusively as the fuel, but now the use of natural gas and mazout is widespread, especially in the lime, cement and glassware industries, and certain branches are therefore becoming increasingly tied, though fuel imports, to foreign trade.

Water consumption is significant in certain processes, e.g. cement manufacture, but despite this water is less of a locational factor than raw materials and fuel.

A further common factor of national economic importance is the need to minimize the transport of finished products. Even so building materials constitute the largest item of freight transport in the country, amounting in 1979 to over one-third of all goods transported. Although the significance of the construction industry varies geographically, the zone in which building activities are likely to be performed is fairly easily defined. The large centres of activity have attracted concrete-unit manufacturing and, where raw-material supply is ensured, the brick and tiling industry also. As a result of the relatively even distribution of the raw materials of the building-materials industry, efforts must be made when taking development decisions to ensure that the main products of the industry are available in the zone of continued demand.

Lastly, most plants of the building-materials industry issue large quantites of smoke and dust into the environment, and the interests of environmental protection have to be observed in their further location and development.

The mining and quarrying of building materials. Hard and semi-hard limestones are quarried for building and decorative purposes at Sóskút, Süttő, Tardosbánya and Siklós, while the foothills of the Pilis Mountains dolomite and dolomite powder are quarried for the manufacture of plaster.

In mountainous areas of volcanic origin large quantities of hard core are quarried for civil engineering purposes and for road and railway constructions, more specifically basalt in the Tapolca basin, and andesite in the Börzsöny and Mátra Mountains and at Tokajhegyalja.

Owing to the rapid development of concrete and ferro-concrete constructions, and more recently the erection of panel-dwellings, large quantities of gravel are needed. The principal source of this is the bed of the

Changes in the production of major building materials (1949–1981)

Product	Unit	1949	1960	1970	1981
Bricks	in millions	388	1710	1953	1967
Tiles	in millions	119	216	309	112
Cement	1000 tons	552	1571	2771	4635
Lime	1000 tons	226	584	653	457
Drawn-sheet glass	1000 m^2	2060	4588	7827	17121
Glass for the canning industry	1000 t	97	209	893	129·9

Danube, from where it is brought to the surface by dredging. The quantity of exploitable gravel has, however, been declining of late following the construction of hydro-electric power plants on the Danube. Gravel is also obtained from the terraces of the Dráva and Danube, and from former river and lake beds, as at Gyékényes, Ártánd, Makó and Nyékládháza.

The quarrying of other types of minerals is difficult to tie to any particular branch as they are utilized in a number of industrial fields. Yet the building-materials industry as one their main users appears to be the must suitable context in which to discuss them. Their geographical occurrence is the mountains of volcanic origin, where valuable deposits, even by European standards, of bentonite and perlite are exploited. Other minerals, mainly special kinds of sand and clay, can be found in areas of sedimentary rocks.

Bentonite, used by the chemical, foundry and food industries, is found in large quantities in the Pétervásár hill region at Istenmezeje, and in the Zemplén mountain range at Mád.

Kaolin used by the pottery and paper industries, is found mainly at Sárisáp and in the Zemplén mountain range at Mád, Rátka, Szegilong and Füzérradvány.

The most significant occurrences of special-quality sands are quarried at Fehércsurgó where sand for glass manufacture is produced, and at Bicske—Felcsút mines for foundry sand. Clay, suitable for the production of vessels for the chemical industry, is mined at Felsőpetény in the Cserhát Mountain. Hungary is the largest producer in Europe of perlite used primarily by the construction industry for heat insulation. It is mined at Pálháza in the Zemplén range of mountains.

The geographical distribution of the main branches of the building-materials industry:

Brick and tile manufacture. Despite the increasing use of panel and concrete-unit structures in the construction of dwellings and industrial buildings and light-weight structures for commercial and educational buildings, brick for wall-building and tiles for roofing material have not lost their significance. True, the growth of production has slowed down, but brick remains the main building material for family houses and for various traditional types of dwellings and agricultural buildings.

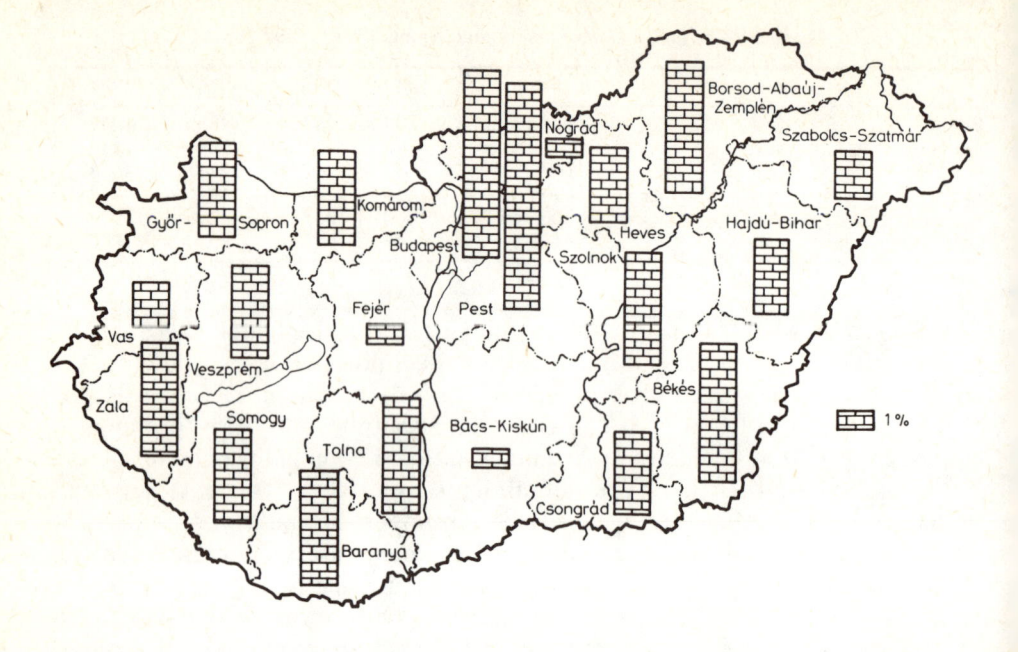

Fig. 31. The spatial distribution of brick manufacture (1981)

Given the geographical endowments of the country, clay is generally ubiquitous, and the branch is therefore quite widely dispersed, although oriented towards the areas of demand. The reconstruction of the brick industry is, however, now under way, and as the number of brickyards declines, so both production and the spatial distribution of the remaining, modernized factories will be more concentrated *(Fig. 31)*.

The largest concentration of the brickyards has developed in the Budapest agglomeration, given the constant demand, and existence of high-quality clay on the north-western and southern peripheries of the capital. Some, however, have recently been closed for environmental reasons, and have been replaced by the modern yards of Solymár, Törökbálint and Őrbottyán, although there are still located in the agglomeration belt.

The Békéscsaba concentration of the brick industry in the Great Plain is based on clay and local demand and all the towns of Szolnok county and the south-eastern part of the plain have their own brickyards. Further significant centres of the industry are Eger, Miskolc, Tatabánya, and Bátaszék, together with most large towns and county seats.

The cement industry best characterizes the material- and fuel-intensive branch of the building-materials industry. Cement is the most important basic substance of the modern construction industry and growth of production is therefore continuous. The demand for cement rises at around 2 to 3 million tons per decade, which means that a new large-capacity cement factory has to be built during each five year plan. Formerly mostly small and medium-sized plants were built, but several of these have now become technically and economically obsolete, owing to their high consumption of energy and low productivity.

During the last five year plan, the capacity of cement industry was expanded with the establishment of new plants on existing locations as at Beremend, Miskolc and Bélapátfalva, which had the advantage of utilizing the existing manpower. The productivity and energy consumption of the new large-scale plants are up to international standards.

The basic raw materials of cement production are either limestone and marl, or limestone and clay [52]. It follows on from this that joint occurrences of limestone and marl, or limestone and clay, are the most suitable sites for the location of cement works, but since these materials occur jointly at many places in the country, locations associated with the third fuel, have proved to be qualitatively the best sites for cement production. Formerly cement manufacturing used exclusively coal for fuel, and plants were based on best-quality raw-material deposits near the coal fuels, for instance, at Tatabánya, Lábatlan, Beremend and Bélapátfalva. The capitalist proprietors of the coal fields were also interested in encouraging such production as the cement works were good consumers of their coal, and those built under capitalism were together with several brick factories in the ownership of coal-mining interests.

As the energy structure of the country was transformed, however, the orientation of the cement industry towards oil or natural gas as fuels was begun. The first cement factory to be built away from the coal basins and located solely upon a raw-material base was sited at Vác. Its fuel is oil, but its location has proved to be far from successful because its raw materials are not satisfactory, the works contaminate the town and the Danube Bend, and the necessary water supply has not materialized. At present the geographical location of cement works, apart from the plainland areas which lack raw materials, is one of approximately even dispersal, yet balanced cement-supplying areas cannot be formed, as plants are not specialized regionally, but on the basis of cement quality, for instance, Vác also produces large quantities of low-quality foundry slag cement. The new works produce mainly Portland cement and, in conjunction with their main users, the concrete-unit and house fabricators, individual cement factories are beginning to develop rational connections with the main consumers.

Gypsum is used as an additive in cement production, and although proportionately a small part compared with the other raw materials, total demand for gypsum has become significant. Workable gypsum deposits occur at Perkupa in the Bódva valley and used partly for cement production and partly for soil amelioration purposes. The fuel satisfaction of domestic demand, however, can only be ensured by gypsum imports from the GDR, Romania and Poland.

Territorially, lime working is closely tied to cement production, as the latter usually have large-capacity lime-burning plants that provide the greater part of lime output. In addition, lime-burning plants independent of cement works operate in the Pilis, Gerecse, Bakony and Bükk mountains.

The production of the concrete and ferro-concrete industry is on the upswing. Its range of products is wide and includes concrete floors, roof supports, concrete pipes and stressed concrete units of load-bearing capacity. The raw materials are cement and gravel, and its geographical location is closely tied to the areas of consumption, with the largest plants operating in the Budapest agglomeration, in the Miskolc area and in Dunaújváros and Szolnok. Special asbetos-concrete elements are produced at Nyergesújfalu. Moulds for the concrete-unit fabrication are manufactured at Kunszentmárton.

The glass-industry has a centuries-old tradition. The traditional small-scale glass-works located in forested areas were replaced at the end of the last century by modern large-scale plants utilizing the gas produced from brown coal. A basic characteristic of the branch is its high energy consumption and, in terms of weight, fuel constitutes a multiple of all the other raw materials, that is why the glass industry is a typically fuel-oriented branch. Consequently, glass factories developed on the various coal fields of Tokod, Ajka, Salgótarján, Sajószentpéter and Miskolc, although they have subsequently changed over to the use of gas as a fuel.

At the same time, oil and natural gas finds have provided new locational possibilities, as with the factory in Nagykanizsa based on the Zala oilfields, and the most recently built ones in Karcag and Orosháza, located on the oil fields of the Great Plain. The demand for glass is rapidly increasing, owing to the expansion of housing construction and of the canning industry, and the glass factories have been modernized and capacities expanded several times. The glass industry is also specialized, with Salgótarján and Orosháza as centres of sheet-glass production, Sajószentpéter and Orosháza those of blow glassware, and Ajka and Parád those of manufacture of fine glassware.

The pottery industry also has long-standing traditions, and is rapidly expanding to satisfy the growing demand. Large plants at Budapest and Hódmezővásárhely manufacture sanitary porcelain, wall tiles are produced at Romhány and industrial porcelain is manufactured at Budapest and Pécs. This industry is also energy intensive.

A special subbranch of the industry is fine ceramics producing artistic chinaware, tableware and fancy articles. After a short period of stagnation, the production of fine ceramics has undergone a rapid development both in terms of the quality and the assortment of its products, and is still increasing. Herend chinaware occupies a prominent place within the traditional branch, while the products of the factories at Pécs (Zsolnay) and Hollóháza are also valued. The youngest large-scale plant at Hódmezővásárhely produces, along with mass products, tableware decorated with folks art motives painted at Kalocsa, while the plant in Budapest produces ceramic articles of commercial quality. The long-standing traditions of folk ceramics survive in the handicraft potteries of Mezőtúr, Karcag and Hódmezővásárhely which manufacture artistic and household articles.

The building industry is a multi-sited branch which changes its locations with construction activity. As such, economic geography does not therefore specifically concern itself with it, although a brief discussion is warranted here.

The building industry is one of the most important branches of the economy. It employs about 7 per cent of all active earners and accounts for 11 to 12 of national income. It contributes to the development of all aspects of the economy, from infrastructure to housing and road development, and disposes of massive investments.

Replacing the former small- to medium-scale, often seasonal, building industry, a large-scale and vertically integrated construction industry has come into being, which has permanent plants in all the large towns as well as operations at large construction sites.

With the development of house construction from prefabricated elements, house-building technology has changed into an assembling and fitting technology. Yards have been established for the production of prefabricated elements, and their siting has been selected according to the criteria of industrial location. Currently, an overall capacity capable of turning out prefabricated elements for 30 000 flats annually is operating in the country, each prefabrication yard having a regional sphere of competence, because the transportation of elements over longer distances would greatly increase building costs. Outside Budapest, with its four yards, yards are operating in the five provincial cities and in several county seats, for instance, in Kecskemét and Veszprém.

The advantage of pre-fabrication yards is the rapid implementation of housing construction, without which it would be impossible to eliminate the still substantial housing shortage in the country. On the other hand, pre-fabricated construction renders the morphology of towns rather uniform and monotonous.

During the past three decades, those regions of the country have been defined where continuous construction will attract the building industry for several decades to come. These are the capital, the five provincial cities, the large industrial complexes, mining centres and the urban redevelopment of towns like Salgótarján and Veszprém. In these regions we can already speak of a building industry of fixed location.

1.9 Light industry

Light industry comprises the textile, clothing, leather, fur, footwear, wood-working, paper, printing and handicraft industries producing primarily the consumer goods demanded by the population. Socialist industrialization, while giving priority to the development of heavy industry, also allowed light industry to expand. Although its share in overall industrial output has declined, production has nonetheless increased over sixfold in terms of value since 1950.

During the past 30 years, as a result of divergent growth rates and development strategies, sectoral shifts and structural changes have taken place within light industry. The paper, furniture, leather and footwear industries have steadily increased in relative production value, while the textile industry has slowly declined, but within it a shift in favour of the knitwear industry has taken place.

The distribution of light industry by social sectors and direction differs from that of the other types of industry. Socialist industry is dominant here, too, but private small-scale industry has remained comparatively common. Within the socialist sector, despite the predominance of ministerial industry, the share of council and particularly co-operative industry is fairly extensive. All this is connected with the tasks that are assigned to light industry in supplying the population. Highly varied activities, closer contact with the consumers, frequent changes in demand and fashion require greater flexibility, which smaller enterprises or those under local and co-operative management are more able to provide.

In 1981, light industry accounted for 15·7 per cent of the gross production value of socialist industry and for 28·6 per cent of the labour force. The utilization of labour by light industry is therefore still very high as it constitutes only 14 per cent when measured in terms of the gross value of its fixed assets and 13 per cent in terms of machinery capacity. Light industry has played a great role in the increase in employment, particularly of female labour, and two-thirds of those employed in light industry are women.

Light industry has undergone great changes both with regard to organization and capital concentration. The clothing industry, which used to be small-scale in character with a few medium-sized plants at the most, has developed into a large-scale industry. Capital concentration has also increased in the footwear industry, although many small and medium-sized plants remain in the council and co-operative sectors. Similarly, the furniture industry has embarked upon large-scale manufacture, as has the paper industry. Despite the multifarious character of the branches of light industry, however, they still have common developmental and locational problems.

a) Light industry has extremely close linkages with foreign trade. Light industry is very import-intensive, and accounts for close to 12 per cent of the imports. This partly derives from climatic constraints, as cotton and tropical fibres have to be entirely imported. Also, for geographical reasons, only a negligible fraction of the country's woodland consists of pine forests, and cellulose production, and the paper, printing and furniture industries are therefore highly import-intensive. In addition, owing to poor pasture, the stock of sheep fed on them is unsatisfactory both in terms of quality and quantity, and can meet only half of the domestic demand. The country also

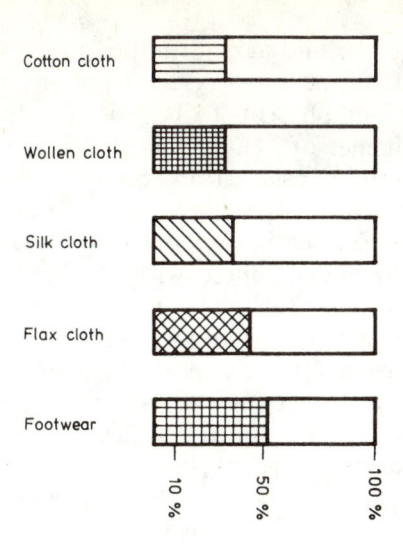

Fig. 32. The export of selected products of light industry (1981)

relies on flax, hide and man-made fibre imports. If we also take into account the constant demand for machine imports needed for technical development – because domestic machine-building for light industry is negligible –, and ancillary imports, it is easy to understand that, as with heavy industry, the development of light industry can only be carried out after due consideration of the possibilities and constraints offered by the external economy. The situation is further aggravated by the fact that the greater proportion of imported raw materials can only be obtained from western and developing countries, i.e. from dollar-accounting markets.

b) Light industry is a significant exporter, with textile, clothing and footwear accounting for 14 to 15 per cent of overall exports. But the economic efficiency of such exports is open to argument *(Fig. 32)*. Products of light industry belong, in general, to the category of cheaper products on the world market, except for a few special articles like luxury ready-to-wear clothing, precious furs and handicraft furniture. Participating in the formation of world-market prices are the developing countries with their low wage-levels, the developed countries with their sophisticated and often automated technology, as well as the other socialist countries. Most products of light industry are exposed to frequent changes in fashion, which also affect the price level. Given these factors, the export-efficiency of the export-oriented branches of Hungarian light industry with their intensive use of labour is often unsatisfactory, despite the substantial technical advances of the past decade.

The greater proportion of the exports of light industry goes to other socialist countries, but they are also significant in overall exports to the West, coming in second place behind agricultural exports. Moreover, since it is in the economic interest of the country to maintain and increase exports to western markets, great emphasis is to be placed on quality and modernity. Decisions of most branches of light industry can only be made after taking international trends into consideration. Some of the large low-wage-level cotton-producers of the developing world, like India, Pakistan, Egypt, and China have themselves become net exporters of mass cotton products, while others export footwear and compete with the light industries of the more developed countries. In the future, it will therefore become necessary to develop strategies, for instance to import rather than to weave cotton yarn or crude cotton fabric, and to re-export them in a processed form, or to seek solutions whereby the labour-intensive production phases are done in the developing countries and only the finished products are manufactured at home; such a possibility is the use of shoe tops made abroad by the domestic footwear industry. These solutions would improve economic relations with the developing countries and also mitigate the manpower difficulties of domestic light industry.

c) On the basis of its traditions, light industry was regarded as a branch of low capital intensity, where the return on capital invested was rapid, the input of labour high and, as a consequence, wage levels were low, for a mainly less skilled female workforce. But, as a result of technical development, the situation has changed, and certain branches of light industry are now highly capital-intensive, as evidenced by the reconstruction of the Hungarian textile and printing industries, and by the investments made in the knitwear and weaving industries as well as in the cellulose and paper industries [56]. Capital intensity still remains low, however, in certain branches of the clothing industry, and of course in the handicraft industry, but these, too, are now using more machinery and other technical equipment than before. It follows from the foregoing that the development or reconstruction of most branches of light industry call for essentially more investment than in the past decades, and a more diversified and selective development is therefore needed in this field, too.

d) When taking economic decisions, it is necessary to take account of that branch for which the available manpower can perform its activity with greatest economic efficiency. Thus it may well be that a significant part of the labour force employed in light industry could be better utilized in other branches, e.g. electronics, and to greater export efficiency. Also given a shortage of labour manpower, it would be expedient to regroup manpower into selected branches, although the implementation of such a policy comes up against several constraints as yet. On the one hand, as a result of recent reconstructions, the labour needed by branches with newly installed machinery has to be secured in the interest of a quick return on the sums invested. On the other hand, owing to the technical lag in various industrial fields, it would not be right, for the time being, to reduce the labour force in those branches that are important from the point of view of domestic supply and exports and redeploy, in other branches which, owing to the present development level and product structure, are, from the point of view of productivity, rather uncertain. Once highly efficiency branches have evolved through the process of selective development, then the redeployment of manpower from light industry will become necessary.

The factors affecting the geographical distribution or the location of Hungarian light industry:

The geographical distribution of domestic light industry is mostly manpower-oriented. The largest spatial concentration occurs in Budapest where, after the First World War, the textile and clothing industries were attracted by low-wage female labour. Manpower-orientation has also been part of socialist practice so as to employ the reserves of female labour in the centres of heavy industry, and light industry has been established by what is called indirect integration in Miskolc, Tatabánya and Dunaújváros, thereby producing a more balanced employment and industrial structure. Under the industrialization programme of the countryside, several light industrial plants were located to use the manpower of the Great Plain and that in other underindustrialized areas.

Some branches of light industry are consumer-oriented, and are therefore attracted to the centres of population as were, for example the clothing, furniture and the printing trades to Budapest with its market of over one million people. The large provincial towns and county seats also have branches of light industry for the same reason.

In the geographical location of light industry the source of raw materials as a locational factor was less important. The so-called fibre industries, processing flax and hemp where loss of weight during manufacture is significant, are oriented towards the producing areas. Hemp requires a warm, dry climate and is grown on bog and alluvial soils in the southern and northern parts of the region east of the Tisza and in south-eastern Transdanubia, while flax demanding a colder climate with more precipitation is found in western Transdanubia and the Little Plain. The processing industries are similarly located. At Szeged, for example, situated in the periphery of the largest hemp-producing area, is also the largest fibre-processing centre. Similar is the location of the leather industry. The slaughter-houses of Budapest as the source of hides attracted the leather industry, while another great concentration can be found in south-eastern Transdanubia, a traditional cattle-raising area.

Transport and transportation routes were locational factors for just a few branches. Some plants of the wood-working industry were located along the Danube and Tisza, because the two rivers provided cheap transport from the forested regions of the country. Other wood-working plants were located near large railway stations and junctions.

As most branches use electricity as a source of power, light industry is generally not attracted to sources of energy. An exception to this rule is the cellulose and paper industry which uses a great deal of steam in the production process and is attracted to locations close to power stations.

In the geographical location of the Hungarian textile industry, capital linkages played an important role. The textile factories of the Little Plain were situated in the vicinity of similar Austrian and Czech enterprises, in a developing region with abundant manpower and enjoying a favourable transportation location.

The role of water as a locational factor makes itself felt only in siting explicitly water-intensive branches, such as the cellulose and paper industry with plants at Csepel, Szolnok, Szentendre and Lábatlan. The fibre and leather industries are also water-intensive. Most light industrial branches have little effect on the environment. Only the wool-washing and fibre branches of the textile industry produce harmful effluents, but are easily degradable. An exception is the cellulose and paper industry which, for lack of adequate water treatment plants, is one of the most serious water- and air-polluting industries.

In summary, the geographical location of light industry in Hungary is characterized, compared with the other industrial sectors, by a balanced distribution. The reasons for this are supplied by the labour-orientation manifested by most of the branches, spatial linkages with centres of consumption and indirect integration. The various government decrees relating to industrial location have tended to urge the provision of job opportunities in underindustrialized areas for which light industry seemed the most appropriate vehicle. In addition, organs of local direction, such as local councils, also made efforts to improve the supply and employment situation in their areas by establishing smaller light industrial plants, while the consolidation of cooperative industry also promoted the process.

Despite these efforts, however, there still remain regional concentrations of light industry and areas where it is less developed *(Fig. 33)*.

The largest regional concentration, though with a declining share, comprises the Budapest agglomeration and within it the capital itself. It is the largest historical centre of light industry in the country, accounting for about 30 per cent of total employment in the sector, and is noted for the textile (cotton), leather, clothing, furniture, paper and stationery, and printing branches. Research and development is also concentrated in Budapest and, what is also a large-city function, the direction of fashion.

Szentendre, Budakalász, Vác and Kistarcsa are significant light industrial centres in the vicinity of Budapest but light industrial plants are to be found in most of the settlements of the agglomeration.

The second traditional region of light industry is the Little Plain, whose share in output has also declined. It amounts to 15 per cent of the wage earners in the branch. The centre of the region is Győr, with such industries as cotton, wool, silk, as well as knitwear, footwear and furniture.

Of the counties in Transdanubia Baranya is worth mentioning with its manufacture of leather, footwear, leather fancy goods and gloves. Less significant and more one-sided is the light industry of Somogy and Zala counties, where furniture and clothing play a dominant role.

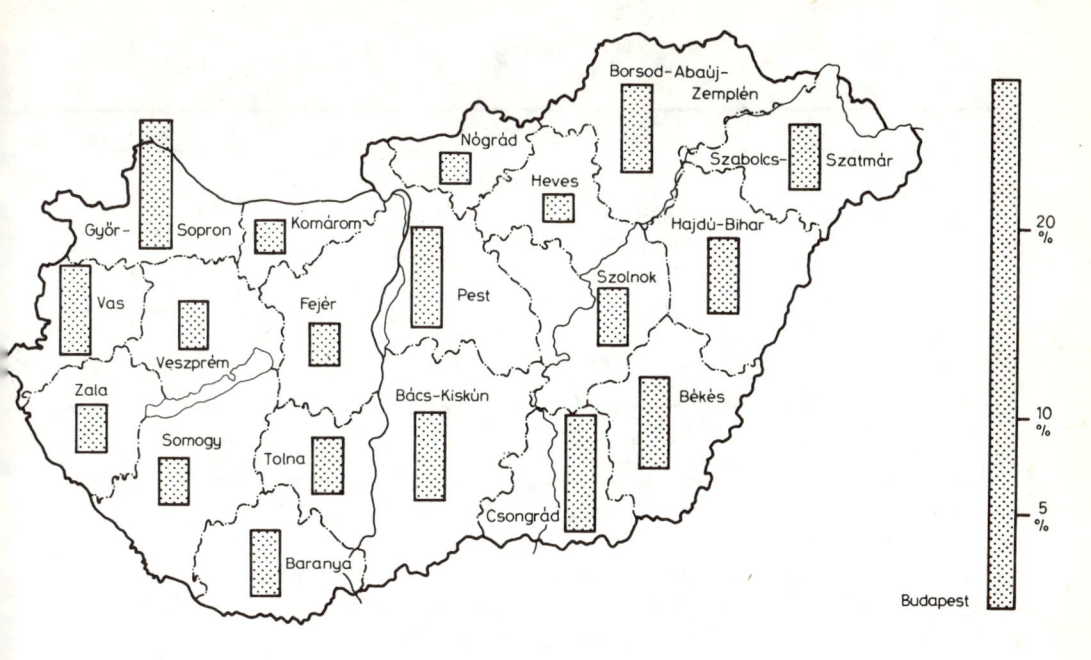

Fig. 33. The spatial distribution of light industry by counties (1981)

While already appreciable, the light industry of the southern part of the Great Plain has exhibited a particularly fast rate of development during the last two decades, and the number of persons employed in the sector in Bács-Kiskun, Csongrád and Békés counties now exceeds the number employed in the Little Plain. Of outstanding significance are cotton-spinning and -weaving, hemp, knitwear, textiles, clothing, woodworking, and furniture manufacture. Important centres are Szeged, Békéscsaba, Gyula, Hódmezővásárhely, Kiskunhalas and Kecskemét. Light industry, primarily clothing and knitwear, is also developing rapidly in the Northern Plain, especially in the Debrecen area of Hajdú-Bihar county.

Formerly, light industry was definitely underdeveloped in the northern counties, but the clothing and textile branches have since become significant, which is not the case in Heves and Nógrád counties.

The geographical distribution and changes taking place in light industry can be summarized as follows:

(a) Textiles appeared rather late in the history of Hungarian industry, but assumed a large-scale character earlier than the other branches of light industry. Since the introduction of economic planning, textile industry has developed selectively. Before the war, the weaving capacity of cotton industry considerably outpaced the capacity of spinning, because the weaving mills owned by foreign capital secured most of their yarn from parent plants

181

Changes in the output of light industry
(1938–1981)

Product	Unit	1938	1949	1960	1981
Cotton yarn	thousand tons	21	25	53	65
Cotton fabric	million m²	146	166	246	319
Woollen fabric	million m²	20	23	32	47
Silk fabric	million m²	12	13	28	59
Knitwear	thousand tons	2	1	7	36
Leather	thousand tons	...	...	20	28
Synthetic leather	million m²		1	7	32
Leather footwear	million pairs	2	4	21	44
Cellulose	thousand tons	...	12	24	32
Paper	thousand tons	55	71	138	457

abroad. In order to restore the balance, new cotton-spinning mills were established during the 1950s in Budapest, Kaposvár, Szombathely, Miskolc and Szeged [3, 87].

Under the influence of internal and external market impulses, the development of the woollen manufacture was speeded up during the early 1960s, and in compliance with international trends, the knitwear industry processing woollen and artificial yarns began to develop. It was also during the 1960s that the use of artificial yarns began to spread throughout the textile industry as a whole, which currently uses man-made fibres to the extent of about 44 per cent.

It is a historical characteristic of the Hungarian textile industry that it was already technically obsolete at the time of its emergence. After the World War I, during the massive establishment of textile mills, the new plants were equipped with spindels and power looms bought from Great Britain, France and Belgium where they had already been discarded, and most were in use up to the mid-1960s. Moreover, even the equipment bought during the 1950s was not of the most modern type. As a result, the Hungarian textile industry was technically the most obsolete in Europe in the mid-1960s, and this situation could no longer be maintained.

In the demand for the manufacture of up-to-date products, the textile industry was faced with great difficulties, as it was impossible for it to produce high-quality products and to improve productivity with its outdated equipment. At the same time, working conditions in the obsolete plants were unfavourable, and owing to the emergence of a general shortage of labour, the textile industry in Budapest and in certain centres of the Little Plain became increasingly understaffed. A comprehensive reconstruction of the textile industry was therefore embarked upon at the close of the 1960s, which culminated during the 1970s, and released about 20000 persons for employment elsewhere. The reconstruction began in Budapest where the situation in the industry was worst, and is still continuing in the large provincial centres, primarily in Győr.

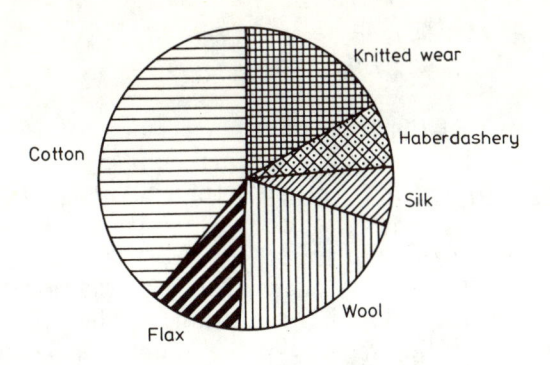

Fig. 34. The structure of the textile industry by major sectors, 1981
(percentage of production value)

The decision to reconstruct the industry in Budapest is, however, debatable. Apart from a few developing countries, the textile industry had been practically removed from large cities, and its reconstruction in Budapest has perpetuated a decades-old situation. In addition, as has already been mentioned, textile exports, especially the exports of cotton products, is still unfavourable and, despite the reconstruction, the structure and quality of textile production have not reached the level of western countries. As a consequence, the reconstruction, instead of leading to an upswing, has brought merely slow progress in a difficult world-market situation *(Fig. 34)*.

The national economy has devoted substantial sums to the reconstruction of textile industry as a high-priority task. As a result, the ratio of automatized machinery has increased, for instance automatized power looms now make up 50 per cent of the total, although it is still unsatisfactory, especially with regard to heavy-duty machines. Following international trends, emphasis has been placed on up-to-date knitting and hooking technologies, and not only have old mills been transformed, but large new mills have been established in the Great Plain at Kiskunhalas and Mátészalka.

The technological cycles of the textile industry are spinning, weaving and finishing, while in the fibre industry spinning is preceded by fibre processing. The integration of the three main cycles in one single mill is rare (it has been realized in the Szeged cotton-manufacturing complex), but the combination of the three phases within one area or centre on a co-operative basis is rather frequent and occurs, for example, in the cotton and woollen industries of Budapest and the Little Plain.

*The main sources of raw material supply
for the textile industry*

The leading branch of the Hungarian textile industry is cotton. The raw cotton, being entirely imported. The leading suppliers are the Soviet Union, Iran, the Sudan, Egypt and more recently the USA. Raw cotton imports are on a significant scale, accounting for about 2 per cent of total Hungarian imports. The sources of cotton yarn imports are Austria, Turkey and Brazil.

The woollen industry boasts a longer historical tradition than the cotton industry. Even before the industrial revolution, woollen-cloth was woven, in the peripheral sheep-breeding regions of the country in Transylvania, northern Hungary, and the Little Plain, and right up to the turn of the century weaving was practiced as a cottage industry in several parts of the country. Reference has already been made to the reasons for the high import-content of the woollen industry, the main source of supply being Australia. Wool is shipped in containers from Australian ports to the Soviet port of Nahodka in the Far East, from where it is transported to Hungary via the Trans-Siberian railway. Further sources of wool supply are Uruguay, New Zealand and Great Britain. Also significant are the imports of so-called woollen tops from western countries, while shoddy is used as well to manufacture products of lower quality. International fashion has shifted towards pure woollen cloths (the Hungarian woollen industry is also a member of Woolmark, the international wool cartel), and it is primarily these high-quality products that are manufactured for export.

Originally, the Hungarian silk industry was based on domestic silkworm breeding in southern Hungary. But silkworm-breeding had already declined before the World War II, owing to a decline in the manpower needed for breeding silkworm and also because of cheaper and higher-quality imports from Japan, China and Italy. For these reasons, silkworm-breeding has come to an end and the last mill producing natural silk in Tolna has closed. The silk industry now relies exclusively on rayon.

The production of rayon began rather early in Hungary, and the Chardonnet rayon acetat factory at Sárvár, which is no longer open, was one of the first factories of its type in Europe. At Nyergesújfalu the manufacture of synthetic silk-type yarn is rapidly growing, although the greater part of the demand is still covered by imports.

In Hungary, just as in most other countries concerned with textiles, the silk industry is the most dynamical branch of textile manufacture.

The flax, hemp and jute branches also have traditions in Hungary and belong to the fibre-processing industry. Raw hemp is entirely produced in Hungary, and although some flax is grown domestically, that of a higher quality is also imported from the Soviet Union and Belgium. The jute industry also uses entirely imported fibres or synthetic threads from Bangladesh and Thailand.

Textile industry also needs large quantities of synthetic fibres, of which less than half is supplied by the Hungarian chemical industry. Artificial fibres are imported from West Germany, Italy, Belgium, Czechoslovakia and the Soviet Union, synthetic cotton-type yarns from Poland and Switzerland and synthetic woollen-type yarns from Switzerland.

A substantial part of the output of the textile industry is exported in the form of fabrics (see *Fig. 32*). The main markets are the Soviet Union, Yugoslavia and West Germany and several countries of the Middle East such as Lebanon and Syria.

The development of the textile industry has taken place parallel with changes in its spatial location. Its two traditional areas, Budapest, including its agglomeration where the vertical integration of spinning, weaving and finishing has evolved in all branches of the industry, and the Little Plain, continue to play a dominant role. Although the first still accounts for over two-thirds and the second for one quarter of the overall output, the number and significance of the provincial centres have also increased. The largest centres in the Little Plain are Győr with cottons and woollens in vertical combination, Sopron where woollens, cotton cloths and carpets are produced, Szombathely with cotton-spinning and -weaving, and the manufacture of household textiles, Kőszeg with the vertical production of woollens, and Szentgotthárd where silk is important.

The largest centre of the textile industry in the southern plainland is Szeged with vertical cotton production and the hemp industry, while the weaving of woollens is also important in Baja. Traditional small centres of silk-weaving are Tolna and Mohács in Trandsdanubia, while Kaposvár with cotton-spinning and Dunaújváros with the weaving of woollens are new centres of the textile industry together with Tata with woollen carpets and Székesfehérvár with cotton finishing. Also worth mentioning is Miskolc where cotton is spinning.

Knitwear industry. This branch belongs partly to the textile and partly to the clothing industry, which justifies its separate treatment. Its technology differs from that of other textile branches, as it concentrates on ready-made products and thus also includes the production cycle of the clothing industry. For these reasons, together with its high productivity, knitwear manufacture has become the fastest-developing branch of textile industry even by international standards. Its development has also been promoted by fashion.

The knitwear industry uses wool, cotton and various artificial yarns of both Hungarian and foreign origin as its raw materials. In geographical location it is fairly widely dispersed, especially when the plants run by local councils and co-operatives are taken into account. The large-scale knitwear industry has traditional and new centres alike. Belonging to the former are Budapest, Vác, Mosonmagyaróvár, Győr, Hódmezővásárhely and Gyula, but the demand for knitwear products has increased to such an extent that new plants have also been established in plainland areas where labour was relatively abundant, as at Kiskunhalas. Indicative of the increased significance of knitwear manufacture is the fact that its products account for one-fifth of the value of the entire output of the Hungarian textile industry. Along with domestic demand, its exports are also considerable with the Soviet Union as the principal buyer.

The clothing industry. During the capitalist period this branch operated as a handicraft industry in the countryside and in the form of medium-sized factories employing 40 to 50 workers in Budapest. In order to use manpower more economically, its reorganization into a large-scale industry was begun as early as the 1950s, primarily by the establishment of several large clothing factories in Budapest. Later on, the clothing industry became an important means of implementing the industrialization of the countryside with the setting up of medium-sized plants employing female labour outside Budapest, and it is in this context that clothing factories have been established in Zalaegerszeg, Kaposvár, Debrecen and Békéscsaba. Otherwise, clothing factories have been created in the heavy industrial towns of Ózd, Dunaújváros and Komló in the framework of indirect integration.

In the development of the clothing industry an important part has also been played by co-operatives, which now embrace the old handicraft industry with its great tradition and superior workmanship. Part of the clothing industry is export-oriented. The most important buyer is the Soviet Union, and sizeable exports also go to western and a few Arab countries. During the last few decades production linkages have also been forged with western department stores in the Netherlands and West Germany and with western clothing firms, for instance Levi's, who commission work from Hungarian enterprises, whereby materials brought in from abroad are processed and exported. Payment is made by the western partner either in foreign exchange or in kind, which has become a significant means of diversifying the supply of the Hungarian domestic market. Another advantage of commission work is that the foreign partner also makes available the necessary equipment, and provides assistance in improving the organizational methods of production.

The *leather industry* used to be one of the country's traditional handicrafts made up of tanners, furriers, saddlers, bootmakers and shoemakers but with the emergence of capitalist production, the leather industry was first to assume a large-scale character.

Currently, the capacity of the leather factories exceeds domestic hide production and the shortfall, especially of raw *oxhide,* is covered by imports from Australia, the FRG, the USA and Canada. Owing to the growing international demand for oxhide, however, imports are increasingly difficult to secure. Sheepskin are imported from Greece and the USA, while most of the materials for the tanning process are also imported mainly from the Argentine. The largest leather factories are located in Pécs, Budapest and Simontornya. The production of artificial leather from a cotton-fibre base is carried on by the Graboplast Works in Győr and its use is spreading rapidly.

The *footwear industry* is a highly important branch of light industry which, along with satisfying domestic demand, also has a significant share in exports. Earlier, the branch was of a typically handicraft character, with a few smaller machine-based shoe-making plants in Budapest and certain provincial towns. The largest shoe factory in the country was built at Martfű in Szolnok county with capital from the Czech Bata firm, its rationale being cheap, mainly peasant female labour.

Since the 1950s, the activity of the footwear industry has expanded with the establishment of new shoe factories, in which co-operatives and local councils have also participated with the result that the branch is now spatially dispersed. The largest centre continues to be Budapest, though his share has greatly diminished. The biggest individual shoe factory remains that at Martfű which is large even by European standards. Kecskemét, Szombathely, Szigetvár and Bonyhád are significant provincial centres of the industry, but shoe factories, over and above the aforesaid, can be found scattered throughout Transdanubia and in the southern and northern parts of the Great Plain. Since the branch exports more than half its output, the main markets being the Soviet Union and Poland as well as several countries of Western Europe, it has become necessary further to improve standards.

The timber, furniture and paper industries. A subbranch of the timber industry is that producing sawn-timber in standard sizes for further processing. The old plants of timber industry date from before World War I, and were based on timber floated down the rivers Tisza, Maros, Vág and Danube or on timber transported as rafts, e.g. the timber-yards at Szolnok, Csongrád, Szeged and Budafok-Háros or on that transportad by railway e.g. the yards at Budapest and Szombathely. The country's largest timber-yard at Tuzsér is based on timber imported from the Soviet Union.

The furniture industry also belongs to those branches of the light industry which have a long tradition of large-scale manufacture. Furniture factories to satisfy consumer demand and using sawn-timber were established in Budapest, Győr, Debrecen and Szeged. At the same time small-scale furniture manufacturing was also at a very high level.

As a result of higher living standards, the explosion in the construction of new dwellings and the changed living conditions and habits of the peasantry, the demand for furniture has increased manyfold. At first industry was unable to meet fully and rapidly the increasing demand either in terms of quantity or quality, but standards have been raised with the reconstruction of old factories and by the establishment of new ones, in most of which large-batch production has been introduced. The expansion of the pre-fabricated construction of dwellings and the demand for built-in furniture have brought about a high-productivity industry. The spatial distribution of the industry has also changed, but Budapest has remained the largest centre. New factories have been built not only in the old provincial centres but also in most large towns of the countryside and in many of the county seats as at Eger, Szolnok, Csongrád, Zalaegerszeg, Nagykanizsa, Pécs and Székesfehérvár.

The *paper industry* is the fastest growing branch of light industry. Its development is justified by domestic consumption with the demand for newspaper and book publications and modern packaging outpacing the pre-war level several times over. Pulp production from imported wood began as late as the 1950s at Csepel, but as it could not be expanded, a solution had to be found by which cellulose suitable for paper manufacture could be produced from raw materials.

The solution is to use straw, although home-grown softwood (poplar) are also utilized. The paper industry, because of its great water demand, is located along rivers or on the shores of Lake Balaton and paper mills are to be found in Budapest, Szentendre, Szolnok, Balatonfűzfő and Miskolc. Other factories that have been built include a straw-cellulose and a corrugated cardboard factory at Dunaújváros, a fine-paper mill at Lábatlan on the Danube and another corrugated cardboard factory at Nyíregyháza. The centre of stationary production is Budapest.

Domestic pulp production is still unable to meet the demand of the paper industry, and substantial imports are therefore still needed from the Soviet Union, Sweden and Finland. Hungary has also taken part in the costruction of a pulp factory at Usty-Ilim in the Soviet Union, which is a joint investment on the part of the CMEA countries. Co-operation has also been established with the paper industry in Slovenia partly by participation in investments in the industry, partly by the export of softwood (again mainly poplar) with paper delivered in exchange. Domestic paper production covers two-thirds of the demand, but the newsprint is almost entirely imported. The sources of supply of the paper industry are the Soviet Union, mainly for newsprint, Finland and the GDR. Owing to the high prices on the world market, paper imports constitute a particularly heavy burden for the national economy. Despite its sizeable growth, however, domestic consumption at 62 kg per capita per year, is still far behind that of developed countries, although it would hardly be sensible to compete with them, given the way in which they squander paper.

1.10 The industrial regions of Hungary

In accordance with the general factors of location, a regional pattern of industry has evolved in Hungary which allows the following types to be identified [30].

(a) The regional industrial complexes are distinctive in terms of the level of industrial development and the internal linkages that encompass the various branches. Although these complexes are smaller than those found in the great industrial countries of the world, yet they share their main characteristics, namely the display of regional linkages derived from the fact that several branches use the same natural resource (e.g. coal, lignite or hydrocarbons), or the processing of products from the same primary industries, for

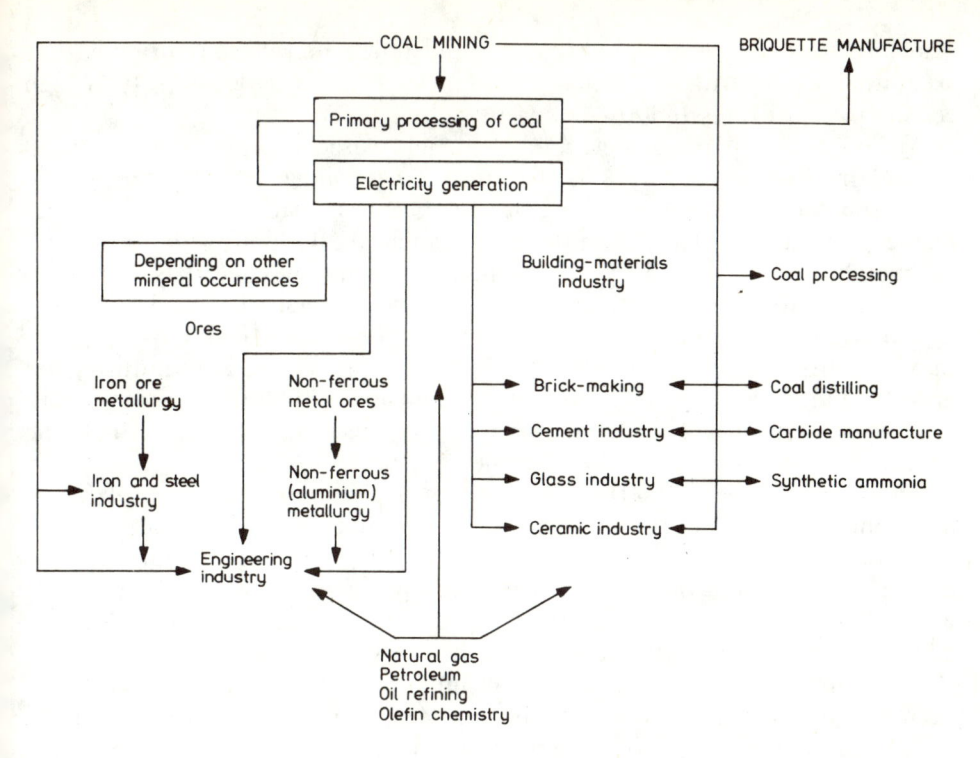

Fig. 35. A scheme for coal-based regional industrial complexes

instance, an engineering industry based on metallurgy, i.e. they are branches of manufacturing industry. It also follows from the regional identity that the various branches comprising the complex make use of the same services (electricity, water, gas and transport), and hence are attached to the same infrastructure network.

Also characteristic of the complexes is the emergence in them of sectoral co-ordination, primarily in the form of vertical and horizontal production linkages, while a tendency towards the integration of production between branches also manifests itself. In the Budapest industrial complex there exist both diagonal linkages, e.g. the engineering and foundry industries are interconnected, and convergent linkages alike. Certain large provincial enterprises also organize component supply for their main products in the latter form (see the Chapter on Engineering industry). Indirect integration makes itself felt primarily in regions of heavy industry.

Most characteristic of Hungarian industrial complexes is the locations of industry on coal field sites (see *Fig. 35*). The pattern emergency from the Figure is clearly recognizable, though not equally manifest in all the various branches. It is mostly the chemical industry and metallurgy, both ferrous and non-ferrous metallurgy and perhaps the foundry industry, that are divergent. Within the silicate industry, glass and porcelain manufacturing appear as mutually substitutive branches. Common to all complexes is their high consumption of fuels and raw-materials.

Although the energy structure of coal field based complexes has changed during the past few decades as fuel oil and natural gas have become dominant, the basic development trends evidenced by each complex have remained unchanged. The heat-intensive branches have uniformly expanded, i.e. metallurgy and especially the chemical and building-materials industries, while manufacturing industry has become more diversified, and less closely linked to the original industrial structure or primary industry of the complex. To promote the employment of female workers, the light industry has also expanded. Within each complex the location of industry forms a distinctive pattern, usually emerging as wedges or in zones around centres. The following complexes can be distinguished:

The Zagyva valley and the Mátra region is a complex where brown-coal and lignite mining, i.e. the basic-materials production of heavy industry, are important. Especially significant are electricity generation, metallurgy, the manufacture of mass metal articles and glass production. Although chemicals are not represented, several branches of the metal-manufacturing industry, engineering, electronics as well as light industry are to be found here, while the food-processing industry, sugar refining and canneries, is a traditional branch. The further expansion of the complex is under way, with the mining of lignite and generation of electricity at Visonta in the east and the mining of non-ferrous metal ores at Recsk in the north. The main centres of the complex are Salgótarján, Lőrinci, Hatvan and Gyöngyös.

The Borsod (Sajóvölgy) complex is noted for its vertically integrated iron metallurgy and chemical industries based on brown-coal mining as well as electricity generation. Further main branches are cement, glass and concrete-unit manufacturing. Natural gas and petroleum have gradually taken over part of the role formerly held by coal in the raw-material and energy base of the region, creating thereby a new situation for the chemical industry. The sectoral structure of the region is one-sided in favour of heavy industry, and the food and light industries are comparatively lacking. The main industrial centres are Miskolc, Ózd, Kazincbarcika and Leninváros.

The industrial zone stretching from Esztergom to Szőny, including the Dorog coal basin, constitutes the basis of the Upper Danube complex. The main branches are coal mining, the building-materials industry (cement, glass, concrete units), paper and man-made fibres, and, on the periphery of the comples oil refining and alumina production. More recently the engineering industry has also become an important branch. The main centres are Esztergom, Dorog, Nyergesújfalu, Lábatlan and Almásfüzitő.

The central Transdanubian complex is based on brown coal found in large quantities in several basins and other mineral raw materials, of which bauxite is the most important. The most significant branches are electricity generation, non-ferrous metallurgy, chemicals and the building-materials industry.

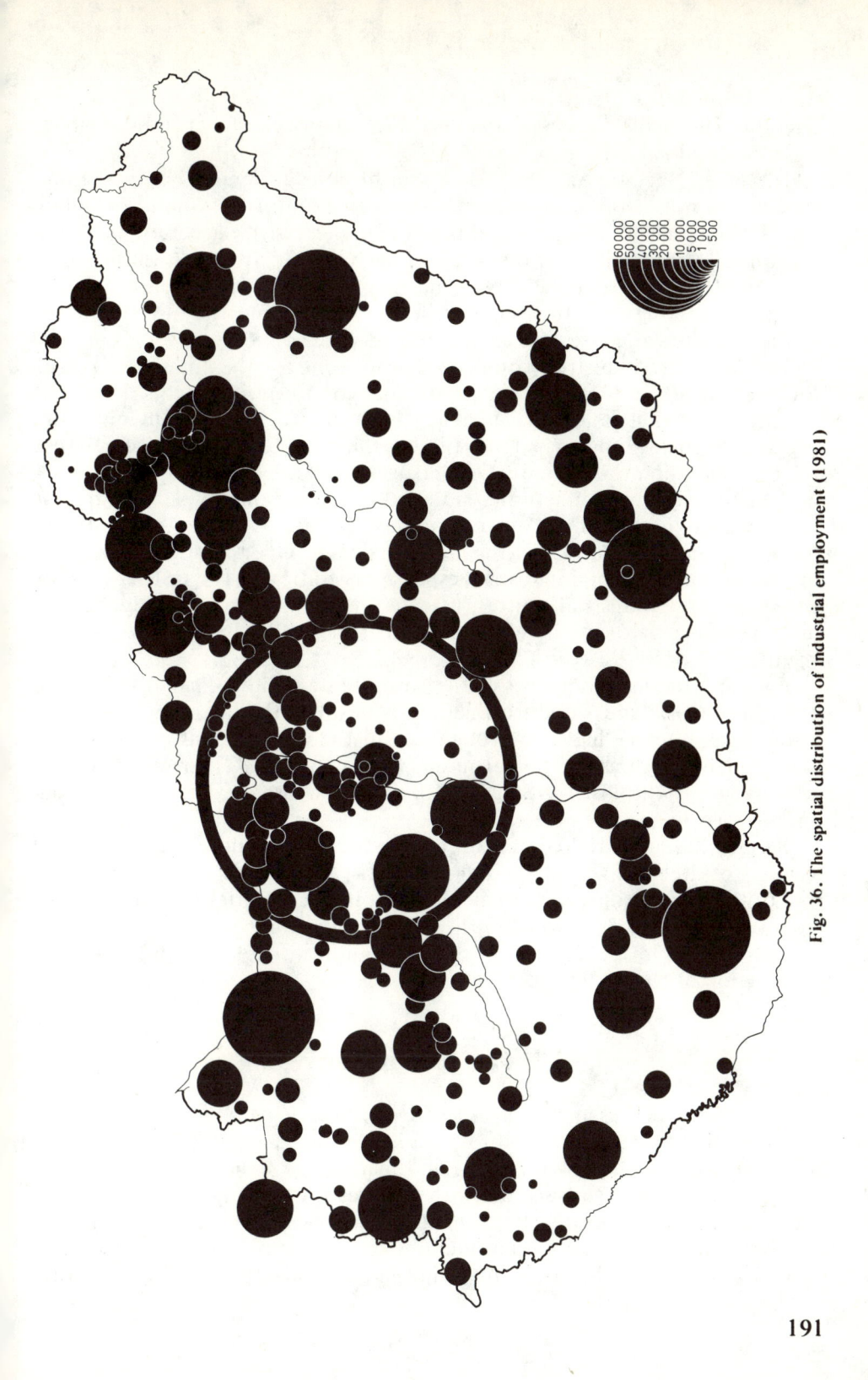

Fig. 36. The spatial distribution of industrial employment (1981)

Another branch of significance is the engineering industry, notably bus production. The main centres are Tatabánya, Tata, Székesfehérvár, Várpalota, Veszprém and Ajka.

The Pécs—Mecsek complex is based on black coal mining, but its sectoral structure is not as onesided as that of the other industrial complexes. Along with the mining of black coal and uranium ore electricity generation and the building-materials industry, the share of such light industries as leather manufacture, footwear, and the timber industry is rather high. Rapidly growing is the engineering industry, but linkages between it and the other branches of the complex are loose. Its centres are Pécs and Komló.

The Budapest industrial complex. The reasons for the emergence of the Budapest agglomeration, the only industrial concentration that is significant by international standards have already been discussed. Especially outstanding are its engineering, paper, textile, clothing and food industries. Within the agglomeration those production linkages have developed.

(b) Districts of manufacturing industry. In this regional type, industry has not emerged in the form of continuous belt but is rather concentrated around industrial centres. Of the industries of the Győr—Little Plain district are the textile and food industries especially significant. The district consists of several large industrial centres, namely Győr, Pápa, Szombathely, Sopron and Mosonmagyaróvár as well as a number of smaller industrialized settlements.

Formerly the main branches of the South-Eastern Great-Plain district were the food, textile and wood-working industries, but the discovery of oil and natural gas reserves has also brought about the development of heat-intensive branches such as the porcelain and glass industries. The most important centres are in the district Szeged, Békéscsaba, Orosháza, Szentes and Hódmezővásárhely.

Besides the industrial complexes and districts, the independent industrial centres of Debrecen, Nyíregyháza, Szolnok, Kecskemét, Dunaújváros and Kaposvár also occupy a prominent place in the spatial structure of the county's industry. Additionally, they exert a great impact on the industrialization of their environs and play a significant role in the industrial production of Hungary (Fig. 36).

2 The food industry

The food industry encompasses the food-producing and -marketing sectors of the national economy. In a broader sense it includes agriculture, the food-processing industry, the purchasing and marketing of their products as well as the provision of these sectors with the means of production and services. In Hungary, with the organization of a modern, large-scale agriculture and the unfolding of mechanized production, new relations have been established among agriculture, the food-processing industry and trade, and the earlier

The share of the food industry in the Hungarian economy
(Percentages)

Share	1950	1960	1970	1982
In socialist product	43	29	25	27
(share of agriculture)	–	–	13	17
In national income	46	30	21	21
(share of agriculture)	37	26	17	17
In number of employed	54	43	27	25
(share of income)	52	39	24	20

one-sided separation is increasingly giving way to co-operation and integration: a modern food industry is taking shape. [41]

In analyzing the territorial division of labour, this process, namely the establishment of a close relationship between the raw-produce and the processing field, has increasingly to be taken into consideration. A significant section of the food-processing industry, i.e. sugar refining, poultry- and egg-processing plants, cheese and butter factories and flour mills, is explicitly tied to large-volume production, with production and processing constituting a territorial production complex. Vegetable and fruit growing and processing, animal husbandry, slaughterhouses and meat-processing plants are developing as definable territorial units. Given this tendency one is justified in discussing the two sectors of the food industry, agriculture and food processing, in conjunction with each other in any consideration of the economic geography of Hungary. At the same time, the spatial approach goes beyond the individual sectors and it is also the intention to analyze the individual components of the territorial division of labour.

A survey of the spatial system of the food industry is complicated by the fact that the individual sectors and enterprises are separated at the administrative level, and one is therefore often compelled to parallel the discussion of the two basic sectors, agriculture and food processing.

The role of the food industry in agriculture. The importance of the food industry in the economies of individual countries is a function of several factors. At given levels of social and economic development, the role of the sector varies with geographical endowments and the size of the available agricultural area. At the same time, at higher economic levels, its relative significance tends to be less, and, for instance, in countries at a medium level of development the share of the food industry in gross national product is generally above 10 per cent, and the proportion of active earners so engaged around 20 per cent. In Hungary, just as in other industrializing countries, output for an industry and its contribution to national income have risen rapidly, while that from the food industry has increased to a lesser extent. Nonetheless, the annual growth rate of 3·4 per cent attained during the 1970s was the highest in the history of the sector and was only just behind the growth rate of industry as a whole. In 1982 the combined share of agriculture and the food processing in the social product was 27 per cent, and in national income 21 per cent.

However, the picture presented by statistical data needs to be corrected, owing to the distorting effect of prices, and if the true achievements of the food industry are to be presented, the role it plays in consumption and foreign trade has also to be examined. Although the quantity of food consumed rises year by year, its share as a proportion of total purchases made by the population shows a slow decline, but still amounts, together with the non-vital articles, to 45 per cent. The Hungarian diet tends to emphasize quantitative satisfaction, and while calorie intake is somewhat more than necessary, the amount of protein consumed is just about adequate. For this reason, consumption habits should be changed from the present relatively high intake of fat, and seasonal consumption of fruit and vegetables to a more healthy diet [95].

The *exports* of agriculture and the food-processing industry are also considerable, amounting to between 20 and 25 per cent of the total exports of the country. More recently, basic foodstuffs have been classified as strategic commodities on the world market, and demand for the more important products, *together* with price levels, are increasing. On the capitalist world market while the price of manufactures rose 1·8-fold between 1970 and 1978, that of agricultural produces, ores and foodstuffs increased 2·2-fold and that of fuel more than 5-fold. Given the dynamic development of the food industry and the moderate growth of domestic food consumption, it is expected that one-third of agricultural output will be exported in the long run, which expresses a heavy export-orientation. A solid foundation for increasing Hungarian exports is provided by the fact products like wines, apples, red pepper (spice paprika), onions, beef, mutton and canned ham are of an excellent quality.

The food-processing industry as an active foreign-exchange earner, has a decisive role to play in maintaining a balance of payments equilibrium with capitalist countries, as industrial raw material and machinery imports from the West are mainly paid for by the export of agricultural produce and foodstuffs.

2.1 Enterprise and ownership relationships in the food industry

The socialist transformation of production relationship in agriculture and the food-processing industry took place at different times and this has had an impact on the development of the two branches.

In the *food-processing industry* socialist ownership relations came into being with the nationalization of industry in 1949, when food-processing plants employing more than 10 persons, small-scale bakeries, dairies, flour mills, and oil-pressing plants were taken into state ownership. Subsequently, practically all the branches of food processing have been characterized by a tendency towards concentration, particularly during the 1960s, when the number of processing plants fell by one-third to 2238, and the number employed in each plant rose from 39 to 99. This tendency was stimulated by efforts to increase economic efficiency and by inadequate investment (lack of capital). This development led to the formation of a heavily centralized, monopolistic enterprise structure, the disadvantages of which became manifest following the introduction of the new economic management system. Excessive plant and territorial concentration caused difficulties primarily when processing was designed to satisfy explicitly local needs, e.g. the baking industry. More recently, decentralization has taken place and more independence has again been given to the individual units making up the trusts and nationwide enterprises. This process has been particularly noticeable in sugar refining and wine production.

Operating now in the food-processing industry, along with close to 200 state enterprises, are nine co-operatives and almost one-and-a-half thousand small-scale private units. To this must be added those agricultural plants, about one thousand, which themselves process their own products.

The establishment of socialist ownership relations in *agriculture*, through the organization of large-scale socialist farms, also began during the late 1940s. First the territorial system of state farms took shape, and then that of farmers' co-operatives. The process of collectivization was completed in 1962, since when state farms and large-scale co-operatives have covered over 90 per cent of the country's agricultural area. 5 to 6 per cent of the arable area is occupied by individual farms of a few hectares in size and by subsidiary activities of a non-agricultural type. They are significant only when the conditions for the organization of collective farming are unfavourable, especially in mountainous, hilly and sandy terrain.

a) One-fifth of the country's agricultural output is provided by *state farms, combines** and forestries whose land and equipment are owned by the state. The 129 state farms and the 15 forest and timber-processing plants occupy close to one-third of the country's arable land and three-fifth of the forested area, respectively. They average 7500 hectares in size, and are equipped with modern machinery.

b) Agricultural co-operatives are voluntary associations of peasants, where the land and equipment are group property. Closely connected with the production of the large co-operative farms are the household plots** of co-operative members, and the two combined constitute the co-operative sector. The 1300 agricultural co-operative farms, with an average size of 4000 hectares, occupy three-quarters of the country's agricultural area, and account for over two-thirds of the gross value of agricultural output.

---

* A combine in the food industry is a large-scale enterprise in which the production, processing and marketing of agricultural produce is vertically integrated. In 1982 they numbered 5.

** Each household plot comprises 0·3 to 0·6 hectares of land, together with animal stock, buildings, equipment serving the activities of the plot.

The social and farm-type structure of agriculture

Designation	Year	State sector	Co-operative sector (including household plots)	Individual and subsidiary farms
Number of farming units	1982	144	1302	1 000 000[1]
Number of active earners (1000 persons)	1982	195[2]	669	189
Distribution of active earners (percentages)	1982	19·0	63·0	18·0
Share of total area (per cent)	1981	30·9	63·7	5·4
Share of ploughland (per cent)	1981	14·4	82·4	3·2
Share of forested area (per cent)	1981	65·5	27·4	7·1
Share of winegrowing area (per cent)	1981	19·3	64·6	16·1
Share of cattle stock (per cent)	1981	16·8	75·7	7·5
Share of pig stock (per cent)	1981	21·5	55·4	23·1
Share of poultry stock (per cent)	1981	7·2	56·2	36·6
Share of total output (per cent)	1981	19·5	70·2	10·3

[1] Estimated figure, of which close to 1 million is the number of subsidiary farms and about 24,000 individual farms.
[2] With the workers of forestries.

	1971	1978	1978/1971
	$/ha		per cent
World	96·0	115·0	119·8
CMEA countries	119·4	148·0	124·0
Hungary	411·4	608·0	147·8
Austria	457·0	521·0	114·0
France	478·0	555·0	116·1
GFR	891·8	981·0	110·0
USA	167·0	191·0	114·0

The above-mentioned dynamic development has brought Hungarian agriculture to a level where it approximates that of the most developed agricultural countries. The importance of agriculture in Hungary as well as its favourable position in the world are well demonstrated by the value of agricultural production per hectare.

The increasing output is shown not only in high yields but in organization of the production as well. During the last 10—20 years not only have production techniques related to the mechanization and use of chemicals in agriculture and factory like production been established, but the effective integration of collective and family farms has been achieved. *Both the division of labour between the co-operative and small-scale sectors* and the implementation of the discipline of market are the most important reasons for the good production results achieved.*

* Including the above-mentioned household plots, individual and subsidiary farms.

During the course of development, large-scale farms have increasingly concentrated on those branches appropriate to mechanization and in 1980, for example, 98 per cent of wheat, 79 per cent of maize and 100 per cent of sunflower cultivation occurred on large-scale farms. By contrast 60 per cent of potatoes, 28 per cent of vegetables, 51 per cent of fruit and 62 per cent of grapes – i.e. the more labour-intensive crops, were produced by small-scale farms. In addition, these also accounted for 31 per cent of all dairy output, 59 per cent of pig meat production, 37 per cent of poultry meat production and 63 per cent from egg production. Such a structure of production contributes greatly towards the profitability of farming, and the rational use of labour and machines. It has been a particularly important social advance, that part-time labour – notably the retired and mothers with small children – can continue to pursue useful work on their private plots. Only 30 per cent of small-scale farms – generally referred to as market gardens in this chapter – belong to co-operative members (household plot), the majority being in the hands of industrial workers, other employees and pensioners (subsidiary farm).

Both large-scale farms and small-scale farms are handled in the same manner by the state. Both receive financial and loan support for specific production purposes, under the same conditions. The prices determined by the state apply to both, although the small-scale farms receive somewhat more favourable treatment over taxation. The owners of small-scale plots can sell their products directly to the consumers or to the state trading units at their own discretion.

Numerous economic interest link the small-scale farms and large-scale farms. The former are provided with seed-grain, breeding animals and fodder by the collective farms. The large-scale co-operatives can help solve the transport needs of the small-scale farms, purchase their produce and offer professional advice as to modern production methods. The mutual connections between the two are organically developing, resulting a wide-scale social satisfaction and increasing agricultural profitability.

2.2 Basic production factors of agriculture

The main production factors of agriculture are *labour, land* and the *means of production,* i.e. *capital.* These three basic factors of production vary with economic development, their relative proportions both modifying and exerting an impact on the territorial division of labour and land use. During the economic development of most countries a decrease in the size of the agricultural labour force is accompanied by increasing capital investment. Although technical development diminishes the impact of the geographical environment, it cannot equalize the impact of different natural endowments in production inputs.

2.2.1 Agricultural manpower

The most important of agricultural production is the working man himself with his production experience and capabilities, and changes in the number and density of population greatly affect the development and territorial structure of agricultural production.

Although the absolute number gainfully employed in Hungarian agriculture increased further during the first half of this century, this number as a proportion of the total earning population nonetheless fell from 60 to 50 per cent, while this relative decline was translated into an absolute fall in numbers by the socio-economic transformation of the economy and rapid industrialization following the liberation. Thus the proportion gainfully employed in agriculture dropped from 52 to 26 per cent between 1949 and 1970. The largest fall, of about half a million, occurred between 1959 and 1965, the period of massive organization of co-operative farms. In 1982 around one million, or 20 per cent of the 5 million active earners in the country worked in agriculture.

Such a proportion engaged in agriculture is typical of medium-developed countries. It is higher than in more industrially developed West Germany, where it is 6 per cent or in France where it is 11 per cent, but lower than in countries at a similar level of development like Poland, where it is 31 per cent, and Yugoslavia, where it is 35 per cent. The figures relate to the year 1976. In Hungary, one agricultural earner produces enough food to supply 10 persons, while the corresponding values for France, Poland and Yugoslavia are 22, 6 to 7 and 6 to 7 respectively.

Occupational restratification of agricultural earners took place in a territorially unbalanced fashion. During the past 25 years the fall in the proportion of agricultural earners was greatest in Vas, Zala and Veszprém counties in Transdanubia, and in Szolnok, Szabolcs-Szatmár and Csongrád counties in the Great Plain, where the agrarian populations declined to as much as one third of their former numbers. At the same time, the number and proportion employed in industry grew faster in these counties than in those of a more industrial character and in this way occupational restratification helped even out the regional extremes in industrial employment. The same, however, has not happened in agriculture, and the differences between the proportion employed in agriculture in Komárom county, the most developed county in this respect, and in Szabolcs-Szatmár and Bács-Kiskun, the least developed counties, has remained unchanged.

The proportion of agricultural earners is higher than the national average in the counties of the Great Plain and also in the majority of those in Transdanubia, being highest in Bács-Kiskun, Békés, Szabolcs-Szatmár, Somogy and Tolna, the counties generally most favourably endowed for agrarian production. In each of these over one-third of earners still work in agriculture today. The lowest proportion is found in Komárom county where it is 16 per cent. In other words, despite the levelling tendencies substantial divergencies still exist in occupational structure, and will continue to do so owing to the variable natural endowments of the contry even though further levelling out is still likely. The low agrarian population density in areas with poor natural endowments calls for a relatively extensive production structure, while employment problems only arise in those micro-regions where unfavourable natural conditions are coupled with a higher density of agrarian population as in the Őrség, South-Kiskunság, and the Nyírség, and where job opportunities outside agriculture are only available in other districts.

Agricultural manpower has declined not only in terms of number but has also changed in age structure with the number of agricultural workers over the age of 60 and entitled to a pension rising from 15 to 46 per cent in earlier years. Although machines have largely replaced manual work, labour shortages nonetheless appear regularly at peak times like harvesting. On the other hand, several farms are unable to ensure full employment for their members throughout the year, particularly in winter.

The picture outlined here of the manpower situation in agriculture in a regional context has to be complemented by noting the changes that have occurred in the skills deployed. Two-thirds of those working in management in the state farm sector and more than on-third in the co-operative sector have university or college qualifications. The number of skilled personnel has thus increased at a rapid rate, but its supply varies considerably between regions and by individual farms. Especially inadequate is the supply of qualified manpower to co-operative farms in areas where conditions are unfavourable, and where qualified labour not only demands a higher income but also living conditions to match its aspirations.

The scientific and research capacity of Hungarian agriculture is up to the best international standards, and the proportion of research workers employed is double that in most countries with a developed agriculture. Human capital, even if it cannot replace the shortage of fixed capital, is likely to become an increasingly important factor in the growth of agricultural output.

Although the overwhelming majority of agrarian manpower lives in the countryside, currently only a minority, 35 to 40 per cent, of the rural population works in agriculture. The majority are employed either in industry or services, and have choosen to remain in rural society, which is in the process of transformation. Many are commuters, who are still tied to some extent to agrarian production partly through their household plot and other subsidiary activities, and partly through family members who continue to live in the village. Moreover, the living conditions and the income relations of the peasantry still working in agriculture have also changed substantially. Some hold the view that with the establishment of agricultural co-operatives the peasantry have ceased to exist, and while this may only become a reality in the long term, it remains, nonetheless, a fact that the manual workers of state farms at least are no longer peasants, and are now classified as members of the working class.

The work performed by the members of agricultural co-operatives has also come closer to that of industrial workers, mechanization and the diffusion of industry-like productions being two examples, and the division of labour in co-operative farms now differs little from that in the other sectors of the economy. Moreover, the income levels of workers employed in state industry and those working in agricultural co-operatives are now more nearly equal. It is the shedding of the peasant character, and the emergence of a new type of worker depending not on property, but on the division of labour and on concrete living conditions that is typical of the Hungarian village today and all its inhabitants.

2.2.2 Land and land use

Land in agriculture is an irreplaceable object and instrument of labour. The size and quality of the land, including its fertility, together with the other factors of production, influence the scale and level of agricultural output. The relatively large proportion of the country's area suitable for agricultural utilization is therefore an important natural endowment. Out of a total area of 9·3 million hectares, only 10 per cent is uncultivated. Land provision is thus favourable, and its productive capacity exceeds domestic demand. Arable land constitutes an estimated one-fifth of the country's assets by value, and the proportion of ploughland, gardens, vineyards and orchards, i.e. the intensive branches of cultivation, ranks second only to Denmark, and the proportion of arable land second only to the United Kingdom in Europe. It is characteristic that while one hectare of agricultural land in Hungary has to ,,sustain" 1·5 persons, in the 16 European countries under review* this ratio is lower only in 4 and higher in 12, among which are Austria with 1·9, Italy with 2·7, the FRG with 4·4, the Netherlands with 6 and Belgium with 6·1 persons.

The country is able to grow all the temperate zone crops that are used for food. It is also characteristic that soil quality differs from one region to another, most being of medium-fertility while about one-third is in need of improvement. The widely differing quality of soils offers different conditions and possibilities for agricultural production. This means that, ceteris paribus, *those farms enjoying more favourable natural conditions will achieve higher yields;* in other words *their input costs are lower and better economic results are achieved than by those working under less favourable conditions.* Under present conditions, this interconnection has remained essentially unmodified by the differing fixed and current assets of individual units and by

---

* The 16 countries included by the Central Statistical Office in its international comparison are Bulgaria, Czechoslovakia, Poland, the GDR, Romania, Hungary, Yugoslavia, Belgium, the Netherlands, Denmark, France, the FRG, the United Kingdom, Italy, Austria and Spain. In subsequent comparisons it is always these countries that are referred to.

Production value of agricultural co-operatives by soil fertility

Cadastral net income (gold crown per ha)	Non-cumulative value per ha of arable land (in forints)	Personal income per member, forints per year
−17·5	14 008	27 887
17·6−28·0	18 866	32 415
28 −	24 992	32 660

other economic factors. The fixed and current capital provision of state and agricultural co-operative farms, and the developmental level of their productive forces are not yet sufficiently high to mitigate the negative effects of unfavourable natural endowments and their impact on crop yields. Co-operatives experiencing unfavourable natural conditions work over one quarter of the country's arable area, and occupy roughly one-third of total co-operative membership. [19].

The effect of soil fertility is so significant that even when analyzed according to the now largely obsolete measure of net cadaster income,* a close relationship emerges between productive level and soil fertility *(Fig. 37)*. Co-operative farms working poor-quality lands, valued at less than 17 gold crowns per hectare, produce per hectare of arable land half the output by value of those co-operatives working the best land valued at over 28 gold crowns. For example co-operatives in the Mezőkovács district in Békés county attain year by year double the production value per hectare of the co-operatives of the Körmend district in Vas county where conditions are less favourable.

A survey of the differentiating effect of soil fertility is given in the table below.

The distribution of land quality is roughly reflected in relief and soil characteristics. Areas with unfavourable natural endowments usually coincide with the heavily leached forest soils in mountainous and hilly areas which have a cool and wet climate. Such areas are the Őrség, Hetés, Göcsej, the lower-Zala valley and the greater part of Inner-Somogy county, Zselic in Western Transdanubia, and the higher parts of the Central Transdanubian Mountains. Poor-quality land also predominates in the Northern Middle Mountains, more precisely along the northern fringes of the Bükk and Mátra Mountains, in the middle sections of the Sajó and Bódva valleys, around the Börzsöny and in the area of the Cserhát Mountains. Finally, mention must

---

* Cadastral net income, as specified in 1875 and 1909, is, assuming average farming conditions, the net income derived from one cadastral acre (0·58 ha), and still constitutes the basis for land taxation. Arable lands were evaluated on the basis of soil fertility on a scale of 0 to 30 gold crowns. Also included in the assessment besides soil quality, were climatic elements and the characteristics of cultivation. This nearly 100-year-old land assessment system can be accepted today only with reservations and needs revision. A new system of land evaluation is now in the process of elaboration, and will classify soil fertility on a scale ranging from 1 to 100.

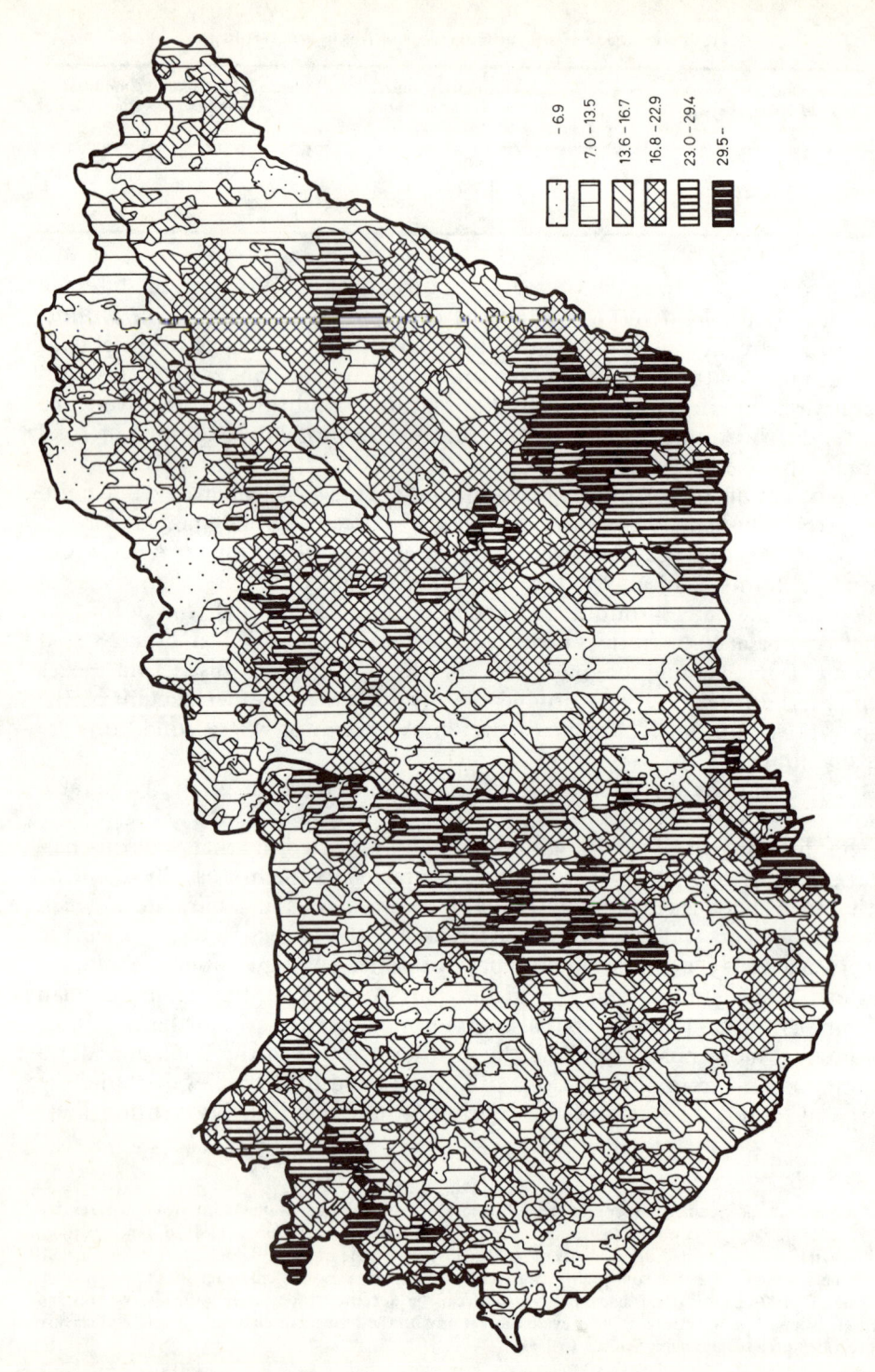

Fig. 37. Gold-crown value per hectare of arable area

The interrelationships among soil fertility, production
value and personal income (selected counties)

County	Cadastral net income	Non-cumulative production value per ha	Personal income per earner
	Percentage deviation from the national average		
Nógrád	− 38	− 40	− 8
Borsod-Abaúj-Zemplén	− 31	− 35	− 18
Zala	− 26	− 37	− 29
Pest	+ 1	+ 75	+ 14
Csongrád	+ 29	+ 3	− 4
Békés	+ 60	+ 8	0

be made of the poor soils of the Danube−Tisza Mid-region and the Nyírség, made worse by the amount of wind-blown sands and alkali soils. Many of the co-operative farms with unfavourable natural conditions can be found in mountain and hill areas of Borsod and Nógrád counties and in the hill regions of Zala and Somogy.

In these areas under question, owing to scarce natural resources, agricultural production tends to be uneconomic and the co-operatives so affected are unable to improve their farming activities and ensure adequate incomes for their members without special state subsidies. The poor relationship between personal income and production value established by soil fertility in the above table is attributable partly to the exclusion of differential land rent and partly to state subsidies. The interconnection between production level and additional investment is also such that returns are higher for co-operatives with favourable endowments than from those with worse than average conditions.

Summarizing, we may say that the effect of soil quality on production level is still an important but not a determining factor. The impact of economic factors, for instance infrastructure, is especially marked in the case of highly efficient co-operatives, but even with those working under less favourable conditions the significance of soil fertility has decreased. In 1967 two-thirds of all co-operatives were regarded as uneconomic, owing to poor soil quality, but by 1972 this ratio has fallen to one half, although it is also true that all the least profitable co-operatives were located in areas with unfavourable natural conditions [19].

The effect of soil quality demonstrably diminishes as development proceeds. This is due, in the case of co-operatives, to significant technical advance with a resulting improvement of farming standards and to conscious economic regulation by the state, which by income withdrawal and subsidization strives to neutralize non-economic advantages and disadvantages (see the Table above).

Land use. The various cultures grown by man produce *distinctive patterns of land uses,* which are distinguished in practice as different branches of cultivation. They are. *ploughland, gardens, orchards, vineyards, meadows, pas-*

Distribution of land-use types

Land use types	1895[1] 1000 ha	%	1935 1000 ha	%	1982 1000 ha	%	Share of land-use type in total value of cultivation
Ploughland	5103	55·5	5601	60·3	4679	50·2	72·0
Gardens	95	1·0	114	1·2	340	3·7	8·4
Orchards	–	–	–	–	121	1·3	9·0
Vineyards	175	1·9	207	2·2	159	1·7	7·0
Meadows	799	8·7	661	7·1	334	3·6	1·6
Pastures	1268	13·8	983	10·6	949	10·2	1·5
Forests	1249	12·9	1099	11·8	1627	17·5	–
Reeds	48	0·5	32	0·3	65[2]	0·7	0·5
Non-cultivated area	528	5·7	603	6·5	1030	11·1	–
Total	9625	100·0	9300	100·0	9304	100·0	100·0

[1] Approximate figures computed for the present area of the country.
[2] Reeds + fish ponds.

tures, forests and reeds. These land uses, together with the areas not utilized for agriculture and forestry, e.g. roads, railways, built-up areas, rivers and canals constitute the total area of the country.

The distribution of land use types is the result of a process of long historical development. The main change following the country's liberation has been the conspicuous decrease in the area utilized by agriculture, primarily ploughland amounting to about 0·6 million hectares. Approximately one half of the area taken out of agricultural use was afforested, the remainder being used by other sectors of the national economy for industrial plants, roads and settlements, often in a wasteful manner. The heavy fall in ploughland, meadows and pastures was accompanied by an increase in the intensive branches of cultivation, i.e. gardens, orchards and vineyards.

When comparing the proportions of the various land-use types with those in other countries, we find a conspicuously high ratio of ploughland, primarily due to the lowland character of the bulk of the country and a comparatively dry climate, which ensure much more favourable conditions for arable farming than other types of land use, like meadows and forests.

A similar picture emerges from a comparison of the total area under cultivation. What is conspicuous, but which in fact is largely due to historical and structural factors, is the relative poverty of forests. For a number of centuries forest land was held to be without value, even hampering development and this is the reason why the forested area has dwindled to the extent that it has. At present forests constitute 17 per cent of the country's area which is small not only relative to the large forested areas of Northern Europe and the Soviet Union, but also to the 25 to 35 per cent forest cover found in neighbouring countries. The proportions of the other land-use types are on the whole similar to those found in other temperate-zone countries with a continental climate.

a) *Arable land* is an area largely under annual plants and ploughed regularly. It is the land-use type most affected by change and is steadily diminishing in extent in favour of other types, notably gardens and vineyards.

Arable crops constitute the basis for agricultural production in all parts of the country, and arable land is generally found in areas of low relief, free from high seasonal precipitation. Proportionately it is most significant in the fertile *lowland areas* of the country, notably in the Békés–Csanád loess regions, where it takes up as much as 80 to 90 per cent of the area *(Fig. 38)*. Good-quality arable land is also to be found on the alluvial soils of the Danube valley. The proportion is somewhat lower in the Danube–Tisza Mid-region, being very low on those areas owing to alkali and sandy soils. In the loess regions of the Trans-Tisza region, especially on the heavy soils around the Körös rivers, a higher proportion of alkali soils is to be found, and pasture slightly diminishes the ratio of arable land. A similar situation occurs in the northern part of the Trans-Tisza region, in the Hortobágy and on the alkali floodplains on the right bank of Tisza, where the ratio of arable land varies between 50 and 70 per cent. In the Nyírség the share of arable land remains above the national average and, despite the sandy soils, the quality is better than in the Danube–Tisza Mid-region. Moreover, the arable land in the north-western part of the Nyírség is the more productive.

In the Bükkalja and Mátraalja of the Northern Mountains that slope down towards the Great Plain, the soils are of medium quality and arable farming predominates. Nor is arable farming entirely insignificant at higher altitudes either, where it averages at least 50 per cent, although the quality of the arable land in the basins and valleys of the hill country is, in general, rather poor.

Arable land covers 50 per cent of Transdanubia. It is, however, the Mezőföld in the eastern part of the region that land quality is best, and the share of arable highest, reaching 70 per cent. By contrast, the proportion of arable is generally average throughout south-west Transdanubia. Of especially poor quality are the arable areas of the Bakony, the Danube Bend and the Mecsek, and indeed of the Transdanubian Central Mountain range in general, where the share ranges from 35 to 50 per cent.

b) The concept of *market gardens* encompasses primarily vegetable gardens, the gardens of family houses and orchards in the inner parts of settlements. More recently, vegetable gardens have been classified as arable land, and orchards now belong to a separate category of their own. The more than fourfold increase in the area under market gardens (together with that of orchards) since 1895 is the most positive trend displayed by this land-use type.

The size and geographical distribution of market gardens are determined by population and settlement density and by relief and soil characteristics. They are most significant in the high settlement-density regions of Transdanubia, on the southern slopes of the middle mountains, in the vegetable-growing districts with sandy soils as well as in the industrial agglomerations.

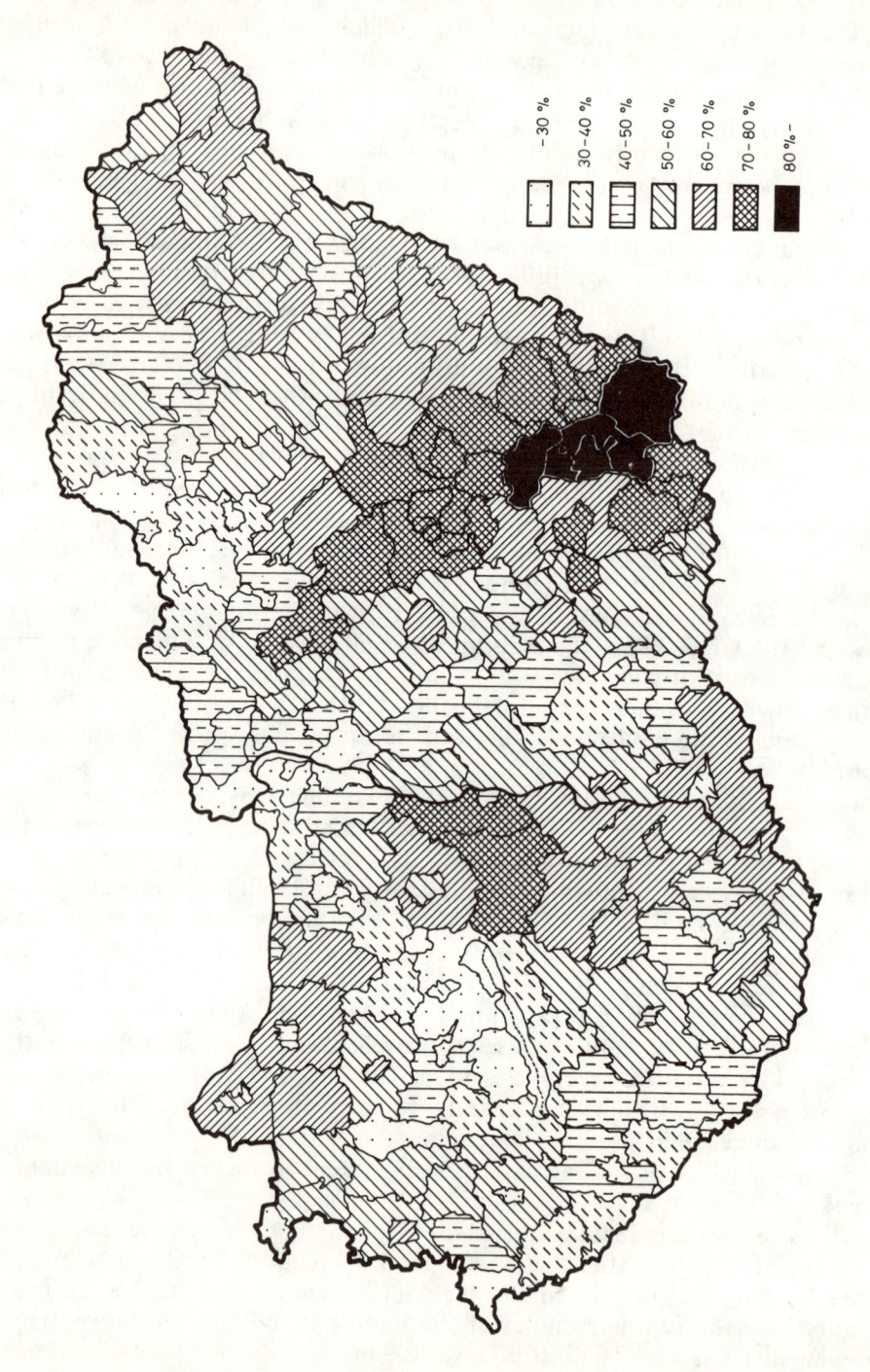

Fig. 38. The distribution of arable land

The proportion of market gardens is extremely high in the greenbelt surrounding Budapest, as well as in the Nyírség and in the Danube—Tisza Mid-region from Cegléd through Kecskemét to Kelebia.

In Transdanubia the higher density of settlements raises the proportion of market garden farming above average in Zala county.

c) *Orchards* account for 1·3 per cent of the total area under cultivation, although the relative value of their production is much greater. The tripling of the area after the war under orchards was therefore an important step towards a more rational utilization of the land. The most important fruit-growing districts are the Nyírség, accounting for one-quarter of the total and the Danube—Tisza Mid-region accounting for another fifth. Along with these two districts fruit growing in Zala county on the southern slopes of the Northern Middle Mountains is also significant.

d) Although the area under *vineyards* is now somewhat smaller than half a century ago, the period has been marked by fluctuations depending on agrarian policy. Typical of the 1970s was again a decreasing tendency, which as regards wine grapes was also experienced internationally. It is interesting that along with the small-scale territorial decrease in wine growing, its geographical distribution has also undergone significant change, with the bulk of cultivation now transferred to the sandy soils of the Danube—Tisza Mid-region. The hilly and mountainous areas, which were important previously, have been occupied for the most part by market gardens and orchards and to a lesser extent by arable land.

The geographical distribution of the country's wine-growing regions is much more concentrated than that of arable land and market gardens, being particularly associated with Bács-Kiskun and Békés counties. Viticulture is discussed in more detail in chapter 2.2.6.

e) Geographical change in the distribution of *meadowland* regularly mowed for hay has been closely connected with water regulation. This is because most meadowland is low-lying, and drainage can make much of it suitable for arable and pasture utilization. A rather large decrease in meadowland had therefore already set in by the turn of the century and this process is still continuing.

Relatively speaking, decrease has been largest in the Great Plain, just in the area where the supply of fodder for the animal stock poses the most serious problems. The most extensive and also best-quality meadowland can be found in Mid-Transdanubia and the Little Plain, where it constitutes the basis for intensive cattle breeding. Outstanding within these regions are the Hanság, Nagyberek, Little Balaton and Sármellék with 20 to 22 per cent of their areas under meadows, although grass quality is rather poor especially in the regions of Little Balaton and Nagyberek.

Another area of substantial meadowland is the Danube—Tisza Mid-region. Although grass yields from the sandy and alkali soils is rather moderate, they nonetheless constitute an important basis for the supply of fodder to the region's animal population as the poor sandy soil and the dry climatic conditions do not favour fodder grain production. Other significant areas of meadowland are the flood plains of the Tisza, Hernád and the Bodrog rivers.

The standard of meadowland utilization is, however, rather low, because the better meadow areas are used for other purposes and the rest are neglected.

f) *Pastureland* is also a constrained land-use type, although no general decrease in area comparable to that of meadowland has occurred. Nonetheless pasture constitutes the most neglected type of land use in Hungary, and utilization has remained at a very low level.

Pastureland occupies one-tenth of the country's area and can be found mostly in the Great Plain, especially on the extensive alkali soils of the Hortobágy and Körös valley. They are, however, of poor quality and cannot support a significant animal stock. Most of the pastures of the Danube–Tisza Mid-region, being on sandy soils, are also of inferior quality, and in places are exposed to the danger of deflation. In mountainous and hilly regions, by contrast, as in South-West Transdanubia and the Bükk Mountains there are usually more and relatively better-quality pastures, although in the highest areas there are barren pastures and poor-quality sheep runs [16].

g) The proportion of *forested area* is, compared with 1935, slowly increasing, a result of the afforestation policy of the last quarter of century, although it is still very low by international standards.

Of all the land-use types forests exhibit the most concentrated geographical distribution, partly due to the relief characteristics of the country and partly due the fact that during the Middle Ages the greater part of the contiguous forested cover of the Great Plain was cleared. Forested areas are located mostly in the Central Mountain range, the most forested counties being Komárom with a 25 per cent cover, Heves with 28 per cent, and Borsod with 24 per cent. Above-average proportions can also be found in Vas, Nógrád, Somogy, Pest and Baranya counties, while the lowest proportions (2–2%) occur in the Middle and south-east Plain, notably in Csongrád and Békés counties.

86 per cent of Hungary's forests are composed of deciduous trees 14 per cent pines, with oak making up 23 per cent, beech 7 per cent, acacia 18 per cent and poplar 11 per cent of this total. The national economy's demand for timber is 10 million cubic metres annually, 75 per cent of which is now covered by domestic production. Today, as forest resources on a world-wide scale diminish and timber becomes more expensive, the principal aim of Hungarian forestry policy is to decrease timber imports, which still make up a significant 10·0 per cent of all imports in terms of value. As part of this policy, forests are being planted with higher yielding trees, while flood plains unsuitable for agricultural purposes are being reforested.

h) The area of reeds and waters suitable for breeding fish and water fowl, or for irrigation purposes, has increased significantly since the turn of the century. In drained and reclaimed areas fish ponds have been established. The exploitation of the reeds that grow around Lake Velence, Lake Fertő and the Little Balaton, and their use for building or their processing for industrial purposes are of great importance.

i) Relative change in the *area of the country not utilized for agricultural purposes* has exceeded that of any other land-use type, and parallel with the decrease in agricultural land use has been a rise in the uncultivated area amounting to 500 000 hectares. Such trends can also be seen in other countries, especially in those with higher population densities than Hungary. In certain heavily industrialized countries, such as Belgium, Great Britain and West Germany, this process has occurred at a very fast rate indeed.

During the period of vigorous economic growth in Hungary, a large-scale increase in non-agricultural land use has occurred as a result of not only positive factors, for instance, the establishment of new industrial and agricultural plants, residential areas and the construction of roads and canals, but also often in the wake of unjustified policies, that squandered land. Thus a great part of the area lost was good agricultural land, despite the need to feed an increasing population and step up agrarian exports. It is for this reason that a law providing for increased protection of agricultural land has been prepared. Additionally the economical use of land is now stimulated by the appropriate economic means of price and rent. But despite these efforts only partial results have been achieved as of all factors of production in Hungary agriculture land is the cheapest. Seen among the cost factors of industrial and infrastructural investment the price of sites usually appears as an insignificant item, and neither the price nor rent of building land are limiting factors. On the other hand, in the case of high-priority state investments, usually covering an extensive area, the cost of the site is charged to the state budget. This is the reason why, despite several prohibitions, agriculture unjustifiably loses more land each year.

This spatial survey of changes in land use has revealed, despite the existence of interwoven and opposing factors, *a general reduction in the regional differentiation of land use and an equalization of regional disparities.*

This trend asserts itself, of course, as part of the general process of agricultural intensification, and results therefore in the spread of more intensive forms of land utilization. The extent to which equalization can go in the longer term is, however, questionable, taking into account considerations of regional efficiency and the persistence of certain differences is desirable.

In this context, *the extent of equalization is generally constrained both by the most economical use of the forces of production* and by such natural endowments as differences in soil fertility, but is not in the least constrained by *specialization in agricultural production.*

The development of agricultural production necessitates a certain modification of the pattern of land use, as the present structure of land use is neither the only nor necessarily the most economical one.

The protection of agricultural land. With technological development the significance of land as a factor of production generally decreases. After a certain level of development has been achieved, technology ensures the increases of yields necessary to maintain the food supply of a given country from an ever smaller agricultural area, making it possible to concentrate production on the best land. At present, however, the main problem facing the world economy is that population is growing faster than the rate of development of the world food industry. Therefore, the demand for agricultural products, along with energy sources, tends further to expand, as does their price level. As regards Hungary, all this *necessitates the maximum use and the increased protection of agricultural land, the country's most significant natural endowment,* for the more and better the land a country possesses, the greater is its growth potential.

In Hungary there is very little agricultural land already in use from which expanded reproduction could not be realized. The growth of production, given average inputs, can only be ensured by a specific production structure even in regions with poorer natural endowments, such as hill areas. Therefore leaving fallow a relatively large proportion of arable land each year, i.e. up to 3 per cent, is, in general, unjustified. The loss of production from arable land left fallow can be replaced only by significant investments elsewhere. The aim is not to leave unused lands with unfavourable natural conditions, but rather to increase the efficiency of production from them. This implies only the exceptional withdrawal of land from cultivation. At the present stage of development it is necessary, firstly, to reduce the loss of agricultural land to the lowest possible level by a rational land-use policy and, secondly, to preserve or intensify the productive capability of all lands available as well as to eliminate or improve their unfavourable natural conditions.

About 20 per cent of the country's area is exposed to soil erosion by water, and 10 per cent by wind. Thus, from among the tasks relating to *soil protection*, the two vital issues invariably in the foreground are the protection of the soil from water erosion and from deflation.

Erosion washes away an annual average of 1 cm of surface soil over an area of about one-and-a-half million hectares, causing damage of the order of billions of forints, and corresponding to 0·1 ton of nitrogenous, 0·05 ton of superphosphate and 0·1 ton of potash fertilizers per hectare. The middle mountains and the hill country of Transdanubia are most heavily exposed to erosion, where considerable damage is caused by run-off to nearly 0·5 million hectares.

The successful implementation of soil conservation programmes calls for a complex regulation of catchment areas, as well as for the application of soil-fixing and run-off-prevention measures, for instance, the construction of terraces, cultivation along contour lines and afforestation.

Wind damages mainly sandy soils loosely bound together by vegetation and poor in humus content, together with loose bog soils. The fixing of nearly 1 million hectares of loose sandy soils in the Nyírség, Danube—Tisza Mid-region and inner-Somogy, and an increase in their productive capacity constitute important aspects of land improvement. One possible method is a change-over from low-productivity pasture or arable farming to more intensive cultures such as vineyards and orchards, and occasionally to afforestation and irrigated market gardening. But even in the perspective of 20 years it is unrealistic to assume that the large expanses of sand of the Danube—Tisza Mid-region or the Nyírség, will be completely transformed. On the one hand, demand will not increase to such an extent and, on the other, the investment cost and other conditions of such a large-scale undertaking will be difficult to ensure.

The utilization of the land is better served by *soil improvement,* which continually transforms the characteristics of the soil and increases productive capability. Assuming a normal level of soil fertility, varied production can be carried on 55 to 60 per cent of the soils of the county. Poor-quality alkali and blown sand soils, amounting to about 40 to 50 per cent of the land area, and certain heavy acidic forest soils poor in nutrients as well as bog soils could be made appreciably more productive by effective amelioration.

More than half the soils with unfavourable characteristics are acidic forest soils found mainly in the region of the middle mountains. Heavy acidic soils needing improvement and amounting to about 1 million hectares are to be found predominantly in Vas, Zala, Somogy, Nógrád and Borsod-Abaúj-Zemplén counties.

The amelioration of the country's alkali soils is an important and high-priority task. Two-thirds belong to the so-called solonetz type of the Trans-Tisza region, and the remainder to the structureless sodic alkali variety, the so-called solonchak soils of the Danube—Tisza Mid-region. Their extensiveness, together with the wide range of types exhibiting different qualities as well as the high cost set rather strict limits on the improvement of these alkali soils. The blown sands, bog, and acidic forest soils covering about eight times the area of the alkali soils, constitute the other types needing improvement. Their amelioration is much cheaper and simpler, and promises more rapid success. For this reason, the improvement of alkali soils can only be of secondary importance from the point of view of the national economy, compared with other soil amelioration tasks.

The task of improving soil fertility only really got underway after the socialist reorganization of agriculture. The overwhelming majority of the soils improved each year, amounting to 35 to 45 thousand hectares, is acidic forest soil, and the geographical distribution of soil improvement thus mirrors the distribution of acidic soils. About half the soil improvement schemes carried out during the past few years have fallen in Vas, Zala, Somogy and Borsod-Abaúj-Zemplén counties.

Irrigation. Along with soil protection and improvement, irrigation also promotes the better, the more efficient utilization of the land area. High-level agricultural production can only be achieved by an equally high standard of water provision. This requirement, increasingly stressed throughout the world, receives special emphasis in Hungary owing to the characteristics of the climate.

Irrigation by land-use types, 1950–1981

Year	Total irrigated area (1000 ha)	Rice	Arable land	Meadows, pastures and others	Market gardens
		Irrigation as a percentage of the total area irrigated			
1950	33	46·0	23·0	15·0	16·0
1970	109	21·0	41·0	17·0	21·0
1975	156	17·0	55·0	22·0	6·0
1981	184	7·0	60·0	30·0	3·0

About a quarter of all agricultural land is subject to drought, and the introduction and expansion of irrigation systems are a precondition for reliable production. Altogether about 2·5 million hectares can be irrigated economically. Of this area less than one-fifth, i.e. 0·4 million ha, is equipped for irrigation, but of that only a third has perennial irrigation plant installed. The area annually irrigated is less than the existing irrigation capacity, but higher than the area irrigated by perennial irrigation plant. Moreover, the area fluctuates widely according to weather conditions.

Vigorous changes have taken place not only in the area irrigated, but also in the geographical distribution of irrigation. While before the end of World War II. the leading role was played, strangely enough, by Transdanubia where precipitation is comparatively high, irrigation has gradually shifted towards the dry regions of the Great Plain over the past decades. The construction of the two dams at Tiszalök and Kisköre has promoted the development of irrigation in the Tisza valley, and Tiszalök, Kisköre, Sajfok, Kőtelek, Millér, Tiszasüly, Ludvár, and Algyő irrigation systems were built one after another. The two dams also generate electric power on a minor scale and in addition, have shipping and reservoir functions.

A further important task of the Tiszalök dam is to supply water through the Eastern Main Canal to the Körös river system. The Eastern Main Canal traverses the basin of the Trans-Tisza region following the fringe of the Debrecen loess plain which separates the Nyírség from the Hortobágy. The Tiszalök dam, together with the Eastern and Western Main Canals, provide irrigation for an area of 120 000 hectares.

When the larger Kisköre dam, adjoining the Jászkunság and Nagykunság irrigation systems is completely filled in 1985, a further 200 000-hectare area will be irrigated.

The area most demanding of irrigation is the *Mid-Tisza region*, and Szolnok county, with its large rice fields, is the most irrigated area of the country. One-fifth of the country's irrigated area and half the area of irrigated rice are located in this county, but proportions of irrigated arable land and pasture are also high. The irrigation systems of the Mid-Tisza region derive water from rivers and canals through pumping. Although the water resources of the area are very restricted, the construction of the second Tisza reservoir and the build-up of the new irrigation systems in the Jászság and Nagykunság will enable irrigation further to expand. The 90-kilometre-long branch of the Nagykunság Main Canal, which connects the Tisza river with the Hortobágy–Berettyó Canal, supplies water to the most drought-prone areas of the Great Plain.

The Upper-Tisza region also needs extensive irrigation, and systems have been built in conjunction with the Tiszalök dam system and the Eastern and Western Main Canals. Dominant among the cultures irrigated are lucerne, maize, sugar beet and rice with a combined share of 50 to 60 per cent of the crops irrigated.

The region comprising the lower section of the Tisza river, the right bank of the Maros river and the Körös valley hardly lag behind the above areas, as regards irrigation. Here climatic conditions, notably high temperatures during the growing season and long periods of sunshine as well as relief and soil characteristics are particularly favourable for market gardening and irrigated rice growing. Two-thirds of the irrigated area is to be found in the Körös valley.

On about 50 per cent of the irrigated area of the *Danube–Tisza Midregion,* which includes part of the Central Industrial District, market gardening is carried on, which makes the region significant in the growing of vegetables. This high-income branch of irrigated agriculture has been made possible by the proximity of the capital. Additionally, contiguous irrigation areas have developed only along the Kiskunság Main Canal between Tass and Akasztó, the remaining areas being isolated and supplied either by canals draining surface water, i.e. the Dömsöd flood canal and the main drainage canal of the Danube valley or by underground sources.

Just as in the Great Plain, a central irrigated area has also developed in Transdanubia, i.e. in the Hanság, where the extensive irrigation of meadows and pastures is carried on and in the Szigetköz of Győr-Sopron county where irrigated vegetable cultivation is to be found.

Irrigation in *the Central Danubian district* is carried out primarily along the Sárvíz canal and in the Nagyberek–Balatonaliga area of Lake Balaton. Here, too, meadow and pasture irrigation is substantial, but market garden irrigation also plays a significant role in supplying the resorts of the Balaton with vegetables.

By contrast, irrigation is of lesser importance and lowest in proportion in the *south-west and south-eastern parts of Transdanubia,* owing to the more favourable precipitation conditions.

In the *Northern Industrial Region* irrigation is less developed than in the lowlands. Along with some irrigation of meadows and pastures irrigated market gardens are to be found at the foothills of the Mátra and Bükk Mountains, often organized as joint co-operative undertakings. The systems established in the Hernád and Sajó valleys are used predominantly for vegetable irrigation to supply the populations of the nearby industrial centres.

Simultaneously with the expansion of irrigation, a considerable change has also taken place in its *structure* and while the irrigation of field crops and vegetables has grown at an average rate during the past few years, the area of irrigated meadows and pastures has increased more rapidly. Another example of change is the beginnings of the irrigation of fruit and grape cultures. By contrast, rice cultivation has been declining since the 1950s. Of the irrigated field crops, the proportion of intensive cultures with a higher yield per unit area has grown at a faster than average rate, particularly with regard to lucerne, sugar beet and maize. While such trends have enhanced the effectiveness of irrigation, its economic efficiency still leaves a lot to be desired.

The maximum water requirement of planned irrigation projects can be fully secured in the *Danube valley*. By contrast, at the time of low water in the *Tisza valley*, supplies will have to be supplemented in 80 per cent of cases. Of the possible supplementary systems, besides local reservoir possibilities, the conveying of water from the Danube through the construction of a *Danube—Tisza Canal* seems to be the most economic solution.

2.2.3 Means of production

The means of production constitute the third production factor of agriculture. Following collectivization, mechanization came increasingly into the foreground as the number of agricultural wage earners abruptly decreased, and the area under cultivation continued to diminish. The replacement of lost agricultural productive forces is still tying up significant investments. During the 1960s, for example, only about half the investments made in fixed assets created new capacity, the rest covering the agricultural assets lost to production, i.e. land, labour and implements. It was only after that investment went increasingly towards the setting up of modern establishments and the creation of technological systems. In Hungary, 1973 was the first year in which the sum spent on machinery purchases approximated the sum spent on buildings.

The main trend of agricultural development in Hungary is aimed at increasing crop output per unit area, and is accompanied by a high asset-use intensity. Four-fifths of the assets of the food industry, which amounts for 18 per cent in terms of value of the total fixed assets of the productive branches of the national economy, fall to agriculture and one-fifth to the food-processing industry.

Of the fixed assets of agriculture, including forestry and water management, the share of immobile assets – buildings, constructions and plantations – is very high at 75 per cent. By contrast, the share of machinery and vehicles, making up 23 per cent, is low. Compared with the agricultural co-operatives, the fixed-asset supply of state farms is one-and-a-half times greater per unit of labour and twice as great per unit of land.

The value of fixed assets per unit area varies widely geographically ranging by more than 100 per cent between Borsod-Abaúj-Zemplén county with the lowest, and Pest county with the highest value. The areas with meadow and loess soils tend to have above average values as do Pest and Komárom counties with their locational advantages, while the fixed assets of farms located on the forest soils of the hilly and mountainous areas of Vas, Zala, Somogy, Nógrád and Borsod-Abaúj-Zemplén counties is lowest. It is worth noting that the regions with extensive sandy territories, that is, with unfavourable soil characteristics, have average levels of fixed-asset supply owing to a high proportion of plantation cultures. On the other hand, as the proportion of grassland increases the asset stock diminishes. The picture presented here is rather distorted by the fact that the most important asset, land, is assumed to have no value. If the land asset were to be evaluated realistically, however, it would certainly modify the territorial picture presented above.

The regional differences in agricultural output and asset supply embrace several interrelationships of an opposed character. Generally *more favourable economic results are attained with a higher than average supply of assets*, their efficient use improving in parallel with the rise of production. But asset supply above a certain level only produces a moderate rise in incomes as demonstrated by the fact that the rise in state farms incomes tends to occur at only half the rate of that of co-operative farms. Moreover, a weak territorial association can be observed between a high supply and unfavourable fixed-asset utilization. The efficient utilization of assets is significantly influenced by land quality and on loess soils, for instance, the net production value per 1000 forints of fixed assets is about one and a half times the national average. Consequently, the utilization of assets is much better on good soils, while their asset supply precisely because of this greater efficiency, is smaller.

On poor land, on the other hand, a larger quantity of assets is necessary because of lower efficiency, but as low efficiency influences investment in a negative direction, poor crop yields are both the consequences, and determinants of the reproduction process. The only way out of this vicious circle is by establishing an asset-specific production structure which can be adjusted to natural endowments. The current system whereby the farms on poorer land are subsidized by the state, although important, is nonetheless unsufficient to generate an economical production structure and therefore cannot be regarded as a long-term programme.

The *energy basis* of agriculture has been completely transformed over the last few decades, and *mechanical traction power* has supplanted the draft animals and manual labour of earlier years. Parallel with this has been the increasing use of grid-transmitted electricity. During the 1960s, the main task was to increase the number of tractors and combine harvesters to ensure the mechanization of cultivation and the harvesting of bread grains, but this has now given way to the needs of complex mechanization, i.e. the evolution of such machine systems as allow the mechanization of all phases, including processing, of the production of a given crop or branch.

The degree of the mechanization in Hungarian agriculture is, by international standards, at a *medium* level only. During the past decades, however, the energy applied to each hectare of arable land, market garden, vineyard and orchard has grown more than threefold in Hungary and Romania, and by two-and-a-half to three times in other CMEA countries. Although the rank order for European CMEA countries as established by this indicator has been modified, Hungary is in a favourable situation comparable with that of Romania and Poland.

Although the number of tractors has remained practically static over the past decade at 55000, tractive power has increased by more than 30 per cent because of the rise in the number of heavy-duty tractors brought about by the expansion of machine systems. Tractor supply and tractor density are at about the world average, but of the 16 countries used for international comparison Hungary ranks last with respect to tractor supply. (It should, however, be noted that the figures for capitalist countries also include small-performance garden tractors, which are not typically found in socialist countries. The different stock composition thus aggravates international comparison.)

There are no substantial regional variations in the level of supply, there being a 25 per cent difference in tractor capacity between Zala and Veszprém counties, on the one hand, the best supplied and Fejér and Borsod-Abaúj-Zemplén, on the other hand, the least favourably supplied. The spread is neither substantial, nor consistent, and appears to depend not on direct needs but rather on the accumulation capabilities of individual cultural units. The 6 to 7 per cent excess tractor capacity of the hilly and mountainous areas in Somogy and Nógrád counties, when compared with the national average, is not in proportion to the 30 to 40 per cent excess need for mechanical power resulting from the 5 to 15 per cent gradients typical of these regions. This above-average need for mechanical power calls for a cost input far above the average, amounting to 20 per cent in areas with slopes of 7 per cent and to 35 per cent in areas with slopes of 11 per cent. Since yields are comparatively low, the high cost level is not accompanied by rising incomes, which helps account for the economic inefficiency of field-crop cultivation in areas poor in natural resources.

Otherwise, the mechanization of the most important field crops and garden cultures is more favourable by international standards. For instance, the mechanization of harvesting is 100 per cent in the case of grain and 96 per cent for sugar beet and 50 per cent for potatoes, respectively. Significant progress has also been made in the complex mechanization of animal breeding and in the market garden sector as well as in loading and transportation.

Chemicals, primarily fertilizers, belong to the non-renewable input assets of agriculture. A direct relationship exists between the use of fertilizers and crop yields, and as their use in Hungary has gradually increased, so have average crop yields. This relationship has been particularly evident since 1970 in the case of wheat and maize. The increase in fertilizer utilization was dynamic and generally well-balanced up to 1975, when consumption per unit area of arable land reached that of countries like Great Britain and France, but since then consumption has tended to stagnate and even fall back as a result of rising fertilizer prices.

During recent years, utilization has come to vary *regionally* also. Specific consumption is highest in Transdanubia, and is about 30 per cent above the national average in the counties of Fejér, Tolna and Komárom. By contrast, consumption is comparatively low on the Great Plain and in the Trans-Tisza region, and is lowest in the Northern Industrial Region where, despite the existence of two fertilizer factories, it is only slightly above a third the level in Fejér county.

The regional differences in fertilizer utilization are generally attributed to natural endowments, notably the distribution of precipitation, whereas the level of fertilizer consumption is primarily connected with the intensity of cultivation, and only secondarily with natural endowments. That the distribution of precipitation utilizable for field crops can nonetheless be identified as a geographical determinant *is due to its greatly divergent efficiency of fertilizer consumption.*[*] *As regards regional differences in the efficiency of fertilizer consumption, they are, basically, a function of the quantity and distribution of precipitation.* For example, whereas in those counties with the highest precipitation, i.e. Győr-Sopron, Vas, Zala, Veszprém and Somogy, efficiency averages 73 per cent, in the plainland counties with low precipitation quantity and uneven distribution as in Bács-Kiskun, Békés and Szolnok, it is only 34 per cent. It is due exactly to these spatial variations in the efficiency of fertilizer utilization that the general relationship between fertilizer consumption and crop yield does not assert itself consistently, and high consumption is often associated only with *medium yields*.

The development of *agricultural infrastructure* has paralleled, although not at a satisfactory rate, mechanization and the use of industrial products. The spread of factory methods to agriculture, especially during the 1970s, set new rural infrastructure requirements as regard to transport, telecommunications, machinery repair facilities, electricity and water supply, and grain and fertilizer storage. The demands have indeed been met in the industrially developed agrarian areas in the vicinity of urbanized regions, for instance, around the capital and in Komárom county, as well as in those parts of the Great Plain which are supplied with good transportation facilities, and has become an important generator of dynamic agrarian development. By contrast, agricultural advance on the loess soils of the country, of crucial importance to overall agricultural production, has not been followed by the development of infrastructure, in other words, the region with the most

---

* Fertilizer efficiency expresses the percentage of surplus yield produced by the use of 1 kg of mixed fertilizer over and above biologically possible crop maximum.

favourable endowments have tended to lag behind agriculturally. At the same time the low level of infrastructure in rural areas with adverse endowments has definitely hampered weak co-operative farms striving not to lag behind their stronger brethren and in their attemps to adjust their production structures to their endowments. [44]

Thus, at its present stage of development, agriculture has generally become infrastructure-sensitive without thereby impending the infrastructural development of individual districts, and of the environmental conditions effecting individual agricultural units, infrastructure has become a crucial factor. This explains why it is not the plainlands with their very favourable soils, but rather the counties of Pest, Komárom and Győr-Sopron with their good market locations, co-operative relations with industrial plants and capacity to satisfy infrastructural demand which rank first in agricultural development.

2.3 Spatial location of the production sectors

The basis of food production is plant cultivation, the products of which can be consumed either directly, or converted by animal husbandry, or processed by industry. Agriculture-plant cultivation, animal husbandry and market gardening – also provides the basic materials for the food processing industry and raw materials (hemp, wool and hides, etc.) for light industry.

The two basic sectors of the food industry, agriculture and food processing, have generally developed in accordance with the demand, but the latter sector at a more rapid rate. Thus the significance of the processing industry within the vertical structure of food production has grown in terms of value from one-fifth before 1945 to two-thirds today. While subsistence economy farming has decreased, the processing of agricultural products has risen to meet increasing consumer demand. This has led to the emergence of new industries like deep-freezing and to the rapid development of others, e.g. the poultry, meat and canning industries. But this development has not always been smooth and the growth in the capacity of the processing branches has not always followed the expansion of primary production. Especially inadequate are freezing and storage capacities, which constitute a source of substantial loss.

An important characteristic of the spatial location of the food-processing industry is the territorial dispersal of individual branches, a fact connected with the relative significance of the various locational factors, i.e. labour, energy, and water but especially *the transportability and transport costs of raw materials and finished products alike*.

Those branches in which the raw material is fully incorporated in the end-product, or which have a high water intake, making the weight and the transport costs of both raw produce and the finished product are virtually identical, are usually located at the consumer market. Such branches are the breweries, bakeries, large dairy farms, and wine and soft-drink bottling plants. However, in the majority of the food-processing industry the raw material loses much of its weight and only a small proportion is incorporated in the end-product: in other words the transport cost of the raw produce greatly exceeds that of the end-product. Such branches, which include sugar refineries, poultry- and egg-processing plants, cheese, butter and milk-powder factories, vegetable- and juice-canning factories, are therefore located at the source of the raw produce. Processing industries located on both a raw material and consumer market basis alike are flour mills, slaughterhouses, meat and canning factories [21]. Despite the fact that regional concentration was least evident in the food-processing industry, over one-third of the active population thus engaged nonetheless worked in Budapest in 1960. Since then considerable change has taken place and the policy of decentralizing from the capital pursued during the last decade and a half thus resulted in a considerable increase in food processing in the provinces especially in the Great Plain. Indeed, this sector has been instrumental in taking industry to backward regions. The regional link-up between the processing industry and primary production has become even closer as „vertical integration" has spread, which has further helped to weaken the territorial concentration of the processing industry. Currently, there are, besides the capital, three counties, Bács-Kiskun, Pest and Borsod-Abaúj-Zemplén, which stand out because of their above-average concentration. Otherwise the food-processing industry has a balanced and evenly dispersed distribution [1].

Along with the even spatial distribution, plant concentration, and enterprise amalgamation has greatly increased following the reconstruction and the establishment of large new enterprises. As a result, the raw produce and production districts of factories have expanded and transport costs have increased.

Another characteristic of the change that has taken place within agriculture is that animal husbandry has developed at a somewhat more rapid rate than crop cultivation. The share of the former in total output has risen to 50 per cent, but nevertheless lags far behind the 60 to 70 per cent share achieved in countries with a developed agriculture and factory methods of livestock breeding. This moderate development is connected with the large investment-intensity of animal husbandry and with the greater expertise that it requires.

Although the relative significance of animal husbandry has increased, the cultivation of crops has a somewhat greater impact on the regional development of agricultural production. This is attributable to the fact that within animal husbandry it is the fodder-consuming pig and poultry sectors, which have mostly developed, i.e. those which are geographically tied to the main crop-growing regions.

With growing production and an expanding technical basis, the *vertical integration* on the farm has increased during recent years, comprising industrial services related to agricultural production, food processing and direct marketing, summarily referred to as subsidiary or complementary activities. This is all the more a welcome development because for a long time economic management interpreted the division of labour and specialization in a one-sided fashion confining agriculture to primary production. Two decades ago, co-operative farms were not allowed to own tractors, to engage in the mixing of fodder, or to sell their products directly. The large agricultural enterprises laid the foundations of their processing activities during the second half of the 1960s, the first combine to concern itself with production, processing and marketing being the Tokajhegyalja Wine Combine founded in 1971. The construction, machine repair and other servicing activities are now organically fitted into the production profile of large agricultural enterprises, and according to the data for 1981, 34 per cent of the net incomes of large agricultural enterprises are derived from non-agricultural activities. These enterprises operate over 2300 units concerned with such things as milk, poultry and egg processing and distilling, 90 per cent of them are also engaged in the construction industry and around 60 per cent in timber processing [41].

It is a pity that, because of a lack of capital, the proportion of subsidiary activities is low precisely in those districts where they would be of great assistance to farms with unfavourable endowments.

The proportionate shifts in the structure of production have also brought about changes in the spatial distribution of individual branches. While livestock breeding was formerly most important in Transdanubia, especially in its western and southern counties, today, while these regions are still of prominent significance, a new area of livestock breeding has now developed in the counties of Békés, Csongrád, Hajdú-Bihar, and Szabolcs-Szatmár, in the Trans-Tisza region. This change is the consequence of an inner structural shift, whereby, pig and poultry rearing has developed faster then cattle breeding, typical of Transdanubia as in Baranya, Tolna, Veszprém and Zala, the structural proportion of the main branches has also changed, primarily again because of a moderate growth of cattle breeding.

The structure of *cultivation* has also shifted towards more intensive forms. The area and production value of fruit and vegetable growing have expanded considerably, while the share of industrial crops and the area under fodder has also grown somewhat. By contrast, the acreage of bread grains, which was dominant in the 1930s, has significantly fallen as a result of higher yields. (The territorial implications of these structural changes are discussed in the section on the main branches of agriculture.)

0·15 per cent of the agricultural area of the globe belongs to Hungary, while the volume of its agricultural production represents 0·7 per cent of world output. Hence, its share in production is four to five times its territorial share. The developmental level of agriculture, measured by international standards, places Hungary immediately behind the agriculturally most developed countries of the world. When the level of agricultural production is compared with that of the 16 European countries mentioned above, Hungary still ranked in 12th place in 1978, as the rate of agricultural expansion has only surpassed the average for Europe during the last few years.

2.4 Bread-grain production, the milling and baking industries

Bread grains and the industrial processing related to them constitute a highly important sector of the Hungarian food industry. Food crops occupy 30 per cent of the arable area and provide 25 per cent of the production value of arable farming. Milling and baking also amount for 20—25 per cent of the output of and workforce employed in the food-processing industry.

The basic food crop in Hungary is wheat and, to a lesser extent, rye. Although Hungary was for long regarded primarily as a cereal-growing and -exporting country, because of the large-scale production of good-quality wheat, such a view is now out of date. With the intensification of production, the area under bread grains fell from 40 to 30 per cent of arable land after the war, but as yields per hectare remained static, the export of bread grains ceased, and the country became a net importer. Indeed, the bread grain issue, i.e. the balanced supply of the country's needs from own production was not solved until the mid-1960s, when the establishment and consolidation of large-scale socialist farms made possible a substantial rise in wheat yields and enabled Hungary again to come a net exporter of this grain.

The area under wheat, amounting to 1·3 million hectares, is now relatively stable in Hungary. It accounts for 0·6 per cent of the total world wheat acreage, but as yields are as much as 1·5 per cent of world output, the output-acreage ratio is double the world average. Hungary's share in CMEA wheat production ranged between 3·5 and 4·5 per cent between the years 1977 and 1980.

Since cold winters without snow cover are rather rare, it is the autumn-sown varieties, making good use of winter and spring precipitation and providing higher yields, that are mosty grown. Indeed, the area sown to spring wheat accounts for only 0·1 to 0·5 per cent of the total acreage, and only rises above this level when unfavourable weather conditions prevent the sowing of winter wheat, or when it was damaged by frost.

Of all the cereals, winter wheat requires the most heat. Its precipitation demands, however, are moderate and are highest in April and May, but while ripening during the second half of June, it likes dry weather. Therefore wheat quality is highest in the warmer and drier parts of the Great Plain where hard wheat with a high gluten content is grown. Given the continental climate of that area, winter wheat is one of the crops that can be grown most extensively and with the greatest safety. It can be relied on even in years when drought causes great havoc among other crops.

Of all physical conditions it is nonetheless *soil factors* that play a decisive role in the geographical distribution of wheat production as precipitation and heat are sufficient everywhere in the country to ensure a good to medium yield. Most favourable for its growth are deep, humus-rich, calcareous soils of medium clay content. It can also be successfully grown in alkali soils. The area sown is therefore usually closely adjusted to soil endowments.

The balanced nature of the area under wheat is connected with production interests, whereby owing to a high level of profit, wheat is one of the most marketable agricultural products. A net income of 3000 to 4000 forints per hectare is usual given the technical conditions of production and good marketing possibilities, and stimulates further development. At the same time, however, income levels are not conducive to the development of greater regional specialization.

The most important production areas for wheat are to be found on the loess table of the Trans-Tisza region, i.e. the Békés–Csanád, Szolnok and Debrecen loess districts, on the former *floodplain areas of the Tisza river* and on the extensive alkali soils of the *Körös region,* where the share of wheat amount for between 25 and 35 per cent of the arable area. In the extensive alkali districts of the Körös region, where it is practically the only crop that can be grown economically, its share is even higher *(Fig. 39).*

Adjoining to these areas to the north is *the second most significant wheat-growing area, the Heves–Borsod plainland at the foot of the Mátra and Bükk Mountains.*

Also prominent wheat-growing districts, with a sown area well above the national average, are *the Mezőföld plain, the Danube valley, south-Tolna and Baranya counties, and the North-Bácska loess table.*

By contrast, the share of wheat in the arable of the sandy areas of the Danube–Tisza Mid-region, the Nyírség and Inner-Somogy county is low because of unfavourable growing conditions. Wheat stands out with its high yields rather than with its area sown in the Little Plain.

For *wheat yields* to reach international levels more than two decades were needed, and two tons per hectare were attained in the mid-1960s. Subsequently it took only six years to reach the 3-ton level, and with an average over recent years exceeding *4 tons,* Hungary now ranks among the first ten countries growing wheat in over one million hectares. Given the present level of output, it is possible to satisfy domestic demand to both bread and fodder wheat and to export between 0·7 and 1·2 million tons per annum. With respect to dollar earnings, wheat is now the most profitable export item of the national economy.

As regards the *territorial distribution of wheat yields,* the highest values are not always associated with the main growing districts, because areas with the optimum natural factors are not necessarily co-terminous with the wheat-growing districts. The highest yields of over 4·5 tons per hectare come from the Mezőföld plain, not so much because of the favourable climatic conditions but rather because of more intensive and varied crop cultivation,

Fig. 39. Wheat production

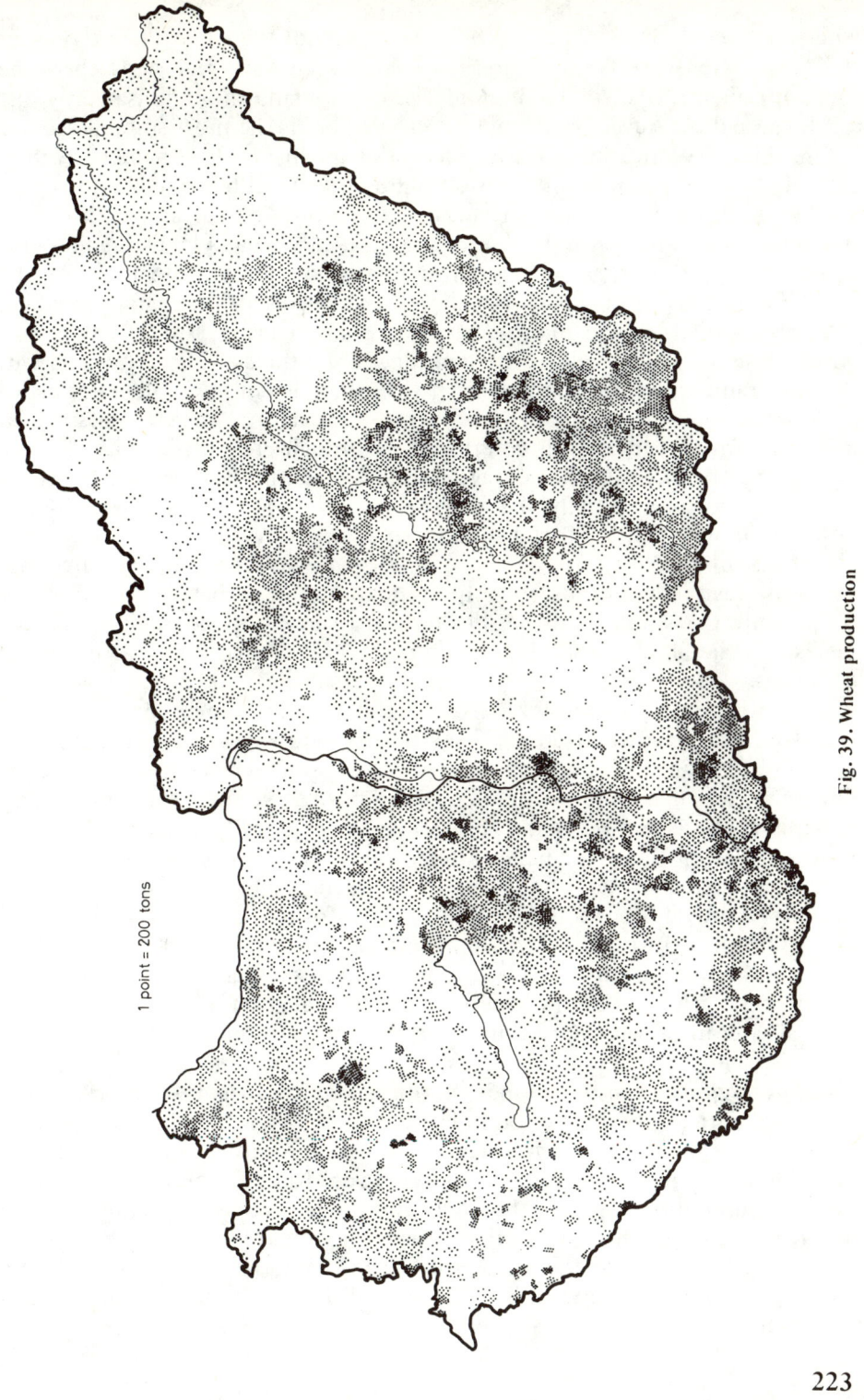

1 point = 200 tons

while the wheat areas of the south-eastern parts of the Great Plain represent the most extensive of arable area with highest average yields. At the same time, although the yields in the Mid-Tisza region and the Hajdúság only just reach the national average, the wheat grown here is the most suitable for the baking industry, and is therefore of greater intrinsic value than the higher-yielding but poorer in quality varieties grown in neighbouring areas for fodder. In addition there are also areas in the Körös region and in northern Borsod county where although acreage is relatively large, yields remain poor, at less than 2·5 tons by hectare. At similarly low level are yields from the Nyírség, south-west Transdanubia, and the basins of the Transdanubian Central Mountains. The main reason for poor yields is that wheat is also grown in areas where soil quality and relief conditions are unfavourable, but the profitability of the sector is such that there is considerable stimulus to grow wheat on a large scale in areas with adverse natural endowments, which leads in turn to further soil deterioration through erosion. Despite the low yields of 2 to 3 t/h, the percentage share of wheat in these areas is above 40 per cent, and is practically the only profitable crop. (This also exemplifies how profitability may distort a sound spatial structure.)

Thus a *comparison between the sown area and average yield* indicates that the most favourable yields roughly coincide with the best production districts. Only two essential disparities remain to be equalized, namely the low yields associated with the alkali soils of the Great Plain and with the hill countries.

The other bread grain, rye, is of secondary importance compared with wheat both as to sown area and yields. The rye-growing area, which amounts to 75 000 hectares, is only one-sixth of the pre-war acreage, because, on the one hand, wheat is more profitable and has ousted rye from the poor-quality rye-growing soils where yields have remained practically unchanged for decades, while, on the other hand, after melioration rye has been almost completely restricted to the sandy soils where wheat cultivation is uneconomic. (Thus rye provides a good example of how former growing districts have been transformed with the development of productive forces.)

Since the *soil requirements* of rye are not as exacting as those of wheat — rye thrives fairly well even on poor, sandy and acidic forest soils — it is, in general, a crop of secondary significance in Hungary and is only sown where the soil is not suitable for wheat growing. *Rye is thus the typical grain crop of sandy regions.* It also demands *more precipitation* than wheat, especially during its critical growing period in late April.

Prominent districts where rye is grown are rather widely scattered throughout the regions unsuitable for wheat cultivation. The most important district, amounting for half the total area under rye, is the Danube–Tisza Mid-region, where in certain districts with poor sandy soils it reaches as much as 20 per cent of the arable total. The second largest rye-growing area with 20 per cent of the total is the Nyírség district, especially its middle and southern parts. It is here that the highest-quality rye is grown. The third significant area is the hill country of *south-west Transdanubia* with its high precipitation and heavily leached forest soils. Here, however, its share of arable cultivation is only between 5 and 6 per cent, ranking behind the growing of wheat. *These three districts constitute 90 per cent of the country's rye-growing area.*

Since rye is grown in areas with poor-quality soils, its yields also lag far behind those of wheat, while methods of cultivation are rather backward. Yields average 1·5 tons per hectare and only exceed the pre-war level by 30 to 40 per cent.

During recent years, however, the cultivation of a new grain variety, *triticale*, has made considerable headway in rye-growing districts. Its endurance is similar to that of rye, but yields are much higher. Although it is officially ranked as a feed grain, the quality of its flour is better than that milled from rye.

Although *rice* is not a staple food crop in Hungary, it can nonetheless be discussed among the bread grains, owing to its role in nutrition. Moreover, it is a relatively new crop, although the first attempts at cultivation date back to the 17th century, during the Turkish occupation. Larger-scale cultivation, however, only began after 1945 when irrigation farming began to gain ground.

The total irrigated area under rice cultivation amounts to about 15 000 hectares, half of which is equipped with modern technical facilities. However, the agro-technology of large-scale production is unsatisfactory, while good yielding varieties needing short growing period are lacking. Therefore, rice is the only crop in Hungary which shows extreme fluctuations between sown area and yields attained.

Between 1950 and 1955 the area under rice cultivation increased from 5000 hectares to 50 000 hectares, mainly in areas with acidic soils which had hardly been utilized before, but as a result of monocropping these areas soon became exhausted, leading to a decrease in both yield and sown area. For this reason, rice has since been grown as part of a rotation.

The geographical distribution of rice cultivation is determined by plant's demand for heat and water. During the growing period, the minimum heat demand for that variety with the shortest growing period is 2600 to 2700 $C°$ and 1300 hours of sunshine, which sets the Barcs–Szekszárd–Kecskemét–Szolnok–Debrecen line as the northern limit for cultivation.

Rice farming is undertaken, as almost everywhere in the world, by irrigation as the plant must be immersed in 15 to 20 cm of water during the greater part of the growing period. On the majority of rice farms, the source of irrigation water is the Tisza and Körös rivers, but use is also made in places of backwaters and reservoirs. Although the *soil requirements of rice are moderate*, the irrigation of permeable soils is impossible. At the same time, the fact that rice can be grown on lime-deficient alkali soils is of great significance, because extensive areas can thereby be brought under intensive cultivation.

The greater part of the rice-growing area is to be found in the region east of the Tisza river *centred on the middle section of the Tisza valley in Szolnok county,* where half of all the rice farms of the country are to be found.

A second extensive growing district is the *Körös valley* in Békés county with a quarter of the overall area sown to rice, while a third significant area is the *Northern Trans-Tisza district* (the Hortobágy along the Eastern Main Canal) with somewhat less than 10 per cent of the total rice-growing area. The *lower-Tisza and Maros irrigation system* in Csongrád county constitutes a fourth area.

In the above-listed areas of the Tisza plain with their warm and dry summers rice output is excellent, especially during drought years when the yields of the other crops are very poor.

However, *rice yields* in Hungary at 1·5 to 3·8 tons per hectare are very poor not only when compared with results achieved in the main European rice-growing countries, but also by international standards. Italy and Spain, for example, achieve double the Hungarian yield. Since the rice-growing districts of Hungary lie at the northernmost limit of the crop, cultivation is risky and yields are subject to extreme fluctuations and a nationwide average output of 1·5 tons in 1980 was followed by a 3·0 ton per hectare in the subsequent year. The best yields are attained in the Körös valley and lower-Tisza region, and are poorest in the upper-Tisza region. Average yields are typical of the middle-Tisza region, which is the largest rice-growing district.

Rice production meets about one-third of domestic demand, and its main significance lies in the saving foreign exchange as exportable surpluses are available only from capitalist countries. However, given the low yields per hectare, domestic cultivation is questionable.

Grain storage capacity in Hungary is approximately 3 million tons, and although its geographical distribution fairly evenly dispersed throughout grain-growing areas, two significant concentrations are to be found in Békés and Szolnok counties, where the high concrete towers of the silos lend a novel feature to the landscape. Existing capacity is, however, about 1 million tons short of demand, and the construction of new storage capacity is an urgent task. Given the existing capacities of agriculture and trade, the best solution is further to develop storage facilities in individual production districts so that the demands of agriculture can be met on the one hand, while storage facilities serving commercial purposes can be concentrated near grain-processing plants on the other. This is because the distance over which grain can be transported economically is at most 15 to 20 kilometres. Assuming the present level of production, efficient grain export requires a much larger storage capacity than that presently existing to ensure that up to one half the amount envisaged for export purposes can be stored if necessary to await favourable cyclical changes in price.

Flour milling is one of the country's oldest industries. With the construction of many flour mills producing for export and with a high level of technical innovation, Budapest developed into one of the world's largest milling centres last century. Besides the existence of large steam mills more than 2000 small mills were also scattered throughout the country, because of the poor road conditions and production relationships of a subsistence economy. After the nationalization of the milling industry, many marginal and loss-making mills were closed and the concentration of the industry began. By the mid-1950s, the number of mills had dropped below 300, while during the 1970s only 163 mills were in operation. Along with concentration, reconstruction was also started, although even today only one quarter of the mills can be regarded as up-to-date. 40 per cent are so obsolete that they endanger the safety of production.

Mills are generally evenly distributed throughout the country, although there is some territorial concentration in the main wheat-growing districts of Békés and Szolnok counties and in Budapest, the large consumer market. The modernization of the industry and the future expansion of its production capacity is not expected to bring about any change in its geographical distribution.

The *baking industry* is market-oriented with a capacity roughly appropriate to the size of the population. Although the output of the 1500 plants of the industry can meet national demand in terms of quantity, this is not the case in terms of quality. Difficulties arise from the concentration of plants and the products of over capacity in certain districts cannot readily be transferred to regions with serious supply problems owing to the distances involved. About two-thirds of dry pastry products are produced by bakeries belonging to the canning industry. The two important centres of the pastry industry are Budapest and Békéscsaba.

2.5 The production and processing of industrial crops

The industrial crops of Hungary may be classified as follows.
— crops with a foodstuff content, for instance sugar beet,
— oil crops, i.e. sunflower seeds, oil flax and rapeseeds;
— textile crops, i.e. flax and hemp;
— tobacco.

Such crops, in general, need nutrient-rich soils, relatively high inputs of labour and, occasionally, specialist machinery and buildings.

Processed products, like vegetable oil and sugar play an important role both in home supply and in helping the balance of payments. Acreages are increasing in parallel with their growing significance, while yields have been rising in recent years with the introduction of factory production systems. The arable area sown to such crops has increased from 2 per cent before 1945 to 9 per cent today. In the following, we shall examine the geographical implications of only the three most important industrial crops, namely sugar beet, sunflowers and tobacco.

Sugar beet, taking up 2·5 per cent of arable land, is the most valuable industrial crop of the country, and during the last few decades, output has tended to rise, although there have been setbacks, in accordance with growing home demand (per-capita sugar consumption has risen from 11 to 35 kilogrammes) and profitability. At the same time, while it was possible to export sugar during the 1960s, stagnant production, based mainly on manual labour and the continued rise of consumption has led to growing sugar imports since then. It was in the 1960s, that the view began to prevail that imported sugar was cheaper than home-produced sugar, but the uncertain world-market position of sugar, during the early 1970s, the abrupt rise in price, and difficulties of procurement proved this view erroneous. As a result, conditions were created for large-scale, mechanized and profitable sugar-beet production to meet the highest possible proportion of demand from home-grown beet. As a result of the technical development of sugar-beet cultivation and the reconstruction of refineries, the profitability of the branch has improved considerably. As a consequence, some 450 to 500 thousand tons of sugar beet have been produced since the mid-1970s, which, complemented by 70 tons of sugar imported from Cuba, covers the country's requirements. Indeed, the sugar deficit had been reduced to 50 000 tons by 1981. The further development of factory methods of mechanized cultivation will create suitable conditions for the satisfaction of domestic consumption from the country's own resources.

The spatial distribution of sugar-beet production, along with the lines of transport and the location of refineries, is determined primarily by soil endowments, the crop preferring lime-rich, meadow-type clay soils. Sugar beet is also sensitive to *climatic conditions,* requiring, by Hungarian standards, a moderate amount of heat, and abundant and evenly distributed precipitation. In addition, *economic-geographical* conditions also affect its distribution, and extensive areas of cultivation have evolved where several sugar refineries are located close to each other. The district with the largest area sown is the region of *Sarkad* and *Mezőhegyes* in the south-eastern part of the Great Plain, where sugar beet amounts for as much as 5 to 6 per cent of the arable area. The second largest beet-growing district is the Little Plain, where there are three sugar refineries and where its cultivation occupies over 5 per cent of the arable land. Three further significant beet-growing districts are to be found in the Great Plain namely, the *Szolnok and Debrecen loess tables* and the *Heves-Borsod* plainland between the Tisza river and the Northern Middle Mountains. Within the confines of *supply district of the refinery at Szerencs,* sugar beet is grown on a relatively small but very significant area *(Fig. 40).* The refineries at Kaposvár and Ercsi in Transdanubia have, of course, also developed their own supply districts, but beet production is dispersed over a larger territory.

Primarily, because of continued increases in yield during the past few years, *average output* has risen significantly from the 20 tons per hectare pre-war to between 38 to 43 tons per hectare today. True, with these results

1 point = 200 tons

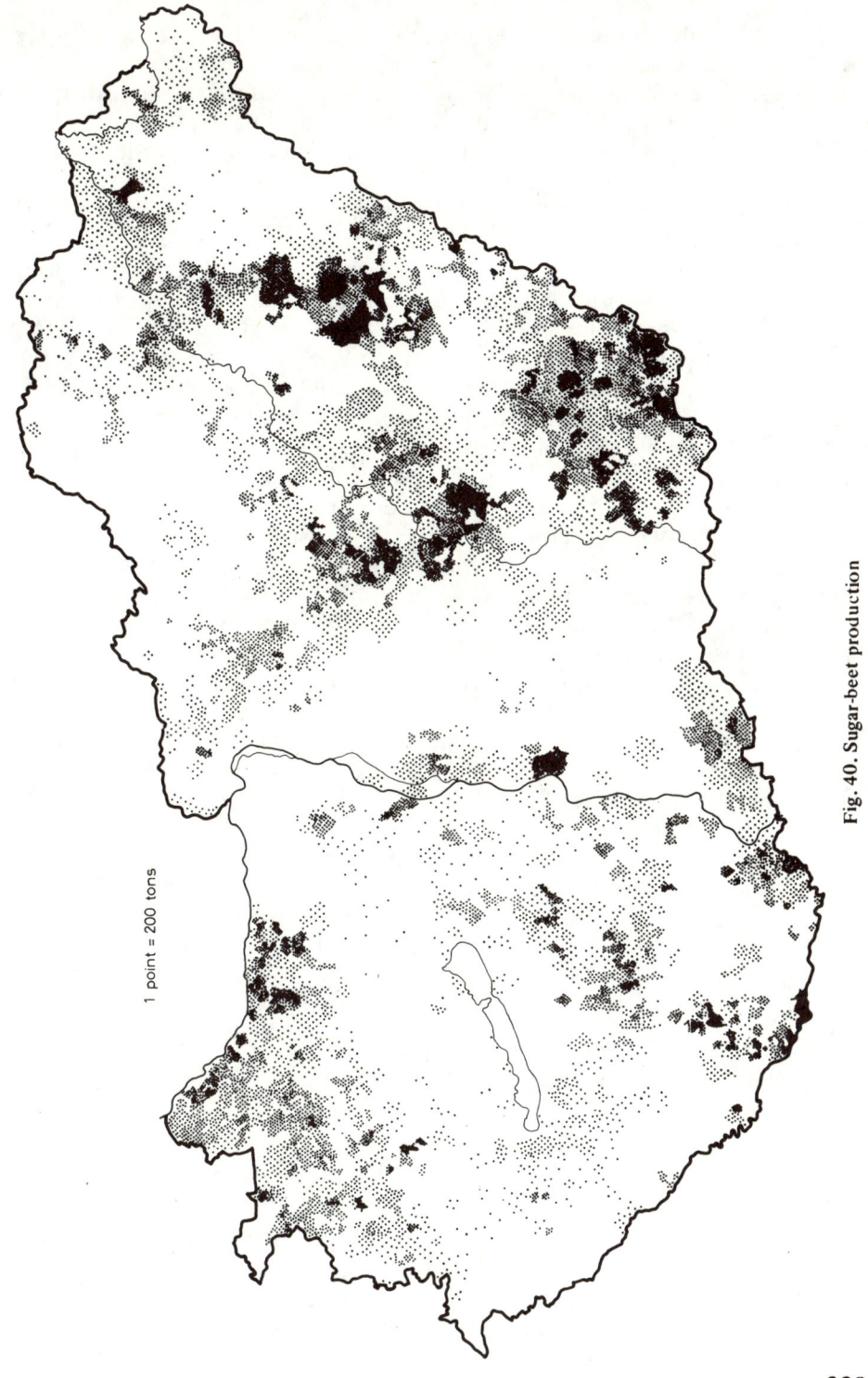

Fig. 40. Sugar-beet production

Hungary still only produces two-thirds of the output per hectare of more efficient beet-producing countries.

The best average yields coincide, for the most part, with those districts with the largest sown areas, but deviations can also be experienced. Especially high are average yields in the Hajdúság with 47 tons per hectare, in the south-eastern part of the Great Plain with between 42 and 45 tons, and in the Little Plain with 42 tons. Yields from the plainland bordering the Northern Middle Mountains are low, although cultivation occupies a large area. By international standards, Hungarian sugar-beet production amounting for 1·5 per cent of world output, is considerable and the country ranks in 15th place in terms of volume.

The territorial distribution of the *sugar industry* evolved a century ago in conformity with the location of the main districts, the large water demand of the refineries, the possibility of the disposal of wester water and the railway and road network. The 12 sugar refineries of the country, with the exception of that at Selyp, are relatively favourably located within the individual districts of cultivation. In order to coordinate production and processing and to cut down transport costs, the sugar refineries first drew upon the production of beet grown in a territory much smaller than that presently surrounding them. Production districts for individual refineries did not exceed 5000 hectares, i.e. the area of a large estate, and transport distances were not more than 30 kilometres. Subsequently the sown area has tripled, and the size of production districts together with *transport distances have greatly increased to an average of 84 kilometres.* Assuming an output of 5 million tons, this means the cumulative task of loading and transporting as much as 10 to 15 million tons of beet because of multiple transsiphments. In this way the economic significance of locational factors is accentuated to such an extent that they may even become dominant in the case of a small country. Long distances increase not only transport costs proper, but also spillage and storing losses resulting from multiple transshipment.

The supply districts of the refineries are quite extensive and as shown from the table below a relatively large proportion of 55 per cent on average stems from districts situated more than 50 kilometres from an individual refinery:

Mezőhegyes	28 per cent	Kaposvár	62 per cent
Szolnok	37 per cent	Ercsi	70 per cent
Sarkad	40 per cent	Szerencs	73 per cent
Sárvár	45 per cent	Hatvan	84 per cent
Petőháza	47 per cent	Selyp	84 per cent
Ács	53 per cent		

Most favourable is the concentration endeavour of the Szolnok Refinery despite the fact that a major programme of reconstruction has recently doubled its daily processing capacity. The Mátravidék refineries, by contrast, are at the opposite extreme with most of their raw beet coming from the

Hajdúság. This not only substantially lengthens transport distances for the factories themselves, but also has a major impact on the national distribution network as well, and was a contributory factor behind the decision to build a new, large-capacity refinery at Kaba in the Hajdúság. With the entry into production of the new refinery in 1979, the growing of sugar beet could be expanded in the Jászság, Hatvan and Gödöllő areas, owing to the economic efficiency of transportation. The case of the Kaba Sugar Factory clearly exemplifies the consequences that can result from the well-thought-out location of a plant for the spatial structure of sugar production and for transport costs. The average distance over which beet is transported to the new refinery is about 40 kilometres, but this also has an impact on the refineries in the plainland as they are compelled better to concentrate production in their supply districts. For this reason, the distance over which beet is carried to the Mátravidék Sugar Factories, — 117 kilometres — has dropped and the mean distance nationally has diminished from 84 to 64 kilometres with the saving of about 30 million forints per annum. A future step that would further increase transport efficiency would be the expansion of the capacity of the Hatvan refinery and the closure of the plant at Selyp, should other factors such as investment and supply make this possible.

There are, however, further significant ways of reducing the distances and thus the losses still inherent in sugar production. If only 10 per cent of the most suitable area were used for beet production, then the entire demand of the refinery at Ercsi and half the demand at the Kaposvár, Szolnok, Sarkad and Mezőhegyes plants could be met by supplies less than 25 kilometres away. The decisive factor in determining the extent to which it is rational to concentrate production within the supply area of a refinery is to identify the areas where the endowments for growing beet of high sugar content and high technological value are to be found. Both characteristics are not always to be found in the vicinity of sugar refineries, and a reduction in transport costs does not necessarily offset a lower sugar content. Given existing railway freight rates, a 1 per cent increase in sugar content compensates for an extra 100 kilometres of transport.

70 per cent of all sugar beet is transported to the factory by rail, and the rest by road (transport by water is, unfortunately, rather rare). Beet is not taken directly to the refinery, but first to a receiving plant 20 to 30 kilometres away, where they are stored for a certain period of time [5].

Of all the oil crops, *sunflowers* are grown on the largest area in Hungary. Cultivation, still insignificant in the early 1930s, expanded greatly as a result of the pre-war boom and subsequently owing to compulsory growing during the war, when it reached 2 per cent of the total arable area. Sunflower-seed oil replaced fat, which was in short supply because of the widespread slaughter of the pig population during the war, and the sown area remained at a high level even after the war. It was only after the pig population had again reached the pre-war level that the area under cultivation began to decline. Vegetable oil consumption in Hungary could not replace animal fats owing to dietry habits. Pig fat constitutes over two-thirds of the 28 to 31 kilogrammes per capita fat consumption per annum, within which vegetable oil consumption is less than 7 kilogrammes. These proportions are reversed in most countries of Western Europe.

The large-scale cutback in the production of sunflower seeds after the Second World War came to a halt because of international rather than domestic demand. In the countries to the north and west of Hungary is no appreciable production, and for this reason, there was increasing interest in Hungarian sunflower-seed oil, espcially as the countries of western Europe can satisfy only half their demand for vegetable oil out of own production. Sunflower-seed oil is a safe export and profitable earner of foreign exchange. For this reason, sunflowers occupy an increasingly significant place among arable crops, and during recent years have come to exceed the area sown to sugar beet (by 6 per cent).

Because heat is the first of its physical requirements, sunflower cultivation is greatest on the poor soils of the warm, sandy areas of the Great Plain. Before 1945 the crop was only grown to any noteworthy extent in the eastern part of Hungary, Szabolcs-Szatmár county, primarily on the large estates of the area. This region, complemented by the rest of Trans-Tisza has continued to remain one of the most important production zones *(Fig. 41)*. Another major growing district is the *Mezőföld* area, while the *North-Bácska loess table* constitutes a third important area of sunflower-seed production. The latter is the centre of a factory system of production, associated with the Bácsalmás State Farm.

Sunflower seed increased yields, however, by only 0·1 to 0·2 tons nationally over the two decades, to the mid-1970s, primarily because it was sown on poor-quality soils. But more recently, with a factory production system gaining ground, yields have increased from 1·2 to 2·0 tons. The highest yields are attained in the Mezőföld and on the Bácska loess table, while the Trans-Tisza region approximates the national average.

Soya beans are an oil crop of the highest nutrition value with a 20 per cent oil and 40 per cent protein content, but are of an exacting character, especially as regards varieties with a short growing period. They are nonetheless successfully cultivated given the humid air and the fertile soils of the country. Experimental production began quite a long time ago, but it was only in recent years that suitable varieties to provide a secure harvest were found. Temperature demands can be met, while that for moisture is satisfied by irrigation. The crop is grown in the sun-rich middle-Tisza region (gestor is on Rákóczifalva near Szolnok) and in the south-eastern parts of the Great Plain. Yields average between 1·5 and 1·8 tons per hectare nationally, and provided a stable 2-ton per hectare production level can be achieved, then the crop can look forward to a very bright future as otherwise the protein requirements of an increasing number of livestock can be met only by steadily growing imports, specifically of soya beans.

1 point = 20 tons

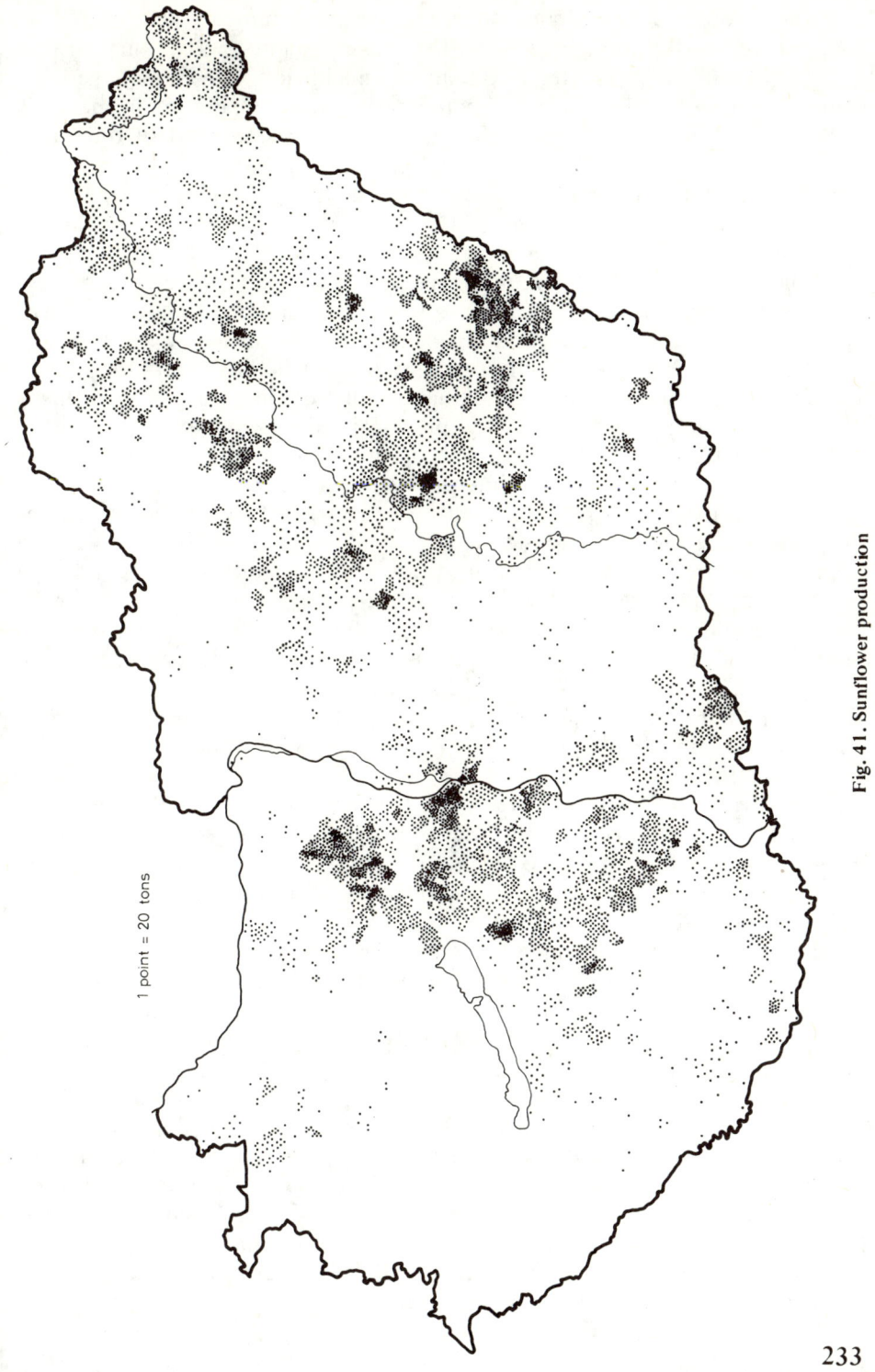

Fig. 41. Sunflower production

233

The location of the vegetable *oil industry* is determined primarily by the raw-produce basis, although the largest processing plants, accounting for half the total capacity, are located in Budapest. In addition, two more large-scale plants are located in *Győr and Nyírbátor,* respectively. Operating in the areas of cultivation, primarily in the Nyírség, the south-eastern part of the Great Plain, the Danube–Tisza Mid-region and in the Mezőföld, are mills satisfying local demand, but some improvement on this adverse locational situation has been attained by the expansion of the plant at Nyírbátor. The expanded production of oil crops and the economic efficiency of vegetable-oil exports necessitated a vigorous increase in processing capacities. A large-capacity factory has been built at Martfű, in the centre of raw material basis at the Tisza border, where factors of water supply and water transport were also of a decisive importance. The capacity of this plant equals that of all other plants combined. From the oil cake, a residual product of the process, the refinery produces large quantities of valuable protein fodder, which has widened the feed basis of the district and may well bring about an appreciable change in the structure of intensive animal husbandry.

Of the industrial crops, *tobacco* ensures the highest production value per unit area, and is the only non-food crop for human consumption which can be grown in Hungary. It is primarily turned into cigarettes, cigars and pipe tobacco, but its effective substance, nicotin, is also used as herbicide and as a basic substance of the pharmaceutical industry. The following varieties classified according to growing districts are to be found in Hungary: *the Debrecen, Szabolcs, Szulok and Heves Virginia varieties.* Distinctive methods of cultivation, soil composition and especially climatic conditions are associated with the individual types, kinds of which *muscutel* and garden tobacco are high-quality varieties.

The growing of tobacco requires warm conditions and reasonable moisture. Preferred soil types differ by varieties, but usually looser soils are favoured. High-quality cigarette tobacco cannot be grown in compacted soils, and heavy clays are absolutely unsuitable for tobacco cultivation. The individual varieties react differently to the soil's chemical properties. Moreover, the unsuitability of heavy alkaline soils is one reason why no substantial tobacco cultivation has developed in the Danube–Tisza Mid-region. By contrast, the brown sandy soils with a loose structure that are to be found on southern and south-western slopes in hilly areas are usually most suitable for growing garden and oriental varieties.

During the 1970s, both sown area and output stagnated, because of low profitability. A significant portion of the crop is grown on co-operative farms working poor-quality sandy soils. Moreover, because of a lack of development funds, these farms are unable to solve their mechanization problems and no longer have a sufficient and adequately skilled labour force. However, measures taken during recent years have somewhat improved the efficiency of production, and with the import of modern tobacco cultivators, the mechanization of the branch has begun.

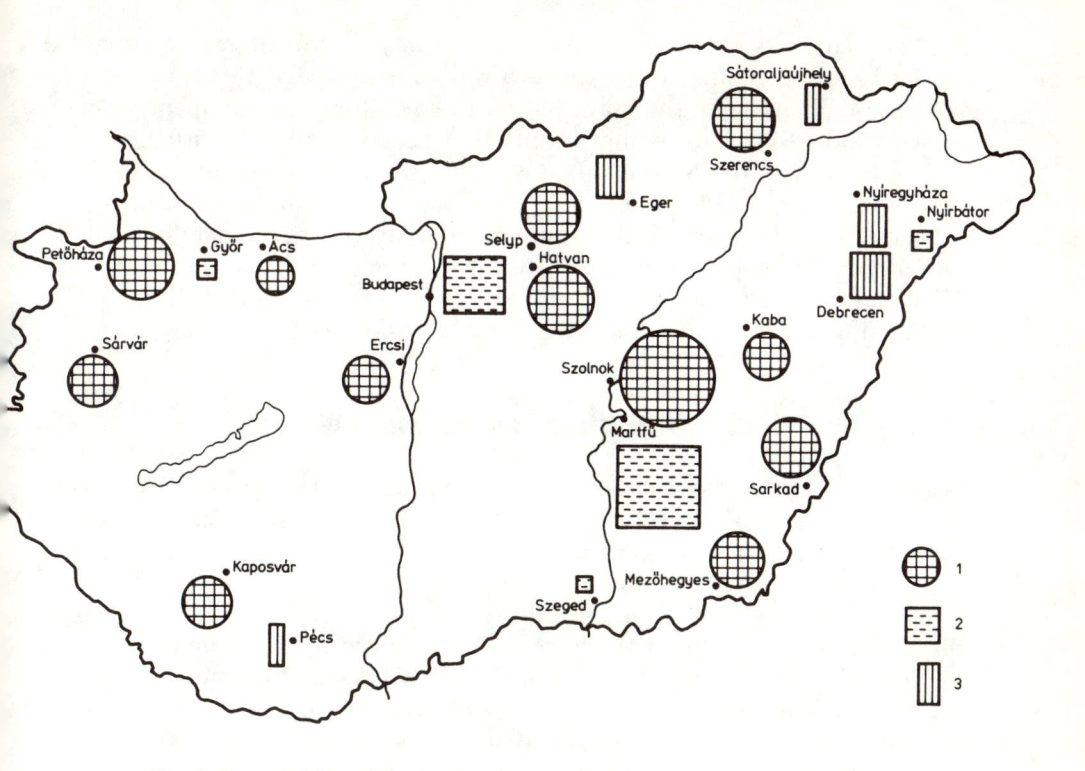

Fig. 42. The spatial location of the sugar, vegetable-oil and tobacco industries
1 — sugar; 2 — vegetable-oil; 3 — tobacco

The main growing region is the *Nyírség*, which accounts for close on two-thirds of national production and more than half output of the good-quality Heves Virginia type. In certain parts of the region the crop occupies as much as 2 to 3 per cent of the arable area. The alluvial slope that forms the northern part of the Great Plain and which runs along the southern foothills of the *Northern Middle Mountains* is the second growing area and accounts for 10 per cent of total output. The cultivation of better-quality varieties, such as Heves Virginia and garden tobacco types, is found predominantly in the Heves sandy landscape. Along with these major districts, two minor districts are located in Transdanubia, namely in South-Somogy where cigar tobacco is produced and in North-Tolna where the emphasis is upon good-quality garden tobacco.

The modernization of tobacco growing has also contributed to *higher yields*. For instance, the introduction of new varieties led to an increase from 1·2 to 1·5 tons per hectare. The best yields are attained in the Nyírség area, where the quality varieties are grown.

As the increase in yield has not been able to offset the fall in sown area, about one-third of the domestic demand for tobacco has to be met by

235

imports. Hungary also imported oriental-type varieties in earlier years too, primarily for blending, but exports always far exceeded this trade. It is an important objective of the branch again to cover home requirement from domestic production, and to import only that necessary for flavouring.

The *tobacco processing* plants are located in the growing districts, with a capacity appropriately adjusted to crop output. The domestic siting of the tobacco industry has been determined primarily by the availability and employment of female labour, and with the closure of the Budapest plant, four tobacco factories remain namely in Debrecen, Eger, Sátoraljaújhely and Pécs, of which the one in Debrecen is the most important *(Fig. 42)*.

2.6 Viticulture and the wine industry

Although only about 2 per cent of the cultivated area of Hungary is devoted to the growing of grapes, this important crop nonetheless accounts for between 5 and 6 per cent of gross agricultural output and for about 10 per cent of agricultural exports.

Grapes belong to one of the oldest cultures in Hungary, dating back to pre-conquest times when viticulture was introduced by the Romans into Pannonia, present-day Transdanubia. In the Middle Ages, Hungary was the main supplier of wine to the neighbouring countries to the north, and although the vine fell back during the Turkish occupation, after their expulsion it steadily increased in area again despite the efforts made by Austria to set barries to wine exports by its customs policy. The present-day high-quality wine-growing areas, the so-called historical wine districts had already evolved by the 18th century, but the phylloxera disease at the close of the 19th century brought the upswing in Hungarian viticulture to an abrupt halt. During one decade and a half, almost half the country's vineyards were wiped out.

The first reconstruction of viticulture carried out at the turn of the century radically changed the territorial proportion of grape production. It was exactly the most valuable vineyards in the hilly regions that fell victim to the phylloxera, while those established in the Danube–Tisza Mid-region for the purpose of binding the soil together suffered hardly any damage and, indeed, *grape growing on these immune** sandy soils was increased by new plantations. Before the phylloxera devastation, the sandy, plainland varieties had accounted for hardly one-sixth of total grape production, but after the completion of the programme of reconstruction before the First World War, this had already increased to two-thirds. One harmful consequence of the reconstruction was the spread of the phylloxera-resistant, direct-growing vine varieties of American origin (Noah, Delaware, Othello)

---

* A sandy soil in which phylloxera cannot survive.

The wine-growing area continued to increase in the years immediately following the Second World War, but as a result of economic measures taken during the first five-year plan involving low delivery prices, and high taxation, the area gradually declined; wine growing was neglected and the state of the vineyards deteriorated. The completion of socialist transformation, however, marked a turning-point. A large-scale method of vine growing was introduced, and although private and auxiliary plots still produced half the total output of the sector, the planting programme has speeded up, and the *second national programme of reconstruction* began.

During the second five-year plan between 1961 and 1965, the establishment of close to 50000 hectares of new vineyards brought the domestic area up to 250000 hectares, and new wine-growing farms, on which large-scale production could begin were organized in the Danube–Tisza Mid-region, in the Izsák, Helvécia and Kiskunhalas State Farms. During the 1960s, large farms gladly planted vines in order to create job opportunities, but since then, the situation has radically changed, and labour has become scarce in agriculture, too.

The asset stock of the sector, comprising plantations, machinery, wine-processing machines, and productive capacity, is markedly high relative to other sectors of horticulture. Owing to increasing mechanization, production costs have been steadily rising, but these are not counterbalanced by increased productivity and higher producer prices. Owing to low profitability and even losses on some farms, the wine-growing area has more recently been dropping on both large and small farms alike, and the sector again shows a declining trend [77]. In 1981 the cultivated area overpassed scarcely the 160 000 hectares.

Hungary is situated close to the northern limit for wine growing. Further north significant and extensive viticulture is hard to find, while no wine growing is undertaken in the same latitude either to the west or east of Hungary, because in the west *cool summers* and in the east *cold winters* exclude economic production. By contrast, in countries farther south, especially in the Mediterranean region, the ripening period is shorter and bouquet is poor, owing to longer and more intensive sunshine, and a significant part of the wines produced there are lighter and softer than Hungarian wines.

The high quality of Hungarian wines is attributable, in the first place, to *climatic endowments*. The large volume of high-quality wines produced is promoted by the *dry, sunny summers and the long, mild autumns* as well as by the fact that the historical wine districts are located on the southern slopes of the Middle Mountains where *radiation* is particularly favourable. The warming up of the soil and of the air immediately above it are so intensive here, that the effective location of the vineyards is equivalent to a plain-land lying in a more southerly latitude corresponding to the angle of the slope. In the sandy region of the Great Plain, by contrast, grapes are affected by a „double" insolation effect owing to the reflection of the sun's rays from the surface of the sandy soils.

The wine districts have been gradually transferred to less steep slopes and to the plains where mechanized cultivation is a more feasible proposition. As a result, the proportion of the total areas in which high-quality vines are grown, is now less than before. The relatively favourable distribution of the 500 to 600 millimetres of precipitation on the southern slopes of the Middle Mountains and in the Great Plain means that *rot* and *fungal diseases* do comparatively little damage to viticulture, while the mild and dry late summers promote fast ripening. Neither very dry years nor those with greatly above average precipitation are favourable for yields. At the same time the relief and structural characteristics of the landscape provide micro-climates which differ from one wine district to another, and which have an important impact on the quality of the wine. Thus the direction and angle of the slope and the existence of nearby water surfaces contribute especially to the formation of a district associated with a wine of specific quality [74].

The vineyards of the Middle Mountains and hill regions occupied the sites of earlier forests, and thus were planted on poor forest soils whereas the detrital products of igneous rocks provide especially good soils. The more recent wine district, of the Great Plain is located mostly in blown sand, where the vines themselves bind the poor soils together, which formerly had at best been suitable for pasturing purposes. Thus average yields in Hungary are much more modest than in the other wine-growing countries of Europe and the 3·8 to 4 tons per hectare average is below the world mean of 5·5 tons per hectare. In other words, the increase in the average yield of grapes lags far behind that of the major field crops. At the same time specific yields per year depend on weather conditions and can fluctuate widely, e.g. from 2 tons in 1965 to 4·9 tons in 1977. Owing to the low yields, the very high input of labour and the considerable assets that are tied into it, the productivity of viniculture is rather poor, and has remained largely a culture of small agricultural units. At current prices, yields ought to be raised to 5 to 6 tons per hectare to ensure that wine growing is economical even without wine making. But offsetting this is the fact that higher growing capacity is usually accompanied by lower quality, although low average yields mean that Hungary cannot compete with the great wine-growing countries in the mass production of table wines. However, high-quality wines accounting for only a minor part of wine growing can still profitably be sold in foreign markets.

For the preservation of the specific character of the various types of wine, as well as for the management of production and the formation of a price structure, 14 special wine districts and good wine-growing areas have been identified, discussed below in which only specific varieties of grape can be grown. Prevailing regulations also prevent the blending of the grapes and wines of the various districts.

The wine district of Tokaj-hegyalja. This is one of the oldest districts producing the best-quality wine in Hungary and indeed in the world as a whole. This district encompasses the vineyards located along the southernmost fringe of the Zemplén Mountains and on the Tokaj hill itself. The area is protected against cold continental air masses by the mountain rim of the Carpathians. Sunny summers are usually followed by long, warm and dry autumns, which promotes the ripening of the grapes and increases their sugar content. The wine district with its 6000 hectares embraces 25 villages centred on the towns of Tokaj, Sátoraljaújhely and Abaújszántó, and also three towns, Sátoraljaújhely, Sárospatak and Szerencs. Most famous of the wine-growing villages are Tokaj, Tolcsva, Tállya, Tarcal and Mád. The bulk of the vineyards was originally to be found between 150 and 300 metres above sea level on loess and friable clay soils of volcanic origin (riolite, andesite) of the southern slopes with excellent insolation conditions. But most of the extensive vineyards planted during the second reconstruction are located at lower levels, on the ,,skirt fringes", in local parlance, where wines were rarely grown earlier.

Two varieties predominate, namely *Furmint*, most suitable for ,,aszú" making and amounting for 63 per cent of the total and *Hárslevelű*, covering 25 per cent of the area. The warm, dry late summer enhance the quality of the grapes, which undergo what is called fine rotting, whereby their sugar content is increased. It is from these grapes that Tokaj ,,aszú", a natural sweet wine is made. Another noteworthy variety is the sweet and dry Szamorodni wine. Similarly well-known are the hard, piquant dessert and sweet wines of the district. The peculiar flavour and fame of Tokaj wine are attributable not only to exquisite natural endowments but also to the species themselves and to their special treatment in the cellars.

Tokaj won its reputation from the quality of its wine and it is this quality that is endangered by the removal of the mountain side vineyards. On the steeper slopes, where cultivation is possible only with the use of manual labour, many of the small producers have discontinued vine growing, while the larger enterprises have lost the initiative to plant new vineyards. Thus the state wine-growing association, which markets the output of both the large and small producers of Hegyalja, is finding it increasingly difficult to ensure the quality that the market is used to as well as maintaining favourable prices in foreign markets. The price of Tokaj wine is comparatively low when compared with that of the world's great wines, and its export is the least economic of Hungarian quality wines.

The Bükkalja wine district comprises the vineyards of Miskolc and 18 neighbouring villages and its *Furmints, Hárslevelűs* and *Ottonel muscatels* have a Hegyalja character.

The Eger wine district encompasses the vineyards located on the southern slopes of the Bükk Mountains, and those in the hill country of the 11 villages surrounding Eger. Soils are mostly clays mixed with gravel, derived from riolite tufa or limestone-based Pannonian clay. The most famous wine of the district is the gently harsh, spicy-smelling, red Eger ,,Bull's blood", which is blended from the *Kadarka, Burgund* and *Medoc noir* varieties. Yet most of

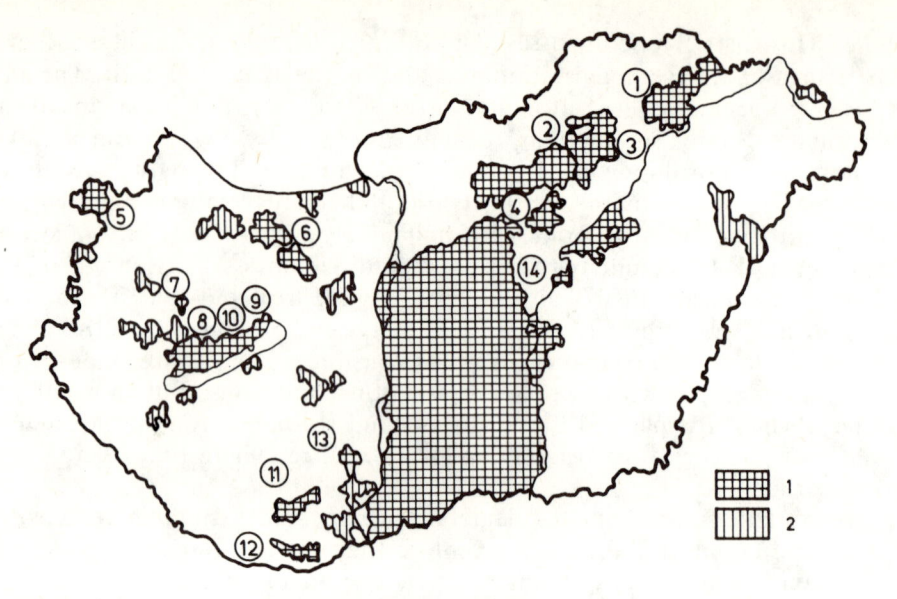

Fig. 43. Wine districts

1. Tokajhegyalja; 2. Eger; 3. Bükkalja; 4. Mátraalja; 5. Sopron; 6. Mór–Császár; 7. Somló; 8. Badacsony; 9. Balatonfüred–Csopak; 10. Balatonmellék; 11. Mecsek; 12. Villány–Siklós; 13. Szekszárd; 14. The Great Plain; 1 — wine-producing areas included in wine districts; 2 — places producing good wines, but not included in wine disctricts

the wines grown in the Eger district, up to 70 per cent, are white wines, the most common being *Olaszrizling* and the best-known *Leányka*.

The Mátraalja wine district is the largest quality-wine district to be found on the southern slopes of the Mátra Mountains around Gyöngyös, Visonta, Aldebrő and Verpelét. The soil is mostly loess based on Pannonian sand and clays or Miocene marl, and at higher latitudes of detritial andesite. 60 per cent of the wines grown here are white, the remainder being *Siller* and red wines. The most important varieties are *Olaszrizling, Mézesfehér, Hárslevelű, Kadarka* and *Othello*, the latter being used as a colourant. A prominent variety, much sought after abroad, is *Debrői Hárslevelű*, a wine rich in bouquet and flavour, and often of a sweetish taste. Also well developed is the table grape production of the district, most of which is exported *(Fig. 43)*.

The Sopron wine district comprises the vineyards around the town of Sopron and the 5 neighbouring villages. It was made famous by *Kékfrankos* – a red wine of low alcoholic content and international reputation.

The Mór–Császár wine district was established by the 1970 Wine Act, which united the earlier independent Mór and *Bársonyos*–Császár districts. It is situated on the sheltered foothills of the south-western side of the Vértes Mountain where it embraces 4 villages surrounding Mór and on the loess, Pannonian clay and sandy slopes of the Gerecse Mountain and the Danube

Knee. The main variety is *Ezerjó*, but *Red Veltelini* and *Tramini* are to be found in the new vineyards and in the Bársonyos–Császár area. The Mór Ezerjó is, thanks to its pleasantly high acid content, exquisite bouquet and fresh flavour, a much sought-after wine in foreign markets.

The Somló wine district embraces the vineyards on the slopes of Somló hill which is of volcanic origin and is located in the western foreground of the Bakony Mountain. It is the smallest wine district, which has lost much of its former reputation. The best-known varieties are *Furmint, Rajna-rizling* and *Tramini*, known for their high alcoholic content and their characteristic bouquet and flavour.

The Badacsony wine district embraces the vineyards on the southern slopes of Badacsony which overlooks Lake Balaton, as well as those on Szigliget, Szentgyörgyhegy and Ecserihegy and around the village of Zánka. These vineyards receive „double insolation" owing to the reflection of sunlight from the surface of Lake Balaton, which is one of the reasons for the good quality of these wines. The soils of the district are varied and are largely made up of Pannonian clays and sands intermingled with detrital basalt from the surrounding volcanic mountains. Wine growing has been carried on here since as early as Roman times. The main variety is *Olaszrizling*, which accounts for approximately 60 per cent of the output of the district. Other exquisite wines, that are well known outside the country, are *Kéknyelű* and *Szürkebarát*.

The Balatonfüred–Csopak wine district, like the Badacsony district, has a micro-climate beneficially influenced by the water surface of Lake Balaton. The soil is largely derived from the detritus of crystalline shales and Permian red sandstone, but in places is composed of Pannonian sands. Of the wines of Balatonfüred and Csopak, *Olaszrizling, Mézesfehér* and *Furmint* are the best-known varieties characterized by their high alcoholic content, and sweet, pleasant flavour. The character of the wines of the two neighbouring places, Füred and Csopak, is basically different. Füred wines are sweety and soft, while those of Csopak, due to their acid content, are more refreshing.

The wine district of Balatonmellék encompasses, in addition to the above area, the vineyards of the hill country between Balatonalmádi and Keszthely.

The Mecsek wine district consists of the vineyards around the town Pécs and the 5 villages located on the southern slopes of the Mecsek Mountain. This is the oldest of all the wine districts, with a history going back to the Bronze Age. Its white wines, *Olaszrizling, Furmint* and *Cirfandli*, have a good flavour and sweet taste.

The Villány–Siklós wine district is located on the loess-covered slopes of the Villány Mountain in Baranya county. Its special, protected red wines are *Cabernet* and *Burgundi*.

The Szekszárd wine district extends around the town Szekszárd and the village of Decs. For the most part, excellent *Siller* and red wines, mainly *Kadarka* and *Kékfrankos* and, to a lesser extent, *Oporto* and *Medoc noir* are grown. Best-known among them is Kadarka with its low acid content.

While it is these historical wine districts that provide the famous wines of Hungary, the greater part of the country's wine output comes from the vineyards on the plains. Of these areas, which produce mainly mass-quality wines, the wine district of the Great Plain is most significant. 95 per cent of the area is located on the phylloxera-resistant, sandy soils of the Danube Tisza Mid-region. To this district belong the wine-producing villages of the southern part of Heves county, and the vineyards along the left bank of the Tisza river in the Jászság and in Szolnok county. The best-known varieties are *Kadarka, Kövidinka, Mézesfehér, Ezerjó* and *Olaszrizling*. In most small-scale vineyards, a great many fruit trees can also be found. A significant part of the grapes grown around Kecskemét is for table, not only for the supply of Budapest, but also for export. The expansion of this production is undoubtedly justified as the total table grape area at present is only 7500 hectares, which can satisfy less than half of domestic consumption. As a result more and more wine grapes are marketed each year for this purpose.

In this district it is primarily light table wines for mass consumption that are grown, but there are also good-quality wines of high alcoholic content. As regards the wines grown on the plains or on sandy soils, it is not their local character, but the type of grape that is decisive. For the champagne production at Budafok and Pécs, for instance, common, sour plainland wines are usually used.

The concentration of vine growing is not satisfactory, owing to the significant proportion of small-scale production, and fragmented areas of viticulture can often be met with on many state and co-operative farms. 36 per cent of the latter are engaged in wine production and of the 60 state farms growing vines there are only 10 in which the vineyard area exceeds 800 hectares.

Wine processing is done partly by the producers, and partly by the wine industry. Both have their advantages and disadvantages. The vertical integration of production, processing and marketing is fairly advanced in the sector, but nearly three quarters of the country's wine output is processed by agricultural producers. The activity of the wine industry also extends, besides actual wine production, over the purchasing, treatment, and the wholesale and retail marketing of wines.

The storing and processing capacities of the wine industry are not satisfactory. 50 per cent of this capacity is located equally at Budafok and in Bács-Kiskun county, and the other half is distributed rather evenly. When there is a good wine harvest, storage capacity is insufficient, especially in Bács-Kiskun and Csongrád counties, as the majority of the co-operative farms here possess neither processing nor storage facilities. On the other hand, at Budafok and in the Eger district, storage capacity is larger than the quantity of grapes that can be procured (see *Fig. 48*).

Hungary ranks among the first 10 to 12 producing and exporting countries of the world. As a result of increasing average yields, the quantity of wine produced surpasses 5 million hectolitres in certain years, two-thirds of which are white wines. Per capita consumption in Hungary is 35 litres as against 100 litres in the great wine-producing countries. Thus, compared with domestic consumption, wine exports are very significant, amounting to 30 to 40 per cent of total production. Hungarian wines are exported to all parts of the world. Four-fifths of the wines exported go to the Soviet Union, the GDR, Czechoslovakia and Poland. The more significant capitalist export markets are the FRG, Switzerland and Austria. Capitalist partners buy exclusively barrelled wine, because high tarifs are imposed on bottled wines. It is unfavourable to Hungarian wine growing that the world-market price has only increased slightly compared with other agricultural products. This is somewhat offset by the fact that bottled wines, which can fetch higher prices, represent a steadily greater share of exports amounting to 64 per cent of the total in 1981.

2.7 Fruit and vegetable production and the preserving industry

2.7.1 Fruit production

Hungary's climatic and soil endowments are particularly favourable for growing the various fruits of the temperate zone, which because of the hot, sunny summers tend to be high in vitamin and sugar content. In Hungary, as in the other parts of Europe with drought-prone, continental climates, the *apple and drupe fruits* are dominant. The various berries[*] (currants, raspberries, blackberries, etc.) also thrive, although their optimum habitat is farther to the north, while drupes (apricots, peaches, walnuts, almonds and chestnuts) are more typical of the countries to the south. The advantages deriving from geographical location make it possible for Hungary to export significant quantities of fruit to western and northern European countries and the Soviet Union as well as to satisfy domestic needs.

Despite the fact that Hungary's natural endowments offer good opportunities for fruit growing, insufficient fruit was produced in the past to satisfy the population's needs.

After the Second World War, increased home consumption, and an endeavour to utilize the growing area more rationally, resulted in the dynamic growth of the sector, and in an upswing in the development of orchards. The fruit-growing area increased rapidly around 1961 owing to the planting of new orchards on 50 000 hectares, and by 1965 approached a total of 170 000 hectares, or three times the area of 1950. Large-scale farms tended to participate in the great national planting programme, if for no other reason than to create new job opportunities.

The extensive phase of development has since come to an end, as the surplus manpower pool has become exhausted, but at the same time, the con-

---

[*] This grouping is an economic classification and does not accord with botanic systematization.

ditions for modern, mechanized production have not yet been created. Compared with other branches of agriculture, inputs of chemical fertilizers, herbicides and energy as in the case of viticulture, have grown faster than yields, and profitability has therefore declined both in relative and absolute terms. For instance, net income per unit cost of production reaches hardly one quarter of that attained in the bread- and fodder-grain sectors. Low profitability has impeded technological development, and the large farms have failed to invest in modernization.

After the plantation peak achieved during the second five-year plan, the orchard area continued to expand slightly for some time, but since 1970 it has began to decline, and the proportion of old, unproductive orchards is now rising year by year. In 1981, the total orchard area was 125 000 hectares, or 1·3 per cent of the arable area, at the same time, however, the branch provides 5 per cent of the gross production value of agriculture. Two-thirds of the country's fruit-growing area comprises commercial orchards belonging to state, but of the 80 million fruit trees, only one quarter are to be found in the state and co-operative sectors, the remainder being in private gardens. Thus fruit continues to be small-scale private culture with half the country's output, or 1·8 million tons, coming from the sector. As for the growing of the most labour-intensive fruits, the role of the small private orchard is even more dominant: 90 per cent of all cherries, both sour and sweet alike, as well as the various berries are grown in family gardens.

Despite the smaller area, the quantity of fruit harvested each year does not decline and, indeed, the output of the two years between 1981 and 1982 exceeded the average of the 1970s by about 25 per cent. Since development is difficult to materialize under conditions of small-commodity production, the increase in *average orchard yields* lags behind that of other agricultural crops, there was only a 25 per cent increase during a decade and yields on most large farms do not reach a level for economic growing. As part of the large-scale plantings of the 1960s, many co-operative farms without adequate endowments, production experience, skilled personnel or equipment were given state support to establish fruit farming, but in most the enterprise has not proved profitable. Even the commercial orchards of the best state and co-operative farms are not always economic.

The phase of production and territorial concentration that co-operative farms went through during the first half of the 1970s, affected specialized fruit growing unfavourably. Fragmented orchards of relatively small size are difficult to fit into the specialized production structure of expanded modern farms, which is quite a problem when one considers that about half the co-operatives engage in fruit growing, but on most commercial orchards are less than 50 hectares in size. It is characteristic that such fragmented growing of up to 6 varieties of fruit produces yields per hectare substantially less than commercial orchards of between 250 and 500 hectares. It is worth noting, however, that four-fifths of all commercial orchards on state farms are over 250 hectares in size, thus making the application of machine systems possible. In these modern orchards yields are 3 to 4 times higher than on smaller ones.

The main task of new plantings, which, by the way, do not fully make up the trees cut down, is to improve the unfavourable composition of the tree stock, largely made up of apple trees and less valuable plum trees. Apples are grown on all farms, because the technology of large-scale growing has been developed, and picking is economical. Cherries, sour cherries and the various berries are much sought after and are highly marketable abroad, but, owing to the very high labour input necessary for picking especially in large orchards, they are somewhat pushed into the background.

Typical of fruit growing is the predominance of certain varieties of individual fruits. For example, 60 per cent of all apple output consists of Jonathans and the case with other fruits is similar. It would be ideal if a great many varieties were grown, thus lengthening the ripening period, ensuring a more balanced supply to the market, reducing fluctuations in production.

About half the annual crop consumed fresh, while 30 per cent is exported and one-fifth is processed by the canning and deep-freezing industries. The greater part of fresh consumption falls within the summer months. Since the period during which fresh fruit can be supplied can be lengthened only to a certain extent and slowly, the demand for canned but particularly deep-frozen products is increasing. Fruit consumption, of 80 kilogrammes per capita per annum still lags behind highest international levels and its increase is therefore justified.

The requirements of individual fruit crops widely differ in terms of temperature, precipitation and soil, but most varieties can be grown in most parts of the country. Nonetheless, the majority have, as a result of natural and economic factors, traditional growing districts, which supply fruit to domestic or foreign markets, or to the processing industry.

The traditional growing districts are, however, subject to geographical change *(Fig. 44)*. For instance, the growing of fruits *suitable for long-distance transport and storage*, for example, the apple, is increasingly shifting away from the domestic consumer market locations towards districts with optimum growing conditions. By contrast, *soft, non-transportable fruits* like strawberries and raspberries, continue to show a strong orientation towards the main consumer market, especially the urban agglomerations. But with deep-freezing technology gaining ground, a further change in the geographical distribution of production is taking place, this time towards the expanding network of cold-storage facilities.

These economically optimal districts do not, however, always coincide with the physiographically optimal growing districts, mainly because areas with optimal endowments for individual fruit varieties also exemplify the best possible conditions for a number of field crops. The outcome of such land use competition is always determined by economic factors such as input–return ratios, the return on fixed-assets and economic efficiency.

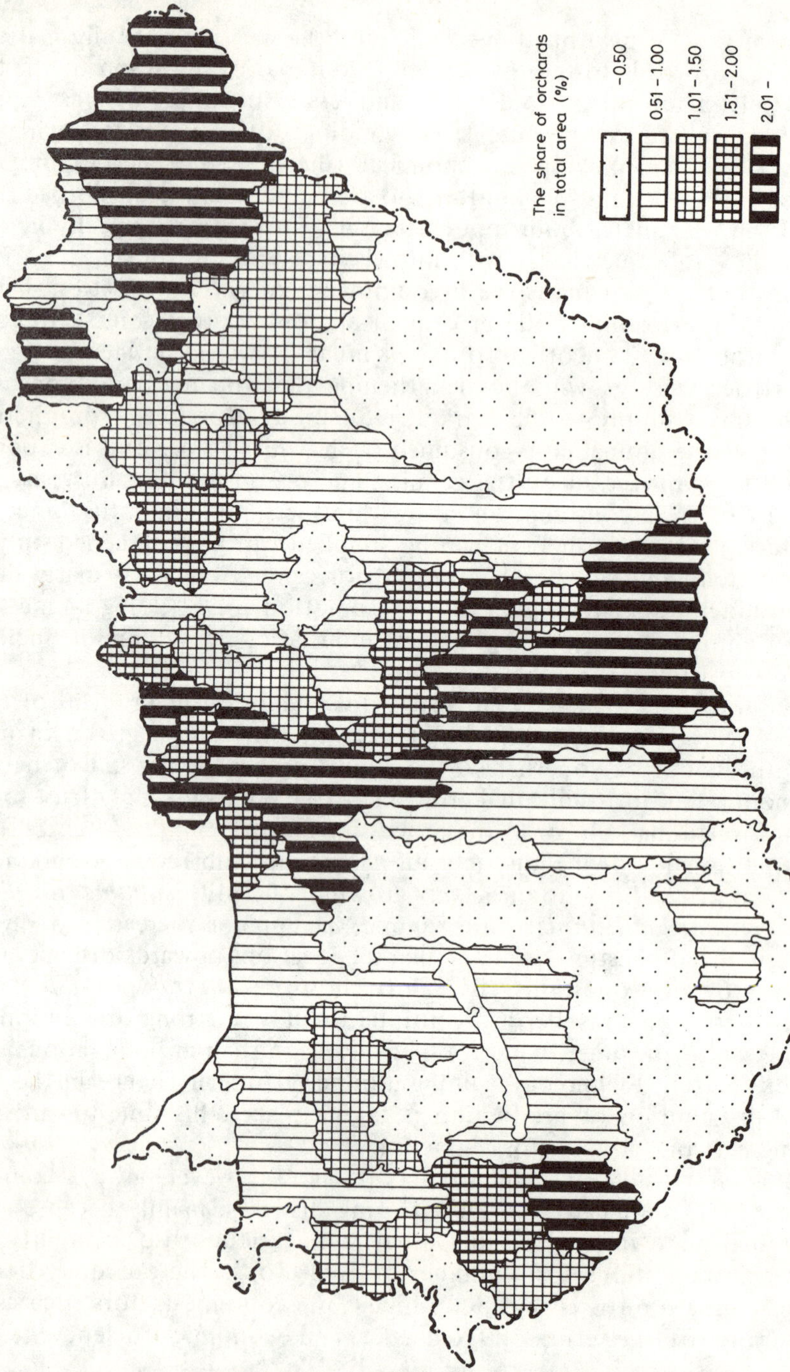

Fig. 44. The spatial distribution of orchards.

As regards the spatial distribution of the total fruit-tree stock, the greatest density is to be found in the Danube–Tisza Mid-region, in the Kiskunság, the Gödöllő hill country, the Danube Knee and the Börzsöny area. A similarly high density is to be found throughout the whole of Zala county and around Lake Balaton. The Mecsek and Villány area of southern Transdanubia is also noteworthy for its high fruit-tree density. In the Trans-Tisza region, only the tree density of the Nyírség and the Szatmár–Bereg plainland reaches that of these districts, although production on the southern slopes of the Northern Middle Mountains, in the Hernád and Sajó valleys and around Ózd is substantial.

The growing districts of the most important fruits are as follows.

Accounting for a quarter of the national stock and two-thirds of total annual fruit output, the apple is one of the most important fruits. In terms of the number of trees, it is behind the plum, but ranks first in terms of quantity and value of production. Hungarian apple growing and export is substantial by international standards, constituting 4 to 5 per cent of world production. The Jonathan, a winter apple grown in the Nyírség, is one of the most tasty and sought after varieties throughout the world.

Both summer and winter apples are common in Hungary. Summer apples are grown in the dryer, warmer regions, and winter apples in the cooler and more vaporous border districts.

The largest contiguous apple-growing district is to be found on the north-eastern border of the country, in the *Nyírség–Szatmár plainland and Bodrogköz*, in which a half of the commercial orchard area is to be found. It is an explicitly winter-apple growing district, with half the entire fruit stock being the Jonathan. This district also accounts for 80 per cent of apple exports. Besides giving a one-sided character to the district, the Jonathan is not an ideal variety for large-scale production. It is very susceptible to disease, to damage during transport and needs intensive fertilization and spraying.

The main fruits of the *sandy area of the Danube-Tisza Mid-region* are also winter and summer apples, but with a more varied production pattern than that of the Nyírség. Along with Jonathan, the mildew-resistant Starking and Golden Delicious varieties are grown in considerable proportions.

The *West-Transdanubian district*, more precisely Zala county, is the third characteristic winter-apple growing district of the country.

Hungary's apple exports, amounting to 1·2 to 1·5 per cent of total export, are increasing year by year. They are directed mainly to the two Germanies, the Soviet Union, the Skandinavian countries and Australia.

Owing to their non-exacting character, plums are the most common fruit of the country, and plum trees account for a quarter of the fruit-tree stock. Plums are grown practically everywhere, except on alkali soils, but yields are low and only 7 per cent of the tree stock is in co-operative or state farm ownership. Still, some typical plum-growing districts are to be found primarily on the floodplains in the *Tisza–Szamos interfluve*. Of more minor significance is the Northern district with small plum-growing areas in Nógrád, Heves and Borsod counties, but intensive cropping is to be found in the *administrative district of Buda*, which supplies the capital directly with fresh plums.

Apricots enjoy great popularity, and can be found in almost all family gardens. As regards their tree stock, they amount for 7 per cent of the total fruit-tree stock and are the second most important fruit in terms of production value. Hungarian apricots have practically no competitors on the European market, because they ripen when Italian and Spanish apricots are already out of the season. Demand is thus great, and they constitute the country's most significant fruit export.

The most important growing district is the Danube–Tisza Mid-region with Kecskemét as its centre, accounting for half the non-private apricot-producing area. The district surrounds the towns of Cegléd, Nagykőrös, Kecskemét and Kiskunhalas and is of a definitely commercial-producing character, with no counterpart in the rest of Europe. A further growing district of less significance is *Fejér county* in Transdanubia.

Apricot exports vary between 300 and 600 waggonloads annually, depending upon production. They are sent mostly to neighbouring countries in the north, but western Europe is also a significant importer. A large quantity is processed by the canning industry, while considerable amounts are exported as Kecskemét apricot brandy.

Peaches require the greatest amount of heat and sunshine of all the fruit crops of Hungary, commensurate with their Chinese subtropical origin. This fruit is rarely grown in countries to the north of Hungary, and exports are therefore considerable.

The traditional growing district is the *Érd, Nagytétény, Budaörs area to the west of Budapest*, which primarily supplies the capital, but from which substantial amounts are also exported. The second most important peach-growing district of the country, developed during the past two decades, is the *Szeged–Szatymaz area*, which has been established on a strictly commercial basis and from which three quarters of annual output is exported.

Cherries and sour cherries, taken together, account for one-tenth of the fruit stock. Their best growing areas are the southern slopes of the middle mountains, but they also extend over the Great Plain. Sour cherries are very common in the plainland, while cherries thrive more on the slopes of the Middle Mountains and in the *Buda, Eger, Gyöngyös and Balaton areas*. Early-maturing varieties, however, are concentrated in the southern part of the Danube–Tisza Mid-region and in the *Szeged–Kelebia district*.

Walnuts grow mainly in *south-western Transdanubia* and in the *north-eastern part of the Great Plain*, along the Upper-Tisza river.

Chestnuts and almonds, of Mediterranean derivation, can be found primarily on the southern slopes of *west-southwest Transdanubia*, and in the *Transdanubian Central Mountains*.

During the past two decades, the production of *berry fruits* has expanded. With their unique colour, flavour characteristics and vitamin content they are regarded as superior to many other fruits and their net production unit value is very high. Export opportunities are outstanding, and their competitiveness in foreign markets is unchallenged.

The production of these soft fruits shows a high degree of orientation towards the consumer market because they are easily damaged during transport. One quarter of the total output is derived from farms around Budapest and in the county of Pest, while the establishment of the cold-storage industry in Debrecen has led to the development of a new growing centre in the Hajdúság.

The most valuable fruit for the preserving industry is the *raspberry*, most of which is grown in Pest, Győr counties and in the northern parts of the country. The bulk of the output of these three districts is deep-frozen by the local cold-storage facilities in Dunakeszi, Győr and Miskolc.

The production of *strawberries*, although substantially expanded during recent years, does not cover domestic and external demands. Production is also concentrated in three areas, namely close to Budapest on Szentendre island, in the Kiskunság and around Szeged.

The demand, both domestic and foreign, for red and black *currants* is too great to be satisfied. Their main growing districts are the environs of Budapest and Mátraalja.

2.7.2 Vegetable production and the preserving industry

Vegetable growing is one of the most dynamically developing and remunerative branches of intensive agriculture, and although occupying a small area, provide a high production value per unit area. Fir instance, they take up to 3 to 4 per cent of the arable area, but account for 6 per cent of the gross production value of agriculture. In a country like Hungary, where population density is relatively high, it is impossible to increase the area under cultivation and for this reason the intensive branches, among them vegetable growing, play a more and more important role. This trend is corroborated by the pattern of food production:

– Per capita consumption of vitamin-rich vegetables (75 kilogrammes) is low, both as regards actual biological need and also by international standards and should be further increased.

– The potential for the growing of most vegetables is good, both in terms of quantity and quality, given the warm summers and abundant sunshine.

– Certain varieties like red peppers and onions can be grown to high quality in Hungary, and offer significant export opportunities both in fresh and canned form.

As a result of these incentives, vegetable production has tripled, reaching 2 million tons during the past few decades. The steady expansion of fresh vegetable supply laid the foundation for a large-scale increase in the canning industry during the early 1960s, which quadrupled its production during a decade and a half. The preserving industry based on vegetable and fruit processing is now a significant branch of the economy. In addition to satisfying home consumption, an increasing quantity of fresh and processed vegetables is exported.

The labour requirements of the vegetable sector, which has developed on large-scale farms, but which is undertaken by small-scale methods, have proved more and more difficult to satisfy in recent years, especially in industrialized areas. Because of a lack of manpower, the vegetable sector began to decline during the 1970s and was unable to compete with wheat and maize production which adopted well-mechanized factory production techniques. The profitability position of vegetable growing is seriously jeopardized by low average yields, which lag far behind the European average. Typical is the fact that tomato and cabbage yields reach only a half to two-thirds of Hungary's main competitors, Bulgaria, Italy and Spain. Fluctuations in average yields, dependent upon the weather, alone account for the uncertainties of the vegetable market, which in turn reacts on production and makes that instable too. In the meantime, the government has taken several measures which have encouraged production, created more secure marketing and have laid the foundations for mechanized large-scale production. In recent years, the large-scale mechanization of green peas and French bean production has been carried out, and significant results have also been attained in the mechanization of onion and paprika production, while the mechanization of tomatoes and root crops is also making progress. Complex machine systems are available for certain crops only, but their procurement prices and operation costs are high. The mechanization of vegetable production for industrial purposes is relatively well developed, but harvesting of vegetables for fresh consumption and export purposes have not been solved anywhere in the world yet. Therefore, vegetable production on private plots, in small and week-end gardens, providing more than one-third of all vegetable output, is of special importance. Compared with the production of agricultural co-operatives, the role of state farms in large-scale production and in diffusion of production systems is significant.

A certain degree of production concentration has also taken place in vegetable growing, but the conditions for specialization, such as complex mechanization, the selection of varieties suitable for large-scale production, sustained levels of profitability level, are still missing. Specialization and concentration are making but slow progress not only in the scale of production but also territorially as well. Nearly half the vegetable-growing co-operatives produce four or more crops, often on an area not larger than a quarter to a half hectare. Even spices, which are relatively concentrated in large, traditional growing areas, are produced in a rather fragmented fashion. Paprika or red pepper is grown, for example, by two dozen farms in the Kalocsa district on an average area of 150 hectares each, and by the same number of farms in the area around Szeged on an average of 50 hectares, but also on as little as 3 hectares on a few farms. Most developed is the concentration of green peas, grown on average of 200 hectares. The degree of production and territorial specialization in vegetable sector is thus determined by momentary profitability, by the availability of labour and by the means of production rather than by long-term decision making with regard to territorial specialization. Often historically established growing districts have lost their local specificity and are disintegrating.

The market plays a special role in the geographical distribution of vegetable growing. The main consumer centres are the towns, the canning factories and the freezing plants. The impact of consumption on the location of production often exceeds that of natural endowments. In the supply belts of urban centres growing predominantly vegetables, the neglect of natural endowments and the attendant cost increments are compensated for by lower transport costs. Low soil fertility is offset by the intensive application of fertilizers, any lack of precipitation is replaced by irrigation, and insufficient heat is overcome by growing in greenhouses and under plastic covers. The pull of the consumer market is not equally apparent for all vegetable crops. Some like cabbages, onions and red peppers can endure transportation and storage and can therefore be grown farther away from the consumer market, provided production conditions are favourable. Most vegetables, however, cannot stand transportation, quality deteriorates, and transport in refrigerated freight cars is very expensive. Such vegetables have to be grown near the consumer market even if optimum growing districts are located elsewhere. Canning factories provide optimal locations when produce can be transported from nearby at minimal costs.

The different vegetable crops grown in Hungary — about 50 in number — require very divergent natural conditions and cultivation methods, and an even greater difference can be experienced in their economic significance. The geographical distribution of the individual crops and the regional characteristics of production will be discussed in Part IV of the book in connection with economic districts. In the following we shall summarize the main vegetable-growing districts of the country, pointing out the proportions and associations of the principle crops *(Fig. 45)*.

a) The historically established, traditional vegetable-growing districts are as follows:

— The capital and its environment which is significant for early vegetables, root crops and mushrooms;

— The North-Pest district, comprising the southern foreground of the Gödöllő hill country where tomatoes are mainly grown;

— The South-Pest district around Vecsés of mixed vegetables and cabbages;

— The Kecskemét–Nagykőrös district noted for its lettuce, cucumbers and tomatoes;

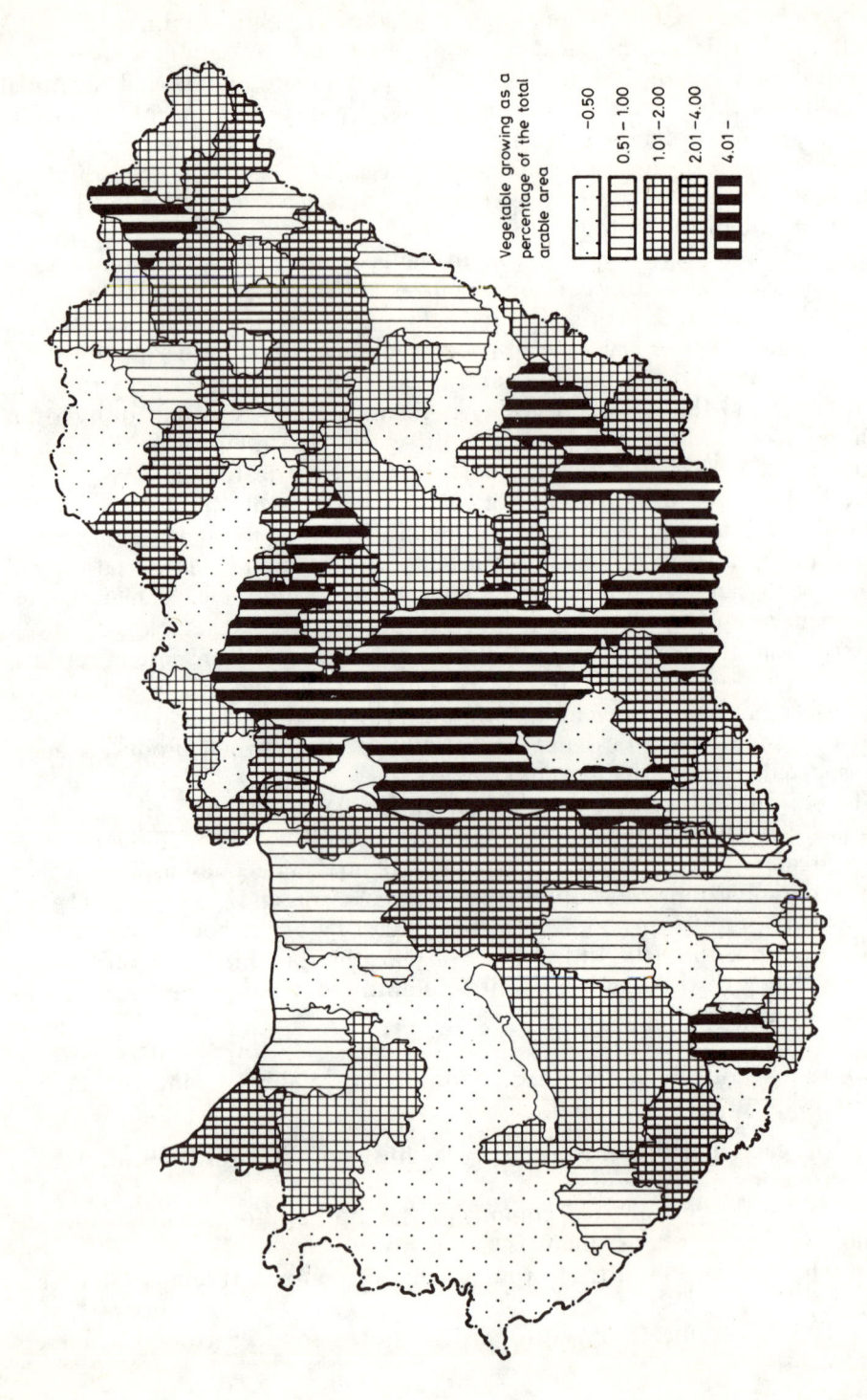

Fig. 45. The spatial distribution of vegetable production

– The Kalocsa district with its red peppers;
– The Szeged district where red peppers, green paprika and tomatoes are grown;
– The Makó district noted for onions, garlics and root crops;
– The Szentes district where the growing of early vegetables under greenhouses heated by thermal water, and green paprika, kohlrabi and tomatoes for fresh consumption are to be found;
– The Mohács district with its cabbages and early green peas,
– The Cece district which concentrates mainly on green paprika.

b) Districts that have evolved around canning factories and cold-storage plants are.

– The Heves district with Hatvan as its centre noted mainly for tomatoes and melons;
– The Békéscsaba–Gyula district with its green peas and French beans;
– The Debrecen district where green peas and French beans are grown,
– The Nyírség district with cabbages, green peas and tomatoes;
– The Szigetvár district noted for its green peas and French beans,
– The Nagyatád district where tomatoes, cucumbers and green peas are grown;
– The Paks district with green peas and French beans.

c) New vegetable-growing districts have been established, and some old districts with small areas have been expanded in the vicinity of industrial and resort areas as follows:

– The Nógrád district,
– The Miskolc district;
– The Balaton district, comprising the southern shore of the lake.

Potatoes

Potetoes are a crop with a wide scope for utilization, being not only a variety of vegetable, but also a valuable fodder and industrial raw material. The consumption of potatoes has somewhat decreased, with the consumption of other vegetables and meat gaining ground, but still about half to two-thirds of the potatoes grown are used for human consumption, Their use for the manufacture of industrial starch has, owing to high production costs, decreased.

The decrease in the potato area and the simultaneous rise in yields is a worldwide phenomenon. In Hungary, however, the large-scale decrease in the sown area has not been accompanied by a rise in yields, and the output of the last few years is thus about three quarters of the output attained a decade earlier.

A characteristic feature is the slow rise in average yield. Average yields are 15 to 18 tons per hectare, i.e. overpassing scarcely the world average, and far behind the yields in European countries with developed potato growing. The low yield has a significant role to play in the relative fall in profitability and the large-scale decrease in sown area.

The *soil requirements* for potatoes can easily be met on the light, gently acidic, sandy terrains of the country, but what is important for them is a balanced distribution rather than the absolute quantity of precipitation. Long, dry summers are not favourable and their production on the Great Plain is therefore insignificant, apart from some sandy regions.

Their most important growing district is the Nyírség with the largest sown area, and accounting for one-sixth of the country's potato output. Potatoes make up more than 6 per cent of the arable area, rising to 10 to 15 per cent in certain parts. The *inner-Somogy sandy hill country* in Transdanubia also stands out with its large-scale production of good-quality potatoes, and is second to the Nyírség in significance. Both districts supply the capital and the densely populated industrial regions, and account for one-third of the country's commercial crop. In addition potato growing in the *Transdanubian Central Mountains* and to the west of them in *Vas county*, in the *Danube– Tisza Mid-region* as well as in certain smaller basins of the *Northern Mountains* is fairly large scale.

As to average *yields*, the highest are attained in Somogy district, where fluctuations are also smallest. In the largest potato-growing district, the Nyírség, average yields reached scarcely the national one.

The preserving industry

The development of both the canning and freezing branches of the preserving industry, has outstripped all other branches of the food-processing industry. Large-scale canning began in the 1960s, while the rapid development of freezing had to wait until the last decade.

The preserving industry account for more than 10 per cent of the output of the food industry and about one half of all vegetables and 30 per cent of all fruit grown are preserved, totalling in an excess of 1 million tons. The industry is heavily export-oriented and three quarters of the canned vegetable and over one half the fruit output is sent abroad. Also exported is more than half the output of the freezing plants.

Canning factories are oriented towards the raw produce base. This locational orientation can be seen in the case of the first canning factories that were built in the Danube–Tisza Mid-region at Hatvan, Nagykőrös, Kecskemét and Szeged as well as in the Transdanubia factories at Paks, Szigetvár, Nagyatád *(Fig. 46)*. Canning factories were also built in Budapest and nearby Dunakeszi where consumption is highest. This one-sided locational situation was, however, transformed in the 1960s, with the setting up of three factories in the Trans-Tisza region at Békéscsaba, Debrecen and Nyíregyháza, all three being sited in areas where vegetable cultivation was underdeveloped, where canned vegetables and fruit were not produced at all, but where abun-

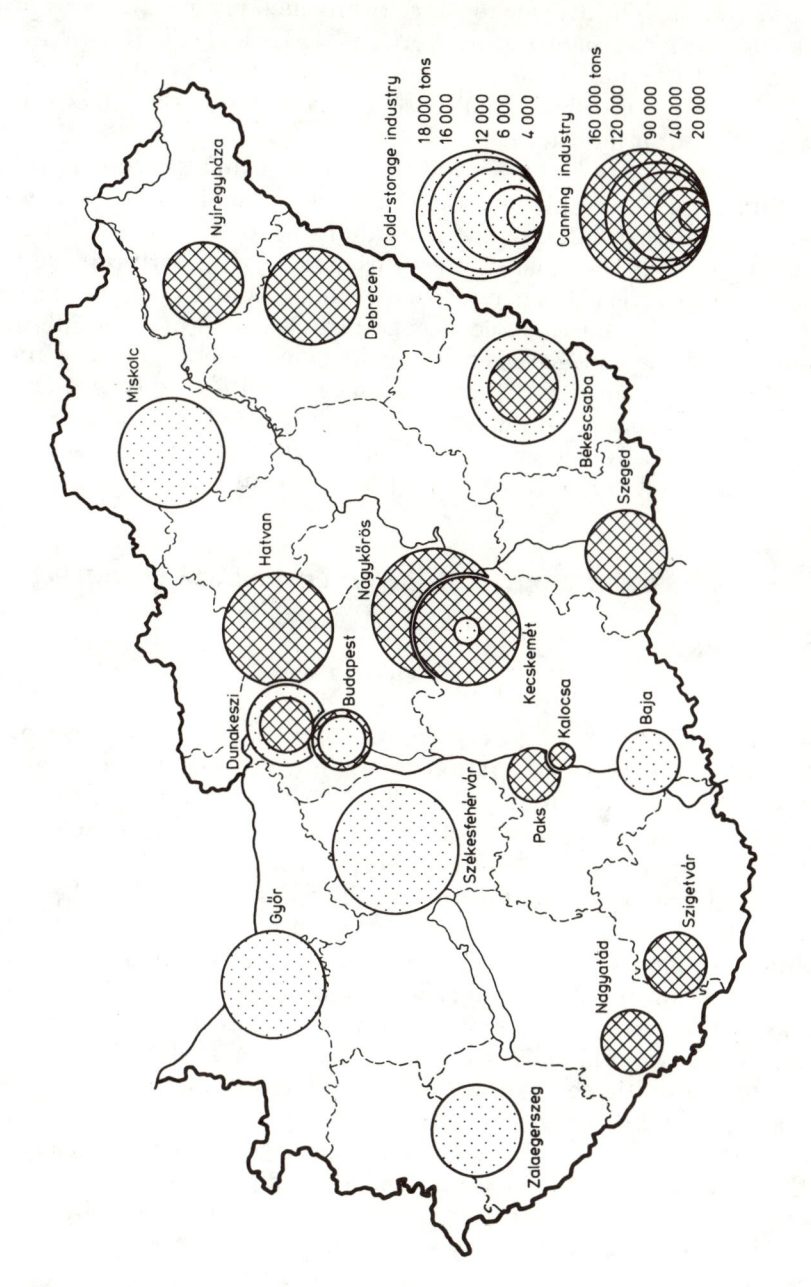

Fig. 46. The spatial location of the preserving industry

dant labour was available. These factories have themselves come to create their own raw-material basis, and function as centres that attract and organize production. The average distance over which raw produce is transported to plants, increased significantly between 1970 and 1975 with the reconstruction of the canning industry, and as a result transport costs now represent over 5 per cent of the total costs of the sector, a value that is only surpassed in the sugar industry.

The network of *cold-storage plants* — using roughly the same raw produce, their perishable nature playing a decisive role — duplicate the locational pattern of the canning industry and is sited in Budapest, Dunakeszi, Kecskemét and Békéscsaba. Beside cold-storage, this industry also performs the function of deep-freezing. The former activity is concentrated primarily in the large consumer centres, and the cold-storage plants located in Győr, Miskolc, Székesfehérvár, Baja and Zalaegerszeg make possible not only the processing and storing of foodstuffs designed to meet local demands, but also enable the storage of products, should world-prices be too low. In the expansion of the national cold-storage chain, new plants will have to be built in southern Transdanubia and in the northern part of the Great Plain [25].

2.8 Fodder crops, and the production and processing of animal products

2.8.1 Fodder crops

Animal husbandry is closely connected with the production of fodder crops and what energy generation means for industry, fodder crop production means for animal husbandry. The nations's animal stock requires over one million tons of various types of fodder per year, reflected in the fact that along with meadows and pastures, which constitute one-sixth of total farmland, nearly 60 per cent of the arable area is also used for the growing of fodder crops. The relative size of the area utilized for animal husbandry is not proportionate to the 50 per cent share of animal products in agriculture, which reacts on the economic efficiency of animal husbandry and the production of animal products. The solution to this problem requires an increase in fodder yield and a more efficient use of feed. This problem is also connected with the breakdown of fodder crops, the composition of the animal stock and the level of livestock farming.

Up to the end of last decade, fodder shortage had been a steady obstacle to the development of animal husbandry, despite the fact that fodder crops were grown on a larger proportion of the arable land than before the last war. The main reasons for this were. the backwardness in the growing of non-grain and succulent fodder crops and the low level of specific feed utilization.

The state of fodder production is shown by the figures in the table below.

Fodder yields in tons per hectare
(starch values)

	Grain fodder (maize, barley, oats)	Mass green feed (arable feed crops other than grain, and yields from meadows and pastures)	Fodder crops combined
Average for the years 1951–55	1·43	0·62	0·99
Average for the years 1961–70	2·02	0·54	1·18
Average for the years 1971–75	3·02	0·62	1·67
Average for the years 1976–80	3·58	0·68	1·96

The development of the feed basis has been uneven. While in grain-fodder production, owing to the steadily rising yields, an increasing trend has prevailed, per-hectare yields of green feed stuffs has remained at the level of the early 1950s despite an expansion of the sown area, a process that has boosted pig and poultry farming, but has hampered cattle and sheep husbandry. Particularly badly affected are meadows and pastures, where hay yields are less than before the last war. The shift in the proportions of the various feedstuffs is closely related to structural changes in the composition of the country's livestock [95].

An inter-country examination of fodder crop yields reveals that grain-fodder yields are about the same as those in the most developed countries, whereas non-grain feedstuff yields lag considerably behind, primarily due to different climatic endowments and to the uneven distribution of precipitation. The vagaries of precipitation constitute a serious retarding factor in the growing of green feedstuffs which require a minimum humidity level and are susceptible to drought. All this of course is reflected in the composition and territorial intensity of animal husbandry in Hungary, which in terms of head of cattle per unit area lags considerably behind that of the neighbouring countries of Czechoslovakia, Austria, Poland and GDR. On the other hand, Hungary is one of the more significant pig-producing countries of Europe.

Fodder output during average years approximately meets actual demand, although the ensurance of the protein content constitutes a persistent problem as the opportunities for the economic cultivation of protein-rich fodder crops, such as fodder peas and oil seed from sunflowers, is limited. Since these sources are expanding more slowly than the demand, the import of protein fodder in the form of fish meal and soya beans from the West has steadily increased, and now amounts to about 250 000 tons per annum with a value of 150 million dollars.

The primary way of developing the production of feedstuffs is to increase yields, by utilizing those parts of the country with optimum natural conditions in terms of climatic and soil endowments. It is common knowledge that through the rational utilization of natural endowments the economic efficiency of production can be improved. At the same time, given the same labour input, higher yields can be attained under favourable natural endowments, and there is hence a close correlation between conditions and labour productivity. In the present-day conditions of a deterioration in the capital efficiency of agriculture, a substantial factor amounting for expensive fodder production is the degree of non-correspondence between areas with optimal endowments and the location of fodder production. In other words, fodder crops, like maize and lucerne, are also grown in areas where their ecological requirements are not met.

a) *Fodder grains*. Fodder grains (maize, barley, oats) now take up a lower proportion of arable land than in the past, largely on account of increased yields per hectare and a consequent rise in the volume of output, with the exception of oats. Indicative of the shift towards intensive production is the fact that compared with the years before the last war a doubling of output has been attained over the past three years from a smaller area.

Maize is the key grain in field crop cultivation. It is grown on an area of more than one million hectares, and yields are among the highest in the world. Its significance stems from the fact that under the given natural conditions of Hungary it is the grain crop that provides the highest nutritional value per unit area, and is the feed basis for pig and poultry raising. Maize, combined with proteins, amino acids and vitamins is also the principal constituent of fodder concentrates. In Hungary, the vertical *chain comprised of maize, pigs and poultry is, owing to its relatively moderate demand for fixed assets and labour, a determinant factor in agricultural production* and an important basis for the country's participation in the international division of labour. At the same time, maize, including the stalk, is an important feedstuff for cattle and sheep also.

Of the various factors of the physical environment climate is the most important determinant of maize cultivation. Like wheat, it requires *hot summers, but its demand for precipitation is much greater*, especially in midsummer, and July droughts can therefore be very harmful. The most significant growing districts lie to the south of the 17 °C isotherm as measured between April and September.

The soil requirements of maize are not exacting: it thrives best on humus-rich clay and alluvial soils, but also grows satisfactorily on sandy soils with sufficient nutrients. Nor is it specifically sensitive to the chemical composition of the soil, only soils with a high alkaline concentration or with extreme acidity (below 5 pH) being prohibitive to its growth. Given these constraints maize can be cultivated in the greatest part of the country, which makes Hungary the northernmost European country with a substantial grain maize production.

The *area sown* to maize has been fluctuating between 1·1 and 1·5 million hectares per annum for the last half century, the precise hectarage being connected with changes in the economic efficiency of maize growing and with pig and poultry raising. The increase during the first half of the 1970s was due to three factors: the significant improvement in yields consequent upon the widespread use of high-yielding hybrid varieties, the rapid growth of pig raising and, last but not least, the expansion of export opportunities. Since the mid-1970s, however, yield improvement has not been able to keep pace with the price rises in fertilizers and herbicides, and the consequent decline in profitability has been accompanied by a temporary decrease in the area sown to maize.

During the first period of improved yields from 1970 to 1974, the area sown to maize increased in all parts of the country, independently of ecological conditions but the introduction and spread of production systems created an undesirable restructuring of the territorial pattern of production. While maize production slightly increased in the traditional growing districts of Békés, Csongrád, Szolnok and Hajdú-Bihar counties on the Great Plain, where optimal natural conditions prevail, its sown area increased most vigorously, by some 25 to 27 per cent, in unfavourable growing districts, as in the upland areas and basins of the Northern Middle Mountains, where the crop does not even ripen in certain years. By contrast, during the decrease in the sown area between the years 1976 and 1980, it fell but moderately in the peripheral areas.

Although the cultivation of maize extends throughout the country, its sown area is nonetheless slightly more concentrated than that of wheat, and two-thirds of total maize output is produced in two major districts *(Fig. 47)*. *The most significant of these runs along the north-south section of the Danube* and comprises the Mezőföld Plain, South-Tolna and Baranya counties, the left-hand floodplain of the Danube and the North-Bácska region. Throughout this district, the area under maize accounts for 35 to 40 per cent of the arable area.

The other principle growing district is to be found farther north in the Trans-Tisza region on the Békés–Csanád loess table and on the excellent dark-brown meadow-type soils of the Szolnok and Debrecen loess regions. The occurrence also of alkali soils in the Trans-Tisza mid-region prevents, however, the formation of a contiguous district comparable to that in the Danube valley.

A third area of cultivation is the Danube–Tisza Mid-region, and despite its rather poor sandy soils, the proportion of arable under maize exceeds the national average. The same applies to *Somogy* and *Komárom* counties, too.

The lowest proportion of the arable area sown to maize up to the 1960s was in Central and Western Transdanubia and in the Northern Middle Mountains, where the cooler climate were less favourable to the traditional strains which had a long growing period; but, with the subsequent spread of new, high-yielding hybrids with a shorter growing period, comparatively good yields have been attained in Western Transdanubia and the sown area extended.

1 point = 200 tons

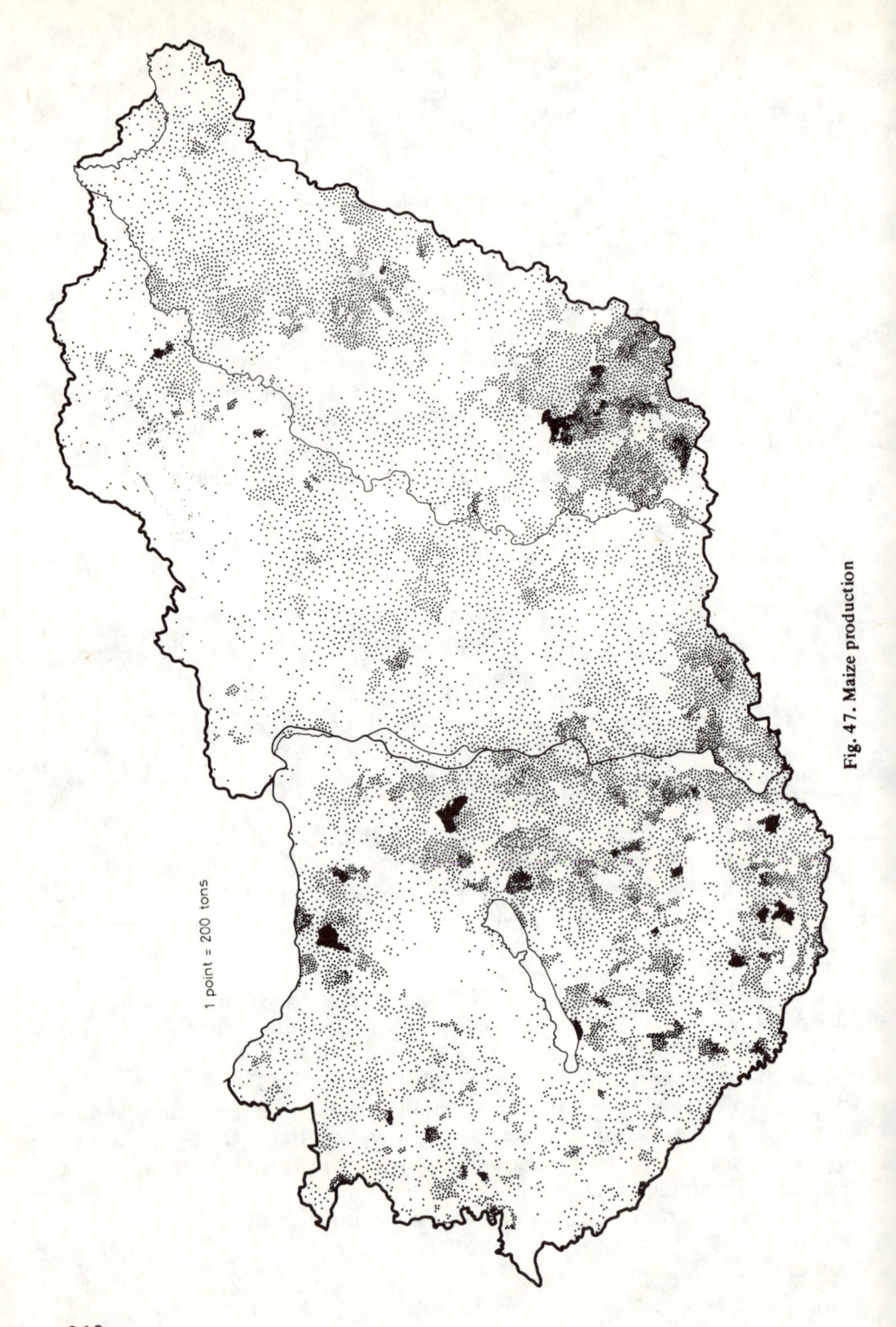

Fig. 47. Maize production

The application of selective weed-killers has also helped to increase maize output in the hillier regions of the country, where earlier the proportion of the area under maize was rather limited owing to *the danger of erosion* from repeated hoeing, to reduce weeds. With the application of super-selective chemical substances and without hoeing, the intercultivation of maize with other crops has in fact became a most useful protective against erosion. With the introduction of modern techniques and the widespread use of high-yielding strains with a shorter growing period, the western countries of Somogy, Zala and Vas with their more abundant precipitation have indeed now joined those districts, where yields are reasonably secure. Increased pig raising in the region has also helped speed up this process. Although the introduction of factory production systems only dates back a few years, by the end of the 1970s, system production dominated two-thirds of the sown area having Bábolna, Nádudvar and Baja centres.

Maize has been in fact one of the most successful post-war crops. The use of hybrid seeds, and the application of weed-killers and chemical fertilizers had pushed yields three times above the pre-war level by the end of the 1970s. As a result Hungary, with yields of 5·8 to 6·8 tons per hectare now belong to the top group of countries in the world in terms of maize production.

From among the most prominent growing districts, the *Danube valley and the south-eastern part of the Great Plain boast the highest yields*, while elsewhere production is below the national average. Indeed, very poor yields were achieved in the Danube–Tisza Mid-region and in the Northern Middle Mountains where a more extensive type of cultivation is pursued although the adoption of production systems would be likely to have little effect. Borsod-Abaúj-Zemplén and Nógrád counties with yields of 3·7 to 4·5 tons per hectare far behind the best areas, and rarely cover the production costs.

Although most of the maize crop is used as fodder, it can also be utilized by *industry* in a number of ways. Along with various starch derivatives, rectified spirit, oil and extracted grits, maize is also suitable for the production of liquid invert sugar. From the technical and economical viewpoints the complex industrial processing of maize is the most practical and efficient, that is the combination of sugar refining and distillation with the simultaneous extraction of protein fodder and oil. A new plant for this purpose has been built at Szabadegyháza, in one of the country's most developed production districts, and where the existing distillation plant ensures an appropriate background for the industrial processing of maize. The experiences of this first factory will be drawn upon in lying the foundations for the development of an up-to-date maize processing industry.

The demand for maize occupies a prominent and reasonably stable place in world trade. Therefore, an alternative of its utilization will invariably remain its secure marketing abroad. It is a crop, which is cultivated on such a large scale that it places Hungary *among the world's significant producers,* coming only after France, Romania and Yugoslavia in Europe in terms of volume of output. Between 1981 and 1982 output averaged 7·3 million tons, and accounted for a quarter of the total production of all CMEA countries combined.

Of the cereals, *barley* is the most important fodder crop, but also important is the industrial utilization, for instance, in brewery, of spring barley. In Hungary, both spring and autumn barley are grown, because winters are sufficiently mild with enough precipitation for autumn sowings to play a substantial role. The ecological requirements and the geographical distribution of the two types, however, differ substantially from one another.

Autumn barley is the more exacting, requires more intensive cultivation, and since it also makes use of winter precipitation, yields are higher than those of spring barley. Nonetheless, prior to the country's liberation, it occupied only a 25 per cent of the area sown to barley, although subsequently, as autumn-sown bread grains have declined, and operations have become mechanized, the area under the more valuable autumn-sown barley has expanded. After maize, barley is the most widespread coarse fodder crop, with great significance in pig rearing, and in the feeding of pigs and piglets, being rich in starch and protein it is also a valuable feed for other animals. The *area sown* to autumn barley amounting to 135 000 hectares, now occupies about the half of the total barley area and is used exclusively for feeding.

The climatic and soil requirements of autumn barley are much the same as those of wheat, but cold areas without prolonged snow cover are unsuitable for its cultivation. Of all autumn grains, autumn barley is the most sensitive to winter frost. The most important growing area of the grain is South-Transdanubia, the broader Mecsek region and the Little Plain as well as the Danube–Tisza Mid-region, where the winter is less severe and the incidence of frost damage less likely. Other significant growing areas are to be found only in the *south-eastern parts of the Great Plain and, to a smaller extent, in the mid-Tisza region*. Its acreage in upland regions is generally insignificant.

The *average yield* of autumn barley, at 3 to 3·7 tons per hectare compares well with other autumn cereals, and its growth rate has improved. The highest yields are recorded in the Little Plain, the Mezőföld Plain and the south-eastern part of the Great Plain, while average yields are to be found in South-Transdanubia.

Spring barley is grown for animal feed and also for the brewing industry. Using the average of the last 5 years, some 5 to 15 per cent is used for brewing. The temperature demand of spring barley is moderate, but it requires more precipitation and, particularly, a more even distribution than autumn barley. Spring barley belongs to the grain varieties with the shortest growing period, during which it requires moderately warm rainfall. Warm, dry or late springs are unfavourable. The *climatic requirement of malting barley is even higher, needing a moderately mild and rather moist, humid and rainy climate*.

Spring barley can be grown in all but poor, loose, sandy, or heavily bound clay, bog and alkali soils. Owing to its short growing period, however, it needs sufficient and easily absorbable nutrients, and therefore *thrives best in deep limey and humus-rich meadow loams*. The crop gains protein in highly nitrogenous soils, which makes it less suitable for brewing and malt production. Nor are acidic soils favourable for high-quality barley. The dependence of the crop on climatic and soil conditions is best shown by the territorial pattern of cultivation. Its main growing districts are to be found in the areas in which the production of malting barley is also concentrated. Two typical brewing-barley districts have evolved. The first occurs along *Rába valley in the Little Plain and the surroundings of Sopron,* where high yields and output indicate that optimum production conditions are fully utilized.

The second is to be found on *the plainland periphery of the Cserhát–Mátra–Bükk and Zemplén Mountains, and also along the Hernád valley* with its good soil. The area sown to spring barley in these regions generally amounts to 9 to 10 per cent of the total arable land.

Feed barley is grown mainly in the upland regions of the western parts of the Transdanubian Central Mountains and patchily in the mid-Tisza region, where climatic and soil endowments mean that maize can be grown less successfully. The cultivation of feed barley, on the other hand, is completely missing in the sandy regions of the country and in Zala county. In recent years, the transitory decrease in the sown area has been accompanied by a large-scale concentration of production in growing districts with optimal conditions. The two typical malting barley districts account for about two-thirds of spring-barley cultivation.

National *yields* have increased significantly compared with the past, although substantial fluctuations still occur, with, for example, 1·7 tons per hectare in 1970 and 3·4 tons per hectare in 1980.

There are also considerable territorial differences in yields. In the Little Plain large-scale output is accompanied by favourable and even explicitly high yields, but yields in the extensive northern growing district are at best medium, and in parts of this district poor.

Breweries are not located in the barley-growing districts but are dispersed throughout the country *(Fig. 48),* reflecting the character of the consumer market. Half of the breweries are concentrated in Budapest where several high-capacity plants are to be found. Two of the four provincial breweries are in the maltery-barley districts of Sopron and Bőcs in Borsod county, while the other two are located in Transdanubia, in Nagykanizsa and Pécs. The establishment of a new brewery at Martfű in the Great Plain is in process would further improve the territorial structure of the industry.

The proportion of the arable area taken up by oats, another important feed grain has declined to *one-eight* of its pre-war value, *a decline greater than the fall in the horse stock, their main consumer*. Contributing to this sharp decline has been the country's erratic and drought-prone climate, which is unfavourable for the growing of oats and which is responsable, along with traditional cultivation techniques, for the extremely low yields and the inefficiency of production.

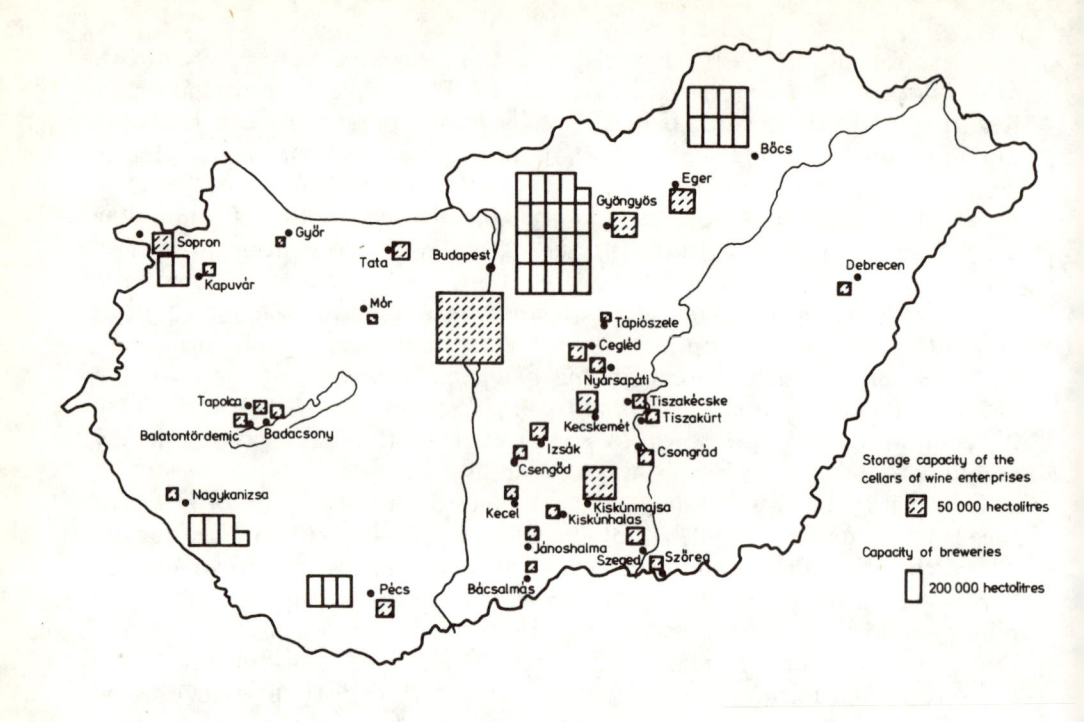

Fig. 48. The spatial location of the wine and brewing industries

Its main growing district can be found in those areas with optimal conditions, namely in Western and Southern Transdanubia, especially in Vas county, where the sown area in parts reaches as much as 5 per cent. During the past decade, a *significant concentration* has been effected in the territorial distribution of production in that more than half the sown area falls within the above districts with optimum endowments.

The average yield of oats, since they are grown on poor soils, is very low, far behind that achieved by the countries of Western Europe. It is in fact the only cereal crop where yields at 2·5 to 2·9 tons per hectare are only just above the pre-war level. The best yields are attained in Western Hungary with its cooler climate and more even precipitation.

b) *Green fodder crops*. While the area sown to grain crops – as we have seen – has hardly changed, the area sown to green fodder crops has grown quite strongly, but this, however, is offset by a contraction in the area under meadows and pastures. Moreover, while changes in the internal structure of fodder grains have generally been accompanied by substantial yield increases, any internal restructuring of green fodder crops has taken place *in the con-*

text *of stagnant average yields*, and the yields of lucerne, red clover and silage maize only just exceed the low values of the pre-war period. Thus the combined output of green fodder crops, including hay, is hardly more than it was at the time of the liberation of the country.

A wide range of green fodder crops are grown as part of the arable rotation, among which the significance and the geographical diffusion of lucerne and red clover are most noteworthy. Silage maize used for cattle feed is also important, but turnips are less so.

Lucerne ranks first among the various arable green fodder crops. It is a papillionaceous field crop with a high nutrient content and rich in protein, which as well as being an animal feed is also useful for soil amelioration purposes. *The significance of Hungarian lucerne production is enhanced by the high quality and exportability of its seed*. In recent years, lucerne has occupied an area of around 350 000 hectares. It is also used as a cheap method of producing protein, and in fact furnishes one quarter of all the protein produced for feeding purposes. Nor is the production of lucerne flour negligible, an important export item to capitalist markets.

Lucerne is very sensitive to natural conditions, which are more dominant in accounting for the geographical distribution of its production than in the care of either wheat or maize. It is best grown in *deep, calcareous soils, rich in nutrients*. Yields in terms of hay are dependent on an even distribution of precipitation, although it can *also endure warm and dry periods*. Its specific climatic requirements, however, exhibit wide differences depending on whether it is grown for feed or for seed, higher temperatures being required for the latter. *Optimum natural conditions* for seed are offered mostly in the middle and southern parts of the Great Plain with their dry and warm summers. It is, in essence, these regions and the western part of the Little Plain and South-Transdanubia which constitute the best districts for growing lucerne as a feed crop.

The production districts of lucerne roughly coincide with the best-growing areas. *Its territorial share is largest in the Great Plain, mainly in the Nagykunság and in the southern part of the Trans-Tisza region as well as further, on the Debrecen loess table and in the southern foothill of the Northern Mountains*. The sown area in the Mezőföld, in Baranya county is also large, as is that in the western part of the Little Plain.

Of the world's significant lucerne-growing areas the Great Hungarian Plain is the driest, and as a result yields are low, at around 5 tons against a pre-war value of 4 tons per hectare. *The highest yields are recorded from the loess-table areas and the Little Plain*. The low average yields stem from the fact that the large-scale system of hay growing is still only in its initial stage. An increase in productivity is of particular significance because the weakest point of Hungarian fodder production is precisely protein shortage, and lucerne yields three times more protein per hectare than maize. Lucerne-seed production, as a result of great fluctuations in output and erratic deliveries is being ousted from western markets, although an attempt to reconquer them with new varieties has now begun.

c) *The production of concentrated feeds and mixtures* began in Hungary in the 1950s and gathered pace during the 1960s. By the end of the 1970s, it already accounted for half the consumption of all fodder grains. Large farms cover the complete feed need of their pig and poultry populations with feed mixtures and concentrates, while the stock on private plots and individual farms depends largely on natural fodders.

In location the concentrates industry reflects the distribution of animal husbandry, usually being directly associated with the large animal raising combines, like those at Bábolna, Mezőhegyes, Nádudvar and Kondoros. About one-third of industrial fodder is also produced by co-operative farms. Feed mixtures, on the other hand, are mostly supplied to the farms by special plants which produce them from stocks of agencies that purchase and store fodder grain. For this purpose the old buildings of former flour mills are used [14].

2.8.2 Animal husbandry. The production and processing of animal products

Following collectivization, agriculture developed at an increasingly rapid rate, an important component of which the faster than average development of animal husbandry. As a result the share of animal husbandry in agriculture has risen from a pre-war 37 per cent to 50 per cent now and although the animal stock has remained largely unchanged, the use of high-yielding varieties, the transformation of farming and the growing application of factory farming methods to animal husbandry has meant about a twofold increase in gross output.

Nonetheless, a further rapid development of the proportionate share of animal husbandry would be desirable. Inter-country comparative analyses provide the evidence that the role of animal husbandry and with it of the processing branches are a function of general economic development as well as of climatic endowments and consumption habits. Typical of countries with a developed agriculture is the high proportion of animal husbandry in the overall production value of agriculture. It is not accidental that, despite growing imports of feedstuffs, this proportion exceeds 70 per cent in the Netherlands, Belgium, Denmark and Great Britain. By contrast, the production value derived from animal husbandry does not reach 50 per cent in such European countries as Romania, Yugoslavia and Spain. If we rank Hungary, taking the proportion of animal husbandry as a yardstick of economic development among European countries, we find that, despite significant progress, it has long ranked in 11th place from among the 16 countries simply because the rate of development was similar in the other countries, too.

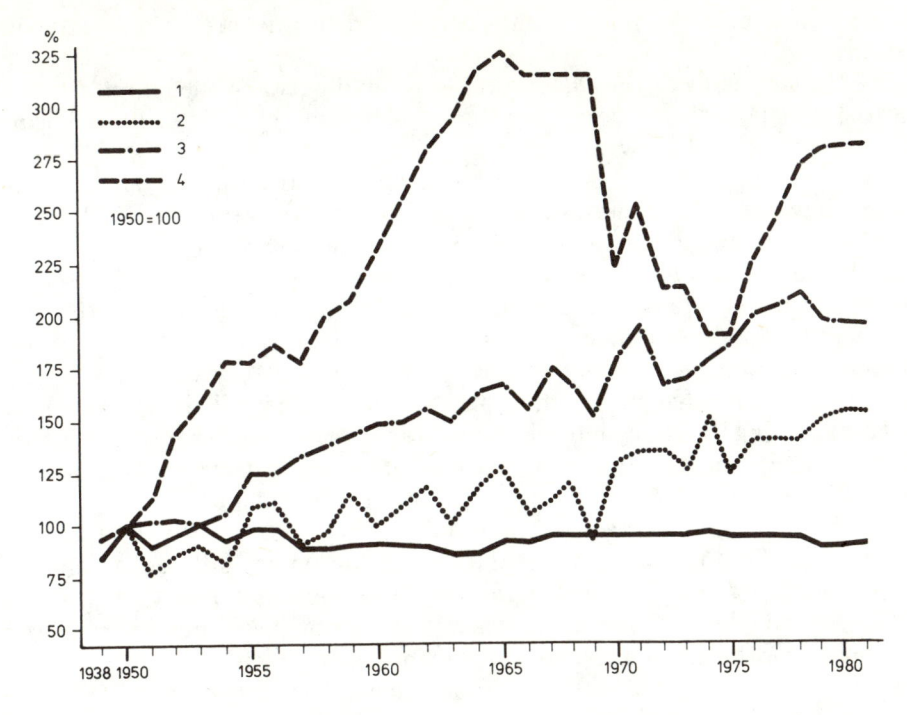

Fig. 49. The development of animal husbandry
1 — cattle; 2 — pigs; 3 — poultry; 4 — sheep

Characteristic of Hungary's animal husbandry is the preponderance of poultry and pig raising. Relative to the number of population, Hungary ranks first in Europe in term of poultry and second to Denmark in terms of pig production. The picture is only marginally less favourable if we relate animal stock to arable land. By contrast, the cattle stock relative to population number is insignificant owing to fluctuations in arable fodder production, which is very sensitive to the uneven distribution of precipitation. Relatively fewer cattle can only be found in Italy, Bulgaria and Spain.

A significant change that has taken place in animal husbandry is the proportionate shift towards the fodder-grain consuming sectors of *pig and poultry raising*. This is largely accounted for by the short period of maturation exhibited by these sectors, by genetic advances and, last but not least, by the wide application of factory methods *(Fig. 49)* to the two sectors.

At the same time, only moderate achievements have been made in *cattle raising*. Moreover, the number of cows is less than what it was before the war, and average milk yields are lower than in Hungary in only four of the 16 countries under review. This stagnation can be traced back to several factors, including the fact that the transfer of the gene stock of superior western cattle types — unlike industrial technology transfer — requires considerable time and, being investment-intensive, the profitability of cattle raising is low because of the combination of relatively high inputs and low returns.

The development of the *sheep stock* was rapid between the end of the war and the mid-1960s. Subsequently, there was a slight setback, followed again by an uninterrupted growth.

The proportionate shifts taking place in the structure of animal husbandry have modified the relative significance of the various animal-raising districts in Hungary, characterized by a *large-scale spatial levelling trend*. Whereas formerly animal density in the Great Plain was only about two-thirds of that in Transdanubia, the structural shift taking place in the past two decades has resulted in the conspicuous advance of livestock breeding in the Great Plain. As a result of various changes, livestock density in Transdanubia has somewhat declined, while that in the Great Plain, owing to the rapidly growing poultry and pig populations now exceed the density in Transdanubia. The territorial intensity of livestock rearing in the northern counties has tended to parallel the experience of Transdanubia.

The levelling process has been due, in no small measure, to the fact that on the completion of collectivization animal husbandry still lacked an adequate range of *large-scale production technologies*. As a result, as modernization set in identical, or at least similar technologies spread throughout the large-scale farms of the country, technologies which, though applicable anywhere, had the disadvantage of not being sufficiently flexible to adjust to, and make use of, local endowments. As a consequence, meadow and pasture farming, natural grazing areas and even arable fodder production were neglected in regions where they could have been a decisive factor in development. Instead, coarse fodder was widely used even where animals could have been fed on grass or arable fodder.

Pig and poultry raising developed on all the large-scale farms of the country, with very little territorial diversification. This process hampered the utilization of local endowments and led eventually to the worsening of efficiency. The earlier traditions of specialization have only tended to survive in small-scale farming.

When examining the territorial differences in animal husbandry, we find that livestock density is highest *in Western Transdanubia, Győr-Sopron, Vas and Zala counties* constituting a unified district, in which about 50 head livestock* per 100 hectares of arable land are to be found. Livestock density in the rest of the counties of Transdanubia, except for Fejér and Veszprém, is above average. Similarly, densities in the counties of the Great Plain east of the Tisza river are around average, and are lowest in the Danube—Tisza Mid-region. Especially marked is the low density of livestock around Budapest, and hence the meat, milk and egg supplies of the capital have to be met from more remote areas.

* Head of livestock is a general term expressed in units of 500 kg of cattle, pigs, horse and sheep, irrespective of animal species.

a) Cattle raising

This is the most important branch of animal husbandry as shown by the fact that it accounts for 55 per cent of total livestock and contributes 30 per cent of the gross production value of animal husbandry. Cattle raising is thus second only to pig raising in terms of production value. In foreign trade, mainly as exports to capitalist countries, *beef cattle* and *beef* play a prominent role.

The cattle population soon recovered from the devastation caused by the war and by 1949 exceeded the pre-war level. Since than, however, and despite all efforts, it has remained around the 2 million mark.

Considering that the population has increased by over 50 per cent since the turn of the century, while the cattle stock has remained static, we can see that this most important branch of animal husbandry has lagged behind the rate of population growth. This lag is counterbalanced by the improved quality of the cattle stock and by an increase in the output of meat and milk.

Milk production accounts for more than half the production value derived from cattle breeding, and in recent years, as a result of the dynamic growth of the second half of the 1970s, is 75 per cent above the pre-war level. Annual output now approaches 4000 litres per cow, constituting a good average by international standards. The rise in milk production is due exclusively to higher annual milk yields per cow as the number of cows has decreased.

The requirements of modern large-scale milk production could not be met by the traditional dual-purpose Hungarian breed, and as a result a programme of cross-breeding domestic stock with imported high-yielding, mainly Holstein-Friesian breeds was begun in the early 1970s, as was the establishment of modern specialized dairy farms. The cross-breed varieties produce one thousand litres more per cow per annum but the completion of the programme still lies somewhere in the future.

In summary, intensive high-yielding cow breeds, giving 5000 to 6000 litres per annum account for 5 to 6 per cent of the overall cow population, while the cross-breed stock with milk yields of 3500 to 4000 litres make up half the cow population.

The remainder of the stock still comprise the traditional dual-purpose grey breed with a milk yield of 3000 litres per annum.

A more intensive production of milk was typical of farms with a large cow stock, but as these have decreased, specific milk yields have also gradually fallen. The territorial differentiation of milk production is characterized by large divergencies, and milk sales per unit of arable land in the counties of the Great Plain run at only half to two-thirds the level of Western-Transdanubia owing to their more meat-oriented specialization.

Beef production, by contrast, presents a more favourable picture. Beef-cattle rearing has shown a more balanced growth and output is now more than double the pre-war level. With respect to the specific indices of beef-cattle production, Hungary ranks as one of the top countries in Europe, which is partly due to the fact that the slaughtering of calves is insignificant, while fat cattle are only slaughtered after they reach a weight of 500 kilogrammes. At the same time, beef production per unit area is poor, owing to the low cattle density. Meat production is still most significant on farms with smaller livestock numbers.

The further development of meat production is also desirable for external economic reasons. Beef exports, accounting for over half the total output, make up 15 per cent of all agricultural exports to the West with hardly any countervailing import demand. The beef-cattle stock is relatively easier to expand than the milk-producing herd, while dual-purpose animals will also have an important part to play. Unfortunately, the meat produced from this breed is very expensive, owing to the high costs of investment in cow-sheds and their exacting feed requirements. To make meat production profitable, the import of, and cross-breeding with Hereford beef cattle has begun. This breed can be kept in the open air throughout most of the year, and can also be fed on by-products. The experiences of the Izsák and Kiskunhalas state farms in the Danube–Tisza Mid-region are favourable with regard to production costs. The new breed also meets the changed requirements of foreign markets. Since the EEC restricted the import of Hungarian cattle, the Middle Eastern market has expanded significantly, although smaller cattle suitable for transport by ship are required.

A positive development of recent years is that large farms with unfavourable physical conditions are placing greater emphasis on an extensive type of cattle breeding. Coarse grain consumption has decreased with the stress being shifted towards mass fodder, which in turn brings meadow and pasture economy to the fore.

A significant change has also occurred during the past two decades in the territorial specialization of beef and milk production, which is closely related to the spatial evening-out of the sector. Despite the fact that the profitability of the branch has been critical for several years, cattle are reared on practically all the large farms of the country. This is, on the one hand, an inheritance from the centralized system of management, and on the other hand, due to the fact that the regulation of agriculture contains very few territorial elements, thus tending towards territorial uniformity. In Transdanubia, which used to have the most developed cattle rearing economy, livestock density per hectare has increased but slightly, whereas significant gains have occurred in the Great Plain. As a result territorial concentration is now on a lesser scale than it was before the liberation of the country. The stagnant or declining trend in livestock rearing has made itself felt most in the vicinity of the large cities, where it has primarily affected the cow population. Milk production in these parts has been neglected in favour of meat production.

Spatial pattern of cattle raising (Fig. 50). Despite the declining territorial concentration of the cattle stock, certain regional differences still remain. Thus cattle density in the administrative districts of Western Hungary is

1 point = 50 head of cattle

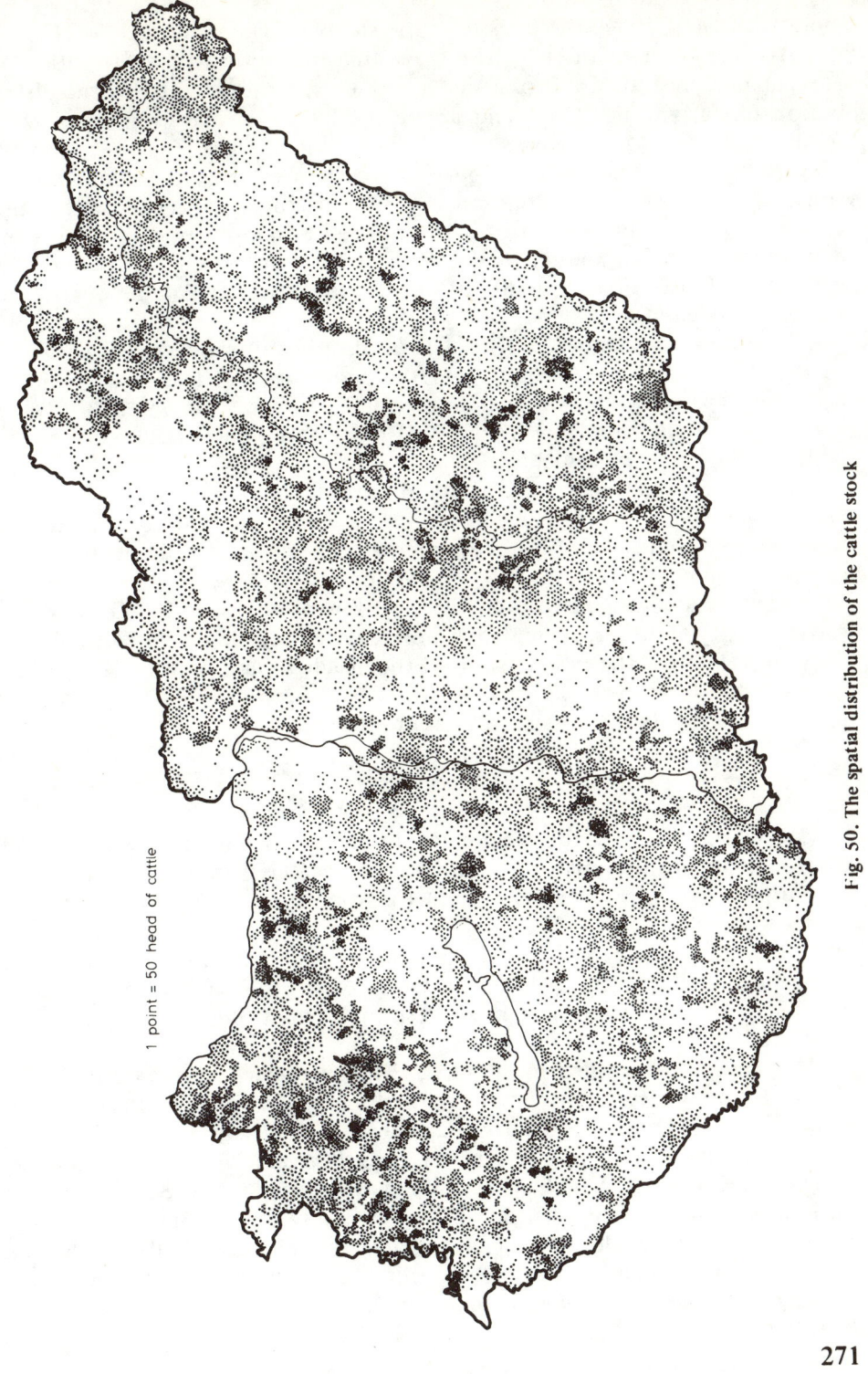

Fig. 50. The spatial distribution of the cattle stock

more than three times the density in the Danube—Tisza Mid-region. The territorial concentration of the cattle stock does not reflect the distribution of ploughlands, meadows and pastures, being more or less linked to the distribution of natural grasslands and arable fodder areas, and even more so to fodder yields from these areas.

Outstanding among the cattle-rearing areas is Western Transdanubia. Contributing to its historical evolution were rich pastures and meadows and the closeness of the Vienna market. The advanced development of the dairy industry, in which the market in Vienna also had a role to play, also exerted its impact. Cattle density is highest in the southern part of the district, in *Vas* and *Zala counties*.

The South-Transdanubian district is of lesser significance and is confined to the *Pécs* and *Mecsek regions* and the *Kapos valley*. The density of the cattle stock is everywhere above average and is only just below that of Western Transdanubia. The large numbers of dairy cattle here are also associated with above-average milk yields.

The *north-eastern district* is third in importance and comprises the *Sajó* and *Hernád valleys* in *Borsod* and *Szabolcs counties* as well as the relatively well-balanced and productive areas of the *Szatmár plain*. The district is associated with both meat and milk production.

In the remaining areas of the country, but primarily in the Great Plain, cattle density is lower, owing to a more extensive type of agricultural production, reflecting the poorer state of the meadows and pastures. Particularly low is the level in the Danube—Tisza Mid-region, where cattle raising only plays a subordinate role in agricultural production.

b) Dairy-farming

The distribution of dairy-farming is closely associated the cow farming as the even, nation-wide distribution of the raw-material source, and with the primarily urban consumer market. At the same time, when milk-processing plants were established in Hungary, the state of the transport network meant that dairying had to disperse its purchasing and milk-collection network throughout the country. The capacity of each processing plant was constrained by the transport system as fresh milk could only be supplied from nearby districts.

Dairying first developed in the Little Plain and came to be associated with the main population centres of the region, including Mosonmagyaróvár, Győr, Kapuvár, Csorna, Répcelak, Pápa and Szombathely. In the other main area of dairying in South-Transdanubia, Pécs, Pécsvárad, Véménd, Szekszárd, Dombóvár, Kaposvár, Nagykanizsa and Zalaegerszeg constitute the centres of an intensive cattle-raising district. The milk-supply belt of Budapest extended across the Mezőföld, embracing the area as far as Lake Balaton and the southern part of Tolna county, eastwards it extends into the northern part of the Danube—Tisza Mid-region including the Jászság.

Since the 1950s, with the improvement of refrigerated transport and the development of processing technology, it can now be guaranteed that dairy products, except for milk, will remain fresh for 8 days or over. As a result the earlier locational principles have been modified. The chief determinant of location has now become economic efficiency, and plants are now centrally situated in the larger towns from which fresh milk can be distributed to the consumers. The milk-processing industry of the capital and of the regional centres as Debrecen, Kecskemét and Veszprém, has grown significantly. The three Budapest plants amount for about one-third of total national capacity, and as the area they supply has expanded, so the average distance over which milk is transported to Budapest has increased. At the same time, more and more associated large plants have joined in the supply of fresh milk ensuring that it is rapidly transported to the processing plants and thence to the consumer within a few hours.

Cheese manufacture is associated with the older dairy plants of small or medium capacity, as at Répcelak, although new, specialized plants have been established as at Zalaegerszeg.

The major *milk-powder plants* in Mátészalka, Nyíregyháza, Berettyóújfalu, Gyula, Kecskemét, Pécs, Dombóvár, Zalaegerszeg, Répcelak and Csorna are located primarily in the more important milk-producing regions although others are to be found away from the consumer markets where the density of the milk-collection network is sparse.

The milk-processing industry is heavily decentralized and the programme of the future development envisages the improvement of economic efficiency through the modernization of about 50 of the 100 plants now in existence.

c) Pig breeding

Pig breeding, both in terms of livestock numbers and of its share in the production value of animal husbandry, is the most significant branch of livestock farming. Indeed, in terms of *the ratio of pigs to the total population of the country*, Hungary ranks second to Denmark in Europe. This intensity of pig breeding is connected partly with the meat tastes of the population and partly with the physical endowments of the country, which, as we have seen, is favourable to the growing of maize fodder grain.

During the past decade and a half, pig breeding has developed faster than any other branch of agriculture, and the pig population increased from 5 million in 1960 to 9 million by the beginning of the 1980s, while the production of pork has roughly doubled. With this rapid growth, its share in animal husbandry has increased to 36 per cent, and its production value is higher than that of the whole of the Hungarian mining industry.

Despite the fact that pig breeding has undergone an impressive transformation, with the evolution of a factory system of production and the introduction of new foreign breeds and hybrids, small-scale production nonetheless still predominates, and 50 per cent of pork output derives from private plots and auxiliary farms. In large-scale production, pig breeding is a typical branch of the state farms, where it accounts for one-fifth of total meat production. By contrast, co-operative farms produce less than 10 per cent. Most of the large-scale, factory-like pig-rearing farms were built between 1969 and 1974 and now provide one-third of the pigs reared for fat. The experiences connected with factory farming methods differ widely, and while they constitute considerable progress in the saving of labour, their economic efficiency is often inferior to those of small farms because of very high investment costs and of a lack of technological discipline. The construction of large-scale pig farms has therefore almost completely stopped.

Typical of pig rearing in Europe in general and in Hungary in particular is the fact that high meat-yielding breeds are coming to the fore. The traditional fat-breeds (mangalitsa) and their crosses have gradually been ousted by the domestically bred large, white meat-types, which now constitute more than half the pig population. Also noteworthy is the percentage share of plainland pigs. Most of white meat and plainland breeds are to be found in Transdanubia, where the rearing of white meat varieties has a long-standing tradition. Pig rearing in the Trans-Tisza region, on the other hand, tends to rely on different breeds. The production of pork is an important element in the domestic supply of meat and in the raising of living standards; about 85 per cent or 1·2 million tons of the annual output of pork is consumed domestically, and more than half the 74 kilogramme per capita annual consumption of meat constitutes pork. More recently, however, the need for more balanced diet has been gaining ground in Hungary, and with it the consumption of protein-rich poultry and beef is now spreading more rapidly than that of pork.

Pig-rearing districts (Fig. 51). The geographical distribution of pig rearing largely coincides with that of maize cultivation, and has become more widely dispersed compared with the pre-war period. The reason lies in the fact that while pig rearing has spread evenly, specialization on the large farms has made but little progress. In the territorial distribution of the pig stock, local differences are still discernible and two major pig-rearing districts can be identified. Most important is the *south-eastern Great Plain*, which also extends northwards into the Nagykunság and Hajdúság. Pig rearing is the most important branch of agricultural production in the greater part of this district where it accounts for some 20 to 30 per cent of total production. Pig density is highest here, and the rearing of fat-pigs is also typical. Piglet rearing, too is on a large scale in the Nagykunság and Körös areas where the pastures are rich.

Although smaller in area, the pig density is very high along the Danube valley in the eastern part of Transdanubia, which largely coincides with the corresponding maize-growing district, and also extends into the Bácska area. The share of pig rearing in gross agricultural production in this area is 15 to 25 per cent.

1 point = 200 pigs

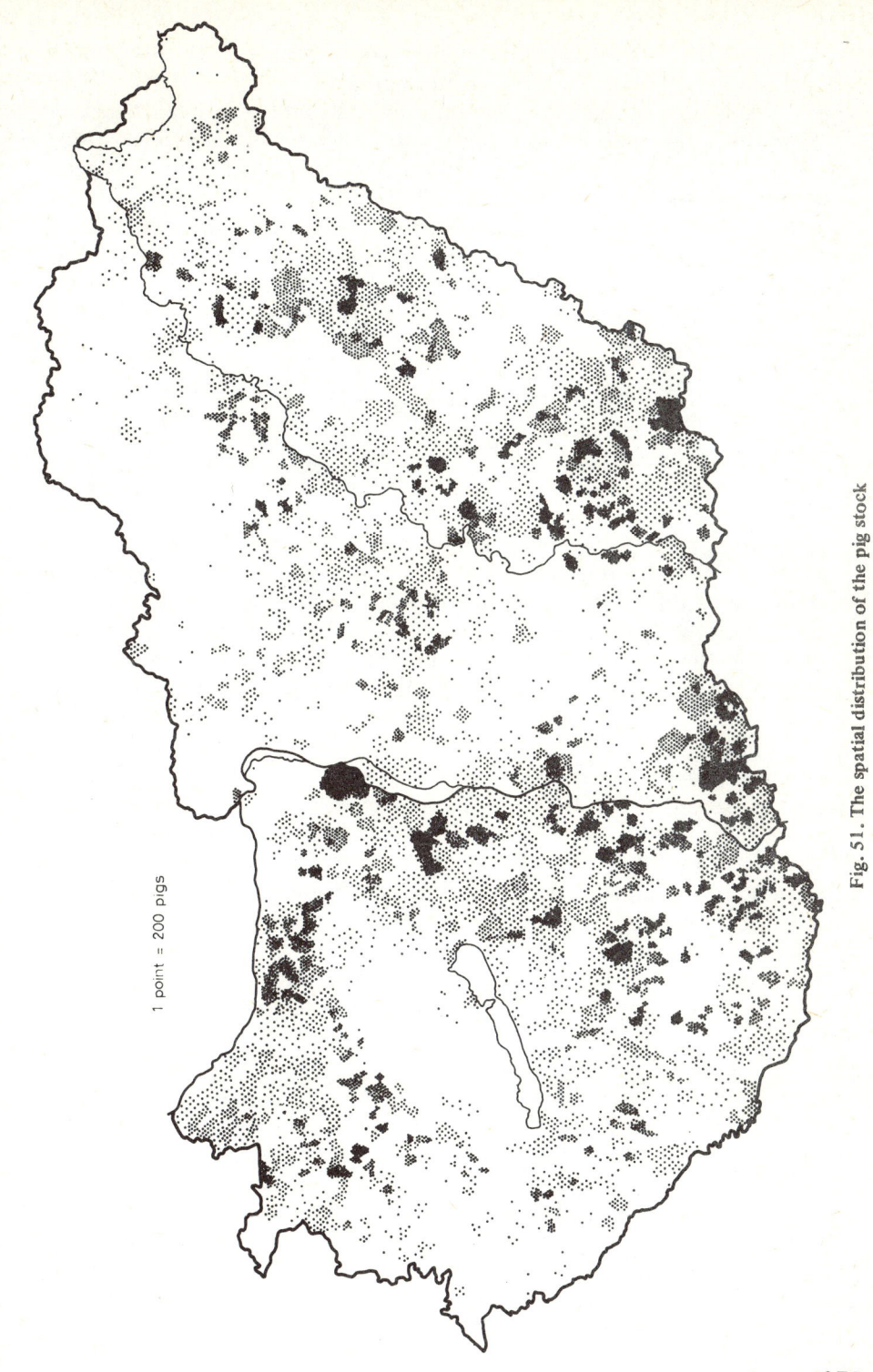

Fig. 51. The spatial distribution of the pig stock

Characteristic of the intensity of pig production in both districts is the fact that over half the pigs for slaughter derive from these districts. Of lesser significance is pig production in the intensive cattle-rearing areas, where feeding conditions are more favourable for cattle. Pig density is also low over the greater part of the Danube–Tisza Mid-region and similarly in the agglomeration area of Budapest, the Mátra and Bükkalja.

As a result of rapid development during the last one and a half decades, the centre of gravity of pig rearing has shifted to the Great Plain for while pig density in Transdanubia has risen only moderately, that in the Great Plain has nearly doubled, and now significantly exceeds the density in Transdanubia.

d) The meat industry

The domestic meat industry was originally located close to the consumer centres, primarily in the capital, and the animals were transported or driven to these places for slaughter. At the time of nationalization, the number of slaughterhouses in the country employing more than 10 persons was 19, of which 10 were located in Budapest. The provincial plants were located in the more accessible centres with the districts specializing in husbandry. Especially well-known were the plants at Pápa and Kapuvár in Western Transdanubia and the sausage plants at Gyula and Békéscsaba in the south-eastern part of the Great Plain as well as the winter-salami plant at Szeged. The modernization of the meat industry began simultaneously with the implementation of the pig programme in the early 1970s. The construction of the slaughter and meat-process plant at Miskolc and the expansion of the salami factory at Szeged also fall within the same period. Indicative of the development of the meat industry is the fact that slaughterhouse capacity has increased by about 70 per cent, although this is still a long way behind the rate of increase in meat production. This has also had its impact on the composition of meat exports, with 25 to 35 per cent of output having to be sold as live animals at lower prices.

While at the national level, an approximate equilibrium has been established between slaughter-livestock production and slaughter capacity, this cannot yet be ensured regionally. With respect to the territorial location of *beef-cattle purchasing and slaughter capacity,* in only three of the six economic planning districts adequate slaughterhouse capacity is ensured, namely in the northern counties with their moderate level of beef-cattle production, in the agglomeration area of Budapest and in South-Transdanubia with its significant fat-cattle stock. But a territorial equilibrium can also be achieved in these three districts by acting on the great inter-county differences in supply levels, shortages and surplus capacity. In the rest of the country, however, the correspondence between livestock for slaughter and slaughterhouse capacity is entirely lacking. The tension in the northern parts of the Great Plain is especially great, where shortage of capacity is experienced in three counties and amounts to about 70 per cent in the district as a whole. Animals have to be transported to the northern counties or to the slaughterhouses of Budapest over a distance of 100 to 200 kilometres. The capacity situation in North-Transdanubia and the southern parts of the Great Plain is much better, where the existence of counties with surplus capacity eliminate the necessity of long-distance transport. This is all the more important as the transport of carcase meat in refrigerated railway cars even over relatively short distances like 100 to 200 kilometres is cheaper by 20 to 25 per cent than the transport of live animals. From this it follows that development favours the transport of meat and not of live animals and, consequently, slaughterhouses must in the future be located at the places of production rather than consumption. Along with the large meat combines, another prerequisite for a rational division of labour is the construction of medium-sized plants.

The territorial imbalances relating to *slaughter-pig production and processing* are even greater. In the largest consumer areas of Budapest and Miskolc huge slaughterhouse capacities have been built without the appropriate nearby rearing of pigs, while in the specialized pig-producing districts of the *southern and northern parts of the Great Plain,* large new slaughterhouses were only recently established at Gyula and Baja to mitigate capacity shortage. The largest imbalance is still in the northern parts of the Great Plain, where the slaughter capacity of the three counties making up the region is only 30 to 80 per cent of what is necessary. It was for this reason that the significant investment in slaughter capacity at Miskolc, in the heart of the Borsod region with practically no pig-rearing activity rather than in the Great Plain, gave rise to much debate. At present, about half a million pigs have to be transported from the northern Trans-Tisza region to Miskolc or Budapest, or to the slaughterhouses of Northern Transdanubia. Thus the developments of the recent past, namely the establishment of the Gyula, Szekszárd and Baja meat combines and the construction of a new plant at Kaposvár at best only mitigate the above problems.

The long-term development and locational programme of the branch, which envisages an expansion in capacity of about 15 per cent up to 1995, seems able to ensure a reasonable territorial equilibrium through the large investments envisaged for the reconstruction of capacity at Nyíregyháza, Debrecen, Győr and Zalaegerszeg. It is a cause of some anxiety, however, that it is also planned to reconstruct the slaughterhouse in Budapest at a cost of thousands of millions of forints, which will entail, along with the unnecessary transport of live animals, the pollution of the environment.

e) Poultry and egg production

Poultry farming is an important branch of Hungarian animal husbandry as is shown by the fact that it accounts for a quarter of the income from livestock breeding, and thus rivals cattle breeding in significance. Its importance is further enhanced by the fact that poultry meat is a significant export item accounting for nearly half the quantity of all fresh meat exports and for about 10 per cent of world exports. In this area, Hungary is second only to the Netherlands. A factory method of poultry farming evolved as early as the 1950s, the foundations being laid at the Bábolna State Farm which originally reared only horses and cattle. Bábolna has supplied domestic farms with millions of eggs for the hatching of broiler chickens for many years, and has come to rival the largest companies in the world. More recently, it has exported whole poultry factories to the Soviet Union and Iraq.

With the diffusion of plants mass-producing selected meat-poultry and eggs, poultry farming has expanded vigorously. Poultry-meat production has almost trebled and egg production has increased two-and-a-half-fold during the last 15 years. Processing has also kept pace with production. Currently, about 500 large farms are engaged in the poultry industry, although the majority of the poultry stock is still kept on the farms of small producers.

The spatial pattern of poultry farming. Poultry farming is concentrated in the Trans-Tisza region, in the Danube–Tisza Mid-region and in Western Transdanubia. *The Trans–Tisza area* embraces the counties of Csongrád, Békés and Hajdú, being primarily associated with their *tanya* areas where poultry farming is the principle branch. High poultry densities are especially characteristic of Békés county. Indicative of the intensity of poultry farming throughout this region is the fact that the three counties provide a quarter of the total value of national poultry production. Egg production in the district is also significant.

The Danube–Tisza Mid-region stands out primarily for its poultry output. In and around Kiskunfélegyháza goose raising and goose-liver production have a long-standing tradition. The *Western Transdanubia region* comprises the tiny villages of Vas and Zala counties, where poultry sales per unit area exceed the national average. Besides the above districts, poultry and egg production in Komárom county is, thanks to Bábolna, disproportionately high.

The poultry-processing network has been built up in line with the evolution of large-scale poultry farming, and is now one of the fastest-developing branches of the food-processing industry. The plants, numbering about one dozen in total, for large-scale poultry and egg processing are scattered throughout the country, with the exception of the northern areas *(Fig. 52)*. Most are to be found in the Trans-Tisza region at Békéscsaba, Orosháza, Szentes, Törökszentmiklós and Debrecen, the area most advanced in producing commercial poultry, and in the Danube–Tisza Mid-region at Hernád, Kecskemét and Kiskunhalas. The plants in Transdanubia are located at Sárvár, Győr, Pécs and Zalaegerszeg. The capacity of these plants, however, far exceeds the poultry production in their immediate environs, and they are therefore compelled to procure birds at more distant locations. Present freight rates do not yet provide any inducement to the bringing about of an optimum territorial equilibrium between production and processing. The processing plants obtain 42 per cent of their live poultry within a distance of

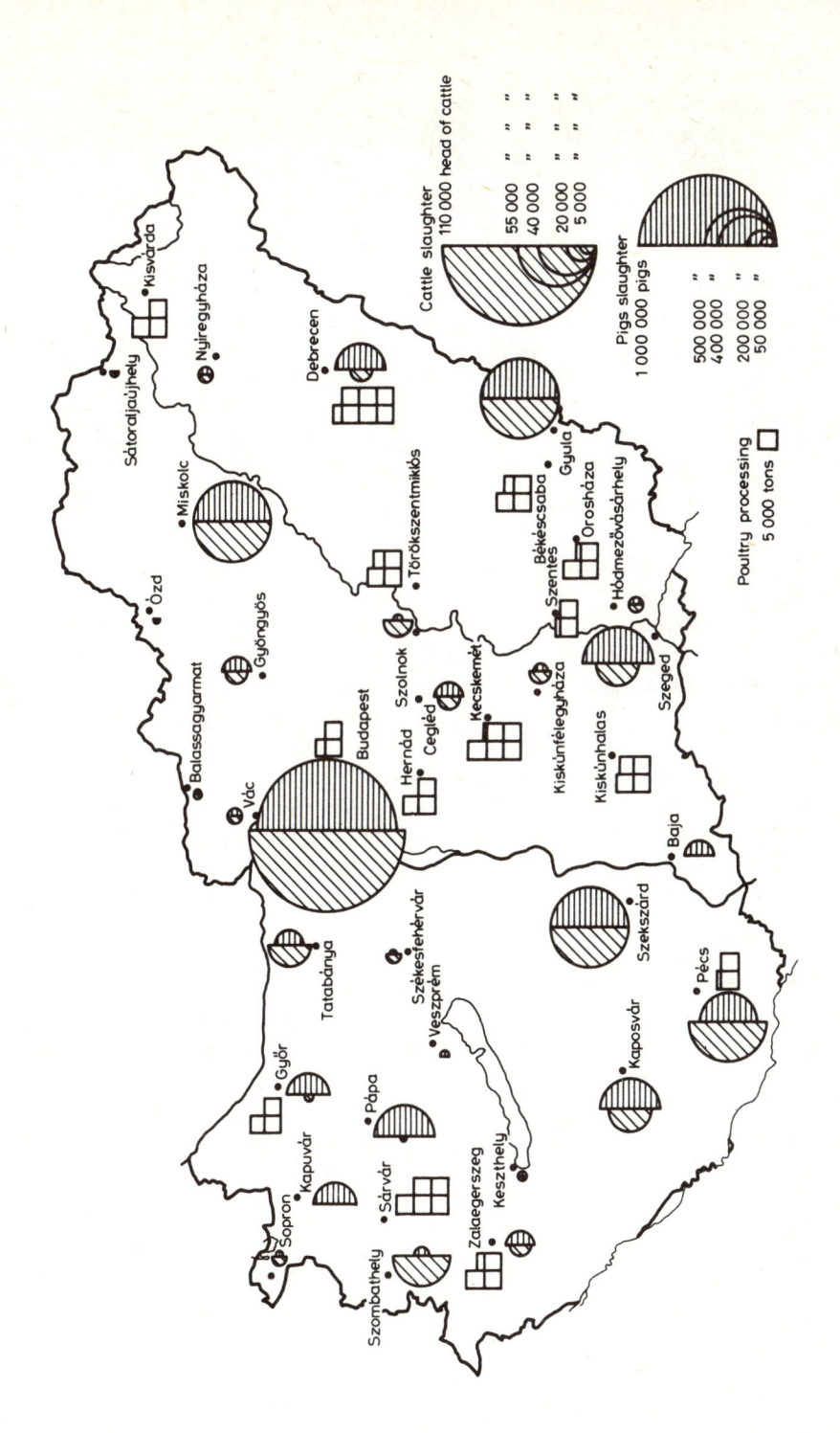

Fig. 52. The spatial location of meat- and poultry-processing

50 kilometres, a distance deemed to be optimal, while 36 per cent come from distances between 50 and 100 kilometres, and the remaining 22 per cent (about 60 million broiler chickens) from distances over 100 kilometres away. About three quarters of the output of the poultry-processing industry is exported, mainly to the socialist countries.

f) Sheep breeding

In the first half of the 19th century Hungary, with its 7 million sheep population, was still one of the largest sheep-breeding and wool-producing countries of Europe. With the intensive development of agriculture, however, the sheep stock fell abruptly and declined to about half its former size by the turn of the century. The Second World War did serious damage to the sheep stock, but subsequently the stock increased to over 3 million by 1965, nowadays the stock is 3·2 million.

In Hungary, the main objective of sheep breeding was traditionally wool production, and therefore meat production was rather neglected until recently. Greater importance is now attached to milk production as well and ewe cheese is an especially favourite dairy product.

The rearing of the traditional ,,racka" and ,,cigája" breeds has practically ceased and the majority of the stock today is made up of the worsted Merino breed. A special advantage of this type is its unexacting character and its fine adjustment to the dry climate of the Great Plain. It is a triple-purpose breed, and produces wool, milk and mutton. Average wool yields per head of sheep amount to 4·1 kilogrammes annually, which is well up to international standards. With a stock 50 per cent more than the pre-war number, sheep rearing today yields only 20 per cent more wool, a fact which is indicative of the extensive nature of sheep rearing, reflecting the scarcity of fodder. Neither the quantity, nor the quality of wool produced meet domestic requirements, and substantial amounts are imported mainly from the capitalist market. Neither does home production satisfy the demands of the Hungarian sheepskin trade. Since lamb and mutton are good export items, their production is more profitable than wool, and sheep breeding has consequently shifted in that direction. In recent years, the foundations of a large-scale meat production, under factory conditions, have also been laid, and with the modernization of production the good export opportunities can be exploited.

Sheep-breeding districts *(Fig. 53)*. Territorial specialization is more marked in sheep breeding than in the breeding of cattle. Regionally, Transdanubia has the least number of sheep per unit area, where less than one quarter of the total stock can be found. By contrast, major concentrations are associated with three districts, of which the largest is the Trans-Tisza region, where sheep breeding is carried out on the rough alkaline pastures of the Hortobágy, Nagykunság and the Berettyó—Körös region, these areas contain more than half the sheep stock of the country. The direction of utilization is increasingly shifting towards lamb production, which requires a

1 point = 50 sheep

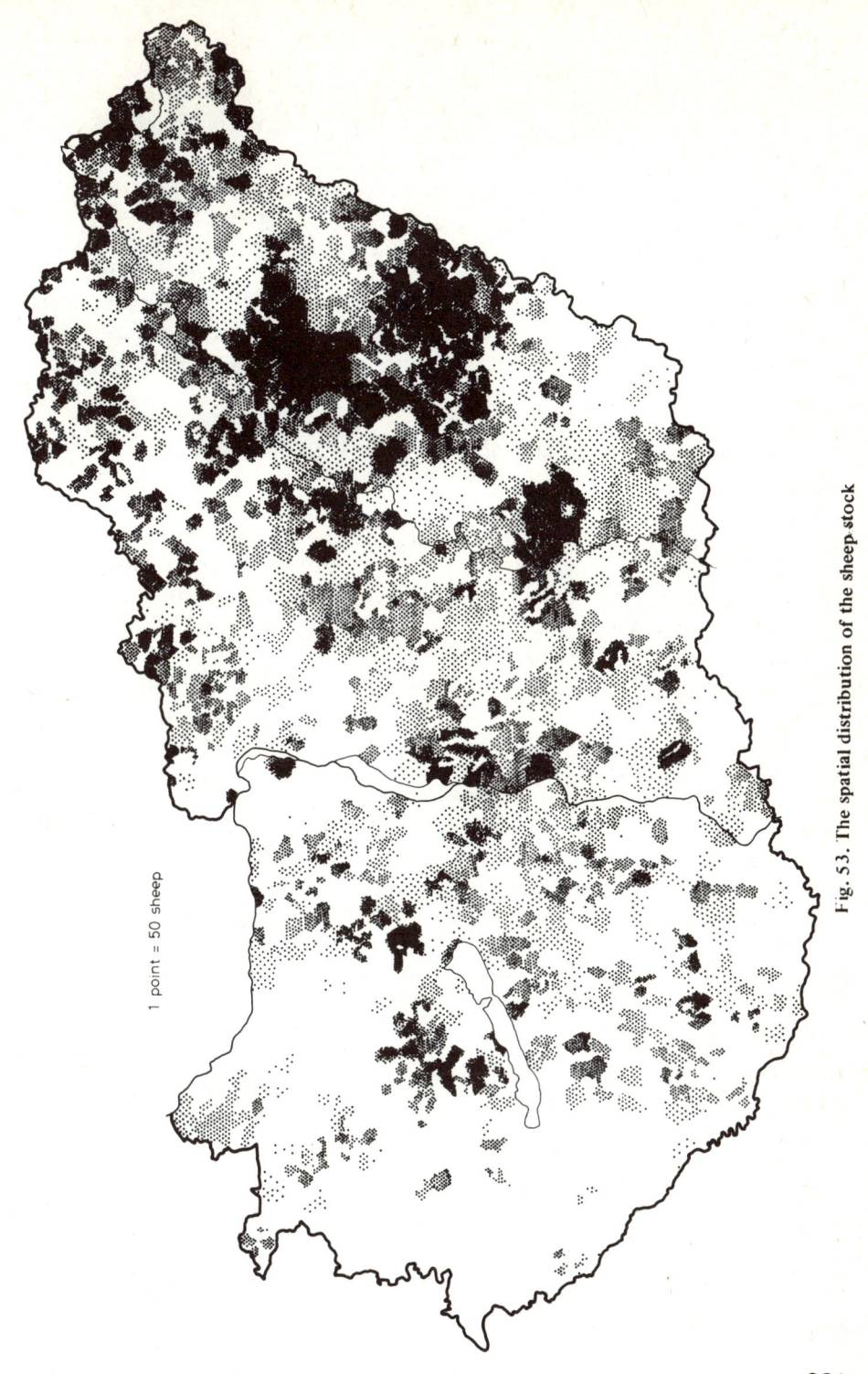

Fig. 53. The spatial distribution of the sheep-stock

more intensive method of rearing than the traditional one. The country's more modern slaughterhouse for sheep has been built in the Hortobágy, and is primarily designed to meet export demands.

In the northern district, on the poor pastures of the Cserhát, Bükk, the Sajó basin and Cserehát 12 to 15 per cent of the country's sheep stock can be found, but the most intensive rearing occurs in south-eastern Transdanubia, most specifically in the Völgység, Hegyhát and outer-Somogy, where, along with rough pastures, arable fodder also plays an important role in the feeding of the stock. It is in this district that the quality of domestic wool production is best, which reflects the more intensive breeding tradition. It was here that the large estates started the breeding of Merino sheep, which yield the finest wool, as early as the beginning of the last century.

2.9 Regions of agricultural production

After surveying the geographical location of the individual production branches and products, we shall now attempt to identify and characterize a system of agricultural regions. The specific nature of each region is determined by the combined nature of arable cultivation and animal husbandry, by the efficiency of off-farm activities, such as processing, the extraction of local materials, and industrial and marketing activities, by the level of production, and by the rate of the individual branches of farming, i.e. by the structure of production [20].

In surveying the geographical location of the individual branches of farming we have outlined their most important production districts. Our aim now is not to study interrelationships, nor identify geographical differences in production structure, as is usually done in a geographical synthesis, but rather to focus attention on objectives and practice and on regional policy. For this reason, we shall establish our agricultural regions on the basis of those ecological circumstances that relate to production and on the level of economic activity. It is to them that we shall subordinate regional specialization. In our view, the region, as a product of the territorial distribution of labour, always comprises a specific production structure.

Hence, the first step to be taken in defining individual agricultural regions is the determination of spatial differences in the level of economic activity, and the examination of the production structure in the areas thus differentiated. The larger region can then be subdivided into subregions on the basis of the production structure.

In determining the level of production besides the usual indicators of economic efficiency, i.e. production value per unit area or per capita, we have also taken into account indices expressing the economic conditions surrounding the activity, i.e. the gold-crown value of land, the value of fixed and current assets and livestock density. We have expressed the level of productive activity per unit area in terms of aggregate number formed out of 10 indices. On this basis we have classified farms and villages into three basic production types, namely high-medium- and low-level production types. Out of these types we have identified homogeneous territorial units, the boundaries of which follow the boundaries of village and urban administrative units, the sizes of individual territorial units vary widely, however [20].

The territorial division is comprised of 19 regions which are broken down into subregions on the basis of internal structural disparities. When the production structure within a homogenous region presents a varied, mosaic-like pattern, however, we have not defined subregions. Specialization according to area and also to production does not sufficiently take into account physical and economic endowments. Even factory-type production systems do not early adjust themselves to specific regional characteristics. For this reason, production specialization does not match the development of the productive forces, and this is why the individual production regions are determined from the production level and not from the territorial structure. The pattern of agricultural regions obtained from this method presents a remarkable picture. Medium-level regions are most prevalent, although the territory they occupy is not that extensive, because the average in this case is not the arithmetical mean of two extreme values, but of a wide band of values dispersed around that mean. Hence, the inner differentiation of the medium-level territories is substantial. Somewhat smaller in area are the low-level regions and the smallest of all are the high-level districts.

A zone of medium-level production regions is to be found in the northern and north-eastern parts of Transdanubia and along the right side of the Danube valley between Budapest and Mohács. Another such zone is the Trans-Tisza area, to which can be added the agricultural area of the Danube–Tisza Mid-region. While the former, as regards production level, is of a uniform character, the latter is heavily differentiated.

High-level regions, surprisingly, are not associated with the loess tables of the Great Plain traditionally judged to be the best agricultural areas of the country, but are found primarily in and around the capital as well as in the vicinity of the main industrial centres and resorts. This corroborates our statement made earlier, that factory-type system reach their highest levels in areas commanding easy access to the consumer market, where they cooperate with industrial plants and help satisfy the more sophisticated demands of the population.

The lowest-level production regions coincide, with few exceptions, with areas of unfavourable soil and relief conditions, which demonstrates that the quality of arable land still significantly differentiates the efficiency of inputs, and influences the level of production. Adverse physical endowments also exert a negative impact on the level of assets, livestock, and the labour force, although it is precisely in this case that better than average supply is desirable. This relationship is both the cause and the consequence of low-level production. A definite correlation between land quality and economic performance can be observed only in this type.

It is clear that there is no relationship between the individual types of region, and the structure and the specialization of production. Thus we cannot say that a high production level requires specialization in animal husbandry rather than in crop cultivation, or vice versa. Districts with the highest production levels stand out mainly for their high proportion of non-agricultural activities.

In designating the individual regions we have used the names of geographical areas or soil types, although the extension and boundaries of our regions generally differ from these. The regions and subregions are as follows (Fig. 54).

The first region is a subalpine region of medium production level overall but also with some unfavourable parts. The Őrség and Vend areas are large territories mostly lacking in co-operative farms, and where such farms do exist, they are concentrated in areas with relatively favourable endowments and their production reaches the general average. In the northern subdistrict (1/A) the typical activities are wine production around Sopron and cattle farming elsewhere, while, in the other subdistrict (1/B) the production of feed other than grain fodder and cattle farming are dominant.

The 2nd region comprises the Little Plain which is divided into three subareas: 2/A is that part of the Little Plain situated in the Danube valley with a production level well above average, 2/B is the Hanság and the Rába Mid-region with a poor to medium level of production, while 2/C is the southern part of the Little Plain of good to medium production level. The structure of production is very similar throughout consisting of high livestock density and varied crop cultivation. Cattle raising is the dominant specialization.

The 3rd region comprises the northern part of the Zala hill country. Production level is around the national average, except in Kemenesalja, the dominant crop is apples, while there are considerable non-agricultural, (industrial, construction, transport and trading) activities.

The 4th region is made up of the Bakony and the Balaton highland, where the proportion of arable land is low and of poor quality. Conditions for viticulture are favourable in the Balaton highland, but even extended wine growing cannot significantly improve the low productivity of the region.

The Vértes and Gerecse mountains compose the 5th region where the basins and foothills are associated with the maize-pig vertical complex of Eastern Transdanubia together with some viticulture. All this renders possible a many-sided and in places, as at Környe, high level of production.

The 6th region is made up of the Mezőföld and the Tolna–Baranya loess tables, an extensive area heterogeneous in both production level and structure. Basically, however, it is a plain area with good-quality arable land, and crop yields above the national average. In the Mezőföld subarea (6/A), the proportion of the arable area under maize is the highest in the country, and although the cattle stock is relatively small, the pig density is high. The Tolna–Baranya loess tables make up a second subarea (6/B) of intensive

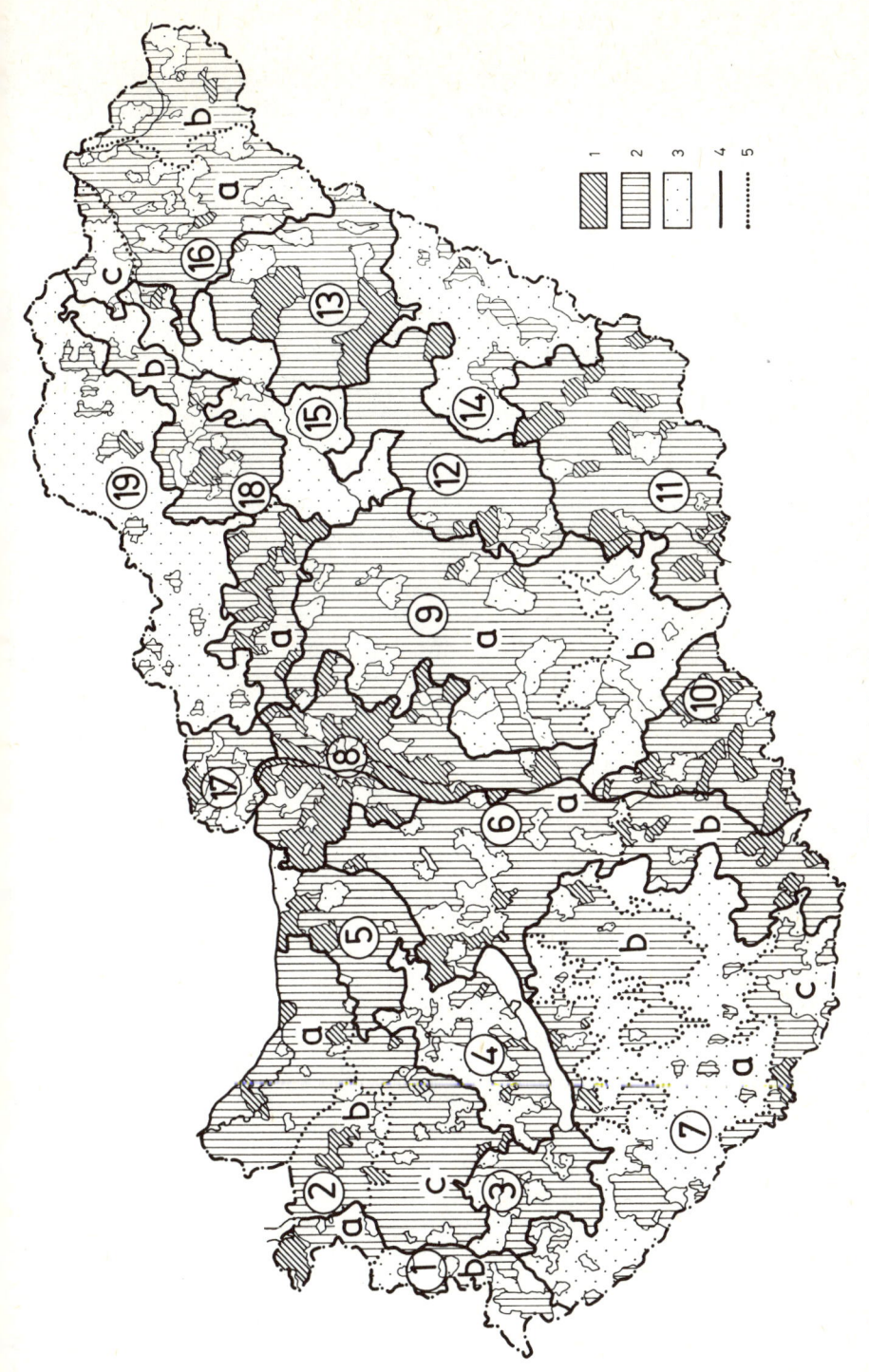

Fig. 54. Agricultural production regions

1 — high level; 2 — medium level; 3 — low level; 4 — boundary of regions; 5 — boundary of subregions

maize production where both cattle and pig raising are also carried out on a large scale.

The 7th region is the Transdanubian hill country. It is, with the exception of the North–Zala hill country which has already been discussed, one of Hungary's most extensive agricultural districts. Soil quality is average overall, although in the Göcsej, inner-Somogy, Zselic, Hegyhát and Mecsek areas, it is even definitely poor, and heavily leached as a result of comparatively high precipitation. Accordingly the level of production is low.

The hill country, characterized by large-scale wheat and maize growing and by a relatively high livestock density, all, however, with lower than average yields, forms the first (7/A) of three subregions. It is a marginal region and it is here that most of the loss-making co-operative farms of Transdanubia are to be found. A second subregion (7/B), made up of two separate medium-level areas extending from Nagyberek and Lake Balaton through Kaposvár to the Kapos valley, is characterized by medium-quality soil, average wheat and maize yields and by a high cattle density, notably in the Kapos valley. With a similar level of production is the third subregion (7/C), the Dráva area, which, in the case of subregion 7/B, can be regarded as a transitory, complementary part of the hill country, with large meadows and pastures and an intensive type of cattle breeding.

The 8th region is made up of Budapest and its broader agglomeration area together with the plainland along the Danube. The larger part of the region is characterized by sandy soils of medium to poor fertility. The existence of intensive vegetable, fruit and flower growing, the proximity of the market as well as large-scale industrial and trading activities result in a high level of production.

The 9th region is the loess table of the Danube–Tisza Mid-region. Subregion 9/A and 9/B differ from each other in production level. Output in the southern part of the Kiskunság (9/B) from a poor loose, sandy soil is at a low level, while in subregion 9/A it is close to average. Outstanding in a varied production profile are vegetables, grapes and fruit in general.

The 10th region is composed of North–Bácska and Mohács island. It is an area of differing soil conditions and also production structure, but a common factor is high productivity. Typical is specialization in pig and poultry farming and grain fodder, as well as vegetables and dairy products.

The 11th region comprises the Körös–Tisza Mid-region, where high levels of production are patchily associated with the loess tables, although owing to good quality soil, the production of wheat, maize, pigs and poultry is well above average throughout the region.

The 12th region is the Nagykunság. It is, properly speaking, a continuation of the previous district, but owing to the existence of sheep rearing it has a somewhat more extensive character. A positive change in the production level is expected to result from the completion of the irrigation system connected with the second Tisza lock system.

Proportionate changes in the structure of transport*
(Freight traffic in ton/kms and passenger traffic in passenger/kms)
(Percentages)

Sectors	Freight traffic			Passenger traffic		
	1950	1960	1981	1950	1960	1981
Rail	89·9	85·0	49·6	93·5	45·2	16·0
Road	1·7	6·3	24·0	5·6	54·3	82·8
Water	8·8	8·3	17·4	0·8	0·3	0·1
Air	0·0	0·0	0·1	0·1	0·2	1·1
Pipeline	0·5	0·4	8·9	0·0	0·0	0·0
Total	100·0	100·0	100·0	100·0	100·0	100·0

* According to the performance of public utility enterprises (state railways, road transport and shipping companies) and non-public utilities (enterprises, public institutions, also including private cars in passenger traffic).

The 13th region is the Hajdúság where the quality of arable land ranges from medium to good. The level of production reaches the highest level in some places but everywhere is above average. The production structure is characterized, as are the two Trans-Tisza regions listed above, by a wheat-maize-pig-poultry combination.

The 14th region is the Körös area. With heavily meadow-type clay soils and extensive alkali patches, it offers unfavourable conditions for production. The extensive wheat production and varied livestock farming reflect a low production level.

The 15th region is composed of the Mid-Tisza valley and Hortobágy, where it has not been possible to raise the low levels of production even by the extension of irrigation farming associated with the Western Main Canal.

The 16th region embraces the Nyírség, the Szatmár—Bereg plain and the Bodrog Mid-region. These three subdistricts are united into a single region by similarity of their production structure. The northern and middle parts of the Nyírség (subregion 16/A) are differentiated by a higher economic level than that of the other two subregions, but the character of all three is determined by the preponderance of fruit, potatoes and vegetables. Associated with fruit are cattle in subregion 16/B, while in subregion 16/C the dominant branch is again fruit in the form of apples.

The 17th region is made up of the Börzsöny and Nógrád basin. The varied production of the Nógrád basin with its good soils is at a medium level, but is lower in the mountainous Börzsöny.

The 18th region follows the southern foot of the Northern Middle Mountains. Only the foothills adjacent to the Great Plain, more precisely the southern fringes of the Mátra and Bükk Mountains, the Sajó—Hernád basin and Tokaj-Hegyalja can be regarded as belonging to this district. Soil quality is varied, ranging from good to poor. The level of production in the western subregion (18/A) is high, owing to the high proportions of vine, fruit and vegetable cultures, but is only average in subregion (18/B).

The 19th region comprises the Northern Middle Mountains. Conditions in this extensive area, which ranges over the Cserhát, Mátra and Bükk Mountains and basins, are unfavourable with a cool climate and heavily leached soils, and thus farming activity is at the lowest level. Arable output varies from area to area, but wheat and maize, despite low yields, are predominant everywhere. A higher livestock density, owing to the low profitability of the sector, cannot compensate for the low level of arable cultivation.

3 Transport

Indicative of the weight of transport in the Hungarian economy are the following data: in 1981, the various branches of transport — including communications — employed 388000 persons and accounted for about 7·5 per cent of national income.

The large-scale increase in all forms of freight and passenger traffic has been due, primarily, to the rapid development of productive forces and also to the marked internal migration of population. Contributing especially to the growth of freight transport has been the development of the transport-intensive sectors of heavy industry requiring the haulage of fuel and raw materials. During recent decades, the growth of freight traffic has also been stimulated by the rapid increase in agricultural activities. The growing separation of place of work from place of residence, together with certain adverse conditions in the main industrial centres, primarily insufficient construction of new dwellings, have given rise to a nationwide system of commuting, with the result that the movement of people has also increased in several places to an undesirable extent. Population mobility resulting from migration, the maintenance of family contacts, visits, and, last but not least, the steady growth of tourism, have also boosted passenger traffic.

The last decades of this century have heralded a new period in the development of transport produced by the many rapid changes that are taking place comparable to those achieved in Hungary at the end of the last century. The developmental level of the country's economy, urbanization, and the close economic relations established with the other socialist countries as well as the obsolescence of the network and of asset provision made the elaboration of a new, comprehensive development plan for transport as a whole necessary. New international trends also called attention to the necessity for change. The basic points of the transport policy introduced in 1968 and still being implemented are as follows: the modernization of the transport system as a whole; the encouragement of the more economically efficient sectors, the channelling of freight towards the more remunerative sectors; the partial transformation of the transport network [100].

Goods transport   Passenger transport

Public and
non-public transport

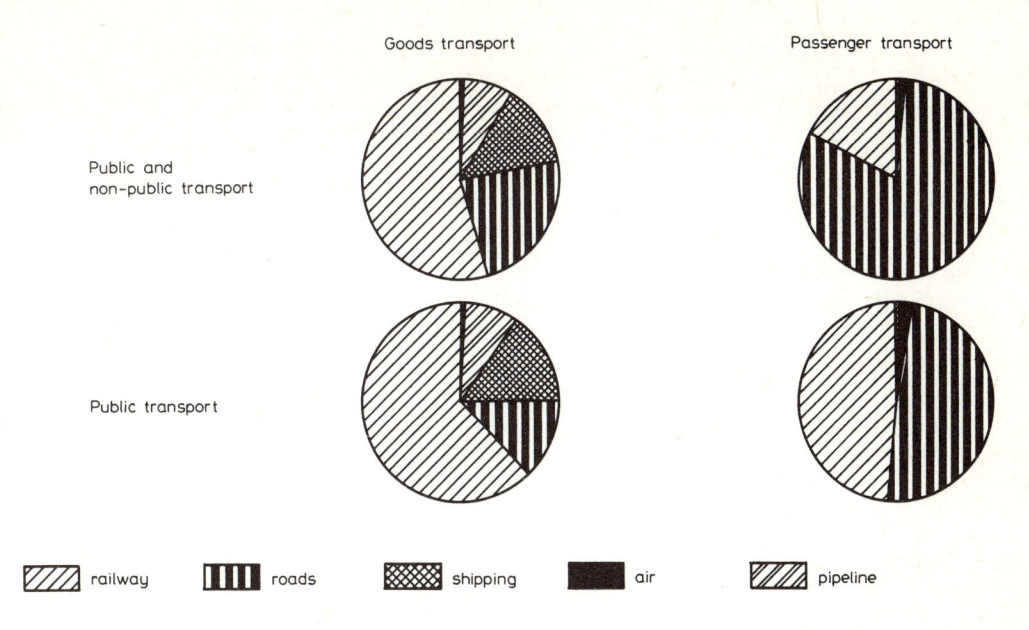

Public transport

▨ railway   ▥ roads   ▩ shipping   ■ air   ▨ pipeline

Fig. 55. The sectoral structure of transport (1981)

During the last three decades, the structural proportions of transport have undergone substantial change. By the end of the 1970s, railways retained their leading role only in freight transport, with passenger traffic being shifted increasingly by buses and private cars. As to volume carried in 1981, 49·0 billion ton/kms of freight and 99·0 billion passenger/kms were moved *(Fig. 55)*.

Within freight, the share of waterborn traffic has only increased slightly, but that of pipelines has risen abruptly, owing to the advance in liquid and gaseous energy sources. The performance of the so-called public utility transport companies differs in many respects from that of the above sectors, and structural change has taken more time to materialize. One of the reasons for this is that a substantial part of road transport is performed not by public utilities but by enterprise lorries, buses and private cars.

Along with the changing structural proportions, transport as a whole needs further modernization. In the post-war development of transport the devastations of the Second World War were part of the cause of slow modernization. (Of all branches of the national economy, transport suffered the largest losses.) During the rapid industrialization of the 1950s, communications could be improved only with great difficulty, as economic policy gave preference to industry. Consequently, the start of modernization had to wait until the 1960s and is expected to take up several more five year plans before completion.

3.1 The main characteristics of the transport network

The transport network of the country, primarily the rail and road networks, is characterized by a strong centralization. The principle arteries radiate out from the capital towards the provincial centres of the country. This pattern was established during the last century in the then larger area of the country, as a result of the conflict of interest between Hungarian and Austrian political and economic policies. The Austrians wanted to build up the railway network throughout the whole empire, including Hungary, with Vienna as its centre (based on the ideas of Friedrich List, the German economist). The Hungarians succeeded in subventing this policy and were able to make Budapest the centre of the railway network of Greater Hungary, which was a significant achievement given the historical situation of the time.

The radial network gave an impetus to the rapid development of the capital, but hampered the establishment of direct economic connections between the various regions of the country. The main characteristic of the geographical division of labour was the relationship between Budapest and the countryside, and the main transport arteries connected the capital with the most significant peripheral areas of the country with their rich agricultural and natural resources. At the same time, the existence of several trunk lines integrated the network with that of the rest of the Monarchy and, thus, with that of Europe.

The lines interconnecting the various regions outside Budapest were few and most were ceded to the neighbouring countries, following the peace treaty concluding the First World War. Between the radial trunk lines only subsidiary connecting links were established. This shaping of this network had been completed by the First World War. Within the new boundaries of the country, the centralized character of the railway network became even more pronounced.

The network was also affected by physiographic factors. Owing to the basic character of the country, the lines, choosing the easiest construction conditions, converged from the surrounding highlands on the economic and political centre of the basin.

Most of the railway lines and the roads built later were constructed along the historical routes of Transdanubia, following the direction of the main fault lines and valleys, for instance the Budapest—Esztergom and the Budapest—Tatabánya railway lines. A similar pattern also characterized the lines built in the north in the valleys of the Zagyva, Tarna, Eger, Sajó, Hernád and Bodrog rivers. The lines in the Great Plain ensured contact only among the market towns which had some significance at the time of construction, and as a consequence, large areas were left out of the railway building programme. This is a characteristic too of certain areas of Transdanubia, where the physical relief also exerted an influence on the pattern of the network.

The network was also little influenced by the impact of urbanization, and the number of towns connected by railways was very small. Indeed an important feature of Hungarian urbanization was that the railways induced urbanization, leading to the rapid development of such towns as Szolnok, Székesfehérvár, Szombathely, Nagykanizsa and Kaposvár.

The railways pushed road construction into the background for at least half a century. Roads functioned only as feeder lines to the railways, or were used to move transport in areas without railways. Elsewhere, they were of local importance only, of primitive construction, and surfaced predominantly with stone or macadam. The trunk roads of national significance, built in the wake of the spreading use of motor cars between the world wars, mostly paralleled the railway lines, and radiated out from Budapest. Transverse motor roads were not built at all, and no direct road contact was established between the large towns of the country. Those primitive macadamized roads which were seemingly built to connect them, could not fulfil, owing to their poor state, the functions of transverse routeways.

The Danube, the country's largest navigable river that passes through the capital, fitted in well with the nodal pattern of the transport network, and its significance was much greater than it is now. Danube freight traffic even over short distances was considerable which is why no north-south railway through Budapest paralleling the river was built, while it handled a significant amount of national and international passenger traffic as well.

Although changes have occurred especially with the construction of new and the modernization of the old roads, the structure and layout of the network does still not meet either the requirements of a rational regional division of labour, nor the needs of rapidly expanding international economic relations and tourism.

Improvements in the transport network can only be carried out gradually, owing to inertia and the size of the investment involved. Therefore the most necessary and the most pressing changes were carried out first which, however, only slightly affected the structure of the network. Improvement is also aggravated by existing spatial linkages because industrial freight traffic is usually handled by the lines running to the north, north-east and south-west of Budapest. The lines in the industrialized areas have remained, despite modernization, largely overcrowded, while the so-called transit lines are also becoming congested.

A primary requirement of the development of the transport network has been, and continues to be, the better reconciliation of the network and junctions with the needs of the regional development of industry and agriculture, with the demands of inland and international tourism and with transit traffic.

Hungary's position in Europe as far as transit is concerned is favourable. The Hungarian network ensures transit contacts among the socialist countries (between the Romanian, Bulgarian, and Yugoslav networks, between the Czechoslovak, GDR, Polish networks and even between the Soviet and the Yugoslav systems). In addition, it is directly linked with several lines to Western and to Southern Europe. Several international express trains and air flights cross the country. At the same time, Hungary's position, from the point of view of the European railway network, is of a peripheral character, because the extensive Soviet network uses broad-gauge tracks. Therefore inter-gauge transfers which increase transport costs, are needed both in bilateral and transit traffic.

The freight traffic between socialist countries, owing to growing economic co-operation, is increasing dynamically, and this increases transit freight movement across Hungary. (In 1981, one quarter of rail freight movements in term of ton/kms were derived from transit traffic.) Transit haulage earns foreign exchange for the country, though the heavy lorries used on the roads are also responsible for the rise in road maintenance costs. International tourism has also increased the number of foreigners in transit. Their transit across the country engages all the various forms of passenger land transport.

3.2 The railways

93 per cent of the railway system, with a length of 8142 kms in 1981, of which 20 per cent was electrified, is open for public use. 97·4 per cent of the system is standard gauge (1435 mm), but only 14·5 per cent is double-track. Narrow-gauge lines use a gauge of 760 or 1010 mm, while in addition, there is a broad-gauge line (1524 mm), the same as used in the Soviet Union, over a 35 km stretch. Railway density is 8·7 km/100 km^2, or 8·0 km/1000 inhabitants, i.e. about average by European standards both in relation to area and number of population. The Hungarian railway network is operated by the Hungarian State Railways (MÁV). In addition, 103 kms of track of the public network are owned by an Austrian–Hungarian joint company (the Győr–Sopron–Ebenfurt Railway Ltd., GYESEV). The Hungarian part of the equity is also state-owned. Besides these, forest managements also maintain a limited public transport (mainly passenger traffic of a tourist character) on a narrow-gauge network.

The railway network is distributed fairly evenly over the country's area *(Fig. 56)*. The extensive flat terrain provides the possibility of a good line layout. Network problems usually arise where the lines prove too sparse to meet requirements, e.g. in the Transdanubian hill country where, owing to the many valleys, there are very few transverse lines. There are only a few steeply-graded lines in the country (e.g. Pécs–Bátaszék and Eger–Putnok), and although bridges are many, tunnels and viaducts are few. The routing of the railway network has been greatly influenced by the country's two large rivers, the Danube and Tisza.

Budapest and its immediate environs, and the Little Plain are best supplied with railways. Sparser are the networks in the Northern Middle Mountains, the middle and northern parts of the Great Plain and in South-Transdanubia. There are no railway lines on the right bank of the Tisza valley between Tokaj and Szolnok, nor on the left bank between Tiszafüred and Szajol, nor

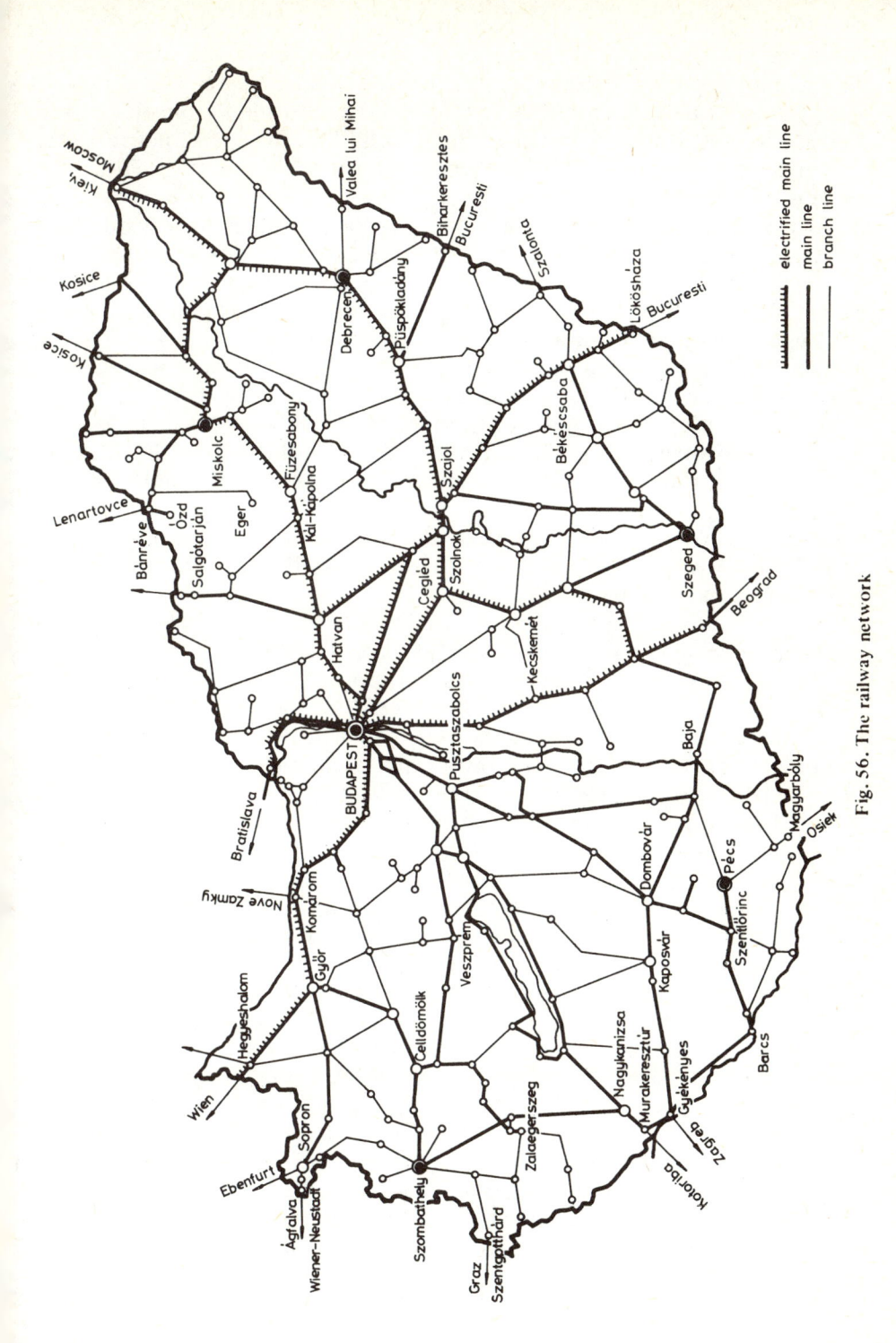

Fig. 56. The railway network

along the Danube between Paks and Mohács or between Dunapataj and Baja. The nodal position of Budapest is further accentuated by the lines that set out in a radial pattern from places 60 to 100 kms distant from it, i.e. from Hatvan, Szajol, Székesfehérvár and Pusztaszabolcs. The sparse network density in certain parts of the Great Plain is only relative as settlement density there is sparse, too.

Two-thirds of rail freight (134 million tons) consists of bulk goods, such as coal, stone, gravel, bricks, cement, refined-oil derivates, metallurgical products, fertilizers, timber, grains, sugar beet and fodder. The above goods, except for agricultural produce, impose an even burden upon the railways throughout the year. The transport of agricultural produce is concentrated in autumn or the beginning of winter, which is therefore the ,,peak traffic" period and often constitutes a serious challenge to the railways.

In the direction and volume of ,,freight flow", there are wide differences between individual railway lines. Traffic intensity is highest on the lines that are most important for domestic industry and for international trade, i.e. between Hungary and the Soviet Union, and between Hungary and Western Europe, which is served by the electrified lines running between Hegyeshalom–Győr–Budapest–Miskolc and Záhony, and between Budapest–Szolnok–Debrecen and Záhony.

Passenger railway traffic is decreasing both in terms of number of passengers carried and in terms of passenger per km. This process is accounted for by three factors: firstly, inter-city bus transport offers several advantages on certain routes (e.g. the frequency of services), secondly, the former passenger traffic of lines now closed has been channelled to road transport, and thirdly, the rapid growth of car ownership (including the significant enterprise and institutional car fleets). The analysis by kilometre zones reveals that railways are used primarily by people travelling daily to their workplaces (in 1981 more than half the total number of passengers travelled within the 30 km zone). Especially high is the number of daily commuters around Budapest, Miskolc, Székesfehérvár, Debrecen, Győr and Pécs. Passenger traffic, disregarding the transport of commuters, is uneven, fluctuating both territorially and seasonally.

Outstanding among the development tasks of the railways is modernization. Of special importance both for traffic and economic reasons is the completion of electrification and dieselization, motivated primarily by the country's energy situation. While the electrification or dieselization of railways has already been completed in the industrially and economically developed countries of Europe, the modernization of traction on the Hungarian system has lagged somewhat behind. (Hungary played a pioneering role in the electrification of trunk railways by electrifying the Budapest–Hegyeshalom line between the two world wars.) Electrification, because of the large investment in overhead cables and expensive locomotives, is justified only on lines where the volume of traffic ensures their economic operation. The electrification of the majority of lines that are significant both domestically and internationally has been already completed, and further electrification could be justified on energy grounds, because electricity generated from domestic coal could be used for traction, while diesel traction requires imported oil. In 1981, 53·1 per cent of all traction on the Hungarian network was performed by electric, 44·2 per cent by diesel and only 2·7 per cent by steam locomotives. There are still few steam locomotives in operation, they only handle branch line passenger traffic and steam traction will completely cease by the mid-1980s.

In order to increase the utilization of freight waggons, the European CMEA countries established a common rolling stock pool (OPW), of which Hungary is a member contributing about 25 000 waggons. In the interests of ensuring the availability of refrigerated cars for export consignments and for more intensive use of domestic refrigerated stock, MÁV also joined the European refrigerated waggon association, Interfrigo. The Hungarian railways has also adopted itself to the use of modern container transport which is an especially economic way of carrying goods as it avoids repeated loading and discharging. MÁV is also a member of several international container associations (e.g. Intercontainer), and container terminals, besides those in Budapest at the Csepel and Józsefváros depots, are being established at frontier stations and in the larger provincial towns.

On several railway lines traffic is so low that revenue does not cover operation and maintenance costs, and to ensure a more economic operation, the policy of MÁV has been to close lines handling an insignificant amount of traffic. Scheduled bus services and freight transport facilities replace such lines. Up to now, railway transport on close to 1400 kms of track (including narrow-gauge plant sidings) have been closed.

The more important inland and international lines are as follows. Budapest—Tatabánya—Komárom (connecting with Komarno—Prague—Berlin—Copenhagen—Stockholm)—Győr—Hegyeshalom and so to Vienna. This is an electrified, double-track line connecting the Hungarian capital with the Tatabánya coal basin and serving the industrial and agrarian territories of the Little Plain, and then on to Western and Northern Europe. The GYESEV line branches off at Győr and runs through Sopron.

Budapest—Székesfehérvár—Szabadbattyán—Siófok—Nagykanizsa—Murakeresztúr—Gyékényes and hence to Zagreb and Rijeka. The significance of this line is especially great in the summer season, as it serves the southern resorts of Lake Balaton, as well as serving through traffic to Yugoslavia and Italy. Szabadbattyán is the junction with the Balatonfüred—Tapolca—Keszthely line which handle the traffic of the northern shore of Balaton.

Székesfehérvár—Várpalota—Veszprém—Ajka—Celldömölk—Szombathely—Szentgotthárd. This trunk line serves the coal- and bauxite-mining area and the aluminium and chemical industrial districts of Middle Transdanubia connecting them with the capital and with the western parts of Transdanubia. Budapest—Pusztaszabolcs—Sárbogárd—Dombóvár—Szentlőrinc—Pécs (electrified) and Dombóvár—Gyékényes (Zagreb). This line connects the southern and south-eastern parts of Transdanubia with Budapest. Its significance is further increased by serving the Mecsek coal basin.

Sopron–Szombathely–Zalaszentiván–Nagykanizsa–Murakeresztúr–Gyékényes–Barcs–Szigetvár–Pécs. This is a less busy transverse trunk line serving the peripheral western and southern parts of Transdanubia. It also links several trunk lines radiating out from Budapest.

Budapest–Vác–Szob and thence to Bratislava and Prague. It was on the Budapest–Vác section of this line that railway transport started in Hungary in 1846. It is the shortest, but in terms of its transit traffic, one of the most significant double-track electrified trunk lines of Hungary. Local commuter traffic is also considerable as is tourist traffic to and from the Danube Bend.

Budapest–Hatvan–Miskolc–Szerencs–Nyíregyháza. This line serves the northern industrial centres and coal basins and connects them with Budapest and the frontier station at Záhony. Through its branch lines it gathers and directs the freight and passenger traffic of about one quarter of the country towards Budapest. Of the branch lines the Miskolc–Kazincbarcika–Putnok–Bánréve–Ózd route serves the industrial district of the Sajó valley, while the Felsőzsolca–Hidasnémeti branch connects with the Hernád valley and Eastern Slovakia.

Budapest–Cegléd–Szolnok–Püspökladány–Debrecen–Nyíregyháza–Záhony and thence to Kiev and Moscow. The significance of this line is particularly great because of Hungarian–Soviet trade exchange. Besides, it is the country's longest and fully electrified double-track railway line, which links the middle and northern parts of the Great Plain with the capital. The Záhony frontier station handles the largest amount of freight traffic in the country and is the point where the Hungarian standard gauge and the Soviet broad gauge meet. An annual freight volume of 15–17 million tons is transshipped here. A branch of this trunk line runs through Püspökladány and Biharkeresztes and hence to Nagyvárad–Brassó and Bucharest.

Budapest–Újszász–Szolnok–Békéscsaba–Lökösháza and thence to Arad an Bucharest. This line is an electrified transit line connecting the eastern parts of the Great Plain with Budapest.

Budapest–Cegléd–Kecskemét–Szeged. This is the busiest electrified line serving the capital, the Danube–Tisza–Mid-region and the southern part of the Great Plain. Owing to Soviet–Yugoslav transit traffic and in the interest of creating a modern connection with the Budapest–Kelebia line, the Kiskunfélegyháza–Kiskunhalas section has also been electrified.

Budapest–Kunszentmiklós–Kiskőrös–Kelebia and thence to Belgrade. This is an electrified trunk line with a slight inland, but a significant transit traffic. Its significance is international, as it connects Budapest with the Balkan countries of Yugoslavia, Bulgaria, Greece and Turkey and beyond them, with the Middle East, too.

Dombóvár – Bátaszék – Baja – Kiskunhalas – Kiskunfélegyháza – Szeged – Hódmezővásárhely–Békéscsaba. This is a circuitous transverse line connecting South-Transdanubia with the southern parts of the Great Plain.

The above enumeration reveals that the country's most important railway junctions handling the largest traffic are: Székesfehérvár, Pusztaszabolcs, Győr, Dombóvár, Pécs, Nagykanizsa and Szombathely in Transdanubia, Hatvan and Miskolc in the north of the country and Cegléd, Szolnok, Szeged, Békéscsaba, Debrecen and Záhony in the Great Plain.

3.3 Road transport

The total road length is around 29 700 kms, of which 98·5 per cent had a dust-free surface (stone, concrete, asphalt, bitumen and macadam surface made dust-free by bituminous treatment) and 1·5 per cent macadam bound by water, and dirt road in 1981. Hungary inherited from capitalism one of the worst road networks of Europe. Apart from the few, relatively modern trunk roads, most of the rest were either surfaced with macadam bound with water and sand, or were dirt tracks. Moreover, a considerable part of the villages were not tied to the national network with built roads.

Continued construction and improvements brought about a significant change in the quality of individual roads and in the network as a whole. Nonetheless, the quality of the road network still lags behind modern requirements, especially the demands of the extremely fast-growing motor-vehicle traffic.

The greatest achievement has been the widening of the busiest trunk arteries to a uniform width of seven metres with kerbs of different colours. In modernizing the roads, bend and gradient corrections also had to be made to enable faster speeds. Moreover, new stretches of road were also built.

Road reconstruction itself brought about changes in the road network. Dust-free roads were first built between the capital and the county towns, and then between the county and the district towns. But the most important change was the emergence of the outline of a transverse road network linking regional centres of the country.

As a result of the geographical position of Hungary, the growth of transit traffic has been extraordinarily fast, especially during the summer holiday season, when motor cars from the socialist countries and from Western or Northern Europe bound for the coasts of Yugoslavia, Bulgaria and Romania cross the country in steadily growing numbers. International lorry transit has also assumed particularly large proportions since the bridge over the Bosporus, opening the way to Asia Minor and the Middle East, was built.

The further modernization of the roads mostly used for tourism and transit traffic has become unavoidable. The international commitments undertaken by Hungary also make it an inevitable task. Of the European transcontinental road network the E–5 (London–Damascus), the E–15 (Hamburg–Bucharest) and the E–96 (Košice–Budapest–Zagreb–Venice) cross Hungarian territory. Of the international roads the section of the E–5 road connecting the capital with the Austrian state boundary was first completed, the section between Budapest and Győr being of motorway quality. South of Budapest, the E–5 road connects with routeway 5, on which as yet only partial corrections have been made. Road 84 between Sopron–Balatonederics shortens the route between the Austrian capital and Lake Balaton, while the transit road 86 cuts the distance for motor traffic between Vienna or Bratislava and Yugoslavia.

The domestic motor-vehicle stock consisting of 1·1 million passenger cars, 662000 motorcycles, 22800 buses, and 156000 lorries (1981) and the increase in inland and international tourist traffic have made the construction of a motorway network indispensable, despite the enormous costs. The plan envisages the construction of a motor-road network of about 500 kms. The first motor road between Budapest and Balatonvilágos has already been completed, while the motor road between Budapest and the Austrian–Hungarian state boundary and between Budapest and Miskolc are under construction. A motor-road ring around Budapest is also envisaged. Domestic motorway construction is faced with two problems: firstly, the time taken for completion which is greater than the international average and secondly, since the planned layout differs but little from the railways serving the same area, or of the old roads, the motorways are unlikely to constitute a new, independent element of the road network. All the motorways will begin independently from Budapest, but a cheaper solution, drawing more on geomorphological endowments, would have been to build two outlet motorways with at least three lines each, with major junctions to serve other centres at a distance of 60 to 90 kilometres from the capital.

Road transport is suitable for the short or medium haul of small loads or of special products. Its advantage over the railway is indisputable because it can carry goods from the forwarder directly to the consigner (door-to-door transport). In Hungary, where, owing to the small area of the country, there are no long distances, and where the main centres of economic life are relatively close to one another, road transport has great potentialities. The long-distance transport of high-value products, like meat, refrigerated goods, confectionery, chemicals and machines, in heavy-duty or special purpose vehicles or containers is also economic internationally.

Road freight transport, according to policy, has fully taken over the domestic carriage of small items, together with many other commodities over short or medium distances. (An appreciable part of mail traffic is also effected by lorries.) The most important items carried by road are construction materials, fuels, metallurgical products, machinery and components, vegetables and fruit, sugar beet, slaughter animals, the retail supplies for towns and industrial settlements, and, in general, the commodities for household consumption. Freight transport between the capital and the other large cities is handled almost completely by road vehicles. Agriculture, which relied earlier mainly on horse-drawn transport, has also changed over to lorries. The weight of commodities carried by lorries is four times the volume of goods transported by rail, but in terms of tons per km it lags behind rail transport, because of the shorter hauls.

The international connections are also extensive. The activities of HUNGAROCAMION extends throughout Europe and the Middle East. It also carries on commission haulage abroad and maintains regular services between Budapest and the large ports of Europe.

Bus transport handles primarily commuter traffic within the industrial regions and meets the daily traffic needs of the administrative, educational and health service centres, markets and shopping centres. Especially important is the function of serving settlements not included in the railway network. Indicative of the growing significance of bus traffic is the fact that while in 1949 railways still carried 12 times as many passengers as long-distance bus traffic, today railways transport only less than two-thirds of the passengers carried by bus. Bus transport embraces over 99 per cent of the country's settlements, and thus the proportion of settlements covered by the transport network, including the railways, is close to 100 per cent. Bus transport by its daily express services between the capital and the major provincial settlements and between the settlements of the individual regional units relieves the railway of considerable passenger traffic. An advantage of long-distance bus transport lies in its ability to establish communications between places not covered by railways. Although still modest in extent, an international scheduled bus transport has also been established with the capitals and major towns of several neighbouring countries. Additionally, buses also handle a large part of domestic and external tourist traffic.

According to international usage, the country's roads have been provided with numbers corresponding to the place they occupy in the hierarchy of the road network. The motorways and motor roads serve exclusively the purposes of motor vehicles. Their designation is the letter M with a one-digit number. The other roads of a non-local character are national trunk roads designated with a one- or two-digit number, of which those with a one-digit number are the more important. Their importance lies in the fact that the entire road network of the country is linked with them, while the two-digit number roads connect with the less significant trunk roads *(Fig. 57)*.

The basic road network of the country consists of two motorways, one motor road and eight one-digit number roads, which with a few exceptions, parallel the most important railway lines. Four of the eight one-digit number roads start from Budapest, from the 0 km post on the Buda side of the Chain Bridge.

The M–1 motor road, Budapest to Győr, is a section of the E–5 European transcontinental network. Its reconstruction as a motorway is at present in progress.

The M–7 Balaton motor road from Budapest through Székesfehérvár to Zamárdi is a section of the E–96 road.

The M–3 motor road from Budapest to Gyöngyös is planned to extend eventually to Miskolc.

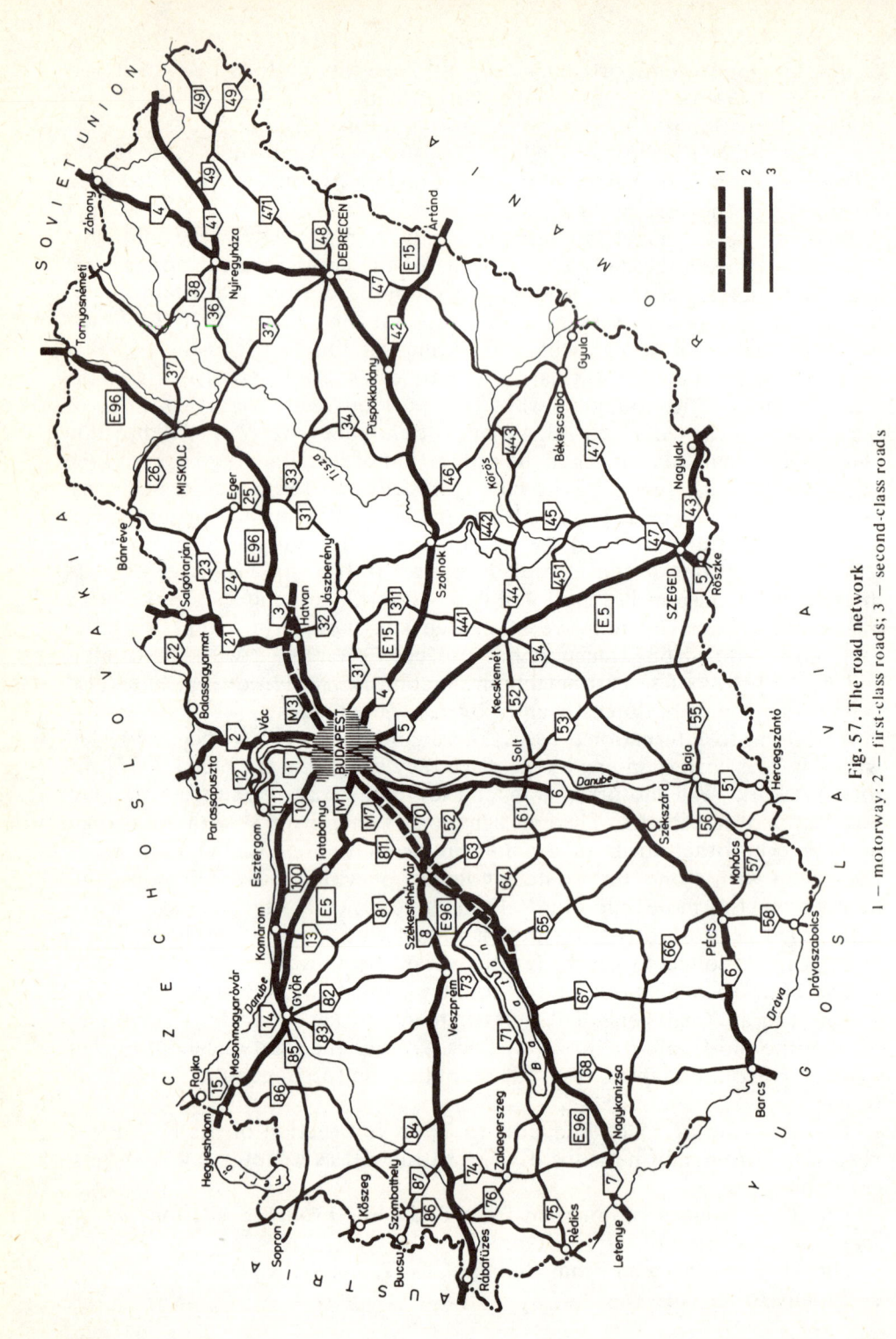

Fig. 57. The road network
1 – motorway; 2 – first-class roads; 3 – second-class roads

The most important trunk roads designated with a one-digit number are listed below:

1. Győr–Hegyeshalom and to Vienna is a busy international trunk road. It is the extension of the M–1 motor road and is part of the E–5 road.

2. Budapest–Vác, Parasapuszta and to Banska-Bystrica and Warsaw is a short but busy inland section of an international route.

3. Gyöngyös–Miskolc–Felsőzsolca–Tornyosnémeti and to Košice is a section of the E–96 road.

4. Budapest – Cegléd – Szolnok – Debrecen – Nyíregyháza – Kisvárda – Záhony and thence to Moscow is a section of the E–15 road, between Budapest and Püspökladány with road 42 which runs to Biharkeresztes and thence to – Kolozsvár and – Bucharest.

5. Budapest–Kecskemét–Szeged–Röszke and thence to Subotica–Beograd–Istambul and Damascus is part of the E–5 road.

6. Budapest–Dunaújváros–Bonyhád–Barcs–Pécs.

7. Zamárdi–Balatonkeresztúr–Nagykanizsa–Letenye leading to Zagreb, Rijeka, Ljubljana and Trieste, is a part of the E–96 road between Zamárdi and Letenye.

8. Székesfehérvár–Veszprém–Jánosháza–Szentgotthárd–Rábafüzes is the main route to Graz.

3.4 Water transport

The length of permanently navigable waterways is 1170 kms, of which 40 per cent falls to the Danube and 34 per cent to the Tisza, while the length of temporarily navigable waterways is 386 kms. The Danube is navigable along its whole length throughout the country. The Tisza is navigable between Dombrád and Szeged where it crosses into Yugoslavia, and at high water between Vásárosnamény and Szeged, the Körös rivers between Kőröstarcsa and Csongrád, the Bodrog between the frontier and Tokaj, the Sió Canal between Siófok and Szekszárd, the confluence with the Danube. The above navigation data are merely possibilities and the actual length of regularly navigable river sections is shorter. Lake Balaton and the section of the Drava constituting the common boundary between Yugoslavia and Hungary are also part of the navigable waterways of the country.

The advantages of water navigation are hard to exploit in Hungary, because the two most important waterways, the Danube and the Tisza, run close and parallel to each other across the country. It is a further impediment to navigation that these two large navigable rivers are not connected by canal in Hungary. The largest volume of industrial commodity traffic is in a north-east south-west direction, connecting the industrial region of the Middle Mountains with Budapest, while the two rivers, except from their frontier sections, run in a north-south direction. The Hungarian enterprise in charge of Danube shipping is called the Hungarian Shipping Company (MAHART).

Competition among the transport sectors has exerted a negative effect on river navigation, although the development of maritime shipping on a new conceptual basis has brought about some growth in river freight transport. River passenger traffic shows a stagnant trend. The utilization of waterways is disproportionate as both passenger and freight traffic are concentrated on the Danube, and this itself is used mainly by foreign shipping. On its domestic section, the materials transported are stone from Dunabogdány and Szob, timber from floodplain forests and gravel from dredging sites. The reasons for the significant amount of domestic traffic are manyfold. After the war, when, because of war losses, the barge fleet was unable to meet the need, several plants located on the Danube channelled their deliveries to other forms of transport, mainly to the railways, and have never since returned to shipping. In the meantime, port facilities have also become obsolete. The low costs of water transport are more than offset by occasional trans-shipment costs. Also lacking is publicity to win over public opinion to make use of shipping facilities. To sum up, the prevailing interest system does not ensure an upswing of water transport. For instance, the new Kaba sugar refinery was located not on the Eastern Main Canal nor have any wharfs been built for new factories located near rivers.

It is worth noting that in some socialist countries, as in the GDR and Poland, water transport is also used for short hauls and with greater intensity.

On the Hungarian section of the Danube, the Csepel National Free Port in Budapest handles the largest traffic including substantial international freight movements amounting to about 1 million tons annually. Other Danube harbours with considerable traffic are Győr, Komárom, the two oil ports at Almásfüzitő and Szőny, Szob, Dunaújváros, Paks, Baja and Mohács.

The bulk of Hungarian Danube freight transport is made up of export and import deliveries [61]. Commodity transport by water is favourable for the economy partly because it saves freight dues payable in foreign currency, and partly because it earns foreign currency by shipping for foreign forwarders. (MAHART handles commission transport on the Austrian and West-German sections of the Danube.) Hungarian ships carry iron ore, petroleum, coal, timber and fertilizers from foreign countries, i.e. primarily raw materials, while finished products predominate in export traffic. Most intensive is the shipping between Hungarian and Soviet ports. Budapest is the headquarters of the Danube Commission controlling international traffic on the Danube.

Passenger transport on the Danube is primarily tourist-oriented. During the shipping season, scheduled passenger transport services only exist on the Danube between Budapest and the Danube Bend, and between Budapest and Paks. Other services have been discontinued, although high-speed hydrofoils ply between Budapest and Vienna, and Budapest and Bratislava.

The development of significant freight traffic on the Tisza is hindered by frequent periods of low water during summer, by the lack of economic relations among the regions along the river, and by all the same negative factors that effect the Danube. Freight transport is confined to construction materials, stone from the Zemplén Mountain range, timber and fertilizers from Leninváros. Formerly, the Triple-Körös was used during the sugar-beet season. The river ports on the Tisza are Tokaj, Szolnok, Csongrád and Szeged.

The Danube-Main-Rhine waterway to be opened during the 1990s also holds out prospects for Hungarian shipping. It will offer a direct link through the Main and the Rhine with the port of Rotterdam, and will enable a part of Hungarian foreign trade to be transferred to water transport [48]. The construction of this waterway raises the need for a Danube–Tisza Canal, which should also have a favourable effect on irrigation in the Great Plain and promote shipping on the Tisza. If the so-called northern alternative – from the Danube south of Vác were to be built, this would shorten the shipping route, and allow the storing of water and the building of a large power plant. Navigation on the Tisza could also be promoted by a system of locks, of which two, one at Tiszalök and the other at Kisköre, have already been completed, while a third at Csongrád will be built in the near future. These locks will ensure a higher water level.

A further possibility is the combined use of barges and seagoing ships. Barges are put on these ships like containers, being off-loaded at their destination where they continue their journey by river. The advantage of this method is the possibility of utilizing the advantages of river and marine shipping without transshipment. For the realization of this a joint Hungarian, Bulgarian, Czechoslovak and Soviet company ,,Interlighter" has been established with its centre in Budapest. Regular traffic with two barge-carrying ships began in 1979.

The Danube is connected with Lake Balaton by the Sió canal, which is furnished with two locks suitable for navigation, one being the flood gate at Szekszárd on the Danube and the other at Siófok on the Balaton. The traffic on this canal is not significant. The goods usually transported are the new ships built at the Balatonfüred shipyard, construction materials and fuels. Passenger traffic between the resorts on the northern and southern shores of Lake Balaton is significant during the summer holiday season.

Mention must also be made of marine shipping, which began as early as the mid-1930s. Ships were operated which could sail equally on the Danube and on sea and there performed a significant traffic, but owing to their size and structure, they were tied to the Mediterranean Sea. They also took a disproportionately long time to sail between Budapest and the Black Sea, while low water in summer and ice during the winter often hindered their movement. This form of shipping was therefore abandoned, and most of the ships sold. In their place a fleet of 5 to 15 000 gross ton ships suitable only for marine transport was built and is being further developed. The home ports for these ships are Rijeka, Trieste and Gdańsk. In 1981, the Hungarian marine fleet consisted of 21 ships with a total capacity of 89 000 tons. Some are used as tramp steamers, others as scheduled carriers (liners).

3.5 Pipeline transport

Carriage by pipelines has several advantages. Apart from construction costs, pipelines need no further large investment. (One pipeline replaces investment in several thousand rail-tank cars.) Manpower demand is very low, and oil and gas are moved almost automatically by pumps. The total length of pipelines in Hungary was 5629 kms in 1981, and 24 million tons were transported by them. For a detailed description of pipeline transport the reader is referred to the section on energy economy, pp. 115—133. The network is used for transporting petroleum, natural gas, oil derivatives and ethylene.

3.6 Air transport

The geographical location of Hungary is favourable from the point of view of European air routes, because of its central position. It is a fact worth noting that the first long-distance transcontinental KLM flight between Amsterdam and Batavia (Djakarta) crossed Budapest in 1932. This advantage, however, can be capitalized on only in the case of flights to and from Budapest, and the idea that Budapest might become a large European transit air centre is now unrealistic for modern, long-range aircraft prefer flights without intermediate stops. It is now less necessary for such planes to land for technical reasons, which certain airports, endowed with a good business sense, can take advantage of and thereby increase their traffic. The number of transit aircraft crossing the air space of the country is steadily rising, and the task of controlling and assigning them free passage along the narrow air corridors is becoming more difficult owing to congestion in these corridors.

The air traffic of the country is operated by Hungarian Airlines MALÉV, with air routes totalling 52 630 kms in 1981. Owing to the small area of the country, it is the significance of international air traffic that has to be stressed, as the operation of inland flights was discontinued in the late 1960s. Owing to the short distances involved, the lack of modern airports in the countryside and the improvement of surface transport, local air transport had become uncompetitive and uneconomic. MALÉV performs an important function within the national economy. It saves foreign currency when carrying Hungarian citizens, and earns it by carrying foreigners and it was with a view to realizing these advantages that MALÉV built up its network. Air traffic also boosts tourism. MALÉV has a modern fleet of TU 134 and TU 154 jets, which has enabled the company to increase the range of its flights.

Technically Budapest's Ferihegy airport conforms with international standards. Thus it is suitable to receive modern jet passenger aircraft and to follow and control their flights by radar. It is also equipped with various technical installations to enable pilots to take off and land in poor visibility (except in dense fog) and also in darkness (ILS). Yet the technical development of the airport still lags behind latest international trends, and can no longer meet the requirements of a growing traffic. Therefore, the complete reconstruction and modernization of the airport has begun and will be completed sometime during the early 1980s.

MALÉV coordinates its schedules with the airlines of other socialist countries, and, as a result, handles flights to the capitals of neighbouring socialist countries at least once a day. During the summer season, there are scheduled flights to Dubrovnik, Konstanza and Varna. With few exceptions, the MALÉV network extends to all the capitals of Europe, and there are even flights to other large cities like Kiev, Leningrad, Leipzig, Erfurt, Milan, Zürich, Frankfurt, Munich and Thessaloniki. Some flights also stop-over in several of the cities of the Middle East, such as Istanbul, Beirut, Damascus, Baghdad, Kuwait and Cairo. The latest development was the opening of the lines to Algir and Tripolis.

MALÉV also participates in international air traffic by co-operating with several western airlines with large world networks, such as KLM, Lufthansa, Swissair, SAS and British Airways, the Budapest flights of which ensure not only more intensive links with the home countries of these airlines, but also enable MALÉV to maintain air communications with America, Africa and the Far East. In contacts with Africa a role is also played by Soviet Aeroflot flights landing at Budapest. During the summer season, MALÉV also receives charter flights from overseas countries, e.g. the USA and Canada. MALÉV is also increasing its freight traffic.

4 Tourism

Tourism has an increasing significance in the Hungarian economy as the growth in purchasing power has enhanced the demand for travels. This demand is realized in foreign travel rather than within the country. Foreigners' visits to Hungary, and to a lesser extent their transit across the country, contribute to foreign-exchange earnings. (In 1981, gross receipts from tourism amounted to 14·1 billion forints, with 50·8 per cent coming from rouble-, and 49·2 per cent from dollar-accounting sources.) Foreign visits and transits contribute to the foreign-currency supply of Hungarians travelling abroad. Along with economic interests, tourism also promotes peaceful coexistence and fraternity among nations, and widens the knowledge and horizon of the participants. It also makes it possible for foreigners to gain firsthand information about the country's economic and social achievements. The geographical assets of Hungarian tourism are, on the whole, less favourable than those of the countries of Europe with long traditions in international tourism. Hungary, for instance, has no sunny coastlines, nor has it high mountains that offer tourist attraction both in summer and winter.

On the other hand, there are geographical endowments that contribute to the development of a realistic tourist industry. Lake Balaton Central Europe's largest fresh-water lake, is situated in beautiful surroundings, and offers to hundreds of thousands of Hungarians and foreigners opportunities for rest and recreation in summer. The unparalleled medicinal water resources of the country also provide a basis for medicinal holidays [57].

Specific attractions of the Hungarian landscape are the plainlands with their changing seasonal colours, the relics of former peasant life, and the Hortobágy and Bugac national parks. The rich fauna of the forests and open areas of the country attract thousands of foreign hunters. The high-quality wines of Hungarian wine-districts, the specialities of the Hungarian cuisine and the international reputation of Hungarian music are also valuable tourist assets. For historical reasons, Hungary is, unfortunately, not as rich in tourist attractions as are many other countries of Europe. Nonetheless, the architecture and religious buildings of the historical towns and the nation's principle museums in Budapest, Esztergom, Eger, Debrecen, Pécs, Veszprém and Sopron have much to offer to the interested foreigner. Tourist interest is also increased by international scientific conferences, fairs (e.g. the Budapest spring and autumn fairs), festivals, artistic events (e.g. the open-air theatrical performances in Szeged) and sporting occasions.

Hungarian tourism began to develop at the end of the 19th century. The attraction at that time was Budapest, a young and modern city with a substantial weight in the economy of south-eastern Europe. It already had a satisfactory hotel capacity, and the attractions of its medicinal baths, thanks to appropriate publicity efforts, reached a peak at that time. A further upswing took place in the 1920s and 1930s when smaller hotels and boarding houses with a family atmosphere were built on the shores of Lake Balaton. After the pseudo-landreform following the First World War, several landowners, using their compensation payments, built jointly with the official tourist agency IBUSZ a hotel network of international standards mainly in the mountainous areas. Despite the results attained, Hungarian tourism was unable to reach a significant level. The Second World War inflicted heavy demage upon tourist facilities, destruction being especially large in Budapest. As a result of the social transformation of the country, the right of the working people to recreation was asserted. Most of the hotels in the recreation areas were taken over as holiday homes by trade unions, socialist enterprises and institutions, while others were used as sanatoria.

During the 1950s, organized domestic tourism also began slowly to develop, although the cold-war climate of those years did not make it possible for international tourism to reach any appreciable level. It is also true that the facilities for it were very limited. In Budapest, for example, only 10 per

Spatial distribution of the capacity and turnover
of the Hungarian tourist industry in 1981

Area	Hotel capacity %	Other accommodation*	Total	Duration of stay by foreign guests
		percentages		
Budapest	28.5	12.8	14.9	38.0
Danube Bend	3.8	2.6	3.0	2.2
Balaton	24.0	47.1	44.0	37.6
Northern Mountains	5.5	7.1	6.9	3.9
Others	38.2	30.4	31.2	18.3
Total	100.0	100.0	100.0	100.0

* Paying-guest service, camping and bungalow and private homes accommodation.

cent of the 1938 hotel capacity existed in 1950, the rest had either been destroyed or had been transformed into offices or student hostels.

Substantial changes took place in the 1960s. After the recognition of the economic significance of tourism and the rise in demand, a multistage development programme was launched. During this period, emphasis was still placed on increasing the capacity of Balaton tourism, but by the end of the decade Budapest had became the centre of development. Hotels were also built in the county towns and the larger cities. The development of tourism based on the medicinal waters of the country started in the 1970s. By the end of the 1970s, development had again turned towards Budapest, a trend promoted by long-term credits extended by the Austrian government for the purposes of tourism.

*Characteristic features
of the Hungarian tourist industry*

a) Tourism is spatially concentrated in the two centres of Budapest and Lake Balaton as shown by the data in the table giving spatial location of hotel capacity and the duration of the stay of foreign guests.

b) For the time being, the spatial pattern of accommodation is not favourable. In the so-called commercial accommodation sector the capacity was 220 000 beds in 1981, the share of hotel accommodation was only 15 per cent for tourist accommodation, 28 per cent for camping and bungalow accommodation, and 57.0 per cent for accommodation in private homes, guest houses and week-end flats providing a paying-guest service.

c) The seasonal character of tourism poses a serious economic problem. The holiday season, for example, only lasts 8 to 10 weeks at Lake Balaton and about 5 months in Budapest. Although in the case of the latter, the utilization of the various forms of accommodation is high throughout the year, seasonality is nonetheless apparent.

d) Particularly low is the average duration of stay, averaging 5·2 days nationally in 1981, but rising to 7·5 days at Lake Balaton.

e) Owing to the geographical location of the country, a high proportion of foreigners entering the country are in transit, majority of whom leave after a minimum stay. The available capacity to handle such traffic is most inadequate as is that for increasing the receipts from longer stays.

As can be seen from the above table, the number of foreign tourists has grown dynamically, although supply was unable to meet their needs adequately. In 1981 the number of foreigners entering the country was 14·8 million, of whom 84·0 per cent came from socialist countries, primarily Czechoslovakia, Yugoslavia, the GDR, Romania and the Soviet Union. The explanation of this biased proportion lies, apart from the high level of mutual interest, in the fact that there is no essential difference either in the respective price levels, or in the conditions of foreign-exchange supply. In addition, geographical proximity is a favourable factor. A large number of international express rail services, air flights, and a dense road network link these countries with Hungary. A substantial number of the visitors from these countries are members of the Hungarian minorities there, who come to Hungary for the purpose of visiting their relatives. The same motivation lies behind the visits of Hungarian citizens to neighbouring countries. Of the western countries it is primarily from Austria that most tourists come, a development helped by the mutual abolition of visa requirements. A significant number of tourists also come from the FRG, Italy and France. Overseas tourists come predominantly from the USA and Canada, and include, to an increasing extent, émigré Hungarians who left the country at various terms, as well as second- or third-generation Hungarians interested in the old country.

In 1981, 5·55 million Hungarian citizens travelled abroad, a relatively high number when compared with the country's population size. 91·0 per cent of these visited other socialist countries. In view of the basic political principles of international tourism, there is also the possibility for Hungarian citizens, depending on the domestic foreign-exchange situation, to travel to western countries either individually, or as a part of an organized group.

Within domestic tourism, an important role is played by ,,social-tourism", that is, recreation organized by trade unions and enterprises. During the last three decades, the capacity of social-tourism has significantly expanded and now totals 3072 holiday homes, which accommodation capacity was 131 473 beds in 1981. Also enjoying the services of social-tourism in 1981 were 1·3 million holiday-makers of whom 71 000 were foreigners in the framework of exchange-holidays. Most of these stayed at Lake Balaton.

The main tourist districts of the country

Budapest. The capital's geographical location, beauty and cultural values constitute a considerable attractive power. In addition, as a city of 2 million inhabitants, it has many tourist assets to offer, including medicinal waters and baths. International scientific, cultural and sports events extend the duration of the tourist season.

The Danube Bend. Located north of the capital, this area offers weekend and summer recreation especially for the inhabitants of Budapest. The beauty of the landscape at Visegrád, the art treasures at Esztergom, Visegrád and Szentendre and other features such as the skanzen at Szentendre also attract many foreigners. The Danube section south of the capital is the centre of water sports.

Lake Balaton. A large number of resorts have been built both on the southern and northern shores of the Lake, notably at Siófok, Balatonfüred, Tihany and Keszthely. With its excellent beaches, the lukewarm water of the Lake attracts hundreds of thousand of domestic and foreign holiday-makers. Of outstanding beauty is the landscape and panorama of the extinct volcanoes of the Tapolca basin at the south-eastern end of the Lake. Located near the Lake is Hévíz, the country's largest and most modern thermal medicinal bath.

As a resort area, the Mátra–Bükk Mountain district has only modest endowments, for instance winter sports opportunities are best here, although not infrequent are the winters when the season is confined to a few days. In adjoining areas there are several medicinal and thermal baths, and the sights of Eger and Miskolc also add to the tourist turnover of the district. Unfortunately, the Aggtelek stalactite cave system, one of the largest in the world, is too inaccessible to be of significance for international tourism.

The Pécs–Mecsek district. Pécs is a city of historical significance. Its beautiful location, art treasures and rich museums make it a remarkable tourist spot. Near Pécs is Harkány, one of the country's most frequented thermal medicinal baths.

Western Transdanubia is, owing to the proximity of the Austrian frontier, the district mostly visited by Austrian tourists. Its attraction is enhanced by the historical towns of Sopron, Szombathely, Győr and Fertőd as well as by the medicinal baths at Balf and Bük.

Besides the districts listed above, mention must also be made of the national parks of the Great Plain, the Hortobágy park near Debrecen and the Kiskunság park near Kecskemét with their characteristic landscapes, flora and fauna, remnants of the former ,,puszta" life, including protected farm animals, like the grey Hungarian cattle, ,,racka" sheep, and stud farms. These, as well as the medicinal baths of Gyula, Hajdúszoboszló, Zalakaros and other local towns are also tourist spots favoured by foreigners.

5 International economic relations and their impact on the spatial distribution of productive forces

International economic relations, based on the international division of labour are of vital interest to the Hungarian economy, and their significance is steadily rising. This statement is justified by the following facts.

a) Owing to the limited availability of domestic natural resources, economically exploitable energy sources and mineral raw materials are insufficient both in terms of quantity and quality, and several raw materials are not available at all. Due to climatic constraints, certain agricultural produce indispensable for the supply of industry and part of the foodstuffs needed for the supply of the population cannot be produced. Such produce can only be acquired from abroad, within the framework of international economic relations.

b) The development of productive forces requires the latest technical equipment and other investment goods, many of which are not produced by Hungarian industry. These also have to be imported. The raising of living standards, a more adequate commodity supply and a wider range of products also necessitate the import of many consumer goods.

c) In addition, the maintenance of international economic relations also has more intricate implications. The development of productive forces has brought about significant productive capacities in the field of material production. Given the small area and population of the country, and the limited size of its economy, the output of Hungarian industry accounts for some 2 per cent of the total industrial output of CMEA countries, it follows that the domestic market is relatively narrow. Resulting from technical progress and so-called economies of scale, several products can be produced economically only in large batches. Also new technologies have been developed, the products of which far exceed the needs of the Hungarian economy. Hence, Hungary faces the choice of selecting either the uneconomic production of small runs of several products, which would be a waste of productive forces, or, the manufacture of these products most appropriate to the economy's endowments, joining in the international division of labour and — by way of specialization — of exploiting the potentialities in the best possible way [66]. The advantages occurring from the international division of labour can best be exploited if products which are more economically produced elsewhere are imported.

By utilizing the favourable natural endowments of the country and by raising the level of technology, agriculture is able to produce surplus goods for export. Thus participation in the international division of labour has increasingly become a precondition for economic growth and has speeded up the development of several branches of industry and agriculture and has increased their efficiency. Hence, the participation of the Hungarian economy in the international division of labour is of a complementary and competitive character.

d) Hungary's society and economy are organized along socialist lines and certain receipts do not therefore figure on the asset side of the balance of payments, such as are available to many capitalist countries, for instance, interest incomes from exported capital. Thus exports are designed not only to earn foreign exchange to cover imports, but also to meet the economy's other foreign financial commitments, for instance, the costs of commodity deliveries abroad.

Owing to its above tasks and its close linkage to all sectors of the economy, foreign trade is of special importance. For national income to be increased by one unit, foreign-trade turnover has to rise by a higher proportion. Increasing turnover is an important factor in the country's economy and brings about increasing specialization primarily in industry. As a result, about 45 per cent of national income passes through the channels of foreign trade, and this proportion is rising. Such a high proportion is unique among socialist countries, and indeed very few other countries have a higher ratio, e.g. Belgium, the Netherlands, Denmark and Switzerland. Also high is the per capita value of foreign-trade turnover which amounts to about 2000 dollars.

The commodity pattern of foreign trade (see *Fig. 58*) reflects not only a country's participation in the international division of labour, but is also indicative of the development level of its economy. The large-scale changes in the economic life and structure of a country are paralleled by changes in the structure of foreign trade. Currently, industrial products account for over 80 per cent of overall exports, including the products of the food-processing industry. Raw materials and fuels constitute the majority of imports, owing to the country's physical endowments.

It follows from the country's social and economic set-up the socialist countries rank first in Hungary's foreign trade turnover. This turnover is laid down in medium-turn trade agreements concluded during each plan period. They ensure the markets from which the most important raw materials and machinery are imported, and those to which Hungarian products are exported. Trade with socialist countries which are contiguous or close to Hungary is favourable also from the point of view of transport as lower transport costs are imposed on the commodities. In the distribution of turnover by continents, Europe comes first accounting for 85 per cent of imports and 88 per cent of exports. Europe is followed in imports by America, Asia and Africa, and in exports by Asia, America and Africa in that order. As regards the destination of foreign trade, the close relationship with the Soviet Union is relatively a new element. The traditional countries of Central Europe, partly socialist and partly capitalist, have remained dominant in foreign trade. Trade with overseas and developing countries is a constantly changing element *(Fig. 59)*.

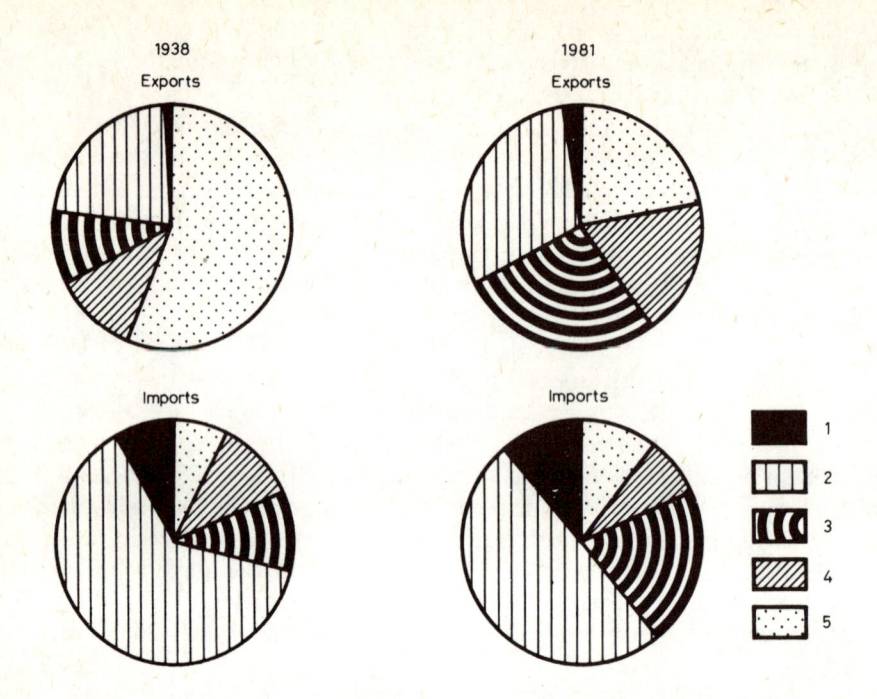

Fig. 58. The commodity structure of foreign-trade turnover in 1938 and 1981
1 — energy sources; 2 — raw materials; 3 — machinery and equipment; 4 — industrial consumer goods; 5 — raw materials for the food processing industry

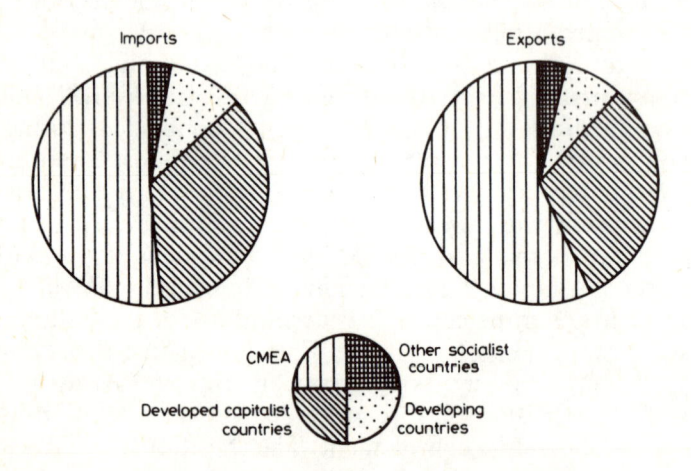

Fig. 59. Foreign trade by destination (1981)

5.1 CMEA integration and its impact on the spatial distribution of productive forces

Socialist international economic co-operation came into being within the framework of the Council for Mutual Economic Assistance, of which the Hungarian People's Republic has been a member since its foundation in 1949.

In view of their increasingly developed and complex economies, the CMEA countries have been determined to set about the realization of new forms of socialist economic integration in the interest of the further and more efficient development of their economies. This determination has found expression in the so-called comprehensive programme approved in 1971. Progress towards integration implies closer economic co-operation over and above the harmonization of medium- and short-term plans, specialization within economic sectors, inter-enterprise co-operation, joint investments and increased scientific-technical co-operation. The improvement of the socialist division of labour makes it possible for the individual CMEA countries and thus also for Hungary to develop their national economic systems so that they may exploit natural resources, productive capacities and the labour force in the most efficient way [62].

The so-called long-term co-operation target programmes, approved in 1979, serve the further deepening of integration. These programmes, with recommendations for the growth of energy, fuel and raw-material production, are designed to ensure the long-term satisfaction of the needs of CMEA countries. They will also promote the improvement of agriculture and food supply. The programme relating to the engineering industry envisages the specialization of production, the deepening of co-operation and the creation of further productive capacities. Participation in the target programme is of great significance to the Hungarian national economy, as it helps in furthering specialization and in transforming the structure, primarily the product structure, of the economy [78].

By taking into account the above factors it is possible to form in individual countries a structure of economic sectors conductive to the strengthening of the world socialist economic system as a whole [69].

The economic branches established within the framework of co-operation are able to meet both domestic needs and also those of the other socialist countries. The participation of the Hungarian national economy in the socialist international division of labour is based on fundamental principles and has several determinants. On the one hand, the Hungarian national economy has, owing to the above-mentioned energy and raw-material problems, to rely on countries which are in a position continuously to satisfy these demands. On the other, its participation provides the possibility of a more rational exploitation of its own natural and economic resources. The importance of this factor is shown by the fact that 90 per cent of imported energy sources, 60 per cent of raw and basic materials and 80 per cent of investment

**Hungarian exports and imports by selected countries
of origin and destination, 1981**
(in per cent)

	Exports	Imports		Exports	Imports
Socialist countries	58.1	51.5	*Capitalist countries*	41.9	48.5
of which			of which		
Soviet Union	33.4	28.6	FRG	8.7	11.9
GDR	6.9	6.7	Italy	3.3	3.0
Czechoslovakia	6.0	4.9	Austria	4.3	5.8
Poland	3.4	3.4	France	1.6	2.7
Romania	2.0	2.0	United Kingdom	1.0	2.3
Bulgaria	1.3	1.3	Iraq	2.5	0.1
Yugoslavia	3.2	2.9	USA	1.4	2.5
China	0.4	0.6	India	0.1	0.1
			Brazilia	0.3	2.7
			Japan	0.3	1.4

goods come from CMEA countries. The country's industrial, agricultural and scientific resources as well as production experience also make it possible further to develop those sectors which can export to other socialist countries as well as meeting domestic needs. Based on the country's climatic and soil endowments, Hungarian agriculture can specialize in those branches which can promote the food supply of socialist countries with less favourable climatic conditions. Owing to the above interrelationships, socialist countries by 85 per cent of machinery and equipment, 70 per cent of consumer goods and about 60 per cent of the products of the agricultural and food-processing industry that are exported by Hungary.

Participation in socialist integration has had, and will increasingly have, an impact on the location of productive forces in Hungary. Participation in socialist economic co-operation is a long-term affair. Consequently, by making use of the advantage of co-operation, the possibility is provided for the efficient location of plants and branches, for agricultural specialization in certain areas, as well as for adjusting the capacity of the transport network to the requirements of co-operation.

The construction of productive capacities in excess of the country's needs makes it possible to build plants that are large in scale and capacity in compliance with the requirements of technical and economic efficiency. (The reader is referred to the section on the chemical industry.) As a result, the benefits from economies of scale can be exploited by the Hungarian economy; at the same time they also constitute advantages for other member countries. Plants of sufficient size to meet the demands of integration can be established in the form of large-scale complexes and combines. And in agriculture, production systems that also meet the conditions of large-scale production can be set up.

As a result of the spillover effects of the branches joining in the process of integration, or those that are developed within its framework, further regional linkages and new location policy may be established. Thus, for instance, in the field of large enterprises it will be possible to set up a system of subsidiary plants in the framework of convergent integration, for the ensurance of a better supply of components and accessories. In addition, manufacturing industry geared to such large enterprises will come into being, which will enable a more complex development of individual areas and the better utilization of labour and infrastructure.

The scientific-research activity that lays the foundations and promotes the development of those branches involved in integration exerts a positive influence on Hungarian scientific life as a whole.

Along with the manifold results of co-operation, there are also problems that hinder further progress. Owing to the duplication of capacities built earlier, there is oversupply of certain products and a shortage equally exist in intra-CMEA trade. There also appear problems in the deepening of interrelations, as, for example, the inability to manufacture standardized subassemblies and components, and the general absence of a background industry for the mostly highly developed sectors of the engineering industry. In this field, as in the more intensive use of the science of economics, there are still a great many unexploited potentialities.

The effect of co-operation on the spatial location of productive forces.

Co-operation in power generation. The harmonization of the long-term energy programmes of member countries had already began during an earlier period. According to its significant quantities of energy from CMEA countries, in the first place from the Soviet Union. In return for these deliveries, Hungary contributes to the development of the Soviet energy industry by extending credits and by sharing in the investment costs of projects, for instance, in the contribution of the 2750 km long Orenburg Gas Pipeline.

The most important forms of co-operation, which also have an effect on industrial location, are the pipeline systems carrying petroleum and natural gas. The pipelines can be directed to energy-poor areas, where they may lay the basis for industrialization. For example, the Friendship Pipeline laid the foundations for the Százhalombatta thermal power station and oil refinery, which play such a decisive role in the supply of Budapest, the largest energy consumer in the country. The Friendship II Pipeline supplies the raw materials of the Leninváros oil-refinery, and indirectly of the Olefine Works of the Tisza Chemical Combine. This has all taken place in an area where the factors of industrial location are available to a limited extent only.

The Hungarian electricity is integrated with the grids of the European socialist countries. The 750 kW grid between Vinyca and Albertirsa and many other grids connect the 100 000 mW electric power system of the Soviet Union with the grids of other European CMEA countries, having a total capacity of 60 000 kW. (Compare the latter data with the performance of the Hungarian electric energy system.) Such co-operation helps supply the great energy users of the country, but also induces new industrial location.

Co-operation in metallurgy. Co-operation in ferrous metallurgy is being realized, in addition to supplying raw materials to Hungary, within the framework of Intermetall. The production of certain rolled-product profiles is increasing in Hungary, while other steel and rolled-steel products are imported from the member countries.

Particularly great is the impact that integration exerts on the development of the Hungarian bauxite-aluminium complex. Bauxite is the only domestic raw material which, along with satisfying the country's own consumption needs, can also be exported to other CMEA countries. The Hungarian bauxite-aluminium vertical system (the reader is referred to the section on metallurgy) has been brought about as a result of close co-operation, since the existing Hungarian energy resources would have permitted the establishment of a small-scale aluminium industry, with consequent loss of economic efficiency. The impact of co-operation on the spatial location of the productive forces found expression partly in the development of bauxite mining, in the opening up of new mines, and partly in the construction of the new, high-capacity alumina factory at Ajka and the continued development of the aluminium rolling mill at Székesfehérvár. Within the framework of co-operation, Hungary, Czechoslovakia, Poland and the GDR are participating in bauxite, alumina and finished aluminium product deliveries. In addition, the question of domestic supply has also been solved most economically.

Co-operation in the engineering industry. In its co-operation with other CMEA countries, the Hungarian engineering industry concentrates its efforts on the development of commercial vehicles, telecommunication and technology. In this way, large-batch production can be expanded and product development accelerated. With the products developed within the framework of co-operation, the Hungarian economy has also tackled the capitalist market. Hungary has created a bus industry with a capacity significant by international standards, which has also stimulated the engineering industries of Budapest and Székesfehérvár. Co-operation in the vehicle industry has required large investments. The Hungarian Railway Carriage and Engineering Works at Győr (RÁBA) has become the centre of the manufacture of diesel engines and rear axles and has established an effective convergent integration by locating several subsidiary plants in the Little Plain.

Within the framework of Hungarian–Soviet and Hungarian–Polish co-operation in the motorcar industry, the engineering industry supplies large quantities of components, which in turn has necessitated the expansion of several engineering enterprises, and the establishment of new industrial plants, for instance, the Bakony Engineering Works for Metal and Electric Appliances in Veszprém and its subsidiary plants in middle Transdanubia.

The development of electronics, the most up-to-date sector of the engineering industry, has also been promoted by co-operation. First, microwave telecommunication and transfer technology began to develop in Budapest and at several plants in the countryside, subsequently, to perform the tasks of the computer technology programme, Videoton in Székesfehérvár has become the centre of computer production. The computer programme (manufacture of computers, peripherials and components) has accelerated the development of many subsidiary plants in Budapest, Székesfehérvár and other industrial centres in Transdanubia. A similar significant co-operation, even if not on the same scale, has also developed within other branches of the engineering industry.

Co-operation in the chemical industry. This is especially significant because it makes the building of capacities of economic size possible, as has been shown by the petrochemical industry. The specialization and the growth of output of the Hungarian pharmaceutical industry have also been motivated by the demands of other CMEA countries. Co-operation in this field is significant because it has made possible highly successful specialization. Co-operation in the production of synthetic fibres ensures the expansion of the product range.

Co-operation in the chemical industry continues to expand. Within the framework of the target programmes it will be possible for the countries concerned to establish either their own or jointly owned chemical plants which have high specific energy demands in the Soviet Union, and also to meet the demands of the participating countries. The Hungarian chemical industry will increase the production of certain highly effective herbicides in return for which the Soviet Union will step up its nitrogenous fertilizer deliveries.

Co-operation in light industry will show up first of all in the mutual deliveries of raw materials and finished products. In satisfying the long-term demands primarily of the Soviet Union, the domestic knitwear, clothing and footwear industries have developed significantly, and several new plants have been established for this purpose.

Co-operation in the food industry. This requires, in the interest of the utilization of natural endowments, the establishment of modern large-scale production so as to meet both domestic needs and the needs of other member countries. The same also holds good for the development of the individual branches of the food-processing industry. Hungarian agriculture supplies considerable quantities of agricultural produce and foodstuffs to most CMEA countries, such as cereals, especially wheat and maize, meat and meat products, vegetables, fresh and canned fruit and wine. As a result of co-operation, vegetable and fruit growing as well as the canning industry have expanded. For instance, the canning factories located in the northern parts of the Great Plain export to the Soviet Union.

Co-operation can take on a number of forms, for instance, the internationalization of production systems. The country's maize-production systems maintain contacts with several such units in neighbouring countries. Over and above the transfer of results and experiences, the conditions for extending co-operation in the field of production systems are also ripe for other plant varieties. The technical development of Hungarian agriculture is a further source of co-operation, such as, for example, the export of broiler strain stock and the installation of large-scale poultry farms, together with selected seeds, especially hybrid seeds.

Co-operation within the food industry can be further expanded. The development of Hungarian agriculture during the past two decades has provided evidence that the reserves are far from being exhausted, and production can be further developed. But the assets required by modern agriculture are very large, reaching, occasionally, the same level as the investment demands of certain branches of basic material production. Therefore, development within the framework of integration justifies the requirement that those member countries which regard the Hungarian food industry as an important source for supplying their own economies should contribute to its development on a bilateral basis.

The effect of economic co-operation on the Hungarian transport network. It follows from the country's geographical position that the commodity flows between the socialist countries impose serious tasks upon the Hungarian transport network. Transit trade among the socialist countries is based primarily on the railway network. To avoid congestion and to ensure a faster passage of transit freight through the Hungarian rail network, substantial development has proved necessary, to which the investment bank of the CMEA has contributed by extending credits. The electrification of several railway lines has also become necessary, primarily for this reason, for instance, of the Budapest–Újszász–Szolnok–Lökösháza of the Cegléd–Kiskunfélegyháza–Kiskunhalas lines.

The construction of the domestic road network and the expansion of long-distance communication systems are being carried out in concert with other CMEA countries. Co-operation in air transport, e.g. in the coordination of timetables is also close.

5.2 Economic co-operation with the developed western countries

The Hungarian People's Republic has established its economic relations with the developed capitalist countries on the basis of equality and mutual interest. Nevertheless, despite its endeavour, it often encounters difficulties [94], such as, for example, recurrent import restrictions and occasional measures of a discriminatory nature, although political détente has also brought about some positive changes in this field. These facts make it difficult to expand, and sometimes even to maintain economic relations. It is particularly the customs duties applied by the European Economic Community against non-community countries, which impose heavy burdens on Hungarian exports, primarily on foodstuffs, but also increasingly on industrial products. The commodity structure of exports also poses problems as it overwhelmingly still consists of agricultural produce. Apart from cotton cloth, clothing articles, gloves and fancy goods and a limited range of industrial consumer goods, i.e. incandescant lamps, television sets and pharmaceuticals, the share of manufacture is very small. The market share of the engineering industry is insignificant in the developed capitalist countries, primarily owing to the comparatively low technical level of its products. The raw-material export potential of the Hungarian economy is restricted, being limited to alumina, rolled products, aluminium, and a few basic materials of the petrochemical industry. Imports from developed capitalist countries consist of machinery and equipment and materials not available in the CMEA market, mainly chemicals, intermediate products, synthetic materials, and man-made fibres as well as standardized components, accessories and consumer goods. Greatest is the trade with the traditional partners of the Federal Republic of Germany, Austria, Italy, Switzerland and the USA.

Besides foreign-trade relations, Hungarian enterprises are also striving to conclude long-term co-operation agreements with capitalist countries as these would contribute to the safety of the country's planned economy. This endeavour, however, faces several constraints, deriving mainly from the cyclical nature of their economies, which make the capitalist partners reluctant to conclude long-term co-operation agreements. Therefore, most important co-operation agreements have so far been of a short-term character, for example, the co-operation in the manufacture of components with the Fiat, Renault and Volkswagen motor companies. Co-operation has been carried on in several forms, the most important of which are as follows:

Co-operation in third markets, comprising major projects, such as the delivery of equipment for power stations, and heavy boilers. Such types of co-operation are usually undertaken with West-German, Austrian and Italian firms.

Production co-operation in the manufacture and delivery of components and spare parts has evolved with Austrian, West-German, French and Swedish firms, but it is also common in the chemical and pharmaceutical sectors too with British, West-German, French and US companies.

IKARUSZ co-operates with several western motor companies in the assembly of foreign components and the marketing of the finished product in western markets. It is usually in the form of building foreign bodies, for instance, Volvo, Renault and Steyer on to self-produced chassis.

Commission work is a form of co-operation that is especially widespread in the clothing industry, and involves mainly West-German, Dutch and British firms, department stores and the Levi Straus multinational corporation.

The establishment of common agencies in Hungary and abroad has recently begun to assume considerable proportions, for instance, Shell-Interag and London Chemicals Ltd. These agencies have promoted co-operation between Hungarian industry and foreign partners, have encouraged the placement of foreign products on the Hungarian market, and have set up servicing networks, for example, Shell, British Petroleum and AGYP filling stations. The number of joint commercial agencies of Hungarian and western trading and industrial firms operating in western countries is already considerable, especially in the FRG and Great Britain. In addition, in order to acquire and maintain foreign markets, there has also began, to a lesser extent, the construction of industrial projects, and the purchase of equity capital, for instance, the building of factories by the United Incandescent Lamp and Electric Company (Tungsram) in Austria, Ireland, Pakistan and the USA, and of small electronic, mainly components-manufacturing plants in Western Europe. The joint venture of the Bábolna State Farm with several American firms in a factory maize production system has proved a successful undertaking.

A most important objective of economic co-operation with the West is the speeding up of domestic technological development and of the transformation of the product structure. Within this framework, Hungarian enterprises are purchasing more and more licences or complete technologies and factory equipment, for example, MAN diesel engines. At the same time, the sale of Hungarian licences is also significant.

Long-term foreign credits play a considerable part in the development of certain branches. Mention must be made of the credits used for the development of the hotel industry as part of the infrastructure for international tourism. Earlier, the Duna Intercontinental, Hyatt and Hilton Hotels in Budapest were built with the participation of private western capital. More recently long-term credits from the Austrian government have made possible the building of six hotels in Budapest and others in provincial towns, which will improve the accommodation capacity of the capital significantly.

5.3 Economic relations with developing countries

The Hungarian People's Republic endeavours both for political and economic reasons to establish and expand economic co-operation with former colonial countries which are, as a rule, at a lower stage of economic development. Hungary also supports the demand of these countries to create a new world-economic order. Moreover, it also extends as far as it can economic assistance to those developing countries which have chosen the path of progressive social transformation. Trade with the developing countries is growing, but economic co-operation has become more extensive than trade. Hungary also extends credits to promote economic growth in several developing countries. Of particular importance are the activities of designing enterprises and expert teams, for example, in Iraq, Algeria and Lybia. Direct capital investment and the organization of joint venture enterprises is also developing in the pharmaceutical industry, the manufacture of incandescent lamps and in food processing.

Hungarian exports to the developing countries are manifold. For example, the export of foodstuffs, poultry-farming technologies, breeding livestock and cold-storage facilities to Arab countries is significant. Machinery, consumer goods, chemicals, pharmaceuticals are also exported to other developing countries. Noteworthy are the efforts of Hungarian enterprises to export complete production units, for instance, alumina factories to India, and minor food-processing plants and canning factories to Middle-East countries.

In the co-operation scheme with developing countries, the Hungarian partner mainly imports various tropical raw materials, like fruit and minerals, as well as appreciable quantities of consumer goods, mostly underwear and knitwear. Further forms of co-operation are in the process of development, for instance, the transfer of certain labour-intensive production processes to developing countries. Greater emphasis has to be placed on increased participation in the extraction of raw materials because the import of several primary or semifinished goods is likely to come increasingly from developing countries in the future, for example, petroleum and phosphate imports. Of the developing countries, it is primarily with Iraq, Algeria, Libya, Kuwait, India and Brazil that significant economic relations have been established.

6 Trends in the spatial structure of the Hungarian economy

Following the survey of the physiographic environment, the spatial distribution of population, the settlement network, the geographical pattern of individual sectors of the national economy and spatial disparities in production, we shall now summarize the main characteristics of the spatial economic structure of the country. Many of these features are connected with inherited spatial endowments, with the development of productive forces, primarily with socialist industrialization and the collectivization of agriculture, as well as with regional development policy. These, in interaction with one another and with other factors like the international division of labour, determine the regional characteristics of the division of labour and the main trends of development.

Without dwelling on the analysis of regional policy and on its main instrument, regional planning, we must first point out the role played by this policy.

The main objectives of regional development policy were realized in the centralized system of economic management through various sectoral and regional plans. The fulfilment of the plans was of low efficiency, because their implementation usually disregarded local physiographic and economic conditions. Over-centralization hindered enterprise interest in production and hampered the implementation of the main objectives of regional development policy.

Since the reform of economic management, the assertion of the main objectives of regional development through planning has declined significantly. The central planning of the regional development of industry has practically been discontinued, although the spatial location of transport and certain service branches continues to be subject to planning. This contradictory situation has come about as a result of the fact that, with the exception of certain high-priority projects, the location of which has remained within the competence of central planning, the right to decide on the choice of industrial location has been delegated to individual enterprises. The same applies to the decisions on the locational pattern of agricultural production units. The locational decisions of enterprises are influenced partly by general economic regulators, i.e. credits, price and taxation policy, and partly by enterprise interests. Since regulators are uniform throughout the country the choice of production locations entails several disadvantages.

Some of these deleterious effects have been made conspicuous by the experiences of the past few years. When located in an area with developed service infrastructural provision, an enterprise obtains, without consideration, an advantage which was brought about by other branches or enterprises, and which another enterprise could perhaps utilize with greater efficiency. Thus enterprise interest may conflict with the interest of the national economy [10]. In agriculture, the differences in income entailed by the prices of different products may one-sidedly benefit farms with lands better suited to certain products, while less economical cultures have to be grown under unfavourable production conditions.

Without an adequate regional policy and its implementation by regulators, the new system of economic management does not ensure undistorted regional development. Moreover, for the implementation of an effective regional policy such decisions are needed as express not only enterprise but also social interests. Social control is ensured by the National Planning Office which, in the context of the five-year national economic plan, sets the current objectives of regional development policy and allocates the resources for their implementation.

As a result of the regional development objectives realized with varying efficiency by the different types of economic management systems of the past three decades (1950—1980), the spatial location of the Hungarian economy has become more evenly balanced. The inter- and intra-regional division of labour has increased, economic relations have become many-sided, and links between towns and villages more intensive. The disparities in industrial and agricultural production between the industrially developed and undeveloped territories have lessened. As a result of the rise in the technical level of agriculture and of the diffusion of factory production systems, industrial and agricultural districts have moved closer to each other economically.

In the division of labour between the industry of the capital and of the countryside, the one-sided role of the latter as the supplier of basic materials and the role of the former as the consumer of finished products has been mitigated. The linkages between districts associated with the extractive and the basic-materials industry have expanded, and in the agglomeration area of Budapest significant industrial bases have been established for the production of basic materials. Spatial differences in living standards and conditions have diminished both regionally and between the basic settlement types.

A levelling tendency is making itself felt in wage levels, individual subsistence costs, and infrastructural provision, although the supply level is still very differentiated.

Alongside this levelling process, concentration tendencies have also manifested themselves and have transformed the regional structure of the national economy. Over the past three decades more than one million persons have settled in the industrially developed areas, and the increase in the urban population has exceeded 2 million. Thus, spatial concentration has become apparent primarily in the increased social and economic weight of the towns. As a result of spatial concentration, the proportion of the active population living in the industrially developed areas has risen from an earlier 55 per cent to about 66 per cent, and the number of daily commuters has also greatly increased in these areas. The spatial concentration of the economy has made possible the more economic utilization and expansion of local natural and social potentials, the exploitation of all the advantages of a more spatially concentrated development and the reconciliation of regional and sectoral disparities.

But this increase in spatial concentration has, along with its advantages, also entailed significant drawbacks, especially the growth in infrastructural inputs at the national economic level. The negative effects have made themselves felt primarily outside the places of work and appear in the high cost of dwelling construction and the overcrowded urban infrastructure, resulting from the massive migration of rural population to the developing industrial centres. The concentration process has also led to a rise in commuting often requiring long travelling times.

The above positive tendencies and the results attained have only diminished the spatial disproportions in the territorial division of labour and productive forces. The basic disproportion in the spatial location of productive forces is still manifest in the different economic, infrastructural, income and cultural levels that exist, with the resulting contradiction between Budapest and its agglomeration belt, on the one hand, and the less industrialized, predominantly agricultural counties, on the other. This is reflected in the unfavourable spatial separation of areas of economic growth from the sources of manpower, calling subsequently for the migration and expensive resettlement of population.

Despite the levelling of differences, the disparities between individual regions, counties are still significant, primarily in industry. As regards the level of industrialization in terms of the proportion of people employed in industry the inter-county range is twofold, and in terms of per capita national income realized from industry the range had fallen from the earlier 14-fold difference to a twofold one by the end of the 1970s. By contrast, with the rising differences in the level of technical equipment, productivity differences between individual counties has hardly changed. An important area of industrial development was, and still is, the industrially developed area, comprising the counties located along the so-called industrial axis — Baranya,

Veszprém, Komárom, Győr, Nógrád, Borsod and Fejér. Their development was also stimulated by the natural resources of the area, primarily coal, which was favourably affected by the 1973 energy price explosion, as they ensure cheaper, more economic production than the marginal exchange products of imported energy. The industrially developed counties have retained their earlier specialization, which, owing to the dynamism of their industries, has further strengthened. For example, Győr and the towns in the Little Plain have become the bases for the commercial vehicle industry, Székesfehérvár for aluminium processing and computer manufacturing and Leninváros for synthetic-material production and processing.

Another centre attractive to industry is Budapest in which the greater part of the country's industry is concentrated, although its labour resources were largely depleted by the mid-1970s. Another factor behind the moderate development of Budapest industry is the conscious relocation of industry. The share of the country's industrial wage-earners working in Budapest has fallen to 28 per cent. This fall is not, however, an unambiguously positive phenomenon as it is also accompanied by the under-utilization of high-value productive capacities [49].

The third area of industrialization embraces the Great Plain and the agricultural counties in South-Transdanubia, in which small industries, handicrafts and the food-processing industry were formerly predominant. In the industrially undeveloped areas new industrial plants, based primarily on the availability of labour, have been set up. The locational policy of extensive industrial development has proved effective in the sense that it has utilized the labour, water and other resources of such areas and has established several industrial centres providing the basis for further industrialization. Although extensive industrialization has promoted the consolidation of provincial industry, the economic results that industrialization was expected to produce have not been attained. The lower efficiency of the industrial bases located in the southern periphery of the country is due, among other things, to inadequate technical provision and to the lower skill level of the available manpower.

As regards the results achieved by industrial development, it may be stated in summary that the spatial location of industry has become more evenly balanced and the differences between industrially developed and industrially backward counties have been reduced. As regards the level of industrial development, however, the country is still differentiated into two distinctive regions — the north and the south of the country.

The changes that have occurred in the spatial structure of agricultural production have been partly due to the rapid increase in cereal yields and the development of orchard cultures, and partly to the dynamic growth of the pig and poultry sectors along with the stagnation of cattle raising. But neither the spatial structure of agriculture, nor the regional specialization in production reflect the technical development and organization of the large agricultural farms. Most of them are engaged in a variety of activities often not in accordance with their given potentialities, and often at a low efficiency. Farms engaging in 16 to 20 different activities is quite typical. Hidden behind this problem is the lack of coordination between the forces of production and the deficiencies in the price structure and interest in agriculture.

It is a new feature of the regional development of agriculture that with the diffusion of factory production systems the demand for regional infrastructural networks has increased, as a result of which the fastest developing agrarian areas of the past decade are today not the districts endowed with the most fertile soils, but those embracing the industrially developed areas.

Another factor in regional differentiation has been the development of the more remunerative industrial, trading and transport sectors, i.e. sectors engaged in non-agricultural activities. In the 1970s, the highest outputs were achieved by the large enterprises and by the areas with a good economic environment containing significant industrial and service activities, i.e. the counties of Pest, Komárom and Bács-Kiskun. Thus the share in agricultural production of the districts endowed with the best soils has gradually declined. This modification of the spatial structure of agriculture leaves un-utilized the potentialities offered by natural endowments, and diminishes the „rent" that could be realized in foreign markets.

The development of agriculture and the strengthening of agrarian-industrial integration, in which the leading role is played by the large co-operative farms, has exerted a significant impact on the development of rural settlements. This impact has manifested itself in the shaping and modernization of both the work and residential environments.

No significant changes have taken place in the geographical characteristics of the transport network. Its geometrical layout is closely connected with the regional division of labour. On the other hand, the division of labour among the various forms of transport has increased. The significance of export-import activities, and of transit traffic and transit routes has grown. Rail traffic is concentrated on the west-east trunk line and in the Budapest area. The rest of the railway network handles just one-tenth of overall traffic. Some minor railway lines have been closed — instead of them cars —, and the construction of stations designed to concentrate the loading of freight traffic has begun. A nationwide bus network serving practically all the settlements of the country has been built up.

The labour and occupational pattern of the country has been affected by the fact that during the past three decades the working population has increased by nearly one million. Although its growth has been continuous, it has also been spatially differentiated, the main sources of the increase being the villages and the north-eastern parts of the country.

The internal migration of population has been connected mainly with the socialist reorganization of agriculture and the demands for industrial labour of individual areas. Migration to the Budapest agglomeration and towns seems to be a lasting trend. Migrants usually come from the industrially poorly developed or slowly developing areas, particularly the northern parts of the Great Plain. Labour movement has exerted a significant impact on the age structure of the population of both areas of in- and out-migration.

In recent years, the concentration of population has slowed down, and the size of most low-order centres has ceased to decline. On the other hand, the population of small- and medium-sized villages which even now is barely sufficient to ensure the most fundamental communal services continues to diminish, particularly in areas deficient in transport and far away from industrial centres.

In conjunction with the changed structure of the national economy, the occupational structure of the population has also undergone a significant transformation. The percentage employed in agriculture has fallen from 50 to 18 per cent, while the proportion engaged in industry rose twofold to the mid-1970s, after which it began to decline. By contrast, the number of people employed in the tertiary sector has risen continuously.

The occupational structure of individual areas and the economic pattern of towns and villages have become more similar. In many villages, the one-sided agrarian function is complemented by industrial or tourist functions. Over 40 per cent of industrial wage-earners now live in the villages.

The spatial concentration of workplaces has only been partly paralleled by the changes in the permanent domiciles of the working population. The spatial separation of place of work from place of residence has become a continual process, and today the number of daily commuters is about one million, and that of the longer period commuters some 300 000.

The most typical change in the settlement network has been the fall in the population of dispersed settlements and of the smallest villages, on the one hand, and the rise in the population of the larger towns, on the other.

As a result of these trends, the population is rather concentrated spatially: 20 per cent live in Budapest and close on another quarter in the Budapest agglomeration. Altogether, more than half of the entire population of the country is concentrated in 109 towns.

Concentration is also apparent in the agglomeration process: besides the Budapest agglomeration the provincial towns of Miskolc and Pécs are also developing their agglomeration belts. But this process can be traced back not to the expansion of the nodal settlements, but rather to their limited intake capacity, which, as a rule, has led to the creation of belts of housing estates.

Another feature of the development of the settlement network is the more even spatial distribution of urban settlements and the fast development of provincial towns. Urbanization in the provincial towns has greatly improved, but there are still substantial differences even between towns of the same order and function. The creation of a modern urban network, especially massive development of the county towns, the development of ,,high-order centres" with small spheres of attraction and the competition of provincial towns in the construction of multi-story buildings, have created other tensions. Villages, especially the dwarf villages, have increasingly come to occupy a disadvantaged situation, which has impeded a well-balanced spatial development and has given rise to social tensions. These tensions are reflected in the concentration of 90 per cent of the investment in the communal sector on the towns, and only 10 per cent on the villages, where half the population live.

The relative levelling out of the population's real income between the two basic social classes of workers and peasants, during the 1960s as well as the more balanced occupational structure of individual areas have tended to narrow the regional gap.

Regional differences in basic infrastructure provision are also diminishing continuously, a trend that speeded up during the 1970s. Nonetheless, there are still significant differences in the provision of basic needs, such as piped-water and mains drainage.

In summing up the changes and characteristics of the spatial structure of the country, we may state that the Hungarian economy has become spatially more concentrated and more balanced, while the regional division of labour has deepened, all constituting a spatially complex system. The levelling out of spatial and structural differences, and the resulting relative saving of social labour are significant.

Bibliography for Chapter III

[1] Abonyi-Palotás, J. (1980): Az élelmiszeripari termelőerők területi egyensúlya (Territorial balance of the productive forces of the food processing industry). *Statisztikai Szemle*, No. 10, pp. 972–984.
[2] Antal, Z. (1977): A vegyipar fejlődése Magyarországon 1945–1975, különös tekintettel a KGST-országokhoz fűződő gazdasági kapcsolatokra (The development of the chemical industry in Hungary, 1945–1975, with special regard to economic relations with CMEA countries). *Földrajzi Értesítő*, No. 2, pp. 179–192.
[3] Antal, Z. and Fülöp, S. (1973): A pamutipar fejlődése és területi elhelyezkedése 1960–1972 között (The development and Spatial location of the cotton industry between 1960 and 1972). *Földrajzi Értesítő*, No. 4, pp. 427–452.
[4] Balogh, B. (1977): *Magyarország építő- és építőanyagiparának szerkezete* (The structure of Hungary's building and building-materials industry). Akadémiai Kiadó, Budapest, 139 p.
[5] Balogh, S. (ed.) (1977): Az élelmiszeripar fejlesztésének területi kérdései. *A Magyar Élelmezésipari Tudományos Egyesület és az Élelmiszeripari Gazdaságkutató Intézet 1977. január 13-i konferenciáján elhangzott előadások és hozzászólások* (Major territorial issues concerning the development of the food-processing industry. Papers and discussions at the conference held on 13th January, 1977 of the Hungarian Scientific Society of the Food Industry and of the Research Institute for the Food-processing Industry).
[6] Barta, Gy. (1978): Hungary's rural industry. In: Enyedi, Gy. (ed.): *Urban development in the USA and Hungary.* Akadémiai Kiadó, Budapest, pp. 393–400. (Studies in Geography in Hungary, No. 14.)
[7] Bartke, I. (1972): A magyar ipar területi szerkezetének hatékonysága (The efficiency of the spatial structure of Hungarian industry). *Földrajzi Közlemények*, No. 2–3, pp. 188–191.
[8] Bartke, I., Bora, Gy. and Illés, I. (1973): Az ipartelepítés hosszútávú területi modellje (Along-range regional model of industrial location). *Területi Statisztika*, No. 1, pp. 472–488.
[9] Bartke, I. (1976): A területfejlesztés hatékonysága (The efficiency of regional development). *Területi Statisztika*, No. 1, pp. 1–8.
[10] Bartke, I. (1979): Az ágazat- és területfejlesztés kapcsolatának változásai (Changes in the relationship between sectoral and regional development). *Közgazdasági Szemle*, No. 4, pp. 413–428.

[11] Bartke, I. (1980): A területfejlesztés irányai és irányelvei Magyarországon (Trends and guiding principles of regional development in Hungary). *Területi Statisztika,* No. 1, pp. 1–8.
[12] Berend, T. I. and Szuhay, M. (1973): *A tőkés gazdaság története Magyarországon, 1848–1944* (The history of the capitalist economy of Hungary between 1848 and 1944). Kossuth Kiadó and Közgazdasági és Jogi Könyvkiadó, Budapest, 281 p.
[13] Berend, T. I. (1974): *A szocialista gazdaság fejlődése Magyarországon, 1945–1968* (The development of the socialist economy of Hungary, 1945–1968). Kossuth Kiadó and Közgazdasági és Jogi Könyvkiadó, Budapest, 236 p.
[14] Berend, T. I. (1975): A szocialista gazdaságpolitika három évtizede Magyarországon (Three decades of socialist economic policy in Hungary). *Gazdaság,* No. 1, pp. 7–29.
[15] Berend, T. I (1977): Current Hungarian economic policy in historical perspective. *Acta Oeconomica,* No. 2, pp. 105–123.
[16] Bernát, t. and Enyedi, Gy. (1961): *A magyar mezőgazdaság termelési körzetei* (Agricultural regions in Hungary). Mezőgazdasági Kiadó, Budapest, 168. p.
[17] Bernát, t. and Bora, Gy. (1971): Változások az egyes gazdasági ágazatok telepítési kritériumaiban (Changes in the locational criteria of different economic branches in Hungary). *MTA X. Osztály Közleményei,* No. 43, pp. 155–159.
[18] Bernát, T. (ed.) (1972): *Magyarország gazdaságföldrajza* (An economic geography of Hungary). Tankönyvkiadó, Budapest, 546. p. (2nd revised ed.)
[19] Bernát, T. (1976): The delimitation and characterization of agricultural areas deficient in physical resources. In: Compton, P. A. and Pécsi, M. (eds): *Regional development and planning. British and Hungarian case studies,* Akadémiai Kiadó, Budapest, pp. 71–81. (Studies in Geography in Hungary, 12.)
[20] Bernát, T. and Enyedi, Gy. (1977): *A magyar mezőgazdaság területi problémái. Termelési körzetek és területi fejlesztés* (Some regional problems of Hungarian agriculture. Production zones and regional development). Akadémiai Kiadó, Budapest, 205 p.
[21] Bernát, T. (ed.) (1978): *Általános gazdasági földrajz* (General economic geography). Tankönyvkiadó, Budapest, 362 pp.
[22] Bernát, T. and Enyedi, Gy. (1978): Rural development in the Hungarian highlands. In: Koutaniemi, L. (ed.): *Rural development in highlands and high-latitude zones.* Oulu, pp. 225–231.
[23] Bernát, T. and Ferenczi, T. (1979). A magyar mezőgazdaság területfejlesztési modellje (A model of the regional development of agriculture in Hungary). *Közgazdasági Szemle,* No. 10, pp. 1234–1248.
[24] Bernát, T. (ed.) (1981): *Magyarország gazdaságföldrajza* (An Economic Geography of Hungary). Tankönyvkiadó, Budapest, 461 pp.
[25] Bernát, T. and Ferenczi, T. (1980): A hűtőipar távlati felépítési programja (A long-term locational programme for the cold-storage industry). *Gazdálkodás,* No. 5, pp. 15–24.
[26] Bíró, G. (1979): An economic policy for the eighties. *The New Hungarian Quarterly,* No. 75, pp. 59–64.
[27] Bíró, F. (1978): A többoldalú hosszú távú együttműködés lehetőségei a KGST-országok élelmiszer-termelésében (Potentials for multilateral long-range co-operation in food production among CMEA countries). *Közgazdasági Szemle,* No. 11, pp. 1201–1210.
[28] Bontó, L. (1976): A magyar vegyipar fejlődése az V. ötéves tervidőszakban (Development of the Hungarian chemical industry during the 5th five-year plan). *Gazdaság,* No. 4, pp. 76–87.
[29] Bontó, L. and Orosz, L. (1978): *Szelektív iparfejlesztés* (Selective industrial development). Kossuth Kiadó, Budapest, 173 p.
[30] Bora, Gy. (1971): Az ipari termelés földrajza (The geography of industrial production). In: Sárfalvi, B. (ed.): *Válogatott tanulmányok a gazdaságföldrajz tárgyköréből* (Selected studies in economic geography). Tankönyvkiadó, Budapest, pp. 300–368.
[31] Bora, Gy. (1976a): Planwirtschaft als Voraussetzung einer wirksamen Umweltpolitik. In: Walterskirchen von M. P. *(ed.): Umweltpolitik in Europa.* Huber, Frauenfeld, pp. 245–255.
[32] Bora, Gy. (1976b): Regional industrial structure and the development of urban systems in Hungary. *Papers of the Regional Science Association,* Vol. 36, pp. 133–145.
[33] Bora, Gy. (1976c): Changes in the spatial structure of Hungarian industry and the determinants of industrial location. In: Compton, P. A. and Pécsi, M. (eds): *Regional development and planning. British and Hungarian case studies.* Akadémiai Kiadó, Budapest, pp. 117–127. (Studies in Geography in Hungary, 12.)

[34] Bora, Gy. (1978): A long-term regional distribution model of Hungarian industry. In: Hamilton F. E. Ian (ed.): *Industrial change. International experience and Public Policy*, Longmans, London, pp. 73–79.
[35] Borai, Á. (1973): A mecseki kőszén felhasználása a kohászatban (The use of Mecsek coal in metallurgy). *Földrajzi Értesítő*, No. 4, pp. 411–425.
[36] Borai, Á. (1979): Neue Industriestandorte und neue Industriestädte in Ungarn. *Mitteillungen der Österreichischen Geographischen Gesellschaft*, Vol. 121, I, pp. 73–93.
[37] Bulla, B. (1962): *Magyarország természeti földrajza* (The physiography of Hungary). Tankönyvkiadó, Budapest, 423 p.
[38] Charvet, J. P. (1980): Mise au point sur le rôle des „systèmes de production industrialisée des céréales" dans l'évolution récente de la culture du maïs en Hongrie. *L'Information Geographique*, I, pp. 21–26.
[39] Compton, P. A. and Pécsi, M. (eds) (1976): *Regional development and planning. British and Hungarian case studies*, Akadémiai Kiadó, Budapest, 233 p. (Studies in Geography in Hungary, 12.)
[40] Csikós-Nagy, B. (1980): New features of Hungarian economic policy. *The New Hungarian Quarterly*, No. 77, pp. 62–72.
[41] Csizmadia, E. (1973): *Bevezetés az élelmiszer gazdaságtanába* (An introduction to the economics of food production). Akadémiai Kiadó, Budapest, 372 p.
[42] Csizmadia, E. (1980): Élelmiszer-gazdaságunk a 80-as évtized küszöbén (Our food economy on the threshold of the 1980s). *Közgazdasági Szemle*, No. 6, pp. 649–667.
[43] Enyedi, Gy. (ed.) (1976): *A magyar népgazdaság fejlődésének területi problémái* (Regional problems concerning the development of the Hungarian national economy). Akadémiai Kiadó, Budapest, 254 p.
[44] Enyedi, Gy. (1976): *Hungary, an economic geography*. Westview, Boulder, 289 p.
[45] Enyedi, Gy. (1977): A falusi életkörülmények területi típusai Magyarországon (A spatial typology of rural living conditions in Hungary). *Földrajzi Értesítő*, No. 1, pp. 67–87.
[46] Enyedi, Gy. (1978): Gazdaságpolitika és területi fejlődés (Economic policy and regional development). *Valóság*, No. 5, pp. 36–46.
[47] Enyedi, Gy. (1978): Die Entwicklung der ungarischen Landwirtschaft nach dem zweiten Weltkrieg. *Mitteilungen der Österreichischen Geographischen Gesellschaft*, Vol. 120, II, pp. 265–279.
[48] Fekete, Gy. (1978): A Duna–Majna–Rajna vízi út közlekedéspolitikai jelentősége a gazdasági együttműködés területén (The transport-political significance of the Danube–Main–Rhine waterway in the field of economic co-operation). *Közlekedéstudományi Szemle*, No. 10, pp. 433–438.
[49] Fodor, L. (1977): A fővárosi ipar fejlesztése a beruházások tükrében (The development of the capital's industry as reflected in investments). *Budapest*, No. 12, pp. 34–35.
[50] Forgács, T. (1977). Relations between industry and commerce in theory and practice. *Quality and Reliability*, No. 10, pp. 639–644.
[51] Hegedüs, M. (1978): *A népgazdaság termelési szerkezetének fejlesztése* (The development of the production structure of the national economy). Kossuth Kiadó, Budapest, 155 p.
[52] Hegyi-Pákó, J. and Vitális, Gy. (1977): *Cementipari nyersanyagaink és kutatásuk módszertana* (Raw materials for our cement industry and a prospecting methodology). Műszaki Kiadó, Budapest, 219 p.
[53] *Ipari Statisztikai Évkönyv, 1978* (Yearbook of Industrial Statistics, 1978). Central Statistical Office, Budapest, 1979, 391 p.
[54] Iványi, A. Sz. (1976): Üzemnagyság és technológiai korszerűség a vaskohászatban (Plant size and modern technology in ferrous metallurgy). *Közgazdasági Szemle*, No. 10, pp. 1238–1244.
[55] Juhász, Á. (1977): Az alumíniumipar központi fejlesztési program néhány kiemelt kérdéséről (On some major issues of the central development programme of the aluminium industry). *Gazdaság*, No. 1, pp. 7–27.
[56] Kapolyi, L. (1978): Hazai energiakincsünk szerepe energiagazdálkodásunkban (The role of domestic energy resources in energy management). *Energia és Atomtechnika*, No. 10, pp. 404–411.
[57] Kemenczei, R. (1979): Megjegyzések a termálvízre alapozott idegenforgalom fejlesztésében (Some remarks on the development of tourism, based on thermal waters). *Kereskedelmi Szemle*, No. 1, pp. 12–23.
[58] Keserű, J. Mrs. (1977): A könnyűipari rekonstrukciók tapasztalata és további feladatai (Experience and further tasks for reconstructing light industry). *Társadalmi Szemle*, No. 3, pp. 12–23.

[59] Kiss, A. (1980): A magyar mezőgazdaság termelésszerkezeti változásai (Structural changes in the production of agriculture in Hungary). *Nemzetközi Mezőgazdasági Szemle*, No. 4, pp. 8–14.
[60] Kóródi, J. and Márton, G. (1968): *A magyar ipar területi kérdései* (Regional problems of the Hungarian industry). Kossuth Kiadó, Budapest, 173 p.
[61] Korompai, G. (1979): A dunai folyami áruszállítás földrajzi kapcsolatai és annak magyar vonatkozásai (Geographical aspects of freight shipping on the Danube and their implications for Hungary). *Alföldi Tanulmányok*, Békéscsaba, pp. 197–214.
[62] Kovács, Gy. (1976): A nemzetközi termelési és kereskedelmi együttműködés szerepe a gazdasági növekedésben (The role of international co-operation in production and trade and its implications for growth). *Gazdaság*, No. 3, pp. 82–91.
[63] Kovács, T. (1974): A vidéki iparfejlesztés eredményei és sajátosságai, 1960–1970 (The results and characteristics of the industrialization of provincial regions, 1960–1970). *Területi Statisztika*, No. 1, pp. 20–27.
[64] Kozma, F. (1978a): Gondolatok a természeti erőforrások hasznosításának hatékonyságáról (Some thoughts on the efficiency of the utilization of natural resources). *Közgazdasági Szemle*, No. 9, pp. 1051–1076.
[65] Kozma, F. (1978b): *Mire képes a magyar népgazdaság?* (What is the potential of the Hungarian national economy?) Kossuth Könyvkiadó, Budapest, 388 p.
[66] Kozma, F. (1980): *A nyitott szerkezetű gazdaság* (Economy with an open structure). Kossuth Könyvkiadó, Budapest, 345 p.
[67] Kőszegfalvi, Gy. (1978): A területi fejlődés eredményei és problémái, a fejlesztés feladatai (Results and problems of regional development and its further tasks). *Területi Statisztika*, No. 3, pp. 234–246.
[68] Kőszegi, L. (1964): *A területi tervezés főbb elvi és módszertani kérdései* (Major theoretical and methodological questions of regional planning). Közgazdasági és Jogi Könyvkiadó, Budapest, 398 p.
[69] Köves, A. (1977): A világgazdasági integrálódás és a gazdaságfejlesztés iránya (World economic integration and trends in economic development). *Gazdaság*, No. 4, pp. 50–63.
[70] Krajkó, Gy. (1973): A gazdasági mikrokörzetek elvi és módszertani kérdései (Theoretical and methodological questions concerning the delimitation of economic microregions). *Földrajzi Értesítő*, Nos 2–3, pp. 259–285.
[71] Kulcsár, V. (1975): A mezőgazdaság szerepe a falvak gazdasági fejlődésében Magyarországon (The role of agriculture in the economic development of villages in Hungary). *Földrajzi Közlemények*, Nos 3–4, pp. 296–305.
[72] Lackó, L. (1975): Az életkörülmények szerint elmaradott területek kutatásáról (Research into areas with disadvantaged living conditions). *Földrajzi Közlemények*, Nos 3–4, pp. 277–283.
[73] Lévárdi, F. (1969): Energiapolitikai koncepció 1964–1980 (Energy policy between 1964–1980). *Gazdaság*, No. 4, pp. 7–23.
[74] Markos, Gy. (1962): *Magyarország gazdasági földrajza* (An economic geography of Hungary). Közgazdasági és Jogi Könyvkiadó, Budapest, 582 p.
[75] Márton, J. (1977): *Az integrálódó mezőgazdaság* (Agriculture in the process of integration). Mezőgazdasági Könyvkiadó, Budapest, 191 p.
[76] Mira, J. (1977): A villamosenergia-felhasználás és a nemzeti jövedelem összefüggésének vizsgálata (Exploration of the interrelationship between the use of electrical energy and national income). *Energia és Atomtechnika*, No. 4, pp. 177–183.
[77] Molnár, I. and Szabó–Medgyesi, E. (1978): Szőlő- és bortermelésünk (Grape and wine production in Hungary). *Statisztikai Szemle*, No. 11, pp. 1112–1127.
[78] Nagy, F. (1979): Magyarország és a hosszú távú KGST-együttműködés (Hungary and long-range CMEA co-operation). *Népszabadság*, 17 January, p. 10.
[79] Nyitrai, F. Mrs. (1977): *Ipari struktúránk: változások, hatékonyság* (Industrial structure in Hungary: changes and efficiency). Kossuth Könyvkiadó, Budapest, 325 p.
[80] Nyitrai, F. Mrs. (1979): *Népgazdaságunk fejlettsége – nemzetközi tükörben* (The level of development of the Hungarian economy – by international standards). Kossuth Könyvkiadó, Budapest, 173 p.
[81] Nyitrai, F. Mrs. (1980): Energiafelhasználás és struktúra a magyar népgazdaságban (Energy consumption and structure in the Hungarian national economy). *Gazdaság*, No. 1, pp. 39–56.
[82] Pánczélos, A. and Fehér, L. (1977): A Duna energetikai hasznosítása (The utilization of the Danube for power generation). *Energia és Atomtechnika*, No. 8, pp. 350–357.

[83] Pécsi, M. and Sárfalvi, B. (1977): *Physical and economic geography of Hungary*. Corvina, Budapest, 198 p. 2nd edition.
[84] Radó, S. (ed.) (1963): *Magyarország gazdasági földrajza* (Economic geography of Hungary). Gondolat, Budapest, 366 p.
[85] Radó, S. (ed.) (1967): *Magyarország nemzeti atlasza* (National atlas of Hungary). Kartográfiai Vállalat, Budapest, 112 p.
[86] Reményi, K. (1978): A hazai lignitvagyon erőművi felhasználásának kérdéséhez (On the use of domestic lignite resources for power generation). *Energia és Atomtechnika*, No. 5/6, pp. 272–280.
[87] Remetei, F. Mrs. (1979): A magyar textilipar szerkezete és perspektívái (The structure of the Hungarian textile industry and future perspectives). *Statisztikai Szemle*, No. 12, pp. 1202–1217.
[88] Romány, P. (1979): Mezőgazdaságunk a hetvenes évek végén (Agriculture in the late 1970s). *Közgazdasági Szemle*, No. 5, pp. 513–528.
[89] Somogyi, S. (1976): A dunai transzkontinentális nemzetközi hajóút megvalósításának feladatai hazánkban (Tasks for Hungary – the Danube transcontinental international shipping route). *Földrajzi Értesítő*, No. 2, pp. 255–263.
[90] *Statisztikai Évkönyv, 1979* (Statistical Yearbook, 1979). Central Statistical Office, Budapest, 1980, 543 p.
[91] Stark, A. (1975): Iparfejlesztésünk három évtizede (Three decades of industrial development in Hungary). *Közgazdasági Szemle*, No. 4, pp. 425–434.
[92] Szekér, Gy. (1980): Iparpolitikánk és a világgazdasági változások (Industrial policy and changes in the world economy). *Társadalmi Szemle*, No. 2, pp. 12–30.
[93] Szili, G. (1978): A villamosenergia-rendszer forrásoldali fejlesztése, különös tekintettel az energiagazdálkodási szempontokra (Development of the sources of electrical energy with special regard to energy management). *Energia és Atomtechnika*, No. 1, pp. 1–9.
[94] Szita, J. (1975): *Az összeurópai gazdasági együttműködés távlatai* (Future perspectives for European economic co-operation). Kossuth Könyvkiadó, Budapest, 345 p.
[95] Szlameniczky, I. (1978): Az élelmiszertermelés szerkezeti kérdései (Structural questions about food production). *Társadalmi Szemle*, No. 1, pp. 21–34.
[96] Szőcs, I. (1980): Energiagazdálkodásunk helyzete és feladatai (The situation and tasks of energy management). *Közgazdasági Szemle*, No. 10, pp. 1159–1171.
[97] Tatai, Z. (1973): A területfejlesztési politika célja és eszközrendszere az iparban (The aim and instruments of regional development policy in industry). *Területi Statisztika*, No. 5, pp. 518–531.
[98] Tatai, Z. (1980): A mezőgazdasági jellegű területek iparosításának egyes kérdései (Some questions relating to the industrialization of areas with an agricultural character). *Területi Statisztika*, No. 1, pp. 9–20.
[99] *Területi Statisztikai Évkönyv, 1979* (Regional Statistical Yearbook, 1979). Central Statistical Office, Budapest, 1980, 400 p.
[100] Urbán, L. (1979): Közlekedéspolitikánk – a közlekedés fejlesztése (Transport policy and the development of transport in Hungary). *Közlekedéstudományi Szemle*, No. 8, pp. 337–349.
[101] Vajda, Gy. (1978): Az energetika néhány kölcsönhatása (Some interactions of power generation). *Energia és Atomtechnika*, No. 3, pp. 97–104.
[102] Zala, Gy. (1977): Vízigényes ipar telepítési lehetőségei (Locational possibilities for water-intensive industry). *Városépítés*, No. 1, pp. 18–20.
[103] Zalai, E. (1978): *Economic problems: Hungary*. Duquesne University, Pittsburg, 61 p. (Duquesne series of international studies, Vol. 1, No. 1.)
[104] Zoltán, Z. (ed.) (1980): *Telephelyválasztás* (Locational choices). Közgazdasági és Jogi Könyvkiadó, Budapest, 350 p.

IV Economic and planning regions — The question of regionalization

We have surveyed the geophysical foundations and population settlement patterns of the country as well as the individual sectors and spatial patterns of the economy. With the development of the territorial division of labour, the productive sectors tend to move towards optimal locations and in so doing become geographically differentiated and form economic regions. But in individual areas, there develop, in compliance with the territorial division of labour, several sectors some of which became dominant. Thus a complex unit of the territorial division of labour, an economic region, comes into being with its characteristic production specialization and close economic integration. The identification, delimitation and characterization of integrated economic regions is a traditional area of research programme in economic geography. The end product of such investigation is usually the identification of homogeneous regions and it stands to reason that having surveyed the individual economic sectors, we must also delimit and describe the economic regions of the country.

Economic regionalization in socialist countries, over and above its scientific value, also provides the basis for formulating prospective regional development concepts and for drawing up regional economic plans. It reveals the territorial types of production, and the economic regions incorporating the characteristic interrelationships of the economy.

But the identification of individual economic regions, even after the methodological principles have been clarified and partial results have been attained is still, in several respects, to be achieved by the science of Hungarian geography. Despite positive initiatives and various regional analyses, the disclosure of economic regions based on the territorial division of labour, through the application of the methodological experience of modern international scientific investigation and based on exact analysis, has not yet been completed. There are several reasons for this deficiency. One of the most important is the fact that the national system of economic planning did not take in the past due account of the requirements of the regional planning of the division of labour and its space-dependent implications, because such a need was not appreciated by the planning organs. Another reason lies in the inappropriate approach of scientific research. Because of its ramification and complex nature, regionalization requires an interdisciplinary approach. In fact, however, efforts have been fragmented, and the problem approached from very different theoretical and methodological angles. As a result, one-sided and occasionally subjective tendencies have prevailed in regionalization. Most differences have involved interpretation: what factors should be chosen to provide the basis for the delimitation of regions. Although all relevant studies emphasized the complex character of regionalization, yet most based their solutions only on the one or two factors deemed to be the most important ones.

There have been several approaches to regionalization and four are discussed in more detail below.

a) The majority of geographers agree that regionalization has to perform two functions: to set out its complexity, the coherent character of the region, and specialization, the specific role it plays in the national division of labour. Because the research methods to meet this requirement were either inadequate or lacking the investigations concerning the delimitation of regions contained many subjective elements, and produced divergent results. This triggered off disputes among geographers, and resulted in the disparagement and misunderstanding of the relevant research by economists and the planning organs.

A pioneer in the regionalization in Hungary was Professor Gy. Markos [44], who divided the country into 13 units *(Fig. 60)*. His scheme was improved on by the Department of Economic Geography and Regional Science at Karl Marx University of Economics, who relying on the experience of earlier regional research, prepared a territorial division of 10 regions [9].

Another model aimed at the delimitation of economic regions by identifying economic centres and associated micro-regions [33]. It claimed to recognize the characteristic features of the territorial division of labour through the investigation of the zones of attraction of settlements, the mobility of population (commuting) and the volume of agriculture produce brought to the market. The attraction zones specified by the investigation of these factors constituted the basis for the identification of economic micro-regions.

These investigations came up against insurmountable difficulties when, after delimiting the areas of individual sectors, specialization, the coherence and complexity of the regions were to be proved. They tended to identify sectoral (industrial or agricultural) districts with economic regions, and established the boundaries separating them on an empirical basis. Over and above the lack of an appropriate methodology, this disappointing outcome was due to a lack of sufficient territorial data and the inappropriate statistical analysis that was applied. Characteristically, sectoral input-output analysis for administrative counties, which takes into account all the transactions among the various counties, has up till now been prepared only experimentally and for only a few counties.

b) A regional division can be derived from the analysis of the settlement network and infrastructure. In the delimitation of regions the urban centres and their spheres of influence as well as the transport network were regarded

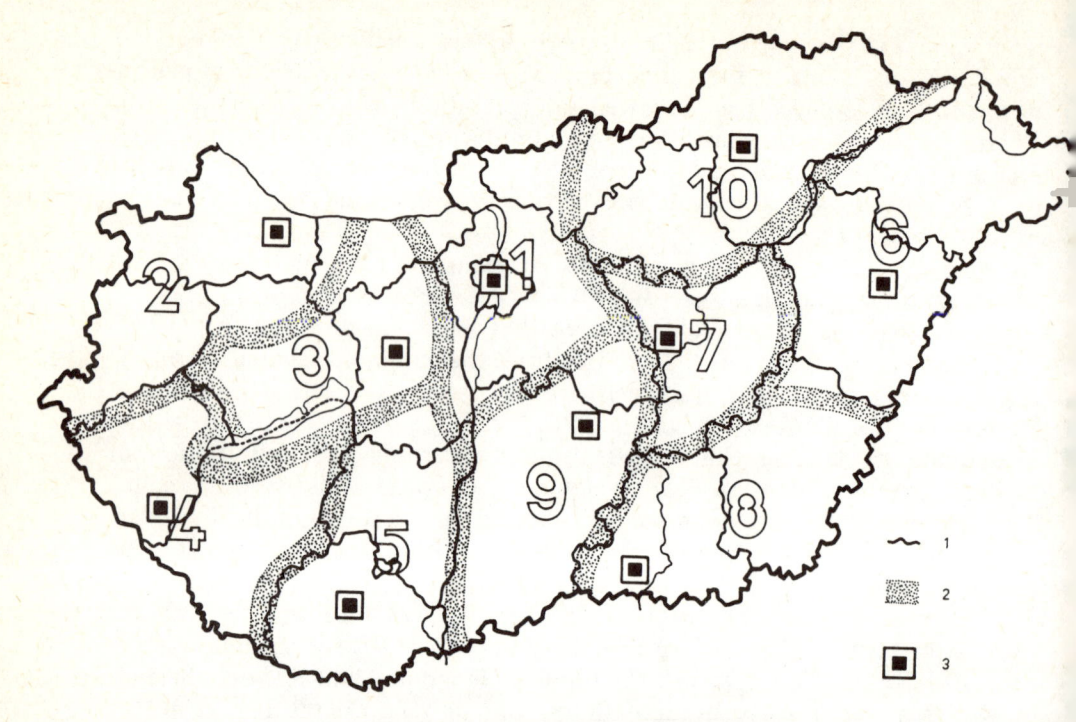

Fig. 60. A regional division of Hungary
1 — county boundary; 2 — region boundary; 3 — regional centre
1. The Central Industrial Region; 2. The Little Plain; 3. The Industrial Region of Central Transdanubia; 4. South-Western Transdanubia; 5. South-Eastern Transdanubia; 6. The Upper-Tisza Region; 7. The Middle-Tisza Region; 8. The South-Eastern Great Plain; 9. The Danube—Tisza Mid-region; 10. The Northern Industrial Region

as decisive. The determination of „core areas" is suitable for clarifying the volume of raw material, energy, finished products and labour flowing between towns and their spheres of influence, and thus helps towards the identification of coherent economic regions. On the other hand, apart from these factors, settlement-based regional research says little about the significance to the territorial division of labour and thus about economic regions, although the existence, economic weight and development of individual towns and settlements are inseparable from the territorial division of labour.

c) Regionalizations established by sectoral planning and administrative authorities set up their territorial units from the specific viewpoints and requirements of individual sectors and associated administrative institutions. The regional divisions used by the railways, the post office and by wholesale trade, for instance, correspond to the aims of the management of these individual sectors, but differ widely from one another. Yet their interrelationships and comparison suggest a regional division of the country into six districts.

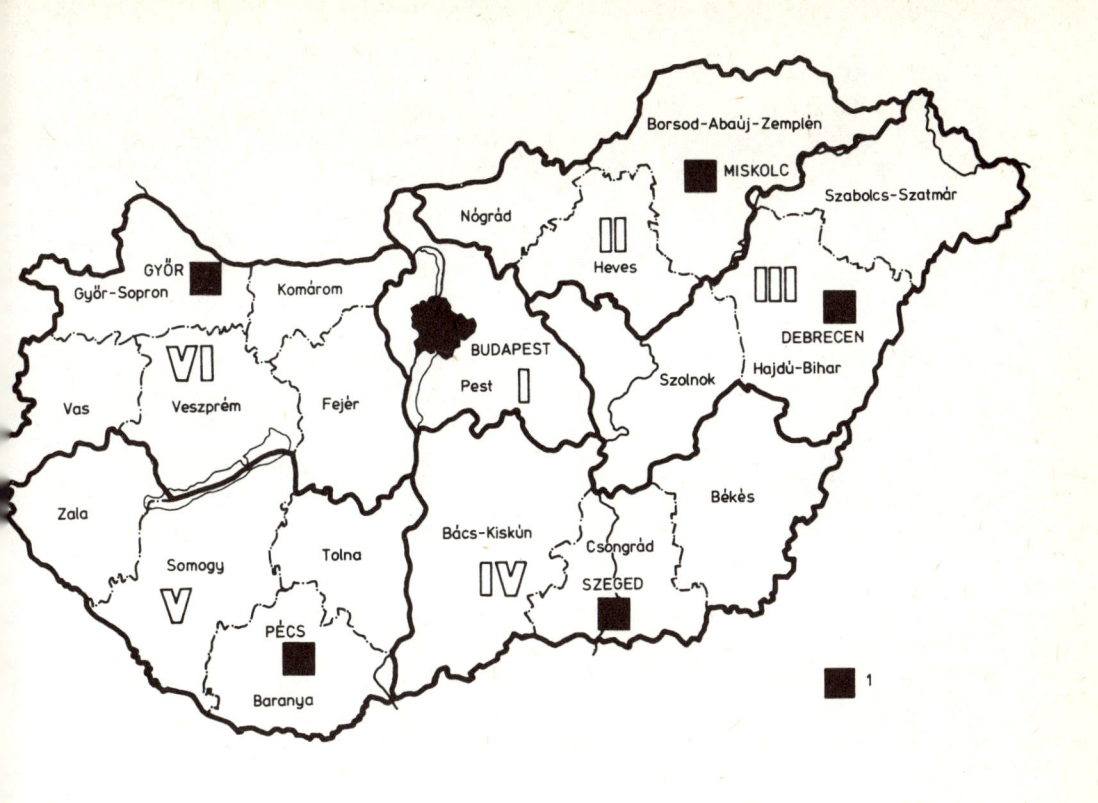

Fig. 61. Economic–planning regions
I — central region; II — Northern Hungary; III — the Northern Great Plain; IV — the Southern Great Plain; V — Northern Transdanubia; VI — Southern Transdanubia; 1 — regional centre

d) Since research had only brought about approximative results in the delimitation of economic regions, a decision had to be taken on which units provided the most appropriate framework for planning when the drawing up of prospective plans of the national economy started in 1967. The National Planning Office had also prepared several variants and the decision was taken to base the system of regional planning on regions much larger than counties, which therefore play, owing to their varied economic character, a significant role in the country's economic life. In delimiting these regions the administrative counties were left unchanged, and a division of the country into six economic-planning regions took place *(Fig. 61).*

This division is based on the principles of economic regionalization and also takes into account the main trends of long-term regional development. The economic-planning regions provide the possibility for drawing up and realizing a rational division of labour between the individual areas of the country, and for eleborating the regional plan of the national economy. Coordination within the individual regions and among the counties makes it possible jointly to formulate the development directions of individual regions and counties and to coordinate thereby the networks that extend beyond county boundaries. As a result, interaction and feedback between the plans of the economic regions and the national economic plan becomes possible. These possibilities can be made full use of only if the authorities within the administrative counties and towns rise above essentially local interests. According to the experience gained so far, the endeavours to emphasize intra-county co-operation have proved stronger than those relating to inter-county co-operation, which is mostly of an occasional character. Hence economic-planning regions are to a large extent fabrications and they have no independent decision-making bodies. It seems necessary to set up a regional advisory organ which, on the basis of the long- and medium-range plans already drawn up, would coordinate inter-county development [24].

The economic-planning regions also contain a great many problematic and disputable elements, and cannot therefore be regarded as the definitive regionalization of the country, but in view of the controversy over the regionalization issue, it is nonetheless practicable to discuss regional issues in this book within the framework of the economic-planning regions. This method, for all its problematic nature, is more suitable for placing the regional division of labour on a realistic and objective basis than previous divisions. This does not negate the requirement that economic geography, with the active participation of other disciplines and by the use of appropriate methodologies, should carry out in the years to come an improved division of the country into economic regions.

1 The central economic–planning region

Although the Central economic–planning region is the smallest with 7 per cent share of the country's area, it is, from an economic and social point of view, the country's most important. It is made up of the county of Pest and the capital, Budapest. Its population is some 3·1 million, or 29 per cent of the national total, and it ranks in first place among the economic-planning regions. Its core is the monocentric agglomeration of Budapest, which includes the capital and whose direct sphere of influence extends over 44 settlements. The Budapest agglomeration comprises 1·7 per cent of the area of the country, but contains nearly a quarter of total population and contributes about 30 per cent of total industrial output.

As regards its geographical location, mention should be made of the fact that owing to the central position of the capital, the Budapest agglomeration is contiguous with three other economic-planning regions, and its weight and role in the economy is greatly enhanced by the nodal position of the capital in the transport network.

The region takes part primarily in the national, inter-regional and international division of labour, and to an increasing extent its manufactures require high professional skills and embody labour-, research-intensive and innovative activities, with a concentration on the higher value of industries and branches. At the same time, it heavily relies on the import of energy, raw materials, semifinished goods and agricultural produce. The structural transformation of the industry and economy of Budapest into a great industrial complex displays a definite regional concentration of those sectors and branches with higher value output and which generate higher incomes.

The agricultural production of the region is highly specialized around the capital. Natural endowments, in terms of relief and soils are favourable and the level of agricultural output of the region as a whole exceeds the national average. The main reasons for this, however, are the proximity of the market, of large-scale commodity production, and of intensive industrial and trading activities as well as co-operation with industrial plants.

1.1 Natural endowments and resources

The northern parts of the region are predominantly mountainous and hilly areas, while plainland, though not completely flat everywhere, is typical of the southern parts. That area of the region lying west of the Danube is made of the Dunazug range comprising the Visegrád, Pilis and Buda Mountains. Another mountainous landscape unit of the region is the Börzsöny, made up of volcanic andesites and riolites. It is, structurally, similar to the Visegrád Mountain, from which it was separated by the fractured valley of the Danube and a large proportion of its rises above 600 metres.

The higher levels of the Gödöllő hill country and adjacent Monor–Irsa uplands are covered by forest. Below 200 metres there is arable land and in places vineyards on medium- to poor-quality soils. Flat is typical of the two large Danube islands and of the lowlands along the Danube and in the Tápió area where soils of very different quality are found.

From a climatic point of view, the greater part of the region is transitional between Northern Transdanubia with its more temperate, and the Trans-Tisza area with its more continental climate. Mean annual temperature is below the national average in the upland areas, and shows smaller fluctuation. The mean annual temperature of the plain and lower hill country is around to the national average of 10·5 °C. The effects of relief and location make themselves felt on precipitation, which ranges between 500 and 800 mm, being highest in the Börzsöny and Dunazug Mountains, and lowest in the lowlands along the Danube, especially the southern part of Csepel island.

The drainage of the region is performed mainly by the Danube, which breaks through the Middle Mountains range at the Danube Bend, where the river has a steep profile, and where the resources provided by its potential energy are easier to exploit. It is here that a hydro-electric generating station will be constructed as part of joint Czechoslovak–Hungarian venture.

Of the tributaries of the Danube, the Ipoly, constituting a section of the Czechoslovak—Hungarian frontier, is a significant river in the region. Its water regime is very erratic, and it often floods large areas. Its regulation is carried out jointly by the two countries. The other water resources of the region, some of which belong to the drainage basin of the Tisza are made up of streams of varying lengths.

Soils are extremely varied both genetically and in quality. Most extensive are brown and red-brown forest soils and meadow soils of poor quality. Best are the soils in the Tápió area while those in the western parts of the administrative district of Buda and to the south where it joins the Mezőföld plain as well as in the Galga area are fairly good. In summary, the soils of the region are below average in quality with very poor natural fertility over large areas. Various soil deficiencies are thus common.

The geographical location communications and physiographic endowments of Budapest and its agglomeration [9]

The role played by certain natural endowments in the evolution and development of the Hungarian capital was significant and can still be recognized. During various historical periods the settlements now making up Buda were attracted by the Danube, and by the large number of thermal springs.

The capital, situated on the Danube between two large islands, lies in an area where mountain and plain meet. Here the Danube disgorges from the mountains and has built up a relatively wide, gently sloping alluvial fan. Since it has cut deep into the accumulated deposits, the area, apart from the occasional very high water, are free from flooding. The relatively narrow river bed has always ensured exceptionally favourable conditions for water transport during the course of history. It is also an important locational geographical endowment of the capital that it is situated in an area where the different economic regions of Transdanubia, the Great Hungarian Plain and the Northern Middle Mountains meet. With this location are associated excellent natural route ways and waterways, which had made the settlement a market town, and a centre of exchange before the period of developed commodity production began. The importance of Budapest as a transport junction became still more pronounced with the construction of the railway network.

Typical of the relief of Budapest is its dichotomous character with the divergent topographical features of Pest and Buda. The heavily fractured Buda Mountains on the west bank of the Danube are part of the Dunazug Mountains, while limestone and dolomite range of the Pilis also extends into the Budapest agglomeration.

The area of the city forming the east bank of the Danube is part of the Pest plain, and is made up of the terraces of the river, which gradually rise eastwards and merge with the Gödöllő hills.

The dichotomous relief of the capital and its agglomeration is also reflected in the climate. The mean annual temperature is 11 °C, but within the city itself substantial temperature disparities develop, due mainly to differences in height, and the morphology of the built-up area. During winter, the temperature of the inner parts of the city is about 2·5 °C higher than that of the more elevated, lying on the Buda side. Of this difference 1 °C is due to urban heating and impeded radiation, and 1·5 °C is attributable to the difference in altitude.

The prevailing wind direction is from the north-west, and clean air moving across the Buda Mountains from the west tends to remove atmospheric pollution. Winds from other directions are rare.

The precipitation of the capital (610 mm) is around the national average. On the other hand, the number of foggy days, which unfavourably affect transport, is rather high. In the case of inversions, when vertical air movement is impeded, air pollution can lead to the development of smog with harmful health and material effects. The control or abatement of air pollution is being effected by modern district heating and by the relocation of heavily air-polluting industrial plants.

The river Danube, regulated during the second half of the last century and First World War forms an indispensable part of the capital's life. It provides water for its industry and households, removes much of the city's waste and is an important transport route. On its banks, a chain of weekend holiday homes and camping facilities has been established.

Budapest abounds in thermal and medicinal springs and over 100 natural springs and 13 artesian wells in 17 places provide lukewarm or hot medicinal waters. These springs and wells are to be found mainly along the fault marking the line of the Danube, and are fed partly by subsurface cold water and partly by hot water coming up from deep layers.

The capital's mineral and medicinal waters are utilized by various health establishments and swimming pools, and constitute significant tourist attractions. An important raw material of the Budapest agglomeration is good-quality clay occurring in large quantities at several places as, for instance, at Kiscell, on which several brick and tile works have been based.

1.2 The economy

The region, including Budapest and its agglomeration, is the most significant industrial and economic area of the country. Budapest and the whole central economic-planning region constitute the heart of the country not only in a political, administrative and cultural sense, but also from the viewpoint of the economy and trade. As a result of economic decentralization, and the development of the settlement network and hierarchy, the overwhelming weight of the capital in the economy of the country has diminished. Yet even today, every region of the country maintains the closest economic relations and co-operation with the central region in general and with Budapest in particular. Since a completely regular urban hierarchy can only come into being in a large country, with a high population density and a developed industry, Budapest, despite significant achievements in decentralization, will remain an unchallenged industrial and economic centre for the foreseeable future, although this will not hinder the economic development of the rest of the country [24].

1.2.1 Industry

Budapest and its agglomeration constitute the largest industrial concentration of the country.

Not only the Budapest agglomeration, but also the urban and even the large-village settlements of the region have made significant progress in industrial development. Nevertheless, the predominant industrial significance of the region is ensured by the agglomeration of the capital, the density of the productive forces of its industry, the transformation of its sectoral structure in compliance with international trends and large-city requirements, and by the integrating role played by large industrial enterprises, mainly through their provincial ancillary plants, in the domestic and international division of labour as well as by the city's nodal position in the country's transport network.

The size and development of the region have evolved as a result of the combined effects of several factors. For instance, as a result of capitalist development during the last third of the last century, Budapest became the largest industrial centre of the country, with the increase in the industrial weight of Budapest and of the region as a whole, the other regions of the country tended to lag behind. There evolved from this a very simple spatial economic structure characterized by extreme regional disparities in productive forces. With Budapest and its agglomeration becoming the central region of the country, owing to their overwhelming preponderance, only a few other towns concerned with manufacturing and heavy industry could develop. Since the liberation of the country in 1945, this preponderance, owing firstly to the increased industrialization of the countryside, and secondly to restrictions on the quantitative growth of the capital, has substantially diminished.

During the course of the industrialization of the central region, particularly of Budapest and its agglomeration, close co-operational relationships have been established within and between most sectors, and several industries have become vertically integrated. With the increase in its economic, political, cultural and commercial weight, the population number of Budapest has also grown at a rapid rate. It has become the country's largest consumer market, where primarily labour-intensive industries, based on domestic and foreign consumer markets, have developed.

Selected data on the industry in the Central region,
1977 and 1981

Designation	Percentage share of the region in the national total	
	1977	1981
People engaged in industry	34	31
Value of gross fixed assets	32	30
Installed motive power (kWh)	25	23
Electrical energy used by industry (kWh)	22	20
Output of selected products		
Electrical energy	44	30
Cement	25	23
Lorries	32	65
Telephone apparatus	100	100
Petrol	58	60
Gas oil	80	80
Film	100	100
Photographic paper	100	100
Canned fruit	34	36

During the century-old development process of Budapest as a metropolitan industrial complex, several factors favourable to industrial location have met and exerted a positive impact on each other and have made the capital and its agglomeration a prominent locational centre of most branches of the manufacturing industry. In this field, the regional integration of industry and of the metropolitan industrial complex have developed in close association with each other.

The main characteristics of the industry of Budapest and its agglomeration *(Fig. 62)* are as follows:

The gradual separation of basic-materials industry from manufacturing industry and the preponderance of manufacturing branches has evolved.

The intensively developed manufacturing industry of the region processes raw and basic materials, as well as semifinished products and components produced in the country or imported from abroad, and also supplies other regions with finished products.

The industry of the capital is in the initial phase of structural change involving technical modernization and product structure.

A shift in the labour force towards the more skill-intensive sectors and towards products which ensure a higher added-value is occurring.

The intensive and selective development of industry, the closure or relocation elsewhere of industrially „outdated sectors" that do not fit into the metropolitan industrial complex is under way.

The rapid development of the science-based branches and a higher concentration on the activities of product development is going on.

Although the vertical structure of manufacturing industry in Budapest is of a high level, its extent has declined as the production of components and spare parts is increasingly concentrated in the plants of large metro-

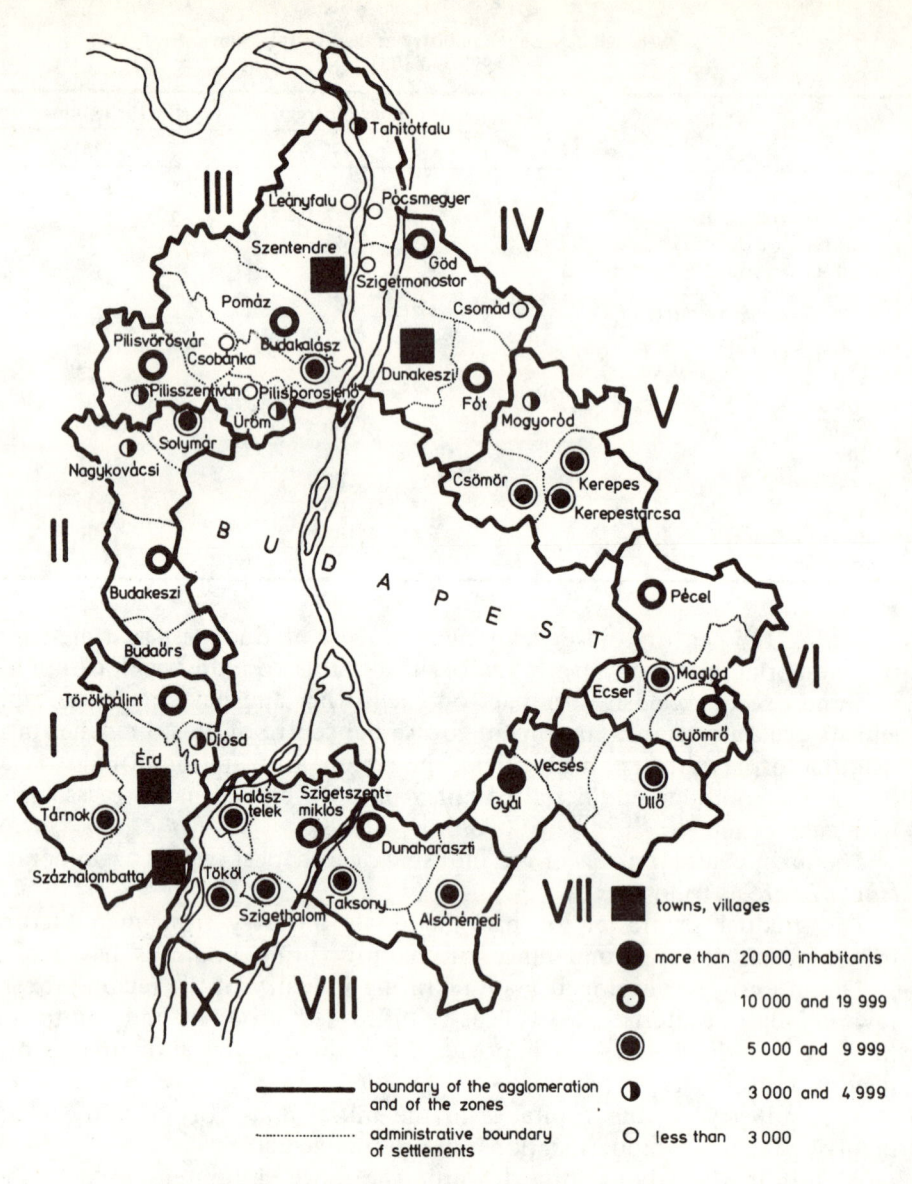

Fig. 62. The Budapest agglomeration belts from I until IX
(number of population on January 1, 1980)

politan enterprises which have been either relocated of newly established in the countryside, and the assembly activities of the capital have greatly increased. This in turn has intensified the territorial division of labour between the industry of the capital and of the countryside.

342

Selected data on the industry of Budapest, 1977 and 1981

Designation	Budapest's percentage share in the national total	
	1977	1982
People engaged in industry	28	26
Installed motive power (kWh)	18	17
Electrical energy used (kWh)	16	15
Output of selected products		
Rail cars	100	100
Passenger lifts	97	100
Cover plates	75	47
B_{12} vitamin	100	100
Chlorocid	100	100
Tyres for passenger cars and coaches	100	97
Paper and cardboard	42	37
Cotton and cotton-type fabrics	60	57
Silk and cotton-type fabrics	87	91
Unprocessed meats	24	20

In the 1970s, the industrial workforce of the capital fell by over 100 000 persons, and the significance of metropolitan industry tends no longer to be represented by the proportion of the national industrial labour employed but by the high level of technical development and efficiency.

With the slowly unfolding development of medium- and small-sized plants, there is an upward trend in specialization, involving the elimination of non-profitable products, more mass production and hence a rise in economic efficiency. But along with specialization, horizontal and vertical diversification is also spreading to the large enterprises of Budapest as, for instance, with the Chinoin and Fékon Underwear Companies.

Budapest and its agglomeration constitute the largest monocentric metropolitan industrial complex in Central Europe. Metropolitan industrial concentration, the so-called industrial complex, is a type of regional unit in which the productive forces occupy a characteristic place.

Typical of the sectoral structure of industry in the region in general and in the Budapest agglomeration in particular is the leading role of heavy industry making up over 60 per cent of the total and within that the increasing weight of the engineering and chemical branches. Otherweise light industry accounts for about 25 per cent, and food processing for some 7 to 8 per cent of the labour force employed in industry. With structural reorganization, with the development of the regional division of labour in the country, the proportion of the basic-material producing branches of heavy industry and mining has dropped, while that of the engineering and chemical industries and, to a lesser extent, of food processing has risen. Conversely, the percentage share of light industry has experienced a substantial fall.

The region has no energy sources of its own, and is supplied with primary energy sources mainly from the nearby Tatabánya and Dorog coal basins and briquet factories, from the Mecsek field with coking coal, and to a lesser extent from other coal basins and imports. Especially significant are briquetted brown-coal imports for household purposes and coke imports for the operation of the Óbuda gas works. Although as a result of the rapid rise in the price of oil and natural gas, particularly of the former, several plants in Budapest and in the region in general have returned to coal fuelling, the basic energy sources have remained natural gas, and heavy fuel oil. Gas is supplied to the capital mainly from domestic fields and from imports through the Fraternity and Orenburg Pipelines, and only to a lesser extent by gas produced from coal. The high-pressure (60 to 75 at) pipelines are attached to the medium-pressure mains surrounding the capital.

The region is the country's most important area for the generation of electricity, and the total output of the local power stations is about 2100 MW, which is somewhat higher than the capacity of the North-Hungarian region. The largest power plant both in the region, as well as in the country as a whole, is the Danube Thermal Power Plant at Százhalombatta with an output of 1920 kW, and which uses heavy fuel oil from the nearby Danube Oil Refinery.

The labour-intensive sector of the engineering industry of the region employs about two-thirds of the region's total engineering manpower. It is these labour-intensive branches that determine the engineering specialization of the region *(Fig. 63)*

The dynamic development of transport equipment production which is one of the traditional industrial branches of the region has been promoted by the central development programme. Especially outstanding is the production of locomotives, buses, ships, bicycles, and various components, such as power-assisted steering gear and tractor parts. Crane manufacturing also belongs to these engineering branches. The favourable structural and technological trends that are taking place have also made themselves felt in the simplification of the product structure, while the international exchange of products and co-operation have developed.

The parent plant of the IKARUS Company at Mátyásföld produces slightly more than half the 13 000 buses of different types turned out annually. With its ambitious foreign-trade policy, the enterprise has not only increased its bus exports to various countries, for instance, the Soviet Union, FRG, USA and Greece, but has also participated in the establishment of assembly plants in the developing countries of Iraq, Angola, Cuba and Mozambique.

As a result of its links with bus production and of CMEA co-operation, new product lines and more precise development tasks have been assigned to the Csepel Motor Works at Szigethalom. It is here that most of the bus chassis and power-assisted steering assemblies are produced.

Ganz-Mávag is the largest railway vehicle engineering plant. It produces diesel, diesel-electric and electric locomotives and rail cars. In co-operation with the Ganz Electrical Works, it has developed the 3000 HP diesel-electric and the 5000 HP electric locomotive types. During the course of product

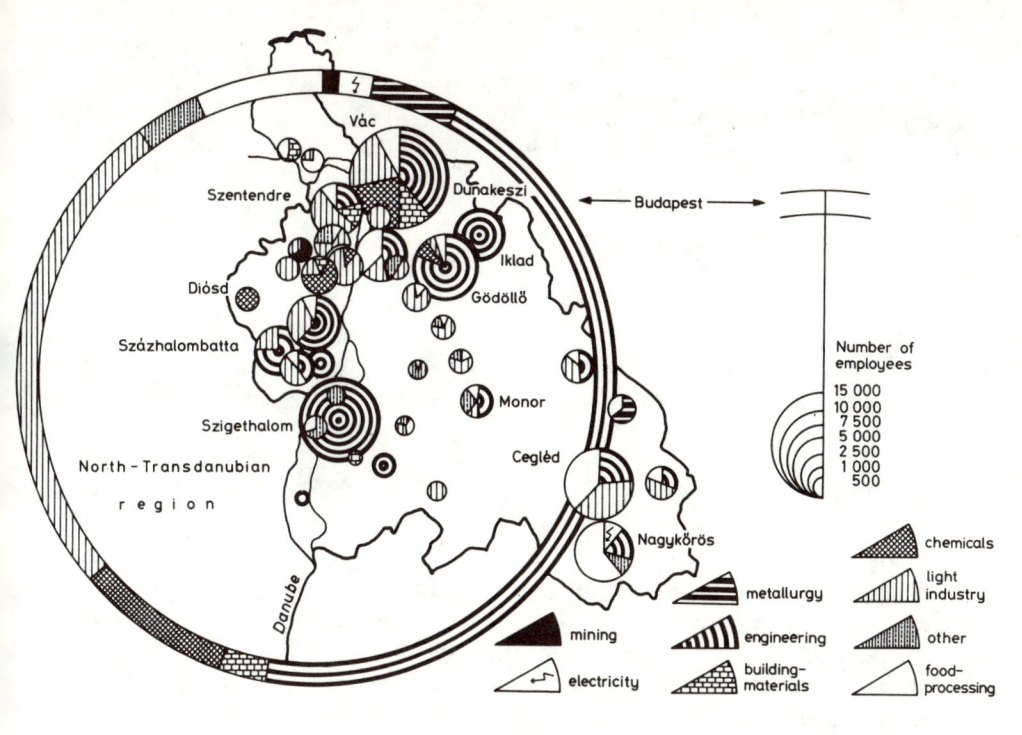

Fig. 63. The spatial location of industry in the central economic–planning region (1980)

restructuring, Ganz-Mávag also started the manufacturing of up-to-date lifts. A significant structural change was the discontinuance of the manufacture of obsolete motorcycles, and its replacement by the mass production of various bicycle types with better marketing prospects.

Ship building is carried on at the Óbuda and Angyalföld yards of the Hungarian Shipyards and Crane Factory. Their most important products are river push- and tugboats, floating, portal and jib cranes, and boilers of various types and sizes. In the Vác yard of the Hungarian Shipyards and Crane Factory, the mass production of different types of containers has been recording favourable sales for some time.

The engineering and machine-tool industries belong to the largest industry groups of the Budapest agglomeration. The largest enterprise in this sector is the Machine-Tool Works, producing in its numerous factories in the capital various traditional and high-precision machine tools, for instance, lathes, grinders, milling machines and numerically controlled single- and general-purpose machines. The Machine-Tool Factory of the Csepel Works is the main producer of radial drilling machines, and of numerically controlled (NC) and computer-controlled (CNC) single-purpose machines.

Of outstanding importance is the Láng Engineering Works, which produces primarily power engines, condenser-type steam turbines of 200 and

345

215 MW and over, boilers for industrial use and household-heating purposes, and tomato-processing and -concentrating production lines for domestic use and export. The April 4 Engineering Works manufactures turnkey factories, boilers, nuclear power equipment and tube fittings. Also significant is the manufacture in the capital of equipment for the chemical and food-processing industries and for the construction industry. Civil engineering products, such as bridges and steel structures for factory buildings, are manufactured mainly by the Ganz-Mávag and the Metal-Working Factory.

The production of electrical machines and appliances is also a traditional industrial branch of the capital, where about two-thirds of the national output of these products are manufactured. The development of the production of this sector, has been stimulated by the gradually rising industrial demand and by increasing domestic and export marketing possibilities. The country's largest enterprises in this field are the Ganz Electrical Works, the United Electrical Engineering Factory, the Electrical Equipment and Appliances Works, the Hungarian Cable Works and the Budapest plant of Kontakta. The Ganz Works produces heavy-duty engines, electric equipment for electric and diesel-electric locomotives, power-plant generators and transformers. The product structure in this industrial branch has been greatly modernized, and the proportion of exportable, economically mass-produced products has grown. Electrical machine production is also carried on in Cegléd.

The telecommunication and vacuum engineering has also developed dynamically and constitutes a major branch of the capital's engineering industry. Although the large-scale industrial development of the countryside has reduced the share of Budapest and its agglomeration in this branch, as regards the number of employees, it is at the same level as the transport-vehicle industry. Owing to intensive investments and technical development, the gap in standards between world and domestic production has been narrowed, and the export opportunities of the branch have expanded both in the capitalist and socialist markets. The development of this industrial branch, requiring relatively small amounts of valuable materials, a highly qualified labour force and a background of scientific research institutes, fits in favourably with the more modern industrial structure of the Budapest agglomeration.

The most important enterprises of the branch are the ORION Company producing black-and-white and colour television sets and micro- and short-wave radio transmitters, the Beloiannis Telecommunication Works turning out crossbar telephone exchanges among other things, the Telephone Factory manufacturing railway signalling and security installations, the Budapest Electro-Acoustic Factory and BRG producing studio equipment, educational equipment, language laboratories, and various accessories, for these products. Also significant are the plants located in the villages of Bugyi and Nagykáta which specialized in manufacturing telephone apparatus. The most important enterprise of vacuum engineering is the United Incandescent Lamps Company, Tungsram, manufacturing and exporting various types of incandescent lamps, motorcar lighting equipment, neon lights, transmitter tubes and the vacuum technology equipment. It is a factory that is significant internationally. It also performs prominent research and development activities, and also has a plant operating at Vác.

The instruments industry has been greatly affected by scientific and technological development. A spectacular upswing has been attained in the sub-branches of automation and computer technology, but developments have also been fast in the production of special geophysical and geodetic instruments, measuring instruments, optical products and business machines. The most important enterprises belonging to this branch are the MEDICOR Works, producing X-ray equipment and medical instruments, the Mechanical Measuring Instruments Company, the Electronic Measuring Instruments Company, the Hungarian Optical Works, Gamma, and the Works of the Mechanical Engineering Company.

The most important plants of the mass-metal industry are the Budapest factories of the Enamel Industry Works, the Arms and Gas Appliances Company and the ELZETT Works of Sheet-Metal Industry.

The region's highly developed engineering industry consumes about one million tons of rolled products, most of which are supplied by the metallurgical industry of the other regions. Steel production in Budapest is carried out at the Csepel Iron and Metal Works, which specialized primarily in high-quality electro-steel and rolled sheets, in response to the needs of the engineering industry of Budapest. The high-quality rolled wire used in electrode production is also an important product. The Lőrinc Rolling Mill, a plant of the Danube Iron Works turns out hot-rolled rough plate. Substantial in the production of basic metallurgy is the Metal Plant of the Csepel Works, where copper metallurgy and the electrolytic processing of non-ferrous metal scrap are undertaken. Its most important product is special quality copper wire. Copper and other non-ferrous metallurgy at the Nagytétény plant of Metallochemia is heavily restricted for environmental reasons. The aluminium-rolling mills may also be ranked as part of basic metal production.

The dynamic development of the chemical industry has been promoted by investment in pharmaceutical, rubber and synthetic-material manufacture as well as in the paint, synthetic resin and oil-refining industry. The largest pharmaceutical factories of the country, the Chinoin Company, the Kőbánya Pharmaceutical Factory and the United Pharmaceutical and Food Factory are located in the capital, as is the parent factory of the Taurus Rubber Company producing tyres for lorries and buses. The production of soap and synthetic detergents is also significant as are paints, varnish and synthetic resin at the Budalakk Paint and Synthetic Resin Factory, household articles, cosmetics and synthetic materials. The FORTE photochemical plant, the only works producing films and photographic papers, is located at Vác.

The country's largest petroleum refinery, processing 6 million tons of crude oil per year, is to be found at Százhalombatta. Its product range has been versified during the course of development and it is now operating

347

special plant for atmospheric and vacuum distillation, catalytic petrol reforming, desulphurizing gas oil, separating BT aromatic compounds and for producing malic acid and malic-acid anhydrates.

The basic inorganic chemistry industry is also considerable with the Budapest Chemical Works producing sulphuric acid, phosphorous fertilizers, chlorine, hydrochloric acid and caustic potash. The product range of the United Chemical Works is also extremely broad and varied.

The size of the construction industry of the region is determined partly by the extensive demands placed upon it and partly by the natural endowments of the region. A large cement factory using the limestone of Naszály is located at Vác, and its output largely satisfies the needs of the Central region, while the wide-spread occurrence of clay provides the raw-material base for brick making. Brick works are to be found at Kőbánya, Óbuda, and Csillaghegy in the capital itself, at Solymár and Pilisborosjenő in the agglomeration. A new, modern and largely automated plant was built at Őrbottyán. Less significant is glass making which largely specializes in the manufacture of technical products, such as test tubes, vacuum bottles and laboratory vessels.

The plants of the Fine Ceramics Works produce porcelain products for the telecommunication industry, high- and low-voltage porcelain insulators, sanitary porcelain, grinding wheels, diamond-tipped tools, and household articles.

The largest plant manufacturing concrete element is the Concrete and Ferro-Concrete Company with factories in Budapest and Szentendre. In Budapest and its agglomeration there are four house prefabrication yards, capable of producing panels for 12 500 dwellings per year. The regional development of the construction industry is no more than average, however, because the endowments for its development are more favourable in areas outside the Central region.

Light industry, overwhelmingly producing consumer goods, employs about one quarter of the regions's industrial manpower, although its share in the sectoral structure of industry is diminishing. Factories are localized, for the most part, in the Budapest agglomeration. The leading branch of light industry, and at the same time the second most important branch after engineering, is textiles. After reconstruction and significant labour losses, it no longer belongs to the least efficient branches. To offset the fall in the labour force and to maintain output, the intensive method of development has come to the fore in Budapest. Despite large-scale reconstruction and technical development, however, both the textile and clothing industries have remained the most critical industrial branch in the Budapest agglomeration. The finishing phase of the technological cycle of textile production is concentrated to a greater extent in Budapest, than spinning and weaving. In the region, all branches are represented, with the cotton industry in the leading position. Outstanding, even on a national scale, are the plants of the Hungarian Cotton Industry, the Kispest Textile Factory, the Kelenföld Textile Factory, the Cotton-Weaving Factory and the Soroksár Textile Factory.

Woollens occupy a similar share to that of the cotton industry of the wool industry and within it especially high is the output of worsted cloths. The plants in the vicinity of Budapest, at Pomáz, Kerepestarcsa and Vác produce only threads, with weaving and finishing being concentrated exclusively in Budapest.

The proportion of the flax and hemp industry, which also uses large quantities of synthetic fibres, is slightly lower, although the Budakalász Flax-Spinning and Weaving Works has carried out a large-scale selective development. The difference between weaving and finishing capacities is greatest in the silk industry. While in the former, the region's participation is rather low, the capacities of cloth making and finishing are concentrated predominantly there. The largest plants of the silk industry are located in Budapest and Vác.

The participation of the region in the production of knitwear and clothing has dropped as a result of the increase in the number of provincial plants. Budapest and Vác are the centres of the knitwear industry, while the country's largest clothing factories, the First of May Clothing Factory and the Red October Clothing Factory, are also located in Budapest.

The Budapest leather and footwear factories contribute some 33 per cent of total national output. The leather industry mainly specialized in the manufacture of soft leather, while the most important footwear factories are the Duna Shoe Factory and the Quality-Shoe Factory, both of which transact substantial export business. In the leather-processing and footwear industry as well as in the textile-clothing industry an important role is also played, especially in Budapest, by the council-owned and co-operative plants which ensure a wider product range in smaller lot sizes. The leather-clothing and fur industries are, following trends in current fashion, in a phase of spectacular upswing.

The cellulose, paper and paper-processing capacity of the Central region is considerable, and this extremely water-intensive branch is located along the Danube. The country's largest paper factory is located in the Csepel suburb of Budapest, while paper and paper-processing plants in Pesterzsébet, Újpest and Budafok are also of significance nationally. In the agglomeration zone is to be found the Szentendre Paper Mill.

The region's timber-processing and furniture industries are significant. One of the country's largest sawmills and veneer factories can be found at Budafok–Háros. Besides the Budapest Furniture Factory, the output of furniture and timber-processing co-operatives is also significant.

1.2.2 Agriculture and food processing

The concentration of large-scale industry in the capital exerts a great impact on the output and structure of the agriculture of the whole region, but mainly on that of the agglomeration. Parallel to its development into a metropolis, there developed around Budapest an extensive area supplying the

Selected agricultural data for the Central region,
1977 and 1981

Designation	The region's percentage share in the national total	
	in 1977	in 1981
Agricultural land under cultivation (including forests, reeds and fish ponds)	7	7
Persons employed in agriculture	10	15
Output of major products		
Wheat	6	6
Maize	5	5
Potatoes	18	18
Green paprika	7	7
Cabbage	20	20
Cattle population	6	5
Pig population	8	7

city with vegetables, flowers, pig rearing and dairying as its characteristic features. This function of supplying Budapest with agricultural produce, though somewhat declining over the past decades, is still discernible in the pattern of land use and animal husbandry.

The economic conditions of agricultural production are still favourable from the point of view of the market situation. But the advantages of market proximity in the sense of a few decades ago have either weakened or disappeared altogether. Agriculture in the Budapest agglomeration also follows international trends and, as a result, the positive role of market proximity has lost, except for a few branches, much of its significance.

The proportion of non-agricultural activities out of the total is very high, amounting to about three quarters of the production value of all activity in agglomeration belt at the end of the 1970s. This is, basically, a favourable phenomenon as it is very difficult to offset the increase in inputs, indispensable for agricultural production, by an increase in productivity only. Thus the large farms of the area have found the growth in revenues accruing from non-agricultural activities indispensable, especially in areas with less favourable natural endowments.

The distribution of land use tends to reflect the endeavour better to utilize the relief conditions and, especially in the agglomeration belt, to adopt more intensive cultures. The proportions of arable land, meadows and pastures are lower than the national average, while those of market gardens, orchards and vineyards are higher. Typical of most of the market gardens is vegetable growing together with fruit and flowers.

Several important vegetable-growing districts have developed around Budapest, of which the northern district on Szentendre island, and the southern area on Csepel island are the most significant. On both islands and in the Monor area, root crops and tomato growing are especially outstanding. Paprika and onions are the main crops on Csepel island, while cabbages are grown around Vecsés and Gödöllő. Additionally the cultivation of green peas, string beans, carrots, cauliflowers, sweet corn, melons is significant, but vegetable supply has, for the most part, to come from other regions. Vegetable growing is particularly developed in and around Cegléd and Nagykőrös producing mainly tomatoes, lettuces, cucumbers and cabbages.

The pattern of arable land use on the collective farms of the agglomeration differs from that of the country as a whole. The proportions of cereals, maize and industrial crops are somewhat lower, while those of vegetables and fodder crops for cattle rearing are higher than the national average. Although vegetables are grown in about 8 per cent of the arable land, they are insufficient to cover the needs of the capital.

10 per cent of the country's orchards can be found in the central region. Peaches are grown in the neighbourhood of Buda, at Budaörs, Nagytétény and Érd, cherries and sour cherries are found in the north and north-eastern part of the region, while raspberries, strawberries, blackberries and other berry fruits are grown in great quantities in the Szentendre, Vác and Nagymaros areas and in the Ipoly valley.

Vineyards occupy, with the exception of the northern part of the region, an area larger than the national average, especially on the sandy soils south and east of the capital on Csepel island, and the neighbourhood of Dabas, Nagykáta and Monor, where they are really part of the northern fringe of the wine-growing district of the Great Plain.

Within arable cultivation, two groups of plants play a major role: grain and green fodder crops occupy the larger part, and bread grains make up about a quarter of arable land. The share of industrial crops is low, although sunflower production is rising significantly. Of the main fodder crops, maize is grown on an area equal to that of wheat, but less than the national average. Average yields are around 4 tons per hectare, which is lower than the national average. The proportion of the arable area under fodder crops for cattle breeding is above the national area especially in the agglomeration belt, with lucerne playing the leading role, followed by silage maize and green fodder maize, with onions playing a subordinate role.

Animal husbandry developed particularly rapidly during the 1970s, as a result of which the animal population density per 100 hectares of agricultural area has reached the national average of 41. This proportion is in the case of cattle below, but in the case of pigs far above the national average, partly owing to the existence of large, industrially organized pig-fattening farms in the region. The function of supplying the agglomeration belt with produce is also apparent in animal husbandry.

The co-operative farms operating in the administrative district of the capital are characterized by intensive land utilization, engage in open-air and extensive hothouse cultivation, and specialize in growing flowers, flower cuttings, propagation materials, garden products and fruit, mainly peaches. Outstanding is the farming activity of the Dunavarsány co-operative which enjoys a nationwide reputation especially for the high milk yields of their

Holstein-Friesian cattle stock. The Hernád co-operative farm, the region's largest broiler chicken producer and processor, also deserves mention.

The regional concentration of the food-processing industry with its orientation towards both the consumer market and the raw-material base is less than the regional concentration in heavy and light industries and the participation of the region in national food processing only slightly exceeds the share of population. But there are considerable differences among the individual branches of the food industry with the less material-intensive but highly skilled branches exhibiting a more dynamic development. To these branches belong, for example, the manufacture of chocolate, salami, margarin, canned meat, rum, liqueur and beer. The country's largest slaughterhouses, meat- and milk-processing plants, flour mills, breweries and deep-freezing plants are located in Budapest.

The region's livestock population covers less than a quarter of the needs of the meat-processing plants, but their capacity for several products exceeds local demand, and some of their meat products are therefore either transferred to other regions or are exported. The renewal and modernization of the meat plants in Budapest that has taken place can be explained by the proximity of the larger consumer market and by the lower costs of reconstruction compared with the greater investment needed for the construction of new plants. On the other hand, the transportation costs of livestock and their loss in weight, let alone the damage done to the environment, would justify their relocation in the livestock-breeding regions. The capacity of the flour mills of the area exceeds the region's needs. The milk-processing industry has substantially enhanced its capacity with the establishment of the East-Pest Plant, and its product range has also been expanded. Typical of the vegetable-oil industry at Rákospalota and Csepel and of the distillery sector is the manufacture of end-products while the country's largest confectionary plants are also located in Budapest. The region's canning and deep-freezing industries are important as represented by the large-capacity canning factories and cold-storage plants in Budapest, Dunakeszi and Nagykőrös. The main output of the Budapest Canning Factory is canned fruit, the Dunakeszi Factory is best known for its canned fish, and the Nagykőrös Factory for its pickles. The Kőbánya Brewery, accounting for half the country's beer production, is one of the largest breweries in Europe. Also significant is the food-processing activity and associated milk and poultry processing of the co-operative farms.

1.2.3 Transport

The transport network of the region as a whole and also its agglomeration zone is more developed than the national network, but as regards the increasing needs of freight, commuting and tourism, it needs to be further developed and transformed.

The region's industry processes large quantities of raw materials and semifinished products derived from other regions and from imports. Nearly all fuels and energy sources and over two-thirds of the food consumed stem from other territories. The greater part of fuels, minerals and semifinished commodities are imported from the Soviet Union or transported from the Northern Transdanubian and Northern Hungarian regions. But the nationwide development of the spatial division of labour has greatly enhanced industrial co-operation and thus transport connections with the industrial areas and towns of other regions have also increased. The origins of the agricultural produces brought to the capital have also become more diversified. Owing to the manufacturing character of the industry of the region, the weight of commodities moved to the capital is a multiple of the weight of commodities transported out of it.

The region's railway network clearly reflects the dominant role that the capital and the agglomeration play in the country's economic life. The capital's connections with the other main economic regions and concentrations of the country is generally good. The main routes of the radially structured railway network are predominantly electrified and double-tracked in the region itself, and in the course of reconstruction the minor re-routing of certain lines has also been carried out. Congestion, on the principal railway lines around the capital is enhanced by the increasing amount of transit traffic resulting from the lack of transverse diversion lines.

The road network of the region is dense and part of the motorway and national trunk systems run across it. The results attained from the modernization of lower-order roads have also been significant, and it is only the northern parts of the region that still have a relatively poor network.

On the Danube it is primarily cheap bulk goods that are transported, although pleasure trips are also significant during the summer season. The Csepel Free Port handles heavy traffic with thousands of ships visiting it each year. Also noteworthy is the harbour at Szob, from which stone is transported in large quantities.

The development of the transport system of Budapest and its agglomeration – in close connection with urban planning – is an investment-intensive but also important socio-political task. In Budapest, the number of daily trips is over 5 million with more than 2 million people participating, over 80 per cent of whom make use of public transport. At the same time, more than 100 million tons of commodities have to be transported in the capital each year. The annual turnover of the warehouses is over 13 million tons, transport thus has a significant impact on industrial production of Budapest as well.

Despite the problems that remain, mass public transport in Budapest, as a result of considerable developments, has moved from its nadir of the early 1970s, and now provides a fairly sound basis from which to tackle the increased tasks facing it. The transport development plan of the capital is a continuous one, and the process of fulfilling it constitutes an organic part of the Area Plan of the Budapest Agglomeration. The radial layout of the underground lines and the network of suburban railway lines joining them have promoted the development of a network pattern, and has favourably influenced urban planning as a whole. As a complement to the three radial underground lines, the building of a semicircular connecting line appears to be a further necessity. The existing transverse road system connecting the radial motorways will be supplemented by a motorway ring road.

Heavy traffic imposes a special burden upon the main central routes of the central public-transport system, which handle over three quarters of total traffic. The insufficient capacity of the eight Danube bridges, during rush hours constitutes a further serious problem. The renewal of individual bridges and the widening of Árpád Bridge to be completed in the mid-1980s will ease the situation, but a final solution will only be provided after the two new bridges to be constructed in conjunction with the motorway ring have been completed together with the likely Danube Tunnel to be built in the inner city.

The most important task in the development of bus and trolleybus systems is the servicing of existing and new housing estates, and the substitution of bus routes with trolleybus lines in the Inner City. The soaring cost of energy demands a sectoral restructuring of the capital's public transport. The trolleybus service, once doomed to be discontinued, has again become competitive, and further development is justified both on economic and environmental grounds.

The choice of the most appropriate public transport service depends, apart from economic factors, on the settlement structure of the individual parts of the capital, on the carrying capacity of the road network, on the size and daily distribution of passenger traffic and on environmental factors.

The underground, tramway and suburban railway systems are, in general, attractive enough in the densely populated urban parts, where they are supplemented by complementary bus and trolleybus lines.

The suburban railway of the capital, of which the Batthyány Square–Szentendre line is the most modern, efficiently connect the greater part of the agglomeration with the capital.

1.2.4 Tourism

The region with Budapest at its centre constitutes the most important tourist area and handles more than half the entire turnover of the tourist industry. Budapest itself is an independent tourist unit with the Danube Bend and the Ráckeve section of the Danube, both of which extend beyond the agglomeration, forming two other tourist areas.

Budapest is characterized by the predominance of international tourism which uses the city's hotel capacity, while the agglomeration belt is used partly by the population of the capital for weekend recreation and partly by domestic tourists of moderate means. Budapest is a year-round tourist centre, contains over half the country's commercial accommodation capacity and accounts for the greater part of the revenue from tourism.

The most important tourist attractions of the capital are its scenic beauty, its medicinal and thermal baths, its cultural, scientific and musical offerings, sports events, entertainment, historical monuments, and the international transit character of the city.

The development of tourism in the Budapest agglomeration, despite the considerable progress made, still lags behind the general level of economic development. Tourist accommodation has been developed primarily in Budapest and the agglomeration, and at the end of the 1970s close to 5000 rooms were available in the 32 hotels of the capital, with total accommodation capacity capable of handling 32000 people. The number beds in the paying-guest sector has increased most rapidly and now accounts for some 60 per cent of total accommodation. The two new hotels on the Danube embankment and other hotels still to be built have increased, and will further increase, the accommodation capacity. Budapest as a thermal and medicinal bath centre has gained considerably from the construction of the Thermal Hotel on Margaret Island and from the opening of the modern Komjádi Swimming Pool.

Contrasting with the slow development of company recreation schemes several thousands of private weekend houses, family holiday homes and angler's cabins have been built on both banks of the Danube to the north and south of Budapest, and in the Buda hills. The settlements of the Danube Bend have increasingly acquired recreational functions and have developed into holiday-type villages. In the south, the middle and lower sections of the 58 kilometre-long Ráckeve branch of the Danube are becoming more favoured holiday areas, which, owing to their proximity to the capital and good transport connections, are frequented on weekends by more holiday makers than is Lake Velence. Several tourist attractions can also be found just outside the region's agglomeration belt.

1.3 Population

The population of the regions increased by 25 per cent during the 1950s and 1960s, but the rate of growth declined considerably during the 1970s. However, while the rate of population growth in the capital fell sharply during the 1970s, the population of the settlements in the agglomeration has continued to rise at an accelerating rate. Some 42 per cent of the population of Pest county lives in the 44 settlements of the agglomeration. For many years before 1973, the rapid population growth of the capital was due exclusively to in-migration, but since then growth has come from natural increase, although the most recent sharp fall in the birth rate may again herald natural decline. At any rate, the great slowdown in population growth resulting from the declining rate of in-migration can be regarded as a significant result in the context of regional development policy.

Largest in number and highest in density of population are the Buda, Gödöllő, Monor and Nagykáta districts of Pest county. It is in these districts that population influx has been greatest in recent years, and from which commuting to the capital is highest. The population growth of the individual settlements of the agglomeration has been influenced, along with natural increase, by such factors as distance from the capital, public transport connections, and housing conditions. During recent years, population growth has been highest in the settlements to the south and southwest of the capital, namely in Százhalombatta, Érd and Szigethalom. The very fast concentration of the population in the settlements surrounding the capital has created mammoth villages like Vecsés, Gyál, Pomáz, Fót and Pilisvörösvár. With populations that may surpass 20 000 they are larger than many minor towns, but their decifient infrastructures cannot yet ensure urban-like living conditions. The main source of population growth in these settlements has tended to be in-migration. Some 60 000 members of the German, Slovak and Southern Slav nationalities also live in the region.

Population distribution and change within the capital are determined by the structure of the built-up area, and increasingly since the second half of the 1960s, by the location of new housing estates and inner-city redevelopment. Hence, regarding population evolution, the districts of the capital can be divided into those with dynamically growing population like Zugló, Óbuda and Rákospalota, and those with diminishing population like Józsefváros. But this distribution cannot be taken to be final as the completion of redevelopment in the inner areas will again lead to a rise in population numbers.

The population density at 442 persons per square kilometer of the region is the highest in the country, but even without Budapest still amounts to 143 persons per square kilometer.

The distribution of population by age shows a metropolitan character, which means that the proportion of children is comparatively low, and that of the elderly much higher than the national average. In the occupational distribution of population there is a marked difference between the agglomeration belt and the rest of the region. The proportion of persons engaged in the manufacturing and construction industries in the agglomeration belt approximates that of the capital, while it is much lower in the rest of the region. The percentage employed in agriculture is the lowest in the country.

During the period 1968–1980, owing to intensive and selective industrial development, the number of people working in industry in the capital fell by about 145 000, and thus the proportion of the industrial population of the country working in the capital dropped to 28 per cent. The Hungarian capital has entered the stage of post-industrial development. The territorial distribution of the active populations does not coincide with the distribution of industrial and other job opportunities, and the number of daily and other commuters is still high. Thousands of working people commute to Vác, Dunakeszi and Százhalombatta and to other significant industrial centres.

1.4 Settlement

The character of the settlement network is determined by the relief, the transport network, the quality of transport facilities and by the local development and diversification of productive forces. The settlement pattern of the northern administrative districts is characterized by small villages, while typical of the plainland areas of the south are widely spaced larger villages which still have significant dispersed populations in their outlying areas. Population density is low at 2·8 per sq km and is indicative of the preponderance of larger villages. The region has, besides the capital, five smaller towns with a combined population of some 230000, which means that the proportion of urban population excluding the capital is the lowest of any region. Although the number of urban population is relatively small, there are quite a few settlements which, given their population size, occupational structure and functions, can be regarded as urban villages or semi-urban settlements. Some of these, for instance, Pomáz, Pilisvörösvár, Szigetszentmiklós and Aszód, are themselves significant industrial and transport centres, while others, like Budaörs, Vecsés, Gyál, Gyömrő and Dunaharaszti, are „dormitory towns" serving the capital.

1.5 Subregions and urban hinterlands

According to the level and direction of industrial and agricultural production and to other economic-cultural and administrative functions, several subregions or spheres of influence may be distinguished. Although each subregion has a definite development trend, the Budapest subregion differs both in size and in quality from the others.

a) The Budapest agglomeration. During the last 100 years, a system of varied and close relationships has evolved between the capital and the settlements in its neighbourhood, as a result of which the Budapest agglomeration has come into being. Budapest arose from the unification of Pest, Buda and Óbuda in 1873 and, developing at an extremely fast rate, there began, even before World War I, a large-scale suburban development which led to the emergency of settlements like Újpest and Kispest. These lived in increasingly close symbiosis with Budapest which until 1950 was much smaller consisting of only 14 districts. The preparatory work carried out immediately after 1945 for the establishment of Greater Budapest, has already formulated and applied the concepts „Budapest neighbourhood" and „Budapest area" [52]. The former provided basis for the unification of Budapest and its suburbs in

1950, when the capital was expanded to encompass 22 districts, while the latter essentially included the territory which has since come into being as a result of the complete amalgamation of the earlier settlement agglomeration. The processes behind the formation of the agglomeration of the Hungarian capital differ substantially from western suburbanization. While western agglomeration extend outwards and absorb the surrounding settlements, in Hungary it was the settlements surrounding Budapest that attached themselves to the capital. This is accounted for mainly by the fact that administrative measures restrict settlement in the agglomeration core, with the result that migration towards the capital increases primarily the population of the settlement ring. Out of the 300 000 inhabitants of the agglomeration, 200 000 are daily commuters to the capital.

The agglomeration of the capital is made up of 44 settlements, of which 4, Szentendre, Százhalombatta, Dunakeszi and Érd are towns and 40 are villages. For the purposes of detailed regional planning, the agglomeration is divided into 9 zones. During the past few decades, many industrial plants, warehouses and depots have been located not in the capital, but in its neighbourhood. Public utilities and transport facilities have been supplied to most of these settlements, and as a result they have become more closely attached to the capital. In this way, a central agglomeration has been established with an area close to 2·5 thousand sq km.

Since the early 1960s, the settlements of the agglomeration belt have rapidly grown from in-migration from practically all parts of the country. Along with the development of industry and warehouses the construction of the Balaton motorway has given a further boost particularly to the settlement making up the South-Buda agglomeration, namely Érd, Budaörs and Törökbálint. A settlement cluster belonging to a similar agglomeration is located around the northern end of Csepel Island, namely Szigetszentmiklós, Szigethalom, Dunaharaszti, Taksony and Halásztelek, with a combined population of about 60 000. A third group of settlements consists of the mammoth villages of Vecsés and Gyál with over 20 000 inhabitants each and neighbouring Üllő. Finally, very rapid population growth has taken place in the Fót–Dunakeszi–Göd area. The industry of the agglomeration is characterized by a strong regional and local plant concentration. Over 60 per cent of the industrially employed population of the agglomeration are concentrated in 11 settlements.

Most of the settlements of the Budapest agglomeration perform a double function. They concentrate, on the one hand, a significant part of the industry of the capital and are therefore important attraction centres for workers, a process which extends along the railways far beyond the boundary of the agglomeration. On the other hand, a substantial part of their inhabitants commute to work in Budapest, and these settlements may thus be regarded as satellite or dormitory towns.

The urban settlements of the agglomeration have gained urban functions and have been granted urban status mostly in the recent past. Szentendre with 17 thousand inhabitants, is a satellite town known for its paper mill and cement-manufacturing industry located at the southern entrance of the Danube Bend. Besides, it is a significant resort and tourist centre, an ,,artists' town", housing painters', sculptors', ceramists' studios and a skanzen. Dunakeszi, with 23 000 inhabitants is an important industrial town with railway-carriage and canning industries. Százhalombatta with 14 000 inhabitants is an explicitly industrial town with its oil refinery, electricity generation and chemical industry and lacks other functions. For a long time, Érd with 41 000 inhabitants was the largest village of the country. It was given town status in 1979, and is now a typical dormitory town.

b) Budapest. Budapest is in every respect the core of a monocentric agglomeration. After the 1950 territorial reorganization, its area was increased to 550 sq km, and its present (1980) population numbers close to 2·1 million.

The structural layout of the city is of a concentric, radial type, which has evolved gradually out of the first development plan for the city by Ferenc Reitter in 1876. At that time the radial-circular road pattern was gaining favour throughout Europe. Subsequent development plans recognized the fundamental significance of the Danube as the capital's axis, and implemented this when building the city. The road network with its radial-circular pattern based on the Danube, the siting of the bridges, the building up of the embankment, the individual parts of the city, and its skyline still reflect this concept in all its essentials. It has been within this framework that the century-old development of Budapest has taken place, and on which the present-day development plans still rely. The correctness and long-term efficiency of the basic plan is shown, for instance, by the fact that the Hungária Boulevard ring, the widening of which is now being actively anticipated, was included in the original plan. At its northern terminal point the construction of Árpád Bridge was completed after the war, and its widening to 35 metres is a task for the 1980s.

With the post-war development of the capital, territorial demands have increased. The prospective development concepts relating to the building up of the empty spaces of the capital have changed several times. First, the ribbon concept came to the fore but around 1960 this was replaced by a plan based on the agglomeration pattern. According to this concept, people wishing to settle in the capital, as well as the city's natural increase, were to be settled not within the boundaries of the city, but in satellite or dormitory towns and villages.

The redevelopment of the city centre is going ahead purposefully and includes the building of hotels and offices, the reconstruction of the palace of Buda Castle, the building of flyovers and the pedestrianization of streets. The urban structure plan also envisages the transformation of Budapest from a monocentric to a polycentric city by the establishment of modern district centres. The building of district centres of metropolitan character in Óbuda, Újpest, Zugló and Pesterzsébet is under way. So far, no single district centre has been fully developed or completed. While the establishment of these centres is designed to relieve congestion in inner districts, their primary function is to improve service provision in the less developed outer districts and to diminish thereby the disparaties between the inner and outer parts of the capital.

c) The spheres of influence of the capital and of the agglomeration extend beyond their boundaries and exert a great impact on Gödöllő, with 28 000 inhabitants, which, owing to its industry, also has an attraction sphere of its own. There are operating in the town an engineering factory, the Ganz Measuring Instruments Factory and an agricultural university. Its environs are an important source of vegetables for Budapest.

In the north, Vác with 35 000 inhabitants, has a definite sphere of influence embracing the Danube Bend and the northern parts of the region. Owing to its differentiated industry (cement, containers, photochemical products, rubber manufacturing, telecommunications and knitwear) it is an important labour attraction centre.

The attraction sphere of Cegléd, with 41 000 inhabitants in the eastern area of the region, is still in its early development stage. Engineering, food processing and wood fabrication have been established in the town, which has also an important railway function. Nagykőrös, with 28 000 inhabitants, is known for its canning industry.

2 The Northern Hungarian economic–planning region

This region extends from the western foothills of the Cserhát Mountain to the Tisza valley, and comprises the counties of Nógrád, Heves and Borsod-Abaúj-Zemplén. It is in this region that the Northern Middle Mountains, with the exception of the Börzsöny, are found, together with the Heves sandy uplands, the Heves–Borsod floodplain, the Taktaköz and the Bodrogköz. In area it comprises 13 430 sq km, or 14·4 per cent of the national total, and has a population of 1·39 million (1980), or 13 per cent of the national total.

Even during the early stages of regional research, the so-called Northern Industrial District was unanimously found to be an undisputed economic region. Owing to the development and inner distribution of productive forces, the easily demonstrable existence of complexity and specialization as well as the close linkage between the economic structure of the region and the natural resources, the Northern Industrial District appeared to match the necessary criteria. Hence it is understandable that the Northern Hungarian economic-planning region and the Northern Industrial District as an economic-geographic macro-region show a closest correspondence [43, 44].

In this explicitly industrial region, specialization is concentrated around the production of the basic materials for heavy industry. The vertically integrated iron and steel industries determine the economic character of the region, while the chemical industry constitutes the main basis for the synthetic-materials industry of the country. The region's coal-mining industry and electricity generation capacity occupy an important place in the energy economy of the country. Another typical branch of basic-material production is the building-materials industry based on the region's raw-material resources. Among the manufacturing branches of heavy industry only engineering has gained an appreciable significance. The structure of industry as a whole is marked by a one-sided prevalence of heavy industry and only food processing, based on local agriculture, and some light industry, mitigate this one-sided structure.

Agriculture, which is unable to meet local demands, lags behind the general level prevailing in the country as a whole. There is, however, significant production and specialization in grapes, wines, fruit and vegetables in certain areas of the region.

The region maintains close economic relations with the central region and the Budapest agglomeration, for which it is the most important supplier of steel and chemicals. As a result of the development of the last decade, more intensive relations have been established with the Northern Plain, which supplies natural gas and foodstuffs, and which receives steel, chemicals, metal products and electricity. International economic relations are also developing at a rapid rate. It will suffice to refer to the co-operation which has evolved with the Soviet and Polish chemical industries, and with the steel industry of Eastern Slovakia. Also intensive are the relations with Eastern Slovakia in bilateral tourism.

2.1 Natural endowments and resources

The greater part of the Northern Middle Mountains is situated in the region. As a result of repeated volcanic activity during the Miocene Period, the main components of the mountains are volcanic in origin. Out of the clay and sandy basement of the Cserhát on the western fringe of the region there emerge eroded andesite and andesite tufa ridges. The Mátra Mountains consist mainly of andesite and andesite tufa, while the Zemplén Mountain range is made up of andesites, riolites, and their tufas.

Situated among these mountains of volcanic origin is the immense Triassic limestone block of the Bükk Mountains which rise to 952 m at the Istállóskő, from a Palaeozoic clay and clay-shale base. They are extremely rich in all forms of the karst phenomena, which are well developed on the extensive plateau. In the North-Borsod karst area, extending north of the Sajó valley, is to be found one of Europe's longest and most beautiful stalactite cave systems near Aggtelek.

The individual parts of the Middle Mountains are separated from one another by river valleys which provide good lines for communications. The southern side of the Middle Mountains is fronted by hills consisting of volcanic tufa and by a series of detrital cones along the Mátraalja and Bükkalja. The flat areas separating the Northern Middle Mountains from the Tisza river are part of the Great Plain.

Owing to its varied geological structure, the region stands out for its abundance and variety of mineral resources. Besides brown coal and lignite, there is iron ore at Rudabánya, lead and zinc in the Mátra and in Gyöngyösoroszi, copper and gold at Recsk, and smaller deposits of natural gas in the Eger—Demjén area. The region is rich in building materials, e.g. limestone, andesite, riolite, clay and gravel. Useful deposits of bentonite are found at Istenmezeje and Mád, of kaolin at Mád and Szegilong, of quartzite at Mád, of silicon at Erdőbénye, of chemical resistant clays at Nemti, of fireproof clay at Felsőpetény, of gypsum at Perkupa and of perlite at Pálháza.

As for the region's climate mean temperature is below the national average, and annual fluctuations are smaller. Winter is longer than in the south of the country, spring comes 2 to 3 weeks later, and summer is somewhat cooler. Precipitation is influenced by the mountains. At higher levels, it averages 800 to 900 mm a year, but the annual total is still above the national average along the mountainous fringe. The western slopes of the mountains receive most precipitation. The impact of the climate on agriculture can be felt throughout the region. Winter is longer, the growing period is shorter owing to the late spring, and the hours of sunshine are less frequent. As a result of the varied relief characteristics, micro- and meso-climates have developed in certain areas. On the southern slopes of the Mátra, Bükk and Zemplén ranges, for instance, favourable insolation conditions can be found, while sunny, dry autumns are associated with Tokajhegyalja.

Brown forest soils and rendzinas in the limestone mountains dominate the region, and soil erosion is considerable. The poor and heavily eroded soils help account for the fact that there are many disadvantaged co-operative farms in the region. On the southern slopes and on the detrital cones along the foothills, however, there are also loess and clay soils rich in eroded volcanic materials, which are suitable for fruit and vine cultivation. Typical of the plainlands are fertile meadow soils, but in places there are also signs of alkalization, as on the Borsod floodplain.

The region is rich in water resources. The Sajó, Hernád and Bodrog rivers rise in the Carpathians outside the country, and their water regimes are decisively influenced by precipitation conditions there. The rivers of Zagyva, Tarna, Eger, Hangony, Bódva, Takta are short in length, and because they drain the local mountains with their rapid run-off, the amount of discharge often fluctuates.

There are several industrial establishments with high water consumption in the region, which has made it necessary to store in reservoirs the surplus precipitation of the regional water economy that falls in spring. Water supply is aggravated by the fact that most rivers, owing to the inadequate treatment of industrial effluents, are already polluted before they enter the country [14].

2.2 The economy

2.2.1 Industry

The region is one of the most important industrial bases of the country. Industry and construction account for over two-fifths of the population engaged in the socialist sector, while the proportion employed in agriculture is less than one-fifth.

The overall level of industrialization is high, but it is heavily concentrated in the coal basins, in areas rich in natural resources, and in the historical and new industrial centres. There are thus districts lacking any industry, as well as economically undeveloped areas in the direct vicinity of the industrially developed territories.

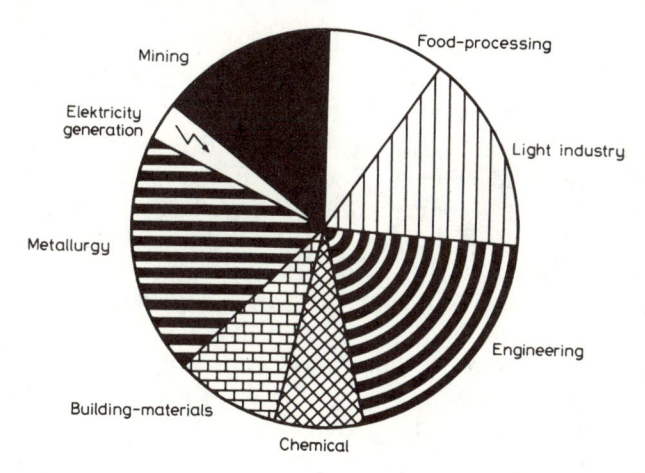

Fig. 64. The industrial structure of the North Hungarian economic-planning region (1981)

The geographical environment has left its conspicuous mark on the region's industry *(Fig. 64)*. The industrial complexes have traditionally been based on coal, and the coal mines made it possible to establish energy- and fuel-intensive sectors, such as electricity generation, iron, steel smelting, and glass and cement manufacture. On their location, other raw materials, such as iron ore, also had their impact on industrial location. With development, however, an industrial capacity far in excess of the region's natural resources came into being, and reliance on imported natural gas and fuel oil has steadily increased. Nonetheless the region continues to exhibit the characteristic feature that mark a coal-based region. These are: a large share of coal mining in the sectoral pattern of industry, high fuel and electricity consumption, large installed mechanical motive power, large-scale raw-material consumption and high volume of output in terms of weight.

The three brown-coal basins of the region have largely unfavourable geological endowments. The coal deposits are widely scattered, the thickness of

Selected data on the industry of the Northern
Hungarian region, 1977 and 1981

Designation	The region's share in the national total, percentages 1977	1981	Designation	The region's share in the national total, percentages 1977	1981
Industrial employment	14	15	Crude iron	71	63
Value of gross fixed assests in industry	20	21	Steel	63	61
			Cement	32	38
Installed motive power	26	26	Drawn sheet glass	48	59
Consumption of electricity by industry	26	28	Nitrogenous fertilizer	60	51
Brown coal	43	45	NaOH	51	86
Lignite	90	85	PVC	100	100
Electricity generation	35	47	Ethylene	100	100
			Polyethylene	100	100
			Sugar	30	23
			Beer	23	18

the seams ranges between 1·6 and 3 metres, and mining, owing to the loose overburden, is hard to mechanize. The coal is also of low calorific value. It is for these reasons that several pits have been closed and the vacated buildings used for the location of new plants. In the mines that remain, it has been possible to introduce more concentrated and mechanized production. The region's share in the country's brown-coal and lignite output is high in terms of tons, but rather low in terms of calorific value.

a) The Nógrád coal basin is one of the oldest fields in the country, and fuel-intensive industries like glass manufacture, foundry-work and electricity generation have been attracted to it. Owing to the closure of many pits, mining is now going on only in the Nagybátony–Kisterenye area. The major consumers of the basin's coal within the region are the thermal power stations, with the surplus going to the capital and the Great Plain.

b) The largest coal field in the region is located in the Borsod and Sajó area, where most of the coal mined is of low calorific value [12].

Mining is concentrated around Kazincbarcika, where the output of the pits of the area is collected for classification. The output of the Lyukó mine in the Miskolc area is the highest in the country, with 1 million tons a year. The leading consumers are the thermal power stations at Kazincbarcika, Miskolc and Tiszapalkonya. The basin also supplies coal to Budapest and the Great Plain and is, in addition, the main supplier of coal to the region's population.

c) The development of industry in Ózd was promoted by the nearby Egercsehi–Királd–Ózd coal field, whose coal is of good quality but whose proven reserves are small. The coal burns well and is suitable for gas production, but the geological conditions are unfavourable. The main consumers are Borsod factories not yet converted to other fuels, the population and the railways.

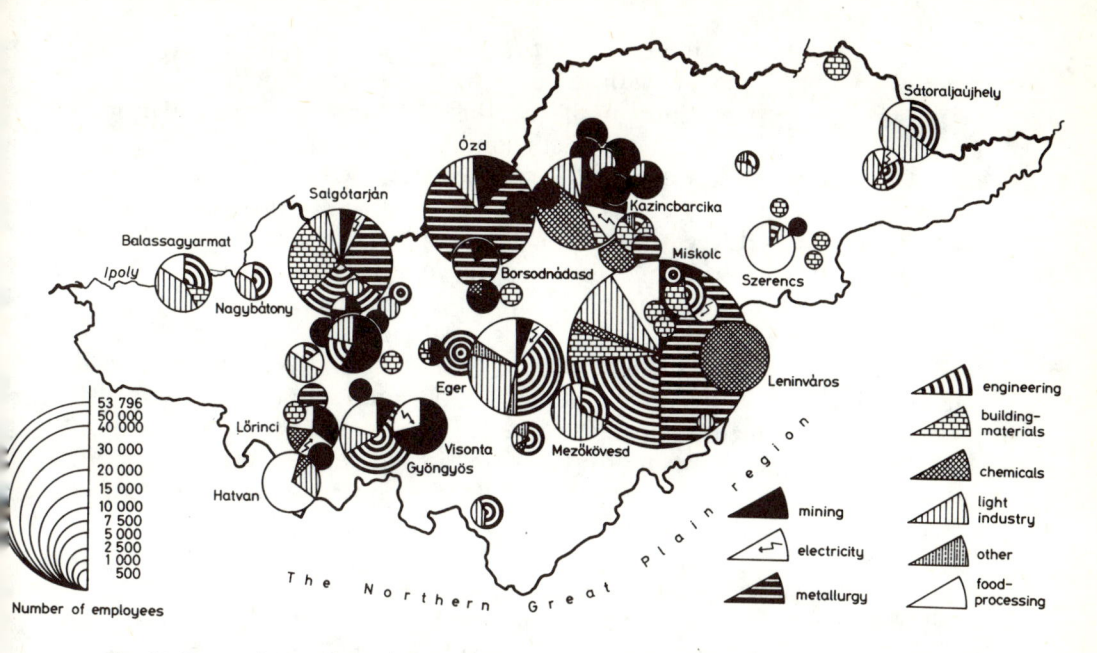

Fig. 65. The spatial location of industry in the North Hungarian economic–planning region (1981)

d) Outstanding among the country's natural energy sources are the lignite resources of the region, which, with few interruptions, extend from the Zagyva valley to the eastern foothills of Bükkalja. The lignite extracted near Visonta by the use of completely mechanized open-cast methods is used exclusively by the Visonta Gagarin Thermal Power Station. Extensive unworked reserves occur between Bükkábrány and Emőd.

As part of the transformation of the energy structure of the region, gas produced from coal has been replaced by fuel oil in steel production. A further change has been brought about by the transmission of Hortobágy natural gas to the region. But the most radical change has been effected by socialist international economic co-operation in that the metallurgy, cement industries as well as electricity generation now use natural gas and petroleum products brought to the region from outside the country by pipeline. Natural gas is also supplied to most of the urban population as well. Electricity generation has developed on the basis of the region's coal and lignite production. The thermal power stations of the Mátra and Salgótarján area based on coal mined at Visonta, Kazincbarcika and Tiszapalkonya, and on fuel oil in Leninváros ensure surplus electricity despite the fact that industries with high specific electricity consumption (chemical industry, and metallurgy) have been established in the region *(Fig. 65).*

The iron and steel industry of the region is most significant for the national economy and has considerable historical antecedents. It was first based on the timber resources of the Bükk Mountains and local iron-ore deposits, and depended on the fast-running mountain streams for energy. Since the end of the last century, local resources have been unable to ensure the supply of industry, especially after the coking process that replaced charcoal was introduced. The increased demand for ore was met by the mines at Gömör (now in Slovakia), and despite the transport of coke over long distances from Silesia and the Ruhr, the location of the Borsod plants did not become detrimental, because the labour needed for modern steel production and brown coal suitable for gas production were available locally. The availability of brown coal suitable for the production of gas was also a decisive factor in the development of the Salgótarján steel industry.

Today, the region can supply just a fraction of the raw materials needed by the industry. Dressed ore from Rudabánya can meet only part of the demand of the smelting works at Ózd and Diósgyőr, and the bulk of their needs is satisfied by imports from the Soviet Union. The region can only ensure the limestone and dolomite demands of the industry.

With respect to the region's metallurgical plants as a whole, a system of regional vertical integration has developed, in which only coke and tube production are missing. The region, even with the construction of the integrated plant at Dunaújváros, continues to be the leading pig-iron, steel and rolled-sheet producer in the country. The two integrated combines in Miskolc and Ózd produce pig iron and steel. The first produces steel by the LD method, and here is located the largest electro-steel, alloyed-steel and fine-steel rolling capacity in the country. Attached to steel making are press and forging plants. Ózd produces primarily mass rolled products for reinforced concrete, but its range of output is supplemented by the Borsodnádasd Plate Factory, which manufactures small quantities of special steel plates. The December 4 Wire Works in Miskolc produces steel wires of special tensile strength, and maintains close co-operative links with the Ózd and Miskolc plants.

An important metallurgical centre is Salgótarján, where a cold-rolling mill and foundry are in operation together with the manufacture of strip-, wire- and other steel products. The Salgótarján ferro-alloy factory plays an important role in the material supply of the metallurgy industry.

Zinc and lead mining and ore dressing are done at Gyöngyösoroszi, and Recsk is known for its small-scale gold an copper-ore mining. The evaluation of large copper-ore reserves at deeper levels is under way, and mining is expected to start in the mid-1980s. The spin-off effect of mining on the region will be substantial.

The region is the base, the country's chemical industry, which has gone a long way towards changing the industrial structure. The raw-material basis of this industry are domestic and Romanian natural gas, the latter having a high CH_4 content, and petroleum and natural gas imported from the Soviet

Union. The oil-refinery at Leninváros also plays an important role in the chemical industry, and supplies the petrochemical sector with low-octane petrol and other refined oil products. When locating petrochemical plants great emphasis was placed on the various technological linkages. For instance, Leninváros is connected with Kazincbarcika by an ethylene pipeline, while international co-operation, primarily with the chemical industry of the Soviet Union, is also substantial.

The Tisza Chemical Trust in Leninváros is the basis of the Hungarian olefine industry and the largest combine in the country's chemical industry. It produces nitrogenous fertilizers, synthetic resins, synthetic dyes and the olefine products of ethylene, propylene, and propipropylene. Also participating in the synthetic material programme is the North-Hungarian Chemical Works at Sajóbábony.

The Borsod Chemical Works in Kazincbarcika specializes in the production of ammonia, nitrogenous fertilizer, caustic potash and PVC. Within the combine, a number of production combinations are effected, for example, capro-lactame is integrated with the manufacture of ammonia. For the satisfaction of the PVC-chloride demand, chloride is produced by the electrolysis of imported rock salt, and from the sodium which is gained simultaneously sodium hydroxide is produced, for use in the alumina factories.

Cement manufacture, brick making and the production of construction elements are based on raw materials found in the region. The two large cement factories at Miskolc and Bélapátfalva were established on the sites of earlier cement plants and utilize the limestone and clay-shale deposits of the Bükk Mountains, while the brick works are based upon the good-quality clays that occur along the foothills of the mountains and in detrital cones. The development of the concrete industry is favourably influenced by the proximity of large users in the region. The gravel pits near Nyékládháza supplies raw material for the production of prefabricated elements for dwellings. Construction panels for flats are produced at Felsőzsolca near Miskolc.

The region's glass manufacture was based on the coal fields as sources of thermal energy rather than on local raw materials. However, almost all factories have now changed over to natural gas. The factories in Salgótarján turn out drawn sheet glass, glass bottles and, on a smaller scale, artistic glass products. Sajószentpéter is a major bottle supplier of the canning industry, while sheet glass for the construction industry in Miskolc and household and artistic glassware are produced at Parádsasvár respectively. In the Hollóháza porcelain factory, which uses the kaolin of the Zemplén Mountain range, household and artistic chinaware are produced, while at Romhány is one of the country's largest wall tile factories.

The most significant of the manufacturing branches of heavy industry is engineering, which plays a relatively less important role in the national economy than the branches discussed so far. This is undoubtedly a negative aspect of industrial development, because the metallurgy base of the region should have permitted the evolution of a much larger engineering industry than the existing one. This was due, partly, to the fact that the region assumed the function of supplying the engineering industry of Budapest with basic materials. After the introduction of the planned economy, this function was further reinforced, while new developments in the engineering industry were channelled mostly towards the industrially undeveloped areas.

With the phasing out of brown-coal mining, the government set up an industrial development fund in order to avoid an economic depression and in order to change the industrial structure of the one-sided, brown-coal mining districts. The greater part of this fund was used in the region, especially in the Nógrád coal field. Small and medium-sized engineering factories, mostly the plants of Budapest enterprises were located in the Sajó valley to absorb the labour displaced by the discontinuance of mining.

The DIMÁVAG Engineering Works, the most important heavy engineering works in the country is linked directly to the Miskolc metallurgy industry. Outstanding among the engineering branches are the large plants of the mass metal industry. the Mátra-Area Metal Works with plants at Sirok, producing aluminium tubes of different sizes, at Salgótarján manufacturing gas- and coal-fuelled stoves, and at Eger, Szécsény and Sátoraljaújhely. Pneumatic elements and compressors for the deep-freezing industry are produced by the Fine Fittings Factory in Eger. A unique plant of the United Incandescent Company is the semi-conductor and chips factory in Gyöngyös, the location of which was based on the pure air of the Mátra region and the availability of labour. The manufacture of telecommunications at Salgótarján, electric automation at Eger and vehicle components also at Eger constitute a turning-point in the region's industrial development. In Sátoraljaújhely bicycles are also manufactured.

The light industry of the region is still insignificant. This important sector is represented by the spinning mill in Miskolc, a few medium-sized clothing factories in Ózd and Salgótarján, the furniture factories in Eger and Encs and the Diósgyőr Paper Factory as well as by plants meeting primarily local demand run by local councils, industrial co-operatives and by the Budapest clothing, knitwear and footwear enterprises.

2.2.2 Agriculture and food processing

Agriculture plays only a secondary role in the region's economy owing to its dominant industrial character and relatively poor physical endowments, although it still adds substantially to the complexity of the region. As a result of relief, soil and climatic factors, a diverse pattern unit of agriculture has come into being. But all in all, the level of the region's agricultural production lags behind the national level.

Owing to the unfavourable physical endowments, the proportion of disadvantaged co-operative farms is rather high. The poor soils of the hill and

Selected data on the agriculture of Northern Hungary,
1977 and 1981

Designation		The share of the country in the national total, percentages	
		1977	1981
Arable area		15	15
Agricultural employment		12	15
Wheat	Volume of output	10	7
Maize		5	6
Spring barley		36	38
Potatoes		14	14
Tobacco		8	7
Grapes		15	16
Cattle	Stock	12	12
Pigs		6	6
Sheep		14	15

mountain areas, soil erosion, alkaline areas, the frequent floods in the Bodrogköz and ground water in the Taktaköz are the main specific factors accounting for this. The labour-absorbing effect of industry also had a detrimental effect in certain areas at a time when the co-operative farms were not strong enough to replace the loss of manpower by machines.

Owing to relief endowments, the pattern of cultivation differs from the national one. Because of the mountains, the percentage of arable is less than 50 per cent of the total area, that of the meadows is low, too, but the proportions of fruit and grapes are slightly above average, as that of pasture. Divergence from the national average is most conspicuous in the relatively high percentage of forest taking up 27 per cent of the area.

In arable cultivation, wheat is the most common crop, but flour milling, except at Selyp and Miskolc, is insignificant. Of the country's grain output barley, especially spring barley in Heves county which favours a cooler and wetter climate, plays an important role. Of the country's two malting barley districts one is to be found in the region, between the Hernád and the Zemplén Mountain range. The Bőcs brewery near Miskolc is oriented partly towards the consumer market, and partly towards the raw material. Maize production is significant in the southern, warmer parts of the region, in the lower valleys of the Zagyva and Tarna rivers and in the plainland between the Tisza and the mountains. In the hill country of Borsod and Nógrád counties potatoes are extensively grown.

Of the two important vegetable-growing districts, the Hatvan area has considerable tradition. The growing of green peas, tomatoes, vegetable marrows, French beans, cucumbers and especially melons is export-oriented, and the Hatvan canning factory processes the products of the region. The Miskolc district has developed only during recent years, as a result of the fresh-vegetable demand of the large industrial population.

Of the industrial crops, sugar beet and tobacco are of national importance. The former is grown in the Zagyva valley, the Hatvan district, Bükkalja, and is particularly important in the Szerencs district. This is also reflected in three sugar refineries operating in Hatvan, Selyp and Szerencs. In Szerencs and Miskolc there are also chocolate factories employing female labour force.

The traditional tobacco-growing area occupies the loose sandy soils of the Tarna valley south of Verpelét and as far as Heves, where the country's best-quality Virginia and garden tobaccos are grown. Of the region's two tobacco factories the one in Eger is the only domestic producer of quality cigarettes and cigars, while the Sátoraljaújhely factory produces mass quality cigarettes.

A characteristic feature of the region is vine cultivation and wine production, and given the favourable relief, climate and soil, as well as long tradition, three historical vine-growing districts producing high-quality wines have evolved.

The wine district of Tokajhegyalja, producing the best white wines in the country well-known throughout the world, is situated on the southern slopes of the Zemplén Mountain range, and has recently been restructured. The Bükkalja district, embracing Miskolc and the sourrounding area, can also be ranked among the historical wine districts.

The restructuring of the Eger wine district only began in recent years with the aim of growing more of the grapes that yield the typical red Bull's blood wine. The Mátraalja wine district, noted for its white wines, extends, with minor interruptions, across the area between the Zagyva and Tarna valleys. Quality varies, and vintage wines are grown mostly in the Gyöngyös area, where dessert-grape production is also significant, and in the settlements of Abasár, Visonta, Domoszló, Feldebrő and Verpelét, east of Gyöngyös.

The processing of the grapes is carried out by the modern wine combines at Eger, Gyöngyöstarján, Gyöngyös, Tarcal, Mád, Tokaj, Tolcsva and Sátoraljaújhely, where excellent cellars for storage can be built in the loose tufas of the area. The region accounts for only 15 per cent of the country's wine-growing area, but the significance of its production, in terms of value, far exceeds this.

A variety of orchard districts has evolved along the foot of the mountains, accounting for 11 to 13 per cent of the country's fruit production. Prominent are the Gyöngyös and Eger districts noted for their cherries, apricots and peaches, the Tokajhegyalja district with its apricots and apples and Bodrogköz noted for its apples.

The importance of animal husbandry in the region tends to be below the national average, the sheep population alone is relatively high, and livestock hardly account for 40 per cent of the gross production value of agriculture. Cattle rearing is only developed in the Zagyva valley and on the eastern fringes of the region. The pig population is relatively evenly dispersed, with higher densities occurring in the maize-growing areas of the southern part of Borsod county. As a result of the establishment of several large pig-rearing farms in the region, slaughter animal output has increased. Sheep are bred primarily on the hill pastures, and show a particular concentration in the poorer karst regions of northern Borsod county.

The region's meat industry satisfies mainly local needs, except for the high-capacity slaughterhouse and meat-processing plant in Miskolc.

As a result of the large forest assets of the region, forestry and timber production are significant. The hardwood stock plays an important role especially in supplying the building industry, and saw mills and timber-processing plants are located around the forest peripheries.

2.2.3 Transport

The region is fairly well supplied with transport routes. The completely electrified railway line serving Budapest, Hatvan, Szerencs, Nyíregyháza and Záhony crosses the axis of the region. The density of traffic on this line is extremely high, and it carries the region's basic materials of coal, steel, building materials and chemicals westwards, to the Budapest agglomeration, and as well as bringing in the raw materials for the metallurgical industry from the Soviet Union. This main line, with its branches, can handle the entire traffic of the region.

The road network is well connected with the national trunk system 3, and within the foreseeable future the M-3 motorway will reach Miskolc from Budapest. Commuter traffic is heavy around the industrial centres.

2.2.4 Tourism

Owing to a variety of natural landscapes, the existence of medicinal springs and the wealth of historical and architectural features, the region's tourist potential is considerable, but before this potential can fully be realized, the trade, hotel and transport infrastructure will have to be further developed, despite the progress made over the last few decades.

The Northern Middle Mountains offer, if only to a modest extent, opportunities for mountain hiking, climatic recreation and cures and, weather permitting, winter sports. The capacity of tourist accommodation is best developed in the Mátra Mountains, where several small mountain resorts can be found as at Mátrafüred, Mátraháza, Galyatető and Parád with its medicinal bath. Much less advantage has been taken of the tourist potential of the Bükk Mountains although their natural beauty, karst formations, the Bükk National Park and the Lipica studfarm attract thousands of tourists each year. The centres of Bükk tourism are Szilvásvárad, Eger and Lillafüred near Miskolc.

The karst cave system at Aggtelek is a rare natural asset even by international standards, but the overwhelming majority of visitors are Hungarians as international tourist traffic is impeded by the poor accessibility of the area. The easternmost mountains of the country form the Zemplén Mountain range, although rich in natural beauties, have been inadequately exploited as yet. The Tokaj wine district which is part of the range has not even been taken into account as a potential tourist attraction. The wine-growing areas of Austria and the Rhine valley bear evidence of the extent, given appropriate encouragement to which such districts can become sizeable tourist centres.

The medicinal baths of the region have undergone considerable development over the past years and the warm water baths of Eger and Miskolctapolca have won great popularity. The saline baths at Bükkszék and the thermal medicinal baths at Mezőkövesd, Kács and Bogács on the southern fringes of the Bükk have also become well-known. In addition to the efforts of state and local council enterprise, the population at large have helped with the development of the infrastructure of these medicinal baths by building weekend houses in their surroundings. In summer and at weekends, many tourists from the neighbouring Slovakia visit these baths.

Along with the tourist assets already mentioned, the historical monuments of the region's towns, particularly Eger, and cultural centres like Sárospatak, as well as the relics of folk art at Palócföld and Mezőkövesd, and folk architecture at Hollókő and Buják also attract significant domestic and foreign tourist traffic.

2.3 Population

With a population density of 102 per sq km, the region is second only to the central region in the country. But whereas the industrially developed areas stand out with their high population densities, the population density of agricultural areas is low. It is especially low in the Bükk Mountains and in the karst district of northern Borsod county.

As a result of industrialization, the region was for a long time an important focus of in-migration, attracted by the opportunities existing in the industrial settlements of the Nógrád basin, the Zagyva valley, the Ózd basin, and the towns to the west of the Hernád river. However, since economic development did not affect western Nógrád, northern and southern Heves, or the tiny village settlements east of the Hernád valley, these areas have tended to lose population. In-migration from the Great Plain was substantial.

More recently, the migration balance of the region has altered and out-movements now exceed in-movements. This is due partly to the fact that the attraction of the Budapest agglomeration has had a strong impact on the western parts of the region, particularly on Nógrád county and even more so on Heves. Moreover, extensive economic development, which used to attract labour into the region, is slowly being phased out, and as a result the number of new jobs has tended to decrease.

2.4 Settlement

The main characteristics of the settlement network comprise an even spread of towns to the west of the Sajó river, and with the exception of peripherally located Sátoraljaújhely and Sárospatak, a lack of urban centres further east, where a dense small-village network can be found. The settlement networks of Heves and Nógrád counties are sparse, especially in the Mátra and Bükk Mountains with their scattered mountain settlements and resorts, while to the south of the main railway line there is a sparse settlement network similar to that of the Great Plain, comprising large villages with extensive hinterlands.

As a result of industrialization and urbanization, a considerable portion of the settlements of the region have undergone a radical transformation, although the proportion of the urban population, at around 50 per cent, is below the national average.

In the vicinity of industrial complexes and mining operations many settlements have rapidly lost their agricultural character, even though agriculture continues to perform a secondary function, and mining and industry have become the determinants of the occupational pattern. In the above „semi-urbanized" settlements the old rural community cores have either entirely disappeared or dwindled in size, and mining or industrial housing estates of multi-storey blocks, or modern family homes can be found in their place. Such processes have occurred at Nagybátony, Edelény, Rudabánya and Hódoscsépány. The settlements of the Mátraalja and Eger wine-growing districts have also undergone radical change, especially those in which families draw their incomes from several sources. Although the infrastructure of urbanizing settlements still leaves much to be desired, it is rapidly improving, particularly with regard to water supply.

The development of the industrial towns and county seats of the region has also been dynamic and varied. Together with the large industrial complexes, two new socialist towns, Kazincbarcika and Leninváros have also been built.

2.5 Subregions and urban hinterlands

a) The Sajó valley agglomeration is the country's largest industrial concentration, outside the Budapest agglomeration, and comprises industrial centres and satellite and dormitory towns alike. Its focus is Miskolc, which is a regional centre, and the second largest city of the country, with a population of 207 000. It developed as one of the market towns on the fringe of the Northern Mountain range, while nearby Diósgyőr was built as a typical company town during the 19th century. Later, the two settlements completely coalesced. Favourable communications in the foreground of the Sajó area and nearby raw materials promoted the industrialization of the city. Until quite recently, the city had a neglected look about it, but extensive development has gone a long way towards remedying this. A great problem for further development, however, is its location in a long valley, which has prevented transverse expansion. As a result, expansion has tended to be concentrated in the mouth of the valley. It has been a primary task of urban development to strengthen both the industrial and general urban functions of the city, and its importance in the commerce of the region is now greater than before. At the same time it has also become a significant centre of higher education with its technical university, and a cultural, health and tourist centre. It has also absorbed such recreational and resort places as Lillafüred along with adjacent areas of the Bükk Mountains and Miskolc-Tapolcafürdő. Kazincbarcika is a satellite town of the agglomeration north of Miskolc, and together these two towns along with the other settlements of the Sajó valley, now constitute a kind of conurbation. Kazincbarcika has grown out of the amalgamation of a few minor settlements to which have been added modern urban districts. It has a population of 37 thousand, and is the centre of coal mining in the Sajó valley as well as serving a highly important role in the chemical industry. Leninváros, with 19 000 inhabitants is another satellite town of Miskolc, and is the centre of olefine chemistry. For the time being, the prime function of both satellite towns is industrial.

The centre of a minor industrial concentration in the northern part of the Sajó valley is Ózd, with 48 000 inhabitants. The town itself originated as a company town, and came about as a result of development of metallurgical activities and coal mining in the surrounding area. With the construction of several new housing estates and the creation of new urban functions, it has undergone a rapid transformation.

b) The Hernád valley subregion. Predominant in the dense settlement network of this area are small and tiny villages. Their economies are determined basically by agriculture but their farms tend to operate under unfavourable physical conditions. Owing to out-migration, their population is on the decrease, and the proportion of the elderly among the inhabitants of the tiny villages has greatly risen. Daily commuting to the industrial settlements of the Sajó valley has grown significantly.

c) The Zemplén Mountain range and Bodrogköz may be conceived of as a subregion encompassing a number of attraction zones and isolated areas. Its economic profile is agriculture, in which a prominent role is played by the fruit, grape and wine production of the Tokaj district and by the agriculture and animal husbandry of Bodrogköz. Quarrying in the Zemplén Mountain range supplies important raw materials to the country's industry.

Sátoraljaújhely, with 19 000 inhabitants, was in a disadvantaged position for a long time, owing to its peripherial location, but industrialization has now largely changed this. The town manages the wine production and wine marketing of the Tokajhegyalja district. Sárospatak, with a population of 15 000 an ancient town, famous for its cultural institution, historical monuments and schools. On the southern fringe of the mountain range is situated Szerencs, a centre of food processing and a railway junction. Typical settlements of the Tokaj wine-growing district, which formerly had wine-trading functions, are Tokaj, Mád, Tállya, Tarcal, and Tolcsva, with their large stone houses and rows of wine cellars caved in the tufa.

d) Eger, with 61 000 inhabitants, is the administrative centre of Heves county, has a significant hinterland extending across the eastern and southern parts of the county. A town of historic traditions, an episcopal seat, a fortress and a market town — these mark the course of its development. Up to recent times, its economic activity was centred almost exclusively on the production of quality wines of nationwide repute, but industrial development has now speeded up, and it has become a centre of the engineering industry. In addition, its other urban functions have also been expanded. Its educational function has been strengthened by an establishment of a college, and its historical, architectural and other artistic relics have made it the best-known cultural centre of the region. Besides these assets, its medicinal waters are also significant tourist attractions. Although it is located off the main roads and railway lines, yet, being the freight and passenger node of the western Bükk, its transportation function is also noteworthy. Eger's geographical location, with the historical town centre lying in the valley of the Eger brook and with residential parts and wine cellars spreading up the sides of the valley, is picturesque, but the expansion of uniform estates of prefabricated housing constitutes a threat to its beauty.

Gyöngyös, with 37 000 inhabitants, is the centre of the Mátra area. As a centre of the Mátraalja wine district, it used to perform purely as a market town, but industrialization has given a boost to its development and it is now an engineering centre. The lignite mining and electricity generation that is carried on near Visonta, whose workers live in Gyöngyös, has exerted a positive impact on the town's development.

Hatvan, with a population of 25 000, is located at the southern end of the Zagyva valley, and is an important transport, trade and industrial centre. Its food-processing industry is of national importance. The transformation of this former agricultural-type settlement into one with urban character is under way.

e) Salgótarján, with 49 000 inhabitants, is the county-town of Nógrád and the centre of the industrial complex of the upper Zagyva valley. The greater part of the smaller settlements around it have now merged with the town. Its economy was originally based on coal mining, and then on the steel and glass industries. Now, as a result of the location of engineering and light industry in the town, its industrial pattern is in the process of transformation. It used to be a typical Hungarian industrial settlement with neglected parts, but following redevelopment, it now boasts the most up-to-date city centre of the country, which is noteworthy from an architectural point of view.

f) West-Nógrád is an area of indefinite agricultural character. It fringes on Pest county and its settlements have increasingly come to form part of the hinterland of the Budapest agglomeration and of the towns of Vác and Gödöllő. Balassagyarmat, of peripheral character, it the only town of the subregion. It is located in the Ipoly valley and has a population of 18 000. For a long time Balassagyarmat stagnated, having lost its former county-town function, but industrialization has given an impetus to its development. It is a school centre and the cultural heart of Palóc land.

3 The economic–planning region of the Northern Great Plain

Administratively, the region comprises the three Great Plain counties of Szolnok, Hajdú-Bihar and Szabolcs-Szatmár. It occupies about one-fifth of the national area, and contains close to one-sixth of the population of the country. Population density, at 88 per sq km, is slightly lower than that of the more industrialized Northern Hungarian and Northern Transdanubian regions, but is higher than that of the other less industrialized regions of Southern Transdanubia and the Southern Great Plain.

The Northern Great Plain shows little variety in relief. Nevertheless, there are significant differences among its western, central and north-eastern parts as regards soils and agricultural land use, and it was for this reason that the region used to be divided into the Middle-Tisza and Upper-Tisza meso-regions. But while the Middle-Tisza area roughly covering the area of Szolnok county, exhibits a more or less homogeneous economic structure, the Upper-Tisza area is more heterogeneous including as it does the Hajdúság and the Nyírség, and this caused quite a few problems when the production profile and economic spatial structure of the region had to be defined. Despite this diversity, however, there are also common features, which make it possible to assess the problems and define the development possibilities of the region as a whole.

Of all the economic-planning regions it is here that the level of industrialization and urbanization is the lowest, and this calls for further accelerated and concerted development. Given its erratic climate with frequent droughts, it has required the elaboration of a comprehensive (regionwide) plan to ensure irrigation for agriculture and adequate supplies for industry and the population.

The region is also characterized by a scarcity of the region's mineral and energy sources, on the one hand, and an excellent agricultural potential, on the other. Its only energy source is natural gas, and for electricity it has to rely on supplies from other regions.

All the significant towns between Szolnok and Záhony lie on a common line of communication which therefore forms a kind of development axis. Moreover, its proximity to the Soviet Union involves advantages in raw-material and energy supply.

The city of Debrecen is located at the centre of the region. Its hinterland extends over the county of Szabolcs-Szatmár and over most of Szolnok county east of the Tisza river. Only the Jászság is problematical from the point of intra-region communication as it is oriented towards the central region rather than Debrecen.

The location of the two regional subcentres, Nyíregyháza and Szolnok is also reasonably symmetrical. Nyíregyháza can exert its influence to the north, and Szolnok to the west of Debrecen, in areas where the central region only asserts a negligible attraction.

The region's industry has developed from a very low level. In the mid-1960s, Szabolcs-Szatmár county and the majority of the towns in the Nagykunság and Kunság, too were still industrially undeveloped. Out-migration was substantial with people searching for jobs in the central or northern regions, where they either settled, or to which they commuted, and even today the region remains the country's most significant area of long-distance commuting with about 80 000 persons travelling to workplaces in other regions.

During the 1970s, the industrialization and urbanization of the region developed rapidly. Several large villages gained urban status and thereby became centres of industrial development. The framework for further development has thus been largely established in the more important settlements.

3.1 Natural endowments and resources

The geological basement of the Northern Great Plain consists of the remnants of a heavy fractured Paleolithic and Mesolithic block structure, made up of gneisses, mudstones, dolomites, limestones and marl lying at a depth of about 1·5 to 3000 meters below the present surface.

A great part of this area was dryland during the Pliocene but from the mid-Miocene the rimes of the basin gradually submerged. In the shallow Pannonian inland that formed between 1 and 2000 meters of clays, marls and sands were deposited in which during the mid-Pleistocene era the Pannonian sea gradually regressed, and the basin was slowly filled up by the alluvial deposits of rivers that flowed into it. The present surface of this area is covered mainly by alluvial and wind-blown formations of Quaternary age [52].

The most important mineral deposits of the Northern Great Plain are the natural gas fields around Hajdúszoboszló and Biharnagybajom. Also significant are the thermal waters found at Hajdúszoboszló, Karcag-Berekfürdő and Cserkeszőlő, which were discovered during the prospecting for petroleum and natural gas and which are used mainly for balneary purposes, while the extensive clay mineral deposits ensure the raw-material base for brick and tile manufacture.

The climate of the Northern Great Plain is more continental than that of the rest of the country and it is here that the range of temperature shows greatest fluctuations. The area is located at the centre of the basin and the air masses crossing it are, to a certain extent, of a főhn character. This usually produces dry, clear weather, erratic precipitation and often droughts, which are likely to occur every few years in the Middle-Tisza section of the region. This physiographic fact explains why one-third of the country's irrigated area, about 300 000 hectares, is to be found in this region.

The number of hours of sunshine is generally high (2050 hours annually), but tends to decline towards the north-east. The mean annual temperature is around 10 °C, dropping to −3 °C in January and rising to 22 °C in June. Predominant among its crops are those that mature in autumn, mainly maize and wheat in the warmer Nagykunság, and tobacco, potatoes and winter apples in the cooler Nyírség.

Winds usually blow from the mountains towards the centre of the basin, and in early spring, the so-called „wind scourge" frequently causes much damage to the newly sown crops of the Nyírség. Green manuring and sand binding are the usual protective methods.

Average precipitation is lowest in the Szolnok area and the Hortobágy where it is below 500 mm. This, in addition to the high temperature prevailing there, means a relative shortage of moisture, which has to be offset by irrigation.

The largest river of the region is the Tisza, which has the erratic regime typical of a plains area. During floods discharge at Vásárosnamény is 90-times that at low-water, and to balance out the flow a series of dam systems have been built that ensure the water needed for irrigation. So far two dams have been constructed, the one at Tiszalök and the other at Kisköre. A large reservoir is attached to the latter. The Tiszalök Dam supplies the large irrigation systems associated with the Hortobágy Canal, the Eastern Main Canal and the Western Main Canal with water. All three are designed to ensure the irrigation of the Hajdúhát.

The Kisköre Dam is associated with a reservoir of 127 km^2. When fully filled, it will hold about 400 million m^3 of water which will ensure the irrigation of 300 000 hectares of arable land, and the operation of 12 000 hectares of fish ponds as well as satisfying the increasing needs of the industrial plants of the surrounding area.

It is possible to irrigate not only water-intensive cultures like rice and vegetables, but also sugar beet, maize, orchards and pastures, while the irrigation canals also contribute to the water supply of the population. For instance, the regional water works at Debrecen obtains water from the Eastern Main Canal.

The Tisza is navigable as far as Záhony, and is used mainly for transporting stone, chemicals, fertilizers and sugar beet. Smaller rivers in the region are the Szamos and the Körös, and these often cause floods. The great flood catastrophe of 1970, which destroyed several villages, occurred in this area.

The Middle-Tisza section of the region is the lowest-lying area of the country — at 85 to 100 metres above sea level, where the extensive alluvial deposits, often covered with loess, form a perfectly flat plain. In the middle of the region is situated a rather large, low-lying grass steppe, the puszta of the Hortobágy, which is roughly at the same level as the Tisza floodplain. After the regulation of the Tisza, the wet land of the Hortobágy — like those in the Nagykunság — were transformed into poor-quality dry pastures. Even now part of this area is used for extensive livestock breeding, although in recent years irrigated cultures have been expanding in those parts outside the Hortobágy National Park.

East of the Hortobágy, the land gradually rises to 90 to 186 metres above sea level in the upper-Tisza area. The first, slightly higher area extending in a north-south direction is Hajdúhát, and the loess table of the Hajdúság; both are covered by a variable thickness of a fertile loess soil.

Characteristic of the Nyírség are its wind-blown sands, which alternate with lower-lying waterlogged areas. The binding of these sands, like those of the dunes of the Danube–Tisza Mid-region, once constituted a serious problem, which has now been solved.

The Szatmár–Bereg plainland was isolated from the Nyírség by subsidence that occurred during the Pleistocene. The plain is still subsiding, and has been filled up by the deposits of the Tisza, Szamos and several minor tributaries.

The soils of the region are variable. The largest part of the area is covered by various kinds of sandy soils. Typical of the northern parts of the Nyírség are brown forest soils, while wind-blown sandy soils characterize the southern parts. But north-east of Debrecen and west of the Jászság, sandy soils of a chernozem type also occur.

Soils of the best agricultural quality can be found on the loess tables of Szolnok and the Hajdúság and in the northern and southern parts of the Jászság, where they are a type of calcareous chernozem. To the north and south of the Szolnok loess table and to the south of the Hajdúhát, there are extensive meadow chernozem soils, which are also of good quality and can be utilized for the growing of sugar beet.

The Hortobágy and the area extending northwards as far as the Tisza are dominated by meadow solonetz soils of low fertility. Typical of the central part of the Nagykunság and the eastern part of the Jászság as well as of the Berettyó area are the meadow solonetz and various meadow and alluvial soils.

3.2 The economy

Traditionally, this area was a typical agrarian region, the production profile of which was basically determined by large-scale agricultural production. As a result of an excessively polarized territorial division of labour, the raw-produce character of the region was later added, and large quantities of grain, livestock, milk and industrial crops like sugar beet, oil seeds and tobacco were mainly sent to Budapest for processing. In addition, the region was — and still is — the main supplier of potatoes and apples to the domestic and foreign market.

As a result of developments since 1960, the agrarian character of the region has gradually lessened, despite the fact that the volume of agricultural output has grown significantly, and specialization has strengthened. In implementing the policy of locating industry in the countryside, more and more factories have been located in the region which have brought about a radical change in its economic structure. In 1979, the number of people employed in industry amounted to 182 000 persons and was more than the number of people engaged in agriculture. The already existing branches of heavy industry have been strengthened and new ones added. Moreover, as a result of the expansion of the food industry, an increasing proportion of raw agriculture produce is now processed in the region.

3.2.1 Industry

During the past three decades of socialist industrialization, the region's economy has been transformed into one of an industrial-agrarian character. This is also borne out by the fact that in 1979 industry employed 43 per cent, and agriculture 32 per cent of the labour force.

Especially high is the participation of heavy industry, with a share of about 50 per cent, while light industry is represented by 33 and food processing by less than 13 per cent.

Such a high proportion of heavy industry may appear to be surprising in a region poor in minerals and energy sources. This is because the plants most characteristic of the region's industrial profile were established as early as the 1950s, when the main priority of economic policy was the development of heavy industry. It was during these years that such enterprises as the Tisza Chemical Works in Szolnok, the Roll-Bearing Factory in Debrecen, the Refrigerator Factory at Jászberény and the Hajdúság Industrial Works at Téglás were located in the region, with the precise aim of dampening its excessively agrarian character.

The significant headway made by heavy industry is attributable to the combined effect of several favourable factors:

— The neighbouring North-Hungarian region, which at that time still had a one-sidedly basic-material producing character, provided the Northern Great Plain with the possibility of easily securing the iron and steel and the electrical power it needed for the creation of an engineering industry.

— As a result of industrialization and higher living standards, domestic demand increased for products such as ball bearings, refrigerators and washing machines, which formerly had not had an independent production base in the country. New plants had to be established to meet this demand, a significant portion of which were located in the Northern Plain.

Selected industrial data for the Northern Great Plain
economic-planning regions, 1977 and 1981

Designation	Proportion of the national total, percentages	
	1977	1981
People employed in industry (number)	10	12
Value of gross fixed assets (milliom Fts)	7	9
Installed motive power (kW)	6	7
Electricity consumption by industry (1000 kWh)	5	6
Output of selected products		
Natural gas	18	13
Ball bearings	86	95
Sulphuric acid	93	88
Superphosphates	70	68
Washing machines	100	100
Spin dryers	100	100
Vacuum cleaners	100	–
Refrigerators (household)	100	100
Electric boilers	90	90
Synthetic detergents	40	48
Penicillin	100	62
Gymn shoes	100	100
Men's shoes	35	45
Ladies' shoes	25	32
Tobacco (cured)	67	100
Cigarettes	25	25
Vegetable oil	26	58

— The proximity to the Soviet Union has been a great advantage in that Soviet imports destined for the central parts of the country move mostly through the region. Thus the manufacture of superphosphates in Szolnok and the further development of the wood-processing and paper industries as well as the upswing of several export-oriented branches, such as the canning and clothing industries, were all due to this favourable location.

While in the 1950s it was usually the large, independent engineering enterprises that were sited in the region, during the 1960s the branch plants of various large Budapest enterprises were established here, most of them producing subassemblies and components in a close co-operation with their parent enterprises in the capital.

Typical of the production profile of the heavy industry located in the region are the labour-intensive manufacturing branches with relatively small raw materials and energy requirements. This is apparent when the specific indicators of industry located in the region are composed with those for other economic-planning regions.

In 1979, the region accounted for only 8·7 per cent of the gross fixed-asset value of industry nationally, while its share of the industrial labour force was 11 per cent.

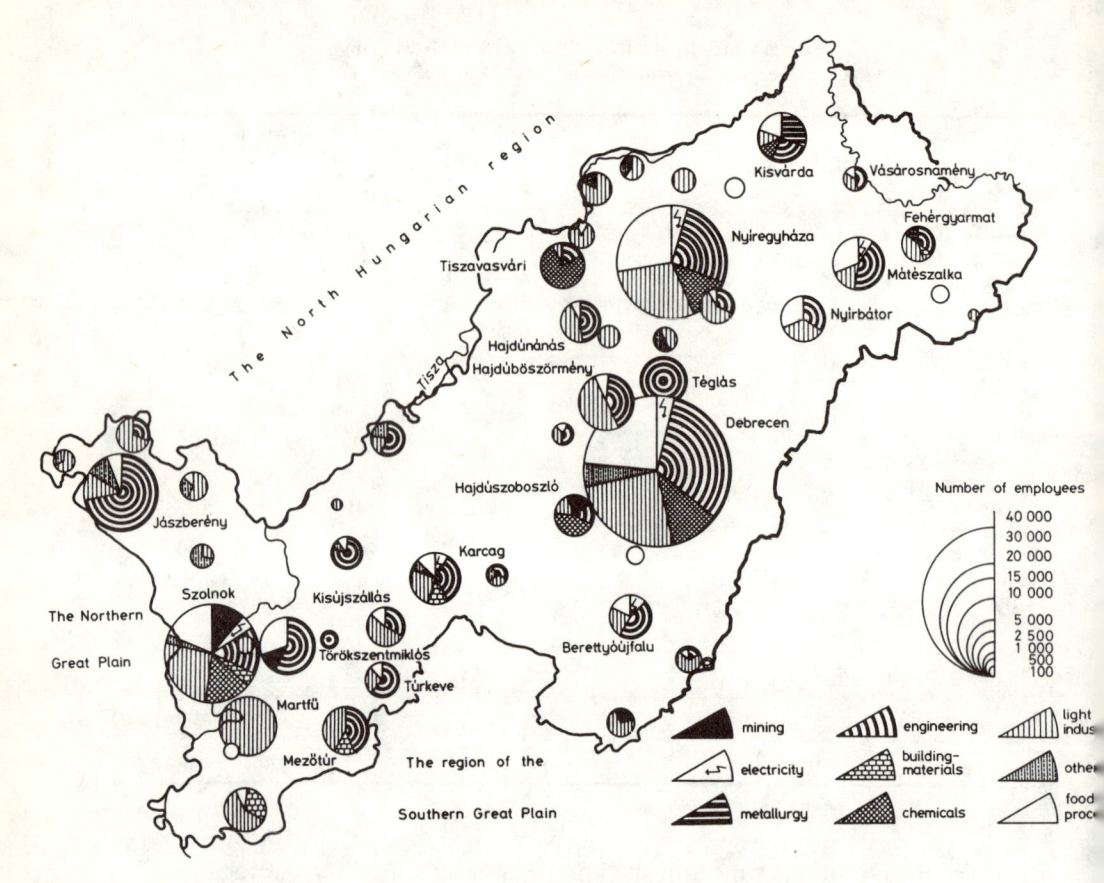

Fig. 66. The spatial location of industry in the economic–planning region
of the Northern Great Plain (1981)

The per capita value of gross industrial fixed assets, 24 000 Fts, is exactly half the national average and barely one-third of that of the North-Hungarian region.

The weight of engineering within industry is significant both in terms of number of employees and volume of output *(Fig. 66),* the most important centre being Debrecen and the nearby Hajdúság.

Outstanding within the engineering industry in Debrecen is its Ball-Bearing Factory, while the existence of a medical university and medical research institute has been instrumental in it becoming the provincial centre for medical instruments manufacture. Moreover, its agricultural tradition was instrumental in bringing about an agricultural machine industry, while its railway-repair shop is of national significance. A telephone-relay factory in the city employs mainly female labour.

It is at Téglás, a village near Debrecen, that the country's largest factory manufacturing electric household appliances is to be found, producing various types of washing machines, spin dryers and electric boilers.

An incandescent filament factory at Hajdúböszörmény, a large metal-processing plant at Berettyóújfalu and a ventillation-equipment factory at Hajdúnánás are other notable industrial establishments.

Jászberény is another significant engineering centre, noted for its refrigerator factory, and a plant manufacturing mineral and coal grinders, presses for brickyards and equipment for the alumina industry.

Along with the Hajdúság and the Jászság, the engineering industry of the Nagykunság and the Nyírség embraces the relatively small and medium-size plants of Szolnok, Törökszentmiklós, Karcag, Tiszafüred, Kisvárda, Mátészalka, Nyírbátor, Fehérgyarmat and Vásárosnamény.

Another significant branch of heavy industry located in the region is the chemical industry, one of its important plants being the Tisza Chemical Works, producing sulphuric acid, superphosphate fertilizers, paints and synthetic detergents. Such locational factors as the relative proximity to the capital, the Tisza river for water supply, good communications, and raw-material import possibilities from other CMEA countries were decisive factors in the siting of this works.

Another sector of the chemical industry involves the manufacture of pharmaceuticals, centred on the Biogal Pharmaceutical Factory at Debrecen, the domestic base for penicillin and antibiotics production. In addition, the Alkaloid Factory at Tiszavasvár produces morphine-based drugs, as well as a range of insecticides and herbicides.

The manufacture of rubber goods is a relatively new sector in the region. Camping articles are produced by a factory in Nyíregyháza built in the 1960s, while of more recent origin is the production of large agricultural tyres. A plastics plant is also to be found in Debrecen, producing pipes and crates as substitutes for non-ferrous metal products.

The largest and most significant light-industrial plant is the Tisza Shoe Factory at Martfű, which is the centre of rubber-soled footwear production. Other shoe factories are to be found at Jászberény, Debrecen and Nyíregyháza, where the main rationale is the employment of female labour.

The timber- and wood-processing industries were once of greater significance than they are now. The Tonett-Furniture Factory in Debrecen, being noted for its deciduous wood products and the manufacture of bent-wood furniture. Nowadays, the Szolnok Paper Factory is based on timber floated down the Tisza, while the Szolnok furniture factory produces mainly kitchen furniture. The Furniture Factory at Mátészalka, and the Wood-Fibre Board Factory at Vásárosnamény are relatively new plants. Also relatively new is the Corrugated Cardboard and Sack Factory at Nyíregyháza, whose location is justified by the demand of the new canning factories of the Trans-Tisza region and the fruit export industry of the Nyírség for packaging materials.

Earlier, the region's textile industry was very undeveloped, but the increasing labour shortage in the capital since the end of the 1960s has induced the location of new textile plants in the provinces where female labour is abundant. The first plants were located in Hajdúböszörmény, and further plants were set up in the 1970s at Újfehértó, Nagykálló and Nagyhalászi, all of which work in collaboration with the textile industry of the capital. As a result of these developments, a new textile manufacturing subregion is emerging in the northern part of the region.

Also the region's excess female labour was responsible for the establishment of two new knitwear factories, one at Mátészalka. The Debrecen Clothing Factory, which produces ladies' wear is the centre of the clothing industry.

The largest brick and tile factories of the building-materials industry are to be found in Szolnok, Mezőtúr, Karcag, Hajdúszoboszló and Debrecen.

3.2.2 Agriculture and food processing

The Northern Great Plain is one of the significant agrarian areas of the country, resulting not only from its favourable physical endowments, but also from its production experience accumulated over many decades, product specialization and the role it plays in domestic food supply and food exports.

The distribution of land-use types, with the emphasis on arable farming clearly reflects the plainland character of the region, which contains close to 22 per cent of the total arable area of Hungary.

The size of its garden, orchard and vineyard areas is second only to that of the Southern Great Plain. While the provision of tractors equals the national average, fertilizer consumption lags somewhat behind.

The average pattern of land use indicates that more than half the arable total of the region is regularly sown to wheat and maize. That wheat occupies the largest sown area of the region, some 26 to 27 per cent of the total, is attributable to fabourable production endowments. More specifically, the proportion in Szolnok county is in excess of one-third, in Hajdú-Bihar county about a quarter, and in Szabolcs-Szatmár county only 17 per cent of the arable area.

The most important areas of wheat production are therefore seen to be the meadow soils of the Nagykunság and the Jászság, i.e. the Szolnok loess table and the adjacent parts, and the Hajdúhát area of the Hajdúság. The wheat grown in these territories is noted for its good baking qualities, due to its high gluten content. The good wheat-growing endowments of the region, however, are not always reflected in the yields, and although the more developed farms on the loess table usually have outstanding records, the average of the region barely reaches half the national average.

Selected agricultural data for the Northern Great
Plain economic-planning region, 1977 and 1981

Designation		Proportion of the national total, percentages	
		1977	1981
Arable land		19	19
Population engaged in agriculture		19	15
Selected products			
Wheat		21	20
Rye		49	45
Rice		60	55
Sunflower seeds	volume of output	28	23
Sugar beet		32	32
Potatoes		28	27
Maize		18	20
Apples		50	59
Tobacco		75	70
Cattle	stock	18	19
Pigs		30	21

Rye is the typical cereal crop of the sandy areas of the region and is mainly grown in Szabocs-Szatmár county where it occupies close 10 per cent of the arable area.

The main bases of the flour-milling industry are located along the Jászberény–Szolnok–Karcag and Debrecen–Hajdúböszörmény–Hajdúnánás railway line, with Törökszentmiklós a major milling centre.

The leading area for rice is Szolnok county, where it is grown on 4 to 5 per cent of the arable land. Rice is the most rational way to utilize alkalide areas, although hours of sunshine, amount of heat and irrigation facilities are also most favourable in these parts. The rice-husking mill at Karcag is the centre of rice processing.

Maize is grown regularly on more than one quarter of the region's arable land, being highest in Hajdú-Bihar county where it accounts for 32 per cent of arable area. It is also high, 28 per cent, in Szabolcs-Szatmár county, despite the rather unfavourable physical endowments, but reaches barely 20 per cent of the total in Szolnok county. However, the average maize output of the region is some 10 per cent lower than the national average.

The cultivation of sunflower occupies fourth place in the region's agricultural land-use pattern, following immediately after wheat, maize and rye. The spread of sunflower growing in the upper-Tisza district was originally related to the regional tradition, whereby the Greek orthodox population consumed only vegetable oils. The largest area is to be found in Szabolcs-Szatmár county where more sunflowers than in the other two counties combined are grown. The sunflowers are processed into vegetable oil at Nyírbátor, which is also noted for producing synthetic detergents. A second vegetable-oil refining plant, the country's largest, was recently built in the etable-oil refining plant, the country's largest, was recently built in the western part of the region, at Martfű, to the south of Szolnok.

Potatoes make up 2 per cent of the region's cultivated land, with Szabolcs-Szatmár being the leading county, and accounting for nearly 30 per cent of the country's area under potatoes.

Sugar beet is one of the region's most important industrial crops, where nearly 30 per cent of all sugar beet is grown. The main areas of cultivation are the Jászság and the Szolnok area as well as the lands south of Debrecen. The good endowments of the region for the sugar beet are borne out by the fact that yields are higher than anywhere else nationally. Until recently, the refinery at Szolnok was the only one in the region, and more than half the beet output had to be transported for processing to other regions. The opening of the country's largest refinery at Kaba, near Debrecen, however has solved this problem.

Tobacco is a characteristic crop of the region, although in area it accounts for only 1 per cent of the region's arable land. 80 per cent of the tobacco-growing area is to be found in the Szabolcs district, whose climatic and soil characteristics are best for the crop. A tobacco-curing plant is located in Nyíregyháza and a research institute of the tobacco industry in Debrecen.

Orchards occupy only 2·5 per cent of the region's arable land, yet, in terms of volume of their production, they constitute one of the most important and the most typical production sector of the region. Four-fifths of the region's orchards are in Szabolcs-Szatmár county, while the other two counties account equally for the rest. In 1935 only 10 per cent of the country's apple trees were to be found in the district of Szabolcs, but this proportion had risen to over 25 per cent by 1975, with most apples being grown in modern large-scale orchards. Szabolcs apples now constitute an important export item. Along with plums, walnuts are another important crop of the Tiszahát with Milota as the centre.

The area under vegetables has expanded significantly over the last two decades, with the opening of two large canning factories in Nyíregyháza and Debrecen in the mid-1960s. Previously, no appreciable fruit processing had existed in the Trans-Tisza area as canning factories had been concentrated predominantly in the Danube–Tisza Mid-region and Southern Transdanubia and up to that time the Trans-Tisza area had largely supplied raw produce to the fruit-processing industry of the Danube-Tisza Mid-region. Vegetable cultivation accounts for close to 2 per cent of the arable area.

It is difficult to define any particular specialization in the region's livestock industry as cattle, pigs, sheep and poultry have equally old traditions and are associated with their own particular districts. This is clearly revealed by an analysis of the various district-specific indices. The cattle density in 1980 was 28 head per 100 hectares of arable land: a higher ratio was recorded only in Transdanubia. Specific pig population was 121 per 100 hectares, ranking third after the Southern Great Plain and the central regions. In terms of standard livestock numbers, the region lies around the national average.

One fifth of the country's cattle population is to be found in the region being particularly associated with the northern and eastern parts of Szabolcs-Szatmár county, the Hortobágy, and the Jászság in Szolnok county. The green fodder area, which could constitute the feed base for intensive cattle breeding, widely varies throughout the region. Although satisfactory in Szabolcs-Szatmár county, it is lucerne, which is less sensitive to drought, that is grown on the largest scale in the region. Yields, however, are below the national average, and cattle density therefore lags behind the desirable standard. The largest milk-processing plants are located in the county towns of Szolnok, Debrecen and Nyíregyháza. In addition, since substantial surplus milk is produced in the extreme east of the region, powdered-milk and cheese factories have also been established in Berettyóújfalu, Mátészalka, Fehérgyarmat and Nyíregyháza.

The region accounts for one-fifth of the country's pig population, with the Hajdúság and Szolnok areas being the most significant. The Nyírség is less important in this respect. The meat-processing industry is mostly to be found in the county towns of Szolnok, Debrecen and Nyíregyháza, but more and more pig-rearing state and co-operative farms operate smaller meat-processing plants of their own, because the expansion of the state meat-processing capacity has lagged behind the abrupt growth in the pig population.

Sheep rearing, owing to extensive alkali pastures, is carried out on a rather large scale, there being about 1 million head in the region. Especially high is the sheep population of the Hortobágy. Lamb exports from the region are significant.

Half the region's poultry stock is to be found in Hajdú-Bihar county, where goose and hen production is particularly developed. Poultry-processing plants operate in all the three counties, at Törökszentmiklós, Debrecen and more recently at Kisvárda.

The region's forestry is of course less significant than that of the mountainous regions, and its timber industry is, therefore, based largely on imported wood. The region's forest assets are poor, consisting mostly of softwood and acacia.

3.2.3 Transport

The region is crossed in an east-west direction by a high capacity transport axis, comprising both road and rail links, which connects the capital via Szolnok, Debrecen, Nyíregyháza and Záhony with the Soviet Union, the country's most important trading partner. The electrified Szolnok–Záhony railway line is the main trunk route of the region, along which several significant junctions have developed, which collect and distribute the traffic handled. The most important junctions are at Szolnok, Szajol, Püspökladány, Debrecen, Nyíregyháza and Záhony.

The main railway running south-east through the region is part of the Budapest–Szolnok–Szajol–Békéscsaba–Lökösháza line, and is also electrified. The branch from Püspökladány to Romania (Northern Transylvania) carries an increasingly significant amount of traffic. The largest railway centre of the region is the transshipment area at Záhony, consisting of several specialized freight yards for transshipment from broad to narrow gauge.

The layout of the road network is very similar, but its development and technical standard for long lagged behind those of the railway. With increasing motorization, however, an intensive road reconstruction programme was begun in the early 1960s, which will result in the completely rebuilding of the network.

The most significant tourist attraction in the region is the Hortobágy, and the romanticism of the puszta attached to it, as well as its thermal baths. To preserve its landscape integrity and specific flora and fauna, the Hortobágy has been declared a national park.

3.3 Population

The region's population is almost 1·6 million, 15 per cent of the national total. The most populated county is Szabolcs–Szatmár with close to 580 000 persons, followed by Hajdú-Bihar county, and then Szolnok with a population of 450 000.

However, the population of the region shows little sign of growth, despite the high natural increase of Szabolcs-Szatmár and Hajdú-Bihar counties because of a traditionally high rate of out-migration in search of job opportunities. The reorganization of agriculture released considerable surplus manpower into the job market which the urban settlements of the region were unable to absorb completely. Only Szolnok, Debrecen and Nyíregyháza, boasting dynamic industries, were able to take up a significant proportion. Although out-migration from the region has since fallen considerably, it has not yet ceased completely, and the migration balance remains negative. Two-thirds of present changes of residence involve movements to urban settlements and half the migrants still settle in Budapest. This can be viewed as an aftermath to the large-scale long-distance commuting which used to exist.

3.4 Settlement

The effects of the physical environment and the specific features of the historical development of the region can still be recognized in the settlement network.

The region's settlement network is dominated by market-town type settlements, particularly in the Nagykunság and the Hajdúság, which represent a special subtype of the Great Plain market town being settlements mainly associated with livestock breeding and grain growing. It is the demands and mainly the development possibilities of these two production sectors that have determined their morphology and provision level, and during the past 100 to 150 years they have therefore had a great many problems to tackle. Since the regulation of the Tisza in the past century, the possibilities of a large-scale extensive livestock breeding have been greatly restricted in the towns of the Nagykunság, such as Törökszentmiklós, Kisújszállás, Karcag, Mezőtúr and Túrkeve. Attempts were made to offset this by increasing grain production, but this only provided an ephemeral solution, because after the grain-growing boom had come to an end, the problems reemerged in even sharper form.

Owing to such long-standing structural problems, the towns of the Nagykunság, even compared with the other towns of the Great Plain, were the least developed with stagnant or declining populations. Even the socialist reorganization of agriculture and regional industrialization were not able immediately to solve this deep-rooted problem, which is why they are still the least developed plainland towns.

The market towns of the Hajdúság have developed along a different path. The so-called Hajduk* evolved as a result of the massive development of the 17th century. Their basic economic activity was also extensive livestock breeding and extensive grain cultivation, but more intensive cultures also appeared. Even so structural problems again emerged which have only partly been resolved by socialist industrialization and agricultural reorganization. Part of the work force thus freed from agriculture have settled in the dynamically growing city of Debrecen and typically, 70 per cent of the people engaged in industry in Hajdú-Bihar county are employed in Debrecen. A similar trend of development has appeared in Szolnok county too, where an appreciable proportion of the surplus labour of the Nagykunság has found employment in the industry of Szolnok town.

The Nyírség displays an entirely different pattern of evolution trend, although Nyíregyháza was forced for a long time to absorb redundant agrarian labour. The agriculture of the Nyírség, however, exactly because of its intensive nature, was not as fast in releasing labour as either in the Hajdúság or in the Nagykunság. Thus, since the mid-1960s, it has been possible to transform the larger district centres performing central functions into settlements of urban rank. Apart from Nyíregyháza, the other towns of the county, Kisvárda, Mátészalka, Nyírbátor, Fehérgyarmat, Vásárosnamény, are relatively new towns. Granting them urban status was justified by the many small villages in their hinterlands, to which they are the supply centres. Nonetheless because

---

* Homeless guerrilla fighters, sometimes highwaymen, who during the Turkish occupation took up arms for the country's freedom, were called Hajduks. They played a decisive role in the victory of István Bocskai, Prince of Transylvania, over the Hapsburgs. It was in acknowledgement of their gallantry that Bocskai settled some 100 000 Haiduks on his estates east of the Tisza.

of a lack of economic centres capable of development, out-migration from these peripheral territories was still substantial.

In the rural settlement network of the region mammoth, medium-sized and small villages are equally to be found. Mammoth villages are especially typical of the Jászság and the northern part of the Nagykunság extending along the Tisza, while certain settlements of the Hajdúság, which have not yet been granted urban status, also belong to this category. A few mammoth villages can also be found in the southern part of Nyírség and along the Tisza, although the latter part of the Nyírség is dominated by medium-sized villages. The so-called Tiszahát and Erdőhát are characterized by small villages.

The disintegrating remnants of the tanya system still exist in the rest of the region, particularly within the hinterlands of the market towns and mammoth villages. In the outlying parts of Szolnok and Hajdú-Bihar counties dispersed tanya types, and in the Nyírség tanya clusters are most frequent. The evolution of these two types is connected with the divergent historical development of the territories in question.

Of the region's population about 40 per cent live in towns, and 60 per cent in villages. This means that the proportion of urban dwellers is below the national average, attributable mainly to the very low urban proportion in Szabolcs-Szatmár county.

3.5 Subregions and urban hinterlands

Given the existing economic structure and production linkages as well as commuter and supply hinterlands, the economic-planning region of the Northern Great Plain can be divided into the following subregions. a) the Jászság, b) Szolnok and its hinterland, c) the Nagykunság, d) Debrecen and its hinterland, e) the Nyírség and f) the Tisza—Szamos interflow.

a) The Jászság has a more or less uniform natural landscape and economy. Its typical agricultural activities are grain, vegetable and industrial crop growing and livestock breeding, centred on the industrial and transport centre of Jászberény with 31 000 inhabitants, which attained a significant engineering function during the 1950s. This was since proved a very viable sector. Its light and food-processing industries are less significant. A considerable part of the agricultural produce of this subregion is processed in Hatvan and Szolnok.

b) Szolnok and its hinterland. Szolnok is the centre of a significant agricultural area, but the production character of the subregion is unequivocally determined by its multifarious and developed industrial activities.

Szolnok, with 77 000 inhabitants, is a high-order centre and a county town. It is also an old an highly important communications centre, which finds expression in the functions it performs as a bridge town, a river harbour and a great railway junction. This has made it possible for Szolnok to become a centre of the vehicle-repair, wood and paper industries, sugar refining and the chemical industry [62]. Here we can also find the petroleum-research institutes and sugar refining of the Great Plain. The town is a cultural centre with several secondary schools and secondary vocational schools. The Szigligeti Theatre and a long-established artists' centre also play a significant role in the town's cultural life.

Apart from its industrial activities, its cultural, educational and health functions are also noteworthy. Szolnok's attraction is particularly strong in a southward direction, where Martfű, a so-called urbanizing mammoth village, is the centre of the region's footwear and vegetable industries. Szolnok's hinterland to the east of the town includes Szajol, a railway junction, and Törökszentmiklós with 26 000 inhabitants, the latter is a major industrial town of the Nagykunság, specializing in flour milling, poultry processing and the manufacture of agricultural machinery. Its granary with a 2000 waggonload capacity stores the grain produce of its area.

c) The Nagykunság subregion encompasses the market towns and mammoth villages that lie east of Törökszentmiklós. Its production profile is still of an agrarian character with wheat and rice cultivation and cattle and sheep rearing. Its industrial activities have not yet developed a definite character, except for the processing of agricultural raw materials, for example, milling, and the manufacture of bricks and glassware. More recently, engineering, wood processing and the production of veterinary materials have also begun to develop.

d) Debrecen and its hinterland. This is the most industrially developed subregion of the Northern Great-Plain region with a high concentration of the engineering and chemical industries, natural-gas extraction, as well as light and food-processing industries. Its agricultural activities are also significant, mainly grain, sugar-beet and vegetable production and pig and cattle rearing. Debrecen, Hajdúszoboszló and the Hortobágy are significant tourist attractions.

With close to 200 000 inhabitants, Debrecen is the third largest city of the country, and the largest city not only of the region but also of the whole Trans-Tisza area. Thanks to its favourable location, it was already a buoyant market town and handicraft centre in the Middle Ages, and its central functions began to develop during the second half of the last century. Of all the towns of the Great Plain only Debrecen has preserved the original plan of the medieval inner town surrounded not by walls but by a moat. With further development, the city has outgrown its former pear-shaped centre, and it has become necessary to free the flow of traffic by building roads parallel with and transverse to the main thoroughfare.

During Hungarian history, Debrecen has twice been the temporary capital of the country. Its functions are varied: it is a significant scientific research and cultural centre, and seat of several universities, for instance, of a university of arts and sciences, a medical university, and several colleges. It also boasts research institutes of nuclear and solar physics and of the tobacco industry. Its health, educational and cultural hinterlands are also significant.

Along with its prominent role in the engineering, light and food-processing industries, it is also the centre of several regional organizations. These together provide the basis for its function as an information, decision-making, market and management centre with an influence extending over the greater part — mostly the Trans-Tisza area — of the region [51].

Hajdúböszörmény, with its 32 000 inhabitants, is the most important of the Hajdú towns, and was, for a long time, a typical market town, associated with grain cultivation and livestock breeding. An engineering and light-industrial function has, however, evolved during the last two decades. Hajdúszoboszló, with 24 000 inhabitants, is noted primarily for this natural-gas output and renowned spa. Its medicinal waters, rich in iodine and bromine, attract a considerable number of foreign tourists. Nádudvar and Kaba are significant centres of the meat-processing and sugar-refining industries.

e) The Nyírség occupies a leading position in the cultivation of potatoes, sunflowers, tobacco and fruit, and vegetables of the region. The centre of the subregion is Nyíregyháza with 108 000 inhabitants, which is both the transport centre and also the major educational-cultural, market and information centre of the upper-Tisza district [6]. Its industry, which is entirely the product of socialist industrialization, has flexibly adjusted to processing the district's agricultural produce, for instance, tobacco curing, deep-freezing, canning and milk processings. At the same time, it also exploits to an increasing extent the advantages deriving from its proximity to the Soviet Union. Its most dynamic phase of development has fallen into the last one and a half decades, when to help resolve the employment problems of the area, several large-scale enterprises were established there. The mammoth villages in the vicinity of Nyíregyháza have gained an industrial character mainly through the spread of textile manufacture.

Kisvárda and Nyírbátor, with 18 000 and 13 000 inhabitants respectively, are small towns increasingly engaged in the food-processing and engineering industries.

f) The Tisza—Szamos interflow. This subregion is a typical small-village area, and a significant role in its production pattern is played by various market-garden cultures, like winter apples, plums and walnuts, and by cattle rearing. Its centres, Mátészalka with 18 000 inhabitants, Fehérgyarmat with 8000 inhabitants, and Vásárosnamény with 9000 inhabitants, are small towns, which have gained urban status during the last ten years.

4 The economic–planning region of the Southern Great Plain

This region embraces the counties of Bács-Kiskun, Csongrád and Békés, and contains close to 20 per cent of the country's territory, but only 14 per cent of its population. Population density, at 80 per km^2, is below the national average.

An earlier regionalization scheme had divided the region into two mesoregions, namely the Danube–Tisza Mid-region and the south-eastern Great Plain. Even now, however, this division has some validity as the region is primarily composed of two areas that are basically different in physical features and economic structure. These are the sand table of the Danube–Tisza Mid-region and the Trans-Tisza area with its loess soils.

Although both territories were for centuries of an agricultural character, which has left its mark on the development of the productive forces and the spatial specialization of production, yet, owing to divergent physical and economic endowments, entirely different development trends have unfolded. Consequently, there are marked disparities in the characteristic features of the Danube–Tisza Mid-region and the southern part of the Trans-Tisza area.

It is difficult to give a definition of the region's economic profile – especially with regard to agrarian production – applicable to all parts of the Southern Great Plain. Nonetheless the endowments, mainly from the viewpoint of the establishment of regional institutions and organizations and their efficient functioning in the three counties, are sufficiently favourable for this area to become an integrated region. Szeged is the regional centre, and despite its excentric location it is here that the main communication axes of the western (Bács-Kiskun county) and eastern (Békés county) parts of the region converge, making Szeged not only the nodal point of the transport network, but also the economic and major organizational focus of the Southern Great Plain. There are no areas of any significant size within the region that are orientated in terms of transport towards other regions.

The locations of the two regional subcentres, Kecskemét and Békéscsaba, are also favourable. They are natural transport and economic nodes, and can perform their tasks in a division of labour with Szeged as the main centre.

Agricultural production was for long the leading branch of the region's economy, although well before 1945 the development towards more intensive sectors had begun, i.e. grape and fruit growing and market gardening in the Danube–Tisza Mid-region and a vertical pig-poultry meat-production system in the southern part of the Trans-Tisza area. These sectors could ensure substantially higher living standards for the population of these areas even on the basis of agrarian production than could the Northern Great Plain with its less intensive production pattern. Therefore, the southern half of the Great Plain was long regarded with respect to both economic and urban development as a relatively advanced plain's area.

The region attained its present characteristic industrial profile largely through the developments of the 1960s, and it was at that time that the first steps were taken to utilize the petroleum resources of the area. The engineering industry also began to develop significantly, while a rubber-, cable-, glass- and porcelain-manufacturing base was created, as a result of which industry began to assume a more pronounced character. In 1979, the industrial labour force accounted for 44 per cent, and agricultural manpower 34 per cent of the region's active earners. Industrial production is increasingly becoming the determinant of the region's profile, although agrarian production and food processing will continue to play a prominent role for a long time to come.

The characteristic sectors of the region's industry are petroleum- and natural-gas production, engineering and the manufacture of building materials, textiles and clothing as well as several branches of the food-processing industry.

The significance of the region's oil and natural gas is shown by the fact that the production of natural gas accounts for 80 per cent and oil for 88 per cent of national output.

4.1 Natural endowments and resources

The geological basement comprises crystalline Paleozoic rocks covered with basin sediments north of the line from Baja to Orosháza and Mesozoic strata, also covered with basin sediment, south of that line. The subsidence of the Great Plain began during the middle-Miocene period, and continued in several stages to a depth of 2000 to 3000 metres. On this basement first the clays, marls and sands of the Pannonian inland sea were laid down, on which rest up to 1000 metres of terrestrial sediments of middle-Pliocene age and younger [52].

The significant petroleum and natural-gas reserves of the region are to be found in rocks of different geological age even over relatively small areas, the actual occurrences depending on rock porosity and the development of the so-called trap-forming factors.

Strata of Pliocene age are the most important source of petroleum resources in the Great Plain. Thus the conglomerate sandstones in the Pusztaföldvár–Battonya area, the so-called Békés and Battonya reservoir, contain petroleum and natural gas, while the Deszk conglomerate at Algyő, in the Ferencszállás–Kiszombor area, petroleum is found in a similar rock formation. The lower-Pannonian sandstones around Makó contain the deepest petroleum reserves in the so-called Makó trench at a depth of over 4100 metres.

Thermal water constitutes a further valuable geological resource of the region, and is used not only for balneological purposes as, for instance, in the town Gyula near the Romanian frontier, but also for heating greenhouses, as, for example, at Szentes. It is in this region, at Tiszakécske, that the country's geothermical gradient is lowest.

Apart from petroleum, mention should also be made of the clay deposits which have long since been used in brick making and the manufacture of tiles and ceramics.

The climate of the region is decidedly continental, but in many respects more favourable than that of the Northern Great Plain. For instance, the zone along the southern state frontier is the country's warmest area, with a mean temperature of -2 °C in January, and over 22 °C in July. The frost-free period lasts for 210 days, which is highly favourable for the cultivation of those plants with a long growing period, such as red peppers and rice. In addition the number of days of frost is lower by 10 to 12 days than in the central parts of the Great Plain, which is advantageous for the growing of early vegetables, especially in combination with thermal-water heating of greenhouses. A further characteristic of the region's climate is the large number of hours of sunshine, ranging from 2000 to 2100 hours annually. The long warm autumns are favourable not only for growing paprika, grapes, fruit, rice and maize, but also for carrying out autumn tillage and autumn-sown cereals.

Temperature differences between the northern and the southern parts of the Danube–Tisza Mid-region are substantial, and can mean as much as a weeks's difference in the maturing of early vegetables, potatoes and fruit. At the same time precipitation is relatively low ranging from 550 to 600 mm per annum, and crops grown on the sandtable usually depend on the abundance of spring water deriving from snow melt. The construction of an irrigation system has been planned for a long time – the idea of the Danube–Tisza Canal first emerged nearly 200 years ago, but has not been carried out as yet.

Annual precipitation in Southern Trans-Tisza is also low, with an average of 120 to 130 wet days a year, which clearly demonstrates the necessity for irrigation. The favourable water economy of the soils of the loess table, in terms of the storage of spring moisture and its slow percolation through the soil, ensures fairly secure crops even during dry periods.

However, flooding can be a hazard during late winter and early spring, and snow melt or heavy spring rain in the river-catchment areas in Romania often lead to floods where river gradients are low.

The water system in the eastern part of the region is fairly well developed with several navigable rivers, such as the Tisza, the Triple Körös and the Maros, while the western fringe is flanked by the Danube. Apart from the Danube, however, no appreciable shipping has developed on these rivers because of the marked fluctuation in their regimes and the absence of appropiate industrial centres. In the previous centuries, however, the floating of timber, and salt and grain transport from Transylvania and the Carpathian Ukraine were significant, and created, for instance, the processing of timber in the towns along the Tisza. Today, the region's rivers play an important role as sources of irrigation and potential, industrial water resources. The development of the region's irrigation systems will be completed with the construction of the Tisza III Dam project at Csongrád, which begun in 1978, while the north-south section of the Danube in the region offers further potential for the expansion of the water-intensive branches of industry.

With regard to surface characteristics, the region can be subdivided into two large meso-regions:

1. The central and southern parts of the Danube—Tisza Mid-region and
2. The Tisza—Maros—Körös region of the Southern Trans-Tisza region.

The sands of the Danube—Tisza-Mid-region lie some 50 metres above the floodplains of the Danube and the Tisza. The highest part of this area is to be found in the south, where elevations of 160 to 170 metres above sea level occur. Most of it is covered with blown sand, but waterlogged marshes and badly drained depressions with saline lakes in places also criss-cross the area. The greater part of the blown sands have already been bound and are utilized for grape and fruit growing, but wedged in between the sandy areas between Kecskemét and Csongrád there is an extensive area of loess, suitable for the growing of arable crops.

The Danube plainland, for the most part, was a marshy area before the river was regulated during the mid-19th century, and dispersed settlements were built on the higher parts. Apart from the young alluvial soils fronting the river, most of the valley comprises meadow soils and poor-quality alkaline soils. Although only a small part of the Bácska loess table belongs to Hungary, its high-quality soils have made it a prominent grain- and fruit-growing area.

In the evolution of the Tisza—Maros—Körös area, a great role was played by the Maros and Körös rivers which, flowing from Transylvania, formed an extensive detrital cone during the late Tertiary, on which fine-grained sediments were later deposited. In addition, aeolian action during the Quaternary led to the formation of the loess cover which is found throughout much of the region, but which is now separated from the blown-sand areas by the young floodplains of the Körös, Tisza and Maros rivers.

The Körös area encompasses a triangular-shaped territory bounded by the Berettyó and the Körös rivers. It is covered, for the most part, with floodplain alluvial fans, which, since drainage regulation, have became alkaline. These areas are utilized today for irrigation cultivation.

The soil types of the region widely vary, with the loess-based meadow soils being the best in quality. As a result of the continental climate, various meadow soils have developed on the higher parts of the sandy tablelands and detrital cones of the southern Trans-Tisza region (the Békés—Csanád loess table) and in the southern part of the Danube—Tisza Mid-region (the Bácska loess table). The best among them are the 2 to 5 m thick chernozem-type, humus-rich brown meadow soils developed on the loess table, which are particularly suitable for growing maize, sugar beet and lucerne [2].

Sandy meadow soils dominate the Danube—Tisza Mid-region. They too are of a fairly good quality, but require additional nutrients, while traditional arable yields are lower than those from the loess-based meadow soils. Sandy calcareous soils which rapidly warm up, are particularly suited for grape and fruit growing.

Owing to the low-lying nature of much of the area, alkaline soils occupy extensive territories, but while calcareous sodic alkaline soils are more common on the sandtable, it is leached alkaline soils that predominate in the Trans-Tisza area where they are utilized for rice growing and as pastures. The best-known alkaline lake of the Great Plain is Fehértó (White Lake) near Szeged, which, owing to its unique assemblage of waterfowl, is a nature reserve. The varied alluvial soils of the floodplains are, in essence, only skeletal soils, although it is on these that the main vegetable-growing areas around Makó, Szeged, Szentes and Gyula have evolved.

4.2 The economy

As a result of the developments of the last few decades, the earlier, one-sidedly agrarian character of the region has undergone a significant change and has increasingly been transformed into one of an industrial-agrarian character. This is also indicated by the fact that during the last few years the number and the proportion of the labour force employed in industry have surpassed those engaged in agriculture.

4.2.1 Industry

12 per cent of the country's industrial population works in the Southern Great Plain region. Although this percentage is lower than the corresponding territorial and population proportions the significant development that have taken place must not be underestimated. In terms of relative industrial weight, the region is about equal to Southern Transdanubia but substantially ahead of the Northern Great Plain.

Within industry, the balance between heavy and light industry is approximately equal in term of employment, which is all the more noteworthy as it was formerly the light and food-processing industries that determined the profile of the region. This has come about entirely as a result of the more dynamic development of heavy industry. At the same time, several plants of the light and food-processing industries have been located in the region, further reinforcing the vertical production systems, which have become particularly marked in food processing.

Selected industrial data for the Southern Great Plain, 1977 and 1981

Designation	Percentage of the national total	
	1977	1981
Persons employed in industry	11	12
Gross fixed-asset value (million Fts)	8	8
Installed motive power (kW)	6	6
Electricity consumption by industry (1000 kWh)	6	6
Output of selected products		
Natural gas	80	79
Petroleum	90	86
Cast-iron bath tubs	95	100
Tape recorders	95	90
Scales	93	90
Semiporcelain household equipment	97	86
Blown glassware (bottles and glasses)	60	64
Drawn-sheet glass	55	50
Winter salami	72	84
Dry sausage (Gyula)	94	100
Red-pepper powder	100	100

As a result of the high proportion of light and food-processing industries, the region's share in the gross fixed-asset stock of domestic industry is only 8 per cent, and still lower at 6.6 per cent, is the region's share of installed motive power and electricity consumed by industry.

Thus we can state that the capital invested in the region's industry encompasses mainly the sectors poor in energy. This follows partly from the specific sectoral pattern of industry, and partly from the energy shortage, traditionally deemed to affect the region. For the lack of necessary energy sources, no significant capacity to generate electricity has been developed so far in the region, although it has had a significant energy base of its own since the early 1960s, when the more vigorous exploitation of its petroleum resources was begun.

Within heavy industry, the production of oil and natural gas at Algyő, Üllés, Szank and more recently Kiskunhalas is worth mentioning. Through the Szeged–Kecskemét pipeline system, the region supplies significant quantities of gas to the national grid, which is transmitted mainly to Budapest and the Central-Transdanubian Industrial District. Except for rubber, no significant branches of the chemical industry have been based on the natural gas resources of the region. It is only the building-materials industry, through such establishments as the Orosháza Glass Factory and the Porcelain Factory at Hódmezővásárhely, that has made any appreciable use of natural gas.

The development of the region's heavy industry was for long characterized by the dearth of energy and the lack of an appropriate professional culture. The development of the engineering industry was concentrated mainly in the central part of the Danube–Tisza Mid-region, and materialized predominant-

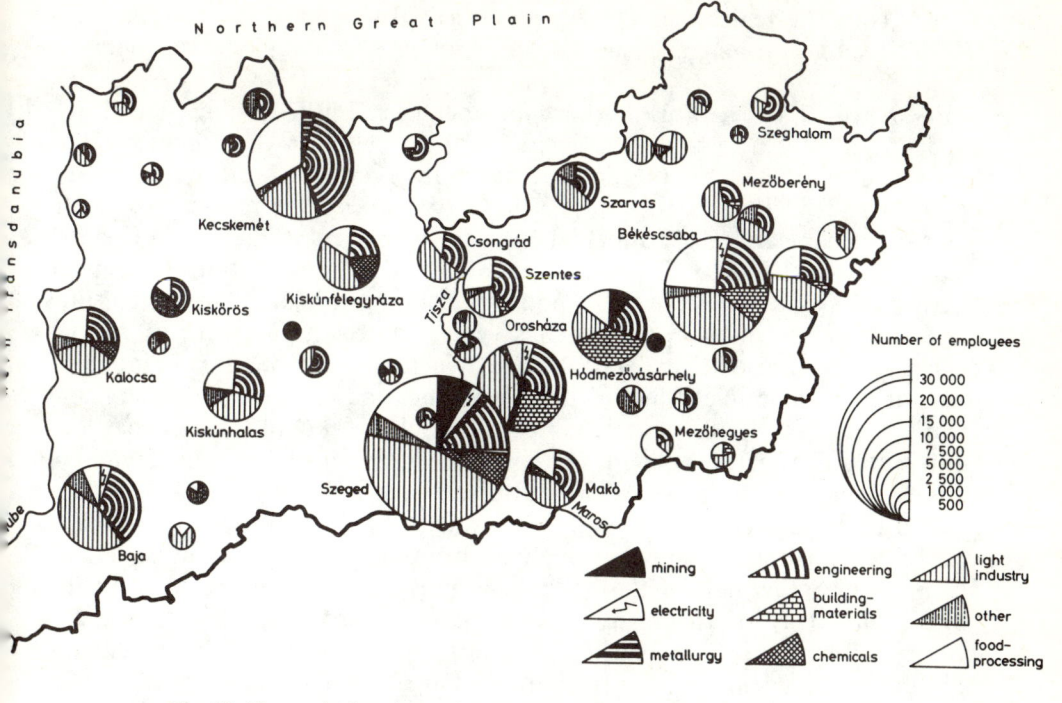

Fig. 67. The spatial location of industry in the economic—planning region
of the Southern Great Plain (1981)

ly in metal-manufacturing branches demanding little energy and no special professional skill or expertise. Such establishments were the Bath-Tub Factory in Kecskemét, the Mining-Equipment Factory and the Metal-Fittings Factory at Kiskunfélegyháza, the cutting Machine-Tool Factory at Békéscsaba and a scales factory at Hódmezővásárhely.

In the 1950s, the profiles of the individual plants were often poorly chosen and had to be modified later. This was a common feature in regions lacking an appropriate production tradition.

In the early 1960s, the location of industrial establishments, for example, factories manufacturing various steel structures, took place roughly in the same manner. Their siting in the Southern Great Plain was justified by the fact that they were designed to serve the development of agricultural infrastructure such as, for instance, supplying water to agricultural farms and villages, and the building of produce-storage facilities and livestock farms. Later, light-structure buildings came into the foreground, which also depended on iron and steel products. Since the mid-1960s, such plants have been established in increasing numbers and testify to the spread of a general technical culture. Such are, for example, factories manufacturing electric motors and other electrical appliances in Baja, Szentes, Kecskemét and

399

Gyula. Thus the region has developed, along with its light-structure industry *(Fig. 67)*, precision engineering, telecommunications and electrical engineering.

In Szeged, a large Cable Factory has been established, which has developed an entirely new and significant production line in the region's industry. The development of the engineering industry was also promoted by the programme to relocate the capital's industry and by the massive establishment of provincial factory units, such as the Compressor Factory in Kiskunhalas, the Hand-Tool Factory in Kecskemét, the Construction-Equipment Factory in Kalocsa and the Gas-Appliance Factory at Makó. The agricultural machine-building industry, which has evolved from the network of discontinued agricultural machine stations and which either specializes in independent machine manufacturing or supplies fittings and components to large enterprises (e.g. in Kecskemét, Hódmezővásárhely, Makó and Békés) has also contributed to the development of the engineering industry. Council- and cooperative-managed industry has also displayed a significant development.

Before 1945, the building-materials industry of the Southern Great Plain was of national significance through its brick and tile manufacture as, for example, in Szeged and Békéscsaba. The basis for this was provided by the good-quality clay of the region. The region was also noted for its peasant-pottery industry. Since the early 1960s, however, a new phase of the region's building-materials industry has evolved. Large enterprises were located in Hódmezővásárhely and Orosháza for the local utilization of the newly discovered natural gas. Hódmezővásárhely exemplifies how a traditional handicraft industry can develop into a modern large-scale industry, provided the other necessary conditions are created. The town had long been famous for its pottery industry, and it was on this basis that the majolika factory had been set up there before 1945. In the mid-1960s, this development continued with the establishment of the Porcelain Factory of the Great Plain, which now has separate divisions for household, sanitary and tile manufacture. The Glass Factory at Orosháza is also energy-intensive having both a blown-glass and sheet-glass plants.

Significant parts of the construction industry are the prefabrication yards in Szeged and Kecskemét, which play an important role in the fulfilment of the region's housing programme.

The chemical industry is represanted in the region by the rubber industry with one of the country's largest factories in Szeged. It manufactures various rubber products for industrial use.

Among the branches of light industry, it was the hemp, timber, carpet and knitwear industries that had attained some importance in the region already before 1945. The textile industry in its classical sense was only represented by a few small plants. They processed mostly industrial crops, primarily hemp.

The Szeged Textile Combine, one of the most important ligh-industrial plants of the region, was established within the industrialization programme of the 1950s. For the substitution of western fibre imports first a cotton-spinning plant was set up, to which weaving and finishing plants were later attached, thus establishing a truly vertical complex.

The Szeged Clothing Factory, also a product of the first period of socialist industrialization, was for long the centre of the domestic manufacture of working clothes, although during recent years it has changed over to the production of higher-quality lines.

The knitwear industry of the region is well developed, having already been based on cheap female labour before 1945. Here are to be found the country's two largest fashion-knitwear factories, the HÓDIKÖT in Hódmezővásárhely, with several plants in the small towns of the Great Plain, and another in Kiskunhalas. Further significant plants are in Békéscsaba, Gyula and Gyoma.

The region is also noted for its carpet-weaving industry, which has developed as a cottage industry mainly in the large villages of Békés county, also based on female labour force. Since 1945, they have further developed in the form of co-operatives and have become significant medium-sized plants. They produce both eastern- and modern-type carpets, in an appreciable volume for export, too.

The significant concentration of the hemp industry in the region is due to the fact that the Southern Great Plain, especially Békés county and the eastern part of Csongrád county, constitute one of the most important hemp-growing districts of the country. For the processing of hemp, plants were established in areas with appropriate water supply quite a long time ago. Most important is the Hemp-Spinning Plant in Szeged, which also processes jute and synthetic fibre.

A significant wood-working industry has evolved on the base of timber floated down the rivers Tisza and Maros, and for the satisfaction of local demand. Wood working in the Szeged area had long been promoted by the demand of the joiner's trade and by the demand of the intensive growing of vegetables and fruit and of the preserving industry for cases and crates as packaging materials. This has made Szeged the centre not only of the timber trade, but also of timber processing, and a vertically complete conifer-processing system has evolved in the town. Furniture, case, and shutter factories and plants of the carpenter's trade also exist in several of the small towns of the region. Szeged is also noted for its manufacture of musical instruments.

The printing trade of the region is based on the old artistic traditions of the firms Tevan and Kner at Békéscsaba and Gyoma, respectively. They have since undergone substantial reconstruction and development.

The woollen industry has a few smaller plants in the Danube–Tisza Mid-region, for instance, at Baja, Bácsalmás and Kiskunfélegyháza.

4.2.2 Agriculture and the food processing

The agriculture of the Southern Great Plain is of greater significance and more advanced than that of the Northern Great Plain. The intensity of its agrarian production is, on the whole, still higher, and is characterized not only by its better adjustment to the endowments of the landscape, but by its superior economic results to those attained in the Northern Great Plain.

This distribution of land use clearly reflects the specializations based on decades of tradition. The proportion of arable land is high, 60 per cent, and more than 80 per cent of all the land is utilized for agricultural purposes. The proportion of forested area is barely 9 per cent.

The nationwide significance of the Southern Great Plain is indicated by the fact that the national proportions of most agricultural crops produced in the region are greater than its proportion of cultivated land.

By contrast, cattle stock per unit area is the lowest in the country, although the density of the pig population is by far the highest.

The technical level of agriculture also presents a favourable picture. The region's tractor stock and fertilizer consumption are on a par with the national average, while its specific fixed-asset value is above it. This is connected with the fact that there are many planted cultures, such as vineyards and orchards, in the region.

In the co-operative farm sector, average monthly earnings are equal to the national average, while gross and net incomes per hectares are 10 to 15 per cent above it.

In the Danube–Tisza Mid-region and the western part of Csongrád county, the calcareous and fast-warming sandy soils, the large number of hours of sunshine, and the long, dry and warm autumns are particularly beneficial to vine and fruit growing. This is because the production value of these cultures is substantially higher in these sandy soils of poor fertility than that of field crops.

Indicative of the national significance of wine growing in the Danube–Tisza Mid-region is the fact that the vineyards of Bács-Kiskun county account for one-third of the country's total wine procurement. The wines produced here are mostly light table wines usually of low alcoholic content, as well as dessert wines.

The region's viticulture displayed a marked upswing at the end of the last century, with the containment of the phylloxera disease and the binding of the blown sands. The old vineyards — both of the small peasantry and the large-scale capitalist farms — were based on traditional manual cultivation. Hence, following the socialist reorganization of agriculture, a significant new planting and reconstruction programme unfolded in the vineyards of both co-operative and state farms. The wide-row planting system, suitable for mechanized cultivation, and concrete props were introduced in large areas. But the vineyards remained under-capitalized and no attempt was made at soil preparation or amelioration, nor were the most appropriate vine species

Selected agricultural data for the Southern Great Plain, 1977 and 1981

Designation	Percentage of the national total 1977	1981
Arable land	20	20
Persons engaged in agriculture	23	20
Major products		
Wheat	25	26
Maize	26	26
Rice	40	43
Sugar beet	25	29
Hemp fibre	70	78
Red peppers — output volume	92	95
Onions	58	68
Tomatoes	32	31
Apricots	50	24
Peaches	33	20
Grapes	37	36
Cattle — stock	21	19
Pigs	20	31

selected. A modern programme of reconstruction began only as late as the 1970s.

The establishment of a specialized co-operative form* in vine areas with traditional narrow-row cultivation made it possible to preserve the old plantations and to maintain their production levels.

The region's major wine-growing and -processing centres are Nyárlőrinc, Lakitelek and Tiszakécske to the east of Kecskemét, and Helvécia, Izsák, Kiskőrös, Soltvadkert, Kecel, Kiskunhalas, Sükösd, Vaskút and Kunbaja south-west of Kecskemét. In these places there are usually not only larger wine cellars, but also wine-bottling plants. Within wine processing, some units also engage in turning out allied products such as champagne, vermouth, cognac and tartaric acid. Wine growing extends beyond Bács-Kiskun county into the Szeged area.

Fruit growing evolved parallel with vine growing, and was indeed grown mainly in the vineyards, constituting a so-called „two-level culture". The varieties grown were not favourable either, with the less valuable summer apple being predominant. Nonetheless, it constituted a significant specialization. In the southernmost part of the hilly terraces, near the country's frontier, early cherries were typically grown. Kiskunhalas and its surroundings were noted for pears, Kecel for sour cherries, Kecskemét and Tiszakécske for apricots, Szeged and Szatymaz for peaches and Bugac for winter apples. After the completion of the socialist reorganization of agriculture,

---

* A specialized co-operative is a production form simpler than the agricultural co-operative. It is an association of small private farms for the joint cultivation of certain crops (grapes, fruit, etc.) or for the joint performance of certain production processes, while the other activities remain within the framework of small-scale private farming.

the establishment of specialized large-scale orchards was begun, in the course of which winter-apple trees were planted over most part of the Bugac plain.

Fruit processing began with brandy distillation, for instance, Kecskemét apricot brandy, during the last century. After the turn of the century, canning factories were set up in the larger towns on the eastern fringe of the sandtable and in Kecskemét and Szeged, which became centres of fruit marketing. Following the introduction of the new economic mechanism, smaller co-operative canning plants, along with large co-operative canning factories, were created. The cold-storage industry also developed rapidly and large cold-storage plants were built in Kecskemét, Békéscsaba and Baja.

The production pattern of arable land reveals that maize and wheat occupy first and second places in terms of sown area, and that the output of both crops is some 10 per cent higher than the national average. The region's maize yield is exceeded only by that of Southern Transdanubia, while average wheat yields are as high as in any other region.

Conducive to an intensification of maize cultivation are the favourable soil endowments, the high temperatures, number of hours of sunshine and an appropriate distribution of precipitation. The most intensive maize-growing areas are to be found within the Szarvas—Makó—Battonya—Békéscsaba—Szarvas square, which roughly coincides with the area of loess meadow soils. This is followed by the Bácska loess table and the lowland plain along the Danube. Closely connected with the region's intensive maize cultivation is pig rearing, which has gained national significance since the middle of the 19th century [22].

The locational endowments and production traditions of the region's wheat cultivation are very favourable, and with the widespread cultivation of intensive varieties, the importance of wheat production has further increased, and now exceeds local demand. Owing to its high gluten content, the quality and the baking value of the wheat grown in the region are excellent.

The highest-capacity flour mills are to be found in Szeged, Hódmezővásárhely, Orosháza and Békéscsaba, i.e. along the rail line crossing the centre of the Békés—Csanád loess table. Unfortunately, the other links in the vertical processing chain, the plants of pastry, cake, waffle wheat-starch production, have not developed in the region. Modern, Italian-type vermicelli manufacture started in the Canning Factory at Békéscsaba as late as the mid-1960s. The scientific centre for grain improvement is in Szeged.

Formerly, sandy soils were largely utilized for rye cultivation, but since yields are rather poor, wheat and a new variety of bread grain, triticale, are now grown even on the sandy soils.

As regards the size of the sown area, lucerne occupies third place and provides a major fodder crop of the region. The lucerne seed developed in Békés county is of high quality, and constitutes a good export commodity.

Red peppers are grown on one-fifth of the area sown to vegetables. Its most typical growing regions lie around Kalocsa and Szeged, where its large-scale cultivation is due, primarily, to the large number of hours of sunshine, and to the production tradition accumulated over decades. The research centre for paprika growing can be found in Kalocsa as can the paprika-processing industry which is also located in Szeged.

The marked expansion of vegetable production on the sandtable of the Danube–Tisza Mid-region is due to the rapidly warming sandy soils and their water content in spring, which has led to the successful cultivation of early vegetables. This area has thus become the cradle of Hungarian market gardening and demands relatively little irrigation. Market gardening in this area began to evolve between the two wars, and has since developed intensively. Since 1945, the centre of potato and paprika growing has shifted increasingly southwards, to the Kecskemét area. Also significant is the growing of lettuce, red radish, green peas and cucumbers. In the Research Institute for Vegetable Cultivation in Kecskemét several varieties for large-scale production have been developed.

Apart from the Danube–Tisza Mid-region important vegetable-growing districts have developed in the southern Trans-Tisza area. Specialized vegetable production areas include Makó for onions, Szentes for green paprika and cauliflowers and Gyula for various root crops and green peas. These districts have also lent traditional „brand names" to the vegetables grown there, which entitles them to a price premium. A corresponding processing industry has also evolved. In Szeged, for example, as well as paprika processing, a canning industry had also developed relatively early on, while in Békéscsaba a canning and a cold-storage plant were set up in the 1960s.

Although sunflowers are grown on about two-thirds of the scale of the Northern Great Plain region, this has not as yet attracted any appreciable processing industry, while intensive sugar-beet production is carried on around the two sugar refineries at Mezőhegyes and Sarkad in Békés county.

Rice is grown in irrigated areas near the Körös rivers, where it mainly occupies the alkaline soils of floodplain. The centre of rice cultivation and processing is Szarvas, where a Research Institute for Irrigation and Rice Growing is located.

Along with plant cultivation, the Southern Great Plain is also a significant area for animal husbandry, especially a vertical integrated system of pig-poultry production and processing. Pig density is 50 per cent higher than in any other part of the country, and pig rearing in the middle and southern parts of Békés and in the eastern part of Csongrád county is especially intensive. Most of the pig farms of this area, based on a factory method of production, have been created during the last few years. Associated with pig rearing are such famous pork-processing centres as the Szeged Salami Factory, the processing plants at Békéscsaba and Gyula, which were already important before the war. They have since undergone significant reconstruction to enable further to increase their exports.

It was a few years ago that the joint efforts of the co-operative farm and state meat-processing industry lead to the establishment of the Meat Combine at Baja, which specializes in the produce of canned ham.

During the 1960s, however, the development of meat processing in the region of the Southern Great Plain — just as in the country as a whole — fell behind consumer demand and the expansion of the raw-produce base, and to bridge the gap, new meat-processing plants had to be built during the 1970s. The joint meat-processing activities of the co-operative farms have also came to play an important role in this process.

In poultry farming, too, the Southern Great Plain is one of the country's most intensive regions with poultry-processing plants operating especially in and around Szentes, Orosháza, Békéscsaba, Kiskunhalas, Kiskunfélegyháza and Kecskemét. Poultry raising is tied partly to grain production, i.e. chickens and hens, and partly to dry, alkaline pastures on which large-scale goose farming was formerly carried on.

Owing to the inadequate production of green fodder and the poor quality of meadows and pastures, the region's cattle population has not been able to attain a level comparable to that of pig raising and significant breeding has only developed on the pastures on the river floodplains. Major dairy farms are to be found in the county towns of Kecskemét, Szeged and Békéscsaba, and in Hódmezővásárhely. To help solve the supply problems arising from the excessively concentrated milk industry, dairy associations made up of individual co-operative farms have been established in certain areas. On the peripheral parts of the region there is some milk surplus, which is processed by the Milk-Powder Factory at Gyula.

Sheep rearing on the poorer-quality pastures of the Danube—Tisza Mid-region and in the area of the Körös rivers has gained some significance but has not attained any manufacturing activity, owing to the poor quality of wool. The fleeces are therefore used mainly by the sheepskin industry.

The relatively large horse stock is accounted for partly by a horse-breeding tradition, as at Mezőhegyes and partly by the needs of the region's significant tanya population, for which horse is still the principal draught animal.

4.2.3 Transport

The layout of the region's transport system is determined by the two main communication axes running from north to south and east to west. To the first belongs the Budapest—Kecskemét—Szeged road, part of the E—5 international motorway, as well as sections of the Cegléd—Szeged and Budapest—Belgrade railway lines. In river navigation, the north-south axis is determinant as is shown by the section of the Danube between Budapest and Baja, and by the Tisza section between Szolnok and Szeged. The east-west transport axes are the roads from Dunaföldvár through Kecskemét to Békéscsaba, from Baja to Szeged and from Szeged to Békéscsaba. Railway lines running from east to west are, however, less developed. The Kecskemét—Szeged and the Szeged—Békéscsaba rail and road links constitute the main transport axis of the region.

The inadequate carrying capacity of the region's bridges poses serious problems for both international and transit transport and to mitigate this, several new bridges have been built across the Tisza over recent years.

In consonance with transport policy several narrow-gauge railway lines with sparse traffic have been closed and their traffic transferred to road vehicles and buses. It is especially difficult to solve the communications problems of the extensive tanya-settlement system.

Whit its open-air theatre and other cultural events and folk art, Szeged constitutes the greatest asset in the region's tourism. Additional tourist attractions are Kecskemét, the Bugac plain and the Kiskunság national park, comprising besides Bugac-puszta several nature reserves. Many tourists visit Kalocsa for its folk art and Folklore Festival.

4.3 Population

The population of the Southern Great Plain is close to 1·5 million and is increasing only slowly, due mainly to a low rate of natural increase, some 60 per cent of the national average.

The population of Békés county has been declining even during the last few years, although that of Bács-Kiskun county has displayed a slight rising tendency. The rate of growth has been greatest in Csongrád county, although it is still below the national average and stems mainly from in-migration.

Population density, at 80 persons per km^2, is the lowest in the country after Southern Transdanubia. The distribution by counties reveals that it is fairly high, 108 persons per km^2 in Csongrád county, but very low, 68 persons per km^2 in Bács-Kiskun county, the most significant tanya county, although it is not much higher in Békés county either.

Internal migration within the region is substantial, and in Békés, the rate of population decrease in the villages is double the national average. A similar rate of out-migration is demonstrated only in Szabolcs-Szatmár county and certain small-village settlement areas. By contrast, the increase in the population of the towns is below the national average, but more so in Csongrád than Bács-Kiskun county.

4.4 Settlement

The spatial distribution of the region's settlement network is fairly even. The proportion of town dwellers is 50 per cent, and although well above the national average in Csongrád county, only a third of the population of Békés and Bács-Kiskun counties live in urban areas.

The towns are located on the peripheries of the Danube–Tisza Mid-region and along the Danube. The number of the large and mammoth villages is particularly large in this area, and two-thirds of the population live in villages.

An even more serious problem is the high proportion of tanya population in both urban and rural settlements alike, as this is the country's most typical tanya region. It is in fact the problem associated with the large-scale cultivation of old-established crops which explains, for all its contradictory character, the long survival of the tanya-settlement form in the region.

The majority of towns in the Tisza–Maros–Körös area are to be found along the rivers fringing the area to the north, west and south and include Gyula, Szarvas, Csongrád, Szentes, Szeged and Makó, while another group is located along the Szeged–Békéscsaba transport axis, i.e. Hódmezővásárhely, Orosháza and Békéscsaba.

The urban network has evolved out of the once agrarian market towns of the region, in which the traditional manual tillage of intensive cultures was dominant. In the 19th century indeed, Hódmezővásárhely and Makó were two of the country's largest towns in terms of population number, rivalling Miskolc and Győr.

In the development of the region's market towns, two basic regional sub-types can be distinguished:

1. The market towns of the sandy plains with Kecskemét the largest.
2. The market towns of the Southern Trans-Tisza area, embracing Békés and Csongrád counties.

On the sandy plains, Kecskemét and Kiskunhalas — together with Cegléd and Nagykőrös which lie outside the region — played a prominent role in creating an intensive form of farming. It was this indeed which boosted their economic development and with it their urbanization. The urban network of the eastern periphery of the region, which only belatedly joined in this development process, is still a much more sparse and for a long time only Kalocsa and Baja were regarded as towns, with Kiskőrös being granted urban status as late as the early 1970s. This is the reason why there are several large villages with populations of 7 to 12 thousand in the area, which, if they had an industrial base, would be eligible for the urban status. Most of them are single-function market towns specializing in viticulture and wine production.

It was the evolution of the vertical integration of pig and poultry farming based on feed-grain and meat processing that laid the foundation for market-town development in the Southern Trans-Tisza area of Békés county and it was primarily this that stimulated the development of such towns as Gyula, Békéscsaba, Szarvas and Orosháza. But the development of the processing industry was on a somewhat smaller scale than in the Danube–Tisza Mid-region, and many functional market towns have not yet attained an urban administrative rank. This concentrated settlement network, however, provides a good opportunity for a more rapid development of the settlement system, provided the necessary economic conditions can be secured.

In the development of the market towns of Csongrád county, the characteristics of these two sub-types have merged. In some, for instance, Szentes, Makó and Szeged, intensive vegetable and/or fruit cultivation provided the foundation for the basis for the food-processing industry, but the pig rearing also contributed to their development. This is why Csongrád county has the most developed urban network in the Great Plain, and the smallest number of large urbanizing villages. With the exception of the county seats, the infrastructural provision of the region's towns is, however, still far from satisfactory.

A further specific developmental problem is also posed by the tanya settlements, whose populations live predominantly in outlying areas [65]. Nonetheless the electrification of both linear and nucleated tanya cluster has made great headway and many hostels have been built for the children from these settlements in the towns and large villages to assist with their education. Efforts are also being made to improve their transport provision.

4.5 Subregions and urban hinterlands

Based on its structural characteristics, communication orientations and co-operation possibilities, the economic-planning region of the Southern Great Plain can be divided into the following subregions: a) the Szeged subregion, b) the Kecskemét subregion, c) the Kiskunhalas subregion, d) the subregion bordering the Danube, e) the town complex in central-Békés county, f) the Orosháza subregion, g) the Körös—Tisza subregion.

a) *The Szeged subregion*. This is one of the most multifariously developed subregions, to which belong, apart from Szeged, the areas of Hódmezővásárhely and Makó in the east and the Danube—Tisza mid-area of Csongrád county in the west. The production profile of the subregion is of a predominantly heavy-industrial character, but in addition, the textile and knitwear industries, vegetable and fruit cultivation, the canning industry and paprika and meat processing are also of significance [35].

Szeged, a county town with 175 000 inhabitants, is one of the country's five provincial centres, and is the transport, economic, cultural and organizational focus of the Southern Great Plain. The present layout of the city owns little to the past as it was completely rebuilt to a new plan with double boulevards and avenues after the great flood of 1879. The housing estates built during the last few decades are attached to those parts of the town that had evolved at the turn of the century. It is, after Budapest, the most planned city in the country which, apart from a few rural-type and poorly supplied parts, is well equipped with public utilities.

Its economic significance derives from the nearby oil and natural-gas resources and its developing industry. It is also a centre of higher education and scientific research, with several universities and colleges, clinics and institutes of the Hungarian Academy of Sciences. It is a cultural centre of long standing with several regional and international cultural events, for instance, the Szeged Summer Festival. Accordingly, domestic and foreign tourism is significant. Szeged is also a developed market, information and decision centre, as well as being the centre of several regional economic organizations.

Hódmezővásárhely, with 54 000 inhabitants, is one of the two significant medium-sized towns of the subregion, with a stagnant population, it was formerly an agrarian town and cultural centre, but has now come to have its own industry. Both in terms of morphology and public utilities it belongs to the group of less developed towns.

Makó, with 30 000 inhabitants, is the other medium-sized town and world-famous centre of Hungarian onion production. In order to change its one-sided agrarian production structure, several smaller plants have been established in it during the course of socialist industrialization, which ensure that the larger part of the population is employed in industry.

b) *The Kecskemét subregion.* This subregion is noted for its wine, fruit and vegetable production and processing and for its engineering industry. The sandtable lying between the Danube and the Tisza rivers is part of the subregion.

Kecskemét, with 93 000 inhabitants, is a county town and the centre of the subregion. The main roads converge on its redeveloped centre in a radial fashion. Besides up-to-date housing estates, it also has parts poorly provided with public utilities, and an extensive tanya area. It is the transport, economic, market, decision-making and information centre of the Danube–Tisza Mid-region, and as a result of the industrial development of the past two decades, its market-town functions are beginning to diminish [41]. There are also colleges for the engineering industry, automation, vegetable growing operating in the town, as well as a Kindergarten teachers' training college. Kecskemét is the research centre for vegetable growing and viticulture [74], and the seat of the International Kodály Seminar.

Apart from food processing, the subregion's engineering profile is also significant with plants in Kecskemét, Kiskunfélegyháza, Lajosmizse and Tiszakécske.

Kiskunfélegyháza, with 36 000 inhabitants, is an important medium-sized town of the subregion. Its engineering industry produces mainly power-station equipment and iron structures.

c) *The Kiskunhalas subregion.* This subregion has become noted for its wine and vegetable growing, but its petroleum-extraction profile is also steadily strengthening. Its centre is the town of Kiskunhalas with 31 000 inhabitants. For a long time, industry was represented in it merely by „Halas lace" manufacture, but today, a cotton-processing plant and a large knitwear factory are also to be found there.

d) *The subregion bordering the Danube* is still of a typical agrarian character with vegetables (mainly red pepper), pig rearing, maize, grapes and wines being significant. Baja, with 39 000 inhabitants, is the subregion's most important town, and the centre of northern Bácska. Along with its former light and food-processing industries, engineering especially has displayed a significant development during the last few decades. Its meat industry is a relatively new development. Kalocsa, with 19 000 inhabitants, is the centre of pepper producing and processing in the subregion. It is noted for its folk art, and constitutes a significant tourist attraction.

e) *The town complex in central-Békés county.* The subregion's production profile is primarily of a food-processing character with plants of the meat, milk, canning, cold-storage and sugar-refining industries, but light industry is also fairly developed. Békéscsaba, Gyula and Békés are its major towns.

Békéscsaba, with 66 000 inhabitants, is a county town, and the transport and economic centre of the subregion. Earlier, it was known mainly for its brick industry, knitwear manufacture and meat processing. Today it has various food and light industries [68].

Gyula, with 34 000 inhabitants, is a medium-sized town and a significant tourist attraction.

Békés, with 22 000 inhabitants, is the least-developed settlement of the town complex [5].

f) *The Orosháza subregion.* Except for the town Orosháza, this subregion is a relatively unindustrialized. Its production profile still has an agrarian character with grain growing, pigs and poultry rearing being significant. The large villages of the subregion are noted chiefly for their cottage industry and their food-processing, flour-milling and sugar-refining activities.

Orosháza, with 36 000 inhabitants, was for long a stagnant agrarian town with a low level of infrastructural provision. The siting of a glass factory there has, however, ensured its long-term development.

g) *The Körös—Tisza subregion.* This is a poorly industrialized and predominantly agrarian area with significant irrigation cultures, such as rice and vegetables. An industrial profile is ensured mainly by co-operative-managed light industry. Major state-owned industrial plants are located only at Szentes and Csongrád.

Szentes, with 35 000 inhabitants, is a medium-sized town and the most industrialized settlement of the subregion.

Csongrád, with 22 000 and *Szarvas* with 21 000 inhabitants, are still small towns with stagnating populations. Efforts are being made to eliminate their backwardness in infrastructural provision. From the educational point of view, Szarvas, with a college faculty of irrigation and a Kindergarten teachers' training college, is important.

5 The economic–planning region of Southern Transdanubia

With an area amounting to almost one-fifth of the country and with a population constituting only 12 per cent of the national total, Southern Transdanubia is the largest and most sparsely populated region of the country.

Southern Transdanubia is a region with a varied, multifarious and open economy. It can be subdivided into a number of meso-regions, which explains why various regional divisions have been proposed, depending on the principles and factors used.

The region contributes to the national economy primarily in the fields associated with the extraction and processing of energy sources, such as black coal, uranium, petroleum and natural gas, and with agricultural and food processing such as grain, canned meat, leather and dairy products.

In terms of economic development the industrial production of the region falls somewhat behind the national level, while the population infrastructure is around the average. The region's endowments are favourable for the development of most sectors, although its labour reserves have been exhausted, and with the available manpower it will be difficult to service further industrial development [71].

5.1 Natural endowments and resources

The region is predominantly an upland area with varied relief and structural characteristics, extending from the southern side of Lake Balaton to the plainland along the Dráva river and encompassing the Mecsek Mountains.

The Paleozoic base mountain and the Mesozoic formations are deeply submerged and only reach the surface in the granites in the Mórágy area. Sediments of Secondary and Tertiary origin reach the surface in several places, as in the Mecsek and Villány Mountains. The Mecsek Mountains are comprised of limestone lying on a crystalline base. It is of a varied structure and mainly forested, and extends over a distance of some 30 kilometres in a north-east and south-west direction, achieving an altitude of between 400 and 600 metres. The most significant mineral resources are uranium-ore occurrences in Permian sandstones and black coal of relatively high calorific value occurring in seams between the northern and eastern Jurassic ranges. Further mineral resources are building stone and sands of marine origin suitable for foundrying and glass manufacture. The cement factory at Beremend is based on the valuable limestone and marl of the small Villány range south of the Mecsek. The pink- and red-streaked limestone, the so-called „semimarble" occurring near Siklós, is also a valuable construction material.

The Mecsek Mountains arising like an island above the surrounding area, are surrounded by the Baranya–Tolna–Somogy–Zala hill country, whose young Pannonian and Pleistocene strata are variably folded and faulted. In the structural anticlines of the Pannonian sediments of southern Zala county oil and natural gas are to be found, and similarly in the traps, formed on the surface of Triassic sediments in central Zala, for instance, at Nagylengyel. As by-products of the extensive exploration, valuable medicinal and mineral thermal waters have also been discovered.

The climate of Southern Transdanubia is the mildest in the country, and is transitional in character between the continental climate of the Great Plain and the more oceanic climate with Mediterranean features of the Sub-Alpine region. The annual amount of sunshine rises from 1800 hours in the west to 2000 hours in the east of the region while mean annual temperatures range between 8 and 11 °C.

The region is one of the areas of the country with the highest precipitation, with declines from 800 mm per annum in the south-west to 600 mm in the north-east. The driest part of the region is the area south of Lake Balaton and the southern part of the Mezőföld, where the risk of drought is rather high. Typical of this part is a second autumn precipitation maximum.

Precipitation conditions are favourable in the foreground of the Mecsek, where an early spring makes it possible to grow early vegetables, while protection from northern winds enables the cultivation of such heat- and light-intensive plants as sweet chestnuts, grapes and figs.

Its major rivers, the Danube, Dráva and Mura run along the fringes of the region. The Dráva, which drains the south-eastern part of the Alps, forms the natural frontier over a distance of 160 kms and for this reason it does not play any significant role in the region's economy, despite its abundant water budget. Its potential energy could be utilized by a power plant built (jointly with Yugoslavia) near the town of Barcs, which would again make it navigable.

The drainage of the northern part of the region is towards Lake Balaton with the exception of the Zala river which flows in a large bend from the state boundary to Lake Balaton and silts up the Keszthely Bay with its deposits. The Sió is the outlet of Balaton, to which the Kapos stream is a tributary. Although the region has significant water reserves, the towns of Pécs, Komló, Kaposvár, Dombóvár and Zalaegerszeg nonetheless suffer from water shortages.

The southern shore of Lake Balaton also belong to the region. The basin of the Lake is a young depression, whose formation began during the Pleistocene and ended in the early Quaternary. With a surface of 600 km^2 it is the largest lake of Central Europe, and given the favourable climate and attractive environs it is one of the most important resort areas of the country. The quality of its water, however, is threatened by serious pollution, and the installation of modern plants for treating sewage is an important task of environmental protection.

The climax vegetation cover is oak and beech forest, connected stands of which can still be found not only on the uplands but also in the arable areas.

22 per cent of the region is forested, a proportion exceeded only by that of the middle mountain areas.

Typically the soils of the region are heavily leached acidic forest soils. Leaching and the inadequate lime content are particularly marked in the south-west, in the Zala hill country and in inner-Somogy county, and fertile arable land is only to be found in Tolna and Baranya counties of Eastern Transdanubia. As one moves eastwards, loess soils become more prominent, however, and in the Mezőföld they are particularly deep. There is a significant correlation between the occurrence of this soil and changes in average crop yields, indeed, even in the production level of agriculture as a whole.

5.2 The economy

The regional equalization that accompanied the great socio-economic transformation after the war also exerted a significant impact on the economic life of the region. The agrarian counties of Tolna and Somogy, however, only embarked upon the path of slow industrial development as late as the 1960s.

It is a consequence of socialist policies that industry now plays the leading role in the region's economy, although not to the extent that it does in the more vigorously industrialized regions. The shift towards oil involving some curtailment of coal mining caused a temporary setback in the region's dynamic development, which was further exacerbated by the slowdown of extraction in the Zala oil fields. The world-economic events of the 1970s, however, directed attention again to a rational economic policy regarding the region's mineral resources, primarily Mecsek coal.

As to the level of economic development, the region occupies fourth place in front of the regions of the Great Plain. On the basis of county development indices computed from the industrial and agricultural indicators, Baranya county can be regarded as the most developed. There is no appreciable difference in the production levels of the other three counties.

5.2.1 Industry

As regards industrial manpower, the volume and specific size of the means of production, the level of industrialization in Southern Transdanubia lags behind the national average, except in Baranya county, thanks, primarily, to its large-scale mining. Most industry is concentrated in the main urban centres of the region and with the exception of the Pécs–Komló industrial concentration, no other interconnected industrial regions have evolved. The leading sector is heavy industry, although its weight has somewhat declined during the last decade; it is followed by the light and food-processing industries.

Selected industrial data for Southern Transdanubia,
1977 and 1981*

	Percentage of the national total	
	1977	1981
Persons employed in socialist industry	10	11
Gross value of fixed assets	9	10
Installed motive power	10	10
Consumption of electrical energy	7	7
Output of major products		
1. Black coal	100	100
2. Petroleum	12	9
3. Natural gas	2	1
4. Incandescent lamps	78	75
5. Oil-fuelled stoves	62	90
6. Cement	23	22
7. Fibre board	100	100
8. Upholstered furniture	15	17
9. Leather (chrome upper leather)	49	67
10. Cigarettes	24	23

* The 1981 data include Keszthely district.

County Baranya is a part of the country with a marked heavy industry associated primarily with basic-material extraction. But since the large coal-consuming sectors, such as iron metallurgy have not evolved there, Southern Transdanubia is a region with an incomplete coal base. Its divergence from the typical regions of heavy industry is also apparent in the relative backwardness of the engineering industry, whose encouragement is an important precondition for the further dynamic development of industry there. All this is offset, however, by the significant role played by the light and food-processing industries.

The spatial distribution of commercially exploitable energy sources is uneven with the mining of coal and uranium ore being concentrated in the Pécs–Komló industrial region. Zala county, with its diminishing petroleum reserves, represents the other pole. High-quality black coal, suitable for coking, is extracted from a field of Lower Lias age which stretches over a distance of 40 km around Pécs–Vasas, Komló and Szászvár. The known coal reserves of the Mecsek field make up more than one quarter of the national total, although unfavourable geological conditions mean that actual output is only one-eighth of the total mined in the country. But this does provide, in the perspective, the possibility of expanding the production capacity of Mecsek coal mining.

Given the unfavourable extraction conditions of Mecsek coal mining, mechanization is difficult to implement and the cost of opening up new faces is higher than the industry average. To offset this disadvantage, large-capacity, heavily mechanized workplaces with massive output potentialities have been established wherever the geological conditions are more favourable.

However, owing to the presence of methan gas, the use of explosives in extraction is small. With its 800-m-deep pits and modern conveyor equipment, Komló has, despite difficult geological conditions, the most developed coal mine in Hungary. Half its output is used by the thermal-electric power station at Pécs and one quarter by the coking plant at Dunaújváros. It was because of its coal that Komló, formerly a large village with a few thousand population only, developed into a socialist town with 30 000 inhabitants.

Uranium-rich sandstone discovered at Kővágószöllős in 1954 is also mined in the region. The sandstone is extracted by modern techniques that ensure radiological protection and after preliminary dressing, the ore is transported to the Soviet Union. The development of Pécs has been greatly promoted by the construction of Újmecsekalja, a modern residential quarter, with some 20 000 inhabitants, locally called „uranium town".

Petroleum, the third mineral resource of the region, is extracted from Lower Pannonian and Miocene strata at Lispe, Budafapuszta, Lovászi and Hahót in the southern part of the Zaia hill country and from Cretaceous formations at Nagylengyel in the Göcsej. The former are oil fields near exhaustion, with oil of a high petrol content, while the latter, which are also declining in output, yield oil of a low petrol content.

Most of the oil now produced is from the Nagylengyel field and from other less significant occurrences discovered during the recent past. Owing to the exhaustion of the oil fields, the technique of sinking vertical pits has been replaced by modern, secondary and tertiary extraction methods (pressing liquids and gases into the storage layers), which have resulted in a 6 to 10 per cent increase in exploitable reserves.

Quarrying constitutes another important sector of the extraction industry. About four-fifths of its output is provided by two large quarries, the andesite quarry at Komló and the limestone quarry at Nagyharsány. The $CaCO_3$ content of the Nagyharsány and Beremend limestone is outstanding, and Nagyharsány is the most important supplier to the country's metallurgy and sugar-refining industries. Gravel is quarried mainly in the Dráva valley, near Gyékényes. Along with the ubiquitous, low-yield sand pits, most of the sand output is provided by the pits in the vicinity of Pécs.

The chalky limestone with its loess or clay-loess cover, making up the Beremend Mountains belonging to the island blocks of southern Baranya county, provides the raw material for the Beremend cement factory. Since its reconstruction, it provides one million tons of good-quality cement annually. After the modernization of the many evenly distributed, small-capacity brick and tile plants (of which several have been closed), the industry has become more concentrated. Up-to-date, pressure-resistant products are produced by plants at Barcs, Bátaszék and Mohács [26].

The manufacture of concrete elements at Pécs and Komló satisfies not only the needs of the housing programme, but also the demands of mining.

The modern glass factory at Nagykanizsa is fired by natural gas, and produces primarily heat-resistant laboratory vessels.

The fine ceramics industry is represented by several plants, of which the Zsolnay Porcelain Factory is of national significance. It manufactures insulators, household porcelain articles, eosin decorative products, as well as products of construction ceramics (pyrogranite).

The bulk of building work in all four counties of the region is performed by the construction industries located in the individual county towns.

The most important consumers of Mecsek coal is the electricity-generation industry, whose largest power plant is the Pécs Power Station with a 200 MW capacity built during the 1960s to satisfy the rapidly growing demand for electricity. The electricity generated in the region, amounting to 7 per cent of domestic output, does not, however, cover the needs of the region, and is supplemented by power transmitted by the Danube Thermal-Electricity Power Station, and the generating stations at Várpalota and Ajka. The putting into operation of the Paks nuclear power station with a capacity of 1760 MW can be expected finally to solve the electricity supply problem. Paks was chosen as the site of the reactor because of the availability of abundant cooling water, and for environmental reasons. The first stage of the pressurized water reactor, operating with an efficiency of about 10 per cent, has been commissioned in 1982.

The metalworking and engineering branches of the region's heavy industry are not linked to the black-coal base as metallurgy is located outside the region. Therefore, the engineering industry was barely represented in the region's industrial pattern in the past *(Fig. 68)*. The role of metalworking and engineering increased as a result of the industrial location policy of the 15 years between 1960 and 1975, when the old-established and dynamically developing plants of Budapest were compelled, for lack of manpower, to establish or relocate certain plants in the countryside. The location was influenced by such factors as manpower, communications, the level of infrastructure, and the degree of urbanization. The United Incandescent Lamp Campany alone established five plants in the region, some employing several thousand persons, such as the Nagykanizsa Lighting and Glass Factory and the Kaposvár Electronic-Tube Factory. Consequently, the number of independent large industrial enterprises is small in Southern Transdanubia. The bulk of the spatially dispersed engineering plants are controlled by, and co-operate with, the parent enterprises outside the region. Their production linkages within the region are at minimum, with only a small proportion of the necessary raw materials and semifinished products coming from the region itself.

Machinery and equipment are produced by the Nagykanizsa Factory for Manufacturing Machinery for the Petroleum Industry, by the Zalaegerszeg plant of Ganz-Mávag, the Barcs plant of the Factory of Construction Machinery, the Tab plant of the Budapest Factory of Chemical Machinery, and the Sophiana Engineering Factory at Pécs.

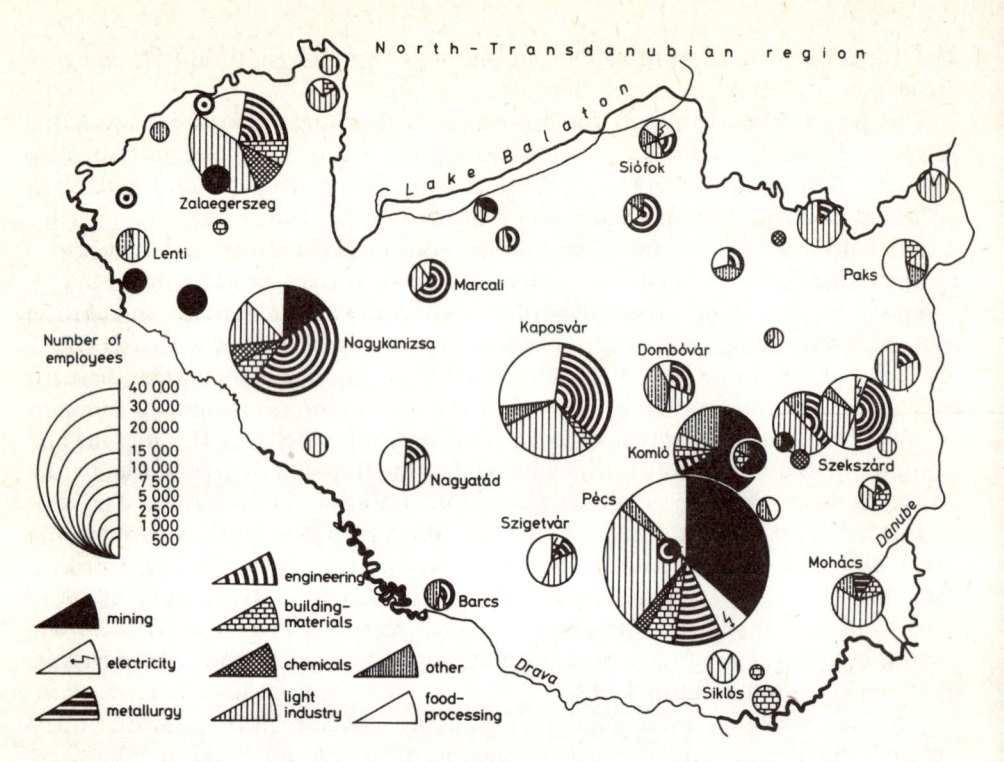

Fig. 68. The spatial location of industry in the South Transdanubian economic–planning (1981)

The vacuum and telecommunications industries are represented by the Lighting and Glass Factory of the United Incandescent Company, the Kaposvár Electronic-Tube Factory producing radio valves and motorcar lights, and the Kaposvár Electric Engineering Factory of the Electric Equipment and Appliances Works, producing transformers and low- and high-voltage electric appliances. A new plant of the mass-metal industry is the oil-fuelled stove factory of the Mechanical Works located at Marcali. The enamel factory at Bonyhád produces enamelled metal articles and household tableware.

Chemicals are the region's least important industry. In addition to the Gas Works in Pécs, there is a plant at Hidas, producing herbicides, and another plant at Zalaegerszeg, manufacturing cosmetics.

The location of light industry, employing close to one-third of the region's industrial workers, has been determined primarily by the available raw materials, such as timber, flax, hemp, wool, silk and leather as well as a skilled labour force and a pool of unskilled manpower. The branch, however, has already long outgrown its own raw-material base, and labour has also become more scarce. Predominant within light industries are the leather, fur and footwear industries followed by the clothing and spinning industries.

Within the textile industry, the cotton and silk sectors process mainly imported raw materials, cotton, synthetic fibre, and only the hemp industry can rely on local raw materials. The cotton-spinning plant at Kaposvár and the thread-processing plant at Nagyatád established after the Liberation are nationally significant enterprises. As silk-worm breeding is no longer economic, the silk factory at Tolna now uses imported man-made fibres, while the hemp-processing plants at Dunaföldvár, Pécs, Szekszárd and Tolnanémedi process hemp grown in Baranya and Tolna counties [17].

Of the two most significant plants of the clothing industry equipped with modern technology, the Kaposvár Clothing Factory specializes in the production of children's wear, and the Zalaegerszeg Factory in the manufacture of men's suits.

The plants of the hide-processing industry are located in Pécs and at Simontornya, while those of leather manufacture are at Bonyhád, Szigetvár, Szekszárd and Pécs.

Timber processing relies, with the exception of the Fibreboard Factory at Mohács, on the hardwoods of the local forestries at Barcs, Csurgó and Lenti. The Kanizsa Furniture Factory at Nagykanizsa and the Zala Furniture Factory at Zalaegerszeg together turn out close to half the country's upholstered furniture.

5.2.2 Agriculture and food processing

The level of the region's agricultural production falls, in general, behind the national level, as shown by the marketing and income indicators per unit area. The two western counties of Zala and Somogy have a lower production level, while the two eastern ones of Tolna and Baranya exhibit an above-average intensity per unit area cultivated. In the hilly area of the two western counties, the majority of the co-operatives are farming on steep, eroded hillsides under adverse natural conditions and one-sixth of the country's weak co-operatives fall into these two counties. Very often even the cost of input is not covered and farming is loss-making and much more risky than in the eastern part of the county. Gross income per hectare of cultivated land on the collective farms in Somogy county reaches barely two-thirds, and in Zala county one half the national average level.

As for output, Tolna county ranks first, with outputs from both crops and animal husbandry at around the national average. But areas with unfavourable endowments are to be found in that county, too. The largest number of large efficient farms are in Baranya county, most located on the Mohács plainland and around the Villány range.

The specialization of the region's agricultural production is characterized by the fact that the volume of marketed bread grain and beef cattle per unit area is higher than in any other economic-planning region. Milk production and pig rearing may also be ranked among the specialized sectors.

Selected agricultural data for Southern Transdanubia,
1977 and 1981*

Designation	Percentage of the national total	
	1977	1981
Cultivated area	19	19
Number of persons employed in agriculture	17	16
Output of major products		
Wheat	19	18
Maize	25	22
Potatoes	18	20
Cattle population	19	19
Pig population	18	11

* The 1981 data include Keszthely district.

Characteristic of the pattern of arable cultivation is the priority given to maize, which far exceeds that of wheat, as well as the significant amount of green fodder grown.

Irrespective of natural endowments, wheat, the most profitable crop, is grown extensively everywhere. Its share is largest on the arable parts of Tolna county, but is also significant on the low-fertility forest soils of the Zala hill country. The average wheat yields of Zala county is one ton less than the high yields of the eastern counties.

The leading crop everywhere is maize, whose share in the sown area is highest in this region. Except in Zala county yields are also very high, 5·5 to 8·0 tons per hectare, and a quarter of the country's maize output stems from the region.

Of the industrial crops, it is mainly sugar beet and sunflowers that are produced on a large scale. Tobacco and hemp are also grown, but their sown area has dropped to half the former acreage.

Among vegetables, French beans, green·peas, cucumbers, green paprika and tomatoes are grown extensively, and their cultivation is concentrated in the hinterlands of the three canning factories at Paks, Szigetvár and Nagyatád.

The cooler, wetter climate benefits the growth of green fodder, those relative sown area ranks third after maize and wheat, except in Zala county, where the two latter crops predominate. Amongst green fodders clover is widespread in the west, and lucerne in the east. The proportionate areas under silage maize and green fodder maize are greater in each county than the national average.

Within the region potatoes are grown particularly in the humus-rich sandy soils of inner-Somogy and Zala counties, and the region is the second largest potato source in the country after the Nyírség. Climatic conditions are especially favourable for growing seed potatoes.

It is due to the varied and intensive character of fodder cultivation that the region has become an important livestock-breeding area, competing with the western parts of the Little Plain in terms of livestock density. The most intensive areas of cattle raising are the Kapos valley and the Zselic, Völgység and Hegyhát areas. Zala county — where the cattle population per unit area used to be the highest in the country — now ranks second after Vas county owing to a sharp decline in small-scale cattle raising. Paradoxically, milk yields in Zala county with one of the county's largest cattle populations do not even reach the national average. By contrast, the county's production of beef is the largest in the country.

As a result of intensive maize production, the region has a large pig population, but only comes third after the two plainland regions in terms of pork production.

One-sixth of the region's industrial manpower is engaged in the traditional food industry, most of the workforce being employed in the canning, milling, milk-processing and sugar-refining industries. The equipment of these industries is, however, not up-to-date. Exports play a substantial role in the commodity output of the three canning factories at Nagyatád, Szigetvár and Paks, processing large quantities of vegetables and fruit. The major milk-processing plants at Dombóvár, Pécsvárad, Tamási, Kaposvár, Nagykanizsa, Zalaegerszeg and Szekszárd turn out a quarter of the butter and over one-third of the cheese produced in the country. The food-processing capacities, which were small compared with the raw-produce base have been expanded during the past few years and highly explorable products are now turned out by the meat-processing plants in Kaposvár and Szekszárd, and the cold-storage plant in Zalaegerszeg.

5.2.3 Transport

In some parts of the region, for instance, in the Göcsej, the Mohács area and the frontier zone, transport provision is inadequate. The network is primarily oriented towards the capital, the only exception being the Sopron—Pécs railway which creates good communication with the Little Plain. The Dombóvár—Bátaszék—Baja—Kiskunhalas line, which is of small capacity, ensures a reasonable link with the neigbouring Southern Plain region but only in a circuitous way. Owing to the limited number of bridges crossing the Danube, the Bátaszék—Baja and the Dunaföldvár—Solt road connections are not free from detours either. Links with Northern Transdanubia are somewhat better. These unfavourable transport endowments impede not only the expansion of relations with neighbouring regions, but also hinder the division of labour and the development of transport within the region.

Railway density is above average, with the exception of Zala county where it is sparse. There are no double-track sections, and no electrified lines. The two international lines, Budapest—Murakeresztúr and Budapest—Pécs—Gyékényes, with their branches establish good communications with the capital. The unfavourable rail situation of a great part of Zala county has been somewhat improved by the reconstruction of existing lines, by the improvement of Zalaszentiván junction and by the establishment of a direct express link between the capital and the county town. The relative number of settlements with railway stations is low, yet traffic is poor and six normal-gauge lines have been closed for being uneconomic.

The density of the road network is around the national average, but there are still villages without a bus service.

Of international and of course national significance is the M-7 motorway, which skirts the southern shore of Lake Balaton as well as its continuation, the trunk road 7. Road 6 ensures communications between Pécs and the capital and, after the rebuilding of the Dráva Bridge at Barcs, with Croatia, too.

The region maintains production relations mainly with the Central region, and thus goods flow, as a rule, in that direction. It is, however, some distance away from the nationally important east-west transport axis, and the region's transport system therefore performs the function of carrying goods up to this axis. The Murakeresztúr–Nagykanizsa–Budapest and the Dombóvár–Pusztaszabolcs–Budapest lines handle the largest amount of traffic.

For the transportation of petroleum and natural gas, a pipeline network has been built connecting the oil fields with Budapest, and the refineries in Northern Transdanubia. With the construction of the Adria Oil Pipeline between Berzence and Százhalombatta, pipeline transport has experienced a further expansion.

5.2.4 Tourism

It testifies to the outstanding significance of tourism in Southern Transdanubia that around one-third of all foreign tourist accommodations, and one-sixth of overall tourist turnover fall into the region. Two areas are of international tourist significance, namely the southern shore of Lake Balaton and the Mecsek Mountains with neighbouring Harkány, Siklós and Villány.

The southern shore of Lake Balaton — unlike the northern shore, whose varied topography provides much of tourist interest — is suitable primarily for bathing resort recreation. Tourism confines itself mainly to the shoreline. As a resort area it began to develop at the turn of the century. First the lakeside settlements nearest to the capital began to develop, among them Siófok, Balatonszemes and Balatonföldvár. Development picked up during the period between the two world wars, and after the Liberation a massive and organized social holiday-making process started. With the building of hotels and company resorts during the 1960s, the tourist capacity of the area expanded significantly.

The first regional development plan for Lake Balaton and its surroundings was drawn up in 1957. It contained a comprehensive concept for the utilization of the settlements. Planned development, however, came to a halt during the second half of the 1960s. Private construction activities expanded, and many week-end cottages, contrary to the plan's provisions and not fitting into the landscape, were built in and even outside the area zoned for such developments. The supply of the rapidly expanding resorts with public utilities constituted a great problem for the local councils which did not have the resources necessary to satisfy the growing demand.

The commercial accommodation on the southern shore – including the Keszthely shore – can cater for 60000 persons, of which 8 per cent is hotel accommodation, but can in no way meet peak season demand.

Insufficient accommodation and service capacities, and infrastructural bottlenecks pose a steadily growing problem as during the last few years tourist flow has far exceeded the planned and realized capacities. A characteristic nature of foreign tourism in this area is its great concentration during the peak season, when the average duration of stay is 7 days. Otherwise, hotels and other accommodation facilities remain unoccupied during a significant part of the year.

The Hévíz and Zalakaros spas also belong to the Balaton resort area. With their excellent medicinal waters, they are attracting a growing number of both domestic and foreign guests.

The second tourist area of the region comprises the Mecsek Mountains and its surroundings. Its attractions include beautiful mountain scenery and the architectural and other artistic treasures of Pécs, the largest town in Transdanubia. A town with a history covering two thousand years, it contains Roman, medieval and Turkish relics, although the architecture of the Baroque and the subsequent periods predominates. Of the springs gushing forth from the tectonic features on the southern side of the Villány range, the Harkány springs where the water reaches a temperature of 62 °C are especially remarkable.

Besides the above two regions, Nagyatád, Csokonyavisonta, Igal, Abaliget, Orfű and Fadd—Dombori are tourist centres of local significance.

One-third of the tourists visiting Southern Transdanubia are foreign citizens.

5.3 Population

12 per cent of the country's population lives in Southern Transdanubia. Between 1949 and 1960, the population grew by 50000, but the subsequent decline in natural increase meant that migration losses were no longer offset and between 1960 and 1970 population of the region has declined. Despite of Tolna county, this process is going on at the beginning of 1980. However, the out-migration process too slowed down during the 1970s, and certain counties are now beginning to show signs of renewed population growth, although only to a moderate extent. In 1980, the region's population was some 30000 greater than in 1970, with Baranya county accounting for most of the increase.

Intra-regional movements have been on a larger scale than out-migration from the region and 70 to 80 per cent of the population changing domicile moved to places within their county. The migration balance of the great majority of villages is negative. Significant migration gains are registered only in the towns and in the settlements on the shore of Lake Balaton. The proportion of urban population has risen from 16 per cent to 37 per cent since 1949, yet the region is still the least urbanized area of the country.

In-migration has been most pronounced to Komló and Pécs. The latter's population doubled between 1949 and 1980. A similar dynamism is typical of the growth of the county towns and also of Nagykanizsa and Siófok. Out-migration has been greatest from the tiny villages of the agrarian districts with unfavourable endowments where even rudimentary services are absent.

The region's natural population increase, compared with that of the other regions, is unfavourable. It is characterized by a high mortality rate and a relatively low live birth rate. During the first half of 1980s, all of the four counties are characterized by the natural popular decrease. In Tolna, Baranya and Zala counties by $0{\cdot}1-0{\cdot}2\ \%_{00}$ decrease is the same as that of the country's tendency. Compared with the above data, Somogy county's natural decrease by $-2{\cdot}4$ per thousand is extremely high, follows that of the capital. Natural increase in the county and other towns of the regions show substantial differences. The county towns, as the centres of in-migration are characterized by natural increase.

The region's occupational structure in 1949 differed greatly from the national average, but the modern transformation of the occupational structure was ensured by large-scale investments in industry, which created a multitude of new job opportunities. By the mid-1970s, industrial employment had become greater than that in agriculture while the proportionate share of employees in the tertiary sector had almost reached the national percentage. Thus the nature of the region's industrialization also finds expression in the large-scale rise in the number of the industrially employed population.

Ethnically, the region is the most heterogeneous area of the country. Apart from the Hungarian population, there are German, Serbian, Šokats, Bunevats minorities in the region's eastern part, Croats and Slovenes in the west and a significant number of Gypsies in all parts.

5.4 Settlement

Physical geography and history have brought about the characteristic settlement structure of Southern Transdanubia. At the beginning of the 1984s, there were 20 towns and about 900 villages in the region.

As a result of the large number of small and very small villages, the settlement network is characterized by a high settlement density and a low level of urbanization.

The size of the region's villages generally rises from the south-west towards the north-east, while their density declines. The Zala—Somogy hillside area — with the exception of outer-Somogy — and the greater part of Baranya county constitute an area of small and very small villages with between a half and two-fifths of the settlements having populations of less than 500. In the Göcsej, there are many dwarf villages, called locally „szer" or „szeg", several of which usually constitute a single community. Dwarf villages, with populations of less than 300 are also characteristic of Baranya county. In Tolna and outer-Somogy counties, in the Villány range area and on the Mohács plain, small villages co-exist with medium-sized and large villages.

Small- and very small-village settlement networks are usually associated with unfavourable environments. They have neither an industrial nor economic basis, their institutional systems are deficient, their infrastructures poorly developed and in the smallest even rudimentary services are non-existent. In such areas, the urban network is also poorly developed. As a result of Turkish rule, which extended over a sizeable part of the region, the number of the long-established towns is small. Before the construction of railways there had been no real towns in the inner part of the hill country. The railway, in fact, played a great role in the evolution of the larger towns like Kaposvár and Nagykanizsa. During the period of capitalism, it was the gaining of county-town functions that gave some impulse to urban development, as in the case of Zalaegerszeg and Szekszárd. The present-day urban network has evolved from the few settlements with more than 5000 inhabitants and which perform modest urban functions, like Bonyhád, Dombóvár, Tamási, Nagyatád, Szigetvár, Marcali, Barcs and Lenti. After such urban nuclei had been provided with some industry, they did not need to grow much more to become central places, performing urban functions. There are very few medium-sized towns in the region, and as small towns are, as a rule, unable to perform the necessary functions, in their place large-scale urban developments are needed. By contrast, a significant agglomeration of production forces can be witnessed in the Pécs and Komló area. Co-operation linkages between these two large industrial and mining centres are expanding, and daily commuting is increasing. Although the all-out development of the county towns has speeded up the growth of population, development of the service network has been unable to keep pace.

5.5 Subregions and urban hinterlands

The economic-planning region of Southern Transdanubia can be divided into the following subregions: a) the Pécs—Komló area, b) the Danube valley; c) Southern Baranya county; d) the Balaton resort area; e) Kaposvár and its hinterland; f) Nagykanizsa and its hinterland; g) Zalaegerszeg and its hinterland.

a) The Pécs–Komló industrial area occupies the centre of the eastern half of the region and is dominated by coal mining and energy generation. In the longer term, a new base sector is likely to develop, which will galvanize the industry already existing. Along with the dominant heavy industry, light industry and food processing, especially in Pécs, are also significant.

The centre of the industrial area and of the region as a whole is Pécs, a provincial centre, with a population of 169 000. It is also the country's fifth most dynamically developing town. With its higher educational, health and cultural services, its hinterland extends, except for the western part of Zala county, over the whole region.

Founded by the Romans (Sopiana), Pécs was a handicraft and market town as well as an administrative and cultural centre during the Middle Ages. Several relics preserve the memory of the town's Turkish occupation. The layout of the central part in the form of an oblong square with rounded-off corners is of medieval origin. With the opening of the coal mines during the period of capitalism, manufacturing industry started to develop rapidly. After the Liberation, with the discovery of uranium, its mining activities experienced a spectacular expansion. ,,Uranium town" built in Mecsekalja, houses about 20 000 inhabitants. Its porcelain, leather and glove industries can be traced back for over 100 years, while the food industry, which includes brewing, champagne, cigarette manufacture, flour milling and meat and milk processing, are largely based on local produce. With its university, colleges, clinics, theatres and other cultural institutions, it is the intellectual centre of Southern Transdanubia. Its growth is exemplified by the fact that the surrounding agglomeration zone includes more than 10 settlements.

The other centre of the industrial area is Komló, a ,,town built upon coal", with 30 000 inhabitants. Over the past 30 years it has developed, thanks to its coking coal, from a backward mining village into a socialist town. During recent years, along with the extractive sector, light industry, especially furniture and clothing manufacture, have also developed at a rapid rate.

b) The Danube valley encompasses those administrative districts of Tolna county that are located along the Danube, that is, the southern part of the Mezőföld and the Sárköz. It is an area with considerable development potential, which has been enhanced by the establishment of the Paks Nuclear Power Station.

The centre of the area, Szekszárd, with 35 000 inhabitants, has lately exhibited a considerable growth. At the time of railway construction it was avoided by the main lines of the region, and its urban status was due entirely to county town functions and its famous wine. Szekszárd's dynamic growth, it had only 16 000 inhabitants in 1949, has been promoted by the new industries there since the 1960s.

Paks is situated on the Danube, and has 20 000 inhabitants. Along with its old industries of canning, brick making and trade, the siting of the country's first nuclear power station now under construction near the town was decisive in its gaining urban status.

Bonyhád, with 15000 inhabitants, lies at the centre of a famous cattle raising area, but already had some significant industries, mainly enamel, crockery and footwear manufacture, before the Second World War.

c) Southern Baranya county encompasses the Baranya hill country south of the Pécs–Komló industrial area, the Mohács island and parts of the area along the Dráva river. It is an agricultural subregion, whose economic character is determined by the large-scale raising of beef cattle and pigs for pork based on extensive maize cultivation. Vegetable growing around Szigetvár and on the Mohács island as well as viticulture which provides the good red wine of the Villány range are also significant.

Mohács, with 21000 inhabitants, situated on the Danube, is the market centre of Mohács island and of the southern section of the Danube valley. It is also an important Danube port. Part of its population is made up of German- and Šokats-minorities. Labour-intensive light industries play a leading role in its economy.

Siklós, with 11000 inhabitants, is the centre of a small area at the foot of the Villány range. The siting of the housing estate serving the Beremend Cement Works there has strengthened its urban functions.

Szigetvár, with 12000 inhabitants, is the centre of the western part of the subregion and a settlement of historic significance. An important role in its development was played by its large footwear and canning factories.

d) The Balaton resort area is, after the capital, the country's most important tourist district. Its significance for both domestic and foreign tourism continues to increase, although its accommodation capacity is inadequate to meet even today's demand during the height of the season. The southern shoreline of Lake Balaton is a relatively highly urbanized agglomeration extending from Balatonszabadi to Balatonberény, with the main resort centres being Siófok, Fonyód and Keszthely. Balatonföldvár is also significant from the point of view of foreign tourism. Boglárlelle and Zamárdi as well as Balatonmáriafürdő and Balatonfenyves, the two latter because of the increasing amount of international traffic of road No. 68, must be further developed.

Siófok, with 20000 inhabitants, is the largest resort of the area with a very significant foreign tourist turnover. Its development into a town has been promoted by the fact that it contains a quarter of the commercial accommodation facilities of the southern shoreline, comprising eight hotels, several camping sites and over 100 holiday homes of various enterprises, and together with institutions related to its resort function and industrial establishments. Its bread factory and meat and milk plants supply the region. Otherwise, its industry is dominated by the pipeline plant of the Petroleum Pipeline Construction Works.

Keszthely, with 22000 inhabitants, located on the south-western corner of the Balaton performs along with its tourist function, a significant educational-cultural function as well. It is the site of a University of Agriculture, of the Helikon Library and of the Balaton Museum. It is the buoyant trade centre of its surrounding area, although its industry is still only moderate with a plant of the Bakony Metal and Electrical Appliances Company, and clothing and food-processing works.

e) Kaposvár and its hinterland. The hinterland of Kaposvár, the region's second largest town, extends throughout Somogy county with the exception of the remoter, peripheral parts. The area is of an agrarian-industrial character, with cereal cultivation and cattle and pig rearing dominant. Vegetable growing is significant only around the Nagyatád canning factory and the vegetable zone supplying the Balaton area is hardly felt in the regional specialization. A relatively developed food-processing industry has, however, been built around the local agricultural production. Heavy industry began to appear during the period of extensive industrialization. Kaposvár, the regional centre with 72 000 inhabitants is increasingly the focus of high-level regional and controlling functions. At the beginning of the last century it was still a rural county town, and subsequently grew to become a rail centre and a market for agricultural produce. Before the Liberation, it had, apart from its sugar refinery and flour mills, no industry, and the first large-scale industrial plant, a textile factory, was set up in the 1950s. This was followed by a period of dynamic growth and with its colleges, a theatre and a museum, it is now the intellectual centre of Somogy county. New housing estates have been built to relieve the housing pressure resulting from industrial development, and the dwelling stock increased by more than 50 per cent between 1960 and 1975.

The medium-order centres of the area grew into towns from small urban nuclei, operating as the centres od smaller subregions, and usually performing the function of district seats. Such a place is Nagyatád, which, with 13 000 inhabitants, is the administrative, economic and supply centre of inner-Somogy. About half of its industrially employed population are engaged in the manufacture of tools, knitting threads and canned foods and commute daily from the surrounding 20 villages.

Marcali, with 13 000 inhabitants, is a minor town on the fringe of Lake Balaton. Its industrialization began in the 1960s with establishments like the Oil-Fuelled Stove Factory, the Precision Instruments Works and the May 1st Clothing Factory, in which, among other things blue jeans are manufactured in co-operation with a western firm.

Barcs, with 11 000 inhabitants, is an important freight centre on the banks of the Dráva river. Besides its nationally known co-operative farm, industry has also taken root with plants like equipment manufacturing for the construction industry, a lime-brick factory, plastics and panel-parquet manufacturing. These industries ensure job opportunities not only for the local inhabitants, but also for the population of surrounding settlements.

Dombóvár, with 20 000 inhabitants, is, in terms of population, the second largest town of Tolna county. Formerly it was characterized by its one-sided railway functions, but today it performs industrial and other urban functions. Here are located plants of the Láng Machine Works and of the Pécs Glove Factory. It has developed a close commuting relationship with nearby Kaposvár, together with which it constitutes an industrial concentration.

f) Nagykanizsa and its hinterland. The hill country with very few urban settlements lies between the two county towns of Nagykanizsa and Kaposvár. It is a typical agrarian area with intensive cattle raising and poultry farming together with supporting fodder cultivation and fruit growing. Half the county's poultry meat and egg production comes from this area.

Nagykanizsa, with 49 000 inhabitants, can only fulfill, despite its excellent location and dynamically developing industry, part of its tasks relating to the organization of the settlement network. During the past century, the town was, owing to the early established railway network, the main produce-collecting and produce-trading town of Southern Transdanubia. Following the First World War, its development was given an impetus by the discovery of the oil fields in southern Zala county. Its relationship with first the extraction and later with manufacturing industry involving such plants as the Lighting and Glass Factory of the United Incandescent Lamp and Electricity Ltd. have shifted the transport and servicing functions of the town increasingly towards industrial functions.

g) Zalaegerszeg and its hinterland. Owing to its relatively unfavourable location, the hinterland of Zalaegerszeg embraces the hill country of central Zala, where, owing to the fragmented settlement pattern, its role is of outstanding significance. The determinants of the rural economy are the large proportion of the area forested and related timber processing. Adverse natural endowments impede the development of agriculture, the main tradition being cattle rearing.

Zalaegerszeg, with 55 000 inhabitants, has been designed as a high-order central place. Yet, owing to its unfavourable location it cannot adequately fulfil its task, despite its dynamic growth and the advantages of being county seat. The growth of the town has been promoted by the rapid and many-sided development of industry. It has a number of modern plants such as a petroleum refinery, a clothing factory, a factory unit of the Ganz-Mávag Works, the Factory of the Cosmetic and Household Chemical Industry and a butter and cheese factory, all offering job opportunities to both the town's inhabitants and the population of surrounding settlements. The modern town centre is representative of the architectural style of many modern Hungarian towns of medium size.

Lenti, with 8000 inhabitants, is the modest centre of an area poor in urban settlements and situated near the national frontier. Its clothing and carpentry industry are based on the labour force of the settlement and surroundings.

6 The economic–planning region of Northern Transdanubia

The economic-planning region of Northern Transdanubia is Hungary's largest economic unit, accounting for about 20 per cent of the country's area and a population close to 18 per cent of the national total. With this percentage it is the most densely populated region after the Central region. It encompasses 5 counties, Fejér, Veszprém, Komárom, Győr-Sopron and Vas.

The region is one of the country's most developed and most complex economic units and is relatively simple to delimit spatially. Its development has been dynamic, which has found expression in its favourable production and employment structures, the rapid development of key industries as well as in the rising level of urbanization.

Owing to the relatively high level and complexity of its economic development, the region plays an important role in the domestic and partly in the international spatial division of labour. Its industry is multi-faceted. The extraction sector, the basic-material and the heavy manufacturing industries, and the light and food-processing industries are represented in the region's economy, and indeed most of them constitute a national specialization. Along with primary mineral raw materials, coal-based electricity generation has been an important rationale behind the location of various branches of the basic-material and manufacturing industries. The economic history of the region has also fundamentally influenced the industrial and general economic progress of the Little Plain.

6.1 Natural endowments and resources

With its varied relief, climate and soil characteristics, the region can be divided into the Transdanubian Central Mountains, the subalpine uplands, the Little Plain, and the rolling hills of the Mezőföld.

1. The Transdanubian Central Mountains, made up of the Bakony, Vértes, Visegrád, Pilis and Velence Mountains, extend in a north-east, south-west direction achieving a length of about 200 kms and a width ranging from 20 to 50 kms. They are composed, for the most part, of sedimentary rocks, limestones, dolomites and marls superimposed on sunked crystalline base. It was Miocene volcanism that brought about such basalt-capped, cone-shaped hills as the Badacsony and Szigliget, which surround the Tapolca Basin as well as the basalt tufas of Tihany peninsula. The fault lines had a decisive role to play in determining the layout of the lines of communication. The mountain ranges and adjoining peripheral parts belong to the most forested areas of the country, and are relatively rich mineral resources, like brown coal, bauxite, manganese, quartz sand, kaolin and construction stone.

2. The other large landscape unit is the subalpine area, connected in both structure rock composition, and relief with the eastern Alps of which it is an

extension. The highest peak of the area and the region as a whole is Írottkő, 883 metres high, in the Kőszeg Mountains. The subalpine area is poor in minerals, the most important occurrences being lignite, talc and limestone.

3. The third landscape unit is the Little Plain lying between the Subalps and the Transdanubian Central Mountains, with a surface formed by both deposition and denudation. It is centred on the Győr basin, the largest contiguous plainland of Transdanubia, while the Szigetköz, the Moson plain and Rábaköz are part of the alluvial fan of the Danube. Southwards are found the Marcal basin with the gravel-covered Kemenesalja, Somló hill and Ság hill emerging like islands from the plain. The Little Plain is poor in minerals, but the carbon dioxide occurrence near Mihályi is the most extensive in the country.

4. The Mezőföld extends east from the Transdanubian Central Mountains up to the Danube. It is similar, in many respects, to the Little Plain, and with its thick cover of different composition fronts the Danube valley with steep loess bluffs 30 to 50 metres in height.

As a result of its geographical location and relief conditions, the region's climate is varied. In the subalpine area and Central Mountains especially in the Bakony, the mean temperature is below average, with minor annual variations. The winter and thus the growing period, too, are shorter, but the annual total of sunshine rises rapidly from west towards east, largely independently of relief. From the point of view of its climate, the Little Plain is one of the country's most balanced areas. The Mezőföld, belonging to the Little Plain's climatic zone, reflects the latter's characteristic features.

Average annual precipitation on the higher parts of the mountains and on the hills of the subalpine area and of South-Vas county varies between 800 and 900 mm. Only slightly less is the precipitation of the western side of the Bakony, and it remains sufficiently high throughout the greater part of the Little Plain excepting the middle part of the Győr basin, to remove any hazard of drought.

From the point of view of hydrology and water management, the economic-planning region can be divided into two parts with sharply differing character and endowments. Its western and northern parts constitute one area with a relatively dense river system, while the watercourses of the Central Mountains and of Mezőföld — with the exception of the Danube flowing along the region's frontier — are sparse, and their water resources are inadequate. The subalpine area and the Little Plain are drained, for the most part, by the Rába river, whose discharge is mainly determined by precipitation conditions in the Eastern Alps of Austria.

The drainage network of the Transdanubian Central Mountains is generally sparse, and the rivers are of insignificant regime. Even the territories with abundant precipitation exhibit a dearth of surface drainage, because of the limestone and dolomite bedrock, although underground streams come to the surface at the foot of the hills and in such basins as that at Tapolcafő.

Of the region's rivers only the Danube represents a significant reserve of energy, and work on the Gabchikovo–Nagymaros Dam, a joint Hungarian–Czechoslovak project, has already begun in the Szigetköz. Among the rivers only the Danube, resp. its Moson branch, is navigable.

The Balaton, Velence, Fertő and Tata lakes are utilized for fishing, irrigation, reed growing and transport, but their recreational and tourist function is the most important.

Soil endowments, like the other natural factors, display a wide variety. The most fertile soils are to be found on the loess terraces of the Mezőföld, and in the Győr Basin where meadow soils predominate. Of greatest extent, however, are the slightly acidic brown forest soils, while gravel skeletal soils predominate on the Vas uplands and Kemeneshát. The decomposed volcanic soils of the Badacsony highlands, coupled with a favourable climate are conducive for vine and fruit growing. The Transdanubian Central Mountains, in general, are quite heavily eroded as are the northern part of the Mezőföld, the Vas hill country and Bakonyalja. In places the soils on limestone and dolomite bedrock as in the Hajmáskér area, have been completely denuded.

The negative impact of society on the environment is particularly apparent in the industrial belt of Central Transdanubia. Ajka and its surroundings and the Veszprém chemical triangle have some of the most polluted air in the country.

6.2 The economy

This economic-planning region is second only to the Central region in its degree of industrialization and general economic development. Its productive forces and population are, however, located in a relatively small area, primarily in the industrial belt of Central Transdanubia, but spreading over into its several large and medium-sized towns.

6.2.1 Industry

Industry occupies the leading position in the region's economic structure as clearly manifested by the fact that it employs over two-thirds of the total labour force. Indeed, industrial employment is, in relative terms, even higher than in the Central region.

Close to two-thirds of those employed by socialist industry work in heavy industry while about a quarter are engaged in light industry and 8 to 9 per cent in the food-processing industry. Within the region, however, quite significant differences exist between counties not only in the level of industrialization but especially in the relative proportions between heavy and light industry.

The number of settlements with an industrial character is large. Although the concentration of the most important plants is high, yet in many of the

Selected industrial data for Northern Transdanubia, 1977 and 1981

Designation	Percentage share of the national total 1977	1981
Number of industrial earners	20	19
Value of gross fixed assets	24	22
Installed motive power	26	28
Use of electricity by industry	35	34
Output of selected products		
Bauxite	100	100
Manganese	100	100
Brown coal	57	55
Electrical energy	19	17
Synthetic fibres	100	100
Alumina	100	100
Foundry aluminium	100	100
Carbon dioxide	100	100
Foundry coke	100	100
Fine steel sheet	90	92
Radio receivers	95	100
Television sets	62	57
Buses	47	49
Fibreboard	76	81
Aluminium semifinished products	80	70
Cement	21	17
Petrol	23	15

smaller settlements the number of industrial employees is substantial, and in the majority of the region's administrative districts the proportion of industrial earners is above the national average.

As a result, there are few backward areas, and non-agricultural job opportunities are generally within commuter reach of most of the population. The southern areas of Vas county are in least favourable position, where living standards and incomes are adversely affected not only by a shortage of industrial employment but also by the adverse natural endowments of agriculture.

In summary, the various characteristics of industry in Northern Transdanubia are listed as follows:

— the favourable proportion of the light and food-processing industries, along with the leading role of heavy industry, and particularly the extractive and basic-material industries;

— the high degree of vertical integration, the existence of closed, or partially closed, production cycles, and the evolution of developed spatial vertical systems;

— the great weight of energy- and electricity-intensive branches;

— the significant role of dynamic key industries, like vertical aluminium integration, transport machinery manufacture and computer technology;

– apart from engineering works manufacturing finished products, the above average proportion of plants producing components, spare parts and subassemblies, which play an increasing role in both the national and international division of labour, and which through socialist integration have led to the development and expansion of the Rába Engineering Works, the Bakony Works, Ikarus and Videoton.

Power generation. Coal has played a major role in the creation of several of the vertically integrated industrial establishments of the region. On the basis of brown coal, a number of sectoral subregions have come into being, for instance, electricity generation and coal-based chemical industry. Although, coal declined in significance during „cheap energy decade", coal mining has nonetheless remained an important sector. A greater part of the region's significant coal reserves (estimated at 2·9 million tons), which developed during the Cretaceous and Miocene periods, is good-quality brown coal. The largest reserves are to be found in the Dorog coal field in the eastern foreground of the Gerecse Mountains, but, owing to heavy tectonic activities and karst-water danger, only part of them can be exploited economically.

The region's largest brown-coal output is derived from the Tatabánya basin where the known reserves are about the same as in the Dorog basin, yet where the economically exploitable reserves are somewhat greater. The danger of karst-water intrusion, however, again makes mining difficult and expensive. With the recent discoveries, the Tatabánya field extends eastwards, towards Nagyegyháza, Csordakút and Mány.

Southwest of Tatabánya are to be found the Oroszlány–Pusztavám coal fields mostly of Eocene origin, which are less exposed to the karst-water peril. A new economically workable field is also located here in the Márkus Mountain area.

The region's fourth coal field is located in Central Transdanubia, and consists of geologically disconnected Cretaceous and Eocene coal basins. Largest among them is the Ajka–Padragkút coal basin, while the Balinka–Kisgyón mines, now under reconstruction and expansion, and located south of the Dudar and Mór trenches on the northern fringes of the Bakony Mountains, will soon significantly contribute to the region's output. Lignite mined at Várpalota has the sole function of supplying fuel to the nearby Inota Thermal Power Station.

The newly discovered lignite field in western Hungary, around the village of Torony, also belongs to the region. About three quarters of the field, with its 1 billion tons of known or probable reserves, belong to Hungary, and one quarter to Austria. Its location in the frontier zone recommends joint exploitation and the establishment of a large-capacity power station.

The principal function of coal mining is power generation, but substantial amounts are still used by the industry and population within the region, and significant quantities are also transported to the capital and south-west Transdanubia. The region's coal mining is now passing through a phase of a vigorous development within the framework of the so-called „Eocene programme". This includes the opening of new mines at Márkus Mountain, Nagyegyháza, Mány and Lencse Mountain as well as the Balinka and Dudar pit reconstructions. The coal will go in increasing amounts to power plants and output will reach 6 million tons by the second half of the 1980s. The implementation of the programme is an extremely important and pressing task not only because extraction costs will be 20 to 30 per cent less than the price of imported coal, but also because the reserves of existing mines will soon be depleted.

Based on its coal production, the region is a significant area of electricity generation, amounting to approximately 1000 MW, or one-fifth of the country's total output. The thermal power stations at Tatabánya, Oroszlány, Ajka, Inota I and Inota II, display the technical parameters of the constructions of the 1950s and 1960s, and the Oroszlány 200 MW station and the Inota II Gas-Turbine Power Station of similar performance are of outstanding significance.

Owing to the great weight of electricity-intensive branches, the region is unable to fully satisfy its electricity requirements during certain peak periods. Although the shortages are not substantial, the great weight of energy-intensive branches in the region has resulted in the decision to construct a new large-capacity thermal power station at Bicske.

Industrial vertical integration *(Fig. 69)*. The region's most developed, vertically integrated and basic industry is the bauxite-aluminium industry. All the production phases — bauxite mining, alumina production, manufacture of foundry aluminium, semifinished and finished-product manufacture are located in the region. As a result of expanded co-operation, regional productive linkages between the individual phases of production have also become increasingly closer. Coal mining and electricity generation may also be regarded as promoting vertical integration in that a significant proportion of their output serves the aluminium industry. Moreover, increasingly reliance has been placed on international co-operation since the 1960s.

The majority of Hungarian bauxite reserves is located in the region, and further discoveries and expansion of capacity may be expected. The largest reserves are to be found in the Bakony Mountains, primarily within the Halimba—Sümeg—Tapolca triangle, where, along with the old mines at Halimba, Szőc and Nyirád — several new mines — Halimba III, Deákpuszta, Darvastó — have been opened the past few years. Prospecting around Fenyőfő, Bakonyszentlászló and in the Sümeg area have also been successful. Moreover, new pits such as those at Rák Mountain and Kincsesbánya have also been opened in the older mining area, and extraction has shifted towards greater depths. Of the 3 million tons of output over 2 million tons are processed in domestic alumina factories, while the rest can be economically exported.

The second phase of the vertical integration process, alumina production, is represented by the two Ajka-based plants and the factories at Almás-

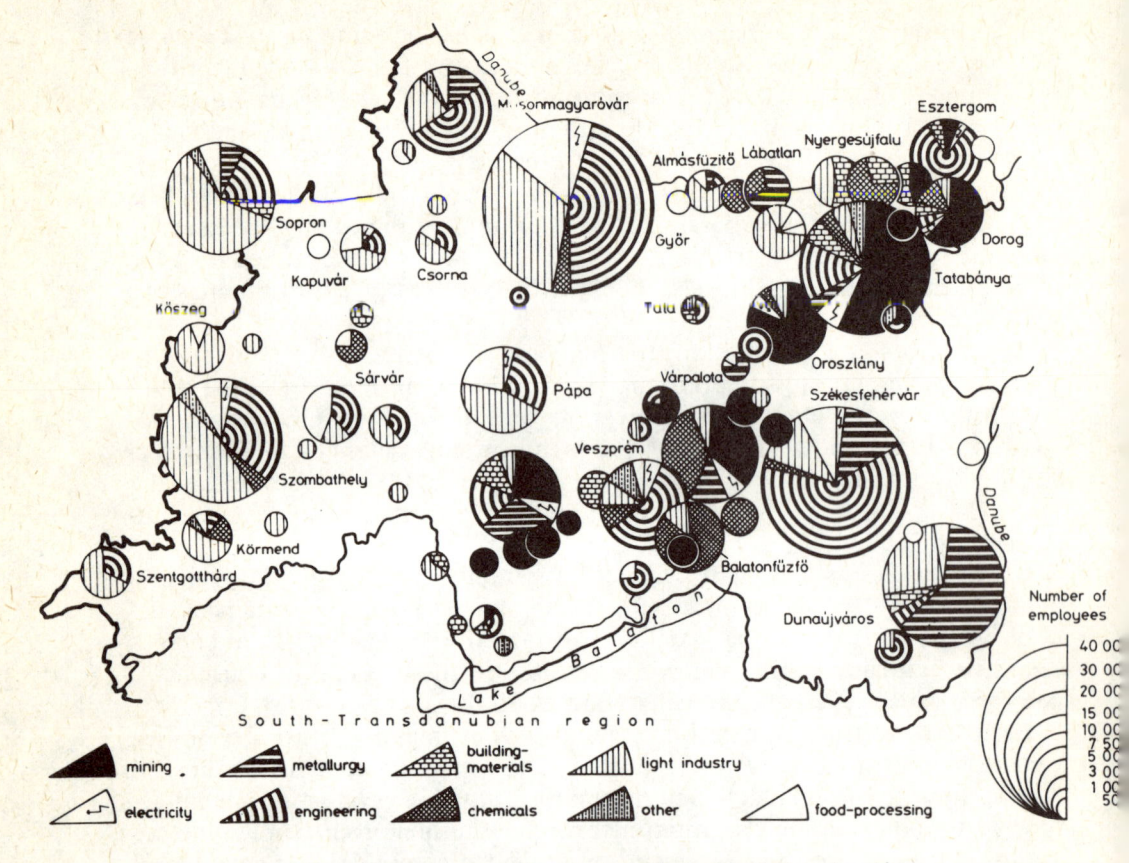

Fig. 69. The spatial location of industry in the North-Transdanubian
economic—planning region (1981)

füzitő and Mosonmagyaróvár. Their combined output is about 800 000 tons annually.

In the Alumina and Artificial Corundum Factory at Mosonmagyaróvár, artificial corundum abrasives, vanadium pentoxide (for manufacturing hot vanadium alloy), zircon-based fireproof materials and moulds (e.g. zircon for the casing of blast furnaces) and aluminium sulphate are produced as weel as alumina. The greater part of the alumina output is used in the international socialist division of labour or is, in the traditional sense, exported, and only one-fifth is used by domestic aluminium foundries.

While close to half the crude foundry output of aluminium was once processed in Budapest, since the mid-1970s the greater part of the various finished products (various alloyed and eloxalized plates, strips, tubes, wires and alloys) have been produced by the Székesfehérvár Light Metal Works, excepting certain semifinished products manufactured in the metallurgical plants. Within the framework of complex development, plants have also been located in the region which utilize large amounts of pre- and semimanufactured materials for manufacturing their finished products.

The region possesses favourable conditions for the further development of the aluminium industry, and given world-market prices it may now be economical to set up a new aluminium furnace with a capacity of 100 000 tons in the Bicske area. This is because the largely coal-based generation of electricity for smelting now enjoys a comparative price advantage over oil-based power stations.

The iron and steel of the region is also vertically integrated in the form of the Danube Iron Works at Dunaújváros. The Iron Works is a completely production closed-cycle and includes pig-iron and steel output, cold- and hot-rolling mills and the manufacture of foundry coke, all based on raw materials brought in from abroad or from other regions.

The Danube Iron Works ranks first nationally in crude iron and soon in steel production as well, concentrating particularly on cold-rolled thin steel sheets. Welded spiral tube production is based on the manufacture of sheet steel, while oxygen-converter unit capable of handling 130 tons is now being built. It may also be suggested that the capacity to manufacture ferro-manganese steels using the region's manganese ores found at Úrkút and Olaszfalu would be a further useful addition to the Works. The manganese could also be used to supply the aluminium-alloy plant of the Székesfehérvár Light Metal Works.

The nitrogen industry constitutes another vertical production process. Although no longer utilize local raw material, like Várpalota lignite, the chemical plants on the north-eastern shore of Lake Balaton constitute a vertically integrated production series in that ammonia, nitric acid and ammonia nitrate are both produced and further processed by the Pét Nitrogen Works, as well as being the feed-stock for the Peremarton Chemical Works and the Balatonfűzfő Nitrochemical Industrial Plants, in turn producing industrial explosives, compound fertilizers and other substances.

After Budapest and its agglomeration, Northern Transdanubia is the country's most significant area of the engineering industry. The development of engineering began in the Little Plain as early as the second half of the last century, first with the production of agricultural machinery and then transport equipment. The majority of people engaged in engineering still in fact work in the transport vehicle sector. Several branches of the region's engineering industry are engaged in close co-operation with one another, and constitute a territorial concentration with the component manufacturing plants. This territorial vertical structure is best exemplified by the Győr-based Railway Carriage and Engineering Works (Rába) and the Székesfehérvár factory of Ikarus.

Most significant is the Győr-based Railway Carriage and Engineering Works, the most profitable large-scale enterprise not only in the region but in the country as a whole. With its ancillary plants located within and outside the region, e.g. at Celldömölk, Sárvár, Mosonmagyaróvár, Szombathely and Budapest, it employs more than 20 000 persons. Most significant of its wide product range are the output of Rába—MAN (Machine factory Augsburg—Nürnberg) diesel engines for commercial vehicles, and the rear axles and transmissions for buses, heavy trucks and trolleybuses. Rear axles are exported to the Soviet Union, Czechoslovakia, the USA and to other countries as well. A new product of the Works is the Rába—Steiger (production co-operation between the Rába and the US Steiger machine factory) heavy-duty agricultural tractor. Heavy trucks and specialist lorries are also produced.

Another large enterprise manufacturing commercial vehicles is the Székesfehérvár Factory Unit of Ikarus, where almost 50 per cent of many varied types of bus (almost 6000 units) are produced and assembled. The factory has extensive co-operation links and builds into its buses chassis engines from the Csepel Motor Works, and rear axles from Rába Engineering, while steel and aluminium plates as well as tubes and castings come from Dunaújváros. Linked to vehicle manufacturing is the Székesfehérvár plant of the Machine-Tool Works, whose main products are, apart from machine tools, brakes for rail and road vehicles. The Main production profile of the Bakony Works for Metal and Electrical Appliances located in Veszprém is the mass production of components and subassemblies for the Soviet Lada and more recently the Polski Fiat 126 cars. The enterprise has an extensive network of plants both in and outside the region.

In connection with the territorial linkages within vehicle production, mention should also be made of the developed foundry industry with major plants in Győr, Komárom, Mosonmagyaróvár and Sopron.

An important new combine producing and processing basic materials for the use of light industry is the Cellulose and Corrugated Cardboard Factory in Dunaújváros. The major products of the combine are sulphate cellulose from straw, corrugated cardboard, and writing and printing paper. Together with other plants, it plays an important role in developing indirect integration in a town with basically a heavy-industrial structure [1].

The construction industry is spatially also of integrated structure. The cement works draw on local sources for the satisfaction of their raw-material and energy demands, and further processing is also fairly well developed. These are, among others, concrete construction elements, asbestos-cement pipes, roofing tiles, and the system housing construction units in Győr and Veszprém. Similar is the situation of the glass industry, at Tokod and Ajka which, like all glass factories of the country, is supplied with quartz sand from Fejérvárcsurgó, while fuel partly comes from the Dorog coal field.

Light industry. Along with the leading role of heavy industry, light industry is primarily represented by the textile industry, although hide- and timber-processing and the paper industry are also significant. As to the geographical distribution of light industry, the Little Plain with its long tradition plays a prominent role; while elsewhere it is generally of recent origin.

All branches of the textile industry are represented, but cotton, followed by wool and furnishings, are the leading branches, while over 50 per cent of the nation's silk industry is found here. The region provides some one-third of the national output of crude cotton cloths, but the weaving capacity is less than one-fifth, and finishing capacity barely more than a quarter of the country's total. The main textile plants are located in Győr, Pápa, Szombathely and Székesfehérvár.

The woollen industry of the region, including the production of wool-type cloth is relatively more important nationally than cottons and more than one-third of woollen threads and over a quarter of woollen cloths are manufactured in the region. The largest plant of the wool industry is the „Richards" Fine Cloth Factory in Győr, which specializes in producing suits and costumes, while the plants in Szombathely, Kőszeg, Sopron and Tata specialize in the manufacture of furnishings like carpets, blankets and upholstery materials. In Dunaújváros, there is only one weaving plant.

The flax-fibre finishing and thread-manufacturing capacities in Komárom, are the largest in the country, but one quarter of finished flax goods are also produced in the region. Half the country's rayon cloth comes from the Szentgotthárd and Sopron plants, while finishing is done in the capital.

The plants of the knitwear and clothing industries are located in Mosonmagyaróvár, Győr, Celldömölk, Sopron and Székesfehérvár. The largest shoe factory is in Szombathely, but also significant is the output of the Tata and Dunaújváros factories. The only artificial leather factory is in Győr, which produces artificial leather from softened PVC powder for home use and for export purposes. The largest plant of the wood and wood-working industry is the Saw Mill in Szombathely, where fibre-board manufacture is the most important production accounting for three quarters of national output. The three large factories of the furniture industry are located in Győr, Székesfehérvár and Veszprém.

6.2.2 Agriculture and food processing

The total output and general level of the region's agriculture and food-processing industry is above the national average. This is shown by the indices of output, mechanization, fertilizer consumption, plant cultivation and animal husbandry, and, more generally, by the marketing indices and income per unit area. This region stands in terms of mechanization at the national average, while in fertilizer consumption it occupies first place.

For several decades the general agricultural level of the region, particularly of the Little Plain, has been among the highest in the country. Despite the catching up of other regions and the strong levelling-out tendencies, the region as a whole, and especially the areas with favourable natural endowments, have remained amongst the most developed agricultural areas. Owing to marked divergencies in relief, to different soil endowments and climatic

Selected agricultural data for Northern Transdanubia,
1977 and 1981

Designation	Percentage share of the national total	
	1977	1981
Cultivated area	20	19
Agricultural employment	18	17
Wheat	20	20
Maize	20	21
Sugar beet	21	22
Lucerne	17	17
Cattle population	23	24
Pig population	18	18

conditions, the level of agricultural activities is not, however, uniform. There are substantial differences between counties, of which Komárom is the most developed, followed by Fejér, Győr-Sopron, Veszprém and Vas. The proportion of areas with unfavourable natural endowments — more than one-sixth of the country — can be found, primarily, in Veszprém and Vas counties.

The most marked specializations of the region are fodder grain and green fodder production and on the basis of their meadows and pastures, cattle rearing, dairy farming, beef-cattle marketing and the growing of industrial crops, mainly sugar beet and flax. Poultry farming and egg production, the production of mixed poultry food as well as grape growing and wine production are also significant.

Varied relief characteristics greatly influence land use with agricultural land accounting for just under 70 per cent of the area.

Wheat is grown extensively everywhere, even in the poorly endowed parts of the Central Mountains. As regards sown area, there are few inter-county differences, but yields vary from 4·7 tons per hectare in Fejér to more than one ton less in Veszprém county.

The area sown to autumn and spring barley is high, especially in Győr-Sopron and Vas counties, due to the high average yields achieved and to the demands of the brewing industry.

The area sown to maize is also rather extensive, being surpassed only by the Southern Transdanubian and the Southern Plain regions. Its area is largest in Komárom and Fejér counties, accounting for 35 to 38 per cent of arable land, where average yields of 4·7 to 5·1 tons per hectare are above the national average. Yields in Veszprém county, however, average only 3·7 tons, and are lower than both the national and regional levels.

The most important industrial crop of the region is sugar beet accounting for close to a quarter of the national output. Some of the sugar refineries regularly contract to process sugar beet from counties Tolna, Somogy, Zala outside the region. Sunflower growing is also spreading in Fejér county.

Apart from fodder grain, green fodder is also significant, with clover being grown in the cooler and wetter western parts, and lucerne in the east, usually with irrigation.

The cultivation of raspberries in the surroundings of Győr and Sokoró, of apricots in Fejér county, of almonds, peaches and mixed fruit in the Balaton Highland are significant. Although there are no vegetable specializations comparable to those in other regions of the country, some development is nonetheless being registered in this field also. It is, however, generally in the form of small-scale cultivation around towns that is typical of the region.

A characteristic agricultural specialization is vine growing. Favourable climatic, soil and relief endowments and long production traditions have combined in the evolution of the so-called historical wine districts of Badacsony, Balatonfüred–Csopak, Somló, Mór and Sopron.

Owing to its diversified and intensive fodder farming, the region is the country's most significant cattle-rearing area, and livestock density per unit area of arable land is highest in the country. In addition, pig rearing and poultry farming has also grown significantly in more recent years. The areas of most intensive cattle breeding are to be found in Vas county, in Rábaköz and around Pápa. The region also leads in the quantity of milk produced and sold per unit area, and milk yields far exceed the national average. Although most of the cattle stock are dairy cows, the region also occupies first place in the marketing of beef cattle as well.

The fodder supply for pig rearing is ensured, apart from maize, by barley and potatoes as well as by the by-products of the food-processing industry, together with imported protein fodder. Although pig density falls somewhat behind the national average, the weight of pig rearing has greatly grown and covers not only the demands of the region's population and meat-processing industry, but also supplies appreciable quantities of pork to domestic and foreign markets. Sheep farming is fairly significant in Fejér and Veszprém counties.

In poultry farming and the marketing of poultry meat the region ranks third behind the two Plainland regions, but lies first in the number of eggs produced and marketed. Although the country's largest „egg factory" is to be found on the Bábolna State Farm, its significance lies primarily in the breeding of hybrids, baby chicks and broiler hens for domestic use and export. The state farm is an important innovation centre for poultry raising, and has delivered complete poultry-breeding systems, together with regular supplies of breeding stock to the Soviet Union, Iraq and other foreign countries.

Food processing is characterized by its diversity — meat and poultry processing, sugar refining, distilling, milk processing and vegetable-oil production. The largest meat factory is at Pápa, while poultry processing is carried on mainly in Győr and Sárvár. Canned ham and the other much sought-after canned foods of the region's meat-processing plants are also exported to Western Europe and the USA. The milk-processing industry has tended to specialize in cheese manufacture.

The sugar refineries located at Petőháza, Sárvár and Ercsi provide nearly one-third of the country's sugar output, while distilling, confectionery, vegetable-oil production and brewing are each represented by one plant in the region. The largest centres of flour milling are Székesfehérvár, Szombathely and Csorna. Canning and freezing are represented by the large-capacity cold-storage houses in Győr and Székesfehérvár.

6.2.3 Transport

The region's transport network is more developed than the national average, since it has to cater for the large-scale transport of mineral resources and basic materials, the development of intra- and inter-regional production co-operation, internal and foreign tourism and international transit traffic.

The density of the region's railway network is above the national average, and ensures good communication with the Central region and Southern Transdanubia, and neighbouring countries. Owing to the closure of many branch lines carrying little traffic, the length of the region's network has diminished, but at the same time the relative share of main, double-tracked and electrified lines has increased. All the major industrial districts, towns and important tourist areas are linked with the national system by trunk lines.

6.2.4 Tourism

Owing to its diverse natural endowments — Lake Balaton, Lake Velence, mountainous areas and spas — and cultural tradition, the region has a significant tourist potential, which could be tapped more efficiently by the large-scale development of the hotel, trade and transport infrastructure. Tourist accommodation capacity made some headway during the 1960s and 1970s, but the utilization of the endowments still lags far behind the possibilities. Two-thirds of hotel accommodation can be found in Veszprém county, mostly in the resorts along the northern shore of Lake Balaton.

The region's two main tourist areas of international significance are the northern shore of Lake Balaton together with the Bakony Mountains and the subalpine area. The deeper water on the northern shore of Lake Balaton is favoured not only for bathing, but also for swimming and sailing. The lake, the slopes of the varied hilly landscapes with their vineyards, orchards and patches of woods, the perpendicular basalt columns of the Badacsony, and remnants of former volcanism present a unique scenery. In addition, the northern lakeside is also rich in historic monuments, and it is here, after Budapest, that tourist facilities have reached their highest level. The Balaton resort area is easily accessible both by rail and road, especially since the Sopron—Balatonederics road was built, which serves tourists coming from Austria, Czechoslovakia and Western Germany.

The subalpine area along the western frontier of the country constitutes a special tourist attraction with its climatic health resorts and spas, in addition to the beauty of its landscape and to the historical monuments in Sopron, Kőszeg, Fertőd, Fertőrákos, Ják, Balf, Bük and Nagycenk.

6.3 Population

The region's industrial concentrations, established during the period of socialist industrial development, constitute one of the strongest attraction zones for internal migrants. The new socialist towns, and the rapidly developing settlement network in the industrial areas of the Transdanubian Central Mountains have absorbed large numbers. The process of out-migration has slowed down since the early 1970s, and some of the areas which formerly suffered large losses are beginning to regain some of their population.

6.4 Settlement

Owing to the large number of small and very small villages, settlement is characterized by a high degree of urbanization. The number of settlements per 100 sq km is higher only in the region of Southern Transdanubia and Northern Hungary. The average size of villages is less than 1300 and thus far below the national average. As in Southern Transdanubia, here, too the size of villages is increasing, and settlement density decreases from south-west to northeast.

With its 24 towns, the region occupies first place in the country as regards urban settlement density. Although the proportion of urban population (46 per cent) is below the national average, it is above the general urbanization level of the provinces, that is, excluding Budapest. The towns belong to the most urbanized settlements of the country because, unlike those of the Great Plain, the proportion of the rural population in them is very low. This also applies to a number of other settlements, for example, Szentgotthárd, Zirc and Vasvár. With the exception of Fejér county, the territorial distribution of towns is fairly even, and, as a result of the planned development policy of the past decade, there are no longer areas without major urban centres. In those areas which are still somewhat deficient in towns, places like Mór, Zirc and Szentgotthárd may develop, given the possibility of increasing their industrial and supply functions, into urban centres within a relatively short period of time.

Urbanization has affected not only the urban centres but industrial development, the opening of new mines, and large-scale tourism have helped many rural settlements to proceed towards full urbanization, in which occupational structure, functional provision, and even outward appearance have undergone radical change. Such semiurbanized settlements are to be found in large numbers in the Balaton resort area, around the Tapolca Basin, and in the industrial belt along the Danube. In the northern part of Komárom county there are a number of urban-like villages, i. e. Tokod, Lábatlan, Nyergesújfalu and Almásfüzitő, which are very important labour attraction centres, and are functionally linked to neighbouring urban centres.

6.5 Subregions and urban hinterlands

a) Győr and its hinterland: Győr, with 124000 inhabitants, is a major provincial centre as well as being the centre of the Northern Transdanubian region. It is the 6th most populous town and the third industrial centre of the country, containing the largest provincial expression of the engineering and textile industries. The town, founded during the rule of the last kings of the Árpád dynasty, has been a production, administrative and cultural centre for 700 years. Contributing to its rapid development has been its favourable geographical location at the confluence of the Danube, Rába and Rábca rivers. It attracts some 20 000 commuters in the zone up to a radius of about 50 kilometres from the centre. One of the main tasks of urban development is to ensure that, along with industry, the other urban and regional functions are strengthened and expanded, and this objective has been helped by the establishment of the Technical College for Transport and Telecommunication. The town's largest industrial establishment is the Railway Carriage and Engineering Works (Rába), while many branches of light industry are also represented in the town.

The small and medium-sized towns within its hinterland are appreciably industrialized, and of their own right are centres of micro-regions. Mosonmagyaróvár, with 30 000 inhabitants, is an important centre of the engineering and textile industries, and its alumina factory was the first to be established in the country. It has a university of agriculture. Sopron, with 54000 inhabitants, is one of the country's oldest towns and is rich in historical monuments. Its most important industrial branches are the textile and clothing industries, but also significant are its foundry, mass-metal manufacture and food-processing industry. The town and its environs with Fertőd, Fertőrákos, Balf and Nagycenk, are much frequented resort areas, and the scenes of cultural arrangements. There is in it a University of Forestry and Timber Processing. Kapuvár, with 11 000 inhabitants, and Csorna, with 12 000 inhabitants, are small towns in a rich agricultural area and have significant food-processing industries and branch plants of the Győr Engineering Works. Pápa, with 31 000 inhabitants, is the urban centre of the Marcal Basin and Bakonyalja, and also an old, renowned school town. Most of its industrial labour force is engaged in the cotton-textile industry, in manufacturing household electrical appliances, as well as in the meat and milk industries.

Celldömölk, with 13 000 inhabitants, is an important railway junction, with branch plants of the Győr Engineering Knitwear Factories.

b) The Mezőföld and Dunaújváros and its hinterland. The Mezőföld is a typical agrarian area with its east-south-eastern part belonging to the hinterland of Dunaújváros and with its western part to that of Székesfehérvár. Along with its large-scale wheat and maize production, sugar-beet, sunflowers and fruit and vegetable growing are also significant. Apart from Dunaújváros, industry is only represented by the sugar refinery at Ercsi, by the distillery at Szabadegyháza and component manufacturing at Sárbogárd. The centre of the subregion, Dunaújváros, with 61 000 inhabitants, is the country's first and largest new socialist town. It is not only an industrial town and an attractive centre for labour, but its urban functions are highly developed, and are most comprehensive of any socialist industrial town. The town's national significance is derived from the fully integrated Danube Iron Works, whose fine-rolled sheet manufacture is of decisive significance for the engineering industry. In addition to metallurgy as its base industry, significant cellulose, paper, textile-clothing and footwear industries as well as watch making and typewriter production have also been established.

c) The industrial belt associated with the Transdanubian Central Mountains occupies the central part of the region, and can be divided into three easily definable parts. The first is the Tatabánya and Oroszlány area, where the character of industry is determined by coal mining, coal-based electricity generation and other energy-intensive branches. Tatabánya, with 76 000 inhabitants, is the centre of the subregion and, being a county town, is also an administrative centre. Dominant in the town's industrial pattern is heavy industry (coal mining, electricity generation, briquette production, carbide, lime and cement manufacture and engineering). Thanks to its functions and good transport facilities, the town's hinterland reaches into quite remote areas. Oroszlány, with 21 000 inhabitants, has developed into a town owing to its coal and electricity generation. Tata, with 24 000 inhabitants, complements the one-sided, heavy industrial character of the two former towns with its light industry. As a result of its natural endowments and historical monuments, it is also tourist resort.

The other area of the industrial belt is the subregion bounded by the lines connecting Székesfehérvár, Várpalota, Veszprém and Balatonfűzfő. This area, in view of the progressive character of the industries located in it and the vigorous development of its urban settlements, can be regarded as one of the country's most dynamically developing industrial subregions. Of its towns, Székesfehérvár, a county town with 103 000 inhabitants, is one of the country's oldest settlements of historical significance. Today it is a heavily industrialized town with a complexity of functions. Besides the industrial branches already mentioned, a large enterprise of outstanding importance is Videoton, the Hungarian production base for the manufacture of television sets, radio receivers and computers. It has an extensive network of auxiliary plants in its hinterland at Veszprémfajsz, Sárbogárd, Ajka and Tab. It is also an important railway and road junction. Veszprém, with 55 000 inhabitants, is a county town and a scientific and cultural centre with a University and a Research Institute for Chemistry. It plays a prominent role as a tourist and distribution centre, but its industry has also developed considerably. The Bakony Works in particular contributed to the town's dynamic population growth. Várpalota, with 29 000 inhabitants, is an industrial town created by the unification of three villages, Várpalota, Inota and Pétfürdő. Coal mining, electricity generation, aluminium metallurgy and the chemical industry are the determinants of the town's economic profile. The Pét Nitrogen Works is the country's largest fertilizer factory. Further important settlements in this area are Balatonfűzfő, Papkeszi, Berhida (Peremarton) with their inter-linked chemical industry.

The third subregion of the industrial belt has evolved around Ajka, a town with 30 000 inhabitants. It is passing through a phase of vigorous growth induced by its vertically integrated aluminium industry, a product of the socialist international division labour. In the course of alumina production, a precious metal, gallium, is gained as a by-product in a volume accounting for some 10 per cent of the world output. Other industrial branches are also developing in the town, which has obtained, among others, an important health function. Tapolca, with its 17 000 inhabitants is a rapidly developing town. Besides performing its earlier trade, transport and tourist functions, it houses the greater part of the workers engaged in the surrounding bauxite mines. In its environs are a number of villages, Zalahaláp, Diszel and Gyulakeszi, whose mining function extends to the quarrying of stone and foundry sand.

d) The Balaton resort area encompasses the narrow strip of the northern Balaton lakeshore and the territory lying immediately behind it. Just as on the southern shore, an almost completely contiguous settlement agglomeration has evolved, extending from Balatonakarattya to Keszthely, and embracing some of the more inland settlements as well. The centre of the resort area is Balatonfüred with 12 000 inhabitants, the third town of the Balaton area with the largest accommodation capacity on the northern shore. Its shipyard and boat-building facilities are significant. Further important resort centres are Balatonkenese, Alsóörs, Balatonalmádi, Tihany, Zánka, Révfülöp and Badacsony.

e) The industrial belt along the Danube embraces the area lying between Esztergom and Komárom. It is, in fact, a linear agglomeration elongated in an east-west direction with a heavy territorial concentration of industry and population.

The largest urban centre of the agglomeration is the ancient town of Esztergom, with 31 000 inhabitants. It was a royal seat for a time and has been the administrative centre of the Roman Catholic church for centuries. Its industrial function with the production of machine tools, laboratory instruments, and optical glass, has greatly developed, but its cultural and health functions also play an important role in its life and that of its hinterland. Komárom, with 26 000 inhabitants, is a developing industrial town on the western fringe of the agglomeration, an important transport junction, and a rail and road frontier station. It is the centre of the commuter traffic between Czechoslovakia and Hungary.

f) Szombathely and its hinterland. Szombathely, an ancient town of Roman foundation (Savaria), is the third largest town, with 83 000 inhabitants, of Northern Transdanubia. Its hinterland extends over the southern part of the Little Plain and almost over the whole of the subalpine area, and population growth was particularly rapid during the 1970s. The growth of the town has been promoted by the rapid development of its industry and central functions as well as by its growing tourism. Industrial plants of outstanding importance are a factory for the manufacture of agricultural machinery, a branch plant of Rába Engineering, a vehicle repair shop, a Remix plant manufacturing radio components, and plants of the textile, shoe and timber industries. It is also an important transport centre. Its direct labour-attraction sphere extends over about 50 settlements, many of them being very small in size.

Centres performing the function of district seats for smaller areas have become towns owing to the development of their industry and other activities. Sárvár, with 15 000 inhabitants, is an economic, administrative and supply centre at the meeting place of Rábamente and Kemeneshát. Its most significant industrial establishment is its sugar refinery. Körmend, with 12 000 inhabitants, is a young town in the Vasi uplands and the northern part of the Őrség. Its important industrial plant is the Factory of Food Preparations and Pharmaceutical Basic Materials. Kőszeg, with 13 000 inhabitants, is a small town of ancient foundation and a centre of the textile industry and tourism.

7 Changes in the spatial structure of the Hungarian economy and society (1982—1987)

The inertia of the traditional regional and settlement network of the spatial social and economic structure is great and slow to change; its modification usually needs several decades. However, in this chapter the authors of the book seek to summarize the spatial processes of a relatively short period that elapsed since the completion of the book (1982). To those who may wonder at this discrepancy we can say that the development of the Hungarian society and economy over the past few years displays such specific new features as the considerably lower dynamism of the economy, of the emergence of new socio-economic phenomena, institutions and tensions that have visibly influenced the spatial structure of Hungary's society and economy. True, the new features originate not so much in the geographical processes as in the socio-economic conditions generating them. Later, however, their cumulative impact will certainly call for redrawing the country's economic map. In anticipation of that we felt obliged to indicate, at least in broad outlines, the new tendencies. Together with this additional chapter, the reader gets an all-round picture of the contemporary situation.

7.1 Changes in the demographic and occupational structure

Due to the steadily negative reproductional figures, the decline of the population, starting in 1981, has continued. On 1 January 1987 the number of the population was 10,622,000, down by 91,000 from 1981. This marks a new era from demographic and occupational aspects.

While our *birth rate,* despite the tendency of decline (13.9–12.1‰) is around the European average, the *mortality rate* started to show extreme values. In 1985 this rate was 13.9‰, the highest in Europe (the GDR having 13.5‰). The proportion of the elderly, which is close to the European average, does not suffice to account for this. The main reason is the increase in the mortality of the 40–60-years-old, mostly male population. The relevant figure is by far the highest in Europe.

It commands attention that Hungary places first among the European countries with its death rates of various diseases. We have the highest rate of cardiac and vascular deaths in the world and in Europe. Regarding tumors, we are placed third behind Austria and England in Europe. Though tuberculosis as a wide-spread disease has been eliminated, the related deaths are still the highest in Hungary after Yugoslavia and Poland.

Last but not least, Hungary has the highest rate of suicides in the world, although this does not modify the death rate significantly.

Apart from Budapest and a few counties (Csongrád, Fejér, Pest, Szabolcs-Szatmár), the *population decline* affects the whole country. As a result of decreasing births and increasing deaths as well as inter-county migration, changes in the number of inhabitants considerably differ from the national average by regions and, more importantly, by settlement-types.

The *natural decline* of the population over the five years studied was concentrated in Budapest and the majority of rural settlements. (The only source Budapest could draw on for the growth of its population was the migration surplus that has so far counterbalanced the annually increasing demographic decline.) Births exceeded deaths, though to a lessening extent, in the country towns.

Out of the 13 counties with decreasing population Somogy, Vas, Zala and Baranya being characterized by small villages (less than 500 inhabitants) as well as Bács-Kiskun, Békés, Csongrád and Heves registered the sharpest decline (2.4–3.8‰) in 1986. The birth rate is still the highest in Szabolcs-Szatmár county, but its intensity is also dwindling (2.4‰).

Inner migration, another factor affecting the spatial distribution of the inhabitants, slightly decreased over the past five years. Migration contributes to the geographical distribution of the population only to a decreasing extent. Three counties, Szabolcs-Szatmár, Borsod-Abaúj-Zemplén and Szolnok, are exceptions, with their outmigration being steadily above the national average. Apart from Budapest, only Pest county profits significantly from the migration, the migrants heading for the settlements of the Budapest agglomeration. The tendency of migration continues to be away from small settlements with less developed infrastructure into larger and infrastructurally more advanced centres or towns, but a slowdown can be demonstrated in this process with fewer people changing their places of residence (outmigration from villages dropped from 134,000 in 1982 to 129,000 in 1986).

The negative demographic trend and the decreasing inner migration affected the changes in the number of urban and rural population to different extent and in different directions within the different counties.

The population of the country towns increased with about 10% since 1982, while that of the villages decreased to the same extent. Due to the high gain from migration, it is the population of the big towns and county seats which grew the fastest among the towns. The small number of cohorts being first empolyed in the mid-1980s will affect the *occupational structure*. The tendency of growth in the 1970s gave way to a basic trend of decline both nationally and in the counties.

With the comparatively low level of economic efficiency and the use of the labour force, and with sources of development to replace manpower becoming limited, the global labour shortage has prevailed despite the decrease of the labour force and the strengthening pressures to economize on labour. The labour shortage started to decrease only in 1987, turning into labour supply in some regions. By then the chances of getting a job in certain occupations and regions had diminished. Hardest hit are the unskilled workers.

Owing to the general properties of the labour market, the chances of getting employed are the best in the capital. This is partly due to the fast upswing of small-scale ventures linked to the existing economic units. In contrast to this, a measurable labour supply structurally different from demand — i.e. unemployment — evolved in the northeastern part of the country (Borsod-Abaúj-Zemplén, Szabolcs-Szatmár) where the economic recession was coupled with a specific demographic trend, notably, the growth in the number of job-seekers. In these two counties, there are 3 jobs for 10 job-hunters.

The regional characteristics of the labour supply and demand anticipate the intensification of tensions in the forthcoming years.

Parallel with the decline in the number of active earners (4,867,000) *occupational restratification* has continued, decisively from material to non-material branches. What underlies this trend is not so much a change of occupations, but rather the sectoral difference between those taking on their first jobs and those retiring. Between 1982 and 1985 the number of the active earners in the socialist sector decreased by some 250,000 people while those in the private sector increased by about just as many. The proportion of the latter came up to 5.8%.

The contraction of the industrial investments and the moderate growth of production resulted in the overall trend of manpower decrease in *industry* and *construction industry* which induced a heavy drop in *commuting*. In agriculture and forestry employment primarily decreased in the joint cooperatives. The drop — 12% in five years — affected employment in the main profile and the subsidiary activities alike. Among the branches of productive infrastructure, transportation and telecommunications faced a loss of emloyment in the majority of the counties and nationally as well.

In the *non-material branches*, nearly two-thirds of the newly employed went to medical care and cultural services. Their spatial distribution was proportionate with the distribution of the population.

With the advancement of the demographic cycle a radical increase can be predicted in the number of young job-seekers for the early 1990s, which will possibly reinforce and geographically widen the scope of employment tensions amidst the economic recession.

7.2 Changes in settlement and infrastructure

The introduction of the system of urban hinterlands to replace the district councils abolished in 1984 and the setting up of local councils in small settlements was basically an administrative move yet it had a major impact on the social environment of individuals, families and institutions and their relationship to it. In 1988 the two-level system of local administration (county and settlement councils) is to be introduced in five counties experimentally, eliminating the intermediary hinterlands.

As part of the transition to the two-level administrative system, 16 large villages in areas short of towns (Bácsalmás, Heves, Kisbér, Sárbogárd, Tiszakécske, etc.) were raised to the rank of town after 1984. In 1987, the councils of 125 towns and 16 large villages transitorily perform the secondary administrative functions of 2933 villages.

The changes of the recent years, the tensions entailed by the real processes and the administrative alterations have pushed the questions of regional organization and administration to the fore in the process of social reform. The problems of local administration of the relationship between sectoral and regional, state and party management and of the financial system of regional and settlement development (central allocations and self-financing) have not been settled conclusively yet.

With the economic growth-rate slowing down in the 1980s, the process of settlement concentration, which incurred much criticism of the policy of regional and settlement development has slackened. The rank of importance among different factors of the living conditions has changed, new needs have emerged, environmental problems have gradually come to the fore.

There have been structural modifications in the *settlement network* that promoted the emergence of new trends in development. They include the process of polarization in the course of which the smallest units of the scattered village network, namely the small villages, gradually lose the majority of their inhabitants. At the other end of the scale — in the towns — quantitative housing shortage could not be eliminated in spite of concentrating the subsidies allocated to urban development in this area.

The *conception of settlement development*, which had been in effect for some 15 years, had to be modified. A new long-term settlement development policy had to be worked out. It was part of the new phase of improved economic management, increasing democracy and emerging local and regional forces.

The competent authorities drafted a new long-term policy and submitted it to debate. The conception entitled *"The long-term tasks of regional and settlement development"* was endorsed by the Parliament in 1985. Besides its numerous disputable points, the main defect of the resolution is that due to the limited time of preparations, it could not rely on the findings of scientific research. It lacks a scientifically verified guiding strategy for practical implementation.

Changes in the urban network. As compared to 1984 (see Fig. 14), the number of the towns increased to 125 with the addition of 16 new towns. The new towns largely differ in size, occupational structure, development of infrastructure, etc. but they all have one thing in common: they are located along the border of their respective counties. More and more areas formerly devoid of urban settlements are getting towns, and through them, a supply of medium-rank services. The urban network of the country started to get its final pattern.

With a few exceptions, the population of our towns was increasing during the 1970s. In the 1980s, this trend changed, as 29 towns were losing inhabitants. The total number of loss (13,000) is not significant (500 people per town). Three towns (Szarvas, Nagykőrös, Törökszentmiklós) lost over 2,000 people.

The population of the majority of towns kept increasing during the 1980s as well. The inhabitants of the *capital* increased with the largest number, with 29,000. However, the pace of inmigration decreased and could not make up for the dwindling sources of labour in the capital. The cut in housing constructions on central funds and the housing shortage of the Budapest residents strictly limited the inflow of active earners with families. The number of people working in Budapest dropped by over 100,000 compared to the previous decade.

The population growth of *county seats* is still a massive tendency with over 100,000 in number. Half of the increase was shared by the five large towns and regional centres. Unlike the capital, the country towns were capable of receiving masses of families and family founders. The economic and social potential of the different groups of the country towns changed to varying degrees and proportions.

The population growth in the youngest towns promoted after 1980 is very poor; it is as little as 8,000. They failed to attract earners as permanent residents, but they widened the choices of jobs for people living in the vicinity and became commuting centres.

The differentiation of the rural settlement network went on, though at a reduced pace. The dynamism of some villages is heightened by their geographical position (nearness of towns or resort areas, main transport lines). The originally populous agrarian villages of the Great Hungarian Plain gradually lose their inhabitants.

The majority of the small villages, mostly located in South-west Transdanubia and North-east Hungary, lost all their functions and local organizations except for the function of dwelling because of the development of new regional centres in the 1970s (school, council, cooperative centre).

The concentration of functions went on in the 1980s, though less intensively. Another 69 productive cooperatives closed down and nearly 100 villages lost their schools. The expansion of the town network and the strengthening of new towns entailed the incorporation of 70, formerly autonomous small settlements.

Small villages with ageing population got into the worst situation, as they were unable to offer suitable jobs to young people.

The number of villagers locally employed plummeted by nearly 100,000 people. In the past five years almost 90,000 active earners left the villages for good.

Though no radical change occurred in migration, the existing jobs in the villages attracted more local young people in the 1980s than earlier, while the appeal of village homes was also enhanced by the modernization of dwellings. Living in town had far less attraction in the 1980s than in the 1970s.

The rate of new *housing* declined both in towns and villages in the 1980s.

There was a considerable drop in the volume and proportion of state-funded housing construction, formerly a basic appeal of larger towns. Between 1981 and 1985 there was a cut of 11,000 flats in Budapest; the towns of county rank had just as big a cut, while the total drop in the rest of the towns was 36,000 flats, compared to the previous 5-year period.

New housing in the villages, most of it being modernization, was reduced only by 6,000 homes. The share of villages in the total national new housing rose from 30 to 34%.

State subsidies effect remarkable growth in housing in the small villages, but they still lag behind the national average. Housing in large villages and small towns increased to an adequate level.

A mainspring of building out the *water-system* is the organization of waterworks on private resources. As a result, 67% of all dwellings and 85% of the population were supplied with water-system in 1986. Besides bringing running-water to as yet unsupplied settlements, the major goal is to replace unhealthy water in certain places with public water works.

The problem of *drainage* is still becoming graver as it lags behind the spreading of water-system; the "public utility gap" between the two is hardly, if at all, decreasing. The rate of dwellings linked to the main drainage is hardly over 40%.

Thanks to developments on decentralized resources (local, private and state credit), a wide range of settlements have been involved in infrastructural improvements. Regarding the main tendencies, a certain degree of equalization can be observed among the various types of settlement in the provision of *basic services*.

7.3 Changes in the development and geographical location of industry

Since the first edition of the book (Chapters 1 to 6) a new situation evolved in the Hungarian economy in general and in industry in particular. The formerly steady and efficient economic growth came to a halt, stagnation ensued with relapses in certain branches. The growth rates of the economy and efficiency plummeted; the badly needed structural transformations of the economy and particularly the industry could not be carried out. The Hungarian industry, insensitive to changes in the world market and slow at streamlining its products, fell at disadvantage on the world market, especially in convertible currency areas, loosing much of its markets or forced to set unfavourable prices. To compound problems, the country's indebtedness to western countries increased rapidly.

The causes of the above-outlined situation are many-sided, including the following.

– The economic reform introduced in 1968 came to a halt in the 1970s, picking up again somewhat belated in the 1980s, when however the economic regulators applied were ineffective.

– As a consequence, the enterprises were little interested in reducing costs and modernizing their product structure, several industrial branches became obsolate, the number of unprofitable enterprises grew. The reduction of foreign debts and interest payments required convertible exports including uneconomical products, which in turn hindered the modernization of the product structure. The government pumped sizeable funds into some unprofitable enterprises and into the production of certain articles; this consumed a growing proportion of the central budget, resulting in the disruption of the budgetary equilibrium. The government tried to reduce the resulting deficit partly with inflationary means.

– The financial management drained an ever increasing amount from the revenues of the profitable enterprises in order to support unprofitable ones; consequently, not even the first ones could make adequate progress.

– Investment funds decreased due to the interest repayments on foreign debts, which limited the drives at modernization.

– Investments with the aim to exploit domestic natural resources, esp. energy carriers, had a steadily high proportion in the total industrial investment, which left insufficient funds to streamline the technical level of the manufacturing industry and to replace old technologies.

– The government made several moves to modify the reform process, e.g. chances opened for setting up small businesses (to improve the background industry, among other things), for the mobilization of private capital; the banking system was transformed (the new banks fulfilling commercial functions); the capital market has been given higher play, etc. These measures, though bringing some partial results already, will only bear fruit in the medium and long run.

– In 1987 the Parliament approved the government's stabilization programme to improve the economic situation. The main targets of the program were to halt the growth of foreign debts, to curb and eventually eliminate the deficit of the budget, to normalize the economic situation and to launch a new economic period in 3 or 4 years' time. Several measures were taken in support of these objectives, e.g.:

– Monetary tools (value-added tax, income tax) were introduced into the economic management.

– Enterprise autonomy increased through a partial liberalization of the pricing system. Enterprise efficiency and profitability became an overriding demand, entailing the rehabilitation and ultimate liquidation of chronically unprofitable enterprises.

– The enterprises were given more authority to decide on changing their product structure by giving more play — though still limited — to the (external and internal) effects of the market.

– Measures were taken to promote the flow of the capital toward the more efficient sectors and enterprises (by bonds, market of bonds, new forms of enterprises, etc.).

– Top-level political and economic institutional systems are being changed gradually.

– Due to the above-said, the fifth — intensive and selective — phase of the industrial development will last much longer than initially expected.

Since 1982, the following industrial changes can be registered.

– There was a slight modification in the sectoral structure of the industry, with the proportion of heavy industry further increasing and light and food industry decreasing. In 1986 the percentage shares of the three main industrial groups in the gross industrial output were: heavy industry — 69.3%; light industry — 13.9%, food industry — 16.8%.

– From 1981 onward there has been a steady decline in industrial employment (by about 105,000 people); productivity remained to be the main source of increasing production.

– Since the mid-1980s no major, centrally-financed investment project has been launched. Industrial development meant reconstructions and enterprise improvements carried out with independent enterprise funds and bank credit.

– The distribution of industrial production by social and economic sectors was modified. The figures for 1986 are: the state industry gave 81.3% of the output, the cooperative industry 5.6%, the agricultural cooperatives and state farms 6.3%, other state-run firms 4.4%, private small-scale industry 1.4%, and small private ventures operating within the state sector (so-called work associations) 1.0%.

– Minor changes occurred in the geographical arrangement of the industry, as well. These were chiefly caused by a drop in industrial employment in Budapest, by further industrialization in economically backwarded areas and by the closure of mostly small industrial plants in the country. In 1986, the spatial distribution of industrial employment was the following: Budapest and Pest county — 28.6% (of this, Budapest — 22.7%), industrially developed counties — 35.3%, less developed counties in Transdanubia — 10.3%, counties in the Great Hungarian Plain — 25.8%. No significant changes can be expected in the spatial structure of the national economy over the next few years to come, either.

Changes in energy management

The modernization of the structure of energy production and consumption made further progress. The composition of basic energy resources (including imported energy resources and electricity) was the following in 1986: coal — 25.5%, petroleum and its products — 33.0%, natural gas — 27.8%, others (nuclear energy, imported electricity, timber, etc.) — 13.7%. The share of coal further decreased over the half decade studied. Responding somewhat belated to the oil shock, the share of oil among energy resources stagnated and then began to decrease. The greatest change came with the start of producing nuclear energy as an energy resource. Imports increased to 51.3% of total energy consumption. In 1986 the country imported 2.6 million tons of coal, 7.6 million tons of crude oil, 4.7 billion m^3 of natural gas and 10.5 billion kWh of electricity.

– The government encouraged energy conservation by increasing the prices of fuels and introducing rationalization programmes, e.g. giving central support for the replacement of outdated and energy-intensive equipment. In order to reduce or slow down oil and gas imports, the power plants fuelled by imported hydrocarbons worked at reduced capacity, and the capacity of power plants fuelled with domestic coal and that of the nuclear power station was better utilized.

– In accordance with the CMEA principle of foreign-trade prices, the price of oil follows the changes on the world market with five-year delay. The phase-lag in oil pricing was favourable for Hungary in the 1970s, but unfavourable in the 1980s. As of 1988, however, oil price cuts can be expected in the CMEA market as well, possibly resulting in improved terms of trade.

– The government's energy policy changed over the past years, not only because the atomic power plant at Paks was put into operation but also because the economic evaluation of the domestic energy resources changed significantly, though not basically. As capital inputs will be limited, no major development projects will be possible in domestic coal mining. A contributory factor is that new mines are highly capital-intensive, they absorb capital for some ten years while they are not yet productive. According to plans, the increase in electricity generation will come from the extension of the Paks nuclear power station for the period up to 2000 (in 1987 the capacity of the plant was 1760 MW). By the mid-1990s, another two reactors of 1000 MW capacity each (not of the Chernobil type) will have been completed and the construction of another atomic station may also begin at another site.

– The past half decade also saw changes in the output of various energy resources and their geographical distribution. The level of *oil production* was kept up and that of the *natural gas* was increased, in compliance with the plans. Geological research explored some newly discovered minor fields and some earlier discovered deposits opened for production (e.g. at Kiskunhalas). The gas deposits in the *Hortobágy* are being slowly depleted with decreasing production. The extraction of oil in the strip from *Szeged to Algyő* has reached the geological and technical peak with a decline in output to be expected. The natural gas reserves are still sizeable. In Bács county (the Danube–Tisza Interfluve) the extraction at the oil fields is shifting northward, while the production in the oil fields in Szolnok county was started. The output of the fields in southern Zala county which were first explored continued to decrease.

Spatial distribution of petroleum and natural gas production in 1986

Field	Oil 1000 t	Oil %	Natural gas million m³	Natural gas %
Hortobágy	37.4	1.9	621.2	8.6
Southern Bács (Szank, Üllés, Kiskunhalas)	190.5	9.5	988.5	13.6
Szeged–Algyő	1404.3	70.2	3774.1	51.9
Békés (Kardoskút, Battonya, etc.)	84.5	4.2	1226.1	16.9
Szolnok county	—	—	517.0	7.1
Southern Zala	213.6	10.7	142.5	1.9
Other areas	70.1	3.5	—	—
Total	2005.3	100.0	7269.4	100.0

International cooperation continues to be important, with some changes though. The exclusive source of Hungary's crude-oil and natural-gas imports is the Soviet Union now. Owing to our large foreign debts and the negative balance of payments, the import of Arab oil stopped (that is why the international "Adria" oil pipeline is used to transfer Soviet oil to Yugoslavia). The expiration of the contract with Romania put a stop to natural gas imports from there, too.

– In order to boost Soviet natural gas imports, the Hungarian energy industry has been involved in the development of Soviet oil and gas extraction with considerable capital input. The exploration of oil fields at Tengiz (on the north-eastern shore of the Caspian Sea) is partly conducted by Hungarian firms. The capital input is to be recompensed by the Soviet Union with an annual 2 billion m³ of natural gas as of 1990. In order to increase the economical use of hydrocarbons, the number of natural gas users was raised, joining more plants and settlements to the national gas supply network. The length of pipelines increased for more economical transport (mainly with new pipelines for natural gas and finished products), amounting to 6700 km in 1986.

– The caloric value of domestically extracted *coal* has continued to decline, to 10,919 kJ in 1986. The fourth phase of coal mining has started and it displays the following features.

– The overriding aspect of developing coal mining is increasing profitability, a major change as compared to the previous phases.

– The so-called "Eocene Programme" devised to modernize the good-quality Eocene brown coal fields in Northern Transdanubia has been completed. Mining shifted to the west by opening the western wing of the *Oroszlány* coal basin and to *south-east* of Tatabánya (new pits were opened at Mány and Nagyegyháza). The opening of the latter mines was hindered partly by karst water and partly by the geological properties of the coal deposits (the seams being horizontal and vertical to each other due to vaultage). In the *Dorog* basin the mine at Lencsehegy took the functions of the depleted pits over.

– The development of the *Mecsek* basin — the country's single black-coal field — in the "Liassic Programme" is being hampered by capital shortage, which resulted in a drop in output.

– Pits were shut down again in several coal basins. The reasons are in part the depletion of the geological coal reserves (in the fields of Mecsek, Ajka, Várpalota, Dorog; while at Tatabánya mining will cease by 1990 in all the pits of the oldest-working basins), and in part the fact that extraction is uneconomical because of the geological context and the poor quality of the coal (in the basins of Nógrád and Borsod), or else vast amounts of capital investment would be needed.

Under the detrital cones at the foot of the Bükk Mountains, near *Bükkábrány*, there is an extensive lignite reserve of the same quality as the Visonta one; its extraction began with an open mine.

Output of coal fields in 1986 (in tons)

Field	Black coal	Brown coal	Lignite
Mecsek	2,325,000	—	—
North Transdanubia (Dorog, Tatabánya, Oroszlány)	—	5,522,600	
Várpalota	—	—	952,490
Mid-Transdanubia	—	2,797,080	—
Nógrád	—	1,012,065	—
Borsod (Egercsehi, Ózd, Sajó valley)	—	4,448,280	—
Visonta	—	—	5,601,262
Bükkábrány	—	—	458,879
Total	2,325,000	13,780,025	7,012,631

With a view to impove the quality of coal and making production more economical (in 1986 2 million tons of bricketed coal was produced) new coal separating plants started to operate at Tokod, Oroszlány and Kazincbarcika and the bricketing factory at Dorog was reconstructed.

The import of various kinds of coal continued (black coal imports for coking becoming steady from the USSR, Poland, Czechoslovakia and the FRG). The use of coal (domestic and imported) has changed. Although industry remained to be the main consumer, there was a further increase in the share of power stations; the second largest consumer is metallurgy (for coking). Several new industrial consumers changed for natural gas. The coal consumption of transport dropped to minimum, but due to the often increased price of heating oil the population's demand for better-quality coal increased.

The radical change in the structure and spatial distribution of *electricity generation* came with the opening of the reactors at the Paks nuclear power station. At the end of 1987, the total generating capacity of the country amounted to 7246 MW. In 1986, the total output was 28 billion kWh, 27% coming from the atomic power plant. Counted in caloric value, the consumption of energy sources by thermal power plants was: brown and black coal — 26.2%, lignite — 12.5%, heating oil — 13.5%, natural gas — 25.2%, atomic energy — 22.6%. Thus the basic energy resources used in generating electricity became more diversified. Even the proportion of coals and oil decreased and that of nuclear energy increased. It has to be noted that some out-of-date thermal power stations with a high coal consumption were shut down (e.g. the thermal plant in the Mátra region). The geographical axis of Hungarian electricity generation is now the Danube valley with two large power stations (at Százhalombatta and Paks), the northern electricity generating district being the other main concentration (Visonta, Kazincbarcika, Leninváros and Tiszapalkonya) and the northern Transdanubian district losing significance.

The drive at boosting nuclear power production was motivated partly by the mentioned constraints on the development of coal mining and partly by the increased threat of acid rains, primarily caused by the SO_2 emission of coal-fuelled thermal power plants. (New thermal plants would further jeopardize the environment.) The results of the Paks atomic power plant are positive both technically and economically. It was built in compliance with the safety-philosophical recommendations of the UN Nuclear Energy Agency, a fact that certainly increased the security of radiation. (NB, the Paks atomic power station is the first in the socialist countries to be constructed this way). Due to the nuclear energy program no coal-fuelled power plants are expected to be constructed before 2000 which means the cancellation of the planned thermal power plant at Bicske.

The construction of the hydro-electric plant system along the common Hungarian—Czechoslovak section of the river Danube between *Gabchikovo and Nagymaros*, a joint Czech—Hungarian project, has accelerated. In Hungary, heated debates preceded the building of the power plant considering the possible environmental risks (a part of which can be eliminated by additional investments). Another concern is that the extremely capital-intensive project is being implemented at a time of unfavourable economic conditions with possibly large opportunity costs. To reduce the latter, the Nagymaros power plant is being built with Austrian credit and the involvement of Austrian construction firms. The credit is to be repaid by electricity exports after completion.

Changes have been numerous in *iron-ore mining and metallurgy*. The sources of raw materials partly changed. The low-capacity iron-ore mine and ore-concentrating plant at Rudabánya were closed down because of low metal content (the precincts of the latter house now an incinerator of hazardous waste), as the high operating costs made the mine unprofitable. Iron-ore imports come chiefly from the USSR, but the import of Brazilian and Indian ore rich in iron started making the raw iron production at the Danube Iron Works economical. To expand the domestic basis of metallurgic coke production, a new coking plant was integrated into the Danube Iron Works with an annual capacity of 900,000 tons.

In the mid-1980s the global steel crisis began to affect Hungarian metallurgy as well since technologies in some plants became outdated; the structure of rolled iron products was not responsive to market demands; the world market prices (mostly of less refined steel products exported by Hungary) were low; and the import restrictions of some western countries. With a view to eliminate the difficulties, several obsolete workshops were shut down (e.g. the last rolling mill to be powered by steam in Europe, a small-capacity iron foundry and a few blast furnaces at Ózd, etc.) and employment was cut back. Metallurgy began to transform its production structure and first and foremost to increase the output of alloyed or higher-quality products. All in all, the level of metallurgical production was stagnant. In 1986 3.7 million tons of steel and 3 million tons of rolled steel were produced (the export share of the latter being up to 1 million tons). The volume of steel produced by the up-to-date converter technology came close to that of blast-furnace steel.

No major changes were displayed by *non-ferrous metallurgy*. New mines opened for bauxite extraction in the vicinity of Bakonyoszlop and Fenyőfő along the western range of the Bakony Mountains. The metallurgical capacity for alumina and aluminium remained at the previous level. The formerly planned aluminium foundry was not built as there was a shortage of capital and besides, the world market price of aluminium had been low for quite some time in the 1980s; which, with domestic electricity costs being high, would make the economical use of a new foundry questionable.

The Hungarian–Soviet aluminium agreement was prolonged, which provides sufficient block aluminium for the rolling mills of which the one at Székesfehérvár expanded its capacity. The Hungarian aluminium industry succeeded in widening its markets, especially overseas. In 1986, bauxite output was 3 million tons, alumina output was 856,000 tons (665,000 tons exported) and crude aluminium output was 74,000 tons.

The capacity of the copper refinery of the Csepel Works in Budapest has been considerably enlarged. The small-capacity Gyöngyösoroszi mines of low-grade lead and zinc as well as the gold mine at Recsk were shut down as the geological reserves had been depleted. At the same time, the mining of the extensive low-lying deposits of relatively low-grade ores has not started yet, as the mine, ore-dressing plant and copper smelter are highly capital-intensive.

The *engineering industry* transitionally lost weight within the whole industry. The reasons were the difficulties of modernization and product structure transformation, which were the gravest here. Several prestigeous factories got into trouble by mismanagement and failed to make good use of the production experience accumulated over the decades under the new international economic conditions. A phase of more differentiated development began in the engineering industry. Well-run innovative enterprises (e.g. in the production of machinery and equipment, vehicles, household appliances, electronic equipment) managed to come out with up-to-date new products gaining new markets. A significant part of engineering firms, however, could hardly keep going.

The difficulties were aggravated by the slowdown in CMEA cooperation in engineering. A favourable change is expected to start with the joint Hungarian–Soviet enterprise agreed on in 1987. Some enterprise managed to import western working capital or to set up new joint ventures, both giving an impetus to upgrading technologies and products. As a new development, trade entered the engineering context: the Skála cooperatives chain and ITT joined forces to assemble colour television sets and video recorders, and to produce components, in Budapest.

Electronic engineering also witnessed progress. A new firm (Microelectronic Company) started to produce, besides components, limited series of high-value electronic equipment in their central plant in Budapest which is mainly engaged in product development. The product structure of the two traditional firms, Orion and Videoton, has also changed.

Both reduced their output of radio sets and increased the production of colour television sets and computer equipment. Videoton began to turn out professional personal computers, with several smaller firms joining in to produce peripherals, printers and other accessories.

In vehicle production, the importance of Rába and Ikarus has further increased, their plants and product structure further improved. The passanger car supply still causes grave concerns and raises the idea of installing an assembly plant in Hungary. Negotiations are going on with Japanese, Soviet and Czechoslovakian partners (Skoda) about this question and other possible ways of cooperation. Car assemblage will probably begin in the early 1990s, widening the possibilities of several Hungarian engineering factories as well.

Regarding geographical distribution engineering industry did not undergo significant changes. The share of Budapest has further decreased, with the weight of northern Transdanubia and the Little Plain growing.

The *chemical industry* was less susceptible to the economic hardships. Its output grew steadily; its capacity was increased with new modern factory units but no new independent plants were built. A few out-of-date environment-polluting or highly energy-intensive plants were shut down (e.g. the sulphuric acid factory in Budapest, the first plant of the Pét Nitrogen Factory built in the interwar period, the oil refinery at Szőny).

The greatest progress was made by the petrochemical industry. A new propylene and polypropylene plant as well as a linear polyethylene plant were completed at the Tisza Chemical Trust at Leninváros. Subsidiary plants manufacturing synthetic materials are also under construction. The plants of synthetic-material production were enlarged in Budapest and Debrecen. The construction of a new acrylic fibre plant and a viscosa-based rayon factory as a Hungarian—Czechoslovak joint venture within the Hungarian Viscosa Company at Nyergesújfalu began.

A major stride forward in synthetic fertilizer production was the changeover to liquid fertilizers. As the production of nitrogenous fertilizers is highly energy-intensive, the capacity is not extended but Soviet imports are used to satisfy surplus demand. The pharmaceutical industry stopped the production of several outdated goods to concentrate on highly effective modern pharmaceuticals.

The major chemical outputs in 1986 were (in 1000 tons): caustic soda: 202; nitrogenous fertilizers (effective substance): 584; ethylene: 269; polyethylene: 80; linear polyethylene: 140; propylene: 178; polypropylene: 101; synthetic detergents: 106; car tyres: 587,000 pieces.

The structural transformation accelerated in the *building-materials and construction industry*. This in part is related to the modified housing policy. The previously predominant state housing gave way to private house construction encouraged by credits and other preferences, producing a rising tendency in family house and condominium construction and a decreasing one in the flats in monotonous pre-fabricated housing estates. Unfortunately, the annual number of new dwellings is also decreasing because of price increases (in 1986 newly built flats numbered 70,0000 with the index of 6.500 flats/1000 tenants);

the country is in the medium category in Europe. Changes in demand shifted interests from concrete elements to traditional building materials (brick, tile). (Two concrete-unit factories were closed down in Budapest and Veszprém, the latter being used now as an industrial park for small plants.) The building materials industry adopted modern western technologies and several products are turned out on licence. In short, a new qualitative trend is emerging in the building-materials and construction industry.

Reconstruction of brick and tile production went on with small outdated plants shut down and up-to-date well-equipped ones constructed. In the cement industry, the obsolete and highly air-polluting Tatabánya cement factory was closed down but no new factory is planned in stead.

Light industry also underwent sectorally and geographically differentiated changes. Despite the several, often detrimental changes in the world market prices and the import restrictions of some countries, the textile and clothing industry kept up its standards and even made progress in quality. To improve profitability, some cotton mills were closed down followed by some wool factories primarily in Budapest. Several plants were updated and the product structure modernized with the help of licences. A major advance was made by extensive cooperation possibilities with leading European fashion houses, department stores, sportswear firms, etc. (Cardin, Adler, Adidas, Quelle, etc.), contributing to enhanced exports and better domestic supply alike. To better utilize export capacities and improve domestic supply, the country increased its imports of raw cotton, underwear and knitwear from, the Third World countries. In exports and raw material imports no major changes occurred.

The *paper industry* testified to great progress. New cardboard and box plants were completed within the *Budapest* and *Nyíregyháza* paper mills to produce up-to-date packaging materials. The Szolnok paper factory was reconstructed with modern equipment and improved capacity. The outdated cellulose factory of the Csepel Paper Factory (Budapest) was shut down for environmental reasons. Despite the growth, the country still needs considerable imports for newspaper and book publication (for a detailed explanation see the relevant chapter in the book, esp. the composition of Hungarian forests).

In 1986 the outputs of light industry were: cotton cloth — 314million m^2, wool cloth — 34million m^2, leather shoes — 42million pairs, paper — 517 thousand t.

7.4 Regional changes in food industry

The 1970s saw a steady growth in Hungarian food production, although the deceleration of global economic growth, the increase of Hungary's indebtedness and the deterioration in the terms of trade gave rise to minor recessions and slowdowns in Hungary's economy including the agrarian sector.

In 1982–86 the pace of growth further decreased. The dynamism of agricultural development came to a halt. Stagnation is born out by the gross produce value if calculated at a constant price. The setback was caused by an array of causes (repeated droughts, steadily decreasing world market prices, slow accumulating capacity).

The previously adopted agrarian policy could not — or could only slowly — adjust to the changed world economic context. One cannot draw definitive conclusions yet as the crisis is not over and it is not clear yet whether we are having a business slump or a fundamental structural transformation. Signs are accumulating to suggest that a global technical transformation is to follow the disorders and setbacks in production and growth.

Technical transformation ensued a structural crisis affecting the entire world economy as it brought about radical changes in production, services and exports and Hungarian food industry cannot adjust to them without major shocks.

State subsidies to agriculture have been dwindling year by year. Payment liabilities to the budget increased, the gap between the relative prices of industrial and agrarian products widened. This, in turn, decreased the profit content of agrarian prices; the price centre tends to adjust to the costs and prices of farming in areas with medium or good endowments. *This enlarged the area considered to have unfavourable conditions and heavily subsidized by the state from one-fourth to one-third.*

Agriculture tried to ward off the pressures and decreasing income with an extension of production, similar to the great depression of the 1930s. Soon, however, it had to be realized that it was an impasse. The newly arisen situation requires the improvement of production efficiency and changes in labour input and costs.

Adjustment to the new price system would have needed a 10–15% cut in specific capital input. Most of the large-scale agricultural enterprises were, however, unable to meet this requirement. Moreover, input kept rising in the farming of the marginal areas. The raised threshold of return put them to an unsurmountable task: the streamlining of their economic activities.

Only a narrow layer of enterprises, a meagre one-third of the large-scale farms managed to grow under the changed conditions with increasing pressures and deteriorating performance. One-fourth of the large-scale enterprises could only carry out simple reproduction and 37% failed even to do so.

a) *The dynamically improving districts with steadily growing income* include the counties of Baranya, Győr, Komárom, Veszprém and Tolna with expanding and high-level basic agricultural performance. Earlier these areas were not among the main agricultural districts of the country and rather belonged to the regions with unfavourable natural endowments. Their dynamic development is due to the nearness of markets, to industrial demand (subsidiary activities) and advanced infrastructural environment. Under more severe economic conditions these areas were better equipped for development than the traditional agricultural regions in the Great Hungarian Plain.

Another dynamically improving district is Pest county and the hinterland of the Budapest agglomeration which owes its advancement, besides the basic activity, to "extra work", to subsidiary activities. The industrial activities of agricultural enterprises mean greater profits and more certain return of costs. This county concentrates one-third of the total revenues from non-agricultural subsidiary activities. By contrast, the returns from agricultural sales hardly exceeded 20% of the total returns. Similarly high is the income from subsidiary activities in Komárom, Veszprém and Bács-Kiskun counties.

A most recent tendency is the deterioration of the profitability of subsidiary activities, principally caused by the rivalry of small-scale production. Several subsidiaries of agricultural farms separated or ceased to exist. This process is especially affecting the areas with unfavourable endowments and low productivity, such as Borsod-Abaúj-Zemplén, Nógrád and Somogy counties.

b) *The development of agricultural regions with unfavourable natural endowments* became polarized by the differentiation in production. A small part managed to offset decreasing profitability of agricultural production by improved processing auxiliary activities and direct sales, making good use of the nearness of markets and the high level of local industrialization and infrastructure. Indeed, in some lucrative units the high income from subsidiary activities was used in part to boost agrarian production. The efficient large-scale enterprises successfully compensating for their unfavourable endowments belonged to the counties of Komárom, Veszprém, Pest and Bács-Kiskun.

Another, larger part of areas with unfavourable soil conditions was incapable of counteracting their handicap of economic backwardness and peripheric position, and fell behind in development. These agrarian enterprises did not have enough income or development funds even to set up processing plants for their own produce, which would have increased their productivity. In this way they failed to align themselves to the profile that best suited them and became unable to adjust to the market conditions already in the beginning of the new process. In the marginal areas, the majority of the enterprises had to limit their production input or cancel developments, which constrained the expansion of agricultural production in the first place. In terms of the national economy this means that the financially unstable, badly-off agricultural units fail to contribute to hoisting the national income with their inputs; on the contrary, they reproduce their low economic performance to the detriment of the nation.

Judging from the agricultural cooperatives balance sheets for 1986, the worst-hit area was Borsod-Abaúj-Zemplén county where net production costs exceeded net produce value, so production ended with deficit. Nógrád and Somogy counties did not fare much better either: produce value amounted to 2.6% and 3.4% resp. on the production value (7.3% nationally). In these three counties the proportion of agricultural companies with unfavourable conditions is 60–90%. The produce value and production level of another two counties — Zala and Szabolcs-Szatmár — relegate them into this category. The amount of net income per earner fell short of two-thirds of the national mean in all these counties.

Between 1982 and 1986 the rate of unprofitable agricultural units rose from 6 to 10%; more than half of the losing farms were in the mentioned five counties. Geographically they are heavily concentrated, too: in Borsod every third, in Somogy every fifth and in the other three counties every tenth agricultural farm worked with higher production costs than income. The increasingly severe economic environment put these large-scale enterprises to a test that they failed to pass. Experiences have shown that the results and the position of the permanently losing companies cannot be improved solely by technical and economic means. Under the current bureaucratic—organizational circumstances these units cannot survive unless they get substantial support from the government. That is why the agricultural management encourages peasants working in such enterprises to choose other cooperative forms, set up specialized producers' groups or pool their interest as private producers.

Development of economically backward areas. In marginal agricultural areas with the poorest endowments population density is relatively high (60–80 persons/km^2). This means that agriculture must support many people for lack of industrialization. Being in the peripheries, they have low-standard transport and telecommunication facilities as well. In order to mitigate the tensions and the problems of employment the government launched a *program to accelerate the economically backward areas* in 1985. Up to 1990 the government appropriated 3 billion forints (c. US$ 60 million) to this effect.

The program stipulates the promotion of 23 microregions in the 7 most severely backwarded and economically least developed counties. The counties are Borsod-Abaúj-Zemplén, Szabolcs-Szatmár, Somogy, and Zala as well as Baranya, Vas and Békés and the microregions are, for example, Erdőhát and Tiszahát in Szabolcs-Szatmár county, Cserehát, Hegyköz and Zemplén Mountains in Borsod-Abaúj-Zemplén. The aim of the financial support is to bring these regions abreast of economic development.

The subsidized 23 microregions amount to 10% of the country's area, 4% of its population and one-fifth of its settlements. These areas are characterized, besides the above-said, by a settlement pattern of small villages, a grave lack of water-system and drainage, a monotonous occupational structure (42% of earners are employed in agriculture) and a steady decline of population due to massive outmigration.

The program gives preference to the development of Borsod-Abaúj-Zemplén and Szabolcs-Szatmár counties, with half of the budgetary appropriation going to them. The financial support to be given from central development funds can be earned by tenders in competition. Applicants must submit a detailed account of available local funds and endowments. As the experiences of the past two years revealed, the subsidy is used principally *to improve the conditions of the basic agricultural activity, boost subsidiary activities and help introduce new jobs by setting up small-*and medium-scale plants. In some counties (Szabolcs-Szatmár) the production infrastructure is also being improved to enable the area to receive industry. In a few counties some cooperatives joined to set up small-scale food industrial units (milk, meat, tinning). In Zala county there have been efforts to incorporate foreign working capital so as to expand exports.

Basic production factors of agriculture — manpower, land and means of production, i.e. capital — are surveyed briefly below.

The number of people employed in both branches of food production continued to decrease from 25% in 1982 to 24% in 1986. The proportion of active earners in agriculture dropped to 19.1%, and of those in basic agricultural activities to 12.7%. The size of decline (50.000 people) is not substantial but marks the termination of temporary reflux into agricultural employment. This, in turn, is a consequence of the changes in the lucrativeness of subsidiary activities.

The regional changes in the labour force can be demonstrated with the changes in the number of those employed at agricultural cooperatives. The geographic tendencies clearly reveal that the changes in manpower closely depend on the income system of subsidiary activities. 50% of the drop of 40,000 in cooperative employment fell to Pest county where the subsidiary activities are the most extensive. There was a massive drop also in Borsod-Abaúj-Zemplén (12%), Bács-Kiskun (8%) and Csongrád (8%) counties. In the rest of the country the outflow from agriculture was minimal or stagnant.

Over the four years studied the *agricultural area* was reduced by a mere 50,000 ha, whereas earlier the annual decrease was of the same order. The extent of the withdrawal of land from agriculture sank to an objectively necessary level. A decisive factor here was the strengthening of enterprise autonomy.

There was a change in land use as well. It was for the first time in many years in 1983 that the area of ploughland did not shrink but increased instead. This trend has been on since then, with an annual increase in ploughland by 5–10,000 ha. As a result of the pressure for economic efficiency, not even the whole agricultural area decreased in some counties (Fejér, Békés, Szolnok and Borsod-Abaúj-Zemplén). It was to the credit of land protection that the size of arable land increased by 2% in Komárom county. It marks the positive trend that in some counties still more land is seized from agriculture than necessary.

Recession entailed a curbing of improvements. The cancellation of capacity-enlarging investments also affected the regional distribution of the *means of production*. The 12% drop in investment against the figure for 4 years earlier is a strong index of the tendencies in the agrarian sector. With investment, capital input not only into constructions but also into machinery and others was reduced. True, the performance of tractors, combines and trucks rose by about half a million kW from 1982, but their technical state further deteriorated, and the proportion of the fully amortized machinery is 47%. The decline in the profitability of animal husbandry did not allow for the replacement or modernization of worn-out fixed assets for animal breeding. Only 60% of planned improvements were implemented. Up to 1983 the consumption of artificial fertilizers rose, then began to drop.

Calculated at constant prices, the *stock of fixed assets* increased in agriculture by 10%. During the same period, the value of gross fixed asset per earner increased faster by one-third in the cooperatives, due to a drop in the number of active earners.

No substantial changes can be detected over the period studied in the regional changes of the fixed assets if the specific indexes of the counties are compared. A comparison of county statistics for the two years shows that not even the extent of divergence between the best- and worst-equipped counties (Csongrád, Hajdú-Bihar, Békés, Fejér and Szabolcs-Szatmár, Pest, Nógrád, resp.) changes.

Spatial structure of production. By the end of the 1970s, as a result of the then-applied system of economic regulation (prices, subsidies, etc.) the production combination of wheat–maize–pig–poultry characterized the specialization of most agricultural regions in the country. Where earlier specialization highlighted cattle (Transdanubia) or the cultivation of some intensive industrial crop or vegetable, the latter line of specialization slackened. From the mid-1970s the spatial spread of the increasingly profitable sunflower production was rapid (from 180,000 to 400,000 ha).

In recent years the number and volume of crops unprofitable to produce and marketed at a loss both abroad and at home increased. Price increases of the energy and the manufactured goods affected various subsectors differently. E.g., the high production costs of maize and sugar beet could no longer be born by less favourably endowed areas, which resulted in a cut in land size available for these crops. The radical shrinkage of the potato area (by 50%) was followed by massive territorial concentration. In the three traditional potato-growing districts — the Nyírség, Inner Somogy, and the Danube–Tisza Interfluve — the area used decreased only to an insignificant extent.

In areas with unfavourable natural endowments where pressure on creating new jobs was not strong, uneconomical ploughland cultivation gave way to grasslands and extensive animal raising (cattle, sheep).

Development of small-scale production. Most of the small-scale producers are not cooperative or state farm members but commuting industrial and other workers living in villages. They number some 1 million.

Despite growing social and economic appreciation, both the number of small-scale producers and the size of land they cultivated decreased in the 1980s.

The main reasons of decrease include such overall tendencies as the ageing of rural population, the thinning of peasantry and migration from villages.

It is a basic feature of small-scale commodity production that relying on large-scale enterprises and functioning as a source of extra income at a low technical level, it is incapable of swift structural changes and consequently, its stability is very poor. There is a basic antinomy between small-scale producers turning out one-third of the agricultural produce and poor stability. The reform conception, the improvement of the political system will have a great say in deciding the role of the autonomous small-scale farms with up-to-date equipment. At present, self-employed farmers have a 4% share in small-scale production, working on hardly over 1% of the total arable land.

In small villages, where the number of small-scale producers rapidly dropped, small-scale farms are one-and-a-half times as big as in large villages and small towns. The urban environment is more favourable for intensive horticultural and animal-breeding activities. They are determined by the scarcity of land rather than by the closeness of markets.

85–90% of small-scale producers belong to the income group in which the returns from sales of agricultural products does not exceed 500,000 forints (c. US$ 10,000) per year. Their activities are not liable to income tax payment introduced in 1988. It is a tax allowance for agricultural families that might play an important role in retaining the rural population.

7.5 Changes in transport network and tourism

Further shifts have occurred toward road traffic both in freight and passenger transport. There was a rise in pipeline transport as well, while railway transport decreased, especially in passanger traffic.

In 1986 the total length of the *railway system* was 8026 km. Uneconomical lines have now all been closed, no further closures being planned. The main direction of modernization is electrification. The electrification of the

Budapest–Dombóvár–Pécs, Budapest–Székesfehérvár–Nagykanizsa lines (the latter largely reducing the air and noise pollution of the resort area along the southern shore of the Lake Balaton) and the main Győr–Sopron stretch of the Győr–Sopron–Ébenfurt Railway Ltd. was completed. Now 29% of the railway lines are electrified. Electrification also entails considerable energy savings. In 1986 a mere 0.1% of all traction on the Hungarian railway network was performed by steam, 40.9% by diesel and 59% by electric locomotives. Steam traction has been eliminated except for a few side lines with little traffic. The high rate of electric traction shows that priority was given to the busiest lines in electrification.

No significant modification was registered in the length and surface distribution of the *road network*. The construction of highways slowed down for financial reasons. The Budapest–Tatabánya track of M1 highway was completed. This and the completion of the motorway between Tatabánya and Győr made road communication between Budapest and the Austrian border faster. The construction of the Budapest–Kecskemét stretch of M5 is going on, a part of it already being opened. At the end of 1987, the total length of highways amounted to 300 km. A major move was to begin the construction of the motorroad ring around Budapest on World Bank credit, which will relieve the inner network of Budapest of the heavy transit traffic already when partially opened.

The domestic *passenger car stock* of the country grew fast to surpass 1.5 million at the end of 1986. Due to import difficulties, no major changes occurred in the composition of the car stock (no foreign currency is available to import western cars, CMEA partners made little increase in their exports, the stock is ageing, with average age being 10 years). This implies that fuel consumption is large and air pollution is high.

A major advancement in *air traffic* was the completion of the reconstruction of Budapest–Ferihegy Airport. There are now two runways, two terminal buildings, repair hangars and storehouses for the expansion of traffic. The reconstruction helped Ferihegy Airport come abreast of the most modern airfields in Europe. MALÉV's network of lines remained practically unchanged, with just a few flights added.

Progress of tourism. Since the first edition of this book the country finished its most successful period of tourism.

– In 1986 the number of foreigners in Hungary was 16.6 million and 6.3 million Hungarians crossed the border. The composition of foreigners by country changed slightly. Since the abolition of entry visa, the number of Austrian tourists considerably increased (2.4 million). Topping the table are still the Czechoslovakian, Polish and East German tourists. The dimensions of earnings from tourism did not grow proportionately with the number of tourists. The reasons are short average stay in the country and reluctance to spend. In 1986, Hungary's gross income from rouble-accounting tourism came to 11.3 billion forints and from dollar-accounting tourism to 16.6 billion forints. Increasing revenues from tourism helped to improve the balance of payments and the foreign-exchange reserves for Hungarians going abroad. Purchasing tourism grew considerably among foreigners coming to Hungary.

– The capacity of accomodations was substantially enlarged. Large modern hotels were built in Budapest and the country centres on Austrian credit for hotel construction. Hotel accomodation capacity grew by 38% between 1981—86, but it is still below demand especially in the peak season.

– The endowments, among others the natural endowments of the country were better utilized with more tourists coming. Hotels, hospitals, spas, sanatoria were built adjacent to thermal hot-springs (Balf, Bük, Hévíz, Sárvár). There is a new thermal spa centre under construction at Zalakaros (southern Transdanubia).

– Tourist traffic at main attraction sites and centres increased in Budapest, the Danube bend and at the thermal spas. Budapest became a renowned international congress centre. In order to restore the water quality of the Lake Balaton, the government allocated large sums to improve water purification capacity, the drainage and running water system, and put a strict ban on construction. Eutrophication stopped, the quality of the water is improving.

Bibliography for Chapter IV

[1] Ádám, L. and Boros, F. (eds) (1979): *Dunaújváros földrajza* (A Geography of Dunaújváros). Budapest, Akadémiai Kiadó, 318 p. (Földrajzi monográfiák, 10.)

[2] Andó, M. and Jakucs, L. (1967): *A Dél-Tiszántúl természeti földrajzi tájértékelése* (A physiographic landscape evaluation of the Southern Trans-Tisza area). A summary report for the Hungarian Oil and Gas Trust. Manuscript.

[3] Baboneaux, Y. (1978): Les problèmes de l'aménagement du territoire en Hongrie. *Acta Geographica*, No. 3, pp. 7–15.

[4] Barta, Gy., Beluszky P. and Berényi, I. (1975): A hátrányos helyzetű területek vizsgálata Borsod-Abaúj-Zemplén megyében (An examination of disadvantaged areas in Borsod-Abaúj-Zemplén counties). *Földrajzi Értesítő*, No. 3, pp. 299–390.

[5] Becsei, J. (1972): *Békés, az átalakuló agrárváros* (Békés, an agrarian town in the process of transformation). Békés, County Council, 99 p.

[6] Beluszky, P. (1974): *Nyíregyháza vonzáskörzete. A város–falu közötti kapcsolatok jellege és mennyiségi jellemzői Szabolcs-Szatmár megyében* (The attraction sphere of Nyíregyháza. The nature and quantitative characteristics of urban-rural relationships in Szabolcs-Szatmár county). Akadémiai Kiadó, Budapest, 118 p. (Földrajzi tanulmányok, 13.)

[7] Beluszky, P. and Enyedi, Gy. (1968): Az Észak-Alföld gazdasági fejlődése (The economic development of the northern part of the Great Hungarian Plain). *Földrajzi Közlemények*, No. 1, pp. 14–32.

[8] Bernát, T. and Enyedi, Gy. (1968): A magyar mezőgazdaság területi fejlődésének néhány kérdése (Some questions of the regional development of Hungarian agriculture). *Földrajzi Értesítő*, No. 4, pp. 407–427.

[9] Bernát, T. (ed.) (1972): *Magyarország gazdaságföldrajza* (An economic geography of Hungary). Tankönyvkiadó, Budapest, 2nd revised ed., 542 p.

[10] Bernát, T. and Viszkei, M. (eds) (1972): *Budapest társadalmának és gazdaságának száz éve, 1872/73–1972* (Hundred years of the society and economy of Budapest, 1872/73–1972). Közgazdasági és Jogi Könyvkiadó, Budapest, 278 p.
[11] Bernát, T. (ed.) (1981): *Magyarország gazdaságföldrajza* (An economic geography of Hungary). Tankönyvkiadó, Budapest, 461 p.
[12] Bora, Gy. (1957): Gazdaságföldrajzi vizsgálatok a borsodi szénmedencében (Examinations concerning the economic geography of the Borsod coal basin). *Földrajzi Értesítő*, No. 3, pp. 303–322.
[13] Bora, Gy. (1960): A rayonkutatás jelentősége és problémája a magyar gazdaságföldrajzban (The significance and problem of regionalization research in the economic geography of Hungary). *Földrajzi Értesítő*, No. 2, pp. 129–141.
[14] Bora, Gy., Hock, B., Mucsy, Gy. and Pintér, J. (1977): A Sajó vízminőségi-műszaki közgazdasági modellje (An engineering-economic model for the water quality management of the Sajó river). *Hidrológiai Közlöny*, No. 1, pp. 27–37.
[15] Bora, Gy. (1978): The Stages of Development in the Industrial System of Budapest. In: Bandman, M. K. (ed.): *Projection of the formation of territorial production complexes*. USSR Academy of Sciences, Siberian Branch Institute of Economics and Organisation of Industrial Production, Novosibirsk, pp. 24–41.
[16] Bora, Gy. (1979): The Stages of Development in the Industrial System of Budapest. In: Hamilton, F. E. Ian and Kortus, B. (eds): *The Spatial Structure of Industrial Systems*, Warsawa, pp. 41–59.
[17] Borai, Á. (1978): A Dél-Dunántúl ipara (The Industry of Southern Transdanubia). In: Marosi, S. and Szilárd, J. (eds): *A Dél-Dunántúl természeti és gazdasági földrajza* (The physical and economic geography of Southern Transdanubia). Manuscript.
[18] Borsy, Z. (1961): *A Nyírség természeti földrajza* (The physiography of the Nyírség). Akadémiai Kiadó, Budapest, 227 p.
[19] Bulla, B. and Mendöl, T. (1947): *A Kárpát-medence földrajza* (A geography of the Carpathian Basin). Egyetemi Nyomda, Budapest, 611 p.
[20] Bulla, B. (1962): *Magyarország természetföldrajza* (The physiography of Hungary). Tankönyvkiadó, Budapest, 423 p.
[21] Deskins, D. R. (ed.) (1980): *Impact of Urbanization and Industrialization on the Landscape*. Proceedings of the American–Hungarian Geography Seminar, University of Michigan, Ann Arbor, 428 p. (Michigan Geographical Publication, No. 25).
[22] Enyedi, Gy. (1964): *A Délkelet-Alföld mezőgazdasági földrajza* (The agricultural geography of the South-Eastern Great Plain). Akadémiai Kiadó, Budapest, 316 p.
[23] Enyedi, Gy. (1970): Az Alföld gazdasági földrajzi problémái (Economic-geographical problems of the Great Hungarian Plain). *Földrajzi Közlemények*, No. 3, pp. 177–195.
[24] Enyedi, Gy. (1978): Gazdaságpolitika és területi fejlődés (Economic policy and regional development). *Valóság*, No. 5, pp. 36–46.
[25] Enyedi, Gy. (1979): Economic policy and regional development. *Acta Oeconomica*, Nos 1–2, pp. 113–126.
[26] Erdősi, F. (1971): A Délkelet-Dunántúl építőanyagipari természeti és gazdasági adottságainak, valamint területi struktúrájának földrajzi értékelése (A geographical evalution of the physical-economic endowments and of the regional structure of the construction industry in South-Eastern Transdanubia). *Földrajzi Értesítő*, No. 4, pp. 443–464.
[27] Erdősi, F. (1980): A dél-dunántúli régió közlekedési hálózatának kialakulása a termelőerők és a településhálózat területi sajátosságaival összefüggésben (The evolution of the transport network of the South-Transdanubian region in the context of the regional characteristics of the production forces and the settlement network). *Földrajzi Értesítő*, No. 1, pp. 61–94.
[28] Fodor, L. (1978): Growth model of the agglomeration of Budapest. In: Enyedi, Gy. (ed.): *Urban development in the USA and Hungary*. Akadémiai Kiadó, Budapest, pp. 131–136. (Studies in Geography in Hungary, 14.)
[29] Illés, I. (1979): Die Regionalisierung Ungarns als Mittel der Raumplanung. *Mitteilungen der Österreichischen Geographischen Gesellschaft*, Bd. 121, I. pp. 66–67.
[30] Kolarik, A. (1970): *A Közép-Tiszavidék agrárföldrajza* (An agrarian geography of the Middle-Tisza region). A candidate's thesis. Budapest, 250 p.
[31] Kóródi, J. (1959): *A borsodi iparvidék* (The Borsod industrial region). Közgazdasági és Jogi Könyvkiadó, Budapest, 281 p.

[32] Kőszegi, L. (1964): *A területi tervezés főbb elvi és módszertani kérdései* (Major theoretical and methodological questions of regional planning). Közgazdasági és Jogi Könyvkiadó, Budapest, 398 p.
[33] Krajkó, Gy., Pénzes, I., Tóth, J., etc. (1969): Magyarország gazdasági körzetbeosztásának néhány elvi és gyakorlati kérdése (Some theoretical and practical questions concerning the delimitation of economic regions in Hungary). *Földrajzi Értesítő*, No. 1, pp. 95–114.
[34] Krajkó, Gy. (1973a): A gazdasági mikrokörzetek elvi és módszertani kérdései (Theoretical and methodological questions concerning the delimitation of economic microregions). *Földrajzi Értesítő*, Nos 2/3, pp. 259–275.
[35] Krajkó, Gy. (1973b): A Dél-Alföld mikrokörzeteinek elhatárolása (The delimitation of the microregions of the Southern Great Plain). *Földrajzi Értesítő*, No. 4, pp. 383–409.
[36] Krajkó, Gy. (1977): A gazdasági körzetek taxonómiai szerkezete az Alföldön (The taxonomic structure of economic regions in the Great Hungarian Plain). *Alföldi Tanulmányok*, pp. 80–92.
[37] Krassó, S. (comp.) (1978): A Dél-Dunántúli Tervezési Körzet (The South-Transdanubian planning region). *Területi Statisztika*, No. 6, pp. 649–667.
[38] Kulcsár, V. and Lackó, L. (eds) (1975): *Magyarország megyéi és városai* (Hungary's counties and towns). Kossuth Könyvkiadó, Budapest, 655 p.
[39] Kulcsár, V. and Perczel, Gy. (eds) (1978): *Vengriya, razvitiye i razmeshtsheniye proizvoditelnykh sil.* Moscow, 480 p.
[40] Lengyel, L. (1976): A II. Tisza (kisköret) vízlépcső és öntözőrendszerei agrárhasznosításának néhány közgazdasági kérdései (Some economic questions concerning the agrarian utilization of the Tisza II. (Kisköre) Dam and irrigation systems). *Területi Statisztika*, No. 6, pp. 591–608.
[41] Lettrich, E. (1968): *Kecskemét és tanyavilága* (Kecskemét and its tanya area). Akadémiai Kiadó, Budapest, 125 p. (Földrajzi Tanulmányok, 9.)
[42] Lukács, J. Mrs. (1975): Kölcsönhatások az aprófalvas körzetek és a gazdaságilag elmaradott területek között Borsod megyében (Interactions between tiny-village regions and the economically disadvantaged areas). *Területi Statisztika*, No. 4, pp. 422–429.
[43] Markos, Gy. (1952): Magyarország gazdasági körzetbeosztása (rayonírozása) (The delimitation of economic regions in Hungary). *Földrajzi Értesítő*, No. 3, pp. 582–634.
[44] Markos, Gy. (1953): Az Északi Iparvidék mint gazdasági körzet (The Northern Industrial Area as an economic region). *Földrajzi Közlemények*, No. 1, pp. 65–78.
[45] Markos, Gy. (1962): *Magyarország gazdasági földrajza* (An economic geography of Hungary). Közgazdasági és Jogi Könyvkiadó, Budapest, 582 p.
[46] Markos, Gy. (1971): *Ungarn, Land, Volk, Wirtschaft in Stichworten.* Verlag Ferdinand Hirt, Wien, 135 p.
[47] Marosi, S. and Szilárd, J. (eds) (1967): *A dunai Alföld* (The Danube plainland). Akadémiai Kiadó, Budapest, 358 p. (Magyarország tájföldrajza, 1.)
[48] Marosi, S. and Szilárd, J. (eds) (1969): *A tiszai Alföld* (The Tisza plainland). Akadémiai Kiadó, Budapest, 381 p. (Magyarország tájföldrajza, 2.)
[49] Marosi, S. and Szilárd, J. (1979): Somogyi tájtípusok jellemzése és értékelése (The characterization and evaluation of landscape types in Somogy county). *Földrajzi Értesítő*, Nos 1/2, pp. 51–86.
[50] *Megyei Statisztikai Évkönyvek, 1979* (County Statistical Yearbooks). Central Statistical Office, Budapest.
[51] Papp, A. (1975): Az agglomerációs fejlődés helyzete és sajátosságai Debrecen környékén (The state and characteristics of agglomeration development in the environment of Debrecen). *Földrajzi Értesítő*, No. 4, pp. 479–488.
[52] Pécsi, M. and Sárfalvi, B. (1977): *Physical and economic geography of Hungary.* Corvina, Budapest, 198 p. (2nd ed.)
[53] Pécsi, M. and Katona, S. (1978): Long-term development of the Budapest agglomeration – an evaluation of the physical-geographical potentials. In: Enyedi, Gy. (ed.): *Urban development in the USA and Hungary.* Akadémiai Kiadó, Budapest, pp. 213–230. (Studies in Geography in Hungary, 14.)
[54] Pécsi, M. (1979): Geographische Forschungstendenzen in Ungarn zwischen 1945 and 1975. *Mitteilungen der Österreichischen Geographischen Gesellschaft*, Bd. 121, I. pp. 46–65.
[55] Preisich, G. (1977): A budapesti agglomeráció kisugárzásában fekvő községek fejlesztése (The development of villages in the attraction sphere of the Budapest agglomeration). *Területrendezés*, 4, pp. 47–49.
[56] Preisich, G. (1979): Entwicklungs- und Planungsprobleme der Stadt Budapest. *Mitteilungen der Österreichischen Geographischen Gesellschaft*, Bd. 212, I. pp. 107–128.

[57] Radó, S. (ed.) (1963): *Magyarország gazdasági földrajza* (An economic geography of Hungary). Gondolat, Budapest, 366 p.
[58] Radó, S. (ed.) (1962): *Ökonomische Geographie der Ungarischen Volksrepublik.* Verlag Die Wirtschaft, Berlin, 235 p.
[59] Radó, S. (ed.) (1974): Magyarország tervezési-gazdasági körzetei, 1–6. kötet (Planning-economic regions of Hungary, Vols 1–6). Kartográfiai Intézet, Budapest.
[60] *Regional Planning in Hungary.* Budapest, 1977, Ministry of Building and Urban Development, 28 p.
[61] Sárfalvi, B. (ed.) (1971): *The changing face of the Great Hungarian Plain.* Akadémiai Kiadó, Budapest, 183 p. (Studies in Geography in Hungary, 9.)
[62] Szabó, F. (ed.) (1974): *Békés megye gazdasági földrajza* (An economic geography of Békés county). Békés County Council, Békéscsaba, 506 p.
[63] Tatai, Z. (1980): Budapest szerepe az ország társadalmi-gazdasági életében (Budapest's role in the country's socio-economic life). *Földrajzi Közlemények,* No. 3, pp. 205–227.
[64] *Területi Statisztikai Évkönyv, 1979* (Regional Statistical Yearbook, 1979). Central Statistical Office, Budapest, 400 p.
[65] Tóth, J. (1979): A külterületi-tanyasi népesség területi különbségei és változási tendenciái a Dél-Alföldön, 1960–1970 (Regional differences and changing trends in the population of the outlying-tanya areas in the Southern Great Plain, 1960–1970). *Földrajzi Értesítő,* Nos 2/3, pp. 247–258.
[66] Tóth, J. (1977): *Az urbanizáció népességföldrajzi vonatkozásai a Dél-Alföldön* (The demographic-geographical implications of urbanization in the Southern Great Plain). Akadémiai Kiadó, Budapest, 142 p.
[67] Tóth, J. (1978): A Dél-Dunántúl gazdasági térszerkezete (The economic spatial structure of Southern Transdanubia). *Földrajzi Értesítő,* No. 2, pp. 205–222.
[68] Tóth, J. (ed.) (1976): *Békéscsaba földrajza* (A geography of Békéscsaba). Békés County Council, Békéscsaba, 541 p.
[69] Tóth, J. (1980): *Mezőberény, a helyét kereső kisváros* (Mezőberény, a small town seeking its place). Békés County Council, Békéscsaba, Scientific Co-ordination Committee, Mezőberény, 206 p.
[70] Vörösmarti–Tajti, E., Pál, A. and Veresházi, B. (eds) (1975): *Szolnok, a Közép-Tiszavidék tájszervező centruma* (Szolnok – the landscape-organizing centre of the Middle-Tisza Area). Town Council, Szolnok, 299 p.
[71] Zala, Gy. (1976): A dél-dunántúli körzet területfejlesztési vázlata (A tentative plan for the regional development of the South-Transdanubian region). In: Enyedi, Gy. (ed.): *A magyar népgazdaság fejlődésének területi problémái* (Regional problems of the development of the Hungarian national economy). Akadémiai Kiadó, Budapest, pp. 226–242.
[72] Zoltán, Z. (1968): Gazdasági erővonalak és csomópontok az Alföld középső vidékén (Economic lines of force and nodal points in the central parts of the Great Plain). *Területi Statisztika,* No. 5, pp. 534–541.
[73] Zoltán, Z. (1976): Az infrastruktúra fejlesztésének elvei és hatásmechanizmusa (The principles and effect mechanism of the development of infrastructure). *Közgazdasági Szemle,* No. 12, pp. 1403–1417.
[74] Zoltán, Z. (1976): Kecskemét mint nagyváros (Kecskemét as a large town). *Forrás,* No. 12, pp. 49–56.
[75] Zoltán, Z. (ed.) (1980): *A változó Alföld* (The changing face of the Great Plain). Tankönyvkiadó, Budapest, 176 p.